Women Writers of the
American West,
1833–1927

Women Writers of the American West, 1833–1927

NINA BAYM

UNIVERSITY OF ILLINOIS PRESS

Urbana, Chicago, and Springfield

Library of Congress Cataloging-in-Publication Data
Baym, Nina.
Women writers of the American West, 1833–1927 / Nina Baym.
p.   cm.
Includes bibliographical references and index.
ISBN-13: 978-0-252-03597-5 (hardcover : alk. paper)
ISBN-10: 0-252-03597-6 (hardcover : alk. paper)
1. American literature—West (U.S.)—History and criticism.
2. American literature—West (U.S.)—Bio-bibliography.
3. Women authors, American—West (U.S.)—Biography.
4. West (U.S.)—In literature.
I. Title.
PS271.B39   2011
810.9'9287—dc22 [B]   2010041878

For Jack, again and always;
and for Shirley Davis and Charles Davis,
our western family, with love and gratitude.

Contents

Women Writers of the
American West,
1833–1927

1

The West as a Woman Writer's Subject

A woman author's name here, another there—in parentheses, a foot-note, a bibliography. How could there be books by women about the Ameri-can West, when everybody knew that the topic was reserved for male authors? Yes, there was Willa Cather. There was also Mary Austin, celebrant of the des-ert whose literary career began in 1903 with *Land of Little Rain,* rediscovered by students of nature writing. Kevin Starr's 1973 *Americans and the California Dream* gave California novelist Gertrude Atherton a whole chapter. Historians of women had recovered and reissued books by wives of frontier army officers. Sarah Winnemucca's 1883 *Life among the Piutes* had become a must-read for those interested in Native American literature. The number grew.

When, at some point, I told colleagues I'd found the names of some forty American women who'd published books about the American West by 1927, they said: write a book about it. I thought: I need to search more thoroughly. If I find a significant array, I can speculate persuasively on the subject's importance to women writers and perhaps even on women writers' importance to the sub-ject in their own day. I chose 1927 to end my quest, because that's when Willa Cather published *Death Comes for the Archbishop*—to my mind one of the very greatest of western books. I went back as far as I could; the earliest book turned out to be the first of Mary Austin Holley's two books about Texas, published in 1833. In all, I've found 343 women publishing books about the American West between those years. I hope my overview of these writers and their books will provoke readers to find out more about them. There are more out there, I'm sure, and I hope also that others will be motivated to find them.

I compiled my set of writers by consulting literary and cultural histories, anthologies, biographical dictionaries, scholarly essays and monographs, book-sellers' catalogs, bibliographies, back-matter publishers' book advertisements, internal references when one woman's book refers to another's, and innumerable Web sites. Colleagues have been generous with their suggestions. In the acknowledgments, I thank those who told me about writers I might not otherwise have found. A few of these authors are known to everybody who works in American literature; others are known to specialists; but many are unknown and the whole array has never been put on the record. I think it's important to show that, once again, where women were supposed to have been silent, they were not. What they were not supposed to have done, they did.

In what follows I use books only. Western material published by women in journals and newspapers is a dauntingly vast archive, much too large for any one scholar to cover. Too, a book makes a different kind of statement from a newspaper or journal article; even now, in the dawning age of the e-book, the print book has iconic status. To publish a book, no matter what the topic, means the woman hopes to make what her preface typically calls a "more permanent" contribution to the record. She doesn't necessarily seek literary immortality, but she does seek access to the public.

Covering so much material, I sacrifice depth for breadth, describing rather than analyzing, though of course description always implies a point of view. Simply placing an author like, say, Willa Cather, among dozens writing about the heroic pioneer woman, is to analyze. I don't engage much with literary criticism, partly because literary criticism is skewed toward a small number of already-known women who would therefore get a disproportionate share of the attention that I hope to disperse more evenly.

My descriptions are governed by three interests. First, how the authors showed women making lives for themselves in the West—what they gave to the West, and what it gave to them. Second, how they represented the West. And third, the author's self presentation, as a western advocate or a western critic or something else. These questions get different answers in all of the almost 640 or so books I talk about. To give something of the books' flavor, I quote and sometimes summarize plots, picking and choosing among myriad details. This means that much is left unsaid. Perhaps another reader of a given book will feel that I left out the most important thing. Much more could be done with these books and writers than I do—I'm opening up a subject, not saying the last word about it. In general, I found these writers showing women making western lives for themselves and their families by achieving domesticity in a new place, improving over what they'd known before but still accepting a domestic agenda. To achieve this end, they had to change the West. The worst fears of the sunset-riding cowboys of the movies are realized as women come in and make the West a settled place. Women are seen to be crucial to the western development of families, farms, and businesses. In exchange for their work, the West made women healthier, more active, more useful, more engaged than their sisters back East.

Second, these writers tried to give detailed depictions of the western places where their accounts were set. There might be an overarching and abstract concept of the West, but on the ground there were many different Wests. To connect the specificity of the place to the overarching concept, to show the achievement of female domesticity and the development of female character in Oregon, Texas, California, Utah, Nebraska, New Mexico, and other parts of the West—each distinct in history, landform, and climate—made the particular West a character in its own right.

And third, these writers were entirely unapologetic about their own work. They hadn't noticed that the West was a subject reserved for male authors. They saw their books as contributions to the record of western settlement. They took political positions. They avoided the violent male plots typical of the dime novel and its successor, the movie western. Norris Yates, whose *Gender and Genre* compared formula westerns by men and by women, found the women's books light on violence and also much more interested in women's stories than men's stories. That stands to reason; a book with a woman's name on the cover would almost automatically make its appeal to women readers. And of course many fewer women than men wrote formula westerns to begin with.

But it's not clear which view of the West was the more realistic. Historians of the American West don't agree about how violent it actually was there, whether it was more or less violent than other parts of the United States (what after all could be more violent than slavery and Jim Crow?), and how this question might be studied objectively. Much, perhaps most, western writing by men was not about violence but was invested in the same domesticating energies as women. That shared narrative, in a somewhat desacralized form, has become labeled Manifest Destiny: the United States was destined to appropriate all the land "from sea to shining sea" not in the name of gunplay, but in the name of peaceful prosperity, in the names of homes, families, farms, and businesses. The "blood and thunder" books so beloved by adolescent boys were mere escape fantasies, not meant to be mistaken for the real.

So the work of women in the West, as the writers showed it, and as their own writing contributed to it, was to act as partners to men in the task of bringing the West to what they saw as its highest development, a space in which they, as women, could flourish and develop. That the outcome of this partnership would be the destruction of the West as they first encountered it was not a problem for them. The sense of shared purpose allowed women to think they mattered. They could merge male and female voices, as in Sarah Pratt Carr's 1907 railroad novel, *The Iron Way,* where a railroad executive delivers a long toast to "Woman" at a San Francisco banquet—a toast, of course, written by the woman author. He refers to generic woman, represented by woman with a capital W, and also to Sally B., a prospector's wife who owns and manages a hotel for railroad people while the husband is away searching for gold. "You ask what Woman has to do with the Pacific Railroad? Everything! Doesn't Woman make the home? Don't home make the nation? Doesn't Uncle Sam protect his nation? And doesn't he need this railroad to do it? . . . Could you build this railroad without woman? Where under the canopy would it get to without Sally B.? Where would be your banquets, your square meals three times a day? . . . What are you building your railroad for, anyway. . . . The supreme reason,—you are building this railroad to carry women, to found homes in the great West" (186–87).

Given this basic structure in books written by "Anglos"—women descended from English, Scottish, Welsh, and Irish forbears—one might have hoped for a significant counternarrative in books by women associated with minority status. Regrettably, I found only nineteen such women, less than 6 percent of the total. These nineteen women, too, accepted Anglo dominance as a historical reality, and sought to place themselves advantageously within it rather than write against it. Identifying themselves with their group and family, they did not cross ethnic lines. Sui Sin Far is interested only in Chinese immigrants, mainly from the merchant class. The three Hispanic women—Maria Ampara Ruiz de Burton, Maria Sacramenta Lopez de Cummings, Adina De Zavala— insist on their pure Castilian genealogies; in *The Squatter and the Don* Ruiz de Burton uses a Castilian-Anglo romance to make ethnicity less important than like-mindedness. Native women identify with their local tribes. The four Cherokee writers claim superiority over Natives who were not affiliated with the Five Tribes because—as Narcissa Owen insisted in her memoir—"the Indians of Indian Territory are civilized, educated Christian people" (134). Three of five African American women—Maud Cuney-Hare, Emma J. Ray, and Delilah Beasley—revised Manifest Destiny to make it culminate in the full citizenship of black people, which they thought would happen in the West. Texans Bernice Love Wiggins and Josie Briggs Hall had other agendas. Wiggins wrote affectionate folklore about black rural populations; Hall attempted to elevate the "race" by presenting examples of black achievement.

* * *

Some women wrote many books, others put down their life experiences (or what they could recall of them, or what they decided to say about them) in a single publication. There were personal and family memoirs—unreliable, of course, as uncorroborated memoirs inevitably are, conveying the writer's ideas about how she ought to present the West and her own life in the West to readers. There were novels, short story collections, histories, biographies (women often published to celebrate a member of their family, to put him or her—usually him—into the record), reportage, descriptive sketches, textbooks, poetry volumes, didactic or amusing works for young people, political and social polemics, and travel books. Some authors had literary ambitions, others didn't. I don't rank the genres according to some idea of literariness, and I don't judge the more obviously literary books according to an idea of better and worse. All contributed to the project of getting women's voices into the western record. Publishers in New York, Boston (Little, Brown; Houghton, Mifflin), Philadelphia (Lippincott), Chicago (McClurg), San Francisco (Harr Wagner), and other urban centers sought out western books, which implies considerable audience interest. Many of these books were illustrated, and the illustrators, too, were often women; the arrival of women as book illustrators is a phenomenon of the 1890s and after, about which more needs to be known.

In addition, an array of local publishers across the West printed books for women who wanted their work to circulate within a limited community that extended beyond the immediate circle. Finding out how all these books got into print would add much to our understanding of book history. Except for a gap in the 1860s, when war shut down much of the publishing industry, the number of books increased steadily from decade to decade: from only 2 in the 1830s (both by Mary Austin Holley) to 170 by more than 100 in the second decade of the twentieth century. But whatever the possibilities for local book publication, professional literary reputations were made in the East, and after the turn of the century, more particularly in New York City. Therefore, ambitious western women with literary ambitions went east as well: Gertrude Atherton, Willa Cather, and Kathleen Norris are prominent examples.

Among women for whom I could find biographical information, perhaps at least two-thirds were literary professionals or semiprofessionals—mainly journalists or women who freelanced for newspapers and periodicals. There were also editors, teachers, community activists, clubwomen, local historians, and novelists. Women's clubs, emerging toward the end of the nineteenth century, encouraged even traditional women to publish on behalf of social and political initiatives. WCTU women wrote on behalf of temperance, missionary women wrote on behalf of Christian evangelism, "Friends of the Indian" wrote on behalf of humane treatment of the Native population, women with land to sell wrote on behalf of real estate. Women often headed the local and regional historical societies; as family historians, many knew how to preserve and circulate an archive. Toward the end of their lives, many women wrote memoirs to contribute to the record of what they called pioneering. Women who visited or toured in the West wrote to tell others what to expect. The place is their reason for writing.

* * *

Working with books only, I had to decide—sometimes to decree—what is and what isn't a book. I've occasionally included something more like a pamphlet than a book, although always a separate publication, because length is not always an indication of purpose. I mostly use books published under the woman's own name, and during her lifetime, so as to ensure that the book in hand was the book she wanted to be known for having authored. In a few cases, where books seem to have been ready for the publisher at the point of the woman's death, I made exceptions. I stayed with "Mourning Dove" and "Sui Sin Far" because these pennames were selected for ethnic identification rather than to conceal gender. Though the women were aware of men's writing, direct engagement with men's books is not the norm. Dime novels and the movie western are scorned, but not for their masculinity so much as for their immaturity and unreliability. Women's books tended to center on women because women readers were their target audience.

I also had to decide what is and what isn't the West. For this I took my cue from the women themselves. Having come, in many cases, from Illinois or Ohio or Wisconsin, they were quite clear that the West was one tier of states over from the Mississippi River; no Louisiana, Arkansas, Missouri, Iowa, Minnesota. The identity of Texas, thought of by some as southern not western—it was after all the only western region to join the Confederacy, and it connected economically to New Orleans—is itself the subject of much Texas writing; as the process of settling moved West, Texas became more western, with cotton fields giving way to cattle ranches. My east-west lines are the current boundaries between the United States and Canada, the US and Mexico. Both the northern and southern borders were in flux and contested; to establish them became the theme of much writing from Texas and the Pacific Northwest.

I divide the West into nine subregions according to the women's sense of place, which I sequence in chapters that are roughly ordered (very roughly, in that settling goes on simultaneously in many places) according to the chronology of Anglo regional occupation. Each subregion has a character corresponding to geographical and historical particularities. Texas/Oklahoma has its Alamo and southern affiliation; the Pacific Northwest has memories of the overland trek and the Hudson's Bay Company, as well as timber and the rain forest; northern California and Nevada have the gold rush, bonanza kings, and San Francisco; Utah has Mormons; Colorado has the Rocky Mountain's conjunction of mining, tourism, and health spas; the Great Plains has Bleeding Kansas, homesteading farmers, and Native hostilities; the High Plains has cowboys and cattle; southern California and Nevada have Hispano-mission history, year-round summer on the coast and year-round aridity in the interior desert; the Southwest has peaceful pueblo people, fear-inspiring Apaches, and Santa Fe. The penultimate chapter covers the perhaps surprisingly small number of what I call "road books" where journey rather than destination is all-important: army narratives (the army was supposed to enable settlement but not to settle, and its forts were erected and dismantled as settlement progressed), overland trail books, railroad books, and motoring accounts. My final chapter contains capsule biographies of the women writers insofar as I could find information.

In general, I work chronologically through this material within the regional chapters, but I also attend to the genres, the more prolific authors, and the overarching themes. I have used the phrase Manifest Destiny, but insofar as that concept is thought to involve the spread of Christianity across the continent, it is not a good description of what the women wrote. Books by missionary women fitted this pattern, but by far the great motive for westering reported by women was simply economic self-improvement. Whatever larger design there might be came into view only by stopping and reflecting. Sarah Raymond Herndon, in her 1902 *Days on the Road: Crossing the Plains in 1865,* recalls that she and her widowed mother and two brothers went West from Missouri to better their circumstances "by gaining wealth" but, she reflects, "The motive does not seem to justify the inconvenience, the anxiety, the suspense. . . . Yet how would the great West be peopled were it not so. God knows best. It is, without doubt, this spirit of restlessness, and unsatisfied longing, or ambition, if you please, which is implanted in our nature by an all-wise Creator that has peopled the whole earth" (9).

For Herndon this plan is peopling the earth not the nation; religion and race are irrelevant. Women who studied any history in school would have learned that history was the movement of peoples, with now one group and now another pressing into new territory to sustain itself: Romans, Vikings, Huns. National fluidity for incoming Westerners was a fact of life. In the 1840s people going to Texas, Oregon, and Utah thought they were leaving the states. Until diplomacy settled the boundary question with Canada in 1846, the Pacific Northwest was jointly administered by Great Britain and the United States. Not only Texas but the entire Southwest including Utah and California became "American" after the Mexican War. Much Texas literature is about making the territory American rather than Mexican, as is the literature of southern California. The Civil War opened a whole new chapter in the question of national identity. Remote Alaska became American soon after the Civil War, and though it did not become a state until 1958, it quickly became a part of the Pacific Northwest. Throughout this period there were initiatives in the air to annex Cuba, Santo Domingo, Nicaragua, Panama, the Virgin Islands, and Hawaii (the Sandwich Islands, as they were then called). By the early twentieth century the distant Philippines had been defined as American territory. Though the boundary with Mexico had supposedly been determined by the Treaty of Guadalupe Hidalgo in 1848, the border remained (it still remains) a vexed territory, and fears about Mexican attempts (with German aid) to retake the lost territories of Texas, Arizona, and New Mexico during World War I had much to do with the American entrance into that war. Individuals, who went west for themselves, not the nation, turned to the nation for protection of their personal interests. Thus the nation is seldom the specific subject of a woman's book—it is, rather the backdrop against which human dramas play out. Implicitly rather than explicitly, the question whether women in the West triumph or fail becomes an inquiry into the national future.

*   *   *

Because specifics of place are so important, some kind of realism is the typical literary technique for western writing. The women who went west were, in the main, the ordinary people realism is designed to be about; readers, too, as Gordon Hutner's recent book about American reading habits has demonstrated, have always been more comfortable with realism than literary experimentation. Because realism imparts an aura of accuracy, because it is designed to make readers think the book is about the real world, plot questions about what human traits can survive, what can be developed, and what is lost in the West resonate beyond the boundaries of the fiction.

As one thinks of the national future and women's contribution to it, it's worth remembering that the settlers' movement was hardly spontaneous but responded to offers and advertisements, many of them grossly exaggerated. Homesteaders went for land offered free by the government and cheaply by the railroads. Railroads especially wanted to populate the territories they were running through to create customers for the goods they planned to haul. Publicists—boosters and boomers, they were called—went to England, to Scotland, to Denmark, offering inexpensive fares as an inducement to emigrate. People beguiled by false promises and unrealistic expectations often encountered crushing disappointment when they arrived on the ground. Many who went to be farmers knew nothing about farming, while experienced farmers often encountered very different terrain and climate from what they knew back home. Women in particular tended to loathe the isolation and drudgery, not to mention the squalor, of farm life; they couldn't wait to get off the farm into town. Many went back home; a surprising number of memoirs were penned later from the friendly confines of Wisconsin, Ohio, Illinois, to which the woman had returned after decades in the West.

Place specificity doesn't mean environmentalism. The settlers' intention of succeeding in the West meant changing the landscape. The overland trails changed the landscape; the railroad changed it; farmers cut down forest and cleared away the native grasses. Eventually the National Park movement, initiated by Yosemite and Yellowstone in the nineteenth century and Glacier National Park early in the twentieth century, helped make scenery into a marketable product. Nor does place specificity necessarily translate into local color as that genre is typically understood. This specialty of female writing was about dying communities and their traditional ways as they were threatened by the modern world with its industrializing, urban, and polyglot populations. Local color looked to the past, while western women's writing looked to the future. In her 1928 memoir,

The World I Saw, Anne Shannon Monroe said of Yakima that "No matter what subject was started, a conversation always ended with the country. Everybody was filled up with it: soil, water, irrigation, country homes, plans for the future. It was just the most *future* place" (15).

Fewer than thirty of the women for whom I have biographical data were born outside the US and only one (Prussian-born Josephine McCrackin) was not from an English-speaking nation; the others were from England, Ireland, Scotland, and Canada. (Some European women published about the American West, but that is not my focus here.) The immigrants from Scandinavia, eastern Europe, and southern Europe, who so markedly altered the demographics of the United States beginning in the 1880s, are seldom featured in these books and did not write English-language books about the West. The US-born came from all over: Midwesterners from Illinois, Ohio, and Indiana, many with New England antecedents; southerners, especially Missourians and—in California and Texas—Virginians; Northerners from New York and Pennsylvania, Maine and Massachusetts. Over the decades, western-born women appeared in the literary ranks as well. But it makes little sense, I discovered, to require these authors to have settled in the West for good—this is a nation of itinerants, and women came and went to and from the West. Nor does it even make sense to insist that they have lived in, or even visited, the places they wrote about. Most women had at least touched down in the places where they set their books but a few had not.

In general terms, the West was seen to allow women to become capable, physically active, independent, honest, and forthright. Ideas of bigness and spaciousness, of freedom from convention, of physical development, contribute to a sense of the western heroine as a new kind of person. The West, with its supposed lack of class distinction, its acceptance of every person on his or her own merits, presumably allowed women without pedigrees to make something of themselves—but only if they also possessed and preserved the delicacy that is taken as foundationally female. It's crucial for women not to lose their femininity, but according to the books, they don't. Western books portray their local heroines in opposition to their overcultivated and too-often manipulative sisters from Boston or New York as the thoroughly American development of true womanhood. Finally! The new woman, like the new man, was to have her opportunity in the United States.

Among political agendas was the franchise, which built on the special public contribution western women were already making. Many western states had active suffragist movements; the first states to give women the vote were in the West (although as Ernest Lee Tuveson demonstrated in *Redeemer Nation,* the motive for enfranchising women was partly to counteract the African American vote). Suffragist Mary Osborn Douthit's 1905 *Souvenir of Western Women,* about

Oregon and Washington, canvasses diverse public activities women are engaged in (while claiming always that this or that suffragist is a wonderful mother and homemaker, thus arguing that women's public enterprises do not conflict with their private duties). Literary activity itself becomes public work. At the least, books demonstrate female abilities; at the most they enter the public arena to engage matters of western interest, showing women as engaged political beings.

Fiction being what it is, novels feature young women who may break a rule now and then but are immovably virtuous. They are seen as raising the tone and improving the morals of a wayward male population—one might say that Huck Finn's worst fears were realized; the cowboy riding into the sunset away from women had to be corralled eventually. In 1891, Fannie E. Newberry, author of Christian-themed books for girls, published *Mellicent Raymond: The Impress of a Gentlewoman,* in which a mine manager's bride transforms the moral atmosphere of a coarse Colorado town by her own genteel kindness and thereby makes it safe for business investment and tourism. The word "gentlewoman" says it all; books for adult readers made the same point in a more nuanced fashion. With little place for the "soiled doves" so familiar in men's western fiction, women's novels find important roles for older women (most of them said to be widowed) who run boarding houses, manage hotels, and carry out other types of homemaking work of a maternal character. They mentor and succor the ingénue female at the center of the story. Except for this model of relationship, there is little close female friendship in these books about women's self-reliance and competence.

* * *

Most poetry remained uncollected, and books of poetry are usually miscellanies, so that western poetry as such is not typical of women's writing. Their poetry consisted mostly of mortuary, consolation, and abstract nature lyrics, along with declamatory odes or praise for local worthies. But these odes are often about national progress, and the local worthies are often Westerners. Place-centered poems appear in books by Ina Coolbrith and Madge Morris Wagner from California; Sharlot Hall from Arizona; Irene Welch Grissom from the High Plains; Belle Cooke from the Pacific Northwest; Virginia Donaghé McClurg from Colorado; and Alice Corbin Henderson from New Mexico. In Utah, strikingly, some eight women published books of poetry with substantial regional content—Eliza Snow, Sarah Carmichael, Augusta Crocheron, Emmeline Wells, Hannah Cornaby, Hannah King, Louisa Richards, and Ruth May Fox. None of this poetry is subtle; diction, versification, and subject matter seldom rise above doggerel. It was poetry for ordinary people.

* * *

Over time, whatever "Old West" might actually have existed gave way to a less rural West, and women's western books in the twentieth century—up to the time when the Great Depression of 1929 and the dust bowl of the 1930s brought that Old West definitively to an end—reflected the changes they had struggled to bring about. In the first of Kathleen Norris's many California romances, *The Rich Mrs. Burgoyne* (1912), she was already describing the town of Santa Paloma with its "drug store quite modern enough to be facing upon Forty-second Street and Broadway, instead of the tree-shaded peace of Santa Paloma's main street. . . . On Broadway, three thousand miles away, the women who shopped were buying the same boxed powders, the same bottled toilet waters, the same patented soaps and brushes and candies that were to be found here. And in the immense grocery store nearby there were beautifully spacious departments worthy of any great city, devoted to rare fruits, and coffees and teas, and every pickle that ever came in a glass bottle, and every little spiced fish that ever came in a gay tin" (9–10). She continues, "In short, there were modern women, and rich women, in Santa Paloma, as these things unmistakably indicated. Where sixty years ago there had been but a lonely outpost on a Spanish sheep-ranch, and where thirty years after that there was only a 'general store' at a crossroads, now every luxury in the world might be had for the asking" (11).

Of course, the vanished Old West produced nostalgia; pioneers who might have been seen as obstacles to progress became objects of veneration. People begin to memorialize it. In her *Rose of the World* (1924) Norris writes that "Up and down the big state . . . went . . . the rodeos, the flower weeks, the pioneer carnivals, Indian medicine dances, blossom jubilees, the pageants and fiestas. The heritage of what was romantic and significant in the old days of the wandering tribes, of the Spanish padres and sheep ranchers, of the hoop-covered prairie wagons and the Orient with its shaking coloured lanterns and yawning paper dragons, was brought forth" (146). There's a good deal of satire in this depiction, as the community organizers search frantically for a bona fide Hispanic woman (they finally discover one in the poor house), but the point is obvious—this New West that has obliterated that Old West still needs that Old West if it is to have any identity of its own.

By the 1890s, when the census declared the frontier closed, pioneer associations had begun to collect and solicit memoirs and histories. Elderly pioneers put down their memories; the younger generation celebrated their parents' and grandparents' achievements; historians and historical novelists went to work full-bore. As the Old West became a fading memory, the New Woman—independent, town-dwelling, professionally employed, tentatively sexual—enters the scene. She turns out to exemplify the New West, to be the reason for all that pioneering, the future realized.

2

Texas and Oklahoma

Texas, the earliest western region settled by Anglos, is also where women's western books begin. Mary Austin Holley, a cousin of Stephen Austin the Texas impresario, was a widow from New England governessing in Lexington, Kentucky. She bought land in Austin's colony and wrote to publicize it in hope of selling her holdings at a profit. Her two books, both called *Notes on Texas* (1833, 1836), already display what came to be typical themes in women's western writing. First, the attractions of the country for settlement; second, a description of the traits needed for success on the social margins; third, celebration of a pioneering kinsman (rarely, kinswoman); fourth, the region's particular advantages and challenges for women; and, in 1836, the Anglo Saxon mission of taking over the territory.

The 1833 book (reissued with an introduction by Marilyn McAdams Sibley in 1985), consists of impressionistic and flowery travel letters describing Texas as a settler's dream. Texas is "adapted, beyond most lands, both to delight the senses, and enrich the pockets, of those, who are disposed to accept of its bounties" (10); her "most sanguine impressions of the natural advantages of the country, both with regard to the salubrity of the climate, the fertility of the soil, and the facility with which the lands can be brought under cultivation, were confirmed" (12). The best settler would be one whose "hopes of rising to independence in life, by honourable exertion, have been blasted by disappointment . . . who does not hanker after society, nor sigh after the vanished illusions of life; who has a fund of resources within himself, and a heart to trust in God and his own exertions . . . who is not peculiarly sensitive to petty inconveniences" (130–31). Although Holley's implied audience of honest toilers have not succeeded where they are, this is not because of an inherent character defect. Almost to the contrary, they are failing because their simple honesty unfits them for success in a complex and sophisticated society. In a place where they may start over, and so long as their expectations are in line with reality, they may bring into being a new and better society then the one they leave behind.

In 1833 she tells readers not to worry that Texas is a Mexican province, but to reject politics and attend to the business of settling. Mexico City is far away, and the government has turned over territorial development to men like Stephen Austin, an example of the "hardy and bold pioneer, braving all the dangers of a wilderness infested with hostile Indians, far out of the reach of civilized society, and all the most common comforts of civilized life" (1833: 108–9). The Texas Revolution of 1836 undercut this part of Holley's sales pitch and necessitated a new book. In 1836 she replaced the epistolary gush with a workmanlike survey of settler possibilities in Texas and introduced the theme of Anglo-Saxon militancy. "The justice and benevolence of Providence will forbid that that delightful and now civilized region should again become a howling wilderness, trod only by savages, or that it should again be desolated by the ignorance and superstition, the tyranny and anarchy, the rapine and violence of Mexican misrule. The Anglo-Saxon American race are destined to be forever the proprietors of this land of promise and fulfillment. Their laws will govern it, their learning will enlighten it, their enterprise will improve it, their flocks alone will range its boundless pastures. . . . This is inevitable" (298).

Holley now represents Mexicans as racially—inherently and inalienably—malign, at once brutal and cowardly, scheming and passionate: the stereotyped Mexican already fully realized. By "Americanizing Texas, by filling it with a population from this country who will harmonize in language, in political education, in common origin, in every thing, with their neighbors to the east and the north . . . Texas will become a great outwork on the west to protect the outlet of this western world, the mouth of the Mississippi . . . and to keep far away from the southwestern frontier—the weakest and most vulnerable in the nation—all enemies who might make Texas a door for invasion" (279). Among potential invaders are those determined to provoke what she calls "a servile war," and here Holley, a Southerner by adoption, addresses southern readers in particular and invites them to settle Texas as a slaveholding territory, not to annex it to the United States but to protect the South.

As for women, Holley appeals to the combination of feminine vanity with opportunity that becomes characteristic of western feminine portraiture. Women in Texas, she says, usually acquire a "hardihood and courage" truly "surprising in the gentle sex"; they often hunt on horseback with their husbands and camp out with them for days; they do all visiting "on horseback, and they will go fifty miles to a ball with their silk dresses . . . in their saddle-bags. Hardy, vigorous constitution, free spirits, and spontaneous gaiety are thus induced" (1836: 145). The silk dresses show that femininity and class need not be sacrificed. Women, she generalizes, "have capacity for greatness" but "require occasions to bring it out. They require, perhaps, stronger motives than men—they have stronger barriers to break through of indolence and habit—but, when roused, they are quick to discern and unshrinking to act" (146). This is the earliest articulation of the generic West's promise to women: here at last they will become the true heroines they innately are.

Holley's books are the entire output of women's western literature I've found in the 1830s. The 1840s also saw only two western books, one about Texas, a second about Texas and California. Jane Cazneau, a militantly expansionist New York journalist committed to the concept of Manifest Destiny (her biographer Linda S. Hudson argues that she actually invented the phrase), published *Texas and Her Presidents* in 1845 after she and her husband acquired Texas land, like Holley, for resale. With the US-Mexican War under way she sees US domination if not annexation of the entire continent as inevitable and desirable, and proposes eliminating both Indians and Mexicans from the territory. As far back as the Mayflower Puritans, she says, the Anglo mission was to clear the continent of Indians so the white race (her term) could establish homes. Mexicans and whites, she says, can't coexist because most Mexicans are part African and white people won't accept blacks on equal terms (15–17).

In 1852 Cazneau published *Eagle Pass; or, Life on the Border,* about the town she and her husband were establishing. With Texas now a US state, she predicts that northern Mexico will secede, opening opportunities for entrepreneurs and especially permitting the building of a railroad through to the Pacific. (The southern railroad theme is reanimated many years later in Ruiz de Burton's *The Squatter and the Don.*) She represents herself as a Lady Bountiful to escaping peons in Eagle Pass itself, finessing the antislavery argument by equating rescued peons with freed slaves. She says the Mexican-hating Comanche could be useful allies (already the Comanche are the only tribe in Texas that matters to Americans), and asks for more aid from the US government to protect the border and flex some American muscle. Amid this bellicosity, she says Texas is Edenic. Nowhere else can a "sober, sensible and industrious man" (the same type that Holley had appealed to) more quickly realize "independence and a delightful home" because "somewhere or other in its vast extent, everyone can find the features and productions that interest him most": the southern prairies—"deep alluvial for sugar, plenty of fish and game, splendid cattle, good horses"; middle Texas—"a rolling, picturesque country, pure and sparkling water sources, and a soil that will return cotton and tobacco as well as wheat and corn"; the Brazos and Colorado—"sublime and exciting" terrain where one can "hunt buffaloes and wild horses"; northwest Texas—mines; the Rio Bravo valley—sheep raising (12–13).

Emma Hart Willard, the New England pedagogue, historian, and geographer, argued in her *Last Leaves of American History* (1849) that the US government had fought the Mexican War not to expand slave power but to secure California and guarantee access to the Pacific. (Today many historians hold the same view.) She saw the war as the locally inevitable product of racial and ideological similarities between Texan settlers and those back home in the United States. New England evangelist Melinda Rankin, who felt a call to convert Mexican Catholics and tried unsuccessfully to get across the border before 1850, settled for teaching Tejana girls in Brownsville and Huntsville. Her *Texas in 1850* (1850) is a town-centered survey describing opportunities for evangelists—the first book to make towns rather than farms the end of settling. In 1875, retired to Illinois, she published *Twenty Years among the Mexicans; A Narrative of Missionary Labor,* in which she recalled her first impression of Texas's natural beauty: it was "one of the most beautiful regions I had ever before beheld. The splendid trees, the verdant plains, and great variety of wild flowers, conspired to make the scene an enchanting one. Instead of a wild and uncultivated population, I found many highly refined and intelligent people, who had but a short time previous emigrated from the Southern States to Texas" (30–31).

Augusta Evans's (later Wilson) *Inez; A Tale of the Alamo* (1855), the earliest western novel I've found, is an overwritten historical fiction centered in San Antonio, developing three love stories within the framework of a fiercely anti-Catholic attack on Mexicans. The novel ambitiously recounts events of the Alamo, Goliad, and the panicked flight of civilians from San Antonio (an exodus known as the "Runaway scrape") in advance of Santa Ana's army. It is dedicated to the "Texan Patriots, who triumphantly unfurled and waved aloft the 'banner of the lone star' who wrenched asunder the iron bands of despotic Mexico and wreathed the brow of the 'queen state' with the glorious chaplet of 'civil and religious liberty.'" The book's chief objection to Catholics is their supposed willingness to follow their priests' orders. Protestants think for themselves. Evans wants Goliad not the Alamo to signify Texan resistance because the massacre illustrates the treacherous Mexican character. "Is there one of my readers who for a moment would attach blame to the noble Fannin? The lives of his men were of far more importance to him than the renown of perishing, like Travis, in a desperate struggle. With the latter there was no alternative. . . . But honorable terms were offered Fannin" (279).

The novel nostalgically describes San Antonio as a natural paradise. "Who that has gazed on thy loveliness, oh, San Antonio, can e'er forget thee! Thine was the sweetness of nature. . . . The river wound like an azure girdle round the town; not confined by precipitous banks, but gliding along the surface, as it were, and reflecting, in its deep blue waters, the rustling tule which fringed the margin. An occasional pecan or live-oak flung a majestic shadow athwart its azure bosom, and now and then a clump of willows sighed low in the evening breeze. Far away to the north stretched a mountain range, blue in the distance; to the south, the luxuriant valley" (27–28).

In Teresa Griffin Vielé's *Following the Drum* (1858; reissued in 1984 with a foreword by Sandra J. Myres) about her two years in Texas as an army officer's wife, the author ignores army life and never mentions her husband, presenting herself simply as an observer of the Texas scene. Her observations are shaped by her sense of Anglos as a recently arrived not a settled population. Unlike Cazneau, who thought the Comanche would cheerfully ally themselves with the Anglos because they detested Mexicans, she says nothing less than their "actual extermination . . . will render many portions of the State of Texas a safe abode for white settlers" (121). The static, impoverished Mexican presence in Brownsville gives "unmistakable evidence of a vanishing people" while Anglo "red brick stores, and white frame shops and buildings of every description" bear "the marks of inevitable progress, or go-aheadativeness, otherwise called 'manifest destiny'" (104–5).

Holley described Texas frontiersmen as true instances of Cooper's Leatherstocking; Vielé calls them "the most daring, adventurous set of men in the world"; their hearts beat "true to the call of friendship"; respect for women "seems an innate principle, while daring and bravery are no second nature, but nature itself" (150). Like Willard she thinks this American type made the Texas Revolution inevitable. "It was not in the nature of things that Texas, in which the Anglo-Saxon blood now predominated, should submit to the arbitrary laws and exactions of this fickle and miserable race. The dissolution of their connexion was the natural consequence of tyranny on the one hand and manly resistance on the other" (238).

*　*　*

In the quarter-century between Vielé's and the next Texas book I found, Mary Wightman Helm's 1884 *Scraps of Early Texas History,* national attention was diverted from the West by the Civil War. But the West became a focus again in the 1870s, when the completion of the transcontinental railroad changed the pace of western settlement and more or less turned the covered wagon overlander into an object of sentimental nostalgia. Helm's book began as a series of articles, written by request in 1878 for the *Texas Clarendon News,* which published them as the "Story of an Old Pioneer." At the age of 77 she collected and expanded them into a book about her life in Texas between 1828 and 1843, correcting and augmenting other histories of Texas, particularly Thomas Pilgrim's 1875 *A Texas Scrap Book,* to which her own title obviously refers. Frequently accompanying her first husband—a surveyor and a founder of Matagorda—as he looked for other town sites (she includes his field notes in her book), she celebrates his contribution to white settlement and makes him into a paradigm of Anglo-

Saxon superiority. "Anglo-Americans are hardy and enduring beyond all other races. Endowed with an incredible and inexhaustible energy, they never turn back or yield to reverses however severe or crushing. On the other hand, the modern Mexicans are, as it were, the debris of several inferior and degraded races; American and Indian crossed and mixed, and even the old Spanish blood was mixed with the Moorish and demoralized by a long course of indolence and political corruption; both physically and mentally they are the very antithesis of the Anglo-Americans" (34).

She recalls the Runaway Scrape: "Had our enemy been a civilized nation, no one would have thought of leaving their homes, for none had any doubt about the final issue. Still to put ourselves in their power was certain martyrdom. Hence the whole country moved at once in as great haste as did the Israelites from Egypt. All prepared, without animals enough to carry provisions and people. The sick and the young and helpless found graves all along the way; they had left comfortable homes surrounded by luxury and abundance" (38). Helm portrays herself as the community's founding mother calmly rising to her obligations during these panicked days, helping those who had neglected to bring money, food, or clothing. That she and her husband left Texas because of his health, and that with her second marriage she had become a resident of Indiana, are matters she doesn't develop.

In 1881, when she was 63, Mary A. Maverick (who had come to Texas from South Carolina with her husband in 1836) began to shape her diaries and letters into a memoir. In her case the usually dubious claim that a book was intended only for immediate family seems convincing, because *Memoirs* appeared in 1895 in just six copies (all now lost). Her son George, who had helped her arrange the materials, also appended documents demonstrating that his father, contrary to popular belief, had never re-branded cattle, branded motherless calves, or even been a serious rancher. A granddaughter, Rena Maverick Green, edited and republished the book for limited general circulation in 1921, apparently with little change from George's text, which in turn—according to Maverick biographer Paula Mitchell Marks—had respected his mother's wording if not her structure. This, then, is a family-produced family memoir mainly authored by Mary Maverick, who says her sources include "family tradition, from letters written contemporaneously, occasionally from books of authority for dates, and I have not failed to consult with many of the survivors of those early days. I have in some instances relied on my memory, but not often" (preface, n.p.).

The account up to 1859 is vividly detailed, describing a socially gendered and leisurely life in San Antonio. "During this summer, the American ladies led a lazy life of ease. We had plenty of books, including novels, we were all young, healthy and happy and were content with each others' society. We fell into the fashion of the climate, dined at twelve, then followed a siesta, (nap) until three, when we took a cup of coffee and a bath. . . . Between two trees in a beautiful shade, we went in a crowd each afternoon at about four o-clock and took the children and nurses and a nice lunch which we enjoyed after the bath. There we had a grand good time, swimming and laughing, and making all the noise we pleased. The children were bathed and after all were dressed, we spread our lunch and enjoyed it immensely" (50–52). There are compelling descriptions of hostilities against the Comanche in San Antonio in 1840, and a poignant narrative of the deaths of two daughters to disease after they returned to the city after five years in Matagorda. "Even now, in 1880, after thirty-two years, I cannot dwell on that terrible bereavement," she writes of the first loss (99); her husband "was ever afterwards a changed man" (100). Disease was always the great killer of migrating Westerners.

Martha E Whitten's 1886 poetic miscellany, *Texas Garlands* (the only volume of poetry I found from Texas), contains mostly mortuary and consolation verse. Among a small number of longer poems on historical or topographical subjects, an apostrophe to the city of Austin contrasts "thy sublime career, / Thy present glory with thy rude frontier," (12); an 1876 New Year's poem trolling for settlers praises "our lovely State! / In vast resources great; / Mark her rich varied soil / Rewarding honest toil; / Her mines of hidden ore . . . / Her climate passing mild . . . Mark well her uncleft sod / Where man has scarcely trod. / Her million acres broad / That well might food afford. . . . / Welcome to Texas! Lo, she stands / Fitting compeer of older lands!" (120–21). A poem on San Jacinto recalls "deeds of valor" by those "who once for our lovely Texas trusty weapons firmly drew" (351); and a melodramatically sentimental anti-Indian poem called "A Touching Incident of Indian Cruelty in Texas" narrates the massacre of a settler family and demonizes the Indians. "The fiends a moment view their bloody work, / Then quick each scalp from off their victims jerk; / Still warm and dripping with their human gore" (168). Neighbors, who massacre the Indians in turn and find the one abandoned survivor, a baby, are exonerated because they understand that "many homes where Texans brave have toiled / Have been laid waste, by ruthless Red Men spoiled" (170).

English-born Amelia Barr, daughter of a Methodist minister and wife of a Scottish businessman, lived in Austin and Galveston. Her husband and a son both died in Galveston during the 1867 yellow fever epidemic. Moving to New York with her surviving daughters, she became a successful author of popular historical novels. Her two Texas novels are *The Hallam Succession* (1884) and *Remember the Alamo* (1888). The first follows the English Hallam family for fifty years, alternating between Yorkshire and Texas, linking present-day Texans with an imagined English racial and high-class past: "Yorkshire is the epitome of England. . . . The men are sturdy, shrewd and stalwart . . . a handsome race, the finest specimens extant of the pure Anglo-Saxon, and they still preserve the imposing stature and the bright blonde characteristics of the race" (3). The piously Methodist novel interprets the Texas Revolution in standard terms as a conflict between predatory Catholic priests who encourage docile obedience and noble, manly, independent-thinking Protestants of English heritage. The novel ends in the beautiful Texas countryside where the English family has made a home "with doors and windows standing open, and deep piazzas on every side," with magnolia and pecan trees, green turf, a multitude of flowers, and "the constant stir of happy servants" (286). Those happy servants are, of course, slaves; as her later memoir discloses, she supported slavery. In line with the vision of a physically emancipated woman appropriate for the outdoors western man, Barr has an English visitor, Elizabeth, take wonderful horseback rides on the prairies, appreciating the possibility "of a real, fresh, natural life"; she sees "with her own eyes, and with a kind of wonder, the men who had dared to be free, and to found a republic of free men in the face of nine million Mexicans—men of iron wills, who under rude felt hats had the finest heads, and under buckskin vests the warmest hearts" (287).

Remember the Alamo opens with a panorama of San Antonio's exotic and multiethnic beauty near the end of its romantic era. But in the colorful crowd, "yet by no means of it," are "small groups of Americans; watchful, silent, armed to the teeth" (5–6), frontiersmen who represent the Texan future. "The royalty of their carriage, the authority in their faces, gave dignity even to their deerskin clothing. Its primitive character was its distinction, and the wearers looked like the demi-gods of the heroic stage of history" (230–31). The family story concerns the Worths, with a Spanish Castilian mother, a New England physician father, and two daughters. One—cool but intense—represents the Anglo strain; the other—flamboyant but shallow—the Hispanic. A villainous priest almost gets possession of the family property through the mother's susceptibility (it's her land—Worth is only one of many Anglo men in women's western literature to marry Hispanics who are invariably pure Castilian). Catholicism doesn't cause the Revolution; it's the Mexican decree that no Texan civilian can carry arms. The good doctor, though too old for combat and temperamentally a pacifist, sides with the revolutionaries, saying heatedly that "a large proportion of the colonists depend on their rifles for their daily food. All of them know that they must defend their own homes from the Comanche, or see them perish. Now, do you imagine that Americans will obey any such order? By all the great men of seventeen seventy-five, if they did, I would go over to the Mexicans and help them to wipe the degenerate cowards out of existence!" (49–50).

The bicultural Worth family persists—one daughter marries a Tejano, the other an Anglo—and is tolerated under the Anglo umbrella. After the war Americans come "by hundreds and by thousands; and those Mexicans who could not make up their minds to become Texans, and to assimilate with the new elements sure to predominate, were quietly breaking up their homes and transferring their interests across the Rio Grande. They were not missed, even for a day. Some American was ready to step into their place, and the pushing, progressive spirit of the race was soon evident in the hearty way with which they set to work, not only to repair what war had destroyed, but to inaugurate those movements which are always among their first necessities. Ministers, physicians, teachers, mechanics of all kinds, were soon at work; churches were built, Bibles were publicly sold, or given away; schools were advertised; the city was changing its tone" (408–09).

In 1913, when she was 82, Barr published *All the Days of My Life*, a memoir asserting that even before she and her husband moved to Texas in 1856, the "gallant, stirring story" of San Jacinto had "made a wonderful impression on me, and I thought how grand it would be to live among men who at least once in their lives scorned the mean god Mammon, and, for the faith of their fathers, and the civil liberty without which life was of no value, offered themselves willingly for their God and their country" (180–81). Her first impressions of Texas were as of "a new world"; "the flowery prairie rolled away magnificently to the far-off horizon, here and there jumping into hills, over which marched myriads of red cattle. Masses of wild honeysuckle scented the air for miles and miles, and a fresh odor of earth and clover, mixed with the perfume of wild flowers, was the joy we breathed. But, best of all was the clear, sweet atmosphere. . . . It lives in my memory green and sweet as the fields of Paradise, with the fresh wild winds gurgling melodiously through all its lovely spaces" (182–83).

In view of the yellow fever epidemic that destroyed her family, this memory is strange, as is her romantic evocation of Austin: "Often, when I am heart and brain weary . . . I smell the China trees and the pine. I hear the fluting of the wind, and the tinkling of guitars. I see the white-robed girls waltzing in the moonshine down the broad sidewalks of the avenue, and the men, some in full evening dress, and others in all kinds of picturesque frontier fashion, strolling leisurely down its royally wide highway" (212). Barr also praises the "real Texan woman" as "brave and resourceful, especially when her environment was anxious and dangerous . . . nearly without exception fine riders and crack shots, and quite able, when the men of the household were away, to manage their ranches or plantations, and keep such faithful guard over their families and household, that I never once in ten years, heard of any Indian, or other tragedy occurring" (211).

Barr complained that on account of the Civil War, she had to do "all the housework that the negroes ought to do" (249). "The daily record of my life at this time is chiefly remarkable for the wonderful way in which it represents men of all ages, and all sorts and conditions taking hold of the heavy housework, thrown upon the hands of the women by the refusal of negroes to work" (253). But she sees states' rights not slavery as the reason Texas joined the Confederacy, because, actually, any slave who wanted to escape could simply take the short, easy journey to the Rio Grande, where he "was sure to be succored and helped by every party of Indians or Mexicans he met. Arriving at the river, he had only to walk across some one of its shallow fords, and touch land on the other side a free man" (218–19).

The best-known Texas writer of her generation was Mary E. Moore Davis, who published as M. E. M. Davis and, with her newspaper-editor husband, eventually left Texas for New Orleans. In *Under the Man-Fig* (1895, reissued with an afterword by Sylvia Ann Grider in 2000) the protagonist has to fend for herself when her father has a stroke; it is set in a fictional town on the Brazos called Thornham but based, according to Grider, on Columbia, Texas. The region is made southern through its numerous minor African American characters—some refusing to be emancipated and others proudly celebrating Emancipation Day—as well as its depictions of yellow fever, sugar cane, floods, returning veterans, "ragged, forlorn, footsore, hungry," and widows: "black-robed women who stole forth to gaze yearningly on the faces of those who came,—asked a few low-voiced questions, and fled weeping back to their lonely chambers" (71). I'll discuss other Davis books, in which Texas is western not southern, later in this chapter.

Elizabeth Brooks's 1896 *Prominent Women of Texas,* a historical-biographical compilation, narrates the state's progress in terms of the increasing influence of women in public affairs. Except for a few Jewish philanthropists among her 153 women, all are of English or Scottish ancestry: political and military wives, frontier women, writers, artists, singers, philanthropists, social leaders. Mrs. Richard King, of the King Ranch, has her own chapter as "The Uncrowned Queen of the West." The words "west" and "western" recur often enough throughout the book to leave no doubt that Brooks's Texas is western. The bravery and endurance of women under Indian threats and attacks gets a chapter, preceded by a critique of humanitarian Indian policy: "The massacres in which the parents of these little ones were martyred were perpetrated by the very Indians who were fed, blanketed and armed by the United States Government, and given homes protected by United States troops in the Indian reservation territory of a paternal government, which in its sentimentality over its 'poor Indian' citizens, neglected its duties to its own blood and race" (69).

Because philanthropists are central to her vision of women's responsibility, Brooks refers to "multitudes" of poor people in Texas. As will often be seen in women's western writing, economic failure in the West is as common as success, notwithstanding real estate hype. Brooks is especially pleased by Mrs. Rice's gift of money to retrain workers sidelined by technological advance: "The progress of discovery and invention has created new industries, and supplanted old ones, and, in so doing, it has created a demand for skilled labor and made vacant many of the places of the unskilled. The consequence of this revolution in the laboring world has been to relegate to idleness and want, multitudes of strong, willing and intelligent workers. The wise and seasonable inspiration of Mrs. Rice proposes a remedy for the evil. Free of cost, the manual laborer may acquire technical training and thus be fitted for his new condition in life. Unspeakable calamities will be averted, and honors untold will crown the work of a public benefactress" (183).

All three African American women who published Texas books identified it as southern, although for different reasons. Josie Briggs Hall's *Hall's Moral and Mental Capsule for the Economic and Domestic Life of the Negro, as a Solution of the Race Problem* (1905), was written under the influence of the "talented tenth" theory. A compound of moralistic essays, poetry, and biographies, its many photographs and drawings of prominent black Texans show what the race can achieve and installs a dignified African American presence in Texas. In 1913, Maud Cuney-Hare published a celebratory biography of her father, *Norris Wright Cuney: A Tribune of the Black People.* (The book was reissued with an introduction by Tera W. Hunter in 1995.) Cuney, who died in 1898, had been the most influential African American statesman in Texas; writing after the Republican Party loss in 1912, Cuney-Hare attributes that defeat to the split between "Lily Whites" and those open to African American political participation. She thinks the Lily Whites—to their discredit—are more interested in southern than national affiliation: "The fight in favor of southern prejudice could not be won as long as a Negro with his following of black voters stood at the head of the party in Texas" (92). And yet, thankfully, Texas is not wholly southern; emancipating it from southern ties is the best recipe for future progress: "It is not necessary for me to remind you of the fact that Louisiana, South Carolina, old Virginia, Alabama, Florida, Georgia and Arkansas are dominated to-day by an oligarchy just as relentless as it was before the late war. We in Texas, outside of a few counties, are relieved of that" (135).

Cuney-Hare praises her father's contributions to Galveston as philanthropist, working class organizer, and example. She traces her lineage from Col. Philip Cuney, a white man who came to Texas in 1842, and her slave grandmother "who bore him eight children and whom he eventually set free. There were extensive areas of cotton under cultivation, while for miles stretched prairies full of grazing herds of buffalo, and woods through which roamed wandering Indian tribes. . . . Here the Cuney clan became part of that great drama by which Texas was made a slave empire and annexed to the United States by the Mexican War" (3). Less politically, Cuney-Hare recalls Galveston as "the garden spot of Texas. For thirty miles the Gulf of Mexico washed the island. The deep white sand girded about by the waves was packed hard and firm. Breezes fresh from the Gulf mingled with odors of oleander, roses, and cape jasmine from the city gardens. The great surf broke upon the beach, fringing the shore with foam. The breakers of deep blue, growing in strength as they neared the shore—high, one above the other, the murmur increasing into a roar, lashed and laved the glistening sands with that endless and fascinating sound of the sea for which an exiled native ever yearns. To-day one must drive far out from the city to see the beach as father saw it forty years ago" (8–9).

Finally, Bernice Love Wiggins's self-published *Tuneful Tales* (1925—a 2002 reissue was edited by Maceo C. Dailey Jr. and Ruthe Winegarten Wiggins.) contains 102 mainly dialect poems describing black people in folkloric terms, with the church central to social as well as religious life. Non-dialect poems of love and piety differentiate the poet from her rustic subjects, and Texas is a remote presence rather than a central character, perhaps appropriate for a highly lococentric population. Only two poems name the Brazos scene, while several passionate antilynching poems, not in dialect, make Texas a southern state.

In 1917 Adina De Zavala, whose grandfather Lorenzo de Zavala had helped write the Texas Republic's constitution and had served for a few months as its vice president, published *History and Legends of the Alamo and Other Missions in and around San Antonio.* (The book was reissued, edited and with an introduction by Richard Flores, in 1996.) The stories bring together history, fiction, and polemic; they want to define Tejanos as Texans not Mexicans, to celebrate a renowned kinsman, and to advocate preserving the Alamo. Her grandfather, a Texan patriot who "openly advocated the separation of Texas from Mexico before many would dare to even think of it" (196), "presents one of the most spotless and exalted characters of modern times, and his memory should be cherished by the children of Texas as one of the purest patriots of this or any other age" (207). As a Texan not Mexican, she says: "The greatest heritage of the children of Texas and America is the noble example of its great men. Let us not forget their deathless deeds. For the moment we begin to ignore the sublime virtues exemplified by the noble souls of our race, our degeneration has begun. Let us save our landmarks and sacred battlefields and buildings as reminders and monuments. No monument that could be erected by the hands of man to the memory of the heroes could be as great or as sacred as the Alamo itself, wherein we are brought face to face with the history and scenes from the lives of the men who made the Alamo immortal" (36). De Zavala's work for the Texas missions is also a function of her Texas chauvinism: "The people of California stress the wonderful labors and long journeys on foot of Padre Junipero Serra, but Texas could perhaps, prove far more wonderful deeds and labors accomplished by Padre Margil if they were more familiar with his life" (144).

* * *

In two novels published before she gave up literature to manage her family's considerable assets, Clara Driscoll portrayed East Texas as western through its missions and its ranches. She dedicates *The Girl of La Gloria* (1905) to her father and the successful ranchmen he represents, defending them against what by now were typical confusions of ranchmen with cowboys and conflation of both with outlaws. These men "know every inch of the ground they own. Night after night of their youth has been spent sleeping in the open, or riding hour after hour across lonely plains on the lookout for cattle thieves. Filled with energy, endurance, honesty that is proverbial, a fearlessness that knows no equal, they have left and will leave records that shall endure forever; battling, not only against evil and wrong-doing; but the law itself, the corruption and injustice of which had forced the cattle-men to become a law unto themselves. It is to these men that the peace and prosperity to-day of the Southwest is due. . . . Those who know the effete East only, cannot understand the quick, deep-seated love that the plainsman born and bred on its mothering fields—not the aliens who have come from the North and settled on its virgin soil—feels for the prairie" (114–15).

The Girl of La Gloria places a melodramatic, tragic romance between an Anglo Easterner (Randor Walton) and a Mexican-Irish woman (Ilaria Benton) in a historical and commercial context. Ilaria dies when the horse she's daringly riding at midnight in order to save Walton's life stumbles and falls. The affinity of western women for horses, the identification of western femininity with athletic skill on horseback, had already emerged in Mary Austin Holley's work, and is seen repeatedly in western women's writing. Because Ilaria has signed her ranch rights over to Walton, he gets moral credit for having truly loved her plus a big financial payoff, which turns the story into a gendered version of the Anglo takeover of Mexican Texas, according to which a feminized and old-fashioned Mexico willingly cedes her property to an up-to-date masculine invader.

But in becoming modern, the West has begun to lose its western essence; a ranch foreman tells Walton that the "'real Wild West' has ceased to exist, except in shows"; he points to "polled Angus stock" and "a small herd of sleek Herefords" to show what has transformed the country. "We had to reform in spite of ourselves. . . . The Longhorn, like the 'bad man,' has been driven from his native heath—shoved out of the ring, by breeding. . . . We used to kill 'em like sheep for the price of the hides and tallow. Now, they've passed away, like the unwashed ranchman of old" (69).

Driscoll's *In the Shadow of the Alamo, and Other Texas Tales* (1906) represents the past, set at various Texas missions, as a series of romantic encounters in exotic settings. The lead (and longest) story is "The Custodian of the Alamo," which publicizes the work of the Daughters of the Republic of Texas in preserving the Alamo: "Could any society have a more worthy, more beneficial object, than that of keeping alive in a country its patriotic enthusiasm, which, after all, is the keynote to a nation's greatness? By the honoring of a glorious past we strengthen our present, and by the care of our eloquent but voiceless monuments we are preparing a noble inspiration for our future (25)."

In these later decades the westernizing of East Texas became a dominant motive in fiction. Harriet C. Morse's amateurish *A Cowboy Cavalier* (1908) involves a New York City woman visiting Texas who falls in love with a rancher and loses interest in urban high life: "She wanted to be on the back of a horse, with the wind blowing through her hair. . . . She longed to hear a burst of hearty, uproarious laughter instead of a conventional titter" (264). Annie Fellows Johnston, whose "Little Colonel" Kentucky books were hugely popular with girls, set *Mary Ware in Texas* (1910) partly in San Antonio and partly in the fictional Bauer (probably New Braunfels). A family in search of health for the oldest son encounters hordes of tourists in San Antonio also there for health reasons, and all looking for the Alamo, "the place where Travis and Davy Crocket and Bowie put up such a desperate fight," as interesting to tourists as "Bunker Hill or Plymouth Rock" (28); "here, for ten days, took place the most memorable, thrilling, tragic, and bloody siege in American history. One hundred and seventy-nine indomitable American frontier riflemen against an army" (31). Bauer, a high, dry hill town, represents its western present; the sheriff's daughter rides around with "a cartridge belt around her waist and a six-shooter in her holster! That's the wild West for you" (59).

Eleanor Porter's 1913 *Six-Star Ranch* has a didactic Pollyanna plot, appropriate for the creator of that series, where a club of five New Hampshire schoolgirls (the Happy Hexagons) summer at the ranch of a Texas classmate and do many good deeds there. The most important of these is to reunite a runaway New England cowboy with his mother. Cowboys are young, respectful, and naive; they and horses are a composite western symbol. As the girls find out when they read Texas history to prepare for their visit (and their knowledge is passed on to the reader), the Alamo is the "Bunker Hill of Texas" (212).

* * *

Textbooks by Texas women made it a western place. First in the field was Anna J. Hardwicke Pennybacker's 1888 *New History of Texas*. Originally written for the early grades, frequently reissued and expanded with extensive footnotes, appendixes, and discussion questions, it became a text for students at every level, including teacher trainees, and remained in print well into the twentieth century. Pennybacker's two main events for early Texas are Austin's settlement and the Alamo. Austin's people "bravely began the work of changing Texas from a wilderness to the grand 'Lone Star' State of our Union" (66), bringing in Americans who were "home-seekers, who came to live and to die in the land of their adoption" (81). The names of the Alamo heroes—Travis, Bowie, Crockett, and Bonham—will "live for centuries" (135). Pennybacker solidified all manner of historical clichés for young people by differentiating degraded Mexicans from elegant Castilians and praising patient Spanish friars for attempting to transform wild Indians into Christian laborers.

Against their will, but for their own good, Indians were "recruited" by the padres to "irrigate the land for miles about the mission, to till the soil until the country smiled like a garden, and to erect the great buildings which are still the pride of every Texan's heart" (16). Yes, she grants in a late footnote, "It may seem very cruel to the young student, when he reads how the Indians were driven from place to place, and hunted down like beasts, but he must remember the provocation his Texan ancestors had. In those dark days no mother on our broad Western prairies ever rocked her babe to sleep at eventide without the fear that the morning would find it torn from her arms and murdered by the red men, who listened to no entreaty, whose hearts knew no such feeling as pity" (216). As always, threats to the polity are conveyed as threats to women and children—to the domestic core of the nation.

M. E. M. Davis's school history, *Under Six Flags: the Story of Texas* (1897—also published as *Texas Under Six Flags*) is mainly military, written with novelistic flair and dash. The Texas Ranger not the Alamo defender now stands for Texas, an innovation that emphasizes the western character of the state through horsemanship. The Ranger's memory "will live forever in song and story, with the brave, the generous, and the noble of all times. . . . Mounted upon a swift horse, with a lariat (rope) coiled about the high pommel of his saddle and a blanket strapped behind him; with his long rifle resting in the hollow of his arm, and the bridle held loosely in his hand; erect and graceful, the brim of his slouch hat hiding the sparkle of his keen eyes,—the Texas ranger is a striking and picturesque figure. But he is more than that. For fifty years and more he has been the terror of Indian and intruding Mexican" (143–44). One notes, of course, how the once-indigenous Mexican is now an intruder. Across the Southwest—Texas, New Mexico, Arizona, and southern California—border clashes across the decades would only intensify the need to interpret Mexicans as, literally, outsiders with sinister intentions where the US was concerned.

Katie Litty Daffan, a locally well-known writer (I haven't been able to read her 1911 collection of poetry, her 1908 memorial to her father, and her 1911 novel, *The Woman of Pine Springs Road*), was a teacher, journalist, and politically active clubwoman whose *Texas Hero Stories* (1908, 1912) followed the mode of celebratory patriotism. It was adopted by the Texas school system. "It has been my purpose in the preparation of these stories to create within the minds of the children a love for our great characters and to stimulate a desire to study carefully and thoughtfully the wonderful history of our State. . . . May the children of Texas become loyal, devoted citizens. May each do his part in keeping bright and ever brighter our Lone Star, as it guides, from every portion of the world, those who seek peaceful, happy homes with a people born of free opinion, free conviction, and free citizenship. Out of these precious, priceless sources has emanated our State, a result of the will of God and the noblest work of man" (5).

Again the Texas hero is embodied in the Ranger: "Our hearts thrill with gratitude when we remember the dangerous rides and raids of our Texas rangers over
the sand and sage of the border, and their personal courage, endurance, their
steady nerve, their energy and in many instances, their great sacrifice. . . . But
for the protection of the rangers who went ahead of the settler, communities and
neighborhoods would have been helpless against the outlaws which visited all
portions of the border" (160). This is a rare reference to western outlawry, but
Daffan makes clear that Indians are even worse; Comanche and Kiowa "were
wild, swift riders, and they would mount their ponies and fly across the prairies
at a moment's notice, attacking villages, and laying waste the country generally.
They loved to kill, the sight of blood was good to their savage hearts, and they
would steal anything" (24). Anglos win out because "quick, personal courage
can get the best of an Indian, and in the presence of this kind of courage the
Indian runs away just as fast as he can, never looking back" (26).

More homage to the Texas Ranger appears in *Taming the Big Bend: A History
of the Extreme Western Portion of Texas from Fort Clark to El Paso* (1926). The
author, Alice Dolan Shipman, was a local historian and daughter of cattleman
and Texas Ranger Pat Dolan, whose biography forms part of the book—another
family hagiography. The earliest Anglo settlers in this part of the state incarnate
a Western ideal of manhood: "that none should be posers, that life should be
unaffected, democratic, that a man's past should count for nothing. This was
a new land. If a newcomer was the son of a titled father, he did not parade the
fact. . . . If a man's past had been a bit too colorful, that was overlooked. . . .
Probably the westerners were a bit rough from society's viewpoint, but those
who are capable of judging true values will appreciate their magnificent souls.
To those whose ideal is of form, scale, and glitter, the westerner, like the West,
will have no appeal" (vi).

Shipman explains that whites settled the Big Bend area to raise cattle to supply the troops, who are there to protect the settlers—a round-robin of motives
until the railroads change history, cleaving the Old West from the New. "The
coming of the 'iron horses' in 1882 heralded the sunrise of the cattle industry
in the land west of the Pecos. . . . The Texas Rangers came as guards during the
building of the two railroads. . . . The Indians were gone, the soil was virgin, the
range was open, awaiting the prospective hordes of settlers. From 1882 to 1885
the settlers rapidly filed in and took up the various watering places" (55). The
book amalgamates Wild West imagery in its anecdotes of outlaws, Indian fights,
Mexican bandits, bringing in an occasional doughty heroine like Alice Stillwell
Henderson around whom "anecdotes and legends are bound to be woven; yet
the real story of her career needs no embellishment. Adventure and desperate
encounters came to her as a part of her daily life" (103). Once "a bullet from one
of the Mexicans' guns clipped Mrs. Henderson's chin strap. She was wearing a

big Mexican sombrero. With her usual calm she stopped to get her hat" (104). The whole point of this book is in its title; the Big Bend has been tamed, which means that the Old West needs historians to memorialize it. "Today, in Marfa and Alpine, luncheons, dinner parties, receptions, bridge clubs, federated literary club meetings, swimming parties, and dances are much the same as in any other town. Though we still have our old time barbecue and rodeo about once a year, the real 'Old West' is only a memory" (170).

Girl Captives of the Cheyennes (1927), in which Grace E. Meredith writes her aunt's story in the first person as the aunt might narrate it (and as she had, many times, the author says), is the only captivity narrative from Texas, written down some fifty years after the events it describes. (In fact, captivity narratives do not seem to be a western woman's specialty.) It's the story of Catherine German, one of four sisters captured in a Cheyenne attack when her family, en route to Colorado in 1874 in a covered wagon, wandered unaware into what came to be called the Red River War. The parents and brother were killed; the girls were divided among families. Recognizing that her captors were poor, starving, and on the run, Catherine is not anti-Indian. She refers to her Indian mother and Indian father and describes Indian life with an open mind. The girls are held for ransom and well-treated, and brought out of captivity six months later by Nelson Miles, to whom the book is dedicated. Here, uniquely, the frontier army not Alamo defenders or Texas Rangers appears as the protectors of Texas.

In 1927 Mattie Austin Hatcher, archivist at the University of Texas, published a scholarly study, *The Opening of Texas to Foreign Settlement, 1801–1821*. She argues that the Spanish unintentionally laid the groundwork for the American invasion when they opened the territory for commercial development and invited the adjacent population to settle it. They prepared "an ideal soil for the planting of Austin's colony of nominal Spanish vassals, but, in reality, of true liberty-loving, home-seeking American frontiersmen who—due largely to the triumph of the movement for independence—were to change the whole history of Texas" (9).

* * *

M. E. M. Davis's short story collection—*An Elephant's Track, and Other Stories* in 1897—and a second Texas novel, *The Wire-Cutters* (1899), are both set in a Texas that is distinctly Western. *An Elephant's Track* contains recognizably local color stories about poor people and their limited lives. In the title story, a Baptist family goes to town one Sunday to see a circus, fretting whether it's a sin to do so; the husband, suckered into a shell game, loses the ticket money so they never make it to the circus after all. "The Groveling of Jinny Trimble" resembles Mary Wilkins Freeman's "The Revolt of Mother": a ne'er-do-well husband takes off, his wife does all the work, he gets in trouble when he returns, they reconcile. "A Snipe-Hunt" features practical joking and West Texas manners.

The Wire-Cutters, set in west-central Texas with its arid climate and corresponding terrain, centers on the so-called fence-cutting wars of 1883, a local example of a kind of violence endemic in the West after the federal government sold previously open range to owners who then fenced it. The narrator says the reckless "disregard both of possible ownership and of propriety" in these actions "excited profound indignation. In some quarters the public roads and familiar byways were closed up; many strong freeholds, belonging to the poorer men, were fenced in; even larger places were practically barred from communication with the common highways. But worst of all, the water supply, scarce at all times in this region, was in many instances cut off; springs, ponds, and water-holes were ringed about with the formidable wire," killing thousands of cattle as a result. "The feeling everywhere inborn in man, that water belong to God, and therefore to all his creatures, was heightened among old frontiersmen by the fact that from the day when the redskin roamed the prairies and the hardy pioneer disputed the ground with him inch by inch, these springs and waterways had been free alike to man and beast" (94–95).

The genteel protagonist, Leroy (Roy) Hilliard, from South Carolina, refuses to participate in night-time illegal fence-cutting operations, although—a man of principle—he openly cuts an illegally erected fence in broad daylight. Standing his ground against extremism from both sides, he is the sort of man Texas needs and, at the end, he prevails in love and war, winning the girl away from the southern villain and getting himself elected to Congress. As though the South produces villains and melodrama, while the West produces heroes and realism, Davis's melodrama involves a nefarious half-brother true to his South Carolina upbringing, while the hero's Texas life is described in terms compatible with literary realism. Roy has left South Carolina on the strength of an advertisement for a ranch, which turns out to be abandoned, rundown, unproductive. Unhampered by class pretensions, he turns the place around, toiling side by side with his two hired Mexican laborers. His evil half-brother is a southern remnant, out of place in Texas.

Kate Alma Orgain's *A Waif from Texas* (1901) contains twenty-two local color stories and sketches, some historical—there's the Civil War, the faithful slave, the great drought years of 1885 and 1886, but no Alamo or Texas Revolution, no Mexicans. The focus is on female endurance and extreme poverty—a signal here as elsewhere in western women's books that the promised land might after all be a scam. The "waif" is the book itself; subtitled "Will you let me in?" it asks the readers' indulgence for these Texas fictions, in which the men drink, commit suicide, or simply decline, while the women keep at it, as is seen in one title: "The Woman with the Hoe—in Texas." These steadfast women are, in reality, settling Texas. Orgain speaks to the cowboy myth—real cowboys are only superficially "roughs and toughs" and are in fact, "your boys, and my boys, many of them from the best families; boys who have given down physically in the confinement of school or business, and must get out into the open air, the life-giving exercise of the prairies of Texas. Or they are boys whose vigor and healthy bodies engender that restless activity which must vent itself, but which afterwards settles and they become our doctors and lawyers, our leaders. They are gentlemanly boys, boys who may drop for a time into the rough life by which they find themselves surrounded, but who take up again the gentleness of home training, as easily as they regain their city complexion and stylish clothing" (121).

Alice MacGowan spent some time in Texas; with her sister, Grace MacGowan Cooke (who hadn't), she collaborated on many popular novels, publishing some under their joint names, some under one or the other of their names, and some (*Wild Apples, The Straight Road*) anonymously. The jointly published *Last Word* (1902) begins and ends in West Texas, contrasting the open plains with the crowded city where the heroine goes to make her way as a journalist, and to which she plans to return at the end after a stint of rest and recreation back in Texas with the friendly cowboys of her youth. Another collaborative novel, *Aunt Huldah: Proprietor of the Wagon-Tire House and Genial Philosopher of the Cattle Country* (1904, second edition 1907), sentimentally evokes the 1880s in West Texas, offering a pleasant view of cowboys and a strong depiction of the widow who mothers the whole town. Huldah Sarvice runs a boarding house and hotel in the town of Blowout, and also takes in orphaned children. "In the remote frontier communities of that day—it was in the early eighties—no provision was made for children orphaned by death or desertion. These are so few in proportion to the population, that some ranchman's wife is usually found willing to take care of them. But to Aunt Huldah, keeping always some sort of stopping-place known as the Wagon-Tire House, wherever she set up her belongings, such children naturally came" (3).

Typical western literature is characterized and dismissed in *Aunt Huldah* via the dime novel, which deals with bad men and entices young boys into the bad life. "The whole story of Huldah Sarvice and her life in the cattle country of the West is a plea for the better understanding of a little understood, and now vanishing, class. . . . The literary material drawn from our Western cattle country has heretofore concerned itself almost wholly with the strenuous aspect of that life. But reflection must show that where there are men and women, birth and death, the cooking and the eating of three meals in each twenty-four hours, the resigning of the body to that glimpse of Nirvana which we call sleep, the rising from it to greet a new day and a new round of petty happenings, there must be much of the simple domestic life common to all mankind. . . . As for Huldah—and many another like her—the pastoral West builds no monuments as yet; and it is hoped that this account of her good works may in some measure fill the lack" (preface, n.p.). Clearly, popular western literature prefers male histrionics to women's quiet tenacity, and the job of women writers is to correct this situation.

Across the book's narrative span, West Texas changes: "Blowout was on a boom. The railroad from above was coming through, and Blowout was to be a city with that mysterious and rather disconcerting abruptness with which tiny western villages do become cities in these circumstances" (150). At the end, Blowout is literally Blowout no more. "Within a year, the name was felt to be out of harmony with its present aims and destiny. A mass-meeting of its citizens renamed it; but not in this chronicle will be set down what "ville" or "burg" they pitched upon as most expressive of the amended and—may one say, the expurgated?—aims of the town" (308–9).

In Alice MacGowan's *A Girl of the Plains Country* (1924), little Hildegarde grows up on a ranch in the Texas panhandle. When her father dies soon after the already motherless family arrives, she becomes the informal ward of the ranch manager, developing into a genteel yet fearless, honest, and direct woman. She heroically rides an almost unbroken horse to the next ranch (many miles away) to bring help before rustlers can make off with cattle; the beauty of this particular kind of landscape is evoked with considerable skill. There are descriptions of cowboys carrying out their daily chores, and enduring the day-to-day hardship of ranch life. The huge ranch could graze many thousand head of cattle on it, but the money isn't there—a dilemma resolved only when a railroad company develops a station on a spur of the ranch.

*   *   *

Changes in literary tone and temper after the First World War involved such technical innovations as focalized narration and stream of consciousness, and such historical innovations as an emphasis on female psychology, a new appreciation of women's angle of perception along with the recognition that the war had permanently changed their lives. From this amalgam come the female romances of the 1920s across the West, wherein modern women confront problems of identity and achievement. Chatty and moralistic, they are not at all modernist in technique, but they do engage with what they see as a modern world. Dorothy Scarborough's east Texas romance, *In the Land of Cotton* (1923), features automobiles, coeds, airplanes, and the USDA. The book follows two children into adulthood, one the daughter of a plantation owner and the other the son of a sharecropper. Cotton shapes and distorts human life, and is itself randomly controlled by drought, flood, insects, and the world economy. This part of the state, and by implication the whole of it, is southern—sometimes the book says "Texas and the South," sometimes "the South" but not once "the West."

Another novel about modern East Texas is Ruth Cross's *The Golden Cocoon* (1924), the first and most successful book she published over a long career. Molly, its poor Texas heroine of Irish background, works hard, gets a scholarship to the University of Texas and marries the governor. His life is threatened by her former boyfriend (it's common in female romance for the heroine to be pursued by a monomaniacal suitor); to protect him she fakes her death and leaves town, becoming a successful New York City playwright before returning. Although Texas seems to be a place to get away from, Molly says she has always loved it, loved "its hugeness, its virility, its colorful history. When we studied about it in school, I used to picture it to myself like a fair white knight—only the knight is mounted on a bucking broncho instead of a charger, with a lasso over the saddle horn and a bowie knife in lieu of a sword!" (173). The gender switch here points to something that had always been implicit in depictions of the Texas woman as Westerner: her assumption of masculine behaviors is part of a more self-expressive femininity.

The Wind (1925), a novel by Dorothy Scarborough set in West Texas in the drought years of the 1880s, is a third-person narrative focalized through the point of view of the main character, the childlike and unskilled Letty. Orphaned and alone, she comes from Virginia to live with her cousin and is totally out of place. The narrator uses the powerful Texas winds—supposedly more powerful in the 1880s than in 1925—as the symbol of a woman-hating West Texas. "In the old days, the winds were the enemies of women. Did they hate them because they saw in them the symbols of that civilization which might gradually lessen their own power? Because it was for women that men would build houses . . . increase their herds . . . turn the unfenced pastures into farms" (3).

To escape her cousin's house (where, actually, her cousin's wife—the older woman figure—gets along just fine, a fact that Scarborough pointed out later when trying to rebut the critical complaint that Letty was meant to be typical of Texas womanhood), Letty marries a sweet-tempered but boring cattleman named Lige, who defines his manhood by his compatibility with the Texas plains. "Seems like I can stand up on my hind legs and look God in the face man to man, you might say. . . . When you lie out in the open at night to sleep, with nothing between you and earth but a blanket, and nothing between you and the sky, you get sort o' chummy with the stars" (53–54). Lige feels that "to be on a horse on these prairies when the spring flowers are blooming" (55) is to own the universe, but Letty shudders at the idea of sleeping outside; she's "oppressed by the solitude of nature, which was so different from the friendly countrysides she had known at home—nothing to see but a few stunted mesquite bushes, and samples of cactus that would repel the touch" (56).

Letty is unmoved by Lige's lessons in Texas history about "the early settlers, the pioneers that had come to this section, not as she had done, in a train, but in covered wagons, across prairies treacherous with Indians, scant of water, and threatened with multiple dangers . . . hardy heroic pioneers that had made possible even so much civilization as the region knew then" (62). Lige makes women—but not women like Letty—key agents on the frontier: "The whole thing depended on the women folks. The women of early days could shoulder rifles and stave off Indians side by side with their husbands. And work—my stars, how they did work! Raised big families, did every lick of work, even to spinning and weaving. I take off my hat to the women of the west" (63). Letty, incapable of this kind heroism, dies by running off into the wind after committing an implausible crime. Like Davis's *Wire-Cutters,* the book rescues Texas from the South by showing a southern character unable to survive there.

*   *   *

If the question of Texas identity as southern or western perplexed and preoccupied many Texas women writers, Oklahoma identity for its women writers alternated between Texan—cattle and ranch—and Kansan—crops and farm, not least because the white population of Oklahoma consisted significantly of emigrants from those two regions. Native Americans constituted a third strand of identity; Indian removal policies had forced numerous eastern and central plains tribes into the region, which they made their own. The state was home to the largest number of Native women writers, but these women, affiliated with the Five Tribes (Five Civilized Tribes, as they used to be called, including Choctaw, Chickasaw, Creek, Cherokee, and Seminole), put at least some of their literary energies into rejecting any pan-Indian ideology that would equate them with their "wild" (i.e., nomadic) cousins.

Whites who wrote about Oklahoma without a consciousness of Native Americans were few. One of these is Eleanor Gates, whose 1907 *Alec Lloyd, Cowpuncher,* is as its title indicates, a cowboy novel—a comic one, a first-person narration by the slang-happy titular character, set among fun-loving Oklahoma cowboys. The story begins when a Boston writer looking for local color comes on the scene. The cowboys, aware that their town has no local color of the sort "Boston" wants, stage a fake kidnapping (of a Hispanic ingénue, but the joke is on the cowboys because she and "Boston" fall in love and elope). Alec explains to his friends that "This liter'toor gent's hired me as his book foreman. As I understand it, they's some things he wants, and I'm to help corral 'em. He says that just now most folks seem t'be takin' a lot of interest in the West. He don't reckon the fashion'll keep up, but a-course a book-writer has t' git on to the band wagon" (204–5).

In 1925 Abbie Hillerman, for many years president of the Oklahoma WCTU, compiled her *History of the Woman's Christian Temperance Union of Indian Territory, Oklahoma Territory, State of Oklahoma; 1888–1925.* Striving to name every woman who was active in the organization during these years, the book refers obliquely to crucial events in Oklahoma history: the founding of Indian Territory after removal, an event of which "no chapter in American history contains so much of pathos and tragedy" (11). The idea of the WCTU as a space for female community and activism is clear in her description of the annual meeting in which the two separate WCTU organizations (Indian Territory and Oklahoma Territory) were merged when Oklahoma became a state in 1907. The event was pervaded by "a note of sadness . . . as the white ribbon comrades realized this was their last meeting as Old Indian Territory. With tearful eyes and sad hearts the unbroken circle was formed" (30). The 1908 convention presented "An Hour with Pioneers" with eleven pioneers—the word echoes throughout Hillerman's narrative—recounting their stories, "a very precious hour as they gave their experiences in establishing the cause of prohibition the early soil of Oklahoma. The roses had faded from some of their cheeks . . . but the fire of a deathless determination to dethrone King Alcohol was still burning on the altar of their hearts" (64–65). The account for 1923 inserts a poem by Josephine M. Buhl, another WCTU activist: "Oklahoma how we love thee / Dearest state of all the West. . . . / In this fair state, this Indian country, / Which from bondage was set free, / By the noble deeds of women / Led by God on bended knee. / 'Law enforcement' is our slogan, /As we give to Thee our best; / Bless us Lord in Oklahoma / Dearest State of all the West" (96).

Also in 1925 Zoe Tilghman, widow of a famous sheriff who'd been shot to death in 1924, brought out her first book, *The Dugout,* a set of six linked tales arranged chronologically and centered on the sod dwelling of the title. Set in an area between the Arkansas and Cimarron rivers, it's a prairie book through and through. "Far scattered over the rolling Western plains, nestling in hollows, burrowed into the sheltering hillsides, the old dugouts tell their story of the past. . . . Within their friendly shelter civilization first took root upon the prairie lands" (1). In the opening story, "The First Tenants," two pards dig into the sloping ground and build "up the low front with earth piled against two heavy logs. . . . Dave drove pegs along the side logs and nailed up a box for a cupboard" (2–3). In the final story, "The Last Adventure," a family returns to the now abandoned dugout with automobile and camera; father tells the children "I promised to show you the old dugout where your grandma fought the Indians, and your mother stood off two men who tried to jump the claim" (107).

Tilghman turned to writing as a means of supporting her family when her husband was killed; she became a professional writer and editor, connected especially with Oklahoma's premier magazine, *Harlow's Weekly.* Her 1926 *Outlaw Days,* celebrating her husband and other famous marshals, drew upon and enlarged her husband's records as they had been redacted by a Richard S. Graves and published by the Oklahoma State Printing Company. Its main purpose, she writes, "besides giving a true history of events, is to impress upon its readers, and especially young men and boys, that there is never an inducement for them to become outlaws. . . . Viewed from the distance of years it may appear to have been picturesque, but in reality it was a life full of terrors and hardships, a mean, low, hazardous, and sordid way of living" (23–24). The lawmen's lives, though often equally mean and hazardous, "had justice and duty on their side"; their job was to make the country "a safe place in which to live" (24). The book's fundamental historical premise is that "Oklahoma and Indian Territories were the last of the frontier and it was here that the bad men of the nation congregated before the country was opened to settlement. . . . They were horse thieves, cattle rustlers, and train robbers, and their operations made the Southwest notorious throughout the country" (i).

The account includes outlaw women like Belle Starr and identifies the cowboy as the type from which the outlaw emerges. The farmer, "a settler committed to the task of bringing into cultivation 160 acres and building a home on it, had little time or incentive for outlawry" (21). Though most cowboys did not become outlaws, "nearly every bandit in the Southwest had been a cowboy before he became a lawbreaker. . . . As cowpunchers they had learned to ride and shoot. . . . As cowboys they had acquired more of the dare-devil spirit than they had originally been endowed with by nature, so when the call came to them to join with other outlaws they were ready" (23). The outlawry that interests Tilghman is a white phenomenon, because "the civilization of Oklahoma Territory was basically white. For in the run of '89 and in subsequent openings, a white population settled an empty land" (21). Indians on reservations had their own culture, their own laws, their own law officers.

*   *   *

Indians are the obsession of other white women's Oklahoma books: Ida Dyer's 1896 *Fort Reno: or, Picturesque Cheyenne and Arrapahoe Army Life* about her life as an Indian agent's wife during the 1880s; Natalie Curtis's study of Native song in *The Indians' Book* (1907); Elizabeth M. Page's 1915 *In Camp and Tepee*, about Reformed Church missionary work among the Comanche, Apache, Cheyenne, Arapahoe, Winnebago, and Omaha; Baptist missionary Isabel Crawford's *Kiowa: The History of a Blanket Indian Mission* (1915); Annie Heloise Abel's three-volume history, *The Slaveholding Indians* (1915, 1919, 1925).

Among these authors, only Dyer (whose account was reissued with an introduction by David Dary in 2005) is programmatically anti-Indian. She calls the Cheyenne and Arapahoe "the worst on the continent" (54) and defends the land rush which in just six years made Oklahoma into "a land of permanent cities, prosperous farms and enlightened people" (214). Married to a former Indian agent, Dyer describes a division between reservation progressives and traditionals that she thinks prevents cultural change: "The more advanced Indians did not dare to favor civilization except in a limited degree, as the wilder element was liable at any time to kill their stock, destroy their tepees, and mercilessly slaughter them" (190). The traditionals, she argues, undermine the cultural work of Indian schools and Indian philanthropists. In anticipation of the imminent vanishing of Native culture, Dyer travels around the reservation to and preserve purchase Native pottery—an unself-conscious example of the way that Native artifacts could be divided from those who produced them.

Natalie Curtis, an early and self-trained ethnomusicologist, looked for correspondence between tribal music and tribal characteristics. Her descriptions of three plains groups removed to Oklahoma—Pawnee, "intrepid warriors, known to their enemies as strong and courageous fighters" who "have always been the friends of the United States government, and their loyal value as government scouts is widely known" (94–95); Cheyenne, "a sturdy, prosperous folk, fighting their enemies lustily, trading with friendly neighbors over a vast territory, and themselves supplying all the needs of their self-respecting and vigorous community life," "truthful, invariably brave, and devout in peace and in war" (147–48); Arapaho, "an imaginative and very devoutly religious people" (198)— are unconditionally admiring.

The two missionary writers were pro-Indian insofar as they saw the Natives as amenable to conversion, but mostly uninterested in the patterns of their culture. Page replaces savage Indians with childish Indians in a book that is really about the missionary careers of her sister and brother-in-law, Walter Roe, who worked around Fort Sill. She believes Christians are obliged to convert the Native: "what if we in our pride leave him to the wreck of his childhood world and go sweeping on our way? Nations like men may be brought to the judgment bar and tried" (9). She also objects, less theologically, to the allotment system's failure to provide tools and livestock while urging if not requiring Indians to become farmers. And she notes that the system ignores the close-knit social texture of Native life by isolating families on scattered holdings.

Crawford, writing from New York some years after she was called back from the reservation on account of a doctrinal dispute, uses her diaries for material on her own labor—both spiritual and physical; on the unpredictable weather; on Sunday services where attendees testify to their new-found faith (their statements are rendered in her own version of "Indian speak"); on constant hunger; and on the long, ultimately successful process of accumulating enough money to build a church. There is no way to vouch for the authenticity of her account, but this book is no different from any other memoir that cannot be corroborated. Whether it happened as she said it did or not, there is interest in the glimpses of white impingement (her own included) on Native lives: cowboys and their herds grazing on reservation land (15), frequent journeys to town for supplies, the allotment process doling out land to Native individuals, and above all the opening of the reservation to white settlers (163–68)—the signal Oklahoma event according to every textbook history. In telling about the land rush her diary format gives way to pure narrative. About the town of Lawton:

"the lonely prairie over which the missionaries had travelled so many times, became a city in a night. There were four hundred places of business and fifteen hundred tents before a lot could be sold, a daily paper the first day and over ten thousand inhabitants before the city was two months old. . . . Our wagon had scarcely stopped when a man pushed up with a basket of doughnuts for sale. A basket of doughnuts! Think of it—for sale on our desolate prairie!" (164).

Annie Heloise Abel's three volumes—*The American Indian as Slaveholder and Secessionist* (1915), *The American Indian as Participant in the Civil War* (1919), and *The American Indian under Reconstruction* (1925)—total over a thousand pages of diplomatic and military history centered on the Five Tribes, whom she defines as sovereign entities entitled to and capable of diplomatic negotiation and treaty rights. Therefore crimes against Indians and abrogation of treaty rights are international crimes. She justifies the alliance of the slaveholding Indians (especially the Cherokee) with the Confederacy during the Civil War, partly because of their shared values—they had, after all, been Southerners before being removed to Oklahoma—and partly by the hypocrisy of the US war government, which left them "to themselves at the critical moment and left them, moreover, at the mercy of the South," and then was "indignant that they betrayed a sectional affiliation" (1915: 14).

The Confederacy, however, also betrayed the Natives, because it wanted Indian country not the "Indian owner . . . for Indian Territory occupied a position of strategic importance, from both the economic and the military point of view. The possession of it was absolutely necessary for the political and the institutional consolidation of the South. Texas might well think of going her own way and of forming an independent republic once again, when between her and Arkansas lay the immense reservations of the great tribes" (1915: 14). Abel, conceding that her interpretation isn't currently popular, believes the government's treatment of Indians "is bound to concern very greatly the historian of the future, whose mental grasp will be immeasurably greater than is that of the men, who now write and teach American history in the old conventional way with a halo around New England and the garb of aristocracy enveloping Virginia. It is in American History rightly proportioned that the present study will have its place" (1925: 10).

* * *

For writers from the Five Tribes—the only group to publish books among the Natives in Oklahoma—the terrain is their obsession, in the sense of protecting their right to it. Having been removed once, at enormous cost, they were unwilling to be removed again. S. Alice Callahan's novel *Wynema: A Child of the Forest* (1891, reissued with an introduction and notes by A. LaVonne Brown Ruoff in 1997), is currently the earliest known novel by a Native woman. Callahan, a Muskogee/Creek who died before she was thirty, published this short novel when she was twenty-three. The novel melds a cross-racial reservation romance, situated in wonderful scenery (Wynema, a reservation child of exceptional talent, marries the brother of her missionary teacher from Virginia, thus establishing a southern connection), with an account of Wounded Knee. The personal and political together bolster an argument for intermarriage on the one side and assimilation on the other, valuing education, temperance, and Christianity.

Four Cherokee women—Mary Jane Ross in *The Life and Times of Hon. William P. Ross* (1893), Narcissa Owen in her *Memoirs* of 1907, Rachel Caroline Eaton in her biography of John Ross, William Ross's nephew (1914), and Mabel Washbourne Anderson in a biography of her grandfather's cousin Stand Watie (1915, rev. 1931)—are concerned with intratribal history, justifying one or another faction among the Cherokee in connection with Removal and then the Civil War, during which some of the slave-holding Cherokee fought for the Confederacy. Jane Ross's memorial volume for her husband collects his letters and speeches and introduces them with an unpaginated biographical essay. Her political aim is to "correct a common report, fabricated for political use, that 'W. P. Ross was an enemy to Southern Cherokees.' He was a friend of humanity, a lover of Northern and Southern Cherokees, united in one nation." He "was no enemy to any part of the Cherokee people. He was no enemy to the Southern Cherokees. He was not the author of the confiscation law passed by the Cherokee council at Fort Gibson in the fall of 1863. He rode no horse of any Southern Cherokee, nor did he ever injure a Northern or Southern man in person or property" (n.p.).

Narcissa Owen (her book was reissued with an introduction by Karen L. Kilcup in 2005) defends the Confederacy, and differentiates civilized from primitive Indians—reminding one that no individual can be safely assigned group traits; in fact to counter Indian stereotyping by her own example is exactly her purpose. An artist recognized in her lifetime for accomplished portraits painted in European style, she objects strongly to a newspaper report about the Louisiana Exposition of 1904, when her painting of the Jefferson family was described in a St. Louis newspaper as the surprising work of an 82-year-old Indian woman. "The facts are the Indians of Indian Territory are civilized, educated Christian people. I myself, the 'Cherokee 82 years old,' was born October 3, 1831, and my painting was not done in a tepee, but on Pennsylvania Avenue, in the Corcoran Building, opposite the Treasury, at Washington city" (134).

Rachel Caroline Eaton's dissertation-based biography of John Ross (she was likely the first Cherokee woman to earn a Ph.D.) presents him as a hero and uses his life to follow the history of the Cherokee as a sovereign nation. While endorsing Cherokee values, especially the tribe's attachment to place—a description of the Tahlequah settlement points out that the site was chosen in part because it resembled the original Georgia homeland—she accepts education (especially literacy) and farming (as opposed to hunting) as signs of progress. She employs pioneer metaphors about the Cherokee transformation of the Oklahoma wilderness: "The proverbial 'lazy Indian' was hard to find among the Cherokee people . . . and, in the course of a few years, there were good farms and comfortable homes with vegetables gardens, and orchards, for the more thrifty, while the most unprogressive full-blood had his log cabin and his maize patch" (162).

When the Civil War makes the Cherokee vulnerable to both Confederate and Union soldiers, the Cherokee align themselves—appropriately, according to Eaton—as self-interest dictates. Ross "joined the Confederacy because he saw destruction ahead if he did not. . . . Likewise, his loyalty to the Union was actuated partly by motives of self-preservation. Why should it have been otherwise?" (198). In this work of passionate scholarship, Eaton alludes to herself and her tribal identity only indirectly, through her prefatory acknowledgment of "Mrs. Lucy Ward Williams, one of the last of the fireside historians of her race, whose vital interest in her people constrained her to repeat their story in season and out of season until it was rooted and grounded in my memory from earliest childhood" (n.p.)

Mabel Washbourne Anderson's biography of her grandfather's cousin, Confederate Officer Stand Watie, shows how the intense internecine conflicts before the Civil War between Treaty and non-Treaty Cherokees (those supporting and opposing Removal) mutated into conflict between supporters of the Union and the Confederacy. Stand Watie, a "Treaty Indian" who accepted the removal of the tribe and argued for reconstructing Cherokee life within its constraints, supported the Confederacy, as was natural for those "born under Southern skies. . . . Many of the Cherokees and Choctaws had inter-married with Southern people, they were all imbued with the same idea of local government that other Southerners possessed" (13). Stand Watie himself "was a firm believer in 'State Rights', a Southerner by birth and breeding. There was no hesitation in his choice, when he cast his lot with the Confederacy" (14). And how lucky for Texas! His troops kept the Union army from entering the state. "Knowing the country and its people as he did, he was able to strike when and where they least expected it, and continually kept them deluded and on the move. . . . His services, in this capacity, to the Confederate Cause and to his own people, as a Nation, can never be estimated" (17). "Sherman's terrible raid, on a smaller scale, might have been repeated through Indian Territory and Texas had it not been for the timely raids, capture of horses, mules and trains of wagons made by General Watie and his men" (27).

Many in Watie's command—in the expanded version of 1931 Anderson names them all—"sleep in unknown and forgotten graves, but the memory of their valiant deeds, in defense of the South, is an heritage that every patriotic Southerner should be proud to cherish. All these Indians, though untrained in the tactics of war, were by nature and habit well-fitted to become ideal soldiers. They were good riders and splendid marksmen, most of them having been athletes from their youth up, trained in self control and endurance. . . . The Five Civilized Tribes lost more men in action, in the Confederate Amy in proportion to the number enlisted, than any other Southern States. These Tribes furnished fully six thousand men to the Southern troops. . . . Most of the Oklahoma text-books, on which the public school children depend for their knowledge of Oklahoma History, give little or no insight into the lives and characters of the leading men of the Five Civilized Tribes, who were the real makers of Oklahoma History. And less has been said and written touching the Indian's part in the cause of the Confederacy than upon any other phase of the War between the states" (28). Anderson complains about the so-called "Dark Treaty" of 1866 whose "most objectionable clause was the unjust one that demanded of the Southern Indian an equal division of their lands with their former slaves and their posterity. . . . The citizens of no other Southern State were forced to divide their inheritance with their former slaves" (32).

The most important Oklahoma historian in this era was Choctaw Muriel H. Wright, whose first book—*The Story of Oklahoma,* a 291-page textbook self-published in 1923 and republished commercially the next year—was enlarged in 1929 and ultimately adopted throughout the Oklahoma public school system. Other textbooks followed, and Wright, editor and contributor for thirty years beginning in 1943 to *Chronicles of Oklahoma,* the Oklahoma Historical Society quarterly, established a narrative in which incoming whites must assimilate to an Indian state. She dedicates the book to the memory of her grandfather, Choctaw chief Allen Wright, whose life and achievements are described at length. A territorial chauvinist, she says in her preface that "the story of Oklahoma is different from that of any other state in the Union" (xvii) because the Indians came first and remain an important political and cultural force. To begin Oklahoma history with Native settlement was not only counter-history (although now it's a standard way to treat US regional history) but rebuts the stereotype that Natives lived outside history. Differentiating the tribes from each other, yet accepting a division between white and Indian, she both is and is not Pan-Indian. She ends the introduction with the future-and-past-based observation that "Life here is teeming with great possibilities—achievements only to be equaled in time to come with the vivid history of its past, which will remain as a spectacular panorama of the 'last frontier'" (xix). Thus, whatever its uniquely Indian history, Oklahoma is also a frontier western space.

3

The Pacific Northwest

Apart from trappers and seamen, the first "American" emigrants to the Pacific Northwest—Oregon, Washington, western Idaho, and eventually Alaska—arrived in the late 1830s. Baptist Jason Lee used a story circulating around St. Louis about Flathead people from Oregon searching for teachers of the Gospel to spearhead a spate of missionary emigration. The overland journey in 1836 of two missionary couples from New York State (Marcus and Narcissa Whitman, Henry and Eliza Spalding) demonstrated the feasibility of overland travel for women. (The Whitmans were killed eleven years later in a Cayuse uprising.) Substantial immigration had to wait until the US and England solved the problem of the US-Canada boundary; a potential war between the two nations, narrowly avoided by diplomacy in 1846, was eclipsed in the national imagination by the actual border war with Mexico.

Having secured a border, the government implemented the Oregon Donation Law of 1850 (precursor to the Homestead Act), granting 640 acres to each individual on the ground to claim it (women included and double for married couples). The Act, presumably intended to fill the territory to keep it firmly under US control, started the overland exodus, whose rigors were far greater than travelers anticipated. Some mishaps were ultimately comic, as Belle Walker Cooke's poem "Crossing the Plains" in her 1871 poetry miscellany *Tears and Victory* reports: "Have you traveled through the sand, / Up the famous river Platte, / Where the bluffs are so romantic, / And the water tastes so flat! / Have you camped out in a hail-storm, / When the wind was blowing high, / Upsetting tents and wagons, / And making children cry? / Did you get up in the morning, / Feeling somewhat water-soaked, / And finding cattle missing, / Did you never get provoked? / And while you hunted cattle, / Did the little muddy creek, / Rise like a second deluge, / And keep you there a week?" (149–50). But there was also loss of cattle and much death from waterborne diarrheic diseases, usually all called cholera. There were Indian scares and occasional incidents of Indian thievery as the emigrants crossed through Indian territory with their herds of cattle, their pots and pans, their knives and tools. In *A Pioneer's Search for an Ideal Home* (1925), Phoebe Goodall Judson wrote simply that crossing the plains in the early days was unforgettable because it was so "terrible" (69). Pioneer narratives, many of them published in old age when the overlanders became objects of sentimental veneration, were more often about getting there and settling in than about the Oregon trail itself, which had to wait for the Lewis and Clark Centennial to emerge as a national icon.

In tandem with the Donation Act came the discovery of gold in California, which was certainly much more newsworthy than the tribulations and tedium of remote homesteading. As Frances Fuller Victor wrote in *River of the West* (1870), "the fame of the California climate, the fascinations of the ups and downs of fortune's wheel in that country, and many other causes, united to make California, and not Oregon, the object of interest on the Pacific coast; and the rapidity with which California became self-supporting removed from Oregon her importance as a source of supplies. Therefore, after a few years of rather extraordinary usefulness and consequent good fortune, the Territory relapsed into a purely domestic and very quiet young State. This change in its federal status was not altogether acceptable to Oregonians. . . . When a rival darling sprang into vigorous life and excessive favor, almost at once, their jealousy rankled painfully" (485–86). In addition, the US government failed to provide military protection against Indians; the more or less endemic hostilities between whites and Natives in Oregon were completely overshadowed by the sensational Comanche, Sioux, and Apache wars of the plains and Southwest. When the military finally did arrive, they were criticized for coming too late and doing too little—in fact for being mercenaries not public servants.

War in the Pacific at the end of the century opened a narrative whose meaning for these writers lay less in the transpacific expansion of US boundaries than the belated recognition by the rest of the nation of Oregon's importance. In 1908, for example, Alice Rollit Coe in her poetic miscellany, *Lyrics of Fir and Foam*, welcomed the US Navy in "Hail to the Fleet" as signifying a new chapter in the history of the Pacific Northwest: "We have won the West for the nation,— / We must hold it in strength, not in fear. / We have whitened the pathless prairie / With the bones of horse and man, / When the painted savages circled / And closed on the lone caravan; / We have fought, in the sand of the desert, / The hunger—the thirst that kills; / We have blazed a trail through the forest; / We have blasted a way through the hills; / The pulse of the Pilgrims beats in us: / Eager to spend and be spent, / We have builded an Empire proudly / On the rim of the continent" (n.p.). On the other hand, Coe's ode to Seattle addresses the city as "Fair city of our hope," and the "Mother of giants yet to be" with "The boundaries of thy power still unset, / The wonder of thy destiny unknown" (n.p.) while in 1900, popular historian Eva Emery Dye opened her textbook, *Stories of Oregon,* with a regional poem announcing that "Deep in her valleys genius waits" (3)—thereby conceding that genius hadn't yet arrived.

Overall, then, women's Oregon literature took the form of complaint. Silent suffering and unsuccessful farming dominated the earliest women's accounts, two autobiographical novels. Margaret Jewett Bailey's two-volume, third-person autobiographical hard luck story—*The Grains; or, Passages in the Life of Ruth Rover, with Occasional Pictures of Oregon, Natural and Moral* (1854)—was published in Portland to defend herself after a nasty divorce and indicts the entire missionary enterprise. The protagonist, a New England teenager who has defied her father to go to Oregon as a missionary teacher, soon discovers that "men may have changed the place, but they have kept their nature" (77). The narrator summarizes: "No mission ever existed which so fully disappointed the hopes of the church as the Oregon Methodist Mission" (136). One missionary "wanted a farm, another an orchard. Another a band of cattle, etc. etc.; another could not go to a remote station for he wanted his children schooled—another could not teach school, for he must attend to his family—another could not build houses, for he had a new plan in his head, he was going to study physic—and another could not accept this or that appointment, for he had no wife—and another could not leave his wife to do this or that, for he had no laundress! . . . Mismanagement and waste both operated to the ruin of the enterprise. There was very little done because there were so few to labor—nobody labored because the work belonged to no one" (137–38). After breaking her contract with the Mission Board to get married, Ruth discovers that her husband is a drunkard, the first but not the last of this type in women's western books.

Abigail Scott Duniway's *Captain Gray's Company,* also published in Portland, in 1859 when she was 24, follows two Midwestern families attracted to Oregon by the Donation Law. One character opines that "This new Donation law will cause thousands to go, who would not otherwise undertake the journey. 640 acres of land would be worth something to a poor man" (42). But Duniway shows that the very poverty that motivates the emigrants makes them unlikely to succeed. Acquiring equipment for a long western journey is expensive, provisions and repairs along the way are costly, establishing oneself in a new place requires cash, and if family members should sicken and die along the way, the arrivals often have no means of support. Women widowed on the trail, and orphaned children, are especially hard hit. (In real life, Duniway's mother had died of dysentery on the trail). One of Duniway's two female protagonists has to go into service at age fourteen and endure the random kindnesses and, more often, cruelties of her employers. Duniway, who later became a prominent feminist lecturer and founded a journal called *The New Northwest,* attributed her feminism directly to her harrowing pioneer experiences.

* * *

Frances Fuller Victor, whose literary career had begun in New York City with dime novels for Beadle and who wrote western history anonymously for Bancroft after her husband died, was the earliest of several Pacific Northwest women historians who tried to insert Oregon into the national consciousness as the true West and encourage patriotism in local youngsters. Without any obvious hero to celebrate, Victor presents Oregon history in *The River of the West* (1870) through the romanticized life story of Joseph Meek, a teenaged runaway from Virginia who trapped, farmed, carried news of the Whitman killings to Washington D.C. (they had been murdered in 1847 by the Cayuse among whom they had settled) in a failed attempt to get government troops to the Pacific Northwest, and was ultimately elected to the Oregon legislature. Victor interviewed Meek at length and used him to represent stages of western settlement. During one man's lifetime Westerners change from "lawless rangers of the wilderness, to law-abiding and even law-making and law-executing citizens of an isolated territory" (265). Here is an example of the female preference for law-abiding rather than lawbreaking men. The preface says Manifest Destiny (she uses the phrase) "seems to have raised him up, together with many others, bold, hardy, and fearless men, to become sentinels on the outposts of civilization, securing to the United States with comparative ease a vast extent of territory, for which, without them, a long struggle with England would have taken place, delaying the settlement of the Pacific Coast for many years, if not losing it to us altogether" (vii).

Victor regretted that Joe had an Indian wife, one of many instances where the supposed ratio in favor of women proved to be a mirage. Her short stories are full of instances of white men who regret the marriages that make connection with a white woman impossible. Moreover, the arriving white women in general were (she claims) of a higher class than the rough mountain men already there. So, in an embellishment drawn from her dime-novel repertory, Victor places Meek in a group of trappers who meet the Whitmans on the trail in 1836; there Narcissa "shone the bright particular star of that Rocky Mountain encampment, softening the hearts and the manners of all who came within her womanly influence. Not a gentleman among them but felt her silent command upon him to be his better self while she remained in his vicinity; not a trapper or camp-keeper but respected the presence of womanhood and piety" (207–8) When Joe becomes dissatisfied with his life "he remembered his talk with Mrs. Whitman, that fair, tall, courteous, and dignified lady who had stirred in him longings to return to the civilized life of his native state. But he felt unfit for the society of such as she. Would he ever, could he ever attain to it now? He had promised her he might go over into Oregon and settle down" (262). And so he does, offering a thoroughly fictional example of the historical effect of female class on rough men.

Urban by inclination and background, Victor became an Oregon booster, publishing two books for tourists and businessmen—*All Over Oregon and Washington* (1872) and *Atlantis Arisen* (1891)—promising that the western future meant towns and cities, businessmen not farmers. *Atlantis Arisen,* which recognizes the involvement of farming in some kind of market economy, says the Donation allotments were too large; "It was impossible, as it was useless, to cultivate a mile square of land, where neither rail-car nor steamboat ever came to take away its produce" (185–86). That the first generation of farmers was unskilled is seen in the landscape's "general air of neglect and improvidence," its shabby farmhouses and unpruned orchards (195). "The farming community of the country was derived originally from the border States, as they were thirty years ago. They had never been *good* farmers in the States of Missouri, Illinois, or Kentucky" (196). Victor's last book, *Early Indian Wars of Oregon* (1894), commissioned by the Oregon legislature to honor the earliest pioneers by construing them as Indian fighters not farmers, says that civilians not the army saved the territory from Indians; many years after the end of Indian hostilities, federal neglect still rankled.

In the next generation, popular historian Eva Emery Dye published a series of books advancing diverse Oregon narratives. The first, *McLoughlin and Old Oregon* (1900), which remained in print into the 1930s, depicted the Hudson's Bay Company, without irony, through metaphors of feudalism, knighthood, Arthurian romance, and saga. The Company reproduced "in the western wilds the feudal age of Europe. The chief of nearly every post had a beautiful daughter who sat behind her casement window, harp in hand, and sang the songs of France" (124). "Oregon slept behind her battlements, waiting for the prince at whose magic kiss the gates should fall, the forest trails expand, and her thousand industries leap to life" (172).

Dye transforms Narcissa Whitman, auburn-haired in real life, into an exceptionally fair-skinned blonde, whom she then calls "snowy Joan" in a clear reference to the Maid of Orleans. The racial implications of this are clear, but to stress the point she says Indian men bowed down to Narcissa "as at a shrine before a golden goddess. The silken cape that encircled her soft, white neck seemed like the fluttering of wings, her golden hair like an aureole of light" (28). In this account, continuing her saga of refinement, McLoughlin (chief administrator of the Hudson's Bay Company) immediately recognizes her as a lady and treats her accordingly. In the end, Whitman and McLoughlin get equal credit for establishing the territory: "Dr. Whitman had risen. Two heroes stood face to face. The early sunset cast its slant shadows across the wall, lighting up the silver locks of the Father of Oregon, and resting in a halo on the brow of the future martyr. Catholic and Protestant, British and American, yet brothers in a common fidelity to God and humanity" (269).

Dye signifies suffering on the overland trail by noting the family relics ditched along the roadside: "The sand scorched, the dust suffocated, the wagons went to pieces. Furniture was thrown overboard; claw-footed tables and carved oak bureaus, the relics of an ancestral time, were left to warp in the prairie sun. Sentinel wolves lay in wait to devour the lagging cattle; Indians hovered in front and rear and ambuscade. . . . Still on the immigrant pressed with the same restless spirit that inundated Europe and broke up the Roman Empire. The migration of races ebbs and flows like the waves of the sea. What if men's hearts died and women wept by the roadside?—the tide swept on" (334–35). Dye's *Stories of Oregon* (1900), a juvenile, described the overlanders as more progressive than Easterners who stayed put, who in turn were more progressive than the English who chose not to leave the old country. There is no one hero, there is the whole group. "Nothing in American history, excepting, perhaps, crossing the Atlantic, equals the crossing of the plains. Three thousand miles by sea came the Pilgrims to Plymouth Rock. Two thousand miles came the pioneers to Oregon. . . . If America was peopled by the specially culled brave hearts of Europe, so Oregon was settled by the picked brave few of their descendants" (121–23). The narrator prods her young audience: "What does not America owe to her Indian-fighters, explorers, hunters, trappers, missionaries, and adventurers? They, before all others, took the land, and held many a dark and bloody ground for civilization. Never, never, did the bold, unflinching heroes yield. They held, in trust, a home for us" (133).

Dye's narrative in *The Conquest* (1902), written for the Lewis and Clark centennial, makes the Pacific Northwest central to US history. Today "five transcontinental lines bear the rushing armies westward, ever westward into the sea. Bewildered a moment they pause, then turn—to the Conquest of the Poles and the Tropics. The frontiersman? He is building Nome City under the Arctic; he is hewing the forests of the Philippines." For this new story Dye makes Sacagawea her heroine, going considerably beyond her source in the Lewis and Clark journals. As a civic activist in Oregon City, she was also instrumental in getting a statue of Sacagawea built in the city center. Sacagawea isn't just any Indian but a princess. "Modest princess of the Shoshones, heroine of the great expedition," she "stood with her babe in arms and smiled upon them from the shore. So had she stood in the Rocky Mountains pointing out the gates. So had she followed the great rivers, navigating the continent. . . . Madonna of her race, she had led the way to a new time. To the hands of this girl, not yet eighteen, had been intrusted the key that unlocked the road to Asia. . . . Across North America a Shoshone Indian Princess touched hands with Jefferson, opening her country" (290). Although Sacagawea ultimately became a familiar historical figure, only one other women writer seems to have featured her at this time; Katherine Chandler's 1905 *Bird Woman of the Lewis and Clark Expedition* retells the journey for first and second graders, and also uniquely finds a place for York, Clark's slave. Sacagawea took hold, York didn't.

Dye's last effort to craft a historical narrative for Oregon was *McDonald of Oregon* (1906), about the son of an HBC factor and an Indian mother; he went to sea, settled in Japan, and taught English, thus making it possible for Perry, when he arrived, to communicate, and closing the immigrant circle insofar as the Indians of the Pacific Northwest were of Asian descent. McDonald, however, never entered the history books; nor did efforts to make heroes of the Whitmans or McLoughlin resonate far beyond the territory's borders.

Canadian-born émigré Agnes Laut is an exception to the work of women who looked for men who made law rather than broke it. She celebrated trapper outlaws; her 1902 *Story of the Trapper* says the trapper "knew only one rule of existence—to go ahead without any heroics, whether the going cost his own or some other man's life. That is the way the wilderness was won; and the winning is one of the most thrilling pages in history" (3). Her 1921 *Fur Trade of America* defends the contemporary fur industry (for which she had become a paid spokeswoman); the 1927 *Conquest of Our Western Empire* militantly extols the pioneers: "What fibre had the people who wrested the wealth from the reluctant soil— people who pulled up home roots in New England and the Middle West; who pitched caution and warnings to the winds; who crossed burning plains . . . the very pick of the finest fibre, the most dauntless souls, in human stock" (336).

Feminist Mary Osborn Douthit, a Duniway follower, tried to write women into Pacific Northwest history by featuring pioneer grit and endurance—transferring the tradition of Patient Griseldas to the frontier. Her *Souvenir of Western Women* (1905) aimed to "record woman's part in working out the plan of our Western civilization; no other civilization, perhaps, bearing so conspicuously the imprint of her hand and brain. In coming to this country through all the perils, privations, and hardships of the longest journey ever made by a migratory people in search of homes, she marched side by side with man. Upon arriving here she could acquire with him equally a part of the public domain (the first instance of the kind on record). . . . To the pioneer woman—without whom permanent settlement could not have been made—the nation owes the very possession of this great Western territory" (3). Douthit celebrates the lonely fortitude of her own pioneer mother, as does feminist Emily Inez Denny, whose *Blazing the Way* (1909) defines women's tenacity as heroism. "The pioneer woman learned to face every sort of danger. . . . Each was obliged to depend almost wholly on herself and was compelled to invent and apply many expedients to feed and clothe herself and little ones" (283).

Katharine Berry Judson's *Early Days in Old Oregon* (1916) used her research in the Hudson's Bay Company files for a textbook that credited English diplomacy not American wisdom for averting war with the United States. Written at the moment when the US was on the verge of entering World War I, it speaks to the kinship of England and the US. "We may all be glad that Great Britain gave up half a state, to which she had as good a right as we, rather than arouse the hatred that always follows a war" (166). She charts three stages of (all-male) pioneering: first, renegades who have little impact because they don't establish towns or cities; next "men determined, honest, hard-working, law-abiding, good husbands and good fathers, seeking better opportunities for themselves and better futures for their children" who "gave the predominant stamp to their country, and by their industry developed it so that it has grown at a marvelous pace, aided by its attractive scenery and delightful climate"; and finally, "other desirable men, bankers, business men, the professional classes who lacked the liking for the rough edge of a pioneer life" who "built up the country" (250). Constance Lindsay Skinner's 1921 *Adventurers of Oregon: a Chronicle of the Fur Trade* adds to McLoughlin's achievements the establishment of farming communities for retired trappers; incoming settlers find the agricultural pattern already there. This is another sign of friendly feeling toward England. In Mabel Goodwin Cleland's 1923 juvenile, *Early Days in the Fir Tree Country,* various adults tell David and Peggy about the early times, justifying the "civilization" brought by whites to Oregon "when men come that are trying to make things better, better roads, better homes, better schools, better food" (188). The children's bemusement about the Oregon history parallels the problems felt by the historian herself.

* * *

Pacific Northwest memoirs added to the developing chronicle of female endurance. A brief memoir by Emeline Fuller, age thirteen when her family left the Midwest in 1860, *Left by the Indians* (1892) was published with corroborating material by a group of Wisconsin patrons. She tells how their wagon train was attacked by Indians and the accompanying soldiers from Fort Hall took off with the best horses, leaving all the other adults to be killed (an example of outrageous dereliction by the frontier army that is offered more as the rule than an exception). "Will the reader of this narrative please to pause a moment and reflect upon my situation. A child of barely thirteen years, and slender in build and constitution, taking a nursing babe of one year, and four other children, all younger than herself, and fleeing for life without provisions and barely clothing enough to cover us, into the pathless wilderness or what is worse yet, across the barren plains of the west" (23). She and her charges get through; a cousin comes to claim her; she marries. The couple farm, take out a timber property, move to Eastern Oregon in 1870 because "the damp winter seasons did not agree with my poor health in the west" (34), rent another farm for two years, take up a second homestead timber claim, buy adjoining railroad land, farm, keep a store, keep a stage inn. At the end, widowed, she has returned to her starting point in Wisconsin. "After the death of my husband our property there was sold and passed into the hands of strangers, and now there is a city on our old place" (34).

Elizabeth Laughlin Lord arrived at The Dalles in 1850 when she was nine, and published *Reminiscences of Eastern Oregon* fifty-three years later. The book, which incorporates narratives from other pioneers, turns her father's life into an example of male endurance. They were poor in Illinois where they started; they were poor in Missouri where they went next. "We have now arrived at the fall of '49, when the reports of gold being discovered in California were exciting the whole of the United States. Father was wild to go" (32). On the road, as hordes of people take the California turn-off past Fort Laramie, father impulsively opts for Oregon. Because there is so much squabbling among the travelers and so much sickness, the family travels on their own whenever possible—not easy when the road is jammed. (So much for images of pioneer community on the trail.) Father decides to stop at The Dalles with the same impulsiveness that sent him to Oregon in the first place. There he contributes to town building, and though much respected and elected to diverse local offices, never becomes prosperous. And he dies at age fifty—of grief his daughter supposes—soon after a beloved son accidentally drowns.

Abigail Scott Duniway's memoir, *Path Breaking* (1914), attributes her feminism to female pioneer life. "To bear two children in two and a half years from my marriage day, to make thousands of pounds of butter every year for market, not including what was used in our free hotel at home; to sew and cook, and wash and iron; to bake and clean and stew and fry; to be, in short, a general pioneer drudge, with never a penny of my own, was not pleasant business for an erstwhile school teacher, who had earned a salary that had not gone before marriage, as did her butter and eggs and chickens afterwards, for groceries, and to pay taxes or keep up the wear and tear of horseshoeing, plow-sharpening and harness mending. . . . My good husband was not idle; he was making a farm in the timber and keeping a lot of hired men, for whom I cooked and washed and mended, as part of the duties of a pioneer wife and devoted mother. . . . I was often compelled to neglect my little children, while spending my time in the kitchen, or at the churn or wash tub, doing heavy work for hale and hearty men—work for which I was poorly fitted, chiefly because my faithful mother had worn both me and herself to a frazzle with just such drudgery before I was born" (9–10).

Mary Jane Hayden's *Pioneer Days* (1915), published sixty-five years after she and her husband arrived in the territory, is mostly about their suffering despite eventual prosperity. After the grueling overland trip, she and her husband farm (they sell produce to the military, the only thing she thinks soldiers are good for), she sews to earn money between crops, the Indian wars of 1855 break out and the only Indian they've ever entertained at dinner joins the other side. He's killed, "thank God" (49). One winter she mostly nurses typhoid victims during an epidemic that kills her daughter. During the Civil War the 14th infantry arrives at Vancouver barracks: "It was well known about New York that we had mines on this coast, and plenty of a certain class who had not the means to take so long and expensive a journey either by land or water were ready to enlist in order to get here, when they would desert and go to the mines, where they could ply their trade (which was gambling and stealing). . . . In less than a week after the arrival of the 14th Infantry . . . it was drinking, gambling, fighting, house breaking and several citizens beaten nearly to death" (53).

Eliza Spalding Warren, daughter of the Spaldings who arrived in Oregon Territory with the Whitmans, padded her brief memoir of 1916, published when she was 79 years old, with family documents about the Whitman massacre. Her mother had died in 1851; as the oldest of four children, "the cares of the home and the children rested on my young shoulders, and being left without a mother, just at the age I most needed her training and careful care and instruction, my school advantages were very limited" (32). Warren praises two overlooked pioneer types: bachelors and "the lone woman that has the courage to file on a homestead to start a home, and probably as is often the case, does not see the face of a person from one week's end to another. I call that grit and bravery. When I meet a frontiersman or a pioneer, I can heartily extend to them my hand of welcome, for we know what hardships are, which seems to bring us together with a feeling of sympathy for each other. . . . Let me say right here I do not think that the pioneer women have ever had the praise and credit that is due them for their part in making this great northwestern country what it is" (41). "If you see an old pioneer now going shambling along, don't say, 'There goes an old moss back;' speak kindly of them any way" (42).

Phoebe Goodall Judson wrote most of *A Pioneer's Search for an Ideal Home* soon after the death of her husband in 1905, when she was 75. It was published twenty years later, when, still alive, she added a brief coda. The book begins with the overland journey but is mostly about life in Washington Territory, as she and her husband settle in four different places—inland, coastal, Olympia, and finally on the Nooksack River four miles from the Canadian border where they establish the town of Lyndon. Like so many others, the Judsons left home (Ohio) with no knowledge of farming and little information about their destination, hoping to get the "grant of land that 'Uncle Sam' had promised to give to the head of each family who settled in this new country. . . . We were willing to encounter dangers, endure hardship and privations in order to secure a home that we might call 'ours'" (9). As for the overland trail, "The only places my memory recalls with pleasure while crossing the plains are the ones where we found pure water and good grass for our cattle, and allowed them to rest over the Sabbath" (48); "for several days we traveled over a country that was too dismal for description. The whole face of the country was stamped with sterility. Nothing under the brassy heavens presented itself to the eye but the gray sage brush and the hot yellow sand and dust" (54).

Once in Oregon, their hopes are "suddenly blasted by an Indian war, which broke upon us like a thunderbolt from a clear sky—that had so disastrous an effect that only a few of the 'advance guard' of pioneers lived to enjoy an advanced state of civilization" (152). Complaints continue: "The inconveniences of our environment and the constant drudgery effectually took all the romance and poetry out of our farm life" (133); "the scene in this place of gloomy solitude, where white women's foot never before trod, was inexpressibly dreary and saddening. A scene more utterly desolate could hardly be imagined" (202).

Louise Gregg Stephens's *Letters from an Oregon Ranch* (1905) describes a different kind of move to Oregon. Lured by a later homesteading initiative from Washington D.C., she and her husband select a house from a huge number of abandoned properties (signifier of massive settlement failure), and try to become rural folk. Shopping is difficult for one "accustomed to the ordering of daily supplies, with the telephone at hand to rectify errors or omissions" (39); milking "is hardly the pleasant pastime once pictured by my imagination,—such a never-ending straining, skimming, and washing of pails and pans! . . . Having neither electricity nor gas-lights, we had to fall back upon the fragrant kerosene" (149). "At home the vegetables we use are brought us from the markets. Here we must ourselves go to the garden for them. . . . There, in the fruit-canning season, the fruit in cases and baskets is delivered at the door; here we must pick it from the trees" (151). Because all the local women are immersed in their own domestic responsibilities, there are—horrors—no laundresses; "being forced to do one's own laundry-work is the worst feature of ranch life. The shadow of the coming event actually darkens my Sundays" (153). Open air and landscape are a partial recompense: "For the first and only time in my life, I am happy and content in my environment. . . . Such a sky as we have here to-day,—blue as a harebell, and much the shape of one, its rim just resting upon this crown of dark firs. . . . A luminous flood of sunshine is in the air, soft, caressing, and sweet with the aromatic breath of the fir trees" (163).

Another homesteader with no knowledge of farming, New England schoolteacher Alice Day Pratt, planned simply to improve her allotment up to the legal minimum and wait for land values to rise so she could sell at a profit. *A Homesteader's Portfolio* (1922, reissued with an introduction by Molly Gloss in 1991) complains when neighbors don't offer help, offer it but fail to follow through, or take money and don't do the promised work. She mistakenly expects neighbor women to be kind and sociable, neighbor men to voluntarily build her cabin and plow her fields. She finds the old pioneers culturally reactionary and hostile to newcomers, while the newcomers don't get along very well with each other either.

Emma Ray's *Twice Sold, Twice Ransomed: Autobiography of Mr. and Mrs. L. P. Ray* (1926) is unique, because Ray was urban, evangelical, and African American. Her book, published in Chicago when she was 67, was designed for sale among fellow Methodists to support the couple in their old age. Originally from outside St. Louis, the couple settled in Seattle when her husband got work as a stonemason. The book recounts a lifetime ministering to drunks, "dope fiends," prisoners, prostitutes, and patients in hospitals. Indirectly, Ray presents a history of Seattle: its virtual destruction in the great fire of 1889, the business downturn in the recession of 1893–94, the razing of hills and building of houses, and the recovery occasioned by the Alaskan gold rush.

The Rays preached, sang, distributed tracts, and brought people to the mission house. They worked mostly among whites, because there were "but a few of our own people in Seattle when we came, and at times I got very lonely" (40). She and a white woman "would go into the slums together and hold meetings, and also into the houses of shame below the 'dead line.' We found the inmates mostly very courteous. Most of the girls were bright mulattoes. The landlady was always willing to stop their dancing and music and to call every girl into the meetings. The Lord gave us good results from this work, and some were saved out of this house" (75). The addicts often "lived under the wharves, upstairs in old deserted buildings, and sometimes they were found in deserted outhouses in the mud flats—anywhere they could hide away in the daytime from the police. About twelve o'clock at night they would come out into the streets to beg and get dope. They told me they had gone for weeks with hardly anything to eat. . . . They would creep along the wharves, or along some back street, and run and dodge around all night long with the fear that they would be arrested. . . . They had come from good Christian homes and had got their start as fiends through the doctors and sickness, and this led them down in sin" (77).

During the depression of the nineties her husband lost his job as a mason but found work as porter in a dry goods store, from which vantage point they witnessed the impact of the Alaska Gold Rush. "As soon as the Alaska boom struck the country, business picked up right away and in a short while the city was full of strangers, preparing themselves to go to the Klondike. Thousands of them outfitted from this business store. With them they took only clothing suitable for that cold climate. Hence they left their old clothing and trunks and such things behind them. The shipping clerk then turned many a parcel over to Mr. Ray to help clothe the poor. I'm sorry to say that many of the men leaving for the North left their Bibles behind, and I suppose many left their salvation also. . . . There was a great opportunity for doing good in the store, as Mr. Ray would hand out tracts to the men and talk salvation to them as they passed through. In about a year or less time the city was flooded with men who had had their feet and arms frozen from exposure" (98–99). "They were from every class . . . all ages of men, but scarcely a woman. . . . Most all had seen better days, but sin and greed had brought them to this place of poverty and want" (158–59).

Leoti L. West went from Iowa to Colfax, Washington, in 1878 and taught in various Washington towns and cities for over a half century; eulogized as the "Inland Empire's Most Famous Teacher," she produced a series of reminiscences for the Spokane *Spokesman-Review*, which she then published as *The Wide Northwest: Historic Narrative of America's Wonder Land as Seen by a Pioneer Teacher* (1927). This town-centered book—reissued in 2005 with an introduction by Brenda K. Jackson—is mostly about the classroom, showing the teacher helping rough children develop into the polished businesspeople the region requires. She recalls: "we represented all classes and grades of human society; we represented also a remarkably high grade of intelligence, much higher than the average in pioneer communities and the beautiful feature of our population was that we were able to amalgamate into one great, integral whole. . . . We were an aggressive and a progressive people; aggressive in the sense that we must take virgin territory and hew out for ourselves a destiny; progressive in that we must build not only for ourselves but for future generations" (277–78).

* * *

Along with Belle Walker Cooke's *Tears and Victory* and Alice Rollit Coe's *Lyrics of Fir and Foam* mentioned above I identified three poetic miscellanies by Alice Harriman, among which I was able to read only *Wilt Thou Not Sing?* (1912), which contains several exclamatory lyrics about the Pacific Northwest. A poem to Seattle calls it "splendid, sired by Destiny" (26) while one to Tacoma effuses: "Tacoma! Water! City of Destiny!" (39). "Songs O' the West" says the West is the land "Of throbbing life invigorating the soul! Thy mountains, glaciers, islands, harbors deep; Thy wide horizons reaching unto God / Uplift, inspire a listening Universe" (57). Irene Welch Grissom's *The Passing of the Desert* (1923) collects fifty-one short poems dedicated "to the men and women who transformed the great American desert into a land of fertility and beauty." The title poem is about irrigation, and says "Now long freight trains speed to and fro, / Where, outward bound, rich harvests flow; / The wires are strung from place to place / That bridge the loneliness of space; / . . . And on the conquered desert sands / A brave young empire proudly stands!" (2). "When the Railroad Comes" imagines a pioneer looking beyond his poor farm "Down years to come, and sees paved street / And noble trees, great gray stone blocks, / And stately homes loom in the heat. / A kingdom's door the steel unlocks!" (35). In "Homestead Land," settlers in tar-paper shacks are "God's chosen ones . . . these who dare / To storm the wild, and wrest it first / From out the grasp of frontier plains; / The leaders brave who go before / To mark the way—whose hard-won gains / Fling open wide a barred, locked door" (42).

*   *   *

Along with her histories, Frances Fuller Victor published a collection of melancholy stories and poems, *The New Penelope* (1877); they are about unfulfilled love, unavailable women, women in legal thrall to exploitative men, abandoned women, widowed women, scheming women, women displaced from the East, and good men who can't marry good women because they have Indian wives. In 1891 Mary P. Sawtelle, apparently the first woman to practice medicine on the Pacific Coast, published *The Heroine of '49: A Story of the Pacific Coast.* Despite its title (and despite a mistaken description by its own publisher), this is about the Pacific Northwest not the Gold Rush, and focuses on the prevalence of forced early marriages inspired by the double acreage allowed to couples in the Donation Act. Sawtelle's protagonist, married off at age fourteen by her parents to a nasty man three times her age, manages to get a divorce and goes East for an education, but Sawtelle says this end to the story is not the norm. Parents, anxious to be free of the burden of many dependents, collude with greedy men effectively to sell their child-daughters into slavery. So much for the pioneer family! Bethenia Owens-Adair, in *Some of Her Life Experiences* (1906), tells a similar story.

In 1905 the Oregon Pioneer Society (whose printing of Narcissa Whitman's letters in 1895 fueled a Narcissa mini-boom) asked Duniway for permission to reissue *Captain Gray's Company*; instead she gave them a new historical novel, *From the West to the West,* showing settler women undone by poverty, the Donation Act's bad effects, and spousal abuse. Two novels by well-known writers of the day, however, endorse and embroider the trail legend: Honoré Willsie (*We Must March*), and Vingie Roe (*The Splendid Road*), both from 1925. Both Willsie and Roe wrote about various parts of the West, as later chapters will show. Willsie went for high moralism and specialized in preachy heroines; Roe liked action and created heroines who were versions of the New Woman in western guise—courageous, athletic, vigorous, bold. Narcissa, Willsie's subject in *We Must March*, is funneled through a strident Anglo-Saxonism; using Dye as her source, Willsie says Narcissa's white and blond beauty is "of the kind that belonged to race, to the fineness developed by generations of gracious living" (107). Narcissa, clever enough recognize the "fatuous" self-assurance of the missionaries (her published letters showed that she had no sense of religious mission and no interest in Indians) wonders what, "without adequate equipment and without knowledge . . . real results could they hope to accomplish among the savages? Between the hostility of the British Company and the hostility of the red men, what could save the missionaries from being crushed?" (102). She tells her husband that Indians are "irresponsible children, with no moral sense whatever! On one side, they are tractable and peace-loving. On the other side, they are fiends" (124). Willsie avoids the job of explaining why Narcissa went to Oregon, or, more particularly, why she married Marcus Whitman, whom she didn't love. Presumably readers are to understand that women at the time had to marry. The romance plot, such as it is, involves her learning to respect her husband if not his beliefs, and eventually coming to love him. This growth in character makes her a true woman and a worthy martyr.

Roe's *Splendid Road* begins when its heroine, Sandra Dehault, along with her three adopted children, drives her own team to the California goldfields; it ends when these four plus an ethnically diverse group of others who have joined her leave California for Oregon. Sandra has "a swiftness and grace which showed her to be fit in every muscle, like a man" (9). Her "wiry strength, her courage, her absolute assurance in the face of trial and hardship" made men respect her (12). Sandra makes the big strike in California that frees her to do what she wants just when an "immense throng" is pouring "across the Klamath, over the Siskiyou range, into the Oregon country—literally the Oregon Trail. These were the lovers of the land who moved this year, the men who carried ploughs and seed, who brought their wives and children. They followed in the wake of the gold diggers, widened the dim traces of their intrepid lead. They, too, were makers of history, these breeders of a hardy type, these rugged visionaries" (293).

Ella Higginson (according to Alfred Powers's *History of Oregon Literature* the best-known Pacific Northwest writer of short stories among eastern readers) collected her tales in *The Flower That Grew in the Sand* (1896) and *From the Land of the Snow-Pearls: Tales from Puget Sound* (1897). These are well-crafted, formulaic local color stories about rural life, involving power struggles among the powerless—mothers and daughters, mothers-in-law and daughters-in-law, young women and their suitors, old women and other old women. In Higginson's one novel, *Mariella of Out-West* (1902), an exceptional female triumphs over sordid surroundings. Mariella, from a poor farming family, lives with her stolid father and half-crazed mother in the coastal town of Kulsha on the outskirts of Bellingham. An incoming railroad creates a boom, classy Easterners arrive, and Mariella has to learn the rules of genteel society without capitulating to social snobbery. There's an unusual description of the railroad boomer, who scouted out sites for railroad stations. "The 'boomer' himself has, like the cowboy, the stage-driver, and the tough character of the mining-camp, passed on; he is no more. As picturesque as they,—and as necessary,—he filled his place, which was an important one at the time. . . . Well-dressed, alive with nervous energy, good-natured, alert, quick to scheme and to act—yet holding something of the power of the sphinx in his narrowed eyes . . . he seemed to carry corner lots in the hollow of his hand, and to sell them without really desiring to sell" (174–75).

Mariella's intuitive connection with nature enables her to assess the social emptiness of the newcomers, who see only a "wilderness of stumps" where she sees ocean and forest grandeur. (Here is an indirect allusion to the ecological damage done by these early settlers.) It's "too awful," says one; "To have been born here in this crude place, and to have lived here always! . . . To have associated only with backwoodsmen; to have heard no literatures, no music" (326). Mariella escapes the town's past and its present—escapes the Pacific Northwest entirely—by marrying a wealthy Canadian and moving with him to England.

Mary Hamilton O'Connor, a film writer originally from Portland, published her young adult novel, *The "Vanishing Swede": A Tale of Adventure and Pluck, in the Pine Forests of Oregon,* in 1905. Sister Gerrie and brother Jack summer in Northwest Oregon—he with a surveying camp, she with a homesteading art teacher. Thanks to his surveying acumen, when they discover stakes "placed at regular intervals" outlining a "strip of land 500 by 1,500 feet, making about twenty acres" they know "that's no homestead nor timber claim, that's the size of a government mineral grant. There's a mine on this land" (184). This turns out to be the lost mine from which the novel takes its title, the "richest silver vein in the west" (200). O'Connor gives a nice picture of Oregon City on claim-filing day, when a crowd "made up, for the most part, of practical woodsmen—squatters on different parcels of land in the upper corner of the State" converges on the land office. "It was probable that all the people about to file today, had been living upon their claims ever since the time they trailed through the forest in the wake of a land-looker and had been shown posts and slashes which, they were told, marked the boundaries of the different quarter-sections. . . . Afterwards he would hold down his claim only by his presence upon it, or it stood a chance of being 'jumped'" (125–26).

Ada Woodruff Anderson published three interesting, ambitious novels somewhat marred by the absolute perfection of its female protagonists: *Heart of the Red Firs* (1908) set in the Yelm Valley; *The Strain of White* (1909), a historical fiction set around Seattle; and *The Rim of the Desert* (1915) about the interconnections between Washington State and Alaska. Her complicated topical plots and subplots center on subjects like timber, homesteading, mining, Pacific Northwest cities, the wilderness, Native people, and alcoholism. In *The Heart of the Red Firs* a schoolteacher homesteads alone, proud to be "a pioneer" and "the daughter of pioneers" (93). The equally noble hero manages a lumber mill in town, keeping people employed through an economic downturn, though what he really wants to do is go into the wilderness and locate his lost mining claim (which she does for him, unbeknownst to him). A subplot is about heavy drinking in the coastal cities and the misery of women whose husbands are drunks. The book contains a fine description of a group ascending Mount Rainier on horseback.

The Strain of White centers on the Battle of Seattle, January 1856. According to its preface, the heroine, Francesca, with a white father and a Native mother, "is drawn from a picturesque figure familiar to pioneers as late as the close of the seventies,—a young Yakima woman, straight as a fir tree, with a proud face, well-chiseled, the skin a clear olive" (n.p.). Francesca goes to town to find her father, who is reluctant to acknowledge her because his wife is horrified by Indian-white marriages. Even so, Francesca, whose best qualities derive from her Indian blood, saves the garrison and the community at some risk to herself, but not (as so many Indian heroines do in this kind of story) for love of a white man. She is simply a heroine, ashamed of her father, his wife, and his nasty blonde daughter (who is transformed by love before the book's end). Indian virtue does not lead to the idea that Natives deserved to win that battle; had they done so, all the tribes would have risen up and "every settlement would have been wiped out—except the Hudson Bay post at Nisqually; and before other immigrants could have ventured in, Canada might have seized the opportunity to take permanent hold" (278). Like many Pacific Northwest accounts, this one is well aware that Oregon almost became part of the British Empire. And like Indian stories nation-wide, it pays homage only to the safely vanished type.

Anne Shannon Monroe's first book, *Eugene Norton: A Tale of the Sagebrush Land,* appeared in 1900. Two other novels are *Happy Valley* (1916) and *Behind the Ranges* (1925). All three take place in the arid regions of eastern Washington, in the process of being irrigated for cattle ranches and orchards. In *Eugene Norton,* the heroine, Catherine, has been bullied into a bad marriage by her father. When she and Eugene meet, though living in "a two-roomed cabin (a mere shack of upright boards one thickness from the weather)" Catherine still sets her table with fine china and solid silver (79). Time passes; Catherine leaves her husband, moves to "Cascadia," finds work singing in a church choir, and gets a divorce. She meets Eugene again; he now directs the city's Insane Asylum, about which the narrator says, intriguingly: "The State of Washington is rich in insane. . . . Many of the inmates come from ranches way up in the mountains, where they have lived in the heavy timber alone and brooded themselves into melancholia. These are mostly women, Germans and Swedes. Others come from the sheep ranches east of the mountains. These are men, sheep-herders. . . . On the Pacific Coast our population is made up partly of people who have lost money or health or good name in the Eastern States. They come West to pick up again, and of course they can't all do it; they become depressed and their brains give way" (143–44).

The novel ends with Eugene's vision of the future, oddly mismatched with the poverty, insanity, and marital unhappiness of the present but entirely in tune with the Pacific Northwest motif of hope deferred. "He sees with those far-seeing eyes throngs of people pouring into his loved Western land. He sees Puget Sound full of ships, ships upon ships plowing the grand old Pacific, the orient and occident closely allied, and all the world open to the people. And he sees, better and grander than all the rest, the era of greed and gain passing away,—and growing out of it, stronger and stronger year by year, man's humanity to man" (290).

Happy Valley is a polemical novel set in the "last West" of eastern Oregon. Billy Blaine, the narrator, is an educated eastern wastrel sent by his grandfather to find—what he does find—hard work, redemption, romance, purpose, the healthy air of the West, and faith in the future. But Billy is surrounded by those who are overmatched by natural and human antagonists: "Always I had thought of the country as new, virgin, and untouched. I now learned that it was an old country over which battles had been fought, nearly every section of which had been wet with human blood. . . . To find this cattleman's Eden was to appropriate it. . . . Settlers were not wanted; settlers fenced; settlers interfered with range and water. In time the powerful cattle companies controlled the whole country" (215).

The novel criticizes government rules and regulations that doom homesteaders, prohibited from cutting wood or hunting game, to failure. "Lumber would have to be hauled over one hundred miles, which made it costly to say nothing of the time and the wear and tear on teams" (95–96). Nor had these neophytes "rightly figured on the cost of getting started on new land"; there were "unforeseen accidents and delays in putting in a garden. The homesteading law would permit the men to leave home to find work, but to hold down their claims the women must remain upon them. No one had wintered in the valley, no one could say whether or not the women would be safe and comfortable in tents" (119). Realizing the connection between farms and markets, Billy wonders: "How will they get their crops out without a railroad? Unless they're bringing in money how will they live till we do get a railroad? You've seen abandoned cabins all over the inland empire—every one a monument to the death of an American citizen's highest hope, his hope of a home and independence. . . . He has to go away and find work and the work just keeps his family on the ranch" (244). The railroad "won't come without settlers; the settlers can't come without a railroad. . . . If that timber belt to the east was open, a railroad would build to timber; but that is shut off from use by the government; if the waterways were open we could have mills, but the water power is tied up by the government; if a canal was dug here, inviting a thousand settlers to irrigated ranches, a railroad might build to that; it would be a feeder; but you can't dig a canal without wood and the wood belongs to the government" (249–50).

Behind the Ranges puts small ranchers in the role of the little guy played by homesteaders in *Happy Valley*. It's dedicated to "those range stockmen of the central Oregon country whose sun has all but set and whose going will remove from America the last remnants of her most picturesque and heroic mode of life." One rancher of unimaginable wealth, crooked politics, and unbridled ambition—bachelor Jim Battles of the Yellow Pines ranch—stands for all rich evildoers; he is opposed by old Ril (Riley) McNab of the oo ranch. The heroine, Helie (or Heliotrope) Grinelli, is a gorgeous free spirit who helps Ril "with every ranch duty—bringing in strayed steers, cutting out the beef stuff, weaning young calves, rounding up wild hogs in the tule marches" (93). The incredible plot turns on Helie's turning out to be Jim Battles's daughter. After he has improbably made her his sole heiress and conveniently been shot in the back by someone unknown, she returns their "paper" to all the ranchers and thereby reorients the community toward the small yeoman. The novel's strength is in its scenes representing ranch buildings, daily and seasonal routines, its rules, and over all, the unpredictable climate and weather.

Irene Welch Grissom set two didactic and political novels about the timber industry in the Cascade Mountains. *The Superintendent* (1910) is also about alcoholism while *A Daughter of the Northwest* (1918) is also a female coming-of-age and new-woman novel—a sign of changed times and changing plot patterns for women's fiction after World War I. Sally, heroine of *The Superintendent,* comes from Kansas; her unfamiliarity with the region sanctions some aesthetic gush, which is both appreciated and quashed by the more practical people around her. She marries an attractive drunkard rather than the mill supervisor, finds she can't reform him, and is freed from her mistake when he commits suicide. At the end she will marry the superintendent and teach in one of the men's clubs that management hopes will keep the men from drink and boredom.

When Sally gets sentimental about the "reckless slaughter of the trees," the superintendent answers: "There are countless homes waiting to be erected from the lumber we make. Great ships must be built to carry on the commerce of our nation. Deep mines need our massive timbers that the ore from far beneath the ground may be brought to the surface to do its share in the world's work. We are ministering to the needs of humanity. The destruction of our forests is only the inevitable yielding to the demands of a great nation" (33–34). Heavy drinking is routine: "To the greater part of the men employed in the twenty-five saw and shingle mills on the harbor, the saloon was the one place where music, good cheer, comradeship, bright lights and an ever-pressing welcome awaited them" (84).

The first-person narrator, protagonist of *A Daughter of the Northwest* is the daughter of a lumber mill owner. She studies architecture at the University of Washington, gets a job and an apartment in Portland, and finally returns to the woods and the right man, Roger, who stands for new principles of forestry. A love story based on forestry ethics is an innovation, but the enormous so-called "Big Burn" of 1910 had brought the subject into public view: "Walking steadily by his side, I could be the silent partner in a splendid work, for I loved and reverenced the great forests, and longed for them to be treated with intelligence and consideration, that they might fulfill their mission on earth in the highest sense" (69).

The most important question about forest use in this novel is how much waste is economically and ethically tolerable. Father thinks waste is necessary for cheap lumber, but Roger disagrees: "An average has been struck for the amount of unused material in every stick of timber logged in the United States, and that it is sixty per cent. Think of this enormous waste! . . . And the loss by forest fires every year is appalling. To labor together to prevent it is every lumberman's sacred duty" (58). This discussion turns out to be more than theoretical when the industry falls on hard times: "A sudden slump in prices, occasioned by a diminishing demand for lumber products, found the company with a huge debt hanging over it, and mills that must be kept running at any cost to meet the interest and make the payments due on the principal. A year of poor crops through many of the Central Western States was blamed for lack of demand. Drouths had prevailed, and the farmer, their most valued consumer, was not buying lumber" (78). But when the Americans enter World War I, according to father, "we shall see an era of unprecedented prosperity in the lumber business" (216). Still, he continues, "we must not forget that great financial gain will bring with it a grave menace to the ultimate prosperity of our nation if the lumberman, in their mad rush to fill orders, cease to practice forestry"; we must serve "posterity by preserving our forests according to the best known modern methods" (217).

Katharine Berry Judson's one novel, *When the Forests Are Ablaze* (1912), was also about the forest and forest fires. Its single (and silly) woman protagonist, Jane, a bored schoolteacher jilted at the altar, homesteads on a timber claim. She quickly sees her unfitness for the life, to which she brings nothing more than banal ideas about scenery. She writes to a friend about the "crude rawness" of the lumber town, "its roughly built shacks, stores with false fronts to give an impression of height, and the grim devastation immediately surrounding it—I never imagined there could be such force in that old saying that God made the country and man made the town" (62). Only the attentions of two men—a businessman and a forest ranger—keep her steady, and an enormous forest fire drives her out of the homestead into the ranger's arms. Western life makes her more self-reliant and more athletic. Solitude teaches her self-knowledge and helps her see, when up against the elements, the usefulness of men. The forest ranger is the hero, and together with the narrator gives the reader pages and pages of information about his duties, training, tests to pass, ways of fighting fires, the damage done by particular fires, and more.

Vingie Roe's 1913 novel, *The Heart of Night Wind: A Story of the Great North West,* says more about lumber mill chicanery and fake homestead claims than the other timber novels, while its highly wrought plot allows for extreme atmospheric effects in the rainy, misty, foggy, frozen Cascade range. Roe westernizes her good woman by making her a white girl who has been raised as an Indian, which gives her health, energy, athleticism, a great love for horses, and an intuitive connection to the landscape without sacrificing her racial superiority. The hero, Walter Sandry, connects the heroine to the landscape: "The mighty trees around them, the eternal majesty of the hills under the intimate grey sky, the girl in her trim, sensible attire of blue shirt, short skirt and boots, with that sudden revelation of the wild about her, combined to suggest the unreal, the mysterious, the lawless, and it struck deep under the veneer of urbanity to the man. She might have been some princess of a forgotten day, the darling of some ancient tribe of the West" (67).

The foil is a scheming eastern writer, Poppy Ordway, visiting the West in search of local color. Poppy, angling for Sandry, discovers manipulated land titles in the rival lumber company; bad as she is, she does good. "You know that all this land was government land. . . . Have you noticed that all of it, or nearly all, belongs to either one or the other of these two lumber companies? . . . Have you noticed that *none of these claims seem to have been taken in good faith?* That none of the filers have complied in spirit with the Homestead Law. I have scoured these hills . . . and at every filing there is the barest hold of tenure,—a windowless shack,—just enough to nail the law by its letter. Nowhere have I seen a cleared field, nor one sign of tillage. Mr. Sandry, I believe we have stumbled upon a huge government swindle, a case of land-fraud gigantic in its proportion" (137). Corruption notwithstanding, West is best; on a trip back East, Sandry wonders: "Was this what he had yearned for, there among the mighty hills? These packed and crowded cities, with their noise and clangour, their trailing smoke, their hurrying multitudes and their dirt-stained, towering piles of stone and mortar?" (259).

Emma Ray and Edith Maud Eaton (Sui Sin Far) are the only two truly urban writers from the region that I've found. The stories in Sin Far's 1912 *Mrs. Spring Fragrance* (her only book, reissued with an introduction by E. Catherine Falvey in 1994) are about urban Chinatowns—mainly Seattle's. They recognize and cater to the Anglo vogue for a slightly risqué Orientalism. "Streaming along the street was a motley throng made up of all nationalities. The sing-song voices of girls whom respectable merchants' wives shudder to name, were calling to one another from high balconies up shadowy alleys. A fat barber was laughing hilariously at a drunken white man who had fallen into a gutter; a withered old fellow, carrying a bird in a cage, stood at the corner entreating passersby to have a foot fortune told. . . . A Chinese dressed in the latest American style and a very blonde woman, laughing immoderately, were entering a Chinese restaurant together" (40–41).

The Chinatown stories in the first part of *Mrs. Spring Fragrance* (the second part contains fables for children) involve discord in well-off merchant families when husbands and wives differ over Americanization. In "The Wisdom of the New" a transplanted wife poisons her child rather than have him learn American ways in school. There are also stories about interracial marriages—especially white women married to Chinese men—and their mixed-race children. Mrs. Spring Fragrance, wife of a successful Chinese businessman, figures in several

stories as a sort of onlooker: "Ah, these Americans! These mysterious, inscru-
table, incomprehensible Americans! Had I the divine right of learning I would
put them into an immortal book!" (20).

* * *

Caroline Leighton's 1883 *Life at Puget Sound* was the earliest book I found that
sees economic value in Pacific Northwest scenery: "To the lovers of the grand
and beautiful, unmarred as yet by any human interferences, who appreciate
the freedom from conventionalities which pertain to longer-settled portions
of the globe" the Puget Sound area "presents an endless field for observation
and enjoyment" (iv). Along with appreciation of landscape, she makes much
of the comfortable, even New England aspect of towns in the Pacific Northwest, and points to the large number of emigrants from Maine. By the time of
Ruth Kedzie Wood's *The Tourist's Northwest* (1917) scenery is well-established
as an economic draw: "To the industries of the Northwest a new one is added:
Multitudes of tourists journey each year down highways of steel or asphalt to
behold the wonders of river, sea and mountain the Creator has performed, and
to praise marvels of city and plain wrought by man" (65).

But for scenery, nothing came close to Alaska. Its identity as part of the Pacific Northwest from the first was evident in advertisements for tourists from
railroad and steamship lines based in Tacoma and Seattle. Eliza Ruhamah Scidmore's *Alaska: Its Southern Coast and the Sitkan Archipelago* (1885), a book that
collapsed three summer visits into one account and worked much Alaska history and geography into the presentation, is the earliest I found. She sees the
Indians, who outnumber whites (apparently in the 1880s Alaska's population of
32,000 included only 430 white settlers), as a population that needs to be managed and also a tourist attraction. "If these fish-eating, canoe-paddling Indians
of the northwest coast are superior to the hunters and horsemen of the western plains, the Haidas are the most remarkable of the coast tribes, and offer a
fascinating study to anyone interested in native races and fellow man" (42–43).
After scenery and natives come prospects for development, which means mining which, in turn, means capital investment protected by laws: "With things
in such an insecure state, capitalists were not willing to venture anything in the
development of these mines, and owners did little boasting of the richness of
their lodes, lest more miscreants should be invited to jump their claims" (84).
Scidmore followed this successful book with a tourist guidebook to Alaska and
the northwest coast, commissioned and published by Appleton in 1893.

Massachusetts resident Abby Johnson Woodman's *Picturesque Alaska* (1889)
is a journal account of a five-week spring tour in 1888. The book brings in the
entire Pacific Northwest by describing the railroad trip through Oregon and
Washington State to Tacoma. And though Alaskan scenery is sublime, the manly

get-up-and-go spirit of Washington and Oregon is better. "The leading business men of Tacoma are, as a rule, young men, ambitious and full of 'public spirit.' The strong and determined will to do, and overcome obstacles in the way of progress—which animated our forefathers upon the eastern shores of our continent—seems to pervade and fill the atmosphere of Tacoma" (56–57).

Septima M. Collis published *A Woman's Trip to Alaska,* a breezy and sophisticated series of letters to her daughter, in 1890; its account of the railroad journey from New York to Tacoma links Alaska to the rest of the nation. Accompanying her husband, a Civil War hero, on a business trip, she attends many social events and relays the life style of the small number of high-status Anglos. She praises the Presbyterian mission school in Sitka for teaching young Indians about order, decorum, neatness, cleanliness, basic literacy, carpentry (for boys), and domestic skills (for girls). These young people can look forward to assimilation into white America as handymen and maids. Like Woodman, Collis is impressed that Washington State is "attracting so much attention that capital and labor are both emigrating there from the East in such abundance that before the echo of the axe has died away in the forest, towns and railways, churches and schools, mills and factories, shops and homes, have taken the place of the stately firs, and a busy community is brought together to increase and multiply, and, I hope, to prosper" (55). The Alaska purchase was good for the rest of the country, not to mention the whole world: in "the peaceable surrender and peaceable acquisition of vast territory without resort to arms" some "five hundred and eighty thousand square miles of the earth's surface passed from the control of the most despotic monarch on the globe into the hands of the most liberal of modern governments; thus the boast of the Englishman, that the sun never sets on her Majesty's dominions, ceased to be without parallel" (94–95).

In 1892, Boston spiritualist Susie Clark published *Lorita; An Alaskan Maiden.* Tourist descriptions of Alaska scenery and settlements from Sitka to Juneau underpin a romance between two perfect creatures. In the Alaska section (there's also a segment about Yellowstone), the book complains about the federal government's foolhardy neglect of the territory. Says Lorita: "If Alaska were better known, perhaps the rulers of our nation would sooner provide for its needs, instead of curtailing the contributions already made toward her educational advancement" (26).

*   *   *

Lyon E. Knapp was governor of Alaska territory for five years beginning in 1889. His daughter, Frances Knapp, worked as his secretary and published *The Thlinkets of Southeastern Alaska* in 1896. (The book is presented as jointly authored with—perhaps ghost-written by?—feminist journalist Rheta Dorr, but constant allusions to "the writer" in the singular present the book as Knapp's alone.) This, the earliest book-length ethnography of that tribe, is also one of the first western Indian ethnographies by a woman. It merges published materials with informants' accounts, and shows the tourist potential of (safe) Indians: "Every year the number of tourists and the volume of enthusiasm increases, and the majority of returned visitors will be ready to testify that a round-trip ticket to Alaska means more unalloyed enjoyment than can be crowded into a similar two weeks' trip in this country or any other. . . . The matchless scenery along the way, the clear brilliancy of the atmosphere, the mild and genial climate, have become celebrated through these summer travellers. . . . In Sitka, the quaint little capital of the territory, the tourist always loves to linger amidst the historic relics of that past which is so rapidly becoming obliterated" (9–11).

Along with culture-bound descriptions of diabolic shamanism and witchcraft, disease, lack of sanitation, alcoholism, and conservative stupidity (the Thlinkit belong to one of the "lower races") is praise of the people's fishing ability and their artistry—the former suggests their aptness as employees in fisheries, the latter encourages tourist interest in native productions. The totem, the potlatch, and an analysis of Thlinkit psychology in terms of (unchristian) pride and retaliation are part of the study. Like Collis, she sees the future of the tribe, after the conservatives have all died off, in mechanical and domestic service. Constant references in all these books to shamanism and disease insist on the way that Natives reject scientific medicine and have no understanding of sanitation.

Mary E. Hitchcock, wealthy widow of a naval officer, went to Alaska in high style, erecting a football-field size tent in the mining camp, throwing lavish parties, and happily recording (or inventing) praise she received from such men as her baggage handler or cook, who intuitively recognize her superior worth in *Two Women in the Klondike: The Story of a Journey to the Gold Fields of Alaska* (1899). Ella Higginson's travel book, *Alaska* (1908), alternately rhapsodizes over landscape sublimity and Indian baskets. Within the terms of her own world view, she takes the Native side when she writes "The recent rapid development of Alaska, and the appropriation of the native food-supplies by miners, traders, canners, and settlers, present a problem that must be solved at once. . . . For forty years these dark, gentle, uncomplaining people of our most northern and most splendid possession—beautiful, glorious Alaska—have been patiently waiting for all that we should long ago have given them: protection, interest, and the education and training that would have converted them from diseased and wretched beings into decent and useful people" (387–88).

Before publishing her history textbook, Katharine Berry Judson had brought out *Myths and Legends of the Pacific Northwest, Especially Washington and Oregon* in 1910 (the book was reissued in 1997 with an introduction by Jay Miller) and *Myths and Legends of Alaska* in 1911. These, the first in what became a six-book set, adapted scholarly anthropology for amateurs, and conveyed an image of Native people as essentially childish. She tells readers she is omitting from these tales what the Pacific Northwest book calls "coarseness" (12) and the Alaska book "low moral conditions" (vii). She leaves out every story with "traces of the white man's religion" (*Pacific Northwest* 12), and rewrites several to recover the supposed "simplicity and directness" that had "been destroyed by attempted witticisms, by philosophical remarks, or by wordy explanations" (*Pacific Northwest* 13). In the Alaska book, even while she says she has not altered "the terse directness of the natives" she admits to leaving out stories that "are very long and tiresome, rambling from one subject to another" (vi). In short, she invents the Natives she claims to be describing—ahistorical, unreflective, unhumorous, prudish, terse, and naively helpless; faced with the Northwest's terrific natural forces, they find explanations in animal examples (mainly the wily coyote and the raven) and are consoled by shamans who pretend to have "power over the evil spirits, those who by incantations and charms of magic, by ceremonial dancing in symbolic dress, can control the designs of those who work ever against these children of the North" (*Alaska,* vi). In 1921, Ella Sterling Mighels in her history of Alaskan Indians (and Pacific Northwest Indians more generally) for children, *Wawona: An Indian Story of the Northwest,* follows the imagined story of a California Indian woman kidnapped by Alaskan Natives who finds her life purpose in keeping history alive, thus celebrating the tribe she'd been abducted from; indirectly, this approach presents Indians as immigrants rather than indigenes and likens their histories to those of Anglos.

* * *

May Kellogg Sullivan's 1902 *A Woman Who Went to Alaska* and Florence Lee Mallinson's 1914 *My Travels in Alaska* record the Alaskan lives of two women who saw themselves as pioneers not tourists. Sullivan's Alaska is a place of meager comforts, extreme weather, alcoholism among miners, lack of sanitation in the camps and consequent illness—it's not only Indians who don't understand the connection between dirt and disease. Nome, "crowded, dirty, disorderly, full of saloons and gambling houses, with a few fourth-class restaurants and one or two mediocre hotels" is a typical new mining camp in every respect (94). "Summer's accumulation of filth in the camp, too young as yet for cleanly conditions . . . brought their sure accompaniment—the fever. Many suffered for weeks with it, and then died" (112).

While hoping to make a strike (she persuades or hires miners to stake claims for her) she supports herself as a cook: "I could teach music; and I could paint passably in water colors and oils; in fact, I had been a teacher of all three, but in Alaska these luxuries were not in demand. . . . Men and women had come to Nome for gold, expected to get lots of it, and that quickly. They had no time for Beethoven's sonatas or water color drawings" (102). She reports that few would-be miners knew anything about Alaska or mining. "Thousands of persons who were ill qualified in these and other respects had journeyed to Alaska, only to return, homesick, penniless, and completely discouraged, who never should have left their home firesides" (166). The narrative stops occasionally to admire the scenery: "This, then, was our new Arctic world. How wonderfully beautiful it was in its purity and stillness! Look whichever way I would, all was perfect whiteness and silence. When I walked the snow scarcely creaked under my feet. . . . It was a solemn stillness, but ineffably sweet and tender. It was good to live. A feeling of sweetest peace and happiness swept over me, and tears sprang to my eyes. Was this heaven?" (264).

In 1910, encouraged by her book's success, Sullivan published *The Trail of a Sourdough: Life in Alaska,* with nine fanciful sketches designed to "picture not only character, but also the vast and wonderful gold producing region, so plainly that even the young may better know Alaska, and learn somewhat from glimpses of the trials, privations and successes of its early pioneers" (5). She again shows the generic Gold Rush pioneer as inexperienced and ignorant. He drinks, quarrels, and—failing to find nuggets lying around to pick up off the ground—quickly departs.

Much like Sullivan, although with a husband, Mallinson went to Alaska to make a fortune. After nine years—one season in Nome and the rest in Fairbanks—she made enough money to treat herself to music lessons in Seattle. "I am one of the pioneer women" of Alaska, she says (16), and her book combines "travel and observation with a discussion of the economic and material progress of Alaska" (56). The book recounts a series of failed mining attempts and heroic struggles to overcome the rigors of an awful climate; Ben Mallinson tries to mine while she works as a cook (cooking again is the one female accomplishment with economic value). Her book is a memoir of a difficult yet exhilarating life and a sales pitch for the territory. She praises Franklin Lane, then secretary of the interior, for his anticonservation politics. Alaska "is a big country and its people at once become stimulated by large ideas. . . . We demand something more than the pinched, dwarfed, conservation-locked pessimism of Eastern statesmen" (22). She makes a point of Fairbanks's amazing growth during her time there and implies that her own presence, which signifies the presence of women, contributes largely to that growth: "What women have contributed to the economic and domestic life of the picture here being introduced constitutes one of its life-giving features" (24).

Esther Birdsall Darling lived in Nome from 1907 to 1917 and, with her husband, ran a kennel that produced prize-winning malamute racers. *Up in Alaska* (1912), a book of twenty-six poems, contained versified banquet toasts, poems about dogs, and poems about Alaska. The title poem has lines like: "The snow is nowhere quite so white / As in Alaska; / And nowhere shine the stars so bright / As in Alaska. . . . / And nowhere is the gold so pure / As in Alaska. / The people—well, we're not so sure / Up in Alaska" (33). The longest, "A Growl from Nome" (pp. 49–54) is a dialect poem about a dog race. "A Wish" hopes that your life may be "as full of brightness / As Alaska's long June days, / where at night the sun just sinks to rest / But leaves his golden rays" (38). Darling also published several dog books for children based on the real inhabitants of the kennel, beginning with *Baldy of Nome* (1916), which has much to say about dogs in Alaska's economy, history, and culture. Dogs "have ever shared the toil of the development of that desolate country that stretches from the ice-bound Arctic to where the gray and sullen waters of Bering Sea break on a bleak and wind-swept shore" (21); "With the departure of the last boats of the summer there is no connecting link with the great, unfrozen outside, except the wireless tele-graph and the United state Government Dog Team Mail that is brought fifteen hundred miles, in relays, over the long white trail from Valdez"; then come the "Dog Days of Nome" when "the town gives itself up completely to the gripping intensity and ardors of this period when all dog men assemble in appropriate places to talk over the prospects of the coming Racing Season" (31).

＊　＊　＊

Ada Anderson's third novel, *The Rim of the Desert* (1915), is densely informa-tive about railroads, highways, avalanches, the Cascade Mountains, Alaska, Se-attle, eastern Washington, town building, mining, orchards, the politics of land deals and territorial status, and home rule agitation. Like Mallinson, Anderson complains about conservation laws requiring the inland settler to "trek back hundreds of miles to the seaport . . . to pack in coal" because cutting timber around his camp is prohibited (251). More than any other Northwest Pacific book, this one demonstrates the codependency of Alaska and the old Oregon territory. Anderson alleges that non-Northwest conglomerations are looting the territory (e.g., the real "Alaska Syndicate" jointly formed by Guggenheim and J. P. Morgan, is represented in the novel by a Jewish family named Morganstein). Alaska needs more white settlers from Oregon and Washington; it needs home rule; and if its climate limits its internal development, then income derived from its mines, fisheries and forests should be used to transform the deserts of Washington and Oregon into blooming orchards. The Pacific Northwest is still the future place.

4

Upper California and Nevada

The Gold Rush and its demon child, San Francisco, dominated women's books from upper California. The author of the earliest such book I found was a woman who never went West. This was New England pedagogue Emma Willard, who drew heavily on John Fremont's accounts in her *Last Leaves of American History* (1849) and proposed that the Mexican War was about controlling California harbors not expanding slave territory. The discovery of gold could not have been anticipated. "California, so lately a poor anarchical territory of an ill-governed state, is now attached as an integral part of the American Republic, and at the moment of her becoming so, discovered to possess immense mineral riches, and a flood of emigration is hastening by sea and land, such as the earth has never seen before" (110). "San Francisco," she predicted, "will therefore probably increase faster than any city of our fast-growing republic." Yet, she continued, it won't be "a healthy growth, unless the immigrants take sober, earnest thought, and resolute action; to suppress vice and disorder, and to uphold law, morals, and religion" (163). The able and enterprising emigrants going to California with "nobler views than the mere love of gold" need to "feel, with a deep sense of responsibility, that they are going to lay the foundations of a new and an important state. Let them look back for an example to their forefathers" (230).

The first woman reporting from the mines—Louise Amelia Clappe—published dispatches in a California magazine that didn't become a book until years after her death. These "Dame Shirley" letters aside, the earliest nonfiction book from an observer on the ground seems to be Eliza Wood Farnham's antimining, profarming *California In-Doors and Out; or, How We Farm, Mine, and Live Generally in the Golden State* (1856, reissued with an introduction by Madeleine B. Stern in 1972). Farnham, a reformer who believed that the world's salvation would be achieved by the superior female, found her approach especially cogent for California. She actually tried, without success, to collect a boatload of virtuous women to go to California and redeem it. "There is no country in the world where the highest attributes of the female character are more indispens-able to the social weal than in California; for nowhere else have the indomitable energies, the quick desires, and the wide-reaching purposes of the Saxon nature been submitted to so severe a test of their self-regulating power" (295). The book ends with an apparent afterthought, a long chapter praising the Vigilance Committee, attributing to the men involved the highest attributes of the Saxon character. But in her novel of 1865, *The Ideal Attained,* Farnham throws in the California towel. San Francisco is "the most wicked city of its size on the globe" (212). Her protagonists move to South America.

Dolly Bryant Bates's *Incidents on Land and Water, or Four Years on the Pacific Coast* (1857) reported on three years (1851–54) spent mostly in the mining town of Marysville. "Persons from all classes were to be found in California, the moral and the immoral, the tempter and the tempted. Well may it call a blush to the cheek of our own sex, when I assert that the immoral predominated, as far as the female portion of the community were concerned" (317). In 1867 May Went-worth (also publishing as May Wentworth Newman) conflated literary culture and high ethical standards, publishing her 400+ page anthology, *Poetry of the Pacific,* to demonstrate California's progress in literature. The book contained work by over 60 poets, some half of them women. A historical poem by Mrs. S. M. Clark tells the westering story (from Europe to New England to the West) and makes wealth a good thing. "California's rock-bound shores" are "Where the 'Lone Star' of the Pacific shines, / To lure the traveler to that land of gold, / Where earth locks up within her secret mines, / For future generations, her vast wealth untold" (287). "Song of the Flume," by Anne M. Fitch, warns the flume (symbolizing mining) to "Pause for a moment in thy swift career. / And dedicate thy strength to *God and Right!*" (319). As an author, Wentworth specialized in children's fables. *The Golden Dawn and Other Stories* (1870) adapted fairy-tale patterns to dark mines and San Francisco in contrast to the sunny gardens of Santa Cruz. Better to be on the ground than under it in the mines or up in San Francisco's fog.

In 1876, Marietta Bell Stow—lecturer, feminist, journalist, and (later) unsuc-cessful candidate for political office—published *Probate Confiscation: Unjust Laws Which Govern Women,* attacking San Francisco juridical sexism. Believ-ing she had been swindled when her husband died intestate and she was pro-hibited from participating in the probate court's proceedings, she assailed the judicial system, the city, and probate judge Milton Myrick. "And behold, the Philistines—the great and impregnable army of Litigites, whose chief is the high and mighty Myrick the Just—pitched their tents over against San Fran-cisco; a city that goes up to the sea on the west, and down to the bay on the east; a city of great renown, far famed for its palatial residences, its hospitality, its magnificent hotels, its Mint, its City-hall expectations, and its Second-street Bridge. Nevertheless it has its fogs, its damps, its winds, its Chinese odors, and municipal government" (191).

Jessie Benton Fremont—wife of the celebrity explorer (whom she helped to write his influential reports) and daughter of Thomas Hart Benton, the senate's most vocal advocate of Manifest Destiny—became a professional writer after her husband's diverse business ventures failed. She published her magazine work in four books, two of them about California. *A Year of American Travel* (1878) recounts her long journey to Panama, across the isthmus, and up the Pacific Coast to rejoin her husband early in the Gold Rush years. So many people were trying to get to California that they had to wait seven weeks in Panama for a ship, during which time many "who had only tents and no resources against the climate" sickened and died. When she and her entourage debark at Monterey, they find almost nothing to eat: "not a fowl left in the northern part of the state, consequently not an egg; . . . no longer vaqueros or herdsmen, and flocks and herds had dispersed. . . . No cows, consequently no milk. Housekeeping, deprived of milk, eggs, vegetables, and fresh meat, becomes a puzzle; canned meat, macaroni, rice and ham become unendurable from repetition . . . while wood was abundant around here, there was no one to cut it" (104). She also describes the couple's decision to support California statehood as a free state: "It was not only the question of injustice to the blacks, but of justice to the white men crowding into the country. Here was a field where labor was amply repaid. . . . It would have been a very poor return for the good fortune that had come to us if we had taken part in shutting it out from these" (146).

Most of Fremont's *Far-West Sketches* (1890) describe two years beginning summer 1858 when, having gone to their Mariposa property for a camping vacation, the family had to remain to protect their land from claim-jumpers. She finds it "unreal—impossible, that in my own country, in the State for which my father and my husband had done so much, on our own ground and in our own home I and my young children should have to face such a condition" (65). Yet, she boasts, in these two years, with her husband mostly away at court defending their claims, she gets their house built, furnishes it, and makes it a center for neighborhood gatherings—the woman triumphs after all. Eventually the ruffian lawbreakers—mainly Australians, who live in a hamlet called "Hornitas, a place of evil fame just below our mountains . . . a place 'where everything that loathes the law' found congenial soil and flourished" (59)—are routed by good American wage-earning miners. These good people also demonstrate the best sort of working-class values: "patient courage in work"; "a brotherhood for maintaining order and the law—quick as the minute-men of our Revolution in united support of the right, and with a largeness of good-humored generosity special to our far-West life" (76). After all, yeoman virtues can be transferred to work in the mines.

Mary McNair Mathews, a widow who went in 1869 to Virginia City with her young son to settle her dead brother's mining claims, published *Ten Years in Nevada; or, Life on the Pacific Coast* (1880, reissued with an introduction by Clark Spence and Mary Lee Spence in 1985) after her return, showing that women can support themselves in a man's world with such respectable work as sewing, nursing, laundering, running a boarding house. There's an implicit critique of mining values in Mallie Stafford's 1884 *"The March of Empire" through Three Decades, Embracing Sketches of California History,* which combines a gold-driven history of Manifest Destiny, gold being "the powerful lever that moves the civilized world" (67), with a narrative about her husband's repeated failures in one Sierra mining milieu after another.

*   *   *

Writing for the World's Fair, Ella Sterling Cummins (later Ella Sterling Mighels, which I'll call her henceforth) published the first literary history of California. Based on newspaper and magazine files, *The Story of the Files: A Review of California Writers and Literature* (1893, reissued with an introduction by Oscar Lewis in 1982) meant to show that California had already developed an impressive literature. She names dozens of women story-writers, novelists, journalists, and poets, among whom poet Ina Coolbrith is "the only woman of these early writers to acquire popular celebrity and a fame that shows no signs of diminishing" (26). Coolbrith is one of only two women I've found to publish poetry books from this part of California. Like many poets of her day, Coolbrith thought poetry—and especially poetry by women—should transcend particularities, voicing lofty sentiments in regular scansion, conventional rhymes, and elevated diction. These ideas are not conducive to poetry of place; the poet Joaquin Miller (née Cincinnatus Heine Miller) wrote blustery epics that epitomized an ideal of manly western poetry. To some extent, Miller and Coolbrith divided the world of poetry between the two genders.

Coolbrith published one book, *Songs from the Golden Gate* (1895—another appeared posthumously) whose California material consisted of a poem on the Mariposa lily, another on the California poppy, and occasional references to fog or sunset in the ocean. A regional poem, "California," opens the volume. This first person narration by California herself thanks the Gold Rush for putting her on the map. For centuries she heard only birds, panthers, and "the savage tongue / Of my brown savage children" who "Chanted wild songs of their wild savage sires / And danced their wild, weird dances to and fro, / And wrought their beaded robes of buffalo." (4). Now, the sound of "the sharp clang of steel, that came to drain / The mountain's golden vein" (5) tells her that she'll "be known! / I shall not sit alone; / But reach my hands unto my sister lands!'" (5). The iteration of the word "savage" suggests that being known means becoming "civilized."

The second book-publishing woman poet is Madge Morris Wagner, who married the San Francisco publisher Harr Wagner late in the 1880s. Her three books of poetry (1881, 1885, 1917) are for the most part conventional miscellanies with flower poems, poems about dead babies, dead love, dead mothers, as well as an occasional political and patriotic foray. The 1917 book, however—*The Lure of the Desert Land and other Poems*—has several place-specific poems, among them poems to the California poppy, the Golden Gate, the Sierra foothills, San Joaquin wheat, and the earthquake, when all the city's "mighty architecture swayed and groaned / With crunch of wrenching beams, and screak and screech / Of twisted steel" (94). A long "legend" of the Carmel Mission shows up in the 1881 and 1885 books, and in 1917 she published a couple of antidesert poems, which I note in Chapter 9.

Mighels's anthology of 1918, *Literary California: Poetry, Prose and Portraits* (1918), again uses newspapers as her main source, and seems to retract its earlier praise, arguing now that the most important California type is the pioneer mother, who "redeemed our California in the Pioneer days" but whose story "has never been told by Bret Harte or any one else, yet it is a vital part of our history" (22). Frona Eunice Wait's *Wines and Vines of California* (1889) promotes the wines of the Napa and Sonoma valleys over those from southern California and praises vintners as "citizens and thorough good fellows in every sense of the word," comprising "the wealth and intelligence" of their communities and "noted throughout the State for their thorough go-ahead principles in business, and their admirable qualities in social life" (88). Wait, a journalist, California's representative to the world's fair of 1893, and northern California booster, also published a theosophical fantasy, *Yermah the Dorado: The Story of a Lost Race* (1897, revised in 1906 when the national theosophical society established its headquarters outside San Diego), and a book about Mount Lassen. *Yermah* adapts the theory, shared by some Native cultures and theosophists, that a great culture (of white people) had once flourished in California. Wait locates its settlement specifically in San Francisco's Golden Gate Park. This culture is destined to return, producing in Northern California a "great center of occult knowledge—the alchemical gold, corresponding to her mineral wealth" (424). Wait's *The Stories of El Dorado* (1904) is pre–Gold Rush California history for young people, distinguishing materialistic Spanish invaders from idealistic American pioneers. In 1922 she was still trying to help California fulfill its destiny; *The Kingship of Mt. Lassen* weaves geology, scenery, and history into a regional history inspired by the mountain's volcanic eruption of 1915 and its designation as a National Park in 1916. The foreword says the "immediate vicinity of Mt.

Lassen is the greatest scenic asset of the entire state" and should motivate the current generation to "live up to California's opportunity for supreme leadership," carrying out God's plan for California to produce "a civilization higher than all that has gone before it" (4).

Adeline Knapp's beautifully printed *This Then Is Upland Pastures: Being Some Out-door Essays Dealing with the Beautiful Things That the Spring and Summer Bring* (1897) is a prose effusion, less restrained than Thoreau but modeled on his botanical excursions, about natural beauty in the country around San Francisco. Luella Dickenson's *Reminiscences of a Trip across the Plains in 1846 and Early Days in California* (1904) and Eliza P. Donner Houghton's *The Expedition of the Donner Party and Its Tragic Fate* (1911) are late-life memoirs. Dickenson, who tells her husband's story not her own, celebrates the aging pioneer generation as "men of intelligence and inflexible honesty; and women of perseverance and determination, combined with a sense of duty, which fitted them for the perilous journey across the plains" (34). Houghton—survivor of the Donner disaster of 1847—extends her memoir beyond winter 1847 to chronicle her life within the framework of California history between 1847 and 1861. Dorcas James Spencer's *History of the Woman's Christian Temperance Union of Northern and Central California* (1913), commissioned by the WCTU State Convention of 1911 (the year women got the vote), is an attractive glimpse of women entering public life by expanding their sanctioned domestic role. Spencer, official superintendent of the Union's organizing efforts and a designated lobbyist to the California legislature, interprets organizing among women as a type of pioneering and narrates "incidents from the labors of early organizers illustrating the conditions under which the pioneering was done" (143).

In 1909, sociologist Mary Roberts Coolidge published *Chinese Immigration* in a series titled "American Public Problems," with a preface suggesting the book's origin in a dissertation. As much a history of California as of the incoming Chinese, it supposes that the state's progress—"the whole history of California"—is the story of how a minority, the "sub-stratum of intelligent, law-abiding American citizens" struggled "to establish order and justice in the midst of a fluctuating population swayed, in varying degree by greed, jealousy, ignorance, and race prejudice, and the primitive spirit of monopoly" (40). The workingmen were like the miners, comprising a lawless and greedy "community composed primarily of adventurers rather than settlers" (39); the unoffending Chinese were "natural victims of ignorant men who were both malicious and cowardly, and of the politicians dependent upon the Labor vote" (117).

I'll talk about Gertrude Atherton's novels later in this chapter. Her *California: An Intimate History* (1914), commissioned by Harpers, is really a history of San Francisco (the 1927 enlarged and revised version gave some attention to southern California as well) governed by her strident and highly gendered

Social Darwinism. The 1850s needed men "strong of body and brain, and only the strong could survive in the face of unparalleled hardships, trials, temptations, and disasters. These men, not all saints by any means, formed a nucleus which enabled San Francisco itself to survive and become the great city of the Western world" (151–52). The stronger, as always, "used their power to the full for the benefit of their own class and laughed at the impotent anger of the weak. There is no lesson so persistently taught by history as this, and it would be well for idealists, utopians, socialists, communists, single-taxers, labor-unionists, and all the rest of them to read it, accept it, digest it, and then either make the best of conditions as they are or find a leader, cultivate their brains, let alcohol alone, avoid windy agitators like plague-bearing rats, sink petty differences, and consolidate. And the best they may do will be as naught unless they find a great leader" (304–5).

Journalist Delilah Beasley's 1919 *Negro Trail Blazers of California* is an African American woman's history of California. For her, black achievement in California and recognition of black citizenship in the West are the aims and ends of Manifest Destiny. The first of the book's three parts is California history from the North African Estevanico on to statehood. California's entrance as a free-soil state, she says, obviously did not avert the Civil War but nevertheless "really was the beginning of the end of human slavery in the United States" (46). The second part of the book collects stories from black pioneers, showing "the wonderful strength of character and energy possessed by the pioneer Negroes of California" (47). Beasley distinguishes black from white miners because "The Negro miners came to California with the one thought of having better days. The allurement of gold was for the white men" (104). Extra cash went to buy freedom for oneself and one's family, or to support abolition. The last section surveys successful contemporary blacks, almost all residing in southern California because the trade unions that "rule" San Francisco have excluded African Americans from gainful employment. "Hence they have gone to make their homes in Los Angeles, where there is open shop, and a chance to make a living" (149).

Lilyan Corbin Stratton went to Reno for a divorce and published *Reno* (1921) as an informal guide to northern Nevada's history, topography, and ambience. She writes about Reno's elegant respectability, its schools, women's clubs, churches, newspapers, residential areas. Day trips to Lake Tahoe and Carson City link Reno to other parts of Nevada and northern California. Rebutting Nevada's bad reputation in the East, she reminds readers that Virginia City gold saved the Union during the Civil War; supposes that divorce does not harm marriage and may even help it; and explains Nevada's lenient laws as understandable attempts to attract settlers.

* * *

The 80-plus books of fiction—more than three times the number of nonfiction titles—include short story collections and novels of varying ambition and ability by writers ranging from the obscure, then and now, to others well known in their day. Earliest is Jennett Blakeslee Frost's potboiler, *The Gem of the Mines* (1866), wherein a young woman from Connecticut discovers her new husband to be an alcoholic spendthrift when they get to San Francisco; after several years of self-support in places like Fresno and Stockton (she runs a small millinery shop among other enterprises) she saves enough money to get back home. The subtext, like that in Mathews's *Ten Years in Nevada,* is about women earning money respectably in California. More than a decade later, her nonfictional *California's Greatest Curse* (1879) alleges that California's moral failings drag down the state's economy: Chinese low-wage work degrades the labor market, speculation keeps the stock market in chaos, monopoly capitalism stifles competition, and—the greatest curse—drink incapacitates huge numbers of white workers.

Ann Sophia Stephens's *The Outlaw's Wife; or, the Valley Ranche: A Tale of California Life* (1874) is the only woman's dime novel about the California Gold Rush I found. A moralistic antimining melodrama set in the Sierra hills, its domestic message couldn't be clearer. Sybil Yates, unhappily married to a professional gambler, schemes to separate the man she truly loves (not her husband, which shows how weak her morals are) from his fiancée. Valley Ranche had once been the "abode of a quiet family, whose cattle were fed on the luxuriant herbage of the valley"; now it's a center for "scenes of strife and dissipation, which destroyed its respectable, homelike appearance entirely" (6). Every Saturday night miners come from the surrounding hills to spend their week's earnings in drink and debauchery (these miners are wage-earners not prospectors); the moon shines on a "repulsive" scene of "men lying stretched upon the trampled grass; poor wretches, wounded in the quarrels, who had dragged themselves under the shadow of the great trees to bind up their wounds or seek the slumber of exhaustion and spent passions" (47). The good couple escapes this contamination by returning East "to the home which now became sacred to them both," and where in "after years the voices of merry children run through the rose-thickets" (115).

The topic of the few San Francisco stories in Josephine McCrackin's three collections, which are mostly set in the Southwest (*Overland Tales,* 1877; "Another Juanita" and Other Stories, 1893; *The Woman Who Lost Him, and Tales of the Army Frontier,* 1913) is always gambling, which for her exemplifies the city from its tycoons to indigents. "La Graciosa," the lead story in *Overland Tales,* weaves a lovely description of the California coast into a humorous courtship narrative, in which a divorced Anglo woman wins the love of a traditional Californio who detests divorce. Jane W. Bruner's melodramatic *Free Prison-*

ers: A Story of California Life (1877), set near the Sierra mining community of Grass Valley, describes gold as a magnet, "the severest tempter of manhood and womanhood" (17). *Tahoe; or, Life in California* by Sallie B. Morgan (1881), meshes its story with Sierra scenery, as the wealthy Heartlands—daughter and widowed father living palatially in Tahoe City—find appropriate mates after being almost swindled by a pair of criminals. Along with Lake Tahoe itself, the author writes about the Yosemite Valley, Sacramento, Oakland, San Diego, the mining districts, the Chinese, the Japanese, the coming railroad, San Francisco, and above all the transformation of the state from wilderness to wealth. Gold is good, yet, says Heartland, "California is full of loathsome adventurers" (79); "We have a dreadful character abroad; we are looked upon as a half-civilized set, unworthy the respect of good and honest men. All the fugitives from justice fly to our borders, and, concealing themselves among our scattered population, under assumed names, commit deeds from which the reputation of our State suffers" (167).

Mary W. Glascock's San Francisco novel *Dare* (1882) describes the city as class-stratified, polyglot, and unpleasantly foggy, a city of temptation although her moral tale shows social climbers losing out, gamblers coming to bad ends, and old-fashioned family virtue winning the day. Maud Howe Elliot's 1884 *The San Rosario Ranch* begins as a social comedy on a California dairy ranch, with a Europeanized protagonist apparently slated to become a western girl; but it abruptly changes direction and sends the protagonist back to Venice, where she dies young. In Louise Taber's *The Flame* (1911), San Francisco is a hunting ground for European aristocrats seeking wives.

Flora Haines Loughead wrote the chapter on California journalism for Mighels's *Story of the Files*. She brought her extensive knowledge of San Francisco to bear in her Dickensian 1886 novel, *The Man Who Was Guilty*. Her protagonist, Philip King, a bank cashier who accidentally embezzled money, insists on pleading guilty and serving ten years in San Quentin. Beginning with the prison population, and working outward and upward, Loughead anatomizes San Francisco from its criminals to its millionaires (some of them in both categories). Throughout the complicated plot runs a simple code of hard work, honesty, patience, kindness, family, and home—a code that flies in the face of San Francisco's values. Loughead brings in upper-class women through their role as social leaders, which they may use for good or ill according to whether their values are domestic or worldly.

Loughead, whose critical survey of California libraries (1878) deplored the intellectual level of the California tycoons, later published two California novels advocating hard work and rural values, *The Abandoned Claim* (1893) and *The Black Curtain* (1898). *The Abandoned Claim* is for young people; a brother and sister homestead in the Oakland hills, working the farm when their widower father has a stroke. The name of the farm is, tellingly although not very subtly, the "Home Ranch." When a younger brother's mine is swept away in a spring flood, sister says: "I don't believe it's a good thing for any boy to have a fortune that he doesn't earn. I'd be gladder and prouder to share the smallest sum made by your own hands' labor than to live in a palace with money that came without effort" (238). *The Black Curtain* is a light-hearted romance; a painter losing his eyesight and a singer who has lost her voice compete for one homestead in the hills east of San Francisco Bay and find love and happiness by uniting their claims. The story is regionalized by accounts of forest fires, water rights quarrels, poor Mexicans, and farmers who don't know how to farm.

Emma Pow Bauder's *Ruth and Marie: A Fascinating Story of the Nineteenth Century* (1895) is a pious San Francisco reform novel advocating temperance, labor, women's property rights and female suffrage. Working girl Ruth (temperance and suffragist lecturer) and wealthy Marie (philanthropist) are San Francisco women doing good for the city according to their means and social standing. Ruth, notwithstanding the evil she confronts daily, is certain that "America is a chosen nation—a God-ordained people whose citizens, from first until now, have been gathered from the great family of nations and appointed to a special mission in the world. That mission is to enlighten the earth and prepare its people for the righteous reign of the Son of God when He shall finally come and set up His kingdom upon the earth" (309–10). *As a Man Lives* (1898) by Mary C. Ferris is a quasireform novel joined to a Cinderella and schoolgirl story; the search by one of the schoolgirls for work in San Francisco meshes with a depiction of Chico, a town with "little honest work for any but miners. . . . The principal trade of the place was in 'pizen' whiskey, appropriately named, and the only amusements were card playing and dancing. When particularly festive, the 'boys' were in the habit of riding furiously down the little street, shooting to right and left, and yelling like painted Indians" (12–13).

Sisters from San Francisco's prosperous Jewish community—Emma Wolf and Alice Wolf—published novels. Two of Emma's five have Jewish characters, all but one are set in San Francisco, and all endorse social responsibility over selfishness. The three non-Jewish novels include *A Prodigal in Love* (1894) about five orphan sisters under the guardianship of the oldest, with a contrast between her and a rebellious second sister. The oldest accepts an obligation to society, the other lives for herself alone and dies violently. There are glimpses of San Francisco's upper-class life, defined by a high culture of museums and concerts. *The Joy of Life* (1896), set outside San Francisco, contrasts a supposed altruistic saintly man to a hardworking businessman, showing ultimately that the saint is a sham while the businessman truly does good for others. In *Fulfillment: A California Novel* (1916) one of two San Francisco sisters becomes a social worker, while the other makes a bad—because loveless—marriage to a good man.

Emma Wolf's *Other Things Being Equal* (1892, revised 1916) is about a romance between a Jewish woman and a Unitarian physician, which is opposed (though not forbidden) by the protagonist's father. The good Jewish daughter is ready to follow her father's wishes, but he abandons his resistance in time for a happy ending. There are glimpses of San Francisco Bay, the weather, seasons, neighborhoods the narrator doesn't approve of: "This quarter is occupied by nothing but Negroes and Chinaman, and foreign immigrants and adventurers, and—and worse" (105). The 1916 revision (reissued in 2002 with an introduction by Barbara Cantalupo) concedes that filial obedience is no longer valued as it had been in 1892, but says the book has merit as testimony to the ways things used to be.

Heirs of Yesterday (1900), her most interesting novel, has for its protagonist a doctor returning to San Francisco after fifteen years in Europe. He moves in with his father but leaves because his father's obvious Jewishness embarrasses him. Then, and quite appropriately from the novel's perspective, he is simultaneously blacklisted from an elite club because he is Jewish and slandered by a jealous journalist (both are courting the same woman) for not being Jewish enough. There are interesting conversations among Jewish characters who attribute their stereotypical traits to their long history as outcasts. One says, "We're first-rate students because no power on earth can beat us in that intensity of purpose—born of the old-time restriction—of doing the best we can with our only unfilchable property—our brains; we are great financiers through enforced specialization; we are thrifty and industrious because we've had to fight for every right of possession inch by inch; we care for our poor as no other poor are cared for, because we were once one in misery, because we can't climb effectually without pulling our weaker ones up with us, and because it was only on the condition that the Jewish poor would not become a burden on the community that the Jews were first granted settlement in the New World. . . . All our civic virtues lie rooted in some hard, grim, ugly fact" (103–4).

From the Jewish point of view, the Spanish-American war is a great opportunity because—as one character puts it without irony—it gives them the chance to wipe out "an old-time unjust accusation—with our lives. On the battlefield all blood flows red" (275–76). Our hero, who has renounced society and dedicated himself to his profession, takes a job in a Manila hospital (where he reunites with the woman he loves, who is also there doing good deeds). The author's rhetoric participates in the war fever: "A strong people felt its great, untried sinews swelling, the young giant felt its unmatched muscles straining and pulling, and spoiling for a fight. 'Manifest destiny' was at work with its hideous means—life went between a hurrah and a sob—there was no longer any individual life—it was all national" (261).

Marrying for security not love is the theme of Alice Wolf's one novel, *A House of Cards* (1896), which shows high society women in San Francisco imprisoned by class values. The needy upper-class protagonist can't find any work to fit her inclinations and training. She lacks the physical strength for factory work (which in any case is below her status); teaching is drudgery; novel-writing means an endless round of submitting and resubmitting manuscripts to eastern publishers. Therefore, she marries a good man she doesn't love: "She was a woman; her hands were tied" (214). But she is punished for this choice: a baby is born dead, the house burns down, her husband's mother turns out to be insane, she falls in love with another man, and she dies young of a heart attack.

Another novel featuring Jewish characters is Florence Land May's muckraker of 1910, *The Broken Wheel,* which draws on the 1908 trial of Abraham Reuf, a political boss who took bribes in connection with the post-earthquake rebuilding of city utilities. In a wide-ranging scandal, only he was sent to jail where—in the novel—he reforms and joins his saintly sister in a later career of good works. The quake as May represents it is simply a new opportunity for greed and corruption—the Gold Rush all over again. May also published a book of poetry, *Lyrics from Lotus Land* (1911), containing among other works eighteen poems in a section titled "Lyrics and Legends of California and the West," consisting mainly of retold Native stories.

The development of the counties around San Francisco for vacationers is the theme of Alice Prescott Smith's 1904 *Off the Highway,* whose overworked physician protagonist unwinds in Contra Costa county; another example of this subgenre is Juliet Wilbor Tompkins's *Dr. Ellen* (1908), whose equally overworked architect protagonist finds sublime scenery in a Sierra town: "All about him towered the peaks of the Sierra, cutting sharply into the pool of thin gold left by the sunset. From the mouths of darkly green canons came breaths of clean, primeval night and the sounds of running water, and down every slope drifted the fragrance of sun-steeped pines" (14). He also finds true love with a woman doctor practicing there, a plot device that allows Tompkins to show rural resistance to women in men's fields.

Amanda M. Douglas added *A Little Girl in Old San Francisco* to her popular "little girl" series in 1905. The story begins in 1851 when Jason Chadsey, a seaman from Maine, becomes the guardian of little Laverne when her mother dies. He takes the child with him when he leaves for San Francisco and a new life. The story then follows the urban history of San Francisco as the two move from neighborhood to neighborhood. Laverne grows up, goes to Europe to acquire some polish, and ultimately marries a Spanish Californian. Douglas's real purpose is to give young readers enormous amounts of information about the city: "The city went on laying out streets, discarding old oil lamps, for now gas was introduced. And in April, a branch Mint was opened by the Government on Commercial Street, which had been a great necessity. . . . There was also an earnest endeavor to awake interest in a through railroad service" (155) and so on:

"The treaty with Japan would open up new ventures. There was to be a line of mail steamers from San Francisco to Shanghai. And all up and down the coast from Puget Sound to the Isthmus vessels were plying, bringing the treasures of other lands" (157).

Pauline Bradford Mackie's *The Story of Kate* (1902) is an Alcott-like tale of three friends from rural California who go to San Francisco and discover their various talents and inclinations. Cora Older's *The Socialist and the Prince* (1903), set in the 1870s, draws on labor leader Dennis Kearney for its male protagonist. The Irish-born Kearney, whose rallying cry was "the Chinese must go," had led a group up Nob Hill in 1877 to protest the nabobs' hiring of Chinese. Older adds a fillip of romance to her story when arrogant heroine Theodosia Peyton, with golden hair and an extraordinary wardrobe (her gowns are minutely described), steps onto her porch on Nob Hill and stares down the Kearney character. At once he decides that what he really wants in life is a woman like that, but he can't win this fight, because Theodosia has no interest in socialism or working for the poor—being, as she realizes, by "temperament and environment" a "dilettante" (273). Labor and capital alike use the Chinese for their own purposes: the demagogue to achieve personal fame and power by maligning them, the capitalists to keep wages down by hiring them.

Emma Frances Dawson's *An Itinerant House* (1897) is a collection of Poe-like stories describing San Francisco as a gothic monstrosity, with Chinatown the source and epitome of evil. In "The Dramatic in My Destiny," opium—the Chinese drug—causes the deaths of the narrator's fiancé and leads him to murder his best friend. Chinatown's fifty thousand people constitute "an alien city" with "narrow, dirty, thronged streets . . . dingy brick piles . . . the lottery-man next door setting in order his little black book covered with great spots like blood; the rattle of dice coming from the half-open basement next to us; the cries of stray vendors of sweetmeats; no sound of any language but the Chinese passionless drone, too cramped for all the changes of life's emotions . . . the only women among the passers-by shuffling along with stiff outworks of shining hair, bright with tinsel and paper flowers, and wide sleeves waving like bat-wings, broad fans, spread umbrellas, and red silk handkerchiefs . . . an endless line of dark mysterious forms, with muffling blouse and flaunting queue, the rank, poisonous undergrowth in our forest of men" (100–101).

A large number of California novels used Chinese cooks or stewards as minor characters; they always spoke an incredible pidgin, had pigtails, and were faithful servants. Other women writers approached Chinatown and the Chinese with a literal missionary spirit, publicizing the work of the mission houses that strove to rescue women and children from the grasp of the Tongs. These books participated in a general missionary project in the US at this time to demonstrate shared humanity the world over—which meant that if you could get to the young and vulnerable in a threatened population, you could convert and redeem them. Among such California books are Mary Bamford's *Ti: A Story of Chinatown* (1899) and her nonfiction *Angel Island: The Ellis Island of the West* (1917), which also encompasses Japanese, Asian Indian, and Korean immigrants and makes the crucial point that wherever they come from, these people are going to become American citizens; Nellie Blessing-Eyster's *A Chinese Quaker: An Unfictitious Novel* (1902) about a young convert who goes back to China to further the good work; Jessie Juliet Knox's juveniles *Little Almond Blossoms: A Book of Chinese Stories for Children* (1904) and her *In the House of the Tiger* (1911), which instruct Anglo children in details of Chinese home life. Lu Wheat's *The Third Daughter: A Story of Chinese Home Life* (1906, shorter version published in 1908 as *Ah Moy, The Story of a Chinese Girl*) shows Chinese Tong leaders using *habeas corpus* to take possession of imported Chinese girls before they get out of the custom house. Wheat attributes Ah Moy's eventual suicide to traditional (and admirable) Chinese moral values; she prefers killing herself to becoming a prostitute or concubine.

Some of the action in *Ah Moy* takes place in China, which is also the case in Mary T. Van Denburgh's *Ye On's Ten Hundred Sorrows and Other Stories* (1907), showing that China is increasingly thought of as an American outpost. "See Wah's New Year" views San Francisco through a Chinese child's eyes: "The rumble of the cable cars and the clang of the bells as they neared the street-crossing added to her desire to see what was going on in the strange outside world" (17); happily for her, she is rescued by a policeman and turned over to the missionaries. Ruth Comfort Mitchell included her one-act play—*The Sweetmeat Game*—in *The Night Court, and Other Verse* (1916) and again in *Narratives in Verse* (1923). In this drama, the woman is abused by three different men: her husband, her stepson, and a drunken Anglo reveler who stumbles into the family's San Francisco apartment.

Two of the thirteen tales in Eleanor Gates's 1910 *The Justice of Gideon,* a collection of mainly California stories (many set in the southern part of the state), treat the Chinese with uncharacteristic respect. "A Yellow Man and a White," set in a mining town, shows a Chinese man who's fled China for political reasons. When a young woman falls off her horse outside his door she speaks pidgin English: "Me fallee off?" she inquires; he replies, gravely, "You were thrown" (223); later, he cures her husband of alcoholism. "Yee Wing, Powder Man" is a San Francisco story about how Yee Wing, whose wife has been kidnapped by the Tong, gets revenge. The story repeats familiar details of the Chinatown setting: "His way led him always through squalid alleys; narrow, dark alleys, where there were no shops, and no coolies going by with heavy baskets swinging from their carrying-poles; but here, from tiny, barred windows, the faces of young Chinese girls looked out—ivory-yellow faces, wondering, wistful" (248).

Miriam Michelson, who grew up in Virginia City and became a journalist in San Francisco, collected several linked previously published stories in *The Madigans* (1904), a delightful comedy about a raucous family of six motherless girls in Virginia City. Their mother is dead; their embittered father (cheated out of his mining claim by a dishonest relative) tinkers at useless inventions all day in his den; Aunt Anne the chaperone mostly stays in bed reading French novels. The children are on their own, and Michelson uses their escapades to draw a wonderful picture of the town. All ends well when an Irish cousin turns up, brings cheer to the father and aunt, reclaims the lost mine, and takes all six girls to the ice cream parlor. Virginia City is a "bare little brown town . . . digging tenacious heels into the mountain's side and propped up with spindle-shanked foothold, the great white inverted cones of steam rising from the mines, the naked and scarred majesty of the gray mountains all about, the desert gleaming like a lake in the east, and Washoe lake gleaming like a desert in the West" (289). In a chapter called "The Ancestry of Irene," sister Irene (nicknamed Split) imagines herself as the daughter of several of the town's characters, giving a cross-section of the population from Paiute Jim to the Irish bonanza king "whose strength was subtlety, whose forte was guile, whose left hand knew not the charitable acts of his right—and neither did the right, for that matter. Thoroughly sophisticated are Comstock children as to the character of the masters of their masters, and Split Madigan knew how foreign to this man's nature a lovable action was" (177–78).

But this ugly town is beautiful to its citizens: "The world seems new-born every summer morning in Virginia City. This little mining-town, dry, sterile, and unlovely, and built at an absurd angle up the mountain, is the poor relation of her fortunate cousins of the high Alps; yet shared with them their birthright—an open, boundless breadth of view, an endless depth of unpolluted, sparkling air, the fresh, shining virginity of the new-created" (282).

Michelson also published two novels about San Francisco women journalists. In *A Yellow Journalist* (1905), the protagonist gets stories by bluff, guile, bravado, and disguise, until her conscience awakens. Set amid moments of San Francisco atmosphere—fog, night, San Francisco Bay—the real interests are backroom state and city politics, rich people behaving badly, and other topics that make San Francisco ugly, evil, and exciting. In *Anthony Overman* (1906), the protagonist falls in love with a social activist she meets in a derelict Sierra mining town where she has gone for a story. "The sweet scents of the country after nightfall, the dim black presence of the forest, the solemn rushing of the river, and the consciousness of the watching heights of the Sierras up among the stars struck a chord in her that seldom vibrated" (20). Like *A Yellow Journalist, Anthony Overman* connects crooked politics to a crooked press; the editor's "contempt for those who ruled the people—a disrespect founded upon the thorough knowledge the journalist gets of politics behind the scenes—was only second to that he had for the people who permitted themselves to be so governed, so cheated, so betrayed" (103). Also like *A Yellow Journalist,* the novel depicts the conversion of an opportunistic woman journalist into an idealist.

Alice Ward Bailey, publishing as A. B. Ward, brought out *Sage Brush Parson,* a novel about a Nevada mining town, in 1906. Supposedly based on the life of California booster George Wharton James, it tells of a Methodist minister who arrives from England, tries to do good, wins the respect of the town's many unsavory characters, and romances a high-class, young, and beautiful widow (unfortunately, his supposedly dead wife turns out to be alive). Amid the surrounding country of alkaline grayness; amid gambling, drinking, and cursing; amid the miners' secret societies, gaudy funerals, and rituals, this genteel widow is totally out of her element.

Sarah Pratt Carr's *The Iron Way: A Tale of the Builders of the West* (1907) is also mostly set in Nevada. It's about building the transcontinental railroad and makes railroad administrators and planners its heroes. They have to overcome the federal government's dilatoriness in issuing bonds, competition, company spies, subversion, dishonest newspaper opposition, and San Francisco itself. "To every thorough-going San Franciscan, California was but a storehouse, a kitchen garden, at most a tribute-bringing suburb of the gay city by the Golden Gate. Nothing outside mattered" (70). Imperfect though it is, San Francisco is where the rustic heroine must go to get smartened up enough to become worthy of the eastern hero. The book is more interested in the challenges of railroad building than the obligatory romance. The great problems are finding workers (hence Chinese labor), and transporting iron, which must be shipped from the East around the horn and then up the Sacramento River because the government refuses to permit importation of foreign iron. Today, the narrator says, "few can realize the problem before these intrepid men, who, with little money and large hostility behind them, hauled their strenuously obtained subsistence and material over nearly a thousand miles of poorly equipped road. They fought mountains of snow as they had never before been fought. They forced their weak, wheezy little engines up tremendous grades with green wood that must sometimes be coaxed with sage-brush gathered by the firemen running alongside of their creeping or stalled iron horses. There were no steel rails. Engineers worked unhelped by the example of perfected railroad building of later times. No tracks or charts of the man-killing desert! No modern helps, no ready, ever eager capital seeking their enterprise! Only skepticism, hatred from their enemies" (299).

Mary Austin, known for her sketches of southern California and the Southwest, published *Santa Lucia* (1908), a novel set in a college town near San Francisco during the early 1890s, about the passing of the great settler generation and the suburbanization of rural California. The novel follows three young women who make a tragic, a comic, and an ordinary banal marriage. The comic plot plays knowingly with gender confusion through an interesting but entirely hetero-sexual woman character named William. The banal marriage is central because it shows California settling into national normalcy, with real estate (the husband's occupation) the contemporary version of California gold. The wife eventually realizes that "his wish to be one with the current interest of his time" is "the rel-ish for life, the undaunted male attitude which begot great achievement on the West"; she is "shamed by its largeness forever out of the complicated futility of her moral conventions" (346).

Novelists active around 1906 worked to represent the earthquake. In Sarah Dean's *Travers* (1908), a pampered heroine lives up to her pioneer heritage by performing many good deeds in the tent cities, while Travers, a ne'er-do-well English younger son, joins her in good works. Two novels by Emma Allen—*The Awakening of the Hartwells: A Tale of the San Francisco Earthquake* (1913), and *Afterwards* (1914)—interpret the earthquake as God's wake-up call. In *The Hartwells,* the earthquake abets a visiting country cousin in her campaign to convert a worldly San Francisco family, but there's as much interest in the fam-ily's earthly fortunes as their new-found faith. "Mr. Hartwell was able to get out of the bank vault, where the small surplus of his lost wealth lay buried in ashes, enough money to reestablish his family in a comfortable home across the bay from the ruined city" (123). In *Afterwards* an eastern woman comes West and laughs at her earlier "stupid ignorance of this wonderful part of my own country, which my romantic fancy had peopled with the picturesque class of barbaric men who stalk through the pages of western novels" (253).

Allen's most interesting novel is about temperance. *The High Road* (1917) at-tacks both the wine and beer industries, dominated by sophisticated French and boorish Germans, respectively. The heroine, a wine mogul's daughter and a col-lege student at Berkeley, ultimately adopts the position of the novel's hero, Phil from southern California, whom she meets at school. Phil's father "had come to southern California from New England twenty-five years previous, broken in health, and had invested his moderate capital in land that had rapidly risen in value with the discovery of high-grade oil. Life in the open, as he bought tracts after tracts of rich fruit-lands in various sections and planted them to orchards of orange, lemon, olive and nuts, beside vineyards of table and raisin grapes, restored his health and made a strong man of him; and a shrewd foresight into the country's marvelous opportunities made him rich in less than ten years and a millionaire before he was fifty" (22). The allusion to oil oddly complicates the vision of an agricultural southland, but the character representing rural values (raisin grapes not wine grapes) is in the right.

In *The Gringos* (1913), B. M. Bower—who published some 40 western nov-els by 1928 and 68 before her death—puts two Texas cowboys, disgusted with

San Francisco in the Gold Rush years, on a hacienda in the Santa Clara Valley. The Don speaks for his rights, while the pioneer point of view divides between these cowboys and some squatters on the Don's property. Bower uses her high plains background (she was originally from Montana) to show how the cowboys win a rodeo. Then, in an image of cross-ethnic solidarity, they take their winnings and the Don's son off to the mines. Bower's 1917 *Lookout Man* contrasts southern with northern California. The protagonist, a pampered mama's boy from Beverly Hills, gets into a scrape and flees to the forests around Mt. Lassen where he works as a forest fire lookout man (and gets the right girl). He returns to southern California transformed into the virtuous and hardy man he was meant to be rather than the effete type southern California had allowed him to be. In *Cabin Fever* (1918), an auto mechanic escaping from suburban life is snowbound for a season with an old miner and an abandoned baby. The plot is deliberately absurd and sentimental (perhaps aimed at the cinema), because suburbia and automobiles not snowbound cabins in the Sierras are what the modern world is all about.

The Dream Maker (1918), a first-person, semiautobiographical novel by Helen Fitzgerald Sanders, takes the protagonist from antebellum Mississippi to southern California to San Francisco in a coming-of-age chronicle. In San Francisco, the protagonist decides she wants to be a writer. The city gives her the knowledge of life she needs to become one. The novel is particularly noteworthy for its account of an enslaved African American woman who accompanies the family and eventually sends her son to medical school—a rare depiction of blacks making lives for themselves in California.

Another semiautobiographical novel is Rose Wilder Lane's *Diverging Roads* (1919). Helen Davies, from Masonville—once a mining town, now a poor farming town—gets a telegrapher's job in San Francisco, marries a fast-talking real estate promoter, and becomes a real estate agent herself when he turns out to be a drunk and a poor businessman. The prologue puts Masonville in historical context. In the early days its story, like California's itself, was an "epic, an immortal song of daring, of hope, of the urge of youth to unknown trails, of struggle, and of heartbreak." Then it subsided into a backwater farming community when "a few discouraged men came down to Masonville and took up homestead claims, clearing the chaparral from their rolling acres, sowing grain or setting out fruit-trees" (n.p.). As a real-estate agent, the protagonist's job is "to find the workman who had saved enough money for the first payment . . . and having found him to play upon his longing and his imagination until the pictures she painted meant more to him than his hoarded savings" (231). The novel makes farming, based on mortgaged land, as much a swindle as the promise of gold. The disillusioned protagonist becomes a successful newspaper columnist, writing guiltlessly about a romantic California that never existed.

The true romance in this book is her friendship with other working women: "In the evenings when they gathered around her fireplace, relaxing from the strain of the day, among her cushions in the soft light of the purring flames, talking a little, silent sometimes, she was so happy that her heart ached" (334). These women—heterosexual of course, in an era when sexual dissidence had no place in mainstream fiction—would like to get married, but "what's the use? We don't need husbands. We need wives" (336). Lane's *He Was a Man* (1925) is based on the life of Jack London, set partly in San Francisco, partly on the Bay (the protagonist works for a time as a fisherman), and mostly in Oakland. Its population of Italian immigrants, crooks, hard-working stevedores, corrupt newspaper editors and reporters, and other dwellers in a big, nasty and yet featureless city shows that the San Francisco Bay area, in becoming modern, has no western identity at all.

Katherine B. Hamill's *A Flower of Monterey* (1921) is a romance set late in the eighteenth century when ease-loving Californios knew neither selfishness nor avarice. "They lived for the day, never anxious over the morrow. They may have learned their lessons from Nature, for she was lavish indeed to her pet protégé—the Californias" (248). But when a Boston visitor compares this population to the climate-hardened New Englander, the Don he's talking to answers that "no country can afford indolence—not even the Californias, where, as you say, the bounties are laid at our feet. If this evil is not dissolved through ambition it will destroy us." As, we infer, it has.

In Rebecca N. Porter's *The Girl from Four Corners; A Romance of California Today* (1920), a naïve country girl moves to San Francisco, where she shares an apartment with two other women. Each has her own story, but all are displaced from a vanished rural past. The city is superior to the country not only because of its cultural life, but also because it welcomes working girls. Porter's *The Rest Hollow Mystery* (1922) is a gothic mystery referring to railroad barons, oil discoveries in Coalinga, and the like. A sort of bodice-ripper romance that mixes California politics with female liberation is Ruth Comfort Mitchell's 1927 *Call of the House,* in which a young woman from the Santa Clara Valley elected to the California State Senate—the fictional first woman senator in California history—wins the day against a political boss, voting her conscience (against the general feeling of her constituency) on reapportionment, even though she therefore cedes much more power to the cities and southern California than her own region. Reapportionment brings in California history and economic divisions among cattlemen, fruit growers, and other coalitions within the state. Her sidekick is a woman journalist, and these two professional women signify the emergence of women into California's public life, with slangy dialogue testifying to the women's up-to-dateness.

∗   ∗   ∗

Mary Hallock Foote, Gertrude Atherton, Geraldine Bonner, and Kathleen Norris all wrote books on many topics set in many places, including substantial contributions to the fiction of northern California. Foote's California work (like her other western fiction) featured genteel eastern women unable to feel at home in the crude West. Rather than elevating the tone they struggle to keep from sliding downward. The title story of *In Exile* (1894) is its only California story and was Foote's first magazine publication (1882). An engineer from Massachusetts and a Connecticut schoolteacher meet in a mining town. He, pursuing a career, is pleased to be in the West, while she, barely making a living, can't go home because the eastern market for refined women's work is glutted. The engineer has a fiancée back home, and our heroine is too timid and too ethical to make a play for him. But the fiancée decides she doesn't want to cope with the loneliness of far western life and breaks her engagement, so all ends well. Foote's historical novella of 1900, *The Prodigal*, is set in San Francisco in the eighties and shows a good woman and a little baby reclaiming a renegade Englishman. The novel is unfortunately laced with slurs against Chinese, Mexicans, African Americans, Native Americans, democratic crowds, and even the New England businessmen who ran the great merchant houses of San Francisco at that time. San Francisco in the '80s, the narrator says, had nothing "that could have been called society" although "a few persons in quiet homes were building up the sort of lives that can save any city" (29).

The title story in Foote's *A Touch of Sun* (1903) has some splendid descriptions of a mining engineer's home with the stamp mill roaring in the background, and brings in the theme of class-bound meddlesome mothers who harm their children. In "Pilgrims to Mecca," a mother taking her daughter east for two years wonders to herself: "why we do cling to that old fetich of the East. Why can't we accept the fact that we are Western people?" (148). She tells her daughter, "If you are going East to ally yourself exclusively with California girls, to talk California and think California and set yourself against everything that is not Californian, we might just as well take the first train west at Colfax" (157). In fact, they are Californians, and they never do get East.

In Foote's *The Valley Road* (1915), San Francisco businessmen—their money derived from mining—decline to fund irrigation projects that might transform waste land into productive farms. The idealistic engineer father in this family novel dies without realizing his dream; the son succeeds only by going to Korea. The mother returns to New England after her husband dies, to live happily ever after with a spinster cousin—here is the feminine East opposed to a masculine West that is now transpacific. In *The Ground-Swell* (1919), a novel set on the coast near Monterey, Foote turns to post–World War I themes, especially the emergence of what she calls the "third sex" as a mother tries to connect her daughter romantically with a working-class Mexican-Dutch youth so as to save her. Sexual orientation is more important than class. The daughter, however, refuses all entanglement with men and goes to Europe as a nurse during the war where she dies of disease; the rejected would-be lover kills himself.

*   *   *

By 1928 Gertrude Atherton had published more than a dozen contemporary and historical California novels. She wrote little about the Gold Rush, but saw it as proving her thesis that successful men had to be strong while successful women had to be beautiful. Oddly enough, however—and I don't think this point has been made much of by those who write about Atherton—her chief characters tend to be failed men and plain women. Perhaps she disliked the historical narrative she believed in.

Atherton's fictions from the 1890s are *Los Cerritos: A Romance of the Modern Time* (1890); *The Doomswoman* (1892); *A Whirl Asunder* (1895); *The Californians* (1898); *The Valiant Runaways* (1898); and *A Daughter of the Vine* (1899). *The Valiant Runaways* is a boys' adventure story about preconquest California. *A Daughter of the Vine* is about female alcoholism (a recurring motif in Atherton's work). In the novella *A Whirl Asunder* (1895) Atherton introduces heiress Helena Belmont, who returns as a foil character three years later in *The Californians*. Helena tells an English visitor that in early California "It was every man for himself. . . . Many succeeded. Some of their methods will not bear the fierce light of history. That savage spirit, that instinct to trample to a goal over anything or anybody, that intolerance of restraint, still lingers in the very atmosphere, and is quick in the blood of many of the present generation" (52). Helena, of mixed Virginian and New England ancestry, hence with "the blood of Cavaliers and Roundheads in her veins" was "born in California, nurtured on its new savage traditions" (53). As a woman, she cannot express this savagery except by scheming for men, preferably men committed to other women.

Los Cerritos, set in the 1860s, is an ugly duckling story, with an atypical concern for exploited workers. The orphan protagonist, "out of place in this commonplace existence" (203), has been raised by peon squatters on the derelict ranch of Los Cerritos where her "latent instinct of caste" and "germs of high intelligence" (34) go to waste until the story's strong man arrives as new owner of the ranch. Thanks to her, he makes it possible for the peons to purchase small—very small, so they don't lose their ambition—plots of land on the ranch. *The Doomswoman,* set in the 1840s mainly at Monterey, depicts the Spanish era as glamorous but fated, perhaps fated because of its glamour. Estenago, the male protagonist, expects to be appointed governor of California, and means to use this position secretly to prepare for inevitable American takeover, because "in American occupation lies the hope of California" (36). Governing as a virtual dictator, he will establish a college, a newspaper, courts of justice, and then surrender the place peacefully to the United States; "My object is to make California a great State and its name synonymous with my own. . . . Shall I say that I have a worthier motive in wishing to aid in the development of civilization? But why worthier? Merely a higher form of selfishness. The best and the worst of motives are prompted by the same instinct" (169–71). History decrees that he'll accidentally commit murder and lose his reputation; he decamps for Mexico with the woman who loves him, Chonita, who until this denouement has done nothing but wear fashionable gowns and fret over rivals for Estenago's affections.

The Californians (1898), Atherton's best-known novel today, is another ugly duckling story, describing fashionable San Francisco in the 1870s and 1880s with its mixed business population of Californios, English, Yankee newcomers, and descendants of the successful forty-niners. Magdalena Yorba is the daughter of a New England mother and a Spanish grandee father who, thanks to his New England brother-in-law, has remained wealthy while other Californios have failed. (He ultimately hangs himself in an American flag—not exactly subtle plotting.) Magdalena is "an unhappy and incongruous mixture of Spanish and New England traits" (17)—her indolent Spanish side is "ever at war with the intellect she had inherited from her New England ancestors" (20). In her glamorous social set of wealthy Anglo daughters, with their full social calendars, huge mansions, and Menlo Park summer homes, she's socially backward as well as physically unattractive. But "in her intimate knowledge of the fact that she was the daughter of a Californian grandee who still possessed the three hundred thousand acres granted his fathers by the Spanish crown, she in all honesty believed no one of these friends of her youth to be her equal" (124). To Trennahan, the jaded man of the world she eventually marries, Magdalena represents old California "as distinguished from San Francisco—with her traditions of luxurious idleness, the low languid murmur of her woods, her soft voluptuous air, her remoteness from the shrieking nerve centres of the United States, the sublime indifference of her people to the racing hours" (159).

The stories in The Splendid Idle Forties (1902), an expanded version of Atherton's 1894 collection Before the Gringo Came, are costume dramas about the American takeover of California, with amours between Spanish women and American men. This pairing ignores the Spanish male, who is feminized by his love for finery; Spanish men are also feminized by their status as victims in the struggle to possess California. Atherton's Rezanov (1906), set in the late eighteenth century, posits a romance between two of her favorite historical characters—the Russian Count Rezanov, posted to Alaska and eager to claim

California for his country; and Concha (Concepcion) Arguella, sixteen-year-old daughter of the Commandante of the Golden Gate Presidio. The wonderfully handsome Rezanov is determined "to take California from the Spaniards either by absorption or force" (38) and has no inkling that the United States is his real adversary, because he has no understanding of a nation without autocratic government. When Rezanov dies en route to Russia, and Concha enters a convent, the gender contrast couldn't be clearer: "So died Rezanov; and with him the hope of Russians and the hindrance of Americans in the west; and the mortal happiness and earthly dross of the saintliest of California's women" (169).

Ancestors, Atherton's longest book and, to my mind, one of her two most interesting novels (the other is *Perch of the Devil,* a 1914 novel about Butte, Montana), is a contemporary, with effective descriptions of the earthquake and its aftermath. Isabel Otis, like Magdalena, is a mixture of Spanish and New England blood—we don't today think of such people as "mixed bloods," but Atherton and other writers of her time apparently did. The love interest, Gwynne (Jack) Elton, is her distant cousin, an impoverished British peer who renounces his title to claim family property in California. Isabel has a mansion in San Francisco and a ranch outside Rosewater—modeled on Petaluma, under the shadow of Mount Tamalpais—where she contentedly raises chickens. Though the novel like most of Atherton's work is obsessed with social standing—especially a standing so high that one can ignore it—and though jingoism is pervasive, at the novel's close Isabel brings back to her ranch several earthquake escapees: a Japanese servant who turns out to be a scholar, and a Chinese family. "Isabel looked at her guests—the Chinese wife and her child . . . the big-footed maid and the husband. . . the Japanese . . . and smiled grimly as she recalled the romantic boat party that escaped from Pompeii. She did not feel in the least romantic, but she felt something greater and deeper" (708). The earthquake that enlarges the view of this snobbish woman also inspires a new generation of strong men who, according to Jack, are "not daunted for a moment, talking already of the new city, of the opportunity this conflagration has given them to make it over in every way. . . . The young business men that have been cleaned out . . . talk only of the enormous possibilities of the future. . . . The higher qualities, those that have inspired the world since it began, are in full possession. And, by Jove, it is going to be the pioneer life over again!" (705). The novel is unusually idealistic for Atherton; in later novels overstressed San Francisco women lose their competitive edge by gambling (*The Avalanche,* 1919), taking drugs, or drinking (*Sleeping Fires,* 1922). The society novel *Sisters-in-Law* (1921) is a sort of farewell to California. With the whole world before her, the protagonist comes to see California as parochial; San Francisco is reduced to its oppressive fog, wind, and ugly mansions built by tasteless millionaires.

* * *

Geraldine Bonner is interested in bonanza kings rather than the business ty-coons who captured Atherton's attention. At the beginning of *Hard Pan: A Story of Bonanza Fortunes* (1900), the protagonist is living in quiet poverty with her father, who had "been a figure in the city from the earliest times, had known San Francisco when it was a straggling line of houses edging the muddy shores of the bay, with a trail winding through the chaparral over the dunes to the Mission Dolores. He had climbed the lupine-covered slopes of what is now California Street, and looked down on the hundreds of deserted ships that lay rotting in the cove. He had seen the city of tents swept by fire, and the city of wood fol-low it in a few months. He had been one of those who had held a ticket for the Jenny Lind Theater on the night it was burned down. He had witnessed the trial of Jansen's assailants, and had served on the two great Vigilance Committees. . . . Of his journey across the isthmus in 49 he could tell thrilling stories. Only those of iron physique and reckless courage had the hardihood to accomplish the trip. The weak in health and feeble in spirit were left behind at the Chagres or turned back at Panama. The fittest survived to become those giants of the far West, the California pioneers" (31–32).

In *Tomorrow's Tangle* (1903), set in the 1870s, Mariposa, the protagonist, moves to San Francisco with her mother. The city is described through her perspective, neighborhood by neighborhood, almost street by street. Later, when she and her mining engineer husband go out to the mines, Bonner de-picts mining operations in highly wrought prose. "Where the pioneers had scratched the surface with their picks, their successors had torn wounds in the Sierra's mighty flank. Where once the miners' shouts had broken the quiet harmonies of stirred pine boughs, and singing river, the throb of engines now beat on the air, thick with the dust, noisy with the strife of toiling men. . . . The expectant hush of Nature awaiting the miracle of sunrise, held this world of huge, primordial forms, grouped in colossal indifference round the swarm of men who delved in its rock-ribbed breast" (451).

In *The Pioneer: A Tale of Two States* (1905), also set in the 1870s, Bonner contrasts two generations of bonanza kings: the noble Sierra miners and the ignoble Nevadans. Early San Francisco "had a distinction, a half-foreign, bizarre picturesqueness, which it soon after lost and has never regained. Separated from the rest of the country by a sweep of unconquered desert, ringed on its farther side by a girdle of sea, the pioneer city developed, undisturbed by outside in-fluences, along its own lines. The adventures of forty-nine had infused into it some of the breadth and breeziness of their wild spirit. The bonanza period of the Comstock lode had not yet arisen to place huge fortunes in the hands of the coarsely ambitious and frankly illiterate, and to influence the populace with a lust of money that has never been conquered" (126). In the winter of '71–'72, "rising excitement in Virginia ran like a tidal wave over the mountains to the city by the sea and there broke in a seething whirl. There was no stock market in the Nevada camp. Pine street was the scene of the operations of capitalist and speculator—the arena where bull and bear met. In Virginia men fought against the forces of nature. . . . Their task was the tearing out from the rock-ribbed flanks of the mountains the treasure that nature had buried with jealous care. . . . In San Francisco men fought with one another. The treasure once in their hands, the battle lost its dignity and became the ignominious scramble of the swindler and the swindled" (192).

In *Rich Men's Children* (1907), a bonanza king and his daughter are trapped by a snowstorm in Antelope, California, for a few weeks. "Confined in a group of rude buildings, crouched in a hollow of the Sierra's flank . . . they were face to face with the nature they thought they had conquered and which now in its quiet grandeur awed them with a sense of their own small helplessness" (109–10). In this interlude, the old-timers tell heroic stories about early California. In *The Emigrant Trail* (1910), five characters on their way to Oregon in the Gold Rush years impulsively decide for California instead. The terrain is described, and mountain men tell their stories. The many characters in Bonner's *Treasure and Trouble Therewith: A Novel of California* (1917) include two orphaned sisters living in a San Francisco mansion with their chaperone aunt and a majordomo, Fong, who becomes the novel's true hero as he employs his network to identify and track a thief. The Chinese are called the best detectives in all California and, because Anglos can't distinguish one Chinese from another, they do their sleuthing in plain view. The many characters in this book come together in a showdown occasioned by the earthquake, which is treated in spectacular prose.

*   *   *

Kathleen Norris was the most successful romance writer from the teens and twenties in California, probably (along with Mary Roberts Rinehart) one of the two most successful American woman writers of her day. In her formula fiction poor, virtuous heroines from impoverished genteel families try to rise socially and economically and, if possible, find true love as well. They struggle against snobbery and petty competition from less beautiful women while contracting and escaping bad marriages. The California setting gives the stories a sense of authenticity, while the formula makes California only one more American locale for female romance. To the working-woman protagonist of *Saturday's Child* (1914), San Francisco is simply a dirty city. *The Story of Julia Page* (1915) follows a mother and then a daughter from the San Francisco mission district as they try to better themselves. In *Martie the Unconquered* (1917), the ambitious heroine has to escape the small town of Monroe, California. *Sisters* (1919) inventories the stores, streets, and people of Red Creek, California, a typical railroad town where nothing ever happens.

The critically best-received of her novels (though not her most popular) is *Certain People of Importance* (1922), a family saga. The grocery store Reuben Crabtree established when he came overland from Illinois to San Francisco in 1849 has prospered, allowing his descendants to live at ease in San Rafael, where daughters try to escape the matchmaking scheming of their mothers. In *Rose of the World* (1924), set in an inland California town called Gates Mill where an ironworks and a flour mill are the two chief industries, the annual California pageant allows the author to satirize the desire to connect with imagined roots: "The dinner and dance to-night were in full costume; Jack and Edith were going as a pioneer-days Chinese and his little Oriental wife. 'Everyone'll be Spanish and early settler and Indian; there'll be twenty senoritas!'" (194). Norris like Foote is dismissive of the Chinese and patronizing to African Americans; only in *Foolish Virgin* (1927) does Hispanic California get any respect, in the shape of a handsome ranch owner whose sexual allure is closely connected to his Spanish traditionalism. But he is Spanish, not Mexican, as the protagonist's mother makes clear: "He may live down there with those Mexican hands of his, but his mother was a fine girl, came of one of the oldest Spanish families in this state, that boy has good blood in his veins! His father was an English gentleman, and *his* father—Gregory's grandfather—was what they call a younger son. He came here a pioneer, no money, but a fine family" (10).

*   *   *

In the forested north of California, natural beauty, Native Americans, and rusticity come into play. Ella Sterling Mighels's frothy *The Full Glory of Diantha* (1909) is a working-girl novel. The protagonist, a New York City bookkeeper, takes a temporary job with her firm's lumber camp near Mount Shasta, looking for the man who matches what she imagines to be her own elemental nature. Nature—steep mountain trails, rock slides, raging rivers—turns out not to be her métier after all. The elemental man she's temporarily attracted to follows her to New York City and makes a fool of himself, sending Diantha into the arms of the right man—her boss. But one of her apartment mates settles down happily with this son of nature and moves to the wilds of California with him.

In the Reign of Coyote, Katherine Chandler's 1905 collection, participates in the vogue for Indian stories through a book of tales supposedly narrated by three California Natives—from southern, central, and northern California, working as nurse, saddler, and blacksmith, respectively, on a ranch near San Francisco. Typically for this kind of book, the supposition is that Indian stories work for children because Indians are childlike to begin with. Typically also, Chandler says her stories are authentic and gives the ethnological provenance for her "elaborated and modified" tales (viii). Beyond this she attempts to convey the sense of ranch life as children of today might experience it, with lessons, amusements, and interest.

Sarah Emilia Olden, an Episcopalian teacher-activist from New England, traveled West in the summer and sometimes lived with reservation missionary families to collect Native folk lore. She followed a 1918 book on the Dakotas (*The People of Tipi Sapi*) with two more in 1923: one of Shoshone tales (now extremely rare) and another of California Karoc stories. The Karoc book begins by describing the gorgeous setting, as the author rides the hundred miles from Eureka to Orleans: "The Silence, the grandeur, the majesty of these ancient forests will fill your soul with reverence and awe. . . . It is all so glorious, the turquoise skies and brilliant sunshine" (11). In her account the miners arriving in 1851 took over Native land, homes, and women. "The Indians were forced to be satisfied with the beads and thimbles offered them for their homes. The white men took their wives, kept them for a while, and when tired of them married the younger women. That is why there are so many half-castes now" (26). She refers to the Wa-gas, mythical white people who preceded the incoming Indians and promised to return; she says the miners were welcomed because they were mistaken for these demigods.

In 1883 northern Paiute Sarah Winnemucca published *Life among the Piutes: Their Wrongs and Claims,* an early and important autobiography by a Native American woman. Her work as a US army interpreter had angered some in her tribe as well as civilian missionary reservation agents. (There was throughout the late nineteenth century an ongoing struggle between what would now be the Department of Defense and the Department of the Interior over reservation administration.) Winnemucca went East to lecture on behalf of her people, displaced from their reservation on account of the Modoc War, and also to defend herself against allegations that she had betrayed her own people. "It is said that I am working in the interest of the army. . . . It is not so; but they know more about the Indians than any citizens do, and are always friendly" (93). Though Winnemucca insists that those who doubt Native abilities and motivation are wrong, she does not stand up for traditional Native culture: "Oh, dear friends, you are wrong when you say it will take two or three generations to civilize my people. No! I say it will not take that long if you will only take interest in teaching us; and, on the other hand, we shall never be civilized in the way you wish us to be if you keep on sending us such agents as have been sent to us years after year, who do nothing but fill their pockets, and the pockets of their wives and sisters, who are always put in as teachers . . . and yet they do not teach" (89). The high point of her service to both Paiute and the Federal government comes in a heroic horseback ride, "the hardest work I ever did for the government in all my life—the whole round trip, from 10 o'clock June 13 up to June 15, arriving back at 5:30 P.M. having been in the saddle night and day; distance, about two hundred and twenty-three miles. Yes, I went for the government when the officers could not get an Indian man or a white man to go for love or money. I, only an Indian woman, went and saved my father and his people" (164).

A less well-known book by a Native woman is Yurok Lucy Thompson's *To the American Indian* (1916—edited by Peter E. Palmquist with an introduction by Julian Lang in 1991); unlike Winnemucca, Thompson makes the case for traditional Native culture, which, however, is more like white culture than most believe. The announced aim of preserving the traditional knowledge which, she claims, is disappearing from tribal life, is directed toward both Natives and white people who have been scammed by Native informants, "the lower classes of the Indians" who give white interlocutors "the fairy tales of the tribe, such as mothers and grandmothers tell to the little children for their amusement; and these are the stories that the white man is made to believe as the true traditions and religion of the Indian. These stories are no more like the traditions and religion of the Indian than daylight is like night" (197). These fakers, Thompson says, are descendants of slaves who want to conceal their low social standing from whites who don't realize that this culture is hierarchical and property-owning. Wealthy families own "lands, hunting territory, fishing places, slaves, flints, white deerskins, fisher skins, otter skins, silver gray fox skins and fine dresses made of dressed deerskins, with fringes of shells knotted and worked in the most beautiful styles, that clink and jingle as they walk and makes one have a feeling of respect and admiration for them" (154). Claiming that she and her father were the only two survivors of a priestly class called the "Talth," she says that when they die, "with us perishes the true name of God to my people. With it has perished from the earth our true Indian laws, our sublime religion, our deeds of chivalry, as rich as the civilized world has ever beheld. Immoral, corrupt, tottering, downtrodden and debauched by a superior race, we have perished in that winter night of the transition period" (74).

5

Utah

Leaders of the Mormon trek to Utah had envisaged an independent, isolated kingdom beyond the grasp of the United States and also far from Mexico, to which Utah nominally belonged. But Utah became an American territory the year of the Mormon exodus. Lying directly on the route to California, it had to deal with hordes of overland travelers. By the time the last spike on the transcontinental railroad was driven at Promontory, Utah, in 1869, mining and railroad enterprises had already brought many non-Mormon residents into Utah as well, and these enterprises wanted to extract Utah from the grip of what came to be called the "ghost government," which simply ignored US rules. The railroad then attracted transcontinental tourists who stopped in Salt Lake City to gape at Mormons and confirm their views of LDS life ways. The flash point for non-Mormons was polygamy, which opened the door to questions about Mormon belief and Mormon fitness for US citizenry. Most historians now believe that polygamy was used to screen economic issues because its sensational appeal made it newsworthy above all other matters. Insofar as the West was to be settled with homes where the wife was partner to her husband, and within which younger women could freely develop their best attributes, the Mormon Kingdom could be represented as a travesty of democratic domesticity. And this was a matter of particular concern to women, who could thus be involved in anti-Mormon campaigns.

Dozens of anti-Mormon books came out in the East, especially in Boston and Hartford where polygamy and slavery were described as twin relics of barbarism. Pro-Mormon books, mainly designed to keep up the morale of the faithful rather than win new converts, appeared mostly in Salt Lake City. When the LDS church gave up polygamy in 1890 and Utah achieved statehood six years later, the main impetus for women's Utah literature disappeared and their books about Utah tapered off. Utah, as Zane Grey's *Riders of the Purple Sage* made clear in 1912, was wonderfully endowed with qualities necessary for nondenominational western literature: it had western landscapes and western industries like cattle, railroads, and mining. But as Susa Young Gates and her daughter Leah Widtsoe noted in their jointly authored little book of 1928, *Women of the 'Mormon' Church*, Mormon women writers chose not to exploit their state's nondenominational endowments. In this book, a "famous Eastern editor" says to an "ambitious and gifted 'Mormon' woman writer, 'if you will drop your militant "Mormon" attitude and just do Western stories straight you will surely succeed.' To this the woman replied, 'Your price is too high. . . . I won't pay it.'" (26).

* * *

The two earliest Utah books by women I've found exemplify pro- and anti-Mormon approaches. Cornelia Woodcock Ferris's epistolary *Mormons at Home* (1856) is an overland travel account with a long middle Utah section, where Cornelia's husband Benjamin served briefly as a Federal Judge. Prevented by Mormon leaders from holding a single session, he left the territory after six months. Cornelia writes in part to defend him from accusations of dereliction. She calls the religion humbug, its "real miracle" consisting in "so large a body of men and women, in a civilized land, and in the nineteenth century, being brought under, governed, and controlled by such gross religious imposture" (48). She says polygamy destroys the bedrock of female character by encouraging female promiscuity: "A dozen women, the common property of one man, some of them divorced from other men, lodged under the same roof, and often more than one in the same room, soon begin to feel that they might as well be the common property each of a dozen men" (306–7). She claims that many disillusioned people wanting to leave are prevented by leaders "very anxious to gain sufficient population to raise the Territory to the rank of a state" who therefore "throw every obstacle in the way" (323).

Eliza R. Snow, already a publishing poet when she went to Utah in the first overland group, brought out *Poems: Religious, Historical, and Political in Liverpool* in 1856. Liverpool was the major center of Mormon evangelism in England, as well as the port of embarkation for the United States. Snow, sealed to (liturgically married to) Joseph Smith in Nauvoo, and later sealed to Brigham Young, eventually became the most influential woman in territorial Utah, known as the "Mormon poetess." Some poems in her book had been written for recitation during campfire evenings on the overland journey, for example, "Let us Go" in which she exhorts: "Let us go, let us go where our rights are secure, / Where the waters are clear and the atmosphere pure, / Where the hand of oppression has never been felt, / Where the blood of the Prophets has never been spilt. / Let us go, let us go where the kingdom of God / Will be seen in its order extending abroad— / Where the Priesthood again will exhibit its worth / In the regeneration of man and of earth" (147).

Snow praised Utah's remoteness from the US and its fitness for agriculture. In "A Journeying Song" the travelers sing: "We go to choice and goodly lands, / With rich and fertile soil / That by the labor of our hands / Will yield us wine and oil. / We go beside the mountain cliffs, / Where purest waters flow— / Where nature will her precious gifts / Abundantly bestow. . . . / We'll find a climate pure and free, / Producing life and health, / Where steady care and industry / Will prove a source of wealth. . . . / And there, again we will surround / In peace the luscious board; / And share the products of the ground / With skill and prudence stor'd" (170–71).

Snow's doctrinal poems make three points. True religion requires a priestly class, a true priesthood gets word directly from God (which means that the Bible is not God's last word before the Judgment Day, a point of great importance for those believing that the Book of Mormon was divinely inspired), and Eve's disobedience led to the deserved subordination of all women. "The New Year," a blank-verse poem from 1852, explains that Utah women don't need the suffrage because Utah's men are fulfilling their God-assigned roles (later, when Utah gave women the vote, she supported this decision). Women elsewhere may seek "to transcend the sphere which God / Through disobedience has assign'd to her" but here in Salt Lake City "are men / Cloth'd with the everlasting Priesthood—men / Full of the Holy Ghost, and authoriz'd / T'establish righteousness. . . . / If elsewhere men are so degenerate / That women dare compete with them, and stand / In bold comparison, let them come *here* / And *here* be taught the principles of life / . . . . Here are noble men, / Whom woman may be proud t'acknowledge / For her own superior, and feel no need / Of female congressmen" (215–16).

As for politics, a July 4 poem argues for the fundamental Americanness of Mormons: "The banner which our fathers won, / The legacy of Washington, / Is now in Utah wide unfurl'd, / And proffers peace to all the world. / We'll here revive our country's fame, / The glory of Columbia's name; / Her Constitution's germ will be / The basis of our Liberty. . . . / Long as the everlasting snows / Upon these mountain tops repose, / Those rights our vet'ran fathers gain'd, / Shall in these valleys be sustain'd" (217–18).

* * *

The title of Elizabeth Wood Kane's *Twelve Mormon Homes Visited in Succession on a Journey through Utah to Arizona* (1874) makes the point that, yes, Mormons have homes. Kane, not a Mormon herself, came from a family of Mormon sympathizers—her father and husband helped the federal government in diverse negotiations with LDS leaders. In her book, assembled by her father from her letters and journals, Kane narrates a three-week trip with her husband and Brigham Young from Salt Lake to St. George, some 300 miles to the South. She debunks the constant refrain of anti-Mormon literature that Mormon women hate polygamy: "it had been one of the accepted beliefs with which my mind was stocked before entering Utah, that every mother would be found to regret the birth of a daughter as a misfortune. This is not so. They honestly believe in the grand calling their theology assigns to women; 'that of endowing souls with tabernacles that they may accept redemption'" (70). Kane describes plural wives cooperating contentedly in neat and clean homes where food is plentiful and much-loved children are well-cared for. A pair of wives "pointed out to me the comfort, to a simple family, that there was in having two wives to lighten the labors and duties of the household"; the wives say they have closer friendships with each other "than could be maintained between the most intimate friends living in different circumstances" (47–48).

Kane asks for "pity and sympathy . . . for those women who have become 'plural wives' from a sense of duty, and who think their lot happy because they deem that God's blessing rests upon its hard conditions" (104). One woman she talked with "rejected with horror the solution of the Mormon difficulty which I advocated: that Congress should forbid any further polygamous marriages, but legalize those that already existed. . . . 'Secure my social position!' she once repeated after me. 'How can that satisfy me! I want to be assured of my position in God's estimation. If polygamy is the Lord's order, we must carry it out in spite of human laws and persecution. . . . How much harder to . . . admit, as I should be admitting, that all I have sacrificed has not been for God's sake!'" (105–6).

Florence A. Merriam's *My Summer in a Mormon Village* (1894), about a vacation in a town northeast of Salt Lake City at the foot of the Wasatch Range, is also less antagonistic than the non-Mormon norm. An ornithologist and botanist, she writes a richly descriptive natural history of the wonderful scenery. But in reporting conversations with older women—some widowed, others running households because their husbands are living with other wives—she reverts to the inescapable subject. "We had become so engrossed in the peaceful side of village life—what with our chickens and cows, and our views of mountain and lake—that we had almost forgotten where we were. One day, however, something was said about polygamy, when some one quietly remarked that our cook was one of the former bishop's *sixty-three* children, and that her mother was one of his seven wives. We awoke with a start, remembering with a sense of shock that we were in Utah" (79).

*   *   *

All the other nonfiction books by non-Mormon women that I've found, including two by apostates whose books, as first-hand testimony, had especially wide circulation, are hostile to the religion and unresponsive to Utah's scenery. Catharine Waite, who published *The Mormon Prophet and His Harem* in 1866, was, like Ferris, the wife of a Lincoln territorial appointee—an associate judge—who stayed on the job only briefly because he was unable to hold any court sessions. For her, the national essence involves the distinction between church and state that Mormonism flatly rejects. She says the religion is popular because most Mormons are ignorant foreigners—not after all truly American, but Europeans accustomed to autocratic regimes. She blames Brigham Young for every evil. The emigration fund fleeces the emigrants, while tithing leaves "families barefooted, women and children nearly naked, destitute of even the necessaries of life, the husband making every effort to meet the day of tithing, fearful of losing his soul's salvation should he fail" (139). Young destroys business initiatives in the name of cooperation, which simply means the same business run by and for Young himself. And finally, Young not Joseph Smith foisted polygamy on his credulous followers.

Nevada, split from Utah at the start of the Civil War and made a state in 1864, is an instructive contrast. It "has made rapid and gigantic strides in all the essentials of a high civilization. Her mines are celebrated throughout the world, and she annually adds millions of dollars to the circulation of the country. Already are her valleys teeming with the life of the husbandman, and her soil yielding up its rich harvests of golden grain, for the sustenance of her brave and patriotic sons. . . . Mark the contrast between loyal and Christian Nevada, and disloyal and Mohammedan Utah! One rushing on to a glorious and happy destiny, and the other falling rapidly back into the habits and customs of heathen nations. The genius of Liberty sits enthroned among the mountains of free Nevada, while despotism of the most hideous character clanks her chains in Utah. May the day of deliverance for the oppressed thousands of Utah soon dawn" (35–36).

In 1882, the year when the Edmunds Act outlawing polygamy passed in the US Congress, Waite returned to the topic in *Adventures in the Far West; and Life among the Mormons.* a novel representing the perspective of one Mrs. Burlingame who discovers valuable mines in the Utah mountains. Waite repeats her earlier room-by-room description of the Lion House, her wife-by-wife description of what she had called Young's harem, and her scene-by-scene representation of the endowment ceremony, ending with the claim that initiates must swear loyalty to Brigham Young personally and enmity to the US government. An appendix asserts that all the Indians are really Mormons, which explains their attacks on US citizens including the raid on Fort Apache; that the assassinator of President Garfield was a Mormon; and most astonishingly that Brigham Young was not really dead but was waiting on a Pacific Island to return and deceive his followers into believing that he had been resurrected. Happily for the United States, she says, after his reappearance he will take all the Mormons to his Pacific hideaway and the country will be rid of them.

The two apostate memoirs by women were Fanny Stenhouse's *Tell It All* (1874) and Ann Eliza Young's *Wife No. 19* (1875). The Stenhouse book expanded her reminiscence, *A Lady's Life among the Mormons* (1872), which had been followed in 1873 by her husband's *The Rocky Mountain Saints* in 1873—full title *The Rocky Mountain Saints: A Full and Complete History of the Mormons, from the First Vision of Joseph Smith to the Last Courtship of Brigham Young: Including the Story of the Hand-cart Emigration, the Mormon War, the Mountain-Meadow Massacre, the Reign of Terror in Utah, the Doctrine of Human Sacrifice, the Political, Domestic, Social, and Theological Influences of the Saints, the Facts of Polygamy, the Colonization of the Rocky Mountains, and the Development of the Great Mineral Wealth of the Territory of Utah*. His book almost immediately became a standard reference, and Fanny's book (published with an admiring preface by Harriet Beecher Stowe) surrounds her first memoir with a good deal of factual material. (Linda DeSimone's 1988 edition usefully compares the two books.) Thomas, publishing as T.B.S. Stenhouse, argued that Young had destroyed every business venture that T.B.S. started; Fanny agrees that Utah's supposed communalism was really a front for Young's private fiefdom, that she and her husband were particular targets because they were successful entrepreneurs. Like her husband she writes about the Danites (the alleged Mormon enforcers), the handcart movement (when emigrants too poor to purchase and equip wagons pulled their belongings in handcarts across the plains to Salt Lake City), blood atonement (the doctrine that some sins could be absolved only by shedding the sinner's blood, executing the sinner), the Mountain Meadow Massacre (when, in 1857, over a hundred people traveling to California through southern Utah were killed by Mormons pretending to be Paiutes), church organization, the initiation ritual at the Endowment House (she describes this in full, disclosing secrets that initiates were sworn not to reveal).

Ann Eliza Young was one of Brigham Young's later wives, the only one to file for divorce (divorces were easily obtained in Utah, which to irate Easterners was evidence of Mormon immorality, and that the plaintiff simply had to pay a fee was evidence of Young's cupidity). She went on the lecture circuit in 1875, after leaving Salt Lake the previous year. *Wife No. 19, or The Story of a Life in Bondage, Being a Complete Exposé of Mormonism, and Revealing the Sorrows, Sacrifices, and Sufferings of Women in Polygamy* enlarged on her lectures. The book—republished with introductory notes by John B. Gough and Mary A. Livermore in 1972—tells her story and rehearses also the handcart expedition, the Mountain Meadow Massacre, and other topics of anti-Mormon discussion. But because her mother had been a Mormon convert, she also writes sympathetically about the early persecution of the Mormons in Missouri and Illinois that drove them to Utah.

Jennie Anderson Froiseth's 1882 *Women of Mormonism; or, The Story of Polygamy as Told by the Victims Themselves,* republished columns from the short-lived *Anti-Polygamy Standard,* which she edited. The anonymous tales combine first-person testimony with fervent editorializing against polygamy, and not incidentally praise the *Standard's* work. One woman (supposedly) writes: "I appreciate the fact that the horrors of the system can never be fully ventilated or truly told, unless we women who have been mixed up with it are willing to put our shoulders to the wheel, and help on the good work by exposing its iniquities to the world. No other consideration on earth could induce me to acknowledge what a dupe, and afterward what a virago I was, except the hope that it may, perhaps, have some influence in preventing another woman from sharing the same fate. I wish only that the *Standard* could be placed in the hands of every young girl in this Territory. Hundreds of them would gladly read it, and profit by its teachings, if it were placed within their reach" (74–75).

Like other anti-Mormon women writers, Froiseth uses polygamy to attack the entire system: "When the people of the United States understand that the leaders of the Mormon church, knowing the utter fraud of the entire institution, employ it as a gigantic political and commercial machine in order to impose upon, rob, and make slaves of the masses; that their weapons toward their people are superstition and ignorance, and toward the world hypocrisy and perjury; and that beyond all, they are doing what they can to overthrow all respect for, and all power of, the United States Government,—then avaricious merchants, soulless corporations, and a subsidized press, will stand aside, even as they did in 1861, and the will of the people must prevail" (285). She argues that the railroad, far from diluting the Mormon population as had been supposed, much increased it: "The iron horse whirls them over that ground in a very few days, and in such numbers that the railroad companies deem them not unprofitable travelers, even at very low rates of transportation. . . . And when it is recollected that a large majority of these immigrants are gathered from the most ignorant and credulous classes of Europe, that they are steeped in superstitious fanaticism, and already shorn of manhood and womanhood by being pledged to obey their leaders in all things, temporal as well a spiritual, it may easily be seen how the system is kept up in Utah by these constant reinforcements" (287).

Froiseth accuses female Mormon activists of cynical hypocrisy, targeting in particular the officers of the Relief Society, the organization formed to encourage and supervise female activities throughout the territory. This society, she alleges, "has two principal objects, the propagation of polygamy, and the gathering of tithes for replenishing the church treasury, especially for the purpose of corrupting members of Congress, and subsidizing the national press. . . . Does any person ask why polygamy is on the increase today in Utah, notwithstanding the counteracting influences brought to bear against it by the establishment of Christian churches and schools, and why young and ignorant girls are every day entering into the unlawful relation? The reason is obvious: Because this female organization is constantly at work, carrying out the plans of a licentious and tyrannical priesthood. But preaching polygamy is not the only way in which these infamous women assist in maintaining the power of the Mormon theocracy. Two sources of that power are, the keeping of the people in ignorance and in poverty" (146).

*   *   *

Among perhaps fifty anti-Mormon novels by men and women published between 1850 and 1900 (not, after all, the enormous number that some literary historians have claimed, given the over 6,000 American novels from those years), seven appeared under the woman authors' own names. In considering these seven I ignore two pseudonymous novels—one by "Maria Ward" (1855) and another by her nephew "Austin Ward" (1857; both have been attributed to Cornelia Ferris but like some others who have written on the subject, although more impressionistically than statistically, I find the Ferris style too unlike the "Ward" style for this to be convincing). I also ignore *The Prophets; or, Mormonism Unveiled*, published "by an American" in 1855 and copyrighted by one Orvilla Belisle, who remains unidentified but seems likely to have been English.

These books feature high-minded female protagonists who are ensnared in the system by appeals to their innate virtue, an important point when sexuality is an issue. They are victimized by gullible and weak-minded men (husbands or fathers to whom they remain true), and evilly charismatic older women (the wicked stepmother type). The protagonist is usually the first wife, whose initiation into the realities of Mormonism involves her husband's taking of a second wife. Earliest is Metta Victor's *Mormon Wives: A Narrative of Facts Stranger than Fiction* (1856—republished as *Lives of Female Mormons* in 1860). The preface frankly says it hopes to stop the movement for Utah statehood. "We conjure every man who has respect for humanity and for progress, to pause over this little record of *one* history, and then, multiplying it by tens of thousands, say if he can find it in his heart to fellowship with such a moral monster as Deseret now is, and will continue to be under the laws and Constitution which she has prescribed for herself" (iii).

In the melodrama that follows, worldly Richard Wilde takes his virtuous, pure wife Margaret to Salt Lake City and, once there, becomes ever more worldly until he takes a second wife—Margaret's best friend Sarah, who has followed them to Salt Lake specifically to marry Richard. Almost from the start, Margaret is horrified by Mormonism. "The whole matter wore to her such a look of farce and trickery played off by a few leaders upon a foolish and devoted people, that she was lost in astonishment that her husband—Richard Wilde—whom she so much admired and honored for his keen and logical intellect—could be, for a moment, duped or influenced" (72). The appearance of a third wife exposes the second wife's fatuous self-deception; Sarah truly believed that Richard had always loved her not Margaret.

In 1865, A. Jennie Bartlett (later Switzer) published *Elder Northfield's Home;* reprinted at least twice, it may have been the best known of women's anti-Mormon fictions. Her preface makes a standard comparison of polygamy to slavery— "Is not this slavery of the West a much more despicable one than that of the South?"—as a lead-in to its political point: "Will our government weakly allow its laws to be trampled under foot? . . . Let it attack this great evil with the energy which characterized the putting down of the rebellion and the blotting out of slavery" (4). The novel begins in England when two orphan sisters, Marion and Elsie, are leaving for the United States to live with an aunt. Marion, however, has already met Mormon Henry Northfield and been converted; she marries him and goes on to Utah, remaining faithful even though she realizes he won't be able to withstand the pressure to take a second, and then a third, wife.

As soon as they get to Salt Lake City Marion recognizes her mistake; she's horrified by the location—the glorious Wasatch Range to her represents incarceration not sublimity. No surprise to her that "the Mormons called this place the 'chamber of the Lord in the mountains,' for it did seem like a chamber or room, so shut in was it from the rest of the world." But her husband says, "thank God that at last we behold this beautiful place, and may we go no more out of it forever" (41)—a remark that fills Marion with dread: "Do not say so! . . . I do not wish to stay here forever" (42). Sentimental descriptions of female misery among Marion's friends are interleaved with analysis of the steps through which Henry Northfield comes to accept and rationalize polygamy. In the second generation, the captivity metaphor turns literal when a Northfield daughter, trying to get out of Utah, is captured and confined to an asylum.

Cornelia Paddock, wife of a mining man who settled in Salt Lake City, was another anti-polygamy activist. *In the Toils; or, Martyrs of the Latter Days* (1879) begins in 1856 and follows Charles and Sarah Wallace from their eastern home to Salt Lake City. Charles's attraction to Mormonism is attributed to a recent bout of brain sickness; nothing else can explain the dramatic change in this formerly good husband. The novel adds many other tales of unhappy plural wives to the main tragedy. This book does not interpret polygamy as an indulgence of male lasciviousness; rather it is a canny strategy for men to acquire cheap labor and keep surplus women safely within the home. Women hate polygamy but accept it out of fear of losing their children. Decent men, similarly afraid, are additionally terrified by the possible consequences should their participation in deeds of blood atonement, the Mountain Meadow Massacre, or other crimes into which they've been manipulated, become known. Some would like to leave but can't afford to, because they don't own anything; they don't own anything because everything is owned communally. In a second novel, *The Fate of Madame La Tour* (1892) Paddock combines a melodramatic thriller with an annotated reference document, writing about the difficulty of enforcing federal laws in a remote territory and asking readers to write to their congressmen opposing statehood for Utah. As long as Mormons are in control, Utah cannot become a western—that is, a capitalistic, individualistic—place.

Jeannette H. Walworth's *The Bar-Sinister: A Mormon Study* (1885) sends fallible John Quinby to Salt Lake on business, where he converts and, in a plot much like Victor's, marries his wife Anna's best friend Effie, a religious zealot. When he next marries Barbara, Anna's maid, Effie dies of shame. Barbara elopes with a miner and leaves her baby behind; Anna conscientiously raises the child as her own. Walworth explicates points of Mormon doctrine, talks like Paddock about the difficulty of enforcing federal law so far from the national center, and denies that woman suffrage in Utah (granted by the territorial legislature in 1870, revoked by the US Congress in 1887—an outcome to which perhaps this book contributed) is something women should be proud of. "Another Mormon outrage! It is the veriest sham on earth. The women are so absolutely under the control of the men, that granting them the franchise was simply multiplying their own votes. When the Pacific Railroad was completed, this city was overrun with Gentile miners, who threatened to sweep the Saints out. By investing their women with the privilege of voting the Saints retained the balance of power in their own hands" (249).

The protagonist of Kansan Mary W. Hudson's 1888 *Esther the Gentile* is a daughter who accompanies her widowed and unworldly father to Salt Lake City. Pressured by the elders until "he was in actual terror of ending his existence upon earth before he had fulfilled every commandment of the Mormon church" (43), he marries the widow Elizabeth, who "never shirked a duty, and yet she stood like a hard, unyielding, silent rock, in the midst of lives that without her would have been smooth and pleasant" (49). At Elizabeth's own suggestion, he marries Elizabeth's daughter Drusilla. Almost alone among anti-Mormon books, this one appreciates the natural setting of Salt Lake City, whose "founders chose wisely this spot from whence the everlasting hills can be seen in such magnificence" (35).

Hudson describes emigration and polygamy as Brigham Young's strategies to increase the Mormon population. She attributes the so-called "Reformation" in Utah—a period from 1856–58 when the arrival of the US army threatened war in the territory and there were stringent investigations into Mormon loyalty by the LDS hierarchy—to Young's "determined resistance to the encroachments of the mining population, the California emigration movement, and the progress of the transcontinental railways" (106). She envisions a future when incoming Gentiles themselves will free Utah from its captivity: "the restless, ever progressive, ever encroaching, native born and rightfully dominant American citizen" has "carried the home, the newspaper, the schools, the arts and the traffic of the United States into the heart of the Land of the Honey Bee, and nothing can stay their influence" (149).

Motivated to counterattack, Helen Mar Whitney—reportedly one of Joseph Smith's earliest and younger plural wives, married to him when she was not yet fourteen—published two pro-polygamy books: the hard-to-find *Plural Marriage* (1882) and the longer *Why We Practice Plural Marriage* (1884). The earlier book rebuts arguments from the Reformed LDS church (headed by a son of Joseph Smith) that the prophet had not instituted polygamy. The second book brings together all the current pro-polygamy arguments via anecdote, polemic, epistolary transcriptions, and other forms: plural marriage is best-suited to fallen human nature; women are needed to produce bodies for the souls waiting to be incarnated (and time is running out); and plural marriage saves women from adultery, prostitution, infanticide, destructive factory work, and puts them securely in the home.

The novel was not a comfortable fit with Mormon ideology, but Susa Young Gates, a daughter of Brigham Young, published *John Stevens' Courtship: A Story of the Echo Canyon War* in 1909—thirteen years after statehood was achieved—when she was 53 years old. This passionately pro-LDS historical novel, using sources including Bancroft and LDS writers, merges a seduction story with military history about the arrival of the US army in Utah. Two women—Diantha and Ellen, sense and sensibility, respectively—love John Stevens, a devout Mormon. Ellen, realizing that Stevens loves Diantha, succumbs to an immoral soldier, elopes to the army camp, and is killed by the soldier's jealous mistress. John frets over Ellen's example of a person tempted "to forsake the simple, honest lives of their people, and to become involved in the sins and corruptions of the outside world" (242). Brigham Young himself, however, enunciating the key Mormon principle of free will, tells him, "You can't keep people virtuous by shutting them up in prisons. The only way that I know of to get men or women to walk in the path of virtue and righteousness, is to teach them correct principles, and then let each one govern himself. . . . Teach all to do right and to live their religion, and give them their agency" (264).

The novel expounds elements of LDS doctrine, presents western history from the Mormon perspective, and celebrates Utah's natural beauty. A group going to a Pioneer Day celebration in Cottonwood Canyon come upon an "emerald-tinted valley with a silvery lake empearled on its western rim . . . cupped in a circle of embracing hills and snow-covered crags. The summits of the eastern and western hills were crowned with pine" (18–19). Salt Lake City, with its neat squares, irrigation, trees, and flowers, possesses "all the goodly evidences of civilization; . . . houses, with blinking windows and comfortable porches; wide streets, flanked on either side with running streams of clear, cold, canyon water, over whose rippling surface drooped in graceful lines the native cottonwood, which had been dug from the neighboring canyon streams and planted along every water-course to furnish shade and rest for man and beast; commodious homes, barns, fences and outbuildings gave this unique city a look of mingled rural simplicity and urban attractiveness. The huge blocks were laid out in large lots, whereon sat with sturdy independence each snug house, its surrounding fruit and vegetable plantations fenced in with poles or cobbles, thus forming a generous combination of orchard and kitchen garden" (190–91). The pro-Mormon territorial Governor says, "these 'Mormons' have done more marvelous things than ever did Moses. And they have even put the Pilgrim Fathers to the blush with their gigantic toil and its marvelous results. They call it the special providence of God . . . but the blossoming desert below may be called, in all reason the result of energy and grit. Yankee grit! Why, sir, you will find that these people down there are mostly of pure New England descent. A very few English and fewer Europeans. Yankees they are, most of them" (168).

In contrast to Salt Lake City is the army camp, shoddily built "of half shacks, half wigwams, and all of them altogether abandoned in their reckless atmosphere of rude frontier conviviality" with "mingled shouts of drunken laughter, oaths of anger, and the shrill cries of ribald woman" (163). Most of the soldiers were "drunken, carousing, miserable wretches, possessed of no impulse but that of a selfish and sensual gratification. Here a coarse woman, with a flaunting air and a ribald jest, passed through the throng, and there a squaw sat beside the road, her eyes red with the whisky she had sold herself for, and her face horrible with the soulless leer of savage, half-drunken invitation" (264). In short, and despite the attacks on polygamy and Mormonism as anti-domestic, Utah is truly a domestic place in the wild west. The novel wants to celebrate the ancestors and wants even more to keep young women in the Mormon fold. Says Diantha, "I am beginning to see things as they are: the glamour and glory and romance which once so fascinated me is fading away, thank God—anyway as it relates to men who drink and carouse or who do wrong. And especially do I begin to see how unsafe we are associating with any man outside this Church and kingdom" (306).

*　*　*

Eight Mormon women, including Eliza Snow, published books of poetry. Their work like most women's western poetry is rigidly conventional, replete with archaisms and unnecessary apostrophes, making its status as poetry indubitable in its own day but compromising its quality for later readers. Sarah E. Carmichael's *Poems*, published with her permission by some friends in San Francisco in 1866, is the only book that resists Mormon apologia, which it does by mostly ignoring doctrine. The book contains twenty-six poems previously published in the *Deseret News*. Two were also anthologized in May Wentworth's 1867 *Poetry of the Pacific*, and one was anthologized again with a different title in William Cullen Bryant's anthology of 1878. Carmichael departed from Mormon teaching by supporting the Northern side in the Civil War (LDS official policy was neutrality) and by proposing that mining revenue should be devoted to the antislavery cause. There are also some antislavery poems about the Civil War; although the inferiority of black people is taken for granted (after all, the poet says, people are not equal) the principle of human brotherhood should prevail.

Other Mormon women poets defended their religion from a female point of view. They wrote with an impressive awareness of the place: the sublime Wasatch Range, the irrigated farmland, the broad streets of Salt Lake City, all of which they saw through the scrim of their biblical understanding. They interpreted their march to the Salt Lake in theological terms—a latter-day exodus—and saw themselves as having, literally, made the desert blossom as the rose. In 1881, English-born Hannah Cornaby, resident of Spanish Fork some 55 miles south of Salt Lake City, published *Autobiography and Poems*, combining a prose autobiography with a gathering of poems. The autobiography explains that she felt called to write poetry because it was her gift, and Mormons are obligated to return their gifts to the commonweal. Key life events are the persecution of Mormons in England, the overland trip, and the arrival at Salt Lake. "When, on the morning of the 12th of October, 1853, we emerged from the mouth of Emigration Canyon and beheld the 'City of the Saints,' we felt more than repaid for the nine months of travel, and all the hardships we had endured. We seemed to inhale the restful spirit of the beautiful city, spread out in peaceful loveliness before us. The neat adobie houses with their trim gardens, the crystal streams coursing along the sidewalks, giving life to avenues of shade trees, all aglow with the lovely tints of autumn, presented a picture that is indelibly fixed upon our minds, and which the greater magnificence of the Salt Lake City of to-day has not the power to efface" (35–36).

The poems include reminiscences, hymns, patriotic and religious songs, occasional poems for particular people and group meetings. "To the Relief Society of Spanish Fork" says "'Tis good that to His *daughters,* God has given work to do, / That not alone his *sons* must toil to bear His Kingdom through. / To us belongs the duty, to relieve the woes we see: / Even minist'ring angels, we always ought to be" (103). She says in "Utah," that "the Lord of all the earth, / In Utah set His throne, / And hence as ruler of the world, / Will have His laws made known . . . / And hither will the honest flee, / Ere the great judgments fall . . . /

And to that band of fearless men / Our noble Pioneers, / Belongs the mead of song and praise / Through all succeeding years" (106).

Cornaby's feckless "The Provo Woolen Factory" extols Mormon business practices: "Thanks to the Factory, old and young, / Now dress in clothes both warm and strong. / There might be imported clothes in the stores, / But their price was fearfully high, / And Utah's productions then were not cash, / So it was little we could buy. / Now, a load of wood will purchase a suit / That will stand the racket and tear, / Or a nice warm shawl, or waterproof dress, / For a wife or daughter to wear. / There's few in this country I guess, / The Provo Factory does not bless" (111). Thanking Brigham Young and the other leaders who established it, she says "we've been too slow to perceive, / The wonderful good which the co-op plan, / In a land like this can achieve" (112).

Also in 1881, Augusta Joyce Crocheron, born in New York City, a Utah arrival by way of California (she came as a baby with her parents in the group sailing around the horn in 1846 under Samuel Brannan's leadership), and a plural wife, published *Wild Flowers of Deseret*. Dedicated to Mormon activist Emmeline Wells, "but for whose untiring encouragement and friendship my efforts would have remained in the obscurity of my desk," the book is woman-centered throughout. The poems say polygamous wives are better at living in female communities than non-Mormon women. This development of womanliness, and their descent from British patriot stock, make them truly Americans, as does their forwarding of the tradition of religious dissent. "Introductory" contrasts the dusty, gray, parched dry valley found by the pioneers to the place where, now, "a hundred streamlets run / With emerald borders . . . / And garden homes reach far and wide— / The tourist's wonder and our pride; / And groups of happy children play / Where first we traced our lonely way. . . . / A new Kingdom's life begun / On freedom's soil 'neath a warm sun / And smiling sky, that yet will be / The fairest house of liberty" (1–2).

Crocheron's long "Women of Zion" celebrates a much-publicized pro-polygamy meeting of Utah women in 1878, "When fifteen hundred women thronged, / To answer back a listening world— / A people by their kindred wronged. . . . / Then we, the hunted, hated, weak, / Something in our own case may say. / Shall it count nothing unto us / That our great grandsires fought and died / For our land's liberty, because / Our creed from theirs may differ wide?" (41–42). She says the early Utah pioneers "left rank aside" and "with bleeding feet crossed deserts wide, / Drawing their hand-carts, day by day, / Through wind, and rain, and bitter snows. . . . / Beside America's dead sea, / Their weary pilgrimage did end. . . . / Then answered to the hand of toil / Fair garden homes and barren fields. . . . / But scarce these blessings are secured, / Ere those we could not dwell among, / Ignoring all we have endured, / With envious eye and venomed tongue, / Survey the scene, and with well feigned / Sense of honor, and of fear / Issue throughout our broad domain / A call for holy crusade here" (43). Envy not ideology motivates these naysayers. In "Salt Lake City" she enthuses: "Though the world now doubt the story / Of thy sacred work and claim, / They shall live to see thy glory, / And their fallen wreck and shame. / Though the world in hate deride thee, / Though the waves of evil foam, / Through whatever ills betide thee, / Thou are Zion—thou'rt my home" (64).

Among the publications of English-born Hannah T. King, which include two small books of poetry and a book about women of the Bible, is her 1884 *An Epic Poem. A Synopsis of the Rise of the Church of Jesus Christ of Latter-Day Saints, from the Birth of the Prophet Joseph Smith to the Arrival on the Spot Which the Prophet Brigham Young Pronounced to Be the Site of the Future Salt Lake City.* This narrative poem, 1800 lines mostly in iambic couplets of four or five beats, opens by invoking Columbia, daughter of Albion, thus claiming English lineage and Puritan descent for the Saints. But "Columbia" is less the land of the free than the designated cradle of the gospel, home of the new revelation in the Book of Mormon. King explains that Joseph Smith was chosen to receive the new dispensation precisely because he lacked formal education: "To this recipient, young, untutored mind, / The mighty revolution God designed. . . . / His mind untaught in all the lore of schools / (Which oft displays a paradise of fools)" (22). Under Brigham Young's leadership (a man "of larger heart and larger brain, / Of stronger will and of enduring frame, / Of higher type yet human in the main; / Undaunted, unimpassioned, formed to bear / Life's grand kaleidoscope, in its wear and tear" [47]), the Saints travel to the Rocky Mountains because Joseph had chosen it "as a place of rest / For saints to flee to, where they should be blest; / Away from Gentile rule and Gentile rod— / And Joseph's word was as the voice of God" (46). In Utah, "the gospel nursery—all the world should see!" they find their promised land: "Blessed pilgrims! Blessed people! / I have traced your journey through, / And have seen you all located / On the land reserved for you. / Years have fled—a mighty city / Stands to-day before all eyes; / Hands and hearts, and brains have labored, / And their work none can despise. / Beauteous city of the Saints! / How I love thee!" (61–62).

The import of Emmeline B. Wells's *Charities and Philanthropies: Women's Work in Utah* (1893), is clear in its title. Thrice-married plural wife, seventh wife of Daniel B. Wells, and a passionate advocate of polygamy, she was second only to Snow in reputation and influence among Mormon women. Her *Musing and Memories* came out in 1896 with a second, expanded edition in 1915. The poems were mostly from earlier years, but even the more recent ones write about polygamy as though it were still church policy. A July 4 poem identifies Mormons as Puritans in principle and by descent: "Within these peaceful vales far in the West, / Guarded by sentinel with snow-white crest, / Are sons and daughters who the truth revere, / Born heirs to liberty, who know no fear; / They are the offspring of those noble sires, / Whose Pilgrim fathers kindled freedom's fires; / Far in the East they lit the sacred shrine, / And lo! its glory in the West doth shine" (82).

"Faith and Fidelity" is part allegory, part first-person narration about a young woman rescued from adversity and nurtured by the Saints. She goes overland to Salt Lake with other "brave women" of whom "little has been told" (215). "At last these travelers reach'd the highest mountain crest, / Though many hardships had their way beset. . . . / And we will leave them in their joy, and glad estate, / Brought safely unto Zion, there to dwell"; here the young woman begins to understand "the great mission unto woman given" (221). "The years rolled on, and many changes came around. / Cities and towns were built throughout the land / Once bare and desolate. . . . / O, how delicious seemed the sweet content and peace / After the toils and struggles by the way; / . . . They loved their mountain home, / 'twas even far more dear / Than all they left behind—full well they knew / The Lord designed His people should build Zion here, / And had a sacred work for them to do" of which nothing is greater than giving "To woman higher place within the realm of thought, / Spreading its influence like a mighty wave" (224).

"Utah and the Pioneers" is about landscape. "These Rocky Mountains stand / A bulwark of great strength, and highest skill . . . / Which only could be wrought by the Great Author's hand" (236). Half a century ago "The savage Indian roam'd at will, and beasts of prey / Abode within these vales, so beautiful today / With all that glorifies the earth, where'er we stray / And everything for man's maintenance grows" (237). In "The Pioneer Jubilee," dated July 24, 1897, she writes that "Fair Utah celebrates with sovereign pride, / And stands today the wonder of the West" thanks to pioneers of fifty years ago, the "stalwarts, who have made this Desert great" (261).

In 1904 Louisa (Lulu) Greene Richards published *Branches that run over the Wall: A Book of Mormon Poem, and Other Writings.* The long "Book of Mormon Poem" partly retells the Book of Mormon in blank verse, and partly comments and embroiders on it in other verse forms, introducing women and romance into the account, and testifying to the book's truth. "Ye who have desire to know the truth, / Take now the Book of Mormon, read it o'er, / And find that it the Bible well sustains. . . . . / Comparing these two *books of books,* / The one establishes the other's truth. . . . / Yet I will add, / That by the Spirit of the Lord in me, / I testify that He had made me know / The book of Mormon is the truth from Him. / And so I say to those who seek for truth, / Take up the book of Mormon, read it o'er, / Yes read it o'er and o'er and o'er again; / The seal of Truth is on it, it is true" (66). Here Richards combines two forms of assent: logical assent, and assent by direct communion with the Spirit.

Richards's poems about babies and mothers call motherhood woman's great work because the mother stands to the child as God stands to the human. There are also poems for children to recite, poems celebrating birthdays or lamenting the deaths of LDS notables both male and female, and other contributions to an archive of public poetry. A few poems seem to refer to those who left Utah (or went to jail) as a result of the Edmunds Act. One, dated 1885, is "Holiday Offerings, to Our Exiled Loved Ones": "And blessed are ye who of sorrow partake, / Imprisonment, hatred, for righteousness' sake; / Or by false accusers denounced and exiled" (156); a second, dated 1896, is "A Call to Latter-day Saints": "He who led our sires to freedom, / Neath the glorious stripes and stars; / He who cheers our friends and brothers, / E'en through prison gates and bars, / He who soothes the hunted exiles, / In their lonely weariness; / Promising the tried and faithful, / He will all their wrongs redress" (151).

The latest book by a Mormon woman is Ruth May Fox's 1923 *May Blossoms,* with 125 poems on religious affirmation, Mormon dignitaries male and female, nature, women, and children. There are several poems to Utah, the "Queen of the Rockies" (14), the place designated by God for the Saints. In the long poem "Utah," Fox makes Utah the divinely chosen place, with hills "full and running o'er / With useful metals—copper, silver, gold, / With iron, coal and wood, and bounties manifold" (112); with towering mountains "From all invaders to protect thy land"; with "flocks and herds . . . emerald fields and waving grain" (113). The poem concludes: "Fulfilled the dream. Proud Utah's in the van / For health and wealth, for intellectual man. / Her cities rise in splendor; on her gates, / Bold opportunity knocks and waits. / The visions of the fathers fast unfold; / Blest Utah's burning sands have turned to gold" (114). "Two Scenes" contrasts the assassinations of Joseph and Hyrum Smith with the present day triumph of the church; the saints left the United States "To find a home where they might thrive and grow / In all the virtues God would have them know, / Toward the West they plodded day by day, / Ending at last their toilsome, desert way, / In a vale enthroned majestically, / Girt with snow-crowned peaks" (78). "Cumorah" dismisses the so-called wise who say "We have one Bible, we'll look no more" (84) in favor of the "meek and lowly" chosen to receive the vision; Joseph gets the plates and "The book goes forth on its shining way, / Nor earth nor hell its power can stay. / An immortal man, a mortal youth, / Destined to flood the world with truth" (85).

Poems about women declare that Utah women have equal political and occupational rights with men. In "The Relief Society" woman gets a separate but equal share in world's progress: "Man's not without the woman in the Lord, / Nor was the Church in Latter-day restor'd / Complete, until the Prophet 'turned the key,' / Which oped the door for sex equality, / And organized our saintly

Sisterhood / A helpmeet to the priestly Brotherhood; / Each in its sphere to forward God's great Cause / Until the world should recognize His laws" (67).

*   *   *

In 1884 Augusta Crocheron published the very important *Representative Women of Deseret: A Book of Biographical Sketches,* collecting brief memoirs from twenty-one leading Mormon women, most from the pioneer generation, who present Mormon history in nondoctrinal terms as a story of hardship, privation, trials, and triumph. Of two well-known Mormon women married to the same man Crocheron writes: "The false assertion made by the world that women of marked character and attainments would never submit to live in the order of plural marriage is disproved by such instances as this one. Both were women of high social attainments, and possessing superior qualities of mind and heart. It is the higher nature that must be aroused to inspire women to carry out practically this exalting, refining principle, and through this crucible many have come forth like gold seven times purified" (65). In connection with another plural wife Crocheron observes that "No tongue can describe, or pen portray the peculiar situation of these noble, self-sacrificing women, who through the providence of God helped to establish the principle of celestial marriage" (30). One of her subjects, Mary A. Freeze, writes that "In the spring of 1871, my husband, a faithful man, desirous of keeping all the commandments of God, saw fit, with my full consent, to take to himself another of the daughters of Eve, a good and worthy girl, Jane Granter by name. It tried my spirit to the utmost endurance, but I always believed the principle to be true, and felt it was time we obeyed that sacred order" (54); says Louie Felt: "I also became thoroughly convinced of the truth of the principle of celestial marriage, and having no children of my own was very desirous my husband should take other wives that he might have a posterity to do him honor, and after he took another wife and had children born to him, the Lord gave me a mother's love for them" (58).

Crocheron's own autobiographical account gently criticizes first wives: "Any woman, no matter how selfish, can be a first and only wife, but it takes a great deal more Christian philosophy and fortitude and self-discipline to be a wife in this order of marriage; and I believe those who choose the latter when both are equally possible, and do right therein, casting out all selfishness, judging self and not another, have attained a height, a mental power, a spiritual plane above those who have not. To do this is to overcome that which has its roots in selfishness, and it can be done if each will do what is right" (107–8).

Occasioned by the panic of 1893 and its effect on Utah life, Josephine Spencer wrote nontheological pro-Mormon stories arguing for LDS communalism against capitalism. The stories in her 1895 collection—*The Senator from*

Utah, and Other Tales of the Wasatch—are set in the Salt Lake Valley, with the Oquirrh mountains as backdrop; they appreciate the scenery of lake and sky, the glorious colors of sunset. In the title story, wealthy capitalists who are also elected officials from Utah try—literally—to drown out a Union meeting by flooding it. "A Municipal Sensation" has a cooperative coal company oppose the Copeland mining operation to lessen the burden on the poor; the Copeland Company is ultimately exposed as deceitful and its officers have to sell and leave Utah. In "Maridan's Experiment" the city abandons city-financed utilities for cooperatively worked and owned utilities. "Finley Parke's Problem" involves the Coxey's army's stop in Ogden. "Letitia" has a young girl temporarily attracted to a real estate boomer; the subtext here is land development, since the agent is interested in lakeside property for a resort. "Mariposa Lilies" involves mining chicanery on Antelope Island.

In 1898 Aurelia Spencer Rogers published *Life Sketches of Orson Spencer and Others and the History of Primary Work,* an autobiography incorporating family history. She had founded the primary school auxiliary of the LDS church, designed to bring after-school discipline to children, boys especially. Rogers uses family letters, newspaper accounts, her journals, and other sources to describe lives of hardship, poverty, and illness as her New England parents convert to Mormonism and join the westward hegira. Her mother dies en route to Nauvoo and when, in 1846, the father is sent on a three-year mission to England, he leaves the children—the oldest a thirteen-year-old daughter—on their own. Protected by Brigham Young, they arrive in Salt Lake, not to see their father again until 1849. Aurelia marries at age seventeen, moves to Farmington (seventeen miles north of Salt Lake City) for the rest of her life, and loses five of her first ten children to diverse childhood illnesses. Throughout, she tries to interpret her life in religious terms and make her book testify to her faith. If she's happy, she's experiencing an influx of the holy spirit; if depressed, God is testing her. There are glimpses of major events in Utah's history—the near war with the US in 1857, Indian conflict in Nevada—but except for noting that her father eventually married three wives, nothing about polygamy. A dedicatory poem by Josephine Spencer, another long poem by Eliza Snow, and many references to Mormon women tell a story of women's work in Utah, including the publication of this book meant, she says, "for the furtherance of primary interests and to the honor and glory of God" (281).

Susa Young Gates's 1911 *History of the Young Ladies' Mutual Improvement Association of the Church of Jesus Christ of Latter-Day Saints from November 1859 to June 1910* traces the society to its Nauvoo origins, with biographies of leading women and many photographs. It says the YLMIA was successor to the early Retrenchment associations, which in turn were preparing to counter the incoming railroad's baneful influence: "The spirit of worldly pleasure and vain fashions was rapidly creeping into the ranks of the daughters of Zion. We women are no better than we should be today, nay, nor half as good; but can the mind picture where we should have been if the training and check of these associations had not been given?" (35). As in her novel, Gates worries about the vulnerability of Mormon women when outsiders settle in Utah. In 1928, collaborating with her daughter Leah D. Widstoe, Gates published the 34-page *Women of the "Mormon" Church*. (By placing of Mormon in scare quotes throughout, she shows the LDS rejection of the term.) The book is for Mormon and non-Mormon readers alike and argues that the doctrine of separate spheres so central to LDS belief is compatible with female equality. In 1930, beyond my cutoff point, she and Widstoe published a celebratory biography of their father/grandfather, Brigham Young, in which polygamy is defended as both chaste and biblical.

Alice Merrill Horne—the second woman elected to the Utah House of Representatives, who worked on behalf of the fine arts in Utah—published *Devotees and Their Shrines: A Hand Book of Utah Art* (1914), introducing the lives and works of several Utah artists from the past and present, with illustrations of paintings, architecture, cabinetry. Her representational painters are inclined to portraiture, landscapes, and pioneer scenes. She begins the book by urging every reader to consult his or her individual talent, referring to the Mormon belief that every soul or spirit is individually endowed with gifts demanding expression as a condition of existence. Perhaps one might take her as a sign that Utah had now matured sufficiently to develop an aesthetic. But the impetus for Utah literature by women had vanished with statehood, and women turned their attention elsewhere.

6

Colorado

Colorado women's writing is about the sublime Rocky Mountains and the transformation of the place in the decade after the discovery of gold in 1858. Prospecting quickly gave way to heavily capitalized mines and turned miners into day-laborers, many of them immigrants. Perhaps partly in defiance of this reality, some Colorado writers were keen to portray the place as manly, traditional, and truly western. How to place women in such a picture was a challenge. As late as 1918, Mae Lacy Baggs, in *Colorado: The Queen Jewel of the Rockies,* approvingly repeated David Starr Jordan's definition of Colorado as a virile state, "one of earth's male lands"; she had "grasped something of the force of the phrase when looking from the summit of peaks upon vast mountain fastnesses stretching without interruption beyond the human eye—knowing that strong men were burrowing far into their granite sides for hidden wealth. But no lesser meanings have I sensed when viewing fields golden in their yield that once were 'dry, monotonous' sand areas. Perhaps it has been this virile male-ness of the land that has forced onward many a faint heart" (233–34).

An equivalence between big scenery and big people, an equation of space with health, made Colorado the epitome of an ideal West: "Colorado does breathe and beget a spirit that sets it apart. Her sons and daughters derive their greatness from the great State which they inhabit, from contact with the great works of nature, from daily visualizing that beauty in which all things live and move. Theirs is the matchless daring that mounts to the heights of human achievement; there is the inspiration of head and heart and hand, the sublime enthusiasm that moves mountains, the giant will to power that throngs the heavens and earth about them. They are poets whose works are expressed in action; poets fired by the rapt contemplation of nature's grandeur; poets that scale the topmost crags of life with their large-hearted love of living, typical of the West in spirit and in fact, for out where the West begins—that is Colorado" (ix). In Colorado "every man stands on his own feet, where he is freed from the cramped and crimped public opinion of congested centers, and has that wide charity and toleration that comes from sound nerves and plenty of mental and physical standing room" (329).

*   *   *

That Colorado was a difficult space for women didn't mean that women gave up on finding places for themselves there and writing about them. Baggs wrote her book for tourists, and though women may have had little to do with mining, they certainly had much to do with touring. The central section of Olive Thorne Miller's three-part *A Bird-Lover in the West* (1894) is about a summer of camping in Colorado to recover from overwork and urban stress; by now the state has become a tourist haven. At Miller's resort the tents are "models of comfort, with regular beds and furniture, rugs on the floor, gauzy window curtains, drapery wardrobes, and even tiny stoves for cool mornings and evenings. . . . The restfulness craved by the weary worker was there to be had for both soul and body. . . . [One] might study the ever-changing aspect of the mountains,— their dreamy veiled appearance, with the morning sun full upon them; their deep violet blueness in the evening" (11). Absence of wildness is not a problem, because the true West resides in such minute details as the western meadowlark's song: "The whole breadth and grandeur of the great West is in this song, its freedom, its wildness, the height of its mountains, the sweep of its rivers, the beauty of its flowers,—all in the wonderful performance" (33).

Miller's book had been preceded by Anna Gordon's *Camping in Colorado, with Suggestions to Gold-Seekers, Tourists and Invalids* (1879). With her husband and children, Gordon vacationed for a month near Estes Park, cooking and eating outdoors, dressing and sleeping in two tents rented on a rancher/farmer's land. Apparently like many others in the mountains who hadn't been able to live off the land, the owner had refashioned the property into an outdoor hotel for Easterners eager to savor the not-so-wild West and in need of rejuvenation after a year of daily grind. "Stock raising, dairying, hunting, trapping, fishing and guiding tourists through wilderness of the mountains, constitute the chief employment of the mountaineer, outside of lumbering and mining enterprises" (95). Because settlers "usually locate in those places which the tourist finds most desirable to visit . . . the tents of the traveller may everywhere be seen" (97); the campers, "usually very socially inclined," are "made up principally of the best talent and most refined intellects. . . . The sick, the adventurer, the explorer, poet, minstrel, artist, student, chemist, geologist, divine, statesman, and historian can all find something in these mountains" (151–52). Those "not fond of adventure" can take a train, stage coach, or hired carriage to just about every place they might want to visit (194). Mountain heights inspire a canned response: "The deeper strung chords of my nature sent forth their first notes of song; while over the whole scale of my being the hand of minstrelsy swept, and the inwrought melody was one that may never be reproduced" (177).

A band of Utes seen from the railroad leads Gordon to reflect that their reservation confinement was necessary, because otherwise there could be no tourism. Here is one of the earlier defensive references to the bitter fighting between Natives and settlers during the Civil War, which culminated in the Sand Creek massacre of 1864, where the wrong tribe—Cheyenne rather than Ute—paid the price in the brutal killing of noncombatants by soldiers under the command of Col. John Chivington. Two years earlier Chivington had led his Colorado volunteers into New Mexico where the battle of Glorieta Pass had stopped the Confederate Army's advance toward California, but that heroism was not enough to stem the reaction of Easterners. (Ellen Williams, spouse of a bugler who served in the Second Colorados volunteer company during the Civil War, strove to correct the image of hooligan miners in *Three Years and a Half in the Army* [1885] by describing their patriotism a couple of decades after the War ended. The book opens with a cheerful scene of mining in 1860 but its interests are with the company not the place they were in when the war happened to start; for the most part, it takes place in New Mexico.)

Chivington's behavior produced a backlash in the form of pro-Indian ("Friends of the Indian") movements among white people nationwide. Colorado writers, for their part, tried to defend Anglo behavior. Gordon, for example, says tourists should not criticize policies that have made their own enjoyment possible. "Inseparably associated with this tribe are many tragedies of frontier life, which are still recited to strangers, as incidentally interwoven with the history of the mountains. Indeed, a generation has passed since this band of outlaws was the terror of every defenseless settler, emigrant, or traveller within their reach. They indiscriminately robbed and murdered every white man, woman, and child, until forbearance with them ceased to be a virtue, and restraint became a necessity, when the men in the white settlements, aided by troops of war, successfully conquered them. They are now considered friendly and peaceably disposed; but it is their want of power to contend successfully against the white man, whom they, perhaps justly, regard as their natural enemy, that assures the settler of his safety" (198–99).

In her *Tales of the Colorado Pioneers* (1884), Colorado-born Alice Polk Hill, a Denver journalist, aimed to memorialize the independent miners whose day in Colorado had been so brief. Hill, appointed the first poet laureate of Colorado in 1919, seems not to have published a book of poetry. *Tales,* inspired she says by a pioneer reunion, is jauntily humorous as it recounts her travels around the state in search of old-timers. Though she enjoys interviewing them—they were "a jovial set" (210)—she sees Colorado's true greatness in the transformation of Denver and Leadville away from mining monoculture. Denver's "rise and progress is a marvel of modern civilization, and in a measure its history is the history of Colorado. . . . Situated in the heart of an empire infested by predatory and cruel savages, at the dawn of a fierce rebellion, in the brief space of twenty-five years it has grown from a small village of tents and log houses to a magnificent metropolis" (94). Leadville is also "a marvel" with "gas and waterworks, telegraph and telephone lines, street railways, the letter carrier system, fine public schools, several large smelting and reduction establishments, stamp and sampling mills, a fine opera house, several extensive wholesale and retail grocery, dry goods and hardware houses; three daily newspapers, the *Chronicle, Herald* and *Democrat;* corner lots for $5,000 to $10,000, and everything that goes to form a full-fledged city" (206–7).

Hill published a second pioneer book in 1915, celebrating an entirely different type from the people she'd interviewed in hotel parlors thirty years earlier. *Colorado Pioneers in Picture and Story,* published by subscription and adorned with photographs of people and buildings (a book obviously meant as a vanity purchase by those featured in it), takes businessmen as its pioneers. A few women—wives of millionaires, club members, or philanthropists—appear in what is otherwise a resolutely masculine set of biographies organized within geographical regions. "The labor of the Pioneers involved the highest type of moral as well as physical courage, and by placing their brave deeds in an historical setting I hope to preserve their intensely interesting human side and show how the isolated settlement, in a dreary desert, found its way into the sisterhood of states" (vii). Hill feels the need, a half century later, to defend Sand Creek yet again, "considered by the philanthropists of the East one of the greatest Indian massacres of modern time. But it brought peace and quiet to the terror-stricken people of Colorado, by crippling the power of the most numerous and hostile tribe of the plains, and men resumed their struggle for daily bread without fear of the savage" (214).

Luella Shaw's *True History of Some of the Pioneers of Colorado* (1909) chronicles the lives of three pioneers to "give an insight into the lives of some of the early settlers who endured the hardships and privations that they underwent for the sake of paving the way to our present civilization, where towns, cities and railroads have sprung into existence as if by magic" (7). Sand Creek is defended: "Look at what this country is today and what it might have been if the Indians had won the Sand Creek fight or if it had never been fought. The Indians would kill the settlers and push them back towards the east and prevent the growth of the nation . . . and instead of this being the land of which we are all so proud, a place of refuge for the oppressed of foreign lands, it would be a heathen and undeveloped land. The Sand Creek fight was the means of pushing the Indians further west and opening up the frontier and showed whether the wheels of progress should turn and make homes for millions of people and raise the standard of civilization and prosperity higher, or if this west of bountiful wealth, health and untold opportunities should remain a wilderness and barren waste. . . . Does not the growth of the West, built by our own fathers appeal as strongly to you as the victory of some foreign lands that are praised by some of our own writers who seem to overlook the struggles, suffering and blood shed in our behalf, by our fathers or grandfathers here at home?" (117–18).

*   *   *

The earliest of several juveniles about Colorado seems to have been Helen Hunt Jackson's *Nelly's Silver Mine,* published in 1878, two years after statehood and twenty years after the gold discoveries. Jackson had moved to Colorado for her health, and her book, launched from a profoundly New England moralistic perspective (and before the Indian issue captured her attention), disparages mining. In the novel, the March family (meant to invoke Louisa May Alcott's characters?) has gone to Colorado for father's asthma; the husband (a minister), wife, and a pair of twelve-year-old twins, feckless Rob and responsible Nelly, hope to farm on rented land. Like other would-be but inexperienced farmers all over the West, they make a hash of it. New England farming practices don't work in the high altitude, so their first crop fails. A second crop is destroyed by grasshoppers. Then it's hand to mouth. Nelly, all pluck and virtue, sells butter and eggs to support the family. She erroneously believes, also, that she has found a silver mine, which she calls the "Good Luck Mine." At the book's end, Nelly and her brother leave Colorado for an eastern education funded by a wealthy woman who has taken a fancy to them; a German immigrant neighbor says: "she haf better than any silver mine in her own self. She haf such goot-vill, such patient, such true, she haf always 'goot luck.' She are 'Goot Luck mine' her own self'" (379). Jackson seems to miss her own mark here by implying that good luck in Colorado consists in being able to leave it; the hard-to-miss lesson for eastern readers is not to expect mining or farming success in Colorado.

Other Colorado books for young people wonder whether and what women (adults and children alike) might bring to the state. One of Jackson's good friends, Sarah Chauncey Woolsey (writing as Susan Coolidge), used Colorado settings for the last two in her five-book series for girls about the Carr family, the first of which, published in 1872, was the immensely popular *What Katy Did.* In *Clover* (1888), Clover Carr, accompanying her ailing younger brother Phil to "St. Helen's" (Colorado Springs), is amazed to find how sophisticated and up-to-date it is, with amenities of an eastern city twice its size (156). Clover turns out to have the attributes of "a first-rate pioneer . . . born to live at the West" (187)—by which the novelist means she has the tenacity and capability to bring Colorado to the point of becoming livable for women and children. At a ranch called High Valley not far from St. Helen's, a Carr cousin, Clarence, is batching it with a young Englishman, Geoffrey Templestowe, aided only by a Chinese cook. Clover rolls up her sleeves and tidies their disorderly cabin, showing girl readers that if they like housework the West has a place for them. The last book in the series, *In the High Valley* (1891), brings the rest of the Carr family to live in the valley, where all are happy to shut out the rest of the world. One minor character explains to an immigrant Englishwoman that America is like a pudding—"plums from one part of the world, and the spice from another, and flour and sugar and flavoring from somewhere else, but all known by the name of pudding" (75). But all the characters are English or Americans of English descent. The conservative messages of this book are that the truest Americans are Anglos, the truest women are homemakers, and the family is the only institution one can trust.

In Fannie E. Newberry's *Mellicent Raymond: the Impress of a Gentlewoman* (1891), a mining engineer's bride goes to a rough Colorado hamlet and, thanks to her combination of refinement and Christian piety, marvelously transforms it in just a few years. The lesson, like Jackson's, is that virtue is the best investment. Moral improvement makes a place safe for capitalists and leads to economic prosperity: "The boom once started, nothing has checked its onward course. From the first weak attempts at refinement started by her own womanly example, has grown absolute luxuriance of grace and beauty. First felt in the home circle, that influence expanded in ever-widening circles until it embraced the valley, which awoke from its long slumber, to strive after better things. Then the railroad came; for, like good deeds, these go where they are called. . . . By the railroad the valley was introduced to the world, and when the world saw what a charming little valley it was, a goodly share of it chose to stop there, and swell the census. . . . By-paths widened into streets, alleys into avenues. Tents folded themselves and stole away before the reign of hammer and trowel. Churches shot up . . . and schools drew in the children" (395–96).

Charlotte M. Vaile's *The M. M. C.: A Story of the Great Rockies* (1898) is a sort of Horatio Alger story in which two young friends—Alice, from New England, teaching school and living with relatives in Colorado, and Lex, an orphan living with an old prospector—try to save a mine from being gobbled up by a syndicate. Though they fail at this, Alice's eloquence so impresses the syndicate manager that he persuades the owners to buy out the prospector at a very good price and give Lex a good job. Her virtue rewarded, Alice returns to New England where she is happy to learn about her friends' success but not, apparently, eager to go back to Colorado. A decade later, Evelyn Raymond's *Dorothy on a Ranch* (1909) is about a group of youths who stay for a summer on a Colorado mountain ranch on their way East from California. They ride horses, talk to bona fide Indians (how exciting, the novel gushes), take excursions, while protagonist

Dorothy rescues a lost boy and does other good deeds. A fourth juvenile, Bertha Cobb's 1920 *Anita: A Story of the Rocky Mountains,* is nominally about mining but in fact about vacationing. Anita and her parents emigrate from Kansas so father can pursue his dream of finding a paying silver mine in the mountains around Boulder. Mother remains in Boulder while Anita goes with father into the mountains and learns about geology, mining techniques, flora and fauna, how to identify arsenic in spring water, forest fires (caused mainly by careless tourists), and miner psychology. She has the fun of camping in glorious natural scenery, participating in the building of a cabin, riding in a mining tram, and playing with her pet burro and cat. Father hits pay dirt, and Anita effuses: "my dreams had all come true. Here on this wondrous mountain I could come each year to live in the heart of nature, with the rocks and running brook, the trees and flowers, the birds and all wild living things" (185).

* * *

Annie M. Green's *Sixteen Years on the Great American Desert; or, The Trials and Triumphs of a Frontier Life* (1887), a memoir about Greeley, is a sort of dark-comedy satire on settler hype reminding us once again that farming was as much a gamble as mining. According to her account, she left Franklin, Pennsylvania, with her husband and two children in 1870 to join the new Union Colony established by Nathan Meeker (agricultural editor of the *New York Tribune*) and endorsed by Horace Greeley in that newspaper. In the memoir's first paragraph, Annie's husband enters their Pennsylvania home, newspaper in hand, to announce, "while an excited expression played o'er his features," that he "can never be contented until we have a home on the far west"; she adds, "I think I am not exaggerating when I say that scores of tears ran down my cheeks 'ere he had finished that which blighted my prospects and filled my soul with gloom"; many other neighbors also "showed strong symptoms of the western fever, and even I found myself reading the New York with unusual interest, especially those highly colored articles so well remembered by every surviving victim of 'Union colony'" (3).

The little book is a year-by-year, month-by-month recital of disaster, beginning with a train wreck on the way out, and moving on to bad weather, locusts, and diverse calamities incidental to farming. Although there is "not a tree, plant nor shrub on which to rest my weary eye, to break the monotony of the sand beds and cactus of the Great American Desert" (13), and although the sublimity of the Rocky mountains does not compare with the brilliant appearance of the sun, moon, or stars back in Pennsylvania (this may be humor), the main fact about the so-called "desert" is the constant rain, which drowns their crops, destroys their roof, soaks their furniture, and ruins their clothes. When, after two years of failed crops, "success had crowned our labor, and the future appeared quite flattering," it turns out that "there was no market for our grain; that the financial crash of '73 had reached our territory at last. No money, no money was the general cry. Yet we were obliged to pay our two per cent interest, taxes, store and threshing bills, besides quite an amount of hired help; therefore the only alternative was to mortgage our grain in order to raise the money" (45). She describes more bad years, during which she becomes a playwright and theatrical impresario to earn money. Regrettably, her play or plays don't seem to have survived. It's quite a surprise to discover that sixteen years later the family has increased its land holdings, that all four of her children (two more having been born in Colorado) and her husband have become true Coloradoans, and that Greeley is now a "handsome little city" (78), a "prosperous city" with "the best of hotel accommodations" (79), two good theaters, "pure artesian water," "electric light," excellent schools and churches (80).

Emma Shepard Hill's two-part memoir directed to her grandchildren—*A Dangerous Crossing and What Happened on the Other Side* (1914)—stitched an overland narrative from late summer and autumn of 1864, when she was thirteen, to letters written over the next decade. The book's theme is the family's successful recreation of their daily Ohio life in Colorado, the point being that the West is won not with outlawry or even heroism, but with children's play, education, party-going, getting married. For this writer the great Rockies barely figure, except in that her father (actually, her adoptive father) goes to Colorado in the first place to manage a mine.

A Tenderfoot Bride: Tales from an Old Ranch by Clarice E. Richards (1920—reissued with an introduction by Maxine Benson in 1988) is a fictionalized memoir about a couple ranching on the plains east of Denver. At first they are ecstatically happy: "In the vast, unbroken silence of the prairies I felt the sense of chaos and confusion give way to peace. . . . We were in a new world, we had a great domain, we faced undreamed of experiences and possibilities. My spirits rose with a bound, and I resolved from that moment to consider our life here in the West, in the midst of new conditions, a great adventure" (19–20). But there are troubles almost from the first. Neighboring ranchers graze their cattle on the Richards's land; because one parcel within the holdings is open range, they can't legally fence any of it, and must struggle endlessly "for the possession and use of what was our own" (104). Then, also on account of open range, homesteaders arrive: "We owned our land and no one could encroach upon us, but after a few years we began to notice forlorn little shacks built here and there on the open range by the poor home-seekers who, attracted by the prospect of free land, had begun 'homesteading.' They built flimsy little houses, scratched up the surface of the prairie for a few inches and raised pitiful, straggling crops. The settlers were coming in! The opening wedge of that great onrush had been thrust deep into the heart of the prairie" (108–9). Finally she accepts displacement to Denver as part of "the evolution of a wondrous plan. We had launched our frail barque in the midst of the prairie sea at the ebb of the tide of the wild, lawless days of the West; with the flow we had been carried through the years of a well-ordered pastoral existence to the era of agricultural productivity, and on each succeeding wave we had seen civilization borne higher and higher toward the ultimate goal set by the Great Spirit" (226).

The narrator claims that western life is completely democratic; "no one in the country cared who you might have been or who you were. The *Mayflower* and Plymouth Rock meant nothing here. . . . The one thing of vital importance was what you were—how you adjusted yourself to meet conditions as you found them" (42). But she shows otherwise; the cultured visitors congregate around the fireplace in the main house, the cowboys keep to their bunkhouse. The guests include "university men who had come West for adventure or investment, men of wealth whose predisposition to weak lungs had sent them in exile to the wilderness, modest young Englishmen, those younger sons so often found in the most out-of-the-way corners of the earth, and who, through the sudden demise of a near relative, had such a startling way of becoming earls and lords overnight; adventurous Scotchmen, brilliant young Irishmen, all smoking contentedly there in the firelight and discussing the 'isms' and 'ologies' and every other subject under heaven" (159–60). The cowboys by contrast are "rough, untutored men . . . whose rules of conduct were governed by individual choice, unhampered by conventions" (42). They reject her plans to "get books for them and to arrange a reading room," in favor of Sears, Roebuck and Montgomery Ward catalogues. "Night after night the boys pored over them absorbed in the illustrations, of hats, gloves, boots and saddles, the things most dear to their hearts, for on their riding equipment alone they spent a small fortune. Improvident and generous, however great their vices might be, their lives were free from petty meanness" (78–79).

* * *

Colorado mining, however viewed, forms the background for much of women's Colorado fiction. Mary Hallock Foote lived in Leadville for a few years and began her novel-writing career with two Colorado novels—*The Led-Horse Claim* (1883) and *John Bodewin's Testimony* (1885). In both, young people from families in mining conflicts fall in love. In *The Led-Horse Claim*, Led-Horse ore is giving out while the adjoining Shoshone Mine is doing very well; the suspicion that Shoshone miners have been breaking into the underground Led-Horse mine is validated when Hilgard, new manager of the Led-Horse who needs the mine to show a profit if he is to keep his job, investigates. Armed violence underground—that the mines are underground signifies the replacement of surface mining by heavily capitalized quartz mining, independent miners by hired workers, and on-site by absentee ownership—temporarily disrupts his romance with the sister of the Shoshone's manager.

Foote, conservative in her social and political values, sees mining as a prelude to the region's real prosperity, to be accomplished by resident businessmen who won't move into a turbulent region. Leadville, for example, "exhibited in its earliest youth every symptom of humanity in its decline. The restless elements of the Eastern cities, the disappointed, the reckless, the men with failures to wipe out, with losses to retrieve or to forget, the men of whom one knows not what to expect, were there; but as its practical needs increased and multiplied, and its ability to pay for what it required became manifest, the new settlement began to attract a safer population. . . . Men of all trades followed the miner. The professions followed the trades, and were represented, generally, by men in their youth. It was, perhaps, this immense, though undisciplined, force of sanguine youth which saved the city. The dangerous elements of the camp . . . were floated and swept onward by its strong tide. The new board sidewalks resounded to the clean step of many an indomitable, bright-faced boy, cadet of some good Eastern family, and neophyte in the business of earning a living, with a joyous belief in his own ability and a clean record to imperil in proving them" (12).

The mining town in *John Bodewin's Testimony* is like the one in *Led-Horse*: "The avenue was straight and wide, as befits the avenue of the hopeful future; but the houses were the houses of the uncertain present. They were seldom more than two stories in height, miscellaneous in character, homogeneous in ugliness, crude in newness of paint or rawness of boards without paint. There were frequent breaks in the perspective of their roofs, where a vacant lot awaited its tenant, or the tenant awaited his house. There were tents doing duty for houses; there were skeleton structures hastily clothing themselves with bricks and mortar that meantime impeded the sidewalk. One-half of the street was torn up for the laying of gas-pipes, and crossings were occasionally blockaded by the bulk of a house on rollers, which night had overtaken in its snail-like progress. The passing crowd was a crowd distinguished by a predominance of boots and hats—dusty or muddy boots, and hats with a look of preternatural age or startling newness. There was a dearth of skirts; and these, when they appeared, were given a respectful, an almost humorously respectful, share of the side-walk" (32–33).

The conflict in this novel is over mine ownership and the villain is reviled for the damage he does to business enterprise; as one businessman says, "We are Western men; we want to encourage Eastern capitalists to seek investments in the West. One way to do it will be to show them that their investments *in* the West can and will be protected *by* the West. The misfortune of one Eastern property-owner will be a warning to a hundred others. It is just such men as the plaintiff in this suit—and not many like him would be needed to do it—who ruin the business of legitimate mining in the west" (291–92). At novel's end the happy couple, who had left Colorado, return, giving the West another chance to civilize itself: "Wind of the great Far West, soft, electric, and strong, blowing up through gates of the great mountain ranges, over miles of dry savannah, where its playmates are the roving bands of wild horses, and the dust of the trails which it weaves into spiral clouds and carries like banners before it! Wind of prophecy and of hope, of tireless energy and desire that life shall not satisfy. Who that has heard its call in the desert, or its whisper in the mountain valleys, can resist the longing to follow, to prove the hope, to test the prophecy!" (344).

In 1888 suffragist Emma Ghent Curtis published *The Fate of a Fool,* a novel set in a Rocky mountain town. It polemicizes against the sexual double standard where men debauch women but insist on marrying virgins; themselves debauched, they carry immorality into the heart of the home. This is to deny that women can influence the developing West by imposing their domesticity on it; they can't impose anything unless men choose to reform themselves. Curtis's *The Administratrix* (1889, a book brought to scholarly attention by Victoria Lamont) has a marvelously improbable plot, and shows much more interest than *The Fate of a Fool* in details of Colorado life. In the first of its three parts Mary, a flirtatious schoolteacher obsessed with clothes and marriage meets Jim, a handsome cattleman. In the middle section Mary, having married Jim, raises the tone of the community by organizing literary evenings for locals and visitors with storytelling, singing, games. This segment, a trove of western lore, is, for at least this later reader, the book's most valuable feature. Mary's effort to bring culture to the town comes to naught, however, because Jim is murdered and mutilated by rustlers who have been stealing his cattle. In just three months Mary puts his property in order and decamps to New Mexico where, in another four months, she becomes a top-notch cowboy. Successfully disguised as a sixteen-year-old boy, she returns to town, gets a job on the rustlers' ranch, and begins methodically to shoot her husband's killers, until, at the end, they kill her. The novel's point seems to be—as in *The Fate of a Fool*—that women's efforts to improve the West through female influence are futile. They need the vote.

Denver journalist Patience Stapleton published two interesting novels in which the glorious Rocky Mountains represent amoral sublimity rather than the divine presence. *Kady* (1888), set in a mountain hamlet, begins with a long, dialect-ridden, local color segment showing that mountain grandeur has no effect on the small-minded people who live there. On the contrary their pettiness is intensified by seven months of winter isolation, with snowslides a constant threat: "As if in judgment on the men who had dared to mutilate a mighty mountain, snow slides each winter cut a portion of the earth above away, like the swath of a huge scythe, sometimes in one place, sometimes another, but always taking a part of this piece of the road, and hurling great boulders, trees, earth and masses of snow down into the ravine" (272). Kady, the protagonist, is one-quarter Indian, representing both a race-blind authorial tolerance and the idea that every young western woman regardless of her ethnicity is in ways both good and bad a "savage." The love story involves Kady with a well-heeled vacationer from Philadelphia; their protracted romance is decorated with an extensive inventory of Colorado types (miner, sheepherder, card sharp, dishonest lawyer, foolish and smart women, confidence men, admirable early pioneers, ferocious Indian mother, spoiled socialite, Philadelphia swells, and more) brought together when the discovery of gold creates a boom. "Cabins, tents and dug-outs crowded the valley. Three saloons came up in a single day, fitted for business. . . . The xylophonic clanking of hammer and wood went on day and night. Mules and burro trains followed each other over a road made into shape almost as soon as they passed by gangs of men working at the highest wages ever known—a workman's paradise. The spade handler might be a millionaire tomorrow. The quiet night air in the settlement was made hideous by loud yells and laughter, the clinking of poker chips, the curses at faro and the chatter over queer three-card games, or the crack of rifles at prize shooting. Policy shops bloomed everywhere like foul weeds, and a big dance hall was crowded every night" (323–24).

Stapleton's *Babe Murphy* (1890) reprises mining settlement through the first-person narration of former Maine resident Lydia Ann Wilder, who, liberated by a small inheritance when she is fifty years old, follows her western dream to Colorado, which she chooses because she has been told women are "well treated there, particularly in the mountain towns" (7). The novel contains unexpected deaths, an apparent murder, and other untoward events, including an interval when the good characters visit flat Texas—land of "wide lands and clear skies, boundless prairie and spring sunshine" (182)—as though to show again that mountains have no impact on goodness or beauty. In the end the good characters take up ranching on Colorado's eastern plains, as close as the mountain-cursed state can get to Texas.

Anna Fuller adapted local color conventions to Colorado with subtlety and humor. *A Literary Courtship under the Auspices of Pike's Peak* (1893) is an amusingly artificial love story in which two New Yorkers, young men of substance—one an author who has published under a woman's name—visit Colorado Springs in search of the woman whose real name it is. Though she turns out to be middle-aged, in the process of finding her the author meets his true love. The protagonists take excursions to Pike's Peak and other sites including Helen Hunt Jackson's grave, and the book has many photographs from around Colorado Springs, making it a tourist souvenir of sorts. As well as beautiful scenery the young men find tennis and polo and parties, showing Colorado a kind of western Newport populated by the well-bred and well-heeled.

Fuller's *Peak and Prairie: From a Colorado Sketch-Book* (1894) collects thirteen stories set around Colorado Springs, here called Springtown. "In its immediate vicinity exists the life of the prairie ranch on the one hand and that of the mining-camp on the other; while dominating all as it were—town, prairie, and mountain fastness—rises the great Peak which has now for so many years been the goal of pilgrimage to men and women from the Eastern States in pursuit of health, of fortune, or of the free, open-air life of the prairie" (iii). In "A Pilgrim in the Far West" a New England woman who went with her son to Colorado for his health and, without funds to return, stayed on after he died, ceases to yearn for New England when a rancher invites her to be his housekeeper: "when at last they reached the ranch, lying like an oasis in the vast barren, with young corn sprouting in the wide fields, and a handful of cottonwood trees clustered about the house, the tears fairly started to the little woman's eyes, so much did this bit of rural landscape remind her of her own far-away New England" (24). And so "the faithless little New Englander passed into the house that had at last taken on the dignity and the preciousness of a home" (35). In "Brian Boru," an Irish Peer is disappointed because his acquaintants "did not wear flannel shirts in general society; they did not ask impertinent questions; a whiskey cocktail did not seem to play a necessary part in the ceremony of introduction; the almighty dollar itself did not stalk through every conversation, putting the refinements of life to the blush. In short, Sir Brian found himself forced to base his regard for his new acquaintances upon such qualities as good breeding, intelligence, and a cordial yet discriminating hospitality,—qualities which he was perfectly familiar with at home" (37).

"The Lame Gulch Professor" is about a mining boom: "In September it was that the bit of quartz was carried down to Springtown; before the winter snows had thought of melting, a town of rude frame huts had sprung up in the hollow below, and Lame Gulch was a flourishing mining-camp. All the rough-scuff of the countryside promptly gathered there, and elbowed, with equal indifference, the honest miner, the less honest saloon-keeper, and the capitalist, the degree of whose claim to that laudatory adjective was not to be so easily fixed. No one seemed out of place in the crazy, zigzag streets, no sound seemed foreign to this new, conglomerate atmosphere. The fluent profanity of the mule-driver, the shrill laugh of the dance-hall; the prolonged rattle and final roar of the ore-chute, the steady pick of the laborer at the prospect-hole;—each played its part to burden and stain the pure, high air that had seemed so like the air of Heaven itself" (156–57). The title character of "Mr. Featherbee's Adventure" is "doing" Lame Gulch, "delighting in every distinctive feature of the rough-and-ready, sordid, picturesque, 'rustling' young mining-camp" (217); "What, to him, were the glories of the encircling peaks, the unfolding wonders of this heart of the Rockies, compared with the actual sight of the mushroom growth of pine huts and canvas tents, straggling sparsely up the hill, centring closely in the valley?" (19).

Anna Maynard Barbour's 1897 *Told in the Rockies: A Pen Picture of the West* (also published as *The Award of Justice; or, Told in the Rockies*) is a long novel with a complicated plot of separated families, supposedly dead relatives, stolen children, concealed identities, and ultimate reunions; it also has two romances and a mining story of fraud and violence. The hero, a Bostonian raised by an aunt and uncle (the latter the president of a large investment company that owns western mines among other properties), is sent incognito to one of these mines to find out why it is not generating profits. He finds romance at his boarding house with a visiting schoolteacher while uncovering a variety of mining frauds: cooking the books, salting the mines to deceive potential investors, tunneling away from the valuable ore to leave it free for surreptitious exploitation. In the crisis/climax, the villains blow up several mines to destroy evidence of their evil-doing. Descriptions of the miners' seedy living quarters and demoralized lives contrast with the beauty of peaks, gulches, lakes, waterfalls, and weather in the Rockies. Gambling is the unifying motif: the big corporations try to minimize mining's inherently speculative nature while the miners gamble their wages away because for them life itself is a gamble: "To most in that community one human life, more or less, was of slight significance. To them, life was but one great game, in which fortune, reputation, character, everything which they possessed, whether much or little, was staked on the high card. No wonder that little thought was given to the losers, dropping out, one by one!" (204). In the end, the good side takes over the mine, improving both its bottom line and the miners' lives: "As one gazes upon the peaceful picture of the mountain town, there is nothing to recall the frightful scene of destruction and ruin of only three years past. . . . On the site of the old boarding house, is a beautiful, wide-spreading stone cottage, so built that its numerous bow-windows take in a view of the azure lake and shining cascades, as well as of the surrounding peaks and the sunset sky; and on the broad, vine-covered veranda, is a well-known group, who come from their distant, city homes, to spend a few weeks of each summer amid the grandeur and beauty of the mountains, to listen to the whispering of the pines and the music of the cascades" (333). One notes that it's not the women, but the men, who effect this transformation of the scene.

∗   ∗   ∗

Four outlier Colorado books from the early twentieth century are Emma F. Jay Bullene's *The Psychic History of the Cliff Dwellers: Their Origin and Destruction* (1905), Alma Estabrook's *The Rule of Three: A Story of Pike's Peak* (1909), Ellen E. Jack's autobiographical fantasy, *The Fate of a Fairy; or, Twenty Seven Years in the Far West* (1910), and feminist Charlotte Perkins Gilman's *The Crux* (1911), one of the few novels she published separately after serialization in her magazine, *The Forerunner* (it has been edited by Jennifer S. Tuttle in a 2002 reissue). Bullene, a spiritualist trance speaker, uses objects from Mesa Verde to argue via psychometry (the art of divination by holding an object) that the cliff dwellers were originally white people from Scandinavia. Estabrook's novel is a drawing room farce set in a summer cabin in the mountains, celebrating the western girl—slim, gallant, chin up, a model of "spontaneity and freshness"—in contrast to female gold diggers and censorious women moralists (101). Ellen Jack, a widow who went to Colorado in 1873, reports on her investments in real estate and mining; her bad second marriage to a man who (fortunately, because she can easily get rid of him) turns out to be already married; her marksmanship such that when men overcome by her beautiful golden hair (this explains the title) accosted her on the street, she could scare them off by whipping out— her phrase, no matter that the pistol weighed over four pounds—her trusty 44. Her iterated point is that the whole of the Rocky Mountain West is one giant con game; people "read novels and wander out West, thinking they can find gold anywhere, and when they get there they find they can get nothing without money to pay for it, and that smart people have been there before them and have played every trick on the western people, as there is not a game thought of that has not already been played" (92).

Gilman's *The Crux* shows two generations of women from a languishing New England town with almost no marriageable men finding useful work and— surprisingly perhaps for the feminist best known for *Herland,* her fantasy of a land without men—good husbands. But that the rejected New England suitor of the protagonist turns out to be syphilitic allows Gilman to write about the double standard and sexually transmitted disease. The point seems to be that when men are scarce, marriage-obsessed women will endure anything just to be married, even destroying their health and their children. Although venereal disease is the novel's overt theme, the novel implies that there are more than enough available men in the West for a single woman to get a good husband.

Other twentieth-century Colorado fiction branched out to take in ranching as well as mining, extending its purview beyond the Rockies to the state's eastern plains. Mary E. Stickney collected four tales in her self-published *Ouray Jim, and Other Stories* (1904). These are polished stories with sentimental trick endings, topographical description, naturalizing details, and lively dialogue about men and the uncertainties of mining or ranching. "Ouray Jim regarded the plains as but a special dispensation of Providence in favor of the cattle man; the scarcity of water but a crowning device of divine wisdom to keep out the hungry horde of settlers who, otherwise, armed with homestead and pre-emption rights, would be coming in with their fences and foolishness to spoil the range" (2). In "A Star-Route" a stage coach company, trying to unload its mail delivery contract, fakes a holdup to persuade the government to switch to the railroad, which is destroying the stage trade anyway. "The railroad hoodooed the stage business. We've been running at a loss for over a year now. We have no passengers, no freight; everything goes by the railroad. . . . And of course the mail ought to go that way too. . . . We've tried petitions and we've tried arguments; it would be twice as convenient for the public to get the mail by train, as a blind man might see; but those fools at Washington just promise to look into the matter" (31). In "An Arizona Speculation" the architect narrator from Denver goes to Arizona to inspect a town site: "when the hard times struck Denver in '93 my business was knocked into a cocked hat. . . . Constructions of every sort stopped as short as grandfather's clock in the song; architects were a drug on the labor market, and I began to cast my eye about for greener pastures. The papers were having a good deal to say about Arizona just then" (45). In "The Jack Pot Mine" one would-be miner advises another to leave Colorado because "in a survival of the fittest you'll get left. Go back to the old folks on the farm and hoe potatoes—it's the work you were cut out for. . . . Hereafter I stick to business and let speculation alone" (84).

Two novels by Hattie Horner Louthan, a Kansan who worked in Denver as an editor and journalist, attach the Romeo-Juliet formula to ranching conflicts. Along with Barbour's *Told in the Rockies,* these are the most fact-packed Colorado fictions. *This Was a Man: A Romance* (1906) connects good girls and wicked men to a story of labor and capital on the great ranches whose employees are underpaid, and often immigrant, wage-earners. The baronial estate of Pierce Eldreth includes mining and sheepherding operations, and the Mexican and Swedish employees are all his tenants. Paul, the noble hero, is a captain of industry who believes himself to be Mexican but—in a cradle-switching, prince-in-disguise turn of plot—is discovered to be Eldreth's son. Paul's charisma averts a possible strike and preserves the class system. Along with an inane heroine whom the narrator calls irresistible, the book is loaded with technical talk about mining, ledges, irrigation, and more. In Louthan's *A Rocky Mountain Feud* (1910), illustrated with photographs, two ranch establishments clash over boundaries, water rights, sheep vs. cattle, and much else. The book is fleshed out with descriptions of the Colorado Rockies around Clear Creek, Georgetown, Berthoud Pass, Valley of the Yampa, and elsewhere, and also by much information about sheep: "Edyth had 'sheep' for dinner and supper as well as for breakfast . . . not in the form of mutton, but of table-talk. Water for the sheep, fresh ranges for the sheep, market quotations, bulletins from the Fort Collins experiment station, statistics of profit and loss" (123); "Upon examination of the library, she discovered whole shelves of such fascinating literature as 'Nature and Treatment of Common Sheep Scab,' 'Feeds and Feeding: an Invaluable Handbook for Students, Sheepmen and Farmers,' 'Craig's

Sheep-raising in the West'" (124). The racial/national aspect of the conflicts in this novel is acknowledged when one rancher says that "ill-feeling with a national basis goes far in this cattle-and-sheep war we're into" (110) by which he means Mexican versus Texas cowboys.

*　*　*

Honoré Willsie's *Judith of the Godless Valley* (1922) is set in the remote Rocky Mountain town of Lost Chief, where cattle is raised on the open range. The book is vague on particulars, making the story represent all cattle ranching. Though settled by descendants of the New England Puritans, the town has become lawless, and its women are forced into the roles of drudge (married) or prostitute (unmarried). Women need law; they cannot impose it on men. Even more, they need religion, insofar as religion means Christian morality. Doug and Judith—foster siblings—struggle with and against each other, until finally he realizes his true manhood by bringing religion to the town in the shape of a new minister. Judith is smart and observant, and what she sees of marriage looks awful: "Marriage is too hard on a woman. Why should I want to cook your meals and darn your socks and wash your clothes for you the rest of my life? Yes, and listen to you swear and lay down the law and spit tobacco juice? And when I'm a little older and beginning to get knotty with the hard work, see you take notice of girls who are younger and prettier than I" (219).

In a flight/pursuit scene the two are helped by a Mormon settler, who explains that Mormons are "building up God-fearing communities all over the West, just like the Puritans once built up in the East. Why? Because we pioneer, inspired by our church and the love of God! What Gentile church is doing this, answering the economic needs of its people as well as the spiritual? Why should a settlement like yours prosper? Why, the most promising young man in it is deserting it to chase after a flighty girl! It has no church. It has no minister. Ha! As long as you Gentiles are so, the Mormons can ride over you and crowd you out!"(344). It's not, then, male vs. female, but godless vs. godfearing that affects the West's future.

Although many of these women writers were urban journalists, and pioneer memoirs made much of businessmen, Marianne Gauss's *Danae* (1925), which merges a female soap opera with political critique, is the only truly urban novel I've found. "Queen City"—i.e., Denver—is defined by political graft and corruption, by working girls, automobiles, and cigarettes. The Rocky Mountains are now merely a backdrop. Criminals lurking on the highways, along with automobile accidents, replace the bandit and the stagecoach in modern life. But the true focus of good and bad is the statehouse, where graft and corruption reign.

In the context of these Colorado books, Willa Cather's *Song of the Lark* (1915)—no mountains, no tourists, no health-seekers, no ranches—is more a plains book, essentially a Nebraska book pushed out onto the Colorado plains, than it is a Colorado book in the sense of a struggle with Rocky mountain terrain. Even more than a plains book, it is a town book; Thea and her family live in a railroad town, and there is little about making a living on the plains. Thea's father is a minister. She walks out into nature to appreciate its beauty and imbibe its message of transcendence. The real plot involves the destiny of a superior artist hemmed in by banality and convention. This, the earlier of its two versions, has much about Thea's life after she leaves home to become an internationally famous opera singer. Nevertheless, the book does use some strategies possibly borrowed from other women's writing about the West: a genteel heroine of exceeding whiteness (a whiteness that somewhat neutralizes the fact of her being Swedish not truly Anglo) with a beautiful voice (many protagonists sing in the choir and aspire to singing careers); a foil woman who is both flirtatious and conventional, and whose ambition stops with the church choir; a set of appreciative men outside the protagonist's social circle, including Mexicans. It is pure fantasy that a railroad man with a crush on Thea, and who is killed in an accident, would leave her enough money to get out of town. It is pure fantasy that one of the Mexican men who appreciate Thea's voice should turn up in the big city to appreciate her operatic triumph. What the book has that no other Colorado book does—what is germane to Colorado that the other books ignore—is its canyon interlude in the southwestern part of the state. This setting reappears in *The Professor's House,* which draws on the Wetherill brothers' discoveries in Utah and Colorado, and reaches its great expression in Cather's New Mexico book, *Death Comes for the Archbishop*—a book, however, that is not about Colorado.

I conclude this chapter with a book published beyond my cutoff date: the poems of Virginia Donaghé McClurg, collected by her husband and published two years after her death in 1931. My rationales here are that many of these poems had appeared in separate keepsake editions before 1910, and that this is the only Colorado woman poet I've found. McClurg was apparently the first white woman who saw the ruins of Mesa Verde. Dedicated to bringing the site to national attention, she lost a bitter fight to keep its ownership at the state level. She lectured around the country and overseas as well on numerous scholarly topics. But the poems in this little book are almost all simply about Colorado. By 1933 their understanding of poetry as elegant diction and archaic syntax was dated. Except for some brief tributes to Colorado wildflowers they imply or assert the usual historical framework from wilderness to domesticated terrain. But in Colorado something always resists that story, something represented by the high mountains and especially by Pike's Peak. McClurg makes this peak represent not masculinity, but a sign of something beyond the human, something timeless.

McClurg's eight-page ode to Pike's Peak begins with the Paleozoic period—
"Th' abysmal void" (18); moves to the Mesaoic—"up-leaps the fire, / Crumbling the riven rock" (18); on through the Glacial—"creeping glaciers wander,
tempest-tossed" (19) when the mountains rise up; then come Indians, pioneers,
miners; all the time, the "peerless Peak" is looking down at events, unmoved.
McClurg's two poems about women—one praising Suffrage, the other written
for the Denver women's club—make Woman into "God's best gift to Earth"
(15), the best thing ever to have happened to Colorado: "Virgin plains of Colorado, mountain silences unbroken / Lie before queen-regnant Woman, as she
westward takes her way, / While the sunset's benediction gilds her pathway as
a token, / That New West, like old world's dawning, bows before her sovereign
sway" (17). "Ode to Irrigation," set to music and apparently sung by the Mormon Tabernacle Choir, moves from desert wilderness to cultivated farmland,
which is the future arrived. "The Future's sweet, stern eyes / Look out in glad
surprise. On lands to be; / Where the world's three in one, / Forest and stream
and sun, / Have wrought a realm well-won / Future! for Thee!" (59).

7

The Great Plains

Kansas, Nebraska, and the Dakotas differ from each other in climate, landform, and details of history, but all are part of the Great Plains that sweep from Oklahoma to the Canadian border. The term "Midwest" was seldom used for the region before the twentieth century—the Midwest before then was Iowa, Illinois, Ohio, Indiana, Michigan, Wisconsin, and Minnesota. Women publishing books about the Great Plains during the years I'm looking at saw the region as western, indeed the heart of the true West. Their work told of failure repeatedly averted by women's pioneer tenacity.

I found only two books of poetry for the Great Plains. Celeste May's 1886 miscellany, *Sounds of the Prairie,* does not specify its setting beyond the title. For her the plains are one continuous space (she lived in Nebraska and Oklahoma, and published her book in Kansas) dominated by homesteaders. A sequence of opening poems shows a family leaving a rented eastern farm to homestead. On the prairie they cope with such natural disasters as prairie fires, blizzards, and droughts, ultimately establishing "cottages neat, and pastures wide, / Flowering gardens and stone walls grand, / Young orchards and field on every side / Pictures of comfort and thrift" (24). "The Cities' Poor" describes the agonies of slum dwellers and the incendiary danger they pose to national security, proposing homesteading as a safety valve. Yes, on the farm they still "rise at dawn, but not to chill and cramp / You hear them singing; for their cheerful toil / Speaks more of lusty life than hard turmoil" (125). Thousands "have plenty now. and some to spare instead, / With homes that are their own, and grown so dear. / The Nation, for her safety, need not fear; / For if she ever needs strong, loyal hands, / She'll find them in these sons who till the lands" (126).

According to Nettie Garmer Barker in her 1915 *Kansas Women in Literature,* the title poem in Esther M. Clark's *The Call of Kansas and Other Verses* (1907—in its first edition unpaginated and with only nine poems), was known to everybody in the state (5). A 1921 expansion contained 66 pages. In "The Call of Kansas" the speaker, on a southern California beach, contrasts the gorgeous scenery— pepper trees, poinsettias, ocean, hills—with the prairies and states that "Sweeter to me than the salt sea spray, the fragrance of summer rains; / Nearer my heart than these mighty hills are the windswept Kansas plains." In "The Man Behind the Gun," Clark praises Kansas men "who shed their blood at the Nation's call for the martyr-state's release" and the women who stood behind them.

* * *

After the Civil War, Kansas celebrants usually claimed that all emigrants from the Northeast had been abolitionist patriots, while all Missourians arriving over the border were pro-slavery ruffians driven by greed. In the 1850s and early 1860s, however, New England women's reports from Kansas boomed the territory for settlement more than they made lofty nationalist arguments. Hannah Anderson Ropes's 1856 *Six Months in Kansas* and Miriam Davis Colt's 1862 *Went to Kansas* were nonideological. Ropes went to live with her son, who was homesteading outside of Lawrence, the center of New England emigration; Colt went with her husband and children to live in a vegetarian commune among like-minded people. Sara Robinson's 1856 *Kansas; Its Interior and Exterior Life* was both ideological and economic in its concerns; Massachusetts abolitionist Lydia Maria Child's novella *The Kansas Emigrants,* serialized in 1856 and collected the next year in her *Autumnal Leaves,* was purely ideological—but Child didn't go to Kansas.

Ropes's initial anxieties in the letters home to her mother she used to produce her book were over dirt and illness among the emigrants—"the sickly look of everybody" (48) and the horrifyingly unsanitary conditions of their lives. Lack of sanitation, a constant among the overlanders and new settlers, is usually ignored in women's books, although their occasional references to terrible conditions imply this. They traveled and slept with their cattle; they washed their clothes, bathed in, and drank contaminated water (when water was available). Much as she was focused on pioneer filth, however, Ropes did note "the dark clouds heaving up over our hopeful sky, from our heartless, poor-apology of a neighbor, Missouri" (201). Six months after her arrival she was back in Massachusetts, publishing for a New England audience and alternately describing the awful conditions of settler life and railing against Missourians, rather for their land greed than their politics. She followed this book with an obscure novel, *Cranston House* (1859), set in an abstract western space that ignored politics and defined the entire West as antiwoman—"in emigration, woman, being most devoted to home, suffers most" (365). Among the enemies are open space, nature—whose "wild utterances" are "new and strange"—Mormons, and the land speculation fueling western settlement at the expense of domestic values: "if no more town sites were offered, to tempt successfully the appetite of land hunger, the holy love of home,—a homestead—might ultimate itself in the great West, with the most happy results" (366).

When Colt arrived with her husband and children at the designated site, they found none of the promised amenities: no houses, no public buildings, no mill. The settlers had been scammed. Within a month the Colts were trying to leave. It took time to sell their goods and put together necessary goods on the wagon for their return trip, on which both her husband and son fell ill and died. Though there were no border ruffians, there were Indians who seemed to feel (as she tells it) that they had the right to pilfer whatever crop the family tried to grow. Much later (1880) Lois Lovina Abbott Murray, returning to Indiana after eighteen years in Kansas, wrote about that time in her life in *Incidents of Frontier Life*. With her husband and three children, she lived in the Cottonwood Valley a few miles from neighbors, helped her husband farm (and after his death in 1866 farmed on her own with her children's help; one of these children marries a Missourian—there is no sign of political commitment in this book), withstood prairie fires, uninvited Indian visits and horse stealing, transient railroad workers (a source of fear but also useful because she boarded many such), illnesses and injuries, crops that failed, and the annual burden of taxes. A piously devout woman who taught Sunday School at a settlement five miles from their home and on occasion led services, she writes at the request of her friends but also to testify to God's goodness. Her view of Divinity is entirely personal, however; Manifest Destiny is nowhere on her horizon.

Robinson used her book specifically for political propaganda; her book tried to reconcile accounts of dangerous settler life with reassuring promises of a glorious Kansas future. Her political interests were ultimately personal, because her husband had organized and directed an emigration party, was instrumental in founding the Kansas Free State Party, had been the first elected governor of the territory (in an election which, since territorial governors were appointed, was extralegal), and was arrested for treason in 1856 and imprisoned for four months outside the territorial capitol of Lecompton. Sarah joined him there. Working from diaries, newspaper accounts, and official documents, she produced an effective propaganda book vilifying the federal government as much or more than Missouri. The Squatter Sovereignty Bill, she wrote, gave settlers "a right to look for such protection to the President of these United States in the very provisions of that bill. How have they been protected? Let his infamous appointees in the territory—the vile tools of tyranny—answer to an enlightened public sentiment. . . . Let the bristling bayonets of the United States army tell how the free settlers have been outraged and plundered, while ruffian bands have been protected by it" (343).

At the same time, because Kansas needs more New England settlers, Robinson calls the landscape—which Ropes founds monotonously oppressive—

beautiful: "When we came to look out upon Lawrence and the surrounding country, as we had nearly run through the vocabulary finding words to express our rapture at the ever-changing beauty of every part of our route, and as this view from our window, and from the hill beyond us, was the master-piece, silence expressed most truly our feelings" (37). For Ropes the poverty and illness of the Kansas immigrants demonstrated their ineptitude; Robinson saw a glorious future ahead of the hardy immigrant farmers. "Being used to the emergencies and the hardships of pioneer life, Kansas will depend on them mostly, in this early settlement, for the ground work, the substratum, upon which to build up a glorious new state. While they, for the most part, settle in the country, and will gather into their garners of the golden treasure so the rich and fertile soil, eastern capital will form a nucleus, around which the young, the adventurous, the enterprising, will gather, and new cities, new towns, will spring up with rapid growth, emulating in thrift and intelligence those of the old states" (88). Robinson like other western boomers sees the first wave of farmers as the pioneers whose groundwork underpins the cities and towns that eventually signify the triumph of "civilization" in the West.

Robinson recommends pioneering to women in familiar terms: "with a constant use of faculties and sympathies, the useless ornament of a city drawing-room becomes the strong, the active, earnest woman" (179). Lawrence ladies "combine the advantages of personal beauty with intellectual merit" more "than in any place I ever lived. Our friends east need have no fears that in this 'roughing it,' not only with the necessary inconveniences, and inelegancies, of a new country, but with the tyrannous acts of a vile administration's tools, that they have lost any of the instinctive gentleness or modesty of woman" (183).

In *The Kansas Emigrants* Child fictionalized a much-publicized shooting of a Kansas settler in the back, funneling it into a formula story of two emigrant couples with two different types of admirable wives. Katie is the capable pioneer, while delicate and timid Alice tries nobly to be a good, supportive wife. When Alice's husband gets shot she goes operatically insane and dies after prophesying the creation of a second New England in Kansas—if, that is, Massachusetts supports the free soilers. The border ruffians are, almost without exception, villains of the deepest dye as well as low-caste ruffians, as in an episode where one of them spits tobacco juice in Katie's face.

*   *   *

Following the Civil War publishing hiatus, the first Great Plains novel I've found is Mary E. Jackson's quasi–dime novel, *The Spy of Osawatomie; or, the Mysterious Companions of Old John Brown* (1881). The cross-dressing heroine in "real life" is Ona Leland from New Hampshire and in her adventurous life is the well-known Kansas male spy, Dickey Deane. Amid its unconvincing derring-do, the novel promotes Kansas as superior to the East for middle- and lower-class people: there are "better opportunities to seek a higher position . . . more land to cultivate, and land that in itself is productive without the aid of fertilizers. . . . Having more land, they have greater scope for their energies, and after certain pressing seasons, they have opportunities of frequently meeting, which develops more sources of amusement and consequent happiness" (387–88). Inconsistently, however, Ona leaves Kansas at the end to enjoy the luxury of her father's New Hampshire home. Jackson's second book, *The Life of Nellie C. Bailey: A Romance of the West* (1886) is a potboiler based on a true story; Bailey was tried (but acquitted) in Wichita for murdering her much older husband. There's a full transcript of the trial proceedings, along with descriptions of Nellie's amorous indiscretions and her wandering life from Kansas to Oregon to California. The attraction of this story to the author of *The Spy of Osawatomie* would be the protagonist's unconventional freedom. Totally unlike these two is Jackson's 1890 *Topeka: Pen and Camera Sketches,* a staid booster book with numerous photographs publicizing Topeka's churches and schools, hotels and transit systems, and its temperance laws, for prospective settlers uninterested in farming. Topeka is "the most delightful country for homes, for business of all kinds . . . one of the most enterprising places on the globe" (9); "For educational, social and business advantages Topeka affords the best to be found in the West" (18).

Mary A. Humphrey's *The Squatter Sovereign* (1883) is a historical novel dedicated to "the pioneers of Kansas. The Noble martyrs who gave up their lives . . . the survivors of that olden time who succeeded in rearing upon her plains, the rampart which turned back the advancing tide of slavery, and the gallant army of works, whose toils and privations made possible the glorious prosperity now enjoyed by her people." Triumph over adversity is the novel's story: "Ah, it was an easy thing, from beds of down in homes of luxury, to echo back the cry 'No more slave States!' but the early pioneers of Kansas with the true spirit of devotion, cast themselves before the iron wheels of the great Juggernaut of oppression, and with their own stout arms stayed his onward march" (346–47). The plot concerns two northern couples with exemplary pioneer wives. When one wife first enters the cabin her husband (who'd stopped in Kansas on his way back from the gold fields where he found no gold) has prepared for them "she gazed upon the rude walls and no shadow clouded the sunshine. She stepped over the door-sill as lightly, and trod the cottonwood floor as firmly, as though her footsteps fell on marble and velvet tapestry" (118). Kansas women transform slovenly shanties into homes and are politically engaged: "Quite a number of ladies were present, it being characteristic of them from the first, to take a lively interest in affairs of state, and seats were furnished them, and in every way their presence made welcome" (123).

The book ends in 1883, the year of its publication, where it now becomes clear that the emigration was not about politics but "material prosperity"; the surviving couple's "brightest anticipations" have been "more than realized. Nature with lavish hand has responded to the 'open sesame' of patient toil," and has given grain, fruits, herbs, in abundance, along with rosy apples, purple grapes, yellow pears, golden corn, new-made hay. Our characters' faces bear "an unmistakable impress of content—content material and spiritual—beautifying and glorifying all the lines left by toil and care, by sacrifice and subordination of things selfish, to the higher motives of patriotism and humanity" (353). No greedy miners, no Northwest Pacific malcontents, but simply the highest western types—highest in part because they don't aim high.

Elizabeth Bacon Custer's three successful books dedicated to silencing criticism of her husband's actions at the Battle of the Little Big Horn—*Boots and Saddles; or, Life in Dakota with General Custer* (1885) about Custer's final command; *Tenting on the Plains; or, General Custer in Kansas and Texas* (1887) about his early posting to the plains; and *Following the Guidon* (1890) about the years 1868–69—take place mostly in the Great Plains. Denying knowledge of, or interest in, military tactics or strategy, she portrays army post life in domestic terms, depicting her husband as a home-loving man. In her view, it's only on army posts that civilized life is possible; frontier towns are quagmires. Hays City, according to *Following the Guidon,* was typical: "A considerable part of the place was built of rude frames covered with canvas, the shanties were made up of slabs, bits of drift-wood, and logs, and sometimes the roofs were covered with tin that had once been fruit or vegetable cans, now flattened out" (153). "The carousing and lawlessness of Hays City were incessant. . . . Our men knew so much of the worthlessness of these outlaw lives that it was difficult to arouse pity in them for either a man's or a woman's death in the border towns. . . . There was enough desperate history in the little town in that one summer to make a whole library of dime novels" (154).

In *Tenting on the Plains,* mostly set at Fort Riley, Kansas, Custer introduces the western theme of women's physical liberation in open space, showing that domesticity and athletic freedom are not incompatible female traits. She writes of "the wild sense of freedom that takes possession of one in the first buoyant knowledge that no impediment, seemingly, lies between you and the setting sun. . . . It is simply an impossibility to describe how the blood bounds in the veins at the freedom of an illimitable sea. . . . Oh, the joy of taking in air without a taint of the city, or even the country, as we know it in farm life!" (242). In this book Custer celebrates ordinary soldiers and pioneers: "As I try to write something of the sacrifices of the soldier, who will not speak of himself, and for whom so few have spoken, there comes to me another class of heroes, for whom my husband had such genuine admiration, and in whose behalf he gave up his life—our Western pioneer" (331). And she contrasts Kansas now to Kansas then:

"I lately rode through the State, which seemed when I first saw it a hopeless, barren waste, and found the land under fine cultivation, the houses, barns and fences excellently built, cattle in the meadows" and "could not help wondering what the rich owners of these estates would say, if I should step down from the car and give them a little picture of KANSAS, with the hot, blistered earth, dry beds of streams, and soil apparently so barren" (382). *Following the Guidon,* a boys' book, defends the battle of Washita in 1868, where Custer's men killed peaceful women, children, and older men (including the great Cheyenne chief Black Kettle) as payback for Cheyenne and Ute raids elsewhere (a sort of reprise of the Sand Creek massacre in Colorado four years earlier).

In 1885 the well-off Alice Wellington Rollins, writer of popular magazine sketches, published *The Story of a Ranch,* using a visit to her brother's spread in Kansas to demonstrate how ladies and gentlemen, especially ladies, can enjoy themselves in that remote spot—and not incidentally making much of her own high level of culture. "Much of my object in writing this story of a ranch is to show that ladies accustomed to every eastern luxury can be both comfortable and happy on a ranch" (49). The book also shows that homesteading is mostly a losing cause, in contrast to large-scale ranching. At her brother's sheep ranch near the town of Ellsworth (he employed some fifty men whose lives, Rollins assures us, he made pleasant and comfortable), guests are treated to horseback riding, "hammocks and piazzas, lawn tennis, a piano, and a billiard-room" (11). The parlor is "brightly lighted with swinging lamps that had all the effect of gas" and contains "an ebonized metal with mirror set into the wall, a piano, books overflowing every chair and table, a Palmer and Batchelder clock, a Rogers group, scrap-baskets, plaques, and Kate Greenaway titles. The ladies—one at the piano playing Chopin, one embroidering . . . and one turning over the leaves of Scribner—had evidently 'dressed for dinner.' Through the open door could be seen a wide hall with laid wooden floor and rugs, opening into a square hall from which led a breadth and a half of carpet to cover it, with a broad landing and Gothic window half way up. On the piazza the gentlemen could be heard discussing the Greek play" (79).

Returning several years later, she finds the country around the ranch much improved, thanks to the examples of her brother and other wealthy settlers who are systematically buying abandoned homesteads to enlarge their own properties. "There is no place where the very poor seem so utterly wretched as on a Kansas prairie. There is nothing to stimulate ambition. . . . Nowhere are the very poor so much in danger of being crushed as in a community of those who are almost as poor" (182–83). But in two years, energized by their well-off neighbors, the poor have made their prairie houses neater while in town "every old house seemed to be having a new bay-window or piazza or porch" (185).

Mary M. North's *A Prairie Schooner; A Romance of the Plains of Kansas* (1902) is set mostly in an early Kansas settlement: "As soon as the 'town' was laid out, the tide of immigration set in, and when this story opens, there were a few general stores, on a small scale, a blacksmith shop, which was a crying necessity, as there were always horses to be shod—those belonging to the Government, or those of people on the 'trail,' and wagons to be repaired. To this embryo town came also a physician, and with the first settlers, there were two lawyers. There were a few houses which were entitled to the name, a number of shanties, and 'dug-outs' of settlers who had come west to try their fortunes, and get rich, as they fondly hoped, by raising cattle or some other method which might present itself. There was also a boarding-house for those who were without a home" (21). The heroine becomes a "fine type of a happy, healthy western girl; was a fearless horsewoman, and many a time had helped her father herd the cattle" (48–49). Curiously, though—or perhaps not, given the drumbeat of pioneer failure that complicates these settler narratives—the opening of Oklahoma produces a huge rush of Kansans out of the state, and she along with everybody else in her family resettles there.

After retiring from public life in 1906, populist organizer and orator Annie L. Diggs brought out a tribute to the populist legislator Jerry Simpson on behalf of his wife, who funded the publication. *The Story of Jerry Simpson* (1908) connects the down-home, wisecracking politician to the state of Kansas as it had been in early times and uses his life to expound the populist philosophy: "Remembering the great beginnings of Kansas—how there had foregathered on her freedom-consecrated soil, men sublimely purposed to live or die for justice, it was surely befitting that the 'People's Party' should have its genesis in that state" (77). "In the late Sixties the people of the Western States were for the most part poor of pocket but rich in ways of industry and of small possessions. . . . The call of husking bee, of spelling match, of singing school, harks back to simple days before big money came to set up glittering things that lure young men and maids to glare and blare of life, and trade them feverish falsities for wholesome, homely ways" (13–14).

Kansas as the expression of agrarian philosophy also controls Sarah Comstock's first novel, *The Soddy* (1912), a tribute to Kansas pioneers, and especially the wife. Idealistic Dexter Hayden starts to build his sod house in a place where for miles "in all directions there was no sign of vegetation save for the corpses of occasional stunted, thorny weeds; the brown buffalo grass, apparently dead in this late November rawness; and here and there a Russian thistle loping madly before the wind. It was the cruelest of mockeries to trace the line of a dry river snaking its way, a broad, sinuous line of sand, across the forsaken earth" (3). Dexter recognizes that he's one in "a multitudinous army, all labouring toward the same end. . . . Suffering untold hardships, accomplishing vast labours, they worked on, patiently, courageously, splendidly—enduring all, that in time to come the desert might rejoice, that the generations to come might reap a glorious harvest—strugglers, sufferers, heroic figures—Pioneers of To-day—nobly carrying out that part assigned them in the Great Design" (51).

But Dexter falters; a barrage of agricultural calamities—scorching wind, blizzard, drought, and the malice of a neighbor—drives him back East. His wife remains, holding down one odd job after another, waiting for his return. The word "home," repeated throughout the novel, is the book's last word. Dexter comes back: "The twilight had faded into dusk, the world was shrouded; in the dusk the Soddy loomed drab, solitary, a somber picture; but within it shone a light unquenchable, eternal, radiant: the light of home" (369–70).

Dell Munger's one novel, *The Wind before the Dawn* (1912), is a Kansas farm saga that rebuts pioneer stereotypes. The book begins during a terrible summer of heat and drought and follows the fourteen-year-old protagonist as she tries to find herself within the constraints of farming's relentless drudgery and dangers; the debts incurred by farmers who try to enlarge their holdings, buy animals and seeds and feed and machinery—an important recognition of how deeply farming is enmeshed in a money economy; and male supremacy (men's ownership of all assets makes wives and daughters into helpless dependents and, therefore, into male possessions). Farming is an endless present defined by drought, debt, grasshoppers, and accidents. And farmers are inherently small-minded petty people even before diverse calamities deplete their emotional resources.

Two well-meant comic novels by Kansas schoolteacher Effie Graham are about African Americans, whose virtual absence from other Kansas books despite its supposed origins in Abolitionist sentiment is striking. (In fact, the Kansas emigrants seem to have been interested in free labor for themselves, not for African Americans; and recent histories of Kansas argue that the amount of blood shed in "bleeding Kansas" was minimal.) In her preface to *The Passin'-on Party* (1912), Graham calls black people "free-tongued freeholders in a western land," and "Kansas 'jayhawkers'—full-pinioned, though of a duskier hue." The patronizing tone might be unacceptable today; but Graham's affection and respect are obvious, as is her sense that these people belong in the record. This story is about two former slaves whose little house has been built from materials scavenged from the river bank and the railroad tracks. The book's gimmick is Aunt June's wish for a party to mark her supposed imminent death, which allows for descriptions of the town's population both black and white, since everybody comes to pay respects. *Aunt Liza's "Praisin' Gate"* (1916) is about another old couple; Aunt Liza hangs a sign on her gate, now that she is too old to go out to work, testifying to her many accomplishments. There are also submotifs about divorce and woman suffrage, which leads Aunt Liza to add to her sign: "Newwmber 5 1912, Loud to Vote."

In 1910 Margaret Hill McCarter, the most popular Kansas woman novelist of her day, began publishing ambitious historical fictions whose pioneers were less earth-stained farmers than Indian fighters. Demonic Indians and strongly gendered models of white manhood and womanhood populate complicated stories requiring several pages of running explanation by characters and narrator alike. But McCarter's intentions are simple. *The Price of the Prairie: A Story of Kansas* (1910), a first-person narration by sixty-year-old Philip Baronet, recalls fifteen years of his Kansas life beginning with his arrival in 1857 at age seven. His newly widowed father wants to overcome grief and take part in the "struggle that is beginning beyond the Missouri. I want to do one man's part in the making of the West" (18). Philip falls in love at once and for life with little Margery Whateley, struck by "the exceeding whiteness of her face. . . . Even in the Kansas heat and browning winds she never lost the pink tint no miniature painting on ivory could exaggerate" (19). There's no mistaking the purport of that whiteness.

Obligatory misunderstandings delay the resolution of the love plot and drive the now grown-up Philip to enlist with the Indian-fighting Kansas 18th and 19th Regiments. This is the start of McCarter's defense of Indian removal. Philip fights because of his "swift, unworded comprehension of a woman's worth, of the sacredness of her life, and her divine right to the protection of her virtue; a comprehension of the beauty and blessing of the American home, of the obedient daughter, the loving wife, the Madonna mother, of all that these mean as the very foundation rock of our nation's strength and honor" (50). McCarter interprets the Civil War in Kansas as an Indian war because the Confederates try to organize Indian uprisings against Unionist settlers: "With the border raiders on the one side and the hostile Indians on the other, small chance of life would have been left to any Union man, woman, or child in all this wide, beautiful Kansas. In the four years of the Civil War no cruelty could have exceeded the consequences of this conspiracy" (109). The novel describes battles and circulates anecdotes of Indian atrocities in Kansas against children, young women, and mothers. Black Kettle, the martyr of Washita, is defined as a hypocritical "good Indian" in winter when he needs help, a murderous savage in better weather, and deserving to die. "In the shelter of the Washita Valley on the twenty-seventh day of November, God's vengeance came to these Indians at the hands of General Custer" (372).

In the novel's present time, which is the reader's present time, the outcome of pioneer sacrifice is clear in the "rippling billows of yellow wheat, orchard, meadow, populous cities and churches and stately college halls, factories, mines, oil derricks, natural gas, and above all, the sheltered happy homes, where little children play never dreaming of fear; where sweet-browed mothers think not of loneliness and anguish and peril—all these are the splendid heritage of a land whose law is for the whole people, a land whose God is the Lord. The brave-hearted, liberty-loving, indomitable people have come into their own, paying foot by foot, the price that won this prairie kingdom in the heart of the West" (487–88).

McCarter's *A Wall of Men* (1912) is a bleeding Kansas novel set between 1854 and 1865, whose demons are Missourians and heroes are the Kansas Abolitionists, with cameo appearances by John Brown (hero) and Quantrill (demon). Southerners "came to seize the land by lawless force and to depopulate it by brute ferocity" (268). The abolitionists are defined by their women: the "sweet-faced Quaker woman, calm, fearless, smiling kindly, with the unconscious grace of her womanhood like a garment about her, and a power of mind and voice—the only real power—that controls men" (32); or the golden-haired ingénue Beth, a "Scotch lassie, with the sweetness and strength of her womanhood that marks the rank of peerage in this prairie kingdom!" (177). In *Winning the Wilderness* (1914) a gracious southern woman and an Ohio man marry against family opposition and make a home on the prairie. Pioneer hardship falls most heavily on the woman, but she triumphs: "Into the crucible out of which a state is moulded, she cast her youth and strength and beauty; her love of luxury, her need for common comforts, her joy in the cultured appointments of society" (86). *The Peace of Solomon Valley* (1911) wherein a tenderfoot is sent to Kansas by his father and learns to love it; *A Master's Degree* (1913) about a Kansas college where farm youth learn culture and cultured Bostonians learn to appreciate Kansas; and *The Reclaimers* (1918), another tenderfoot novel with a New Woman protagonist who learns to love Kansas; vary McCarter's typical themes of the necessity for violence in Kansas and the inspirational role of women.

* * *

Almira Cordry's *The Story of the Marking of the Santa Fe Trail by the DAR in Kansas and the State of Kansas* (1915) describes how the idea of marking the Santa Fe trail germinated among DAR members and evolved into engagements with the state legislatures, the Kansas State Historical Society, newspapers, schools, and other civic institutions. McCarter was an active speaker in this enterprise too, and her *Vanguards of the Plains* ends with praise for it. The trail, Cordry says, made more than Kansas history; it was "the connecting link between the settling of the West by the people of the East. And as those early travelers prized the old Trail as a road to the future, we hope the people of years to come will use it and keep its early history in remembrance" (133). Not only does this book acknowledge the twentieth-century movement by which the West became more and more a tourist spectacle, it also supposes that because for so many, Kansas was now Midwestern not Western, attaching it to Santa Fe would reanimate its western identity. The little book also shows how these female associations (like the WCTU or, in Texas, the Daughters of the Confederacy), however conservative their intentions may seem now, were occasions for female community and participation in public life.

Anna E. Arnold, teacher and public school administrator, published two textbooks to help Kansans become—as the subtitle to her 1912 *Civics and Citizenship* expressed it—"worthy of their heritage." *History of Kansas* (1915) says knowledge of "the difficulties that have been met and conquered in building the State" will "create in the minds of the boys and girls a greater respect for the sturdy qualities of the pioneers, . . . give them a wholesome sense of the great cost at which the ease and comfort of to-day have been purchased" and "stimulate in them a desire to live up to the past" (5). The chapter on "Pioneer Life" says frontier life was harder in Kansas than elsewhere because of all the "strife and warfare" (104); and says, again, that "the privations, the sacrifices, and the loneliness of pioneer life fell most heavily on the women" (105).

Annie Abel, a professor of history whose study of the slaveholding Indians focused on Oklahoma (see Chapter 2), mentioned Kansas in the first of her three volumes (1915): "Never in all history, so it would appear, has the insatiable land-hunger of the white man been better illustrated than in the case of the beginnings of the sunflower state. The practical effect of the Kansas-Nebraska Act had been to lift an entail, a huge acreage had been alienated that before had been sacred to Indian claims; white men had swarmed upon the ceded lands; and the Indians had retired, perforce" (1: 23–24). Emma E. Forter's seven-pound, 1000+ page, *History of Marshall County, Kansas: Its People, Industries and Institutions* (1917) is a booster book, giving county history by city, town, village, along with individual and family biographies that make town-formation the ultimate aim of pioneering: "The growth, development and prosperity of the county are due solely to the thrift, industry and honesty of the pioneer men and women who endured every hardship, even death itself, to build up a law-abiding community. In less than ten years the sentiment of the country had changed from the reckless, happy-go-lucky frontier manner to that of earnest effort in building up a strong and forceful community. The county has grown in wealth and prospered until it now ranks sixth in the state. But its greatest growth has been along educational, moral and religious lines, and its greatest wealth today is splendid citizenship" (102).

In Margaret Lynn's historical novel *Free Soil* (1920) a New England couple with young children emigrates for principle's sake. Ellen, fresh and fragrant, always gracious, always giving, never complaining, "found the usefulness she had planned beginning from the very outset. Almost every guest meant an amusing difficulty of some sort in the primitive housekeeping, and an amusing joyous expedient on Ellen's part" (43). John, for his part, "reflected tenderly on the amazing adaptation of women who came to this country—women whose whole habit of mind before this had been as remote as could be from brutality of life or need for physical courage" (112); "they could bring the charm which leisure and ease had developed in another world, into this—and yet lose nothing of practical usefulness in it" (121). Lynn's juvenile, *The Land of Promise* (1927), reprises the bleeding Kansas story through the perspective of a plucky, curious, outspoken little girl. Mother explains that despite the violence, making homes "is more our business than the fighting is. That's the solid thing we're doing, dear. We are to be the solid ground of a free state. After the fighting is all over and everything like that passed, we'll have our home here" (232).

*   *   *

The earliest Nebraska book I found is Frances Fuller Victor's dime novel *Alicia Newcome; or, The Land Claim, a Tale of the Upper Missouri* (1862). The story opens with a description of the prairies as the Indians depart. "Away, away toward the almost trackless plain stretched the rolling prairies. The Indian Territory had given way before the advancing hosts of civilization, and surveyors, speculators, locators, squatters, traders and adventurers gathered where the red-man had been, to found new States. Nebraska and Kansas became familiar names; and, as the Pawnees, the Owahas, the Ottoes, the Kickapoos, the Puncas, disappeared like shadows, the tide of restless, eager, insatiable 'pale-faces' poured in to make the Indian wilderness to blossom with a new life. The grand old river, coming from the unexplored and mythic regions of the Rocky Mountains, poured its flood through plain and forest, through bluff and bottom, to bear on its bosom the new civilization which it was to serve with the best elements of health, wealth, and peace. From its sides spread the avenues of settlement, and villages spring up like magic to stand as buoys guiding the settler to the new regions beyond, where plains were still unstaked and timber bottoms still unclaimed" (5). The domestically inclined Alicia makes a home for her widowed father where, "though every thing was most unpoetically new, rude and ungraceful about the cabin home, an air of neatness and propriety were everywhere visible, which spoke volumes in favor of its youthful mistress" (8).

In 1884 Frances Fulton published her diary travelogue, *To and Through Nebraska, by a Pennsylvania Girl*. She went to claim a homestead on behalf of her young brother, but found the sites reserved by the Nebraska Mutual Aid Colony, which had been organized in her Pennsylvania hometown, unsuitable. Since she couldn't write about homesteading, but wanted to publish a book, she produced an impressionistic account of Nebraska settlements as she observed them from the railroad while returning. She reports that people coming to their designated homestead sites were often disappointed, that the best claims were usually taken, and that the sand hills and isolation led many, like her, to return almost as soon as they arrived.

The women's books about Nebraska report even less success than the Kansas books. Elia Peattie, journalist and long-time Chicago resident originally from Michigan (a collection of her journalism was edited by Susanne George Bloomfield in 2005), lived in Omaha for eight years beginning in 1888. Her seven-story collection, *A Mountain Woman* (1896), contains two Nebraska tales, a comedy—"The Three Johns," in which a widowed woman homesteader finds romance and happiness (although she and her baby almost perish in an awful snowstorm prior to this happy outcome); and a tragedy—"Jim Lancy's Waterloo," about the human toll of prairie life. Jim Lancy, a good man trying to succeed at farming, becomes a labor-dulled bumpkin while his city-raised wife can't rise to the challenges of pioneer life and leaves. "The farm-houses seemed very low and mean to her. . . . The door-yards were bleak to her eyes, without the ornamental shrubbery which every farmer in her part of the country was used to tending. The cattle stood unshedded in their corrals. The reapers and binders stood rusting in the dull drizzle" (41). What she sees as shiftless, Jim explains as poverty: "sheds are not easily had. Lumber is dear. . . . It takes some money for a man to be economical" (42). When the crop is good, shipping costs are so huge that the farmer can't sell it profitably; says Jim "It's been a conspiracy from the first" (54). Then comes a summer of heat and drought: "The sun came up in that blue sky like a curse, and hung there till night came to comfort the blistering earth. And one night . . . a blast of air struck her in the face. . . . The wind blew for three days. At the end of that time every ear was withered in the stalk. The corn crop was ruined" (60–61).

Another journalist, Kate Cleary (Bloomfield collected some of her works and provided a biography in 1997), created vernacular characters in short stories that gave her some reputation as a humorist. She lived in Hubbell, Nebraska, from 1884 to 1898. *Like a Gallant Lady* (1897), despite the comic relief of Mrs. McLelland, wife of the local undertaker and spinner of yarns and malapropisms, has little good to say of pioneering life. Place and people are seen through the eyes of a Chicago girl who goes to Bubble, Nebraska, looking for her absent fiancé. The motive is unconvincing, but it gave Cleary an excuse to get a well-bred, single, urban woman with no need to earn a living out to the prairie. One character tells her, "I've been in the farmhouses and talked with the women. Such isolation! Such monotony! Such drudgery! And the hopelessness of ever escaping from these conditions accentuates the horror of them" (63). Farmers without capital who must depend "upon the benignity of the skies from one season to another" face "slow starvation" and "mental malady" (64, 65). Another character tells the heroine (who doesn't find her fiancé but gets a good substitute): "the only people who associate solitude, romance and all that sort of thing with the plains are those who write about them without having had any personal experience. You have seen and studied Western women—those of the small towns and farms, I mean. The young women are sometimes pretty, generally vulgar, always foolish. The middle-aged women are the old women, a set of drab-colored, toothless, petty-minded old crones" (267–68).

Cleary's description of drought resembles Peattie's: "July came in with skies of brass, fierce, scorching winds blowing up from the south, winds that drove fine, white, stinging dust in billows before them; winds that even at night did not cease, but shrieked and whined, and mockingly puffed its hot breath in the faces of gasping humanity. Men looked out with haggard eyes over the land they had plowed and planted and saw how, with each day, the green ranks were becoming more dwarfed and yellow. The creek was dry. Cattle died along its banks. The leaves of the oaks and cottonwoods no longer rustled—they rattled. . . . Desperation lived in many hearts. July was almost merged in August, and still no merciful rain had fallen. Disease became epidemic" (248–49).

Elizabeth Higgins, yet another journalist, published *Out of the West* (1902), a populist novel in which soil and climate and exorbitant railroad freight rates almost defeat the farmers, until the hero gets himself elected to the US Senate and sponsors legislation to regulate the railroads. Columbia Junction, Nebraska, is the "deadest town between Omaha and Ogden. It is the crossing of two railroads of a western prairie . . . three miserable straggling streets, two grain elevators, and a few hundred frame houses" (3). "This year, after the freight rates were paid, the margins left would not as much as compensate the planters for the hauling of the grain-cars. Lumber was something beyond their means, and the building of granaries out of all question. . . . Wood in many localities is as scarce as coal. . . . Corn is commonly used for fuel, but many homes must depend for warmth upon the burning of stalks, manure, or twisted withes of buffalo grass" (69–70).

Frances Elizabeth Janes Budgett, publishing as Elizabeth Dejeans, wrote popular female romances about independent working girls attracted to married men, or bored married women looking for freedom. Coming late on the scene, she calls Nebraska midwestern not western. In the opening to her 1915 *The Life-Builders,* a group of men is said to be "all of the Middle West, that fertile producer of virile men and women, outgrowth of its rich soil, one with the miles of waving wheat, the river-bottoms' rank output of corn, the sweet-scented fields of timothy and clover—and the capable schoolhouses with windows looking east and west, tempting the spirit of youth to the beyond. Brain and brawn and energy a-plenty it produced, that great Middle West, and in spite of—or was it possibly because of?—its solidly material prosperity" (1). In her 1917 romantic farrago, *The Tiger's Coat,* the part Native, part Mexican, part Anglo heroine is out of place in a very different Midwest from that in *The Life-Builders.* Says one character "It's in the middle-western town that the Puritanism which makes a hypocrite, more or less, of every American, really flourishes. It's been pushed out of the East by Southern European ideas—which are anything but Puritanical—and trekked westward, but never really reached the Pacific Coast. It was scared by the wide expanse of nature. It got lost in the sands of the desert. It lodged in the middle-western town, a residue that mingles funnily with bald commercialism and an entire lack of subtlety" (149).

Mary K. Maule, who wrote in many genres during the teens and twenties, contributed *A Prairie Schooner Princess* to Nebraska fiction in 1920. The carefully researched historical novel opens in 1856, when nine members of the Peniman family leave Ohio to escape the coming war (they're Quakers not cowards) and settle on the Little Blue River in Nebraska territory. The story brings in blizzard, fire, bison, prairie dogs, Indians (good, except for the Sioux). The trajectory, interrupted by the Civil War (for which the boys enlist despite their parents' pacifism), is onward and upward until a little community has coalesced around them. All ends happily except for the Indians, one of whom gives the standard vanishing speech in a version of Indian-speak: "My people are as the leaves on the trees in the winter, yours as the grass in the fields. If we rebel we get kill. If twenty your people fall, hundreds of mine must pay. No hope. The Indian must go. His day is ended" (218).

* * *

Willa Cather's three Nebraska books, artistically many levels above all this fiction, are no less committed to the mystique of pioneering. Their protagonists succeed in an atmosphere of general failure that goes to emphasize their success. That a woman in *O Pioneers!* (1913) tames the land is understood within an ideology that sees conquering the land as inevitable and good. Though Alexandra is a Swede, thus—according to contemporary race theory—not Anglo-Saxon, she is characterized (like Thea in *The Song of the Lark*) by her blonde hair and white skin. In Cather's deeply romantic presentation, Alexandra's love for the land, which her brothers don't feel, is what makes it fertile. The grueling farm labor depicted in other Great Plains fictions is absent. Alexandra says, "The land did it. . . . It woke up out of its sleep and stretched itself, and it was so big, so rich, that we suddenly found we were rich, just from sitting still" (194). Cather's wonderfully efficient descriptions of change embody typical ideas: at the start "The great fact was the land itself, which seemed to overwhelm the little beginnings of human society that struggled in its somber wastes" (144); sixteen years later "The shaggy coat of the prairie . . . has vanished forever. . . . A vast checker-board, marked off in squares of wheat and corn; light and dark, dark and light. Telephone wires hum along the white roads, which always run at right angles" (174).

My Antonia (1918), Jim Burden's first-person narration, is like *The Song of the Lark* (see Chapter 6) essentially a town book, whose greatest contribution to western literature may be its representation of the many ethnicities forming modern Nebraska. But the novel has an ethnic/national hierarchy, with the Burdens from Virginia at the top and the traveling entertainers—the Italians who run a dancing school and Blind Tom, the black pianist—at the bottom, Swedes and Bohemians in an undifferentiated middle. The novel begins with Jim on his way from Virginia with Jake, the hired hand sent to bring him to his grandparents in Nebraska. Jake, who loves dime novels—as always, dime novels are the reservoir of Wild West stereotypes—reads to him about Jesse James, so that Jim sees the ranch hand Otto waiting for them at the depot as a desperado. These western clichés are gently satirized as the fantasies of little boys and uneducated ranch hands (who in their own way are little boys themselves). The Bohemian Shimerdas, who know nothing about farming, represent all the emigrants who fail on the prairie, while Jim's grandfather combines practicality and idealism to make the best kind of pioneer. "The cornfields were far apart in those times, with miles of wild grazing land between. It took a clear, meditative eye like my grandfather's to foresee that they would enlarge and multiply until they would be . . . the world's cornfields; that their yield would be one of the great economic facts, like the wheat crop of Russia, which underlie all the activities of men, in peace or war" (156). Grown up, Jim becomes "legal counsel for one of the great Western railways" (x) loving "with a personal passion the great country through which his railway runs and branches. His faith in it and his knowledge of it have played an important part in its development. He is always able to raise capital for new enterprises in Wyoming or Montana, and has helped young men out there to do remarkable things in mines and timber and oil. . . . Jim is still able to lose himself in those big Western dreams" (xi).

Cather's fondness for pioneering tropes is especially clear in *A Lost Lady* (1923). Set in a western railroad town (Sweet Water) between Omaha and Denver, the novel identifies two social classes in the prairie states: "Homestead and hand-workers who were there to make a living, and the bankers and gentlemen ranchers who came from the Atlantic seaboard to invest money and to 'develop our great West,' as they used to tell us" (3). The scare quotes seem to imply irony, but there's no irony in the depiction of the book's real hero, the railroad man Forrester, who explains that the "great West" has developed from dreams: "the homesteader's and the prospector's and the contractor's. We dreamed the railroads across the mountains, just as I dreamed my place on the Sweet Water. All these things will be everyday facts to the coming generation" (29). The dream motif is repeated in an elegiac mode from the focal character Neil's point of view as he thinks of how a second generation of grasping businessmen like the novel's nemesis, Ivy Peters, has spoiled the western heritage: "The Old West had been settled by dreamers, great-hearted adventurers who were unpractical to the point of magnificence, a courteous brotherhood strong in attack but weak in defence, who could conquer but could not hold. Now all the vast territory they had won was to be at the mercy of men like Ivy Peters, who had never dared anything. They would drink up the mirage, dispel the morning freshness, root out the great brooding spirit of freedom, the generous, easy life of the great land-holders. The space, the colour, the princely carelessness of the pioneer they would destroy and cut up into profitable bits, as the match factory splinters the primeval forest. All the way from the Missouri to the mountains this generation of shrewd young men, trained to petty economies by hard times, would do exactly what Ivy Peters had done when he drained the Forrester marsh" (58–59).

Bess Streeter Aldrich, the most productive of the Nebraska novelists, didn't start publishing until the 1920s; like Elizabeth Dejeans she calls it a Midwestern state. But her Midwest is definitively western in its constant connection of the contemporary with a pioneer heritage. Her first novel, *Mother Mason* (1924), pulled together stories published between 1918 and 1920 about a family living in Springtown, Nebraska. Mother—an old woman at age 52: fat, with thinning gray hair, and false teeth, but entirely domestic—is at the center. As is appropriate in these two-generation stories, the Masons have given up farming and moved to town, but they retain their family values. "They were good folks, kind folks, simple-hearted folks—and God give us more!—to whom it would not have mattered greatly if, instead of the big comfortable house with its ample rooms and sunny porches, there had been but a poor wee hut tucked away somewhere out of the wind and rain, for with willing hands and loving hearts, they would have made of it—HOME" (268–69).

In one story, Katherine invites her professor to dinner and is mortified when countrified grandpa drops in. But the professor says grandpa is "just what I've been looking for, an intelligent man who has lived through the early history of the state and whose memory is so keen that he can recall hundreds of anecdotes. I am working on a history of the state, and my plan is to have it contain stories of vividness and color, little dramatic events which are so often omitted from the state's dull archives. From the moment he began to talk I realized what a gold mine I had struck" (67–68). To him "these old pioneers . . . were the bravest, the most wonderful people in the world. . . . To have changed an immense area of Indian-inhabited wild land into this!" This "is our heritage from the pioneers. From sod houses to such beautiful homes as yours!" (69–70)

Aldrich's more ambitious *Rim of the Prairie* (1925) is about a young writer who has published some mean-spirited anonymous stories about the West, and is now in Nebraska trying to recover from writer's block. He finds romance with a young woman living with her uncle and aunt, a farming couple; he overcomes his block when he develops respect for the pioneers whom he sees embodied in them. Meditating on the grasshopper invasion, he thinks of the "hardihood, the faith, the courage of the people who stayed and saw the thing through.

What a stupendous thing they had done for the country. It was war, wasn't it? The whole frontier was a battleline. They fought for civilization" (141–42). He continues, "Nebraska is conquered. . . . Like a huge giant it lies with man's foot on its supine body. Fields are fertile. Orchards are fruitful. Pastures yield their heavy gifts. There are cattle on a thousand hills. Great consolidated schools, substantial and comfortable, flags without and libraries within, center in many districts. And all in one man's lifetime! What a heritage your Uncle Jud and his coworkers have given to the new generations" (143).

In *The Cutters* (1926), another loosely connected set of family stories, Gramma is the important pioneer figure. "When I was in my twenties . . . and the mother of two babies, we moved on again to the West. I've gathered my babies up to me and prayed that we'd get through the night without the Indians coming. I've lived in a sod house and shared the last of our family supplies with rough strangers. I've seen the grasshoppers take all our crops and a tornado lay every building low. I've seen the raw prairie with its long wild grass turn to mellow farm land and towns and cities. I've seen saplings grow to giant trees, and little boys to manhood" (46–47).

A Lantern in Her Hand was published in 1928, one year after my cutoff date. I include it because it was Aldrich's best-known novel. The center is again the pioneer mother, whose lantern lights the way for the next generation. After the sudden death of her farmer husband she stays on while her children grow up to become professors, statesmen, prominent businessmen. Through her, Nebraska retains the pioneering roots that continue to nourish the state. She says to her granddaughter in language much like Cather's: "We old pioneers . . . dreamed dreams into the country. We dreamed the towns and the cities, the homes and the factories, the churches and the schools" (280). At the book's end, Nebraska itself is interpreted as a monument to the pioneers. "Omaha and Lincoln are great centers for commercial, industrial, and educational interests. Where once the Indian pitched his tepee for a restless day, there are groupings of schools and churches and stores and homes" (84).

✳ ✳ ✳

In books set in the Dakotas there is more about Natives—including three Native-authored books—and there are Badlands, cattle ranching, and towns full of outlaws. Two white women—Sarah Larimer in 1870 and Fanny Kelly in 1871—published captivity accounts about the same incident (and the two got involved in an unsavory legal quarrel over priorities). Though Larimer escaped with her son after a few days, her book describes Indian customs at length, catering to a reader interest that, she frankly acknowledges, she could not satisfy by first-hand observation. She praises the "founders of Western empire—the hardy sons of toil . . . braving the vengeance of the savage, and turning the dreary wilderness into a garden, causing the desert waste to bloom like the rose" (13–14). She repeats many hearsay accounts of "women and children who became victims of Indian cruelty" and opposes the arguments of the group calling itself Friends of the Indian. If these humanitarians were to be "subjected to a journey across the plains, where a visit from their savage neighbors would result in poverty and a narrow escape from death, or in a life of bondage, they would probably modify their flattering opinion; and when subsequent observation would reveal gross indolence, uncleanliness, ignorance, deception, and cruelty, they would inevitably arrive at the conclusion that, instead of the Indian being a noble lord, holding a patent of nobility from heaven, he, in truth, too often embodies the most repulsive, lazy, and unprincipled habits and attributes" (128).

Kelly, held captive for four months, claimed that she helped the army by alerting them to an impending attack and wrote her book as part of a campaign for compensation from Congress. Although she had time enough for first-hand observation, many incidents in her story could not be corroborated by later historian-editors Mary Lee Spence and Clark Spence who published an annotated edition with an introduction in 1990. Even a nonspecialist might wonder how someone unfamiliar with the Native language could speak eloquently to Sioux chiefs, teach English to Natives from a book that just happened to be lying around one of the tepees, and enjoy many special privileges. "For hours I had sat with the book in my hands, showing them the pictures and explaining their meanings, which interested them greatly, and which helped pass away and relieve the monotony of the days of captivity which I was enduring. Moreover, it inspired them with a degree of respect and veneration for me when engaged in the task, which was not only pleasant, but a great comfort. It was by this means they discovered my usefulness in writing letters and reading for them" (119).

Frances Chamberlain Holley's *Once Their Home; or, Our Legacy from the Dahkotahs; Historical, Biographical, and Incidental from Far-off Days, down to the Present* (1891) combines Sioux history with Dakota boosterism including a full canvas of the amenities in every Dakota town, celebrating the railroad that brings "this great domain within easy distance of every son and daughter of the Union" (342), praising the climate, assuring readers that the Dakotas's resources are "beyond computation" (391). Particularly interested in those Sioux who want to improve Indian-white relations, she gives one chapter to Charles F. Picotte and another to Mrs. Picotte-Galpin; "in consideration of all that she has done for her family, her people, and for the whites and their Government, herself a full-blooded Sioux, I regard her as one of the most illustrious women of her time" (311). She points to the white double standard: if Indians win "by good generalship and a preponderance of numbers . . . even it if be in defence of their homes and children, then the cry goes over the land: 'Another Indian Massacre!' Yet, should victory perch on the other limb, loud prolonged huzzas ring out;

promotions follow in rapid succession, while the War Department chronicles another brave battle in which the United States Troops were victorious!" (314).

Helen Cody Wetmore's account of her brother's life, *The Last of the Great Scouts: The Life Story of Col. William F. Cody, "Buffalo Bill"* (1899), moves from Kansas where Cody was born and grew up, to Nebraska where he first established himself, and then to the Dakotas where he achieved his scout's reputation before opening his Wild West show, making her book a survey of the Great Plains as well as a hagiography. Cody is understood as a home-loving man not an Indian-fighting roughneck, deeply devoted to his mother and generous to his sister. Wetmore says he became a scout specifically to prepare himself for the show he had planned to open since boyhood. As a participant in Indian wars, he understands "injustice on the part of the United States government and a violation of treaty rights" (214) but still recognizes "the old, old drama of history" such that "the inferior must give way to the superior civilization. The poetic, picturesque, primitive red man must inevitably succumb before the all-conquering tread of his pitiless, practical, progressive white brother. . . . The total extinction of the race is only a question of time" (293).

In *The People of Tipi Sapa* (1918), Sarah Emilia Olden says she is putting into print Tipi Sapa's (Philip Deloria's) oral account, and wants to retain the "childlike simplicity in his manner of relating the incidents to me" (21). Olden is vague about whether this supposed simplicity corresponds to Tipi Sapa's essential childishness, his limited English, or the limitations of the Natives he wants as readers—not to mention, of course, her own idea of Native mentality. He hopes "when his little book appears in print that it will have a wide circulation among all those of his own people who can read the English language. The English vocabulary of the majority of Indians is naturally limited, and they would not readily understand a book written in elaborate diction" (21). The narrative describes traditional Sioux practices and endorses the missionary enterprise. The preface enthuses about the beautiful land: "We cannot begin to realize the greatness of this United States until we have seen the prairies—broad, vast, limitless, with innumerable 'cattle upon a thousand hills,' with herds of horses grazing on the plains and in the picturesque valleys; and with camps nestling in the bits of timber that fringe the edges of creeks and rivers. They extend into space on every hand as far as eye can reach; and, just as they blend with the circle of the horizon, present the appearance of countless blue billows rolling over some mighty ocean" (xv).

The account begins with Tipi Sapa's parents, and analyzes then-contemporary Indian life, making whites chiefly but not entirely responsible for Native decline. Native men have been "grossly corrupted by the intoxicating liquors handed over to them by the white man" and are "decreasing in numbers from the diseases contracted through our civilization . . . barely subsisting on the wretched rations furnished them by the government," but they also refuse to work because they've "been brought up to regard work with the greatest contempt" (22). Native women who once worked hard now have nothing to do and are "deteriorating in their morals on account of their indulgence in gossip and scandal of the grossest kind" (22). In a coda, Tipi Sapa speaks in the first person: "I know full well that some of you who read this will smile at a simple people's simple beliefs. I beg you to remember that the Dakotas saw quite as far as it was given them to see in their time and on that plane of development" (153); "My people are an essentially religious people. When once they understand Christian teaching, they prove to be devoted and faithful followers" (155); "The church, and the church only, is able to solve the future of the Indians" (157). (In 1999, his descendant Vine Deloria Jr. published an annotated rebuttal, *Singing for a Spirit*.)

Josephine Barnaby (an Omaha graduate from Hampton posted to the Standing Rock reservation as a missionary's assistant), Gertrude Bonnin (half Sioux, publishing as Zitkala-Sa), Marie McLaughlin (one-quarter Sioux, wife of and translator for a white Reservation Agent) are the three Native women who published books. Extracted from the journal of the Bible House of the American Missionary Association and separately published, a brief pamphlet rather than a book, Barnaby's undated but pre-1890 *The Present Condition of My People* is mainly a plea for distributing the Christian Bible among Native people, but it is also a defense of the allotment policy of the Dawes Act. Contrasting a feast and dance at the Standing Rock reservation with Christian services, she writes that "As an Indian woman working among my people, I see the need of each man having his own piece of land, and not being allowed to go dancing and begging from one tribe to another. If taught by some earnest Christian white men to farm and plant their fields, then they would be men" (5). The Indian is "naturally a religious being, but his old religion is full of degrading superstitions; his fear of the different gods is his only law. If we take the old religion away, we must give him a new one in its place" (6). She thanks "those two dear good men, fathers Riggs and Williamson, who gave the Dakotas the Bible in their own tongue. When I hear the men talk and read the Bible in Dakota, I regret that we had no one to make an Omaha Bible for my tribe" (8). Equally important as her affirmation of the Christian Bible is her wish that the Standing Rock people would reject their reservation dependency; "This depending on rations takes all the manliness out of the Indian, and after awhile if it continues, we shall not have brave, fearless Indians to look back upon as our honorable race, but a demoralized set of paupers" (5–6).

In *Old Indian Legends* (1901), Zitkala-Sa collected fourteen children's stories: "The old legends of America belong quite as much to the blue-eyed little patriot as to the black-haired aborigine. And when they are grown tall like the wise grown-ups may they not lack interest in a further study of Indian folklore, a study which so strongly suggests our near kinship with the rest of humanity and points a steady finger toward the great brotherhood of mankind" (vi). Zitkala-Sa's 1921 *American Indian Stories*, a work for grown-ups, consists of ten items previously published in *Harper's* and the *Atlantic* at the turn of the century. There are three autobiographical essays: "Impressions of an Indian Childhood," "The School Days of an Indian Girl," and "An Indian Teacher among Indians." "The Great Spirit" is revised from an essay originally called "Why I Am a Pagan"; "The Soft-Hearted Sioux" is about a Christianized Indian whose fatal soft-heartedness is his Christianity; in "A Warrior's Daughter," a young woman absorbs the warrior spirit of her father and rescues her lover from captivity among the enemy. "The Widespread Enigma of Blue-Star Woman" is about young Indians who scandalously take advantage of federal Indian policy to cheat the traditionals: "Incongruous as it is, the two nephews, with their white associates, were glad of a condition so profitable to them. . . . They thrived in their grafting business. They and their occupation were the by-product of an unwieldy bureaucracy over the nation's wards" (276–77).

Zitkala Sa's autobiographical sketches show her developing from a Native girlhood centered on her mother and the reservation through indoctrination into white ways to her decision to make her way as a writer—a decision that bridges her bicultural selves by allowing her to express both of them. Going East means leaving the Indian world; mother and the West equally symbolize Indianness. Returning to the reservation from school, she finds she can't go home again: "I was neither a wee girl nor a tall one; nether a wild Indian nor a tame one" (234). And this is the story of her whole generation: "No more young braves in blankets and eagle plumes, nor Indian maids with prettily painted cheeks. They had gone three years to school in the East, and had become civilized. The young men wore the white man's coat and trousers, with bright neckties. The girls wore tight muslin dresses, with ribbons at neck and waist. At these gatherings they talked English" (235).

Marie McLaughlin, collecting stories from tribal elders whose language she speaks, associated the West with the maternal, like Zitkala-Sa. She dedicated *Myths and Legends of the Sioux* (1916) to her mother. The preface, dated 1913, defines the author as a "progressive," that is, as an assimilationist. Although the stories she relates were always meant for children, she doesn't propose as Lucy Thompson had that the tribe's really important stories are concealed from white people. And though a Native herself, she distances herself from the people by construing adult Indians as childlike; the stories reflect "a simple, grave, and sincere people, living in intimate contact and friendship with the big out-of-doors that we call Nature; a race not yet understanding all things, not proud and boastful, but honest and childlike and fair," affording "an intimate insight into the mentality of an interesting race at a most interesting stage of development, which is now fast receding into the mists of the past" (ix). The book's three dozen or so tales, some very short "just so" animal stories, others about ghosts, witches, dead people brought back to life, people dismembered and made whole, are placed in a Nature of woods, lakes, and hills, and contain incidental information about making arrows, preparing meat, erecting a tepee. There are stories about intertribal hostilities and warfare, running off of horses, taking scalps, etc., and many on the lines of a Grimm fairy tale involving a poor young man in love with a wealthy girl.

Another view of Natives is Alice Fletcher's *The Omaha Tribe* (1911), still a source for Omaha tribal information material and a foundational contribution to the view of traditional Native behavior in terms of religious ceremony. Her 600+ page book, based on interviews with older Natives as interpreted by her collaborator, Omaha Francis La Flesche, ends with a brief account of the tribe's postcontact history as she sees it, or wants to see it: "To-day, towns with electric lights dot the prairies where the writer used to camp amid a sea of waving grass and flowers. Railroads cross and recross the gullied paths left by the departed game, and the plow has obliterated the broad westward trail along the ridge over which the tribe moved when starting out on the annual buffalo hunt. The past is overlaid by a thriving present. The old Omaha men and women sleep peacefully on the hills while their grandchildren farm beside their white neighbors, send their children to school, speak English, and keep bank accounts" (30). For all her interest in supposedly timeless religious ceremony, Fletcher points to much history in Native behavior; for example she says Natives weren't originally hunting people, but stopped crafting items more easily bought from whites and began commercial hunting to acquire cash. "The stimulation of hunting as an avocation weakened the influence of the old village life, created different standards of wealth, enhanced the importance of the hunter, and greatly increased the labors of the women in preparing pelts and skins for the market. There is good reason to ascribe to the last-named condition an impetus to the practice of polygamy among the Omaha. There was no special working class in the tribe nor could labor be hired" (615). Because Fletcher thought Natives had to become modern or die, she supported the allotment policy embodied in the Dawes act; she worked for the federal government on Nez Percé allotments.

Drawing partly on Fletcher (who also published on nonwestern Native Americans), partly on other anthropological sources, Katharine Judson extended her project of constructing a white man's—a white woman's—Indian through Native tales. Most of the stories in *Myths and Legends of the Great Plains* (1913) are drawn from the Omaha and Pawnee and are couched in a supposedly childish prose corresponding to Native simplicity. "Standing far out on the plains with no hint of the white man or his work," she writes in her preface, "one sees the earth somewhat as the Indian saw it and wonders not at his reverence for the Mysterious One who dwelt overhead" (n.p.).

* * *

Among western mining towns, Deadwood acquired a particular cachet. Long without a railroad, it had to freight out its ore in wagons that were vulnerable to outlaw attacks. But its reputation began when white people entered the Black Hills to find gold in defiance of government rules. Annie D. Tallent, whose son and husband both served as president of Deadwood's Pioneer Society, was the only women among twenty-nine people in the so-called "Gordon party," the first group to defy the federal government by entering the Black Hills in search of the gold that Custer said was there. In later years a teacher and school administrator, she compiled *The Black Hills, or Last Hunting Grounds of the Dakotas* (1899) for the Pioneer Society, proceeding chronologically, naming every country, town, and mining settlement, with information about civil organization, transportation, businesses, newspapers, infrastructure, and mining. (The book was reissued in 1974 with a scathing introduction by Virginia Driving Hawk Sneve.)

She recalls the Gordon party's journey: "At any time we were liable to be met or overtaken by roving bands of Indians, who we felt sure would look with no favor upon our aggressive movements. On the other hand, we were still more afraid of the authorities we had secretly defied" (25). She interprets their lawbreaking as a popular uprising: "Miners became clamorous for what they regarded as their rights, which they were determined to have at all hazards—if not with, then without, the consent of the government" (96). The book is strongly anti-Sioux, more as a matter of policy than morality, because gold not yeomanry is driving the illegal influx: "The spirit of adventure and aggression was then abroad in the land; the handwriting was on the wall. The gold-ribbed Black Hills were to be snatched from the grasp of savages, to whom they were no longer profitable even as a hunting ground, and given over to the thrift and enterprise of the hardy pioneer, who would develop their wonderful resources and thereby advance the interests and add to the wealth of our whole country" (9).

The white desperadoes of Deadwood in the early days were "even more to be feared than the Indians" (210). After miners and basic suppliers arrive, there come the "gamblers and all kinds of crooks and sharps, and with them those fixed facts in the moral or immoral economy of nearly all mining camps and municipalities, those human leeches that remorselessly feed on the earnings of weak men—the courtesan. By the latter part of August, Deadwood had become a vast seething cauldron of restless humanity, composed of virtue and vice in about equal ratios, engaged each in his own way in the mighty struggle for gold" (259). Most mines fail; "nine-tenths of the stamp mills erected throughout the Hills during the early years of their quartz-mining history were failures and a detriment to the reputation of the entire Black Hills, and more, their erections were stupendous blunders on the part of mine owners and mine operators" (346). "I often wonder," she reflects early on, "if any of the little band of pioneers, who sat dreaming around that camp fire on French creek that night, have ever yet realized their hopes. . . . I am quite clear on one point, and that is, that the author of this story has been reaching out for more than two decades after that delusive 'will-o'-the-wisp' and is still employed in the same fruitless occupation" (44).

Stella Gilman, who moved to the Dakotas as a child in 1878, published one novel for girls—*That Dakota Girl* (1892)—and a story collection, *A Gumbo Lily* (1901). Both feature the western American female ideal: innate gentility and high-mindedness combined with courage, frankness, and athleticism. The heroine of *That Dakota Girl* is "a slender girl of seventeen, who sits in her saddle as though it were a rocking chair, and who rides with the easy, cool, and collected air of one perfectly at home on horseback"; her flexible figure is clothed in a neatly fitting habit, her "sun-browned face, perfect in contour" is shaded by a "big cowboy's hat tilted jauntily"; her position on the horse is one of "extreme carelessness, though wondrously graceful" (5, 6). When two of her schoolmates visit, they spend their days in "riding, hunting, shooting, and boating," their evenings in "music, songs, private theatricals" (145). Schooling completed, she lives with her adoptive father, who has chosen to reside on a ranch "safe alike from the corruption of Eastern civilization and the wild lawlessness of frontier life, for this portion of South Dakota has become quite generally settled, and already enjoys the facilities of railway and telegraph, while the frontier line has been advanced hundreds of miles to the westward" (26–27). In "Barbed Wire," one of the stories in *A Gumbo Lily*, the eastern (male) narrator, a writer in search of local color, boards with a South Dakota family whose high level of culture surprises him. "Except for that elegant rifle in the corner and those antlers over the door, I might safely have remained in New York City to write up a description of the interior of a South Dakota dwelling" (52). When he meets a ridiculous low class character, he decides to put him into print as an average Dakota man because he's "the style that takes among Eastern readers" (47).

Eleanor Gates grew up on a South Dakota ranch, the setting for two novels: *Biography of a Prairie Girl* (1902) and *The Plow-Woman* (1906). *Prairie Girl* is an episodic juvenile set in the 1870s near the Yankton Sioux reservation. Born the day her father dies in a snowstorm going for the doctor, the unnamed little girl grows up with her mother and three older brothers. In early childhood she has her pet animals, and later she plants and herds with her brothers; after her mother dies she takes on household duties and teaches school. Besides that first snowstorm there are prairie fires and droughts, thieving Indians, assassins in town, July 4 and Christmas celebrations, the arrival of the railroad and the telegraph. When she is dying, the mother sees a future when the plains will have been domesticated, when "every quarter-section will hold a house, and there will be chimneys in sight in every direction," when "churches and better schools will follow. The roads will be planted with trees. There will be fences about the fields, and no Indians to thieve and kill," and this valley "will no longer be the edge of civilization" because "the frontier will have moved far to the west." But the future is not yet here; she tells her daughter "one woman in a family is enough to sacrifice to the suffering and drudgery of frontier life. So I want you to go East, to go where the sweetest and best influences can reach you. The prairie has given you health. It has never given you happiness" (286). *The Plow-Woman* takes place near an army fort in the Bismarck area, mixing Indians and soldiers with a plains romance about homesteading and claim-filing, pitting honest toil against legal chicanery. There is also the threat of a breakout from Sioux imprisoned in the fort; the plight of an Indian shamed by his tribe for weeping at the Sun Dance; an Evangelical; and a Shantytown where soldiers spend their time and money.

Sarah Comstock brought out her Dakota novel, *Speak to the Earth,* in 1927. The story, set in the Badlands, is premised on the government's plan after World War I to relocate unemployed veterans in the West as homesteaders. "In a land so difficult, where the utmost skill can hardly bring about profitable results short of five years, it was rash to expect a group of young men without capital—former dentists, icemen, salesmen of dry goods or groceries, soda-fountain servitors, waiters, chauffeurs, milkmen, or stenographers—to achieve success. . . . Their tragedy is as brave and pitiful as that of the more spectacular and famous heroes of the old West" (9–10). The novel also brings the New Woman and sexual freedom into the narrative design, asking whether the West can solve this generation's problems as it has solved those of earlier generations. The answer is no. There are Indians, a country dance, a visiting paleontologist, and pioneers from Europe, "peasants from faraway lands" who "know the soil as we never know it" (129). The novel says that most of the failed farmers are deracinated Americans, going West because they're rootless and remaining so. The female protagonist, confused New Woman though she is, does seem to understand the earth intuitively as she deals with dilemmas that "had assailed thousands of pioneer women before her. The first covered wagons that blazed a trail across the plains sheltered women who lay awake at night . . . racking their brains to devise a camp-fire substitute for the boiled dinner and pie of home tradition" (121).

Kate Boyles (later Bingham), working with her brother, Virgil D. Boyles, is the period's major woman Dakota novelist. According to historian Ruth Ann Alexander (the one scholar to work on the Boyles) Virgil, a court reporter, did the research while Kate did the actual writing. *Langford of the Three Bars* (1907) involves cattle rustling and courtroom drama and features a small-time rancher and his daughter Mary; Paul Langford, a big-time rancher and his trusty cowboy assistant; a judge, his niece Louise (a court reporter coming West to support herself), and a prosecuting attorney. Louise's outsider view becomes that of the novel; she falls in love with the prairie, reveling "in its winds; the high ones, blowing bold and free with their call to throw off lethargy and stay from drifting; the low ones, sighing and rustling through the already dead grass—a mournful and whispering lament. It was the strength of the wind and the freedom . . . that enthralled her imagination. It came about that the bigness and loneliness of this big country assumed a like aspect. It was not yet subjugated. The vastness of it and the untrammeled freedom of it, though it took her girl's breath away, was to dwell with her forever, a sublime memory" (146–47).

Amid this scenic grandeur, history is against the "small and independent ranchman" caught between "the wealthy cattle owner, whose ever-increasing wealth and consequent power was a growing menace" and the "boldness, cunning, and greed of the cattle rustlers who harassed all the range country of the Dakotas and Nebraska" (12–13). Mary, her father's right-hand man, is a great shot and kills at least one man, possibly two before the novel is over. In the end, when Mary and Paul get together, the father will become foreman on Paul's ranch, amalgamating his herd with Paul's and capitulating to history by giving up his ranch. Among other sensational events are a courthouse fire and a freeze that brings the cattle into town: "Mingled with the howl and bluster of the wind, and the swirl and swish of the snow drifting outside during the small hours of last night, sometimes had been distinguishable the solemn sound of heavy steps running. . . . To some to whom this sound was borne its meaning was clear, but others wondered, until daylight made it clear to all. . . . The town was full of cattle" (226). "During the second night the wind fell away, the snow ceased. Then such a sight greeted the inhabitants of the little town as perhaps they had never seen before. . . . Every dead spear that had lived and died in the protection of the sidewalk . . . had been ravenously nipped—Every heap of refuse, every grass plot had been ransacked" (227–28).

The book calls for strong women characters, but they are said to be exceptions in this "hard country on women, a hard, treeless, sun-seared, unkindly country. Men could stand it—fight for its future. . . . And after all it did not prove to be the undoing of men so much as it developed in them the perhaps hitherto hidden fact that they were already wanting. . . . Down in the southern part of the State, and belonging to it, a certain big barred building sheltered many women, when the sun of the treeless prairies and the gazing into the lonesome distances surrounding their homesteads seeped into their brains and stayed there so that they knew not what they did" (195–96).

In *The Homesteaders* (1909) a brother and sister homesteading in South Dakota suffer from the malice of a bad neighbor, enjoy the friendship of a good one, and benefit from the protection of a young, part-Sioux woman, who takes on the characteristics of the ideal western woman, shooting, riding, and covering the territory without fear. This cast, along with a few ranch-hands, contributes to a story of cattle rustling, horse stealing, and cattlemen's hostility to homesteaders. *The Spirit Trail* (1910) is a historical fiction set on the Sioux Reservation between the Treaty of Laramie and the Dawes Act, with Custer's expedition into the Black Hills and the Little Big Horn battle as defining off-screen events. The main characters are an Episcopal Minister, the second-in-command at the Reservation agency, the daughter of the Reservation agent, and a romantic Indian couple. Along with the idea that the Sioux must become Christians if they are to cease being savages is an emphasis on Indian rights and Indian humanity. Most interestingly, the white female protagonist spends fifteen months in a friendly Sioux camp and becomes virtually Indian, an event seen as entirely good for her and also exemplifying a woman's version of the fantasy of "playing Indian."

A Daughter of the Badlands (1922) is set at the turn of the century. Boni-bel, daughter of a Sioux woman and a white man who ranches on his own in the Badlands, attends college in the Northeast and, living with her aunt, has taken the name Sherwood. Only at commencement does her boyfriend Allan Sprague learn that she's part Indian. Bonibel assumes that Allan will now re-ject her, so she takes off; but Allan searches for her. In the Badlands he meets a cowboy known as Bat, foreman on a ranch for sale. "A typical cowboy—the breed really did exist then. It was not a figment of fancy, held over from a former generation. Allan awaited the moment of meeting with a queer little anticipatory thrill, very much akin to the kind that used to chase each other up and down his spine when he had surreptitiously gloated over the tales of Deadwood Dick and Wild Bill and their ilk" (26). On account of Bat he de-cides to buy the ranch and stay on. With Bat's help, Bonibel is found by page 33, and though it takes a while for the two to tie the knot, they are a couple. Among several good things are the novel's descriptions of the Badlands, ac-counts of cattle raising and trailing, depiction of Allan's father as he learns to appreciate Bonibel's worth, and adroit handling of the cowboy stereotype. The novel's midsection is given over to a long hunt for missing cattle and a huge round-up: "When one remembers that on this particular Round-up every inch of ground from the Missouri River to the Black Hills and from the sand-hills of Nebraska north to the Cheyenne and farther was to be covered; and that it required seventeen outfits, the output of seventeen organizations all meeting simultaneously, independently of each other but working in perfect harmony, to accomplish the covering of this vast region; that each outfit consisted of eighty or ninety riders, each rider furnishing at least ten riding horses, and all the camp equipment of blankets, tarpaulins . . . wagons, grub, cook-wagon and cook, one begins to appreciate what a man-sized job in the aggregate was the organizing, the financing, and the putting into execution of such a gigan-tic affair" (174–75). The novel ends when Allan imagines Bonibel "riding with him over illimitable solitudes; sometimes in the bright sunshine; sometimes scudding before high winds . . . or walking her horse side by side with his after a frolic of wild riding on the prairie, when the coyotes . . . began their mournful sounding serenade, and when now and then one caught the gleam of the river through the trees that surrounded the little home. 'We are of the West, Bonibel, you and I. Here is home'" (257–58).

8

The High Plains

Women's books about the High Plains—Wyoming, Montana, and Idaho—mainly ignored Owen Wister's adulation of the heroic Wyoming cowboy in his wildly successful 1902 novel, *The Virginian*. They did put cowboys in their work, recognizing (as Wister did not) that after the disastrous winter of 1886–87 the cowboy had simply become a ranch hand. They saw the area as underpopulated, underdeveloped, and underappreciated. Winters were fierce, the plains were arid, its absentee-owned mines a cauldron of labor trouble. As the National Park movement emerged and High Plains spaces—Yellowstone, Glacier—became apt candidates for recognition, tourism began to emerge as the region's major drawing card, and this was an angle particularly attractive to women. The cowboy himself could be thought of as a tourist spectacle, an eroticized symbol of the West itself.

In fact, *The Virginian* is narrated from the perspective of a dude ranch visitor. But more important for women writers is that tourism had become a basic fact of the High Plains economy when the US government made Yellowstone into the first national park in 1872. Alice Wellington Rollins (see Chapter 7 for her Kansas book) published *The Three Tetons: A Story of the Yellowstone* in 1887. Her book complains about the absence of tourist luxuries that had become standard by the time Grace Gallatin Seton-Thompson and others published their tourist books. Seton-Thompson's *A Woman Tenderfoot* (1900), set in the northern Rockies, is "a tribute to the West. . . . The events related really happened in the Rocky mountains of the United States and Canada; and this is why, being a woman, I wanted to tell about them, in the hope that some going-to-Europe-in-the-summer-woman may be tempted to go West instead" (n.p.). Women, she says—provided someone else does the cooking—need not "be more uncomfortable out in the mountains, with the wild west wind for companion and the big blue sky for a roof, than sitting in a 10 by 12 whitewashed bedroom of the summer hotel variety, with the tin roof to keep out what air might be passing. . . . The usual walk, the usual drive, the usual hop, the usual novel, the usual scandal— . . . do you not get enough of such life in the winter to last for all the year?" (19–20). Thanks to the trip, "I know what it means to be a miner and a cowboy, and have risked my life when need be, *but,* best of all, I have felt the charm of the glorious freedom, the quick rushing blood, the bounding motion, of the wild life, the joy of the living and of the doing, of the mountain and the plain; I have learned to know and feel some, at least, of the secrets of the Wild Ones. In short, though I am still a woman and may be tender, I am a Woman Tenderfoot no longer" (360). Her sequel, *Nimrod's Wife* (1907), urges the reader to "give your starved soul a chance—the road to the outdoors is open to all" (17).

Alice Harriman's comic romance of 1907 narrated through diaries (*Chaperoning Adrienne: A Tale of the Yellowstone National Park),* follows a tourist party through the Yellowstone, with notes on bears, mud geysers, Old Faithful, and other icons of this park. The comedy hinges on the remarkable obtuseness of the main narrator, an aunt who's supposed to shield her niece from a persistent suitor but is completely hoodwinked by the pair while finding romance with a former suitor of her own. Though this may not have been the author's intention, the book shows that any sort of unprepared person can have a tourist vacation in the once-wild West. The book's drawings and photographs make it an apt tourist souvenir.

In 1910 Helen Fitzgerald Sanders, who had moved from California (see Chapter 4) to Montana, published an essay miscellany, *Trails through Western Woods,* in which tourism romanticizes and domesticates the vast spaces of the High Plains. Though dedicated to "the West that is passing; to the days that are no more and to the brave, free life of the Wilderness that lives only in the memory of those who mourn its loss" (n.p.), the book proposes that a visitor can recapture this lost world and that, in fact, such imaginative play is the reason for coming—temporarily—to the High Plains. In "Above the Clouds," for example, "The world-rush calms into the great stillness of untrodden places, the world-voices sigh out in the murmuring breeze, the petty traffic of the cities is forgotten in the soulful silence of the trees. . . . The love of adventure thrills into being, together with the fine scorn of danger and the resolve to do that which we set out to do no matter what the cost or the peril. . . . This spirit is the faint, far-off echo of the hero-bearing days of the early west" (246–47).

Mary Roberts Rinehart's 1916 *Through Glacier Park: Seeing America First with Howard Eaton,* urges readers to "Throw off the impediments of civilization, the telephones, the silly conventions, the lies that pass for truth. Go out to the West. . . . Let the summer rains fall on your upturned face and wash away the memory of all that is false and petty and cruel" (24–25). But go soon, she counsels, because "There is little of the Old West left. Irrigation, wheat, the cutting-up of the Indian reservations into allotments, the homesteader, all spell the end of the most picturesque period of America's development. Not for long, then, the cow-puncher in his gorgeous chaps, the pack-train winding its devious way along the trail. . . . The old West is almost gone. Now is the time to see it" (85). The passage suggests that settlers in the High Plains are destroying it while tourists may preserve it. In *Tenting To-Night: A Chronicle of Sport and Adventure in Glacier Park and the Cascade Mountains* (1918), she says vacationing women should never be required to do housework. "Much as I love the mountains and the woods, the purple of evening valleys, the faint pink of sunrise on snow-covered peaks, the most really thrilling sight of a camping-trip is two cooks bending over an iron grating above a fire, one frying trout and the other turning flapjacks" (110). Agnes Laut's *Enchanted Trails of Glacier Park* (1926), distinguishing national parks from national forests, said the forests were for development, especially as "pulp woods and big timber and water-power become scarcer and scarcer in the east" (180), while the parks should be kept as a "No-Man's-Land of dreams and play and majestic calm" (182).

Elinore Pruitt Stewart ostensibly went to Wyoming to homestead. She agreed to do housework for her neighbor, rancher Clyde Stewart, and married him six weeks after arriving. She persisted in describing herself as a homesteader, however, in two books of literary letters to a former employer in Denver who saw to their publication in the *Atlantic*. *Letters of a Woman Homesteader* (1914) and *Letters on an Elk Hunt* (1915) both imply that Stewart had literary intentions from the start. She did not "allow Mr. Stewart to do anything toward improving my place, for I want the fun and the experience myself. And I want to be able to speak from experience when I tell others what they can do" (216). Homesteading solves "all poverty's problems. . . . Any woman who can stand her own company, can see the beauty of the sunset, loves growing things, and is willing to put in as much time at careful labor as she does over the washtub, will certainly succeed; will have independence, plenty to eat all the time, and a home of her own in the end" (216). Stewart says that nothing would give her more happiness "than to bring the West and its people to others who could not otherwise enjoy them. If I could only take them from whatever is worrying them and give them the bracing mountain air, glimpses of the scenery, a smell of the pines and the sage,—if I could only make them feel the free, ready sympathy and hospitality of these frontier people, I am sure their worries would diminish and my happiness would be complete" (220–21). In *Letters on an Elk Hunt* her project is no longer to attract emigrants or even visitors, but to amuse readers at home. People on a hunting party tell their stories, characters from *Woman Homesteader* reappear, and set pieces include a stampede, protective cowboys, stray animals, thieving Indians, a fat and friendly Mexican couple. Says a new-comer, Elizabeth, "I never saw such a country as the West;—it is so big and so beautiful,—and I never saw such people. You are just like your country; you have fed me, cared for me, and befriended me, a stranger, and never asked me a word" (82–83).

*   *   *

In a different way from tourist effusions, histories of Wyoming and Montana were also High Plains publicity. Alice Harriman's *Pacific History Stories, Montana Edition* (1903) calls the state "one of the stars of first magnitude in the galaxy of the union" (68). She also testifies to the disappearing cowboy: "The necessity of breaking up the endless ranges as more and more the settlers come into Montana, is sending the cowpuncher into the shadowy past as surely as the railroads and other conditions did the trappers, Indians, and buffalos" (96). In 1909, Katharine Berry Judson of the University of Washington (see Chapter 3) published her textbook *Montana: The Land of Shining Mountains*. "Montana as we see it to-day with its great ranches, fragrant apple orchards, and gleaming wheat fields, is very different from the strange land, covered only with beautiful wild flowers or prickly pear cactus which the early pioneers saw. Our great cattle ranges bear no resemblance to the vast brown herds of hump-backed buffaloes which wandered over the plains, nor do the well-kept cities with comfortable houses, lawns, and restful parks look at all like the shacks and cabins which used to occupy the same land" (130).

In 1913, Helen Fitzgerald Sanders published a three-volume boomer *History of Montana* praising Montana's pioneers and publicizing the state's attractions. The book, still cited in historical research, features statistics and documents including the papers of her father-in-law Wilbur Fisk Sanders, an important figure in early Montana: a member of the vigilante group that hanged numerous outlaws in the early days, a radical republican active in state politics, and ultimately a US Senator. Though her account is partisan, she goes beyond partisanship to imagine Montana progressing toward an agricultural future, after its apprenticeship in trapping, mining, and stock raising. This future requires irrigation and more people: "When the plans are perfected and tens of thousands of acres are watered, Montana will take its place as one of the great agricultural sections of the United States" (1, 534); it will be "thickly settled with thrifty men and women who will exploit her vast virgin areas, promote her countless industries, manufacture her raw materials and populate her farm lands and cities. Indeed, the country but waits for the people. The opportunity is here for him who comes to claim his reward" (1, 793).

Grace Raymond Hebard, on the University of Wyoming faculty, published history texts praising the state and extolling the railroad for opening it to settlement. Her earliest, *The Government of Wyoming: The History, Constitution, and Administration of Affairs* (1904), says that the state, lacking navigable rivers, is "entirely dependent" on the railroad; "With the coming of this sign of civilization we needed a fixed form of government and we needed our public lands surveyed and we needed different tribunals than the Vigilance Committee" (45). Next came *The Pathbreakers from River to Ocean: The Story of the Great West from the Time of Coronado to the Present* (1911), beginning with the military: "The white man could not bring his family to the western plains and the Rocky Mountains, among the fierce Indians, until some protection was given by an armed force of men. The time for the actual settler had now arrived" (181), and moving on through the brief cowboy era to the present: "The buffalo has been driven to the zoological garden, the Indian to the reservation, and the cowboy to the 'Wild West Shows' and 'bucking bronco contests.' The open range has given way to the irrigated farm, and the cowboy is speedily being obliged to abandon his free, happy, and independent life to be placed in history with the explorer, the trader, the trapper, and the early pioneer" (215–16). To all this admirable destruction the railroad is key: "When the East needed the loyal support of the West during the trying days of the civil strife, and the wealth from the mines was eagerly sought to refill a depleted national purse, when our statesmen began to fear that those Americans so far away, so isolated from the national center, so rich and self-sufficing, might do as the South had done and set up an independent government, no sacrifice seemed too great, no labor too arduous that promised to bind that isolated region to the rest of the Union. We must remember this when we contemplate the generous aid that our country gave to the first builders of transcontinental railroads" (228).

Finally, Hebard, collaborating with E. A. Brininstool, brought out *The Bozeman Trail: Historical Accounts of the Blazing of the Overland Routes into the Northwest, and the Fights with Red Cloud's Warriors* (1922). This was a clear effort to replace other overland stories with an account of the High Plains. "Our national expansion has been a western movement, one that was the most romantic and most epochal in all of our written history. Change is the immutable law of progress. Men and women of energy, courage, and determination are the ones who have sought in the broad expanse of the west a refuge from social stagnation felt in the localities from which they have migrated. . . . It is the frontiersman with the pioneer spirit that builds a nation and founds commonwealths within that nation" (266).

*   *   *

Four books by army women certainly boost the territory (after all, the military was there to lay the groundwork for settlement by protecting railroad workers, restraining Natives, and the like), but mainly celebrate army life and justify the presence of officers' wives in the forts. Two women memorialized the so-called "Fetterman Massacre" (December 1866), when Sioux under the leadership of Red Cloud ambushed and killed eighty men from Fort Phil Kearny under the command of two captains, one of them William Fetterman. The soldiers were on a mission to cut wood; their stripped and mutilated bodies were discovered only a few hours after the carnage. Margaret Carrington's husband had been the commanding officer at the fort, and she wrote *Absaraka, Home of the Crows* (1867) both to defend him and to boom Wyoming (which she insisted on calling by its Crow name) for whose future he had worked. She denied Sioux ownership to the land and implied that since the Crows were the territory's real owners, their alliance with the whites had effectively constituted white people the heirs. But Carrington also complained about the small number of inadequately armed soldiers, and their inappropriate work of building and maintaining their own fort. If not for the need to acquire wood, the soldiers wouldn't have been out that day. The government was as much to blame as the Indians who, after all, were only doing what Indians do. But because the army was out there to enable the building of a railroad, which in turn would bring in settlers, Carrington could move from defending her husband to boosting the territory. The land's "natural charms . . . will in the future have equal beauty for those who seek homes in a new and hitherto undeveloped land" (26). In a situation where female qualities might seem to be superfluous, she praises the officers' wives as they learn to roast, boil, bake, stew, and—when on the road—make their tents "neat and genteel" (175).

Decades later, Frances Carrington, widow of a lieutenant killed in the Fetterman episode, who later became General Carrington's second wife (Margaret died in 1870 at the age of 39), published *My Army Life and the Fort Phil. Kearney Massacre, with an Account of the Celebration of "Wyoming Opened"* (1910). With the Indians now safely neutralized, she can praise them as well as white soldiers for martial bravery. "At the time of my arrival it had become apparent to any sensible observer that the Indians of that country would fight to the death for home and native land, with spirit akin to that of the American soldier of our early history, and who could say that their spirit was not commendable and to be respected?" (45). Women's social rounds on the fort are most pleasurable: "With a coterie of five ladies at the post, each had four places to visit, and the most was made of it in comparing notes upon the important matters of cooking, sewing. . . . There was often an all-round social dance, games of cards, the 'author's game,' and other contrivances for recreation and amusement, in addition to the receptions at headquarters, which were spirited and congenial, and, with a band having the deserved reputation of being the finest in the army, their choice music was no small feature in the cheer on the frontier" (102–3). Returning to Wyoming after many years, she finds evidence in the "undulating plains with verdure clad, waving wheat, barley and other grains" (234) that the sacrifice wasn't in vain. "Our own brief function of solemn and almost heart-rending service during the constrained, forcible opening of the original, historic Bozeman Trail . . . was only that of simply unlatching a door for an intelligent and progressive generation to grasp" (315–16).

Two other army memoirs praised the High Plains for the challenge and purity of its open-air life, especially for women. In *Prairie Sketches; or Fugitive Recollections of an Army Girl of 1899,* (1837), Mary Katharine Jackson English, a captain's daughter, recalled a summer at Fort Washakie, Wyoming after two years at boarding school. "It was with a feeling of absolute content that I looked forward to our life of the prairies, with many additional delights connected with an army post adding to our amusements. . . . The great stretches of prairie and the sublimity of the mountains impart strength and reality. Honest and true are the people of the great outdoors, and pure are their lives" (76). She calls the Shoshone "old friends" and says it's no wonder "that a race of brave fighting people have often rebelled and tried to right their wrongs in blood. . . . It will take many long years of patient teaching of the younger generation . . . to outgrow their hereditary instinct of fighting, and to learn the art of cultivating land—an art seemingly unnecessary, when one realizes they had all Nature's gifts at their command" (39).

Frances Roe's epistolary *Army Letters from an Officer's Wife* (1909—reissued in 1981 with an introduction by Sandra Myres) says army life was exhilarating for a woman. Some "yawn and complain of the monotony of frontier life, but these are the stay-at-homes. . . . If they would take brisk rides on spirited horses in this wonderful air, and learn to shoot all sorts of guns in all sorts of positions, they would soon discover that a frontier post can furnish plenty of excitement" (42). Familiar social activities acquire new significance in the remote setting: "Last evening we gave a delightful little dance in the hall in honor of the officers and their wives who are to go, and the officers who have come. We all wore our most becoming gowns, and anyone unacquainted with army life on the frontier would have been surprised to see what handsome dresses can be brought forth, even at this far-away post, when occasion demands" (109). Roe says the "very presence" of the officer's wife "has often a refining and restraining influence over the entire garrison, from the commanding officer down to the last recruit. No one can as quickly grasp the possibilities of comfort in quarters like these, or as bravely busy herself to fix them up" (81). "We know, if the world does not, that the part we are to take on this march is most important. We will see that the tents are made comfortable and cheerful at every camp; that the little dinner after the weary march, the early breakfast, and the cold luncheon are each and all as dainty as camp cooking will permit" (166).

Mary MacLane published her memoir of 1902, *The Story of Mary MacLane,* when she was nineteen years old. (The book was reissued by Riverbend Press in 2002 with an introduction by Julia Watson, and has been collected with other works by MacLane in later editions.) The first page of this happily narcissistic account tells readers that the author is "distinctly original innately and in development," possesses "a quite unusual intensity of life," has "a marvelous capacity for misery and for happiness," and is, in short, "a genius" (1). For western purposes, that MacLane had grown up in Butte, Montana, graduated from high school with nothing to do, and therefore took long walks every day, allowed her to declare that "Butte and its immediate vicinity present as ugly an outlook as one could wish to see. It is so ugly indeed that it is near the perfection of ugliness" (10). The book became a sort of scandalous success in its day, and earned her enough in royalties to leave Butte and the West forever. Laughably pretentious though it is, the book makes a point that recurs in other chronicles of small-town western life (including Willa Cather's The *Song of the Lark*): the settled West does not welcome artists, intellectuals, or nonconformists.

Kate McBeth's missionary history, *The Nez Percés since Lewis and Clark*— (1908, reissued with an introduction by Peter Iverson and Elizabeth James in 1993)—is a story (like Isabel Crawford's, see Chapter 2) about finding a home away from home. The narrative's heroine is the author's sister, Sue McBeth, who was already at the Nez Percé mission when Kate arrived. Sue's controversial activities centered on teaching the men of the tribe, whose conversion she saw as paramount. Sue also believed that Christian life required a renovation of the outer as well as the inner man. Once again, there is an endorsement of the Dawes Act. According to Kate, Sue believed that "there could be no Christian citizenship in any tribe, until the tribal relations were broken up, and that churches could not long exist that were not established on the purity of the home. The two objects to be attained were clearly before her. The first, the power of the chiefs over the people must be broken, and the man must feel his individuality, instead of feeling he was a part of a band. Second, the moral tone of the people must be raised" (89).

*   *   *

The earliest High Plains fiction seems to be Josephine White Bates's Montana mining novel, *A Blind Lead* (1888), about three sisters in the little town of Colusa trying to manage. The book observes that the few who get rich also run the place because they own it and proposes that poverty and hardship are opportunities for women to show their mettle. She contrasts the town's masculine business street to that street, "quiet and orderly as a New England village" (19), where "women and children lead the same helpful, holy lives that are lived in homes the world over" (20). Two of Bates's eight *Bunch-Grass Stories* (1895)—"Taken in at Oare's" and "A Transferred Town"—are set on the High Plains, praising western women, censuring western men. "Taken in at Oare's" equates the West with its fresh-faced, virtuous, and outspoken young women, "the ideal of our West, our young, rude, glorious West" (139).

Caroline (Carrie) Marshall published two High Plains books about homesteading for girls: *The Girl Ranchers of the San Coulee* (1897) about Montana, and *Two Wyoming Girls and Their Homestead Claim* (1899). They both ask whether the girls (acting on behalf of their families) can hold on to their claim against the machinations of people who covet it. The answer is yes. In the Montana book, the ailing father buys a sheep ranch without knowing anything about sheep or the hostility between cattlemen and sheep men. Thanks to their own hard work and a clever ruse in which friendly Mexican and Native Americans participate, the girls salvage their first season and then wisely decide to turn the ranch into a fruit farm, which they can do because they have saved enough money to invest in trees, and because their sterling characters have so impressed a neighbor that he gives them water rights to his irrigation ditch. In *Two Wyoming Girls,* irrigation figures again as the key to High Plains success, as the girls struggle against a neighbor who wants their claim because it has water. Both books are packed with information about homesteading law, sheep, water, and other matters germane to High Plains settling; and both moralize about the practical advantages of goodness, which makes powerful others like you and do good for you.

May Arkwright Hutton's *The Coeur d'Alenes; or, A Tale of the Modern Inquisition in Idaho* (1900) is a passionately pro-union fiction about the 1899 miners' strike. Dedicated to her husband "who, an innocent man, was arrested and confined in the 'bull-pen' for days in an effort to coerce him into giving testimony, knowing his reputation for probity and honor in the community, where he has resided for years," it has photograph illustrations and polemicizes like a newspaper editorial. In the story, Jock Hazelton is trying to make his fortune in Idaho after his father has committed suicide owing to the (supposed) collapse of his mining stock—although the stock hasn't collapsed at all, which saves Jock at the end rather than any triumph of labor over capital. "Many there are among the miners of the Coeur d'Alenes of education, many of fine physical proportion and some of high morality, but the combination of the three in the person of Jock Hazelton made him known far and wide in that country among mine-owners and miners alike. But none of these noble qualities availed to save an innocent man from the machinations of the Standard Oil Company, which has the wealth to call to its aid the bayonets of the United States Government with which to down the working people" (297). Hutton argues for fair wages and tries to advance the union cause among formerly independent prospectors whom capitalism has transformed into wage-earners in the underground mines. To achieve this, "The working people of this land must become a unit on this subject of the oppression of the masses by the money classes" (380);

and when it does "this latest gem in the crown of Idaho will shine forth in splendor" (400).

Mary Stickney's *Brown of Lost River: A Story of the West* (1900) is a tender-foot novel whose protagonist Edith is summering on her brother's Wyoming ranch while she thinks about an engagement proposal. She is impressed by the elegance of the ranch house: "I came expecting to 'rough it,' and find silk portieres and Persian rugs, high-art furniture and the latest books. I feel that I have been a victim of misplaced confidence; that 'the wild and woolly West' is a myth" (47). Edith is contrasted to two types of failed womanhood: her spoiled, indolent sister-in-law who makes no effort to keep a pleasant home, and a selfish schoolteacher who, augmenting her salary by working in summers as a maid, cares only for personal advancement. Edith, whose claim to female superiority is rather asserted than demonstrated, falls in love with Brown, a local "cowboy"—actually a ranch owner—whose good breeding surprises her. He asks if she'd looked "for Indians in war paint, and cutthroats clothed as cowboys, to stand in the foreground of every landscape, firing guns and flourishing knives. . . . That is rather a common Eastern conception of the wild and wooly West, I believe. But you will discover, the sentiment in favour of dying with one's boots on is rather out of date in Wyoming; while it is not considered good form to snuff the candles with six-shooters in these days" (12).

Frances McElrath's *The Rustler: A Tale of Love and War in Wyoming* (1902) is another summering story, an improbably plotted novel about a spoiled eastern woman vacationing on a ranch who turns social reformer when she is kidnapped by a rustler, a former cowboy with whom she had foolishly flirted. Transported to his rustler hideaway, a fully functioning western town, she redeems herself by nursing the community's sick and educates the children, and continues to do so after his death in a shoot-out frees her from captivity. As Victoria Lamont has noted in her introduction to the reissue of 2002, the novel is partly powered by the sort of late-nineteenth-century feminism that underwrote women's entrance into public life by claims about their inherently moral maternalism.

Frances Parker's debut novel of 1903, *Marjie of the Lower Ranch,* features an incredibly beautiful ingénue who undergoes a number of ridiculous trials through which her character "was gradually developed" (26)—impossible, because she was already perfect. Parker's *Hope Hathaway: A Story of Western Ranch Life* (1904), an improvement, opens with a segment in which Hope's rancher father reflects that "The old-time cowboy was fast disappearing, customs of the once wild West were giving way before an advancing civilization"; the open range is filling up with "offensive bands of sheep and small cow-ranches" (2). Hope is "of the West. Its vastness filled her with a love that was part of her nature. Its boundless prairies, its freedom, were greater than all civilization had to offer her" (44). Later in the book she goes to New York

City and dislikes it; a return to the West is the novel's happy ending: "We are going back to our West—*home* again, away from all this fuss and foolishness. . . . Oh, I am wild for my horses and the prairie again!" (406). Parker's third novel, *Winding Waters: The Story of a Long Trail and Strong Hearts* (1909), is better still: a strongly pro-Native historical fiction about Chief Joseph and the non-treaty Nez Percé. The heroine is Nanaiha, a study in blended identity: brought up by a white couple, she thinks she's a Nez Percé but is actually white. (Hutton had used the same device for Jock's love interest; the free although virtuous physicality of western white women is seen as a borrowing from Native life. And the trope appears in fiction by Vingie Roe and Kate Boyles as well.) At the end, Nanaiha, knowing now that she's white, still goes with Chief Joseph and the others on their long march: "In her heart she bade good-bye to the white race forevermore. If her people were to be slaves—prisoners of the Government,—they had need of her. It was for her to pave the way so that these children of Nature might not feel the cruelest stings" (151).

Grace Livingston Hill, author of over sixty novels and said to have invented the "Christian romance," set much of *The Girl from Montana* (1908) on the road as the heroine, an orphaned wild mountain girl, makes her way—on horseback—from Montana to Philadelphia in search of her grandparents. The novel exemplifies the formula in which a country girl becomes a fine lady—becomes outwardly, that is, what she is already inwardly; and additionally she becomes a Christian. (I take up Hill's southwestern novels in Chapter 9.) Therese Broderick's *The Brand: A Tale of the Flathead Reservation* (1909) is set on the Montana Reservation among cattle ranchers; its villain is the white Indian agent Davies, a seducer and betrayer of women who almost marries the (white) protagonist Bess except for her last-minute discovery of his immoral character. The hero is the half-white, half-Indian college-educated ranch owner, who literally brands Davies in an act of violence that Bess attributes to his Indian blood. (The letters RW on the brand stand for "respect women.") The novel ends when Bess "forgets" this action, paving the way for an interracial marriage in which the romantic West is incarnated in a partly Indian man. Mourning Dove attacked this novel in her *Cogewea*, which has made it moderately interesting to students of Native American literature.

In Mary K. Maule's novel for boys, *The Little Knight of the X Bar B* (1910), a child brought to a crude Wyoming ranch by the owner, his uncle, is raised by cowboys. This poor little rich boy formula takes place in a region bounded by the Big Horn mountains to the West, the Black Hills to the East, and the Laramie Mountains to the South, with much of the action represented through a child's viewpoint. At the end he has grown up to inherit the ranch, and assures the cowboys that "just as soon as my education is completed, it's me for the ranch and the West. The East is all right for some things, but give me the West every time. I grew up here, and I love it, and now that the old X Bar B is mine, I mean to make it my home" (459).

In *A Man of Two Countries* (1910), Alice Harriman wrote about the backroom intricacies of Montana politics, as the high-minded protagonist—an Englishman who's left Canada to settle in Montana and raise cattle—is elected to the Senate and maneuvers among schemers, manipulators, dishonest lobbyists, and those who buy and sell votes. At this time, US senators were elected by the appropriate state legislatures, a situation corrected by the 17th Amendment to the United States Constitution in direct response to the scandal in Montana that forms the background for Harriman's novel. To the hero, who values issues over party, it all seems "but a continuance of the days of fur and whiskey smuggling" (231); "That we are Democrats or Republicans, Labor or Fusion, should not figure in this contest. Instead, each man should consider whether we, a young State, shall enter Washington tarred with the ineradicable pitch of bribery or shall we send a man who will show the elder states that Montana is proud of her newly acquired statehood, and that no star in the Northwest firmament shines more pure?" (287). Love for the West competes with self-love, and Montana's open spaces create a loyalty that contrasts with the self-seeking opportunist who wants to leave the West for the fripperies of eastern social life. Social life, relegated to women, introduces a contrast between a woman who, excited by the political game, uses her charms to buy votes; and another who, steadfast and true, gets the hero in the end.

Agnes Laut's *The Freebooters of the Wilderness* (1910) is another political novel, with a forest ranger hero standing for people against the Plutocrat. Among events, a herd of sheep is driven over a precipice to save land for cattle, and dummy homesteaders take money for "settling" on nonarable land that's good only for timber. In her preface Laut complains about "the wresting of self-government from the people into the hands of the few. . . . It seems almost incredible that such lawlessness and outrage and chicanery can exist in America" (x). The story has two villains. One is Senator Moyese ("foreign," but with nationality unspecified) to whom every poor man is simply "a damned incompetent unfit swinish hog, too lazy to plant and hoe his own row" (244); the other is a sycophantic newspaper editor. There are also two heroes: Ranger Wayland, who dreams "of the day coming when all the national Forests would be a great park, the people's playground, yielding bigger annual harvests in ripe lumber than the wheat fields or the corn; yielding income for the state and health for the Nation" (358), and Matthews, his old frontiersman sidekick whose impenetrable vernacular in a court trial carries the day for justice. The woman's role in this novel is to stay home and pace the floor thinking "vague womanish thoughts that women have thought since time began of finding that magic vein of heroism in the Man . . . the gentle womanish hoping-against-hope thoughts that women have worn out their lives thinking and enslaved their bodies and pawned their souls" (272).

Katharine Hopkins Chapman's *The Fusing Force: An Idaho Idyll* (1911) uses the tensions of 1907, when the assassination of Governor Steunenberg and the trial of "Big Bill" Haywood and other union men affected mining all over the state, to plot exciting summer adventures for Charlotte Bondurand, a college graduate from Mobile, Alabama, camping with her brother and sister-in-law on his mining property. A nasty mine manager dares to kiss Charlotte on the cheek—and, as might be imagined from someone who performs such a dastardly deed, turns out to be an embezzler and murderer. The novel describes Ketchum and its history: "a mushroom mining town which had sprung up in boom days and as suddenly withered away in the silver depression of '93, when young Idaho suffered an attack, an epidemic of bull-pens, stockades, and bomb-throwing which would have been fatal to a less vigorous State. Even this young and virile scion of the West had not escaped unscathed. In 1907 Idaho was still stunted in growth and scarred in places, while the Haywood-Pettibone trial in Boise threatened to throw the whole State into a relapse of anarchy. In Ketchum many houses were vacant, while pretentious residences were occupied by humble tenants in order that the absentee owner might collect the insurance in the highly desired event of a fire" (21).

Helen Fitzgerald Sanders, unable to work Natives into her business-booster history of Montana, gave them space in *The White Quiver* (1913), a novel illustrating Piegan (Blackfoot) myths and ceremonies. She says the Blackfeet were "a people of dances, festivals and songs" that she has tried to represent faithfully; she has also "endeavored to preserve the old form of speech; the curiously dignified and impressive phraseology of the Indian. And the reader will understand the spirit of the story better if he bears in mind that every description of mountain, lake, love and battle is from the Indian viewpoint and is seen through the medium of his fancy" (x).

Gertrude Atherton set *Perch of the Devil* (1914) in Butte, where, she explained in her autobiography of 1934, she went to see first-hand what no longer existed in California—great captains of industry in the fullness of their powers. Her hero, Gregory Compton, "had grown to maturity in the most romantic subdivision of the United States since California retired to the position of a classic. Montana, her long winter surface a reflection of the beautiful dead face of the moon, bore within her arid body illimitable treasures, yielding it from time to time to the more ardent and adventurous of her loves" (16). In Butte strong men—pirates, effectively—may still triumph over the recalcitrant terrain and, even more, over "those hostile millions, whose brains so often are of unleavened dough, always devoid of talent, envious, hating, but . . . fooling themselves with dreams of a day when mere brute numbers shall prevail, and (human nature having been revolutionized by a miracle) all men shall be equal and content to remain equal" (15). In the woman's story, Gregory's wife, Ida, a good-natured country girl, suits him in his early rise to power but begins to bore him when he succeeds. He falls out of love with her until she smartens up.

As with Atherton's California fiction, the only field open to female enterprise is competition for men. Atherton says flatly, through Ida, that this story is a poor second to a man's, but women are to blame because they're not able to live without men. "The extraordinary woman hasn't been born yet, in spite of the big fight the sex is putting up. . . . When women really are extraordinary they will be just as happy without men as they now want to be with them. . . . Inside they are just one perpetual shriek for the right man to come along—that is all but a few hundred thousand tribadists. But they've made a beginning, and one day they'll really be able to take men as incidentally as men take women. Then we'll all be happy. Don't you fool yourself that that's what I'm aiming at, though. I'm the sort that hangs on to her man like grim death" (367).

New England academic Mary Ellen Chase published two novels about a Wyoming ranch girl sent to a New England boarding school. *The Girl from the Big Horn Country* (1916) is an episodic fiction contrasting the Wyoming heroine, Virginia, epitome of the western female character—direct, open, generous, and brave—to her eastern schoolmates. Virginia's Thanksgiving oration defines the pioneers as updated pilgrims: "they crossed a sea of land, our great prairies, where there were even more perils than those of the Atlantic—perils of Indians, wild animals, cyclones, and blizzard. They crossed the mountains, cutting their own trails before them, protecting the tired women and helpless children from danger; and those who went to the Far West crossed the great deserts, suffering great hunger and worse thirst, and sometimes leaving their bones upon the sands" (151). The book praises the vigilantes, who become the model for a girls' club committed to justice and fair play: "We take our name from the vigilantes of the West—those brave men, who in the early days of our Western States, bound themselves together in the endeavor to stand for fair play, and to preserve law and order" (264). In *Virginia of Elk Creek Valley* (1917) the girls summer at Virginia's ranch: "So this was Virginia's country! It was a big land! She understood now what Virginia had meant by talking about the bigness of everything. The plains, stretching on and on, gray-green with sagebrush, the gaunt mountain spurs, the far-away real mountains, blue and snow-furrowed, the great, clear sky over all!" (14).

Katharine Newlin Burt, who with her husband Maxwell Struthers Burt (also a writer) operated a Wyoming dude ranch, wrote many successful female formula romances including three with western backgrounds within my time period: *The Branding Iron* (1919), *Hidden Creek* (1920), and *Q* (1922). A few critics have found crypto-feminism in these romances, but I find in them the formula that glorifies female suffering at the hands of masterful men rather than the formula in which persecuted women outmaneuver and rise above their enemies. A key moment in *The Branding Iron* is the literal branding of the protagonist by her enraged husband (the branding metaphor is seemingly appropriate for a cattle culture). But at the end, after an amazing hegira that takes her to New York City and fame as an actress, she rejects her intellectual mentor by telling him she prefers physical branding to his moral and mental control. In *Hidden Creek,* a wayward young woman gets work as a barmaid in an unnamed western town, eventually to find true and masterful love. *Q* is a different kind of story; a handsome and virile cowboy goes East in pursuit of one woman only to fall in love with another, the woman who is tutoring him in social niceties. The outcome of moving the cowboy out of his western setting is to make his westernness more obvious and more attractive.

In Margaret G. Young's well-received Idaho novel, *Homestead Ranch* (1922), Harriet Holiday is yet another eastern schoolteacher visiting a brother for the summer. Rob is homesteading on the Camas Prairie, which is described in its beautiful vastness, its terrifying badlands, and its general promise as "the foundation for as great a romance as the world has ever seen: the transforming of the waste places of the earth into a garden of plenty" (37). Rob persuades her to file on an adjoining homestead claim and gradually, with many mistakes along the way, she becomes a Westerner—learning to bake pies, ride a horse, hoe a row, and more. Diverse episodes convey an array of homesteading challenges: filing a claim, building a house, keeping house, dealing with sheep, cattle rustling, horse stealing, dishonest neighbors. The brother-and-sister duo survives, facing on the one hand craftier and wealthier ranchers who want to run them out of the country, and on the other small time poachers. Because Harriet applies New England grit, courage, honesty, and intelligence to her new situation, the ideal western type becomes an updated New England type. The most important lessons come not from Rob but from a farmer's wife whose homespun dialect puts her outside the circle Harriet would normally travel in. But her friendly competence exemplifies the type of older, wiser, woman of the land whose guidance the neophyte welcomes.

The irrigation-obsessed Honoré Willsie set one of her eight western novels, *The Exile of the Lariat* (1923), in Wyoming. Hugh is a paleontologist devoted to his irrelevantly selfish work; Jessie is his unhappy wife trying to get him to become the important man she rightly thinks he ought to be. The conflict plays out over land called the Old Sioux Tract in which there are both a cave of magnificent dinosaur specimens and a river with enough water to "electrify half of Wyoming" if a dam is built there (91). Hugh is finagled into running for governor in a state where politically powerful women have the vote; he comes to recognize what might anachronistically be called his sexism. Accepting his responsibility to the general welfare, he sacrifices his fossils and wins the election. There's a great deal about Wyoming politics in this novel, with Wyoming standing for the interior West as a whole with vast spaces, beautiful skies, a cattle economy, mixed attitude toward dudes and tourists ("Being a foreman on a dude ranch . . . I get homesick for real western life. So as soon as the dudes begin to come in, I begin to load up on western novels" [44]). Hugh is a good candidate: "After all, this still was a frontier state. Men still delighted in the single gun holdup. And Hugh, standing alone against the great Eastern Electric Company and against the ring at Cheyenne . . . independent of spirit, iron of will, held his followers in a fever of enthusiasm" (197–98).

Mary Roberts Rinehart's *Lost Ecstasy* (1927) is a cowboy romance whose well-bred heroine pursues and marries her cowboy in the fading years of the type, to her own and his regret. "Take a cowboy off a horse and what was he? A field hand! She had married him out of some sort of romantic idea of him, but where was the romance now. . . . How would it work out, with her eternally trying to make him like the men she knew, and Tom dragging her down to the level of his own small-town girls" (203). They separate; she returns east while he gets work in a Wild West Show, a plot development implying the Old West's future in self-reenactment. The distance between this rough county lad and the sophisticated woman would seem to be unbridgeable, but Kay manages it by reanimating her romantic idealization of the cowboy type—an analog perhaps to the East's continuing love affair with an imagined West. "She saw him only as the apotheosis of all that she had remembered, the sublimation of her dreams" (181); through "a life of grinding hard work, adventure and escape, had he come to her; against this backdrop he once more loomed young and strong and god-like" (228).

Like *The Brand*, Mourning Dove's *Cogewea, the Half-Blood, Given through Sho-pow-tan with Notes and Biographical Sketch by Lucullus Virgil McWhorter* (1927, reissued in 1981 with an introduction by Dexter Fisher), is set on the Flathead Reservation. Although the exact contributions of McWhorter to this book are unclear, he certainly added much to it, but the plot seems to have been Mourning Dove's. A fan of dime novels, she fashions a plot in which Cogewea, with a white father and an Indian mother, is beset and misled by the smooth-talking white reservation agent, rescued by a faithful brotherly suitor—a reservation cowboy and another "breed" like Cogewea herself—and ultimately enriched by a bequest from her absent father. This story is interestingly decorated with traditional Indian ceremonies and diversions, along with pointed stories about recent events narrated by Cogewea's grandmother—a strategy implying that Native tales are not children's how-to stories but told to influence immediate outcomes. There is also cowboy humor and practical joking with slang dialect dialogue and highly oratorical prose about the injuries done to Indians by white men in general and the BIA in particular. Cogewea has both obvious "white" and obvious "Indian" traits according to the novel's own classification scheme, although she has none of the evil qualities that are exclusive to the novel's whites. "Breeds" are the novel's protagonists; the book's best chapter, in which Cogewea acts out her "breed" nature, involves her participation in two women's horse races, one astride like an Indian and one sidesaddle like a white woman. She wins both.

*   *   *

The four most important woman authors of High Plains fiction are Marah Ellis Ryan, Mary Hallock Foote, B. M. Bower, and Caroline Lockhart. Ryan, whose many novels eventually spanned the West from Canada to Mexico, began her novel-writing career with two Montana books (where, apparently, she had never been at the time). In *Told in the Hills* (1891), set near the Canadian border, Rachel, visiting her sister and brother-in-law, longs to be a useful woman and eventually becomes one after an almost-romance ends in the hero's death. Among characters are an old mountain man, a novelist searching for material, good Indians (Kootenai), bad Indians (Blackfeet), good military men (Major Dreyer, who wants to save human life), and bad military men (Captain Holt, who wants to exterminate the Indians). A "squaw man" (Genesee Jack) becomes the hero, a man with a secret. "A squaw man!—well, what if he is?" Major Dreyer asks: "What difference does it make whether the man's wife has been red, or white, or black, so long as she suited him? There are two classes of squaw men, as there are of other men on the frontier—the renegades and the usual percentage of honest and dishonest citizens. . . . So far as I've noticed, the sneak who abandons his wife and children back in the States, or borrows the wife of someone else to make the trip out here with, is the specimen that is first to curl his lip at the squaw man" (348).

Squaw Elouise (1892) is set near the US border in British Columbia in the Selkirk mountains, and continues Ryan's thematic interests in Native people (here, the Colvilles) and what whites have done to them. The book like many others from the High Plains and Pacific Northwest accepts the fluidity of the Canadian-US border as a fact of life. All the novel's "good" characters are mixed, while the wholly white characters tend to be shallowly vapid or downright evil. *That Girl Montana* (1901) uses a Cinderella motif in its story of runaway Montana Rivers, a girl dressing as a boy for safety's sake. When Montana saves a little Native boy from drowning, she comes to the notice of miner Dan Overton. Working together, they strike a rich lode, from whose profits Montana is sent to New York City and turned into a lady although she eventually returns to Dan and life in the mountains.

Mary Hallock Foote's Idaho stories and novels, like those I've discussed set in Northern California and Colorado, are saturated with a resigned melancholy.

As critics (Foote is one of the more-written-about western women authors) have observed, her work deals repeatedly with refined women who experience the West as an assault on their gentility and judgmental women who assess everybody by what they think of as eastern standards. Those who are in the West as dependents of a father, brother, or husband long for the East but don't dare return, because leaving their men is something one just doesn't do. Often they can't afford to return. Foote's heroes tend to be engineers and mine managers, along with a few cultured businessmen. These men are usually in the West on a temporary job like building a dam or plotting the path of a railroad. Sometimes they are the objects of misplaced crushes by mountain girls, as in "A Cloud on the Mountain" from the collection *In Exile* (1894), where a lovelorn girl saves a camp of engineers from a flood but loses her own life in doing so. Bad women are usually lower-class, and the novelist cold-bloodedly brings them to various violent ends with no regret.

Each novel has its obligatory love story, but Foote is more interested in men's than women's work. Her Idaho novels about irrigation and mining ask how best to accomplish the necessary transformation of the land, pitting money-making and corner-cutting pragmatists against idealistic engineers. Her earliest Idaho novel, *The Chosen Valley* (1892), opposes the American businessman, Norrison, to the Scottish engineer, Dunsmuir. Both want to irrigate a valley by building a dam; but while Dunsmuir wants to build an expensive, impermeable dam of solid masonry, Norrison wants to build quickly and cheaply. His son Philip is more like Dunsmuir than his own father, while Dunsmuir's daughter, Dolly, operating on a separate track, fears that her isolated upbringing has unfitted her to marry into the class to which she rightly belongs back in Scotland.

Ultimately, ousted from his claim by Norrison, Dunsmuir goes to work for him and builds the requisite shoddy dam, which cracks and collapses—killing Dunsmuir—the day before its scheduled opening. The dam is then rebuilt to his specifications; Philip and Dolly marry. The novel ends with a temporizing meditation about ideals and compromises couched in almost biblical language: "The ideal scheme is ever beckoning from the West; but the scheme with an ideal record is yet to find—the scheme that shall breed no murmurers, and see no recreants; that shall avoid envy, hatred, malice, and all uncharitableness; that shall fulfill its promises, and pay its debts, and remember its friends, and keep itself unspotted from the world. Over the graves of the dead, and over the hearts of the living, presses the cruel expansion of our country's material progress: the prophets are confounded, the promise withdrawn, the people imagine a vain thing. Men shall go down, the deed arrives; not unimpeachable, as the first proud word went forth, but mishandled, shorn, and stained with obloquy, and dragged through crushing strains. And those that are with it in its latter days are not those who set out in the beginning. And victory, if it come, shall border hard upon defeat" (313–14).

"The Watchman," an Idaho story from *In Exile*, opposes builders of an irrigation ditch to farmers who fear the diversion of their water. Foote uncharacteristically sets the story among working people—her couple is the watchman Travis and the farmer's daughter Nancy. Says Nancy to Travis, "You don't know the trouble my father has had; how many years he has worked, with nothing but his hands; and now your company comes and claims the water, and turns the river, that belongs to everybody, into their big ditch" (233). Travis responds: "Companies save years of waiting. This one will bring the railroads and the markets, and boom up the price of land. The ditch your father hates so will make him a rich man in five years, if he does nothing but sit still and let it come. As for water, why do you cry before you are hurt? Nobody can steal a river. That is more politicians' talk, to make out they are the settlers' friends. . . . I've got land of my own, but I can see we farmers can't do everything for ourselves; it's cheaper to pay a company to help us. They are just peddlers of water, and we buy it" (233–34).

In 1895 Foote collected four long Idaho stories into *The Cup of Trembling*. Each is set in a different part of the territory and matches its story to landscape: mining in the title story, where an eloping couple hide out in an elegant cabin during the winter months; lava beds in "Maverick," whose protagonist, trying to escape her awful home life, deliberately loses herself in the equally awful landscape; the railroad in "On a Side-Track" where a Quaker maiden and her father are going to join a sister for the father's health; the borders of the Bannock reservation in "The Trumpeter," with its mixed population of natives, civilians, and soldiers, about a doomed romance between a noble Indian maiden and a much less noble army bugler, Henniker. The title story features Foote's stagey speechifying, as a spoiled beauty tells her paramour (mine manager) at length (even though they've been living together for months) just why she originally chose the inappropriate husband she's fleeing (mine owner) and how it comes that such a refined—in this case overrefined—woman is out there in the West. Only crude, rough woman with flexible morals seem appropriate to the place—but in this story, atypically, gentility is nothing to be proud of.

"The Trumpeter" is significant for its display of Foote's social conservatism as she complains about Coxey's army through the bugler Hennicker, who, his term in the army expired, becomes a labor leader. "It need hardly be said that when Henniker raved about the inequalities of class, the helplessness of poverty, the tyranny of wealth, and the curse of labor; and devoted in eloquent phrases the remainder of a benighted existence to the cause of the Poor Man, he was thinking of but one poor man, namely, himself. He classed himself with Labour only that he might feel his superiority to the laboring masses" (247). Coxey's army was "begging and bullying its way eastward, and demanding transportation at the expense of the railroads and of the people at large" (248); the men "were parading their idleness through the land as authority for lawlessness and crime, and . . . our sober regulars had to be called out to quell a Falstaff's army" (251).

Foote's *Coeur d'Alene,* also from 1895, is a novel about the miners' strike of 1892. Some critics say it shows a conflict between good owners and bad union-izers; but in actuality all the owners are absentee Englishmen and all the good characters are managers and others who mediate between these owners and the anonymous workers. Darcie is sent from England on the owners' behalf to spy on Bingham, the dishonest mine manager, whom he exposes. Bingham's daughter, the "adorable" Faith (4), recently arrived and deeply hostile to the crude West, comes to love it; she stays on to marry Darcie. "Therefore Darcie came to America as manager of the Big Horn, and the intrepid young pair went westward on their conquering way, and left age and opposition behind them. . . . Faith celebrates in her letters the wonderful wild flowers of the Coeur d'Alene, the grandeur of its mountains, the softness of its sudden spring" (238). The rhetoric swerves from politics to nature when it takes on the feminine angle of vision.

Foote's 1902 *The Desert and the Sown* is a weak novel about parents and chil-dren, with unusually melodramatic trappings and her usual strong descriptions. *Edith Bonham* (1917) is a romance along the lines of *Jane Eyre,* narrated by the title character. Edith sets off for Idaho to help her dearest friend raise her chil-dren; arriving, she finds that her friend has died, but loyally stays to raise the children since the father is usually away at his mines. When he proposes to her, she is horrified and returns East with the children for five years of needless mis-ery. On her first journey Edith sees a county "vast and broken, not by man with dynamite and steam-shovels, but by the agency of rivers and ancient glaciers and lava-flows. Through rents in the mountains that came down to the high plain we were crossing, you saw bluer mountains, snow-capped, flat against the sky. . . . But the wind! . . . It was this earth-stillness, manifest in subtle unfamiliar sounds, that gave me my first thrill—the 'feeling' of the West. . . . The voice of it is that desert wind, soft, insistent, secret, that is known only in the heart of a great continent" (77–78).

Five years later, the West is transformed. Boise, for example, is now "forward-looking, a brilliant little center for a country waking up—you would hear of enterprises now that sound like fairy-tales. They were conceived and worked out by men of unusual parts at various times separated by long intervals of harrowing patience. . . . The town has kept on with its fight for homes in the desert, and all manner of lesser fights have been lost and won in between the physical fight with nature—some of them very great little victories on questions of principle that strike hands with good citizenship the country over and the credit of the whole nation" (328).

The premiere High Plains novelist is B. M. Bower, whose enormous output of popular fiction began with Montana, where she grew up and married a rancher.

All her books that I read for this project—some two dozen out of the 40 she'd published by 1927, many of them republished so often that to assign a correct date to their publication constitutes a true bibliographical puzzle—are comedies in the formal sense of the term. They have generally upbeat assessments of human nature, along with happy endings in which opposing forces are reconciled. Their view of the West is fundamentally democratic. They choose trickery over violence, as time after time her good-hearted cowboys find ways to outwit the opposition. She's sometimes said to have published under a penname, but her maiden name was Bertha Muzzie and her first husband—eventually she had three—was named Bower; hence, B. M. Bower. But to publish under initials was of course to allow readers to suppose she was a man, and in the early years of her career she much preferred male to female characters. Still, her dislike of violence is a distinctly feminine trait.

Bower's pre-1920 novels involve such local High Plains features as drought, fire, homesteading, cattle, sheep, alcoholism, cowboys, ranch wives, schoolteachers, male camaraderie, rustlers, and the ambiguities of "progress" as the range is fenced and the cowboy becomes obsolescent. She claimed, with some justice, to know real cowboys better than other writers of cowboy fiction. As one of her foremen says to a dude writer in *The Lure of the Dim Trails:* "Well, there's a lot in this country that ain't ever been wrote about, I guess; at least if it was I never read it, and I read considerable. But the trouble is, them that know ain't in the writing business, and them that write don't know. The way I've figured it, they set back East somewhere and write it like they think maybe it is; and it's a hell of a job they make of it" (41–42).

Bower's best-known books in her day were about a group of good-natured and well-behaved young cowboys from the Flying U ranch who call themselves the Happy Family. The device of the Happy Family allowed her to add or subtract characters from time to time while continuing their group adventures across several novels. Hired hands, they rebut the stereotype of independent cowboy loner; they are intensely loyal to their employer J. G. Whitmore, "the Old Man." In *The Lonesome Trail and other stories* (1904) mostly about the Family member nicknamed Weary (Will Davidson), Weary's romance with a schoolteacher is overshadowed by his love for his horse Glory (this may have been a dig at *The Virginian's* schoolteacher-cowboy amour*). The story of meeting, losing, and getting the girl is also complicated by the appearance of an earlier love, red-headed Miss Forsythe from Iowa. When Weary decamps to Portland to escape female finagling, the rain depresses his spirits; he imagines the plains, "scarred and broken with sharp-nosed hills and deep, water-worn coulees gleaming barren and yellow in the sun. The blue, blue sky was bending down to meet the hills, with feathery, white clouds trailing lazily across. His cheeks felt the cool winds which flapped his hat-brim and tingled his blood. His knees pressed the throb and life, the splendid, working muscles of a galloping horse. . . . Now he was racing over the springy sod which sent a sweet, grassy smell up to meet him. Wild range cattle lumbered out of his way, ran a few paces and stopped to gaze after him with big, curious eyes. . . . The rope corral was filled with circling horses half hidden by the veil of dust thrown upward by their restless, trampling hoods. Now he was in the midst of them, a coil of rope in his left hand; his right swung the loop circling over his head. And the choking dust was in his eyes and throat, and in his nostrils the rank odor of many horses" (94). Weary goes back—to the Flying U, not to the schoolteacher.

Bower's *Chip of the Flying U* (1904), the most popular of the series, centers on the romance between Chip the cowboy (a sensitive young man with artistic talent) and the Old Man's younger sister, Della Whitmore, a lady doctor who tends to horses and cowboys alike. The gender bending here is obvious, and to this are added misunderstandings based on supposed class difference between cowboy and lady; and beyond this, one Dr. Cecil Grantham, coming to visit the lady doc, is imagined by Chip ahead of time to be a competing suitor but turns out to be a woman. In the end Chip, marrying the lady doc, leaves the bunk house and makes room for a new entrant.

After a gap of ten years in which she wrote other westerns (she wrote westerns only) Bower returned to the Happy Family with *Flying U Ranch* (1914), about the transformation of the cattle industry from range to ranch. In this novel the old man is hospitalized in Chicago after an automobile accident, so Chip and Little Doc leave the Happy Family—now augmented by Native Son, a part-Spanish Californian—to run the ranch. The story, involving the sale of a neighboring ranch to sheepmen, takes up the problems of sheep vs. cattle on the partly open and partly closed range, and the plot question is how the Happy Family will get rid of the sheep and the new owners without violence. "They were cattlemen to the marrow in their bones, and they gloried in their prejudice against the woolly despoilers of the range. . . . The Flying U range had been kept in the main inviolate from the little, gray vandals, which ate the grass clean to the sod, and trampled with their sharp-pointed hoofs the very roots into lifelessness; which polluted the water-holes and creeks until cattle and horses went thirsty rather than drink; which, in that land of scant rainfall, devastated the range where they fed so that a long-established prairie-dog town was not more barren. What wonder if the men who owned cattle, and those who tended them, hated sheep? So does the farmer dread an invasion of grasshoppers" (77–78).

In *The Flying U's Last Stand* (1915) the Happy Family copes with homesteaders, whose advent on the open range really does signal the end of the Old West. The villain is a woman real estate agent, Florence Hallstead, who is brokering parcels of arid land to naive would-be farmers. Misreading the honest face of Andy, the Happy Family's prize liar, she tries to recruit him for her nefarious work by recounting her scheme. When Andy asks her what line of talk she gives to possible clients she says she tells them what they want to hear whether about potatoes or dairies. To stop her, every Flying U employee takes out a homestead claim on the best land, to all appearances without collusion and certainly without the Old Man's knowledge. Hallstead schemes to counteract their plotting, but her plan backfires badly when a prairie fire she has paid someone to start burns out the homesteaders but not the more astute cowboys who have built fire ditches around their properties. An attractive schoolteacher-homesteader finds the lost son of Chip and the Lady Doc, thereby resolving the apparent conflict between ranch and homestead.

Among non–Flying U books is *The Range Dwellers* (1906), a first-person narration by a young, wealthy San Franciscan ne'er-do-well sent to his father's ranch to be reformed. In another book of 1906, *Her Prairie Knight,* a woman tenderfoot succumbs to the witchery of the West and rejects the proposal of a British lord. In 1907 Bower published *The Lure of the Dim Trails,* a tenderfoot novel about a Montana-born writer raised in the city and returning to the range to brush up on the local color that his editors want. Two weeks suffice to change him: "In his story of the West—the one that had failed to be convincing—he had in his ignorance described a stampede, and it had not been in the least like this one. He blushed at the memory, and wondered if he should ever again feel qualified to write of these things" (71). "He had come to stay a month, and he had stayed five. He could ride and rope like an old-timer, and he was well qualified to put up a stiff gun-fight had the necessity ever arisen—which it had not. . . . By all these signs and tokens he had learned his West, and should have taken himself back to civilization when came the frost. He had come to get into touch with his chosen field of fiction, that he might write as one knowing whereof he spoke. So far as he had gone, he was in touch with it; he was steeped to the eyes in local color—and there was the rub. The lure of it was strong upon him, and he might not loosen its hold. He was the son of his father; he had found himself, and knew that, like him, he loved best to travel the dim trails" (143).

Also in 1907 (two or three novels a year for her is typical) Bower published *Rowdy of the Cross L* which begins when Rowdy, a cowboy looking for work, gets lost in a snowstorm along with the new schoolteacher, Miss Conroy. They part, he gets a job, and in the cowboy assortment is one named Pink—an absurdly effeminate name for an absurdly effeminate man with no interest in women who turns out, however, to be both tough and a splendid shot. This is as far as Bower went with sexual dissidence among cowboys—love between men for her is the deeply romantic yet nonsexual friendship Axel Nissen has written about in *Manly Love.* Pink later joins the Happy Family, and the love interest promised in Miss Conroy fades away. Bower's 1909 *The Long Shadow* is about the end of the open range and the cowboys who disappear along with it. The protagonists are the cowboy Billy and the would-be ranch owner Mr. Dill from Michigan who is bamboozled into buying a ranch at the worst possible time. Dill hires Billy as his foreman, everything goes wrong with both love and ranching, but in the end Dill, seeing the future, sells the ranch, starts a general store, connects with railroad, and gives Billy work on a horse ranch.

Bower's 1912 *Good Indian* introduces Native Americans via a quarter-blood protagonist brought up as a son in a white family. He loses one white girl (a flirtatious visitor who is really afraid of him) but gets a much better one, the telegraph operator Miss Georgie Howard. Two novels from 1913 (*The Lonesome Land*) and 1914 (*The Uphill Climb*) are about alcoholism. In *The Lonesome Land* a prim and cultivated eastern woman marries a man who turns out to be an alcoholic cattle-rustler. The novel painfully portrays female suffering even as it chronicles the protagonist's gradual toughening up. At the novel's end the husband, trying to escape the sheriff, accidentally drowns; the heroine is going back East, funded by the friendly woman hotel keeper, but will probably return to take up with a better specimen of western manhood than her husband. In *Rim O' the World* (1919) Bower moved her scene to Idaho, a territory not yet reached by progress, for a nastier and talkier novel than her norm, in which owners of two adjoining ranches try variously to destroy each other. In this presentation the remote region denoted by the title has been settled by fugitives trying to be lawful ranchers who are always tempted to go back to their old ways.

The Quirt (1920), also set in Idaho, is a tenderfoot story with a twist. It is one of several novels in which Bower, having left Montana for southern California and script-writing, plays with the disjunction and overlap between the movie West and the real West. The protagonist, Lorraine, a film actress, goes to Idaho to live with her father and interprets everything through her cinematic knowledge. The local cowboys lack "the dash and the picturesque costuming of the West she knew. They were mostly commonplace young men, jogging past the house on horseback, or loitering down by the corrals. They had offered absolutely no interest or 'color' to the place" (88)—and here Bower makes a statement about the western's bad faith glorification of violence: "In her fictitious West Lorraine had long since come to look upon violence as a synonym for picturesqueness; murder and mystery were inevitably an accompaniment of chaps and spurs. But when a man she had cooked breakfast for, had talked with just a few hours ago, lay dead in the bunk-house, she forgot that it was merely an expected incident of Western life. She lay in her bed shaking with nervous dread, and the shrill rasping of the crickets and tree-toads was unendurable" (200). In *Cow-Country* (1921) Idaho serves again as the refuge of criminals whose activities are more and more firmly relegated to the past.

*   *   *

Four of the six novels Caroline Lockhart published before 1928, more town than range novels, are set in the High Plains (the other two were southwestern). Her major theme is western small-town snobbery. Following the success of her southwestern novel *Me—Smith* (1911), Lockhart set her second novel, *The Lady Doc* (1912), in a town much like Cody, Wyoming, where she had settled. Three plots converge in the town of Crowheart: one about a manipulative swindler, one about a vicious lady doctor, and one about foundling Essie Tisdale who works as a waitress and becomes the object of the lady doc's special malice when she rejects what was most likely a lesbian approach—malice and justified paranoia being two characteristics of a Lockhart fiction. All ends well when Essie's long-lost uncle arrives to declare her a lady and to help pay her way to becoming one.

Lockhart's next High Plains novel, *The Man from the Bitter Roots* (1915), is an Idaho mining story that begins with a tremendous snow storm and bitter cold, setting the scene for landscape and climate. In *The Fighting Shepherdess* (1919), Lockhart's most popular novel, Kate Prentice, brought up by her slatternly mother who runs a roadhouse, flees from Joe Mullendore, a "breed" with (as it turns out) some negro blood as well, who propositions her. She is taken in by, and made a partner of, the shepherd "Mormon Joe," whose mysterious murder deprives her of her last support. The town of Prouty snubs her, the banker tries to cheat her, and she is left with only her sheep and an occasional helpful sheep-hand. Driven by hate, energy, and inner strength, Kate nevertheless succeeds, thanks to the market opened by "Troubles in Europe" and the quality of her sheep. The town is beginning to accept her, but what really happens is that she discovers her long-lost father on a trip to Omaha and he turns out (but of course!) to be a millionaire. Now, given the chance to ruin the town (her father will or won't buy into it and thereby save it), she declines to do harm and therefore rises above her own weakness. In the background are banking, shepherding, duding. But also in the background is a racism or cultural chauvinism attributing Mullendore's "savagery" to his being a "breed," and explaining his superstitious nature through his quotient of negro blood. The book is also extreme in its depiction of female meanness. The women are all nasty to Kate, and the author is nastier still about these women.

Finally, *The Dude Wrangler* (1921) is a self-destructing slapstick novel aiming indiscriminately at eastern snobs, western bullies, and conventions of the generic western. Opening in a posh Atlantic seaside resort peopled by caricatures, it follows the Dude—Wallie Macpherson, an effete Easterner dependent on his wealthy aunt—as he goes to Wyoming and tries first to homestead and then, after a short interval during which he becomes an outstanding rider and shooter, to run a dude ranch. The book is powered by the desire to pillory Easterners and rich people, elevating the Westerner strictly in his character as one who rejects the East. By 1921, Lockhart recognizes, the dude ranch is installed as a fantasy reenactment of an Old West that never existed anyway, and the unreality of it all gives her satiric sense free rein. From the perspective of the westerner, the dude ranch is nothing more than a source of income; as Wallie's foreman and best friend (Pinkey, no doubt a name appropriated from Bower, as is Lockhart's name for the group of Easterners—the Happy Family) says: "If we could winter—say—ten head of dudes at $150 a month for seven months, that would be $10,500"; "Look at the different ways we got to git their money. Two bits apiece for salt water baths and eight baths a day. . . . Then $10,000 apiece every time they go to town in the stage-coach" (177); "We shore got a good dudin' outfit! But it's nothin' to what we *will* have—watch our smoke! The day'll come when we'll see this country, as you might say, lousy with dudes! So far as the eye kin reach—dudes! Nothin' but dudes!" (179).

Southern California and Nevada

Helen Hunt Jackson's *Ramona* (1884) was more than a historical romance about southern California's early triracial culture; it was a historical event itself, with immense implications for the literature of that region. Realizing that her *Century of Dishonor* (1881) had failed to shame the nation into making amends for its history of treaty-breaking with Native tribes, she wrote the novel to create sympathy for the displaced California Indians. The settled farming life of this population made them look safer and more civilized than the warrior cultures of the plains; in fact Jackson had little respect for Native cultures that deviated from what she understood as an agricultural, Christian norm. Ramona herself is a devout Catholic.

In *Glimpses of Three Coasts* (1886), a posthumous collection of previously published travel essays, she said bluntly that most San Diego Indians "are miserable, worthless beggars, drunkards of course, and worse. Even for its own sake, it would seem that the town would devise some scheme of help and redemption for such outcasts. . . . It must be done speedily if at all, for there is only a small remnant left to be saved" (91). That she was assembling this collection before her death suggests that, post-*Ramona*, her views had not changed. *A Century of Dishonor* saw no future for Natives other than becoming "civilized," which is also what she supposes the Indians themselves wanted. "Had the provisions of these first treaties been fairly and promptly carried out, there would have been living to-day among the citizens of Minnesota thousands of Sioux families, good and prosperous farmers and mechanics, whose civilization would have dated back to the treaty of Prairie du Chein" (143).

But whatever her intentions, *Ramona* had no impact on Native cultures. *Uncle Tom's Cabin*, whose aims she hoped to achieve for a different population group, seems truly to have inspired abolitionist sentiment; but Hispanics not Indians attracted *Ramona's* readers, in particular the supposedly pure Castilian type with little relevance to the ethnic realities of the Hispanic peoples of the US Southwest. The glamorous hacienda life she portrayed, taken as factual, started a tourist vogue for visiting the "real" sites where the imaginary heroine had lived, and opened the door to California histories that were frank inventions.

As late as *Ramona's Homeland* (1914), Margaret V. Allen, President of the San Diego Pioneer Society, praised *Ramona* (which she called the greatest book by an American woman) for its San Diego authenticity. Hacienda culture as channeled through books about southern California reanimated the fantasy of English lords on their great estates rescuing underappreciated heroines, with an exotic twist in the darkly handsome hero. The sadness of Allesandro's death is greatly mitigated by Ramona's second marriage to the ever-faithful Castilian Felipe, who takes her to a Mexico that, unlike southern California itself, resists the tide of Gringo modernization.

Following quickly after *Ramona,* and no doubt hoping to catch some of the spillover interest in southern California, *The Squatter and the Don* by Maria Amparo Ruiz de Burton (1885), is also set in and around San Diego. Beginning with the first reissue of this novel in 1997, with introduction and notes by Rosaura Sanchez and Beatrice Pita, the novel's Castilian class-consciousness has been downplayed by critics appreciating its defense of the dons accompanied by its attack on Anglo squatters and the cultural invasion they represent. But Carrie Bramen has pointed out the author's conservatism, and Vincent Perez has written about the book's attack on northern business interests (i.e., San Francisco railroads) from a perspective identifying hacienda culture not with the exploited Chicano but with the plantation owners of the Old South. Like Perez, I see the book as much more about the failure of the Texas Pacific Railroad's attempt to get a line across the South to San Diego in 1881 than about mistreated Hispanics.

In some ways, also, Ruiz de Burton's book accomplishes the *Ramona*-inspired task of turning attention from Native Americans toward a particular kind of imaginary Hispanic. In fact, *The Squatter and the Don* has little to say about Indians and poor Mexicans—until, that is, the novel's protagonist, Don Mariano Alamar, becomes a poor man. The dons are pure Castilian, and Indians are wild people civilized by the hacienda rather than the mission. Natives employed on the ranchos "began to be less wild. Then in times of Indian outbreaks, the landowners with their servants would turn out . . . to assist in the defense of the missions and the sparsely settled country threatened by the savages. Thus, you see, that it was not a foolish extravagance, but a judicious policy which induced the viceroys and Spanish governors to begin the system of giving large land grants" (163). Women don't interest her; she includes them in her fiction only for the obligatory love story.

The protagonist, who knows that the squatter invasion dooms his days as a Don but hopes to be on history's winning side, invests in a railroad not only for himself but for his people and his city. Railroads and squatters are part of the same phenomenon, because the Anglos squatting on Alamar's rancho have put their money into town lots, expecting that San Diego will soon have "a railroad direct to the Eastern States" so that "land will increase in value immediately" (57). Which is to say, squatters are speculating in real estate; they farm and raise cattle on Alamar's land to pass the time until they can make a bundle selling their urban lots. They farm without fences, destroy Alamar's cattle encroaching on their crops, and pay no taxes because they don't own the land. As the Don puts it, laws to protect agriculture mean "to drive to the wall all owners of cattle ranchos" (65). Alamar says, "California was expected to be filled with a population of farmers, of industrious settlers who would have votes and would want their one hundred and sixty acres each of the best land to be had. As our legislators thought that we, the Spano-American natives, had the best lands, and but few votes, there was nothing else to be done but to despoil us, to take our lands and give them to the coming population" (162).

The question isn't whether there'll be a railroad to San Diego—there will be—but which company will get government support and which route, accordingly, the railroad will follow (and who will profit thereby). The Don and his creator endorse the Texas Pacific, as should "every honest man in the United States, for it is the thing that will help the exhausted South to get back its strength and vitality. . . . Don't we see here in our little town of San Diego how everything is depending on the success of this road? Look at all the business of the town, all the farming of this county, all the industries of southern California—everything is at a standstill, waiting for Congress to aid the Texas Pacific. Well, the poor South is in pretty much the same fix that we are" (274). The railroad Alamar wants is not a creature of northern monopoly capitalism, but one to cement southern California to the South. The failure of the railroad enterprise, not the spoliation of Alamar property, drives the family into bankruptcy.

A different sort of Ramona-influenced book is self-trained anthropologist Constance Goddard Du Bois' pro-Indian novel—A Soul in Bronze. First serialized in Charles Lummis's Out West magazine in 1898, and separately issued in 1900, the book was dedicated to Helen Hunt Jackson. It argued, like Jackson, that the settled mission Indians of southern California deserved respect and admiration. Far more than Alessandro, an untutored noble savage well suited to the piously childlike Ramona, this Native hero embodies the highest qualities of civilization. The complicated plot of A Soul in Bronze features the ladylike Dorothea Fairfax arriving in southern California to live with a widowed aunt who teaches at the Indian school. Dorothea's horror of Indians quickly changes to admiration, and then something close to love, on account of Antonio Lachusa, a college-educated Cahuilla out of place on the Reservation but with no future in the white world. Dorothea is attracted to Antonio: "I could love such a man. . . . In spite of myself, I can not feel when he is near me that he is an outcast simply of another race. I can not shut my eyes to the beauty of his nature, the finest, most unselfish, nature I have ever known. . . . I shall carefully obey the conventions which men have made, do not be uneasy about that. . . . But in my heart I despise and defy these narrow rules" (173).

She says this to Harry Burke, a lawyer in love with Dorothea but opposing her in a court case on behalf of a mine owner laying claim to reservation land. Ultimately Antonio takes the blame for a murder actually committed (unbeknownst to Dorothea) by her criminal father. His willingness to go to jail for life shows his innate nobility and also takes him out of contention as a lover. Having lost the case, Burke contributes to regional development by establishing a vineyard while Dorothea, enriched by a huge inheritance, finances a gold mine on the reservation that employs Native workers. These two represent a future for southern California from which the possibility of Indian-White romance has been raised and eradicated.

*   *   *

The many newcomers to southern California, including a large number of retirees and invalids there for the climate, along with would-be farmers and colonizing groups, gave rise to monitory guidebooks and dreamy historical fictions. Yda Addis Storke's massive *Memorial and Biographical History of the Counties of Santa Barbara, San Luis Obispo, and Ventura, California* (1881) is a statistic-heavy and history-laden boomer book, insisting that prior settlement has made the regions safe for business investment. Mary Cone, a Boston spiritualist, published *Two Years in California* (1876) for Easterners thinking about going to southern California after the Panic of 1873. She rejected mining; said there were already too many "clerks, book-keepers, teachers, civil engineers and professional men generally" (166); and affirmed the mystique of the yeoman by calling the place "truly a paradise for farmers" (176)—who, she said, would be protected from loneliness and hardship if they emigrated with an organized colony. Canada immigrant Caroline Churchill's *Over the Purple Hills* (1877) warns about dishonest land agents, says year-round camping (recommended for invalids by some tourist companies) is actually disastrous for health and comfort because of winter rain and fog, and warns that railroads control every aspect of southern California life. Behind this comment are facts that it would take another quarter century for Frank Norris to nail in *The Octopus*—railroads not the government owned much of the desirable land, setting passenger and freight fares as high as the traffic would bear. Even more than other regions, it seemed, southern California was an artifact of railroads.

Ohioan Emma H. Adams's *To and Fro in Southern California, with Sketches in Arizona and New Mexico* (1887, expanded to include the Pacific Northwest in 1888) warns that too many incurably ill are already wintering in rainy Los Angeles; she says that misinformed invalids often bring clothing too light for the weather, go without knowing anybody, and often die alone. Her message for invalids is: don't go; her message for others is to join colony associations dedicated to town formation not farming.

Massachusetts-born Kate Sanborn's *A Truthful Woman in Southern California* (1893*)* concurs. "With snow-covered mountains on one side and the ocean with its heavy fogs on the other, and the tedious rain pouring down with gloomy persistence, and consumptives coughing violently, and physicians hurrying in to attend to a sudden hemorrhage or heart-failure, the scene is not wholly gay and inspiriting" (24). Like many post-*Ramona* books, Sanborn's says Jackson's Indians were romantic inventions. She also thinks Jackson overdid the hacienda era; she herself contrasts the "Hispano-American era of adobe, stage-coaches, and mule teams" to the "purely American" era as a vast improvement. She likes Los Angeles, with its "brick, stone, vestibule trains, and all the wonders of electricity" because it is equal to "the best environs of Eastern cities" (58). Pennsylvanian Mary Wills's *A Winter in California* (1899), written after the 1893 panic punctured the real estate bubble in southern California, says real estate was as much a swindle as farming, exhibiting "the old story of covetousness, its tardy recognition and subsequent punishment, for the land did not become worth its weight in gold as they formerly imagined it would, but is left upon their hands, with taxes still accumulating, still untilled" (25).

But people kept coming. Sara White Isaman's *Tourist Tales of California* (1907), *Sophisticating Uncle Hiram* (1912), and *Uncle Hiram in California* (1917), written in the form of vernacular letters, satirize the adventures of rustic Uncle Hiram from Nebraska, as he and Aunt Phebe visit, look around, and eventually settle in San Diego. Uncle Hiram says—and we are meant to believe him—that southern California is populated by retirees and run by women. Along the same lines, Mina Dean Halsey contributed *When East Comes West* (1909), a minimal revision of a book pseudonymously published the previous year as *A Tenderfoot in Southern California,* with letters from old Uncle Eben to Bill back on the Ohio farm, who is advised to rescue his wife from the hardships of farm life by bringing her to southern California. Ruth Kedzie Wood's *The Tourist's California* (1914) criticized *Ramona* but accepted its view of the Hispano-Indian past: "Standing before the sun-tinted walls raised by Indians' hands, we picture scenes of arrival at Mission doors. We see the gleam of wet flanks, the flash of inlaid bridle, and dark slim hands lifted to the lips in halloo and greeting; we hear the answer of swarthy helpers and hurrying monks, the creak of doors opening into cool bare rooms, the scurrying of fowls, the hum of the kitchen, and, if it be night, the far-off strum of Spanish strings to the drone of neophytes about the *patio* fire" (35).

Histories of southern California, with an alternative California history to one centered on the Gold Rush and San Francisco, started their narratives with the romanticized Hispanic mission and hacienda past that *Ramona* had put into circulation. A few anthropologists examined the California Indians, but always from the standpoint of their aptness for white civilization. In 1901 Constance Goddard Du Bois' pamphlet, *The Condition of the Mission Indians of Southern California,* argued that few Indians are as little known as this group, few had been so neglected, "and yet there is in no other case better material for producing all the fruits of civilization by building up out of their past, where already a good foundation had been laid" (3). The padres' success "shows what wise statesmanship could devise and devoted Christian purpose accomplish with no previous preparation in an incredibly short space of time toward building up an Indian civilization 'as beautiful as it was transient.' Evil days began for the Indians when the rule of Spain was exchanged for that of Mexico" (4).

Bad as Mexico was, Anglos were worse: "crowding settlers, crazy with greed of gold and greed of land, came pushing in"; to them Indians "were no more than herds of wild deer, to be driven back" (4). She accepts the view that the Indian is "driven to despair, since he is willing and eager to work" (6); in an argument showing her preference for the settled tribes she says that if the California Natives "were bloodthirsty savages" they'd be coddled, "but little is being done for these peaceful wards of the nation, who are every way more deserving than the savage tribes who have received so much of the nation's bounty" (11).

Du Bois followed this pamphlet, an outgrowth of the so-called "Friends of the Indian" enterprise located in southern California, with her *Religion of the Luiseño Indians of Southern California* (1908), a footnoted report on her own field work. Always approaching her topic from the perspective of the superior race to which she belongs, and always accepting the ethnological focus on Native religion, she says that "acquaintance with Luiseño mythology reveals a loftiness of conception, a power of definition and of abstract thought, which must give these people claim to a place among the dominant minds of the primitive race" (75). She defines primitivism as belief in witchcraft, magic, and shamanistic medicine—the same line taken by Knapp in her Alaskan book about the Thlinkets (see Chapter 3), and echoed in Lucile Hooper's *The Cahuilla Indians* (1920), the only book by this student of Alfred Kroeber's.

Between 1903 and 1925 Harrie Rebecca Piper Smith Forbes (Mrs. A. S. C. Forbes), who with her husband established the California Bell Company and designed the mission bell replica that decorated (and still decorates) the Camino Real, self-published eleven editions of *California Missions and Landmarks, and How to Get There.* Celebrating the padres, she wants to "draw the wavering sentiment of this day of golden lust to an appreciation of the work accomplished by a band of noble pioneers, and at the same time to mark the historic road of California in such a manner that a stranger need but follow the Bells of El Camino Real and find the way from San Diego to San Francisco over the best and most direct route" (267). Forbes's narrative stops at statehood. It says the padres treated the Indians well and kept them happy; it attributes the secularization of the missions to Mexican greed. That the padres were Spanish not Mexican, that California dons were all pure Castilian, are truisms of this literature as she encountered and then elaborated on it. Forbes augmented her crusade to give urbanizing southern California a glamorous past with a book of romantic stories, *Mission Tales in the Days of the Dons* (1909), showing the padres as especially concerned for their women wards both Indian and Mexican.

Helen Elliott Bandini's 1908 textbook began California history long before the Gold Rush in the southern part of the state. She praised climate and scenery, endorsed mission restoration, defended the padres, and grieved over the post-secularization decline of Native people. (That the population declined drastically under mission conditions is something none of these books acknowledge.) Bandini, daughter of a founder of the Indiana Colony that settled Pasadena, had married into a Californio family and thus had southern California history from both sides in her background. She describes the dons' lives as idyllic: "In this land of balmy airs, soft skies, and gentle seas there lived, in the old days, a people who were indifferent to money, who carried their religion into their daily pleasures and sorrows, were brotherly toward one another, contented, beautiful, joyous" (106). "Each rancho was miles in extent, its cattle and horses numbered by thousands. . . . In the better class of homes several feet of the space in the courtyard next the wall were covered with tile roofing, forming a shaded veranda, where the family were accustomed to spend the leisure hours. Here they received visitors, the men smoked their cigaritos, and the children made merry. In the long summer evenings sweet strains of Spanish music from violin and guitar filled the air, and the hard earthen floor of the courtyard resounded to the tap-tap of high-heeled slippers, the swish of silken skirts, and the jingle of silver spurs, as the young people took part in the graceful Spanish dances" (109).

Bandini says it was easy for Easterners to dispossess the Californio, who, "seldom a man of business after the standard of the Eastern states, was forced into the distressing necessity of fighting for what was his own, in courts, the law and language of which he did not understand. . . . The way in which unprincipled men got the better of the rancheros would fill a volume" (183). But she tacks on a conventional pioneer ending: "People in the East had begun to find out that southern California had a mild, healthful climate and that, though the sands of her rivers and rocks of her mountains were not of gold, still her oranges, by aid of irrigation, could be turned into a golden harvest, and that all her soil needed was water in order to yield most bountiful crops. . . . Many never gained wealth, while some lost lands and savings; but it was these earnest, intelligent men and women who developed the rich valleys of the south land and to whom we are indebted for the bloom and beauty found there to-day" (213–14).

Two outlier histories are Katherine Tingley's *Lomaland* (1908), a well-illustrated tourist book giving a history of the American Center of Theosophy, established at Point Loma in 1900 to attract Theosophists to southern California, and Delilah Beasley's *Negro Trail Blazers of California* (1919—see Chapter 4), which argues that San Francisco hostility to black workers made southern California, especially Los Angeles, the best place for black people to live because "there is open shop, and a chance to make a living" (149). Beasley makes the only mention in this literature of the all-black southern California town of Allensworth.

* * *

Mary Austin built her reputation on desert essays. The earliest collection, based on her life around Bishop and Lone Pine, was *The Land of Little Rain* (1903), containing fourteen sketches. This book and the collection *Lost Borders,* reissued together as *Stories from the Country of Lost Borders* in an edition by Marjorie Pryse in 1987, have been the subject of most critical work on Austin. This focus doesn't encompass the whole of what Austin did with the West, nor is it meant to. Aside from its stylistic skill, Austin's successful replacement of the populous and urbanizing southern California coast with the desert as a way to make the place more "western" is central to regional perceptions. Austin probably knew the translation of Pierre Loti's *The Desert* (1895), and certainly knew art historian John D. Van Dyke's *The Desert* (1901), both of which circulated widely around the turn of the century. But she is much more interested in desert detail than these two writers, and as much interested in human life in the desert as in its setting. Although her depictions of desert life—her own included—are highly imaginative (this is "creative nonfiction" taken to the utmost), her sense of necessary interaction between people and place has endeared her to environmentalists. She writes, "Not the law, but the land sets the limit" (9); "The land will not be lived in except in its own fashion" (57).

The Land of Little Rain opens with sketches that begin close to the ground, describing the almost invisible signs of desert flora and animals. Then they move out and around, uncovering human networks, hidden lives (to Anglos) of Indians, Mexicans, shepherds, failed prospectors. The stereotypical Mexicans in a town Austin calls Las Uvas "keep up all the good customs brought out of Old Mexico or bred in a lotus-eating land; drink and are merry and look out for something to eat afterward; have children, nine or ten to a family, have cockfights, keep the siesta, smoke cigarettes and wait for the sun to go down. And always they dance" (144).

Austin identifies herself with Native people, claiming in "Shoshone Land" that Winnenap—a displaced Shoshone medicine man in Paiute country—taught her secret rituals and myths, claiming in "The Basket Maker" that old, blind Seyavi satisfied "The keen hunger I had for bits of lore and the 'fool talk' of her people" (96). Critics and scholars have wondered, respectfully, how these interchanges happened, since Austin spoke no Native language nor did the Natives she communed with speak hers. This was a problem for reviewers in her own day, and her later books rationalized the claim by insisting on her intuitive (and therefore authentic) connection with non-Anglos through a shared feeling for the land. In *The American Rhythm* of 1923, for example, she writes "Better than I knew any Indian, I knew the land they lived in. This I held to be a prime requisite for understanding originals of whatever description. It was only by such familiarity with the condition under which a land permits itself to be lived with that I was able to overcome the difficulty of language" (38–39). While insisting that her own work was trustworthy, she dismissed popular western writing by men as overblown, inaccurate, and too fond of violence. In "Jimville" she says, "Bret Harte would have given you a tale. You see in me a mere recorder, for I know what is best for you" (68); western writers "smack the savor of lawlessness too much upon their tongues" (71).

The Basket Woman: A Book of Fanciful Tales for Children (1904, later republished as *Indian Tales for Children* and reissued in 1999 with a foreword by Mark Schlenz), collects fourteen stories centered on Alan, a child who lives with his homesteading family. At first he is dismayed by the dirt and indolence of an Indian camp and frightened of the people. But in his dreams Seyavi (not the same character as in *Land of Little Rain,* because this one does the laundry for Alan's family) instructs, protects, and even rescues him. Because she comes in dreams, there's no language problem. Austin's earliest southern California novel is *Isidro* (1905), a historical adventure-romance whose cross-dressing foundling heroine, Jacinta, has been raised by a shepherd. There are murders, captures, false accusations, a forest fire, Mission Indians and renegade Indians, faithful Mexicans, with the Carmel mission in its heyday at the center. When romance beckons, Jacinta becomes a woman by virtue of "a man's need of womanliness to love"; once in proper clothes, her beauty "grew apace like a flower" (419)—and she turns out to be the daughter of a Monterey naval officer.

In her collection *The Flock* (1906) Austin rewrites the silent Basque shepherds of *Land of Little Rain*—"superstitious, fearful, given to seeing visions, and almost without speech" (89)—as wonderful storytellers: "Once you get speech with them, of all outdoor folk the minders of flocks are the most fruitful talkers; better at it than cowboys, next best after forest rangers. . . . They have in full what we oftenest barely brush wings with, elemental human experiences" (61). The book's opening chapter, "The Coming of the Flocks" exhibits Austin's splendid style, intimates how unusual it is to write finely about sheep, and establishes her credentials: "By two years of homesteading on the borders of Tejon, by fifteen besides the Long Trail where it spindles out through Inyo, by all the errands of necessity and desire that made me to know its moods and the calendars of its shrubs and skies, by the chances of Sierra holidays where there were always bells jangling behind us in the pines or flocks blethering before us in the meadows, by the riot of shearings, by the faint winy smell in the streets of certain of the towns of the San Joaquin that apprises of the yearly inturning of the wandering shepherds, I grew aware of all that you read here and of much beside" (12).

The final essay, "The Shade of the Arrows," invokes the Paiute proverb that "no man should go far in the desert who cannot sleep in the shade of his arrows" to identify the desert as the source of true religion. This is the context for Austin's explanation, in *The Man Jesus* (1915) that Christianity came about because Christ was a man of the desert. "It is impossible not to conclude that to the circumstances of great light and space in which he received it, quite as much as to the compulsory co-operations and interdependence of poverty from which he came, we owe the spacious social character of the teaching of Jesus" (87–88).

Austin's 1909 *Lost Borders* presents its fourteen short desert tales (fourteen seems to have been her favorite number for collections) as stories gathered from informants. They tend to be about women who love men passionately and men who love the desert in the same way—a twist on the truism that women love men and men love abstractions. "It is men who go mostly into the desert, who love it past all reasonableness, slack their ambitions, cast off old usages, neglect their families because of the pulse and beat of a life laid bare to its thews and sinews" (159). Again she alleges that standard western writing is fanciful and uninformed: "There was a man once who skidded through Lost Borders in an automobile with a balloon silk tent and a folding tin bath-tub, who wrote some cheerful tales about that country, mostly untrue, about rattlesnakes coiling under men's blankets at night, to afford heroic occasions in the morning, of which circumstance seventeen years' residence failed to furnish a single instance; about lost mines rediscovered, which *never* happens, and Indian maidens of such surpassing charm that men married them and went out of the story with intimations of ever-after happiness" (195). Three stories are about Indian women abandoned by white lovers. In the collection's final, the stoically tragic and much-anthologized "The Walking Woman" a deserted woman whose child was born dead walks restlessly and endlessly.

The eight long travel essays in Austin's ambitious and beautifully illustrated *California, Land of the Sun* (1914) are mostly about landscape and history. "Few people understand why Californians so love their Missions, the meagre ruins of them, scant as a last year's nest. But two priests, a corporal, and three men in the unmapped land with eight hundred angry savages—it is the mark of the Western breed to love odds such as that!" (19). (This is a reference to the voyage of Gaspar de Portola in 1769 with the monks Junipero Serra and Juan Crespi along, and its reference to "savages" ought not to be overlooked, because Austin was much less concerned with consistency than artistic effect.) Rounding out her circle tour of California, she ends with the desert, "open country, great space of sky, what the inhabitants of it call 'eye-reach,' treeless except for a few cotton-woods and willows along the sink of intermittent streams, and stippled with low shrubs of artemesia" (163) and observes that "A man may not find wealth there, nor too much of food even, but he often finds himself, which is much more important." (173).

The Ford (1917) is a novel not about the beauty of the desert and its fitness for soul-formation, but, surprisingly, about the necessity for irrigation as the precondition for farms and real estate. Set in the area around Bishop in the Owens Valley (whose water was about to be diverted to Los Angeles), its two villains are a heartless and amoral capitalist who means to appropriate the water supply; and, taken en masse, the local ranchers who are too stupid and parochial to unite against him. At the end, the capitalist backs out, opening the way for a cooperative and local movement headed by one of the protagonists. Settlement will be in the hands of his sister, a real estate agent who tells him that "land doesn't mean crops to me. . . . It means people—people who want land and are fitted for the land, and the land wants—how it wants them!" (199). A New Woman character in the novel, involved in theater and radical politics, plays "the Spirit of the West" for her arty friends in the only key they recognize, "the key of Owen Wister and the Sunday Supplements" (242).

*　*　*

Idah Meacham Strobridge, a transplant from Nevada mining terrain to southern California, brought out three Austin-influenced collections in beautifully produced editions from her Los Angeles bindery. (They were republished in one volume called *Sagebrush Trilogy* with an introduction by Richard A. Dwyer and Richard E. Lingenfelter in 1990.) Strobridge accepted Austin's argument that the source of life in southern California, paradoxical though it might seem, was the desert not the fruitful coast. *In Miners' Mirage Land* (1904) theorizes that prospectors who devote their lives to searching for lost mines don't expect or even want to find them; artist-adventurers, they relish the mirage, the lure of the desert, the joy of the quest. The stories in *The Loom of the Desert* (1907) are startlingly violent, as befits the landscape in which they transpire. In "An Old Squaw" a Paiute woman, cast out by the tribe as is their custom with the elderly, dies neglected in a garbage heap. (Perhaps this sketch was meant to counter the common belief that Natives were deeply respectful of old people.) In "The Vengeance of Lucas" an old, cuckolded man ropes his employer/cuckolder to a wild horse, causing him to be dragged to death. For comic relief, "The Revolt of Martha Scott" has a long-married drudge leave her husband for a year, live it up with a rake in Hawaii, and then return home, take up her duties, and live (apparently) happily ever after. The twelve sketches in *The Land of Purple Shadows* (1909) are dedicated to those who live in and love the West, with subjects ranging from landscape and weather to ethnic and occupational types: stage-drivers, Indians, Californios, Chinese.

Florence A. Merriam's nature sketches in *A-Birding on a Bronco* (1896) extol the scenery of southern California and implicitly rebut the idea that the area was wholly given over to real estate development. With only a field guide, field glasses, and a horse, she finds birds in their natural habitat all around the ranch near San Diego where she summered. "It was a beautiful quiet morning. The night fog had melted back and the mountains stood out in relief against a sky of pure deep blue. The line of sycamores opposite us were green and still against the blue; the morning sun lighting their white trunks and framework. The songs of birds filled the air, and the straw-colored field dotted with hay-cocks lay sunning under the quiet sky" (68). Kate Douglas Wiggin's *A Summer in a Cañon: A California Story* (1889), a girls' book memorializing her youth in southern California, follows a group of students in a summer-long camping adventure. The story dwells much on the beautiful climate and flora. It provides occasional glimpses of Franciscan friars, senoritas with fiery dark eyes, and splendid Spanish horsemen. There are campfire stories about the forty-niners, the overland trek, and the cattle ranches of yore. "Perhaps California isn't really so interesting since she began to learn manners; but she is a land of wonders still, with her sublime mountains and valleys, her precious metals, her vine-yards and orchards of lemons and oranges, figs, limes, and nuts; her mammoth vegetables, each big enough for a newspaper story; her celebrated trees, on the stumps of which dancing-parties are given; her vultures; her grizzly bears; and her people, drawn from every nook and corner of the map,—pink, yellow, blue, red, and green countries. And though the story of California is not written, in all its romantic details, in the school-books of to-day, it is a part of the poetry of our late American history, full of strange and thrilling scenes, glowing with interest and dramatic fire" (63–64).

In *The White Heart of Mojave* (1922, reissued with an afterword by Peter Wild in 2001), wealthy Cleveland resident Edna Brush Perkins describes a journey through the Imperial Valley to the edge of Death Valley followed by a transfor-mative month in Death Valley itself. Perkins says desert California is entirely unlike the southern California of "charming bungalows with date palms . . .

square orange groves all bushed and combed for dress parade, the picturesque missions, and the white towns with streets shaded by feathery pepper trees" (15). She notes, however, the abandoned mines, borax installations, shacks, and litter they find in the desert—"Like all desert watering places the surroundings were littered with tin cans, old shoes and rusty iron" (157).

* * *

Evelyn Hunt Raymond, a writer of girls' books, who contributed novels to Stratemeyer's "Dorothy" series (see Chapter 6 for one of these), published at least six non-Dorothy books about southern California. These include such attractively titled books as *Monica, the Mesa Maiden* (1892), *The Little Lady of the Horse* (1894), *A Daughter of the West* (1899), *A Yankee Girl in Old California* (1901), *Jessica Trent: Her Life on a Ranch* (1902), and *Polly the Gringo* (1905). All these books, designed to showcase the ideal western girl, compare and contrast the Northeast to southern California; within California they contrast Hispanic and Anglo cultures, throwing in an occasional Indian. They use the same formula: the family is poor; the young girl—sometimes Anglo, sometimes Hispanic but always plucky, resourceful, independent, and honest—supports not only herself but her family. Athletic nimbleness makes her western; Raymond says in her preface to *A Daughter of the West* that the western girl is now the national ideal: "There is no sweeter nor nobler human creature than a typical American girl; and such, as we comprehend her, is Patience Eliot, that Daughter of the West, herewith presented. Born and reared in the freedom of great spaces, she early learned to regard the stern verities of life rather than its polished trivialities; which she disdained because she recognized beneath them a need that was more vital" (5); "In every sense she was a patriot. She realized that American girlhood was to the girlhood of older civilizations as America itself was to older nations. Strong in this faith, yet without vanity, she was constrained to keep herself simple and modest, yet courageous, and, if need be, daring. Like her native land still, she respected her own dignity, which should not be the less because of its youthfulness" (6).

Monica's protagonist is a poor Hispanic who guides tourists with her burro. In *The Little Lady of the Horse,* the protagonist moves from southern California to Pennsylvania, where she helps support her suddenly impoverished family by opening a riding school for neighborhood children. In *A Yankee Girl in Old California,* the New Hampshire heroine Edith Hale is sent to southern California at age sixteen to live with her Hispanic grandmother and family on a decaying rancho outside San Diego. Full of New England capability, with a sprightly disposition and willingness to work hard, Edith revivifies the family by anglicizing (or New Englishizing) it. The book contributes to the southern California scene with descriptions of lemons and olive harvesting and curing, and it depicts tourists unkindly as snoops who interpret everything as spectacle for their benefit. There's also much about the importance of water and irrigation in realizing the California dream. "Water! . . . Without which California is a desert; with which she is an inexhaustible treasure-house" (380). In *Jessica Trent,* the eleven-year-old protagonist learns to manage a big ranch after her father dies. A range of minor and amusing characters converge in a fantasy of the West where tired, hungry, and poor gentlepeople of the earth can become productive citizens growing beets, raising ostriches, or mining coal. One character says "This big West is like a romance, a fairy tale; not the least of its marvels to find a little girl like you riding alone on such a steed up such a desolate Canyon, yet not in the least afraid" (14–15).

In Raymond's historical *Polly the Gringo,* Polly represents a modern world of educated girls. Patrician Californios won't let their children attend mission schools, which are for Indians; mothers "trained their children to be notable housewives, so that no matter how large the establishment, its mistress might have an eye and hand ready for any part of it or any duty that arose. But books? Of what use were they? Even Don Santiago, said to be the very wealthiest ranchero in all that region, could neither read nor write" (147). In *A Daughter of the West* Patience Eliot befriends an Indian maiden, Tulita, who gets an education and brings her once-degraded Indian village into the modern world: "to-day, where was once the humble Indian village by the arroyo, stands a beautiful town. The houses are no longer built of adobe mud, but tastefully and conveniently arranged 'model homes,' such as one sees everywhere in thrifty New England towns, sheltering busy and happy households. The people who dwell in these homes are still Indians, but Indians who command the respect of their white brothers the world over. Nowhere in all America are better tilled farms than theirs; nowhere richer orange groves and vineyards, while their culture of the olive, in which the earliest mission padres instructed tem, bids fair to rival that of Southern Europe. . . . They have churches for all; and for all, as free as the air they breathe, is that education which Tulita so longed for and so thoroughly achieved. Tulita herself is at the head of the great agricultural college, and the zeal with which she inspires her hundreds of students is due to her infinite love for them" (344–45).

Margaret Collier Graham, who with her brother and husband developed land in Riverside County, collected seven previously published tales in *Stories of the Foot-hills* (1895). They are about health-seekers and homesteading emigrants— poor, rural, unlettered vernacular folk who are wry, tyrannical, kindly, eccentric, wise, or bull-headed like local color characters in other regional literatures. The lives seem identical to the lives they left behind. They don't adapt to the land, nor the land to them, and they remain as poor as they were in the East. But the landscape is gorgeous, and now and then Graham stops her action to describe it. "The afternoon was steeped in the warm fragrance of a California spring. Every crease and wrinkle in the velvet of the encircling hills was reflected in the blue stillness of the laguna. Patches of poppies blazed like bonfires on the mesa, and higher up the faint smoke of the blossoming buckthorn tangled its drifts in the chaparral. Bees droned in the wild buckwheat and powdered themselves with the yellow of the mustard, and now and then the clear, staccato voice of the meadow-lark broke into the drowsy quiet—a swift little dagger of sound" (48). In a second collection, *The Wizard's Daughter and Other Stories* (1905), a homesteader's field is described: "The barley-field that stretched about the little redwood cabin was a pale yellowish green, deeper in the depressions, and facing almost into brown on the hillocks. There had been heavy showers late in October, and the early sown grain had sprouted. It was past the middle of November now, and the sky was of that serene, cloudless Californian blue which is like a perpetual smiling denial of any possibility of rain" (213).

Mary Stewart Daggett, prominent in Pasadena society, published *Mariposilla* in 1895, a first-person narration by a wealthy woman boarding with her daughter for a season at the home of a Castilian family outside Pasadena. "So intoxicating is the air that the saddest invalid beams with renewed hope, almost forgetting his burden beneath the delicious blue of the peaceful sky" (31). The book contains episodes of Pasadena social life and American-Spanish interactions according to which even the purest Castilian is lower on the class scale than any white person. Pasadena is already "an established and aristocratic nucleus for its surrounding towns" (32), whose fashionable young women enjoy cotillions, tennis, and horseback riding. When Mariposilla tells the narrator that she's unhappy because she's not an American, the narrator says: "You only desire to be an American because you have perceived that they are more in touch with the times than your own nation, who, from loss of fortune and other causes, are not what they once were, or what they will some day be again. . . . It is perfectly right that you should admire the superior attainments and polished manners of a race not your own. It means . . . only the desire for a broader life and a higher culture" (93). There is no trace of the wild west: "Mrs. Wilbur laughingly owned that her only opportunity for enjoying a peep of the notorious 'wild and wooly' was one afternoon when she had gone into Los Angeles to a wild and woolly show from New York. The show pretended to represent the common peculiarities of the West, whereas she blushed to acknowledge it an embarrassing portrayal of Eastern conceit and prejudices" (196).

Daggett's second novel, *The Higher Court* (1911), about a defrocked priest who marries the woman he had loved before taking orders (and subsequently has a nervous breakdown), also deploys the southern California landscape, climate, and the social doings of rich visitors and residents. Using the fictional mission of St. Barnabas, she asks whether missions are aesthetic spectacle, tourist attraction, or true representation of the soul's need. Of topical interest is her account of the earthquake's effect on southern California: "At last reliable news was beginning to come in from the ill-fated city, still burning, yet under absolute martial law. Thousands were now reported to be safe, though homeless, in the parks and upon higher, undamaged ground, beyond the region of flames. Relief trains had gone out on all the railroads; a few of them were now returning, packed with frightened, hungry refugees. And every one in the South seemed to be helping. The call for clothing for unfortunates had been answered generally" (203).

Daggett's last book, *The Yellow Angel* (1914), collected a novella and three stories, hoping to "dispel Occidental prejudice" (8). The titular angel, Sue Chang, a cook for wealthy southern Californians, is followed through the decades as he works, visits China, and finally goes back permanently to help bring it into the modern world. Chang's radicalization and return result from his exposure to American enlightenment ideals, while the employer's initial attitude—"What good will a change in the law do us, when once we have lost our cook? . . . We simply cannot get along on the Coast without Chinamen" (89)—becomes more enlightened: "Soon Chang would go to his own home a new man—with new ideals. . . . What reforms might he not institute? . . . He linked us as a family with the uncertain destinies of his nation. . . . For the first time, she was able to regard the Yellow Angel's flight with composure" (165). The three previously published stories in the collection are "The Redemption of Hop Lee," "The Awakening of the Dragon," and "The Black Lily." In the first, Hop Lee is called back to China to marry his designated bride although he "loved the land of his adoption. A mission school had broadened the celestial angle of vision, while his awakening mind hopelessly repudiated the claim of unreasonable, deadhead ancestors" (171). In the end, his mother and Chinese wife are killed in the Boxer rebellion, freeing him to come back and resume the Americanization process. "The Awakening of the Dragon" is about a man who loses everything, including his wife, to a gambling shark; but in the end his wife has twins, the shark is killed, and the couple is reunited under the double blessing of the Chinese New Year's dragon and the visit of President McKinley. "The Black Lily" is about a dying prostitute who gives her slave to the Salvation Army, hoping to make her white (235). All these grapple with a racial chauvinism that can't be overcome, but at least is acknowledged.

Clara Spalding Brown had reported to San Diego newspapers from Tombstone during the two years she lived there with her miner-husband. Her only references to the gunfight at the OK Corral disapproved of such outbreaks of lawlessness because they threatened outside business investment. Back in southern California, she set ten of the twelve stories in *Life at Shut-In Valley, and Other Pacific Coast Tales* (1895) there. The longest, "The School-ma'am of Mineral Hill," takes the route of stereotype, contrasting a noble miner to a nasty mustachio-twirling villain. The schoolteacher reforms the miner, and he rescues her from insult. The other stories mostly follow neglected, lonely, refined wives who droop and fail in this unlovely environment drudging from dawn to dusk—images challenging the going idea of the beauty and fertility of the southern California coast.

Emma Mersereau Newton's *The Veil of Solana* (1902) is a first-person zesty narration by a modern woman who comes to San Luis Obispo to find the mysterious veil of Solano, alluded to in her grandfather's papers. The historical and geographical information in this 120-page diversion, which moves on up to Mount Shasta, makes it read more like a scrapbook of Californiana than a novel; the author traverses standard history including suppression of the Indians by the padres, secularization, mountain men, gold discovery, and Fremont. San Luis Obispo: "Such a whimsical old town! Modern American shops jostle antique Spanish abodes, and Chinese hovels bask in the radiance of electric streetlamps" (21).

In 1906, Caroline H. W. Foster published *Little Stories of Yesterday,* with Mexican characters, mission towns, abandoned haciendas, and border villages, whose seven stories inscribe the standard explanation of Californio displacement by what are called "Americans": "When the gold excitement broke out, and Americans began to invade California . . . piece by piece, the property slipped out of their hands; and the shrewd American purchasers always contrived, by honest means or otherwise, to get the best of the bargain" (54). Madeline Deaderick Willard's *The King's Highway* (1913), published in Los Angeles and using Forbes as its source, is a historical recreation whose pious and idealistic priests are Spanish while those intending to secularize the missions are Mexicans, who—as one priest puts it—intend to "rob the Church of everything that she possesses, and then claim that it is done in the name of justice and the welfare of the people they have defrauded! . . . They are thieves and robbers, and their eyes are on the fat of the land" (152). He continues: Indians "are the veriest children—they are not strong men—except a few. In the hands of their spoilers they will be as dead leaves in a winter wind!" (153).

* * *

Marah Ellis Ryan published two novels about southern California and a third in which the region figures briefly but fundamentally. For her, the key to southern California was its underlying, persistent Mexican-Indian identity. *Miss Moccasins* (1904) opposes the all-Anglo wealthy heroine Anchor Darrett to her part-Mexican, evil half-brother, Felipe, who has rushed a dam through to boom his land, which causes a flood. Anchor impulsively saddles a horse and rides to save a threatened Mexican-populated village, earning the townspeople's gratitude. Over time she buys much local property, keeping the land intact for its

Mexican inhabitants. Childlike Mexican villagers need this kind of patronage, once received from the dons. Despite its nostalgia for the imagined California of yesterday, the book makes the point that though the past is gone, Mexicans are very much still there.

Ryan's *For the Soul of Rafael* (1906), a gorgeous piece of bookmaking, every page decorated, every chapter introduced by a notation of Mexican music, dedicated "a mis amigos de Califonia," is a historical novel of southern California at the time of Anglo arrival. In this novel nobody in southern California is pure Castilian, because all men in this culture take Indian mistresses; in just one generation, therefore, all Californios are part Indian. Ryan's plotting shows an interest in archaic religion—in this case, Mesoamerican religion with its priesthood and human sacrifice. The protagonist, unbeknown to herself, is one-quarter Indian, which fact explains her killing her husband's mistress as a way to fulfill a promise to his mother that she'll preserve his soul. At the start of *The Woman of the Twilight* (1913) the heroine Monica, adopted by a Don in southern California but pure Anglo herself, struggles on the one hand to get out of the region, whose pietistic Mexicans reject her as a heretic, and on the other to find a place in New England culture, which is too conventional and superficial. At the end she disappears from the book, at once running from and running to, unable to find a place for herself in the world. The early part of the book is set in southern California and features landscape and a lost (highly romanticized) past: "The cool air of sunset was coming down from the mountains, soon the stars would be shining, and the men of the ranges would be a picture worth seeing—Indian and Mexican in the glow of their roasting fire" (25). But the reality behind this picture is one that "these new Americans will never know" (28).

Cora Older, journalist and wife of a prominent San Francisco editor, attacked the railroad monopoly in a book about southern California oil, *The Giants* (1905), making San Francisco and New York City into tentacles of the same evil octopus but imagining an outcome in which the California hero wins over a New York mogul by forceful eloquence. The twelve stories in Amanda Mathews's *The Hieroglyphics of Love: Stories of Sonoratown and Old Mexico* (1906) are about newly arrived Mexican immigrants in Los Angeles, seen from the perspective of a mission schoolteacher. This is one of the few books to consider Mexican immigrants rather than long-standing Hispanic residents of southern California; the preface describes them as "a dark and lowly people who are yet rich with the riches of the poor, and wise with the wisdom of the simple." The title story collects many stereotypes of slum Mexicans: drunken stepfather; stupid, coarse mother; unintelligent daughter—the point being that even among such people true love can flourish. In "The Christmas of Esperanza," one sees social workers who are neither dark nor lowly. The district nurse, "slight and delicate for such work" is doted on by the children even in her blue and white uniform, "but today when she had donned for them a bewildering silk gown of the glowing red flaunted by the pomegranate blossom, she was a blessed miracle, and little brown fingers stole out for shy, awesome contact with her magnificence" (28).

The six tales in Pauline Wilson Worth's 1909 *Death Valley Slim and Other Stories* are set in desert towns with names like Green Gulch Camp and Pineville and try to make Death Valley into a version of Wyoming. It has pards who fight and reconcile, an old bachelor raising the golden-haired little girl who has been entrusted to him, a loving sweetheart almost forced into marrying for money. Along with stories of upper California, Eleanor Gates's 1910 collection, *The Justice of Gideon,* has a few tales about small town desert life, including the title story, where Gideon saves people and gets the girl; "Doc," who rescues a kidnapped child; "The Boomerang" where the bad husband and good "lover" and woman (who knows the bad husband means to poison the lover) go out to re-locate a claim.

Two novellas are Rose Hartwick Thorpe's *The White Lady of La Jolla* (1904) and Phebe Estelle Spalding's *The Tahquitch Maiden: A Tale of the San Jacintos* (1911). The first, by the author of "Curfew Must Not Ring Tonight," who had moved from the Midwest for her husband's health, compiles short lyrics, legends, and tourist information. Spalding, a Professor of English at Pomona College, originally from Vermont, recounts a legend that has "undergone numerous changes of form and interpretation, until it is become one of the most interesting and significant of the many blended fancies of the red man and the white, which go to make up the unique poetic lore of California" (Preface, n.p.). Lu Wheat's 1908 Utopian *Helen, A Story of Things to Be* (see Chapter 4 for her San Francisco novel) is set in the foothills where the heroine inherits a wonderful ranch and, ultimately, chooses life there rather than in the city. "It was predicted many years ago that the great mountain ranges, the leagues upon leagues of untrammeled space, and the evanescent color of the landscape in southern California would write themselves upon the characters of those who wrought there; and the prophecy seems to be coming true. The out of door life, the never ceasing marvel of bloom, the evening glow, all seem to conspire with each other to evolve in the beholder new modes of thought. Perhaps thus grown, one is not so rugged as the blizzard-defying man, nor so ultra-respectable as those whom we designate as 'Yankee,' but he is large with faith in humanity and untiring in the service of the commonwealth. . . . Nowhere else does humanity grope so surely toward sunlit mountain peaks; nowhere else does the mind answer to the stimulus of the beautiful as it does there" (n.p.).

In *Their Mariposa Legend: A Romance of Santa Catalina* (1921), Charlotte Herr connects past to present through two related stories. The old story is set in the time of Francis Drake when an Indian princess falls in love with an aristocratic English mariner but marries somebody more local; the second part features a romance between an art teacher and a writer, both interested in the legend, who turn out to be descendants of the original pair. Herr's *San Pasqual: A Tale of Old Pasadena* (1924) fictionalizes the history of Pasadena from hacienda culture to Indiana colony. "Their lands gone and, with them, their wealth and prestige, the old families, many of pure Castilian blood who had once ruled with such splendid, happy carelessness the Californias, were dropping out of sight, engulfed by the ever increasing wave of American speculators and business men" (83–84). In the Indiana Colony, there are many hardships, and many give up. "But to their credit it must also be said that most of the colonists had proved themselves of sterner stuff—of that pioneer breed, indeed, of whom it is so truly claimed that they furnish not only the brawn but the brain of mankind. By far the larger portion of them had bravely fought failure and loneliness and homesickness and had won out, so that now . . . the little town of Pasadena, though as yet scarcely more than a village, had begun to lay aside some of the crudeness of its frontier days and to acquire with every season that passed more of the homelike appearance of a settled community" (47).

Maria S. Lopez de Cummings's *Claudio and Anita: A Historical Romance of San Gabriel's Early Days* (1921) uses George Wharton James and Harrie Forbes for its facts. Apparently Claudio Lopez, the author's great-grandfather, came directly from Spain; his mien, we're told, bore "that indescribable stamp of distinction that seems to be the peculiar quality and exclusive privilege of aristocratic families" (22); he had, she says "all that high and formal breeding which runs with pure Castilian blood, and by his manner showed that at one time he had lived among the festivities of life" (51). Why he is working as major domo in the construction of the mission San Gabriel isn't explained. After secularization and the loss of his lovely Anita, Claudio goes to Los Angeles and marries the author's great-grandmother. As for the mission, within a short time "San Gabriel, once the hive of industries, rich in gold derived from the trading of its abundant resources, the toil of the neophytes, from the numberless herd, and the boundless zeal, toil, and sacrifices of our heroes,—all came to naught through the secularization, and, in the same degree that we admire those zealous heroes, we must stamp with ignominy the men and the policy which destroyed the work of the Missionaries and drove their inmates, the neophytes, back to a state worse than barbarism" (136).

Rose Ellerbe collected eighteen previously published stories in *Tales of California Yesterdays* (1916), touching on missions, padres, neophytes, and renegade Indians, native Californians of diverse ethnicity—Castilian, Mexican, Indian—whose customs differ from "ours" and who all share the same relaxed, expressive, performative life style. The action in her ambitious historical novel about southern California and its triracial population, *Ropes of Sand* (1925), takes place between 1832 and 1846, and involves the secularization of the missions, the inevitable takeover of California by "Americans," and the development of

Los Angeles. Its racially chauvinistic protagonist, the trapper James Woods, matures into a man who can accept both his "half-breed" son Isleto (by an earlier marriage) and his Californio wife Mercedes. Mercedes hates Isleto, Isleto thinks he can never be the man his father wants him to be, but at the end everybody comes to love everybody else—a denouement promising a happily diverse future for the nation.

Mae Van Norman Long, theosophist novelist and short-story writer, set her most popular book, *The Wonder Woman* (1917), in an abstract rural space. *The Canyon of the Stars* (1926), by contrast, insists on a southern California of languorous climate, floral profusion, starry nights, and mission architecture. The protagonist Alma Craig, who has come from Michigan to settle in the Simi Valley with her ailing little sister and father (the father dies before the action opens), is rescued from misery by the arrival of two wonderfully handsome men: a commercial gardener and a rancher. The setting is used for its unearthly beauty; within a week Alma has fallen passionately in love with "the land of her adoption. A week of starlight nights articulate with mockingbirds and thrush, a week of golden days, looking off toward the Simi Hills and the rose-flushed mountains, followed by lavender twilights" does the trick (69). "California has driven me quite mad with its beauty." she says (197).

*   *   *

Elizabeth Dejeans' *The Heart of Desire* (1910) wraps an early vision of Los Angeles around a female romance melodrama. The novel begins on a transcontinental train trip in 1893 from New York City to Los Angeles; it follows the growth of Los Angeles (and some of the passengers introduced on the journey as well) over fifteen years. The male protagonist says the city's financial possibilities are "quite sufficient to turn one feverish—if one is inclined that way. Of course socially it is chaotic and will be for many a long day—it is only natural that it should be. What I like is that here one stands with one's face turned to the future" (58). Fifteen years later he says "It is unfair for others to judge us, or for us to judge ourselves by the antics of a few millionaires who come to a smiling climate to play about for a season. . . . They actually sit as an incubus on its progress, because the atmosphere they create kills anything like public spirit" (88). His final judgment of Los Angeles is "hurry and bustle without geniality or laughter, a collection of units, strangers to each other in most part, but bound together by the compelling chain of possibilities. A town of possibilities sprung by bounds into a city of greater potentiality; a combination of crudities, sunned into virile life by a sky of infinite blue, swept clean by the sweet, dry breath of the desert, or touched in turn by the foggy fingers of the ocean, but possessing in full the essential power of crudity; a marvel of the present, a still greater marvel of the future" (267).

Ednah Aiken's novel *The River* (1914) is about irrigating the Imperial Valley in 1905, when the Colorado River burst out of its channels in a great flood. The book covers the flooding and destruction of rancher/farmer property, settlers who have been duped by land promoters, the railroad, and more. The story is highly gendered—men are trying to control the Colorado to enable the valley's settlement while the women visit each other, flirt, and sometimes fall seriously in love. One woman character says: "The real work of the world is man-work; no matter how she or other women might yearn, theirs not the endurance. All they can do is negative; not to get on the track!" (387–88). The inanity of female desert lives affects one character so seriously that she goes crazy, shooting and killing her husband as some sort of outgrowth of her fear of Indians. The novel says much about the workforce, which—since there is no steady population (everybody who "lives" there is a boss, a rancher, or a farmer)—consists of border-crossing Mexicans, itinerant white hoboes from New Orleans and Los Angeles, and Natives from seven tribes. A subplot set in Mexico recognizes that this is a border community; one can walk into the Mexican town from the dry American side to get alcohol, and the Colorado River is a two-nation concern. Along with depictions of the social and business life of this little tent city as it swelters in the stifling heat, the book allows an expert on desert empires to explain that all great civilizations emerged in the desert.

In 1916 Grace Sartwell Mason, collaborating with John Northern Hilliard, published *The Golden Hope,* about a conflict between private corporations and the federal government over a retaining tank that could irrigate thousands of acres and turn the valley into the breadbasket of the world, make jobs for millions of immigrants, and more. Wheat, the aptly named bank-officer protagonist, cooperates with a man he thinks is a government employee, only to find out that the man is really working for capitalists in the town of San Lorenzo, to which the water will be diverted. The book includes a married but independent heroine (her husband is always out prospecting but never finding a mine), a stereotypical lazy and irresponsible Mexican family, and a stereotypical stoic Indian. There are many oratorical passages on the future of southern California if irrigated; "she saw the desert valleys waiting for water, for the magic touch of water that would change their arid acres to the gold of wheat, of alfalfa, or orchards; and she saw the ranch-houses growing larger, the children being sent away to school, the women's faces becoming happier" (105).

Janie Chase Michaels, who in 1895 had published a short romantic novel set in Phoenix (see Chapter 10), published a second schoolteacher romance, *Polly of the Midway -Sunset* (1917) set in the oilfields of southern California. Its bank-cashier hero writes in a letter back home that he finds the landscape of derricks beautiful: "While the alluring breeze brings no odor of sweet flower or blooming tree, it comes laden with the pungent, healthy tang of oil. The drilling of the wells, the chug-chug of the machinery pumping the heavy, black liquid into tank, or 'sump,' and the loading of the long trains at the tracks, have a fascination all their own" (37). He also admires the "panorama" that the writer herself depicts in appropriately painterly language. "In the near distance could be seen the bustling little oil-city, humming with its varied life; beyond, and on every side as far as sight could reach, he saw the forests of oil derricks, guarding, as it were, the dwellings necessary for housing the workmen who make possible this miracle of the elusive desert—the oil industry. Surrounding all this were the smooth, curving hills, now robbed of their early spring dress of green, but showing plainly across their tawny surface the sinuous winding pipe-lines which bear away to the Pacific seacoast this black gold of the desert" (42). Michaels dedicates the little book to oilfield workers, "whose toils release the black gold of the desert and make possible a newer and better age of commerce." Another reference to oil occurs in Rose Wilder Lane's *Diverging Roads* (1919), which though mainly about upper California (see Chapter 4) portrays workers in the oil fields as apt clients for agricultural real estate.

By 1915 B. M. Bower was writing about the Southwest and, also—having begun a screenwriting career—about the differences between the real West and the movie West, which was superseding it. She was also beginning to use women protagonists, although here she was feeling her way. In *Jean of the Lazy A* (1915), Jean, trying to exonerate her father from wrongful imprisonment while working his ranch, gets a job doubling for a film star (whom she eventually replaces) and moves from Montana to Los Angeles along with Lite Avery, the ranch's former manager and her protector. The film's director, having "never, in all his experience in directing Western pictures, seen a girl mount a horse with such unconscious ease of every movement" (62), and later learning about her literary abilities (she writes to assuage her loneliness—this may be an uncharacteristic autobiographical aside) uses her stories for a series called "Jean of the Lazy A" and makes her the series star. The novel's exceptionally plain and direct language implies a youthful audience that would see Jean as a model of the western heroine: independent, active, upright. Toward the end of the novel the book detours into Nogales; watching a newsreel about the Mexican Revolution, Jean recognizes among the ranks of General Kosterlitzky's soldiers the man she thinks committed the murder for which her father has been found guilty and sets off in pursuit; having turned life into art, Bower now turns art into life. But after all, as Bower well knew, the novel form was also a genre that blurred reality and fantasy. Politics and the personal merge when the supposed miscreant, having joined the Mexican army, turns out be innocent and returns to Montana with Jean and Lite to see that justice is served. Films (and fiction, and imagination) are a necessary part of reality.

Bower's *The Parowan Bonanza* of 1923 alternates between the gold country of southern California/Nevada and Santa Barbara, making the inland desert the true West, typing Santa Barbara as a weak imitation of the East. As in her earlier *Lookout Man* (see Chapter 4), the idea is that coastal southern California is not really Western. Its handsome young prospector-hero makes a great strike in the mountains near Goldfield but abandons it to take his new wife to Santa Barbara for social life. When those he left in charge of the mine turn out to be crooks, he has to start over—as does his wife when she sees the shallowness of the society she thought she wanted. The author/narrator sets the scene and displays her own values at the start when she writes of the desert's "magnificent distances, always beautiful, always changing their panorama of lights and shadows on uptilted mesas and deep, gray-green valleys . . . wonderful, translucent tints of blue, violet and purple on all the mountains there against the sky" (3–4).

In Bower's *The Bellehelen Mine* (1924), the aptly named Helen Strong decides to reopen the mine that her dead father started but never had a chance to develop. Another Bower novel from this year is *The Eagle's Wing*, a counterfactual fantasy in which a family living along the Colorado River on the Nevada-California border plans to dam the river to claim the gold they believe must lie on its floor. They're helped at first by the young hero Rawley King, a mining engineer; but the war intervenes and when Rawley returns he explains that a government dam is going to be built at exactly that spot (the Hoover Dam, though it isn't named). The overt theme is the role of the federal government in the West, with Bower siding with the government against private capital on behalf of the common good. Her southern California novel of 1925 is *Desert Brew*, about bootlegging. In this story, an author goes to the California desert incognito and has adventures involving a ranch family trying to get father to give up booze while he is secretly helping a ring of bootleggers export liquor hidden in sacks of ore from the mines. All comes out well; again Bower contrasts the sophisticated California coast with the primitive California desert, a raw place where anything can happen.

Between 1914 and 1920, Margaret Turnbull published more than a dozen popular novels and wrote photoplays for more than fifty films. *The Close-Up* (1918), about the movie business, describes a film colony of decent, hard-working, good-natured, wholesome, and unpretentious people. Kate, a legal secretary from New York City, goes west with her bosses to work in the film industry, is conscripted to act, and becomes (briefly) a star. A chapter titled "In which Kate meets the real west and falls in love with it" distinguishes Los Angeles from the country—the "real west," which is not, cannot be, urban. "She had seen trees that took her breath away, so huge were they! All day long mountain after mountain had unfolded its beauties as they toiled up or circled round it, and pine forest after pine forest held out to hem vast green arms. The camp, when they reached it, was the loveliest thing of all. A lake, vast, cool, and placid, set in the midst of a great pine forest; . . . On the other side of the lake were lush green meadows on which cattle ranged, standing. . . . 'The real West!' Kate said, softly" (192). "A long, lean man with pleasant blue eyes, sunburnt face, and cowboy clothes . . . made Kate think of the illustrations in *The Virginian*. He was handsome and looked unobtrusively efficient in a 'horsy' way. Kate realized that he was the type of Westerner she had been looking for ever since she had come to California, forgetting that a suburban Western town is, after all, the complement of a suburban Eastern town and not the place to look for romancer and picturesque Westerners. Kate, who had almost lost faith in the romantic West and the Westerner of the adventure novels and stories, found them both here" (193). This attractive Westerner does not become Kate's love interest, however; this is an Easterner, Jeff, who comes to southern California on a secret mission to uncover German espionage in California in connection with World War I.

This novel, like some other southwestern novels (see Chapter 10) refers to rumors of an impending invasion from Mexico of German-armed and German-funded Mexican soldiers, perhaps to recover for Mexico the entire Southwest that had been lost after the war of 1846–47. These rumors (which had some truth to them) had much to do with the US entrance into World War I. Jeff points out that in California, Japan is close, Europe "too far away" for political awareness; "you could plant any kind of scare about the Mexican border, or Japan, and we'd swallow it here; but Germany against us? Never! She is our friend, and so we play right into her hands" (284–85).

Sarah Comstock's romantic *The Valley of Vision* (1919) is incidentally yet crucially about southern California, where the New Woman heroine Marcia (who has achieved independence by training to be a nurse) and the unhappily married man she loves meet for three days of chaste romance. Says Marcia, "It's all so big, this world of the West. . . . It almost frightens me" (348); "There's something in the very air that's different from other places. . . . It seems compelling you to expand, to be free" (349). They climb a mountain, walk along the shore, and stumble into a sheep ranch, "one of the old-time ranches of early California, almost the last of its kind" where Indians are shearing: "I know that I'm dreaming I'm Ramona, and that I'm going to wake up!" Marcia exults (365). Her boyfriend just happens to have the book with him, and they read the relevant chapter: "Can you believe that was written for another generation, and not for to-day? Or that we are living in 1912 and not in Spanish California of old? The sheep, the hills, the Indians; everything" (366). They lunch at a Spanish hacienda and then a mission: "They stood before the altar arch, subtly awed by the spirit that hovered, that can never desert the spot where once it strove—a spirit fired by love for blind humanity, consecrated to all toil, all privation, all endurance—the spirit of the Padres. Their religion remains not as dogma . . . but as the labour of man for brother man, spiritualized by a childlike love of God"

(371). Refreshed by this excursion into tourist dreamland, the couple returns East where Marcia, discovering that the wife is pregnant, sacrifices romance to virtue but is promised, via the narrator's foresight, useful work in her profession when the world war arrives.

The title of Ruth Comfort Mitchell's *Corduroy* (1924) refers to the cultural change that transformed the cloth of kings into work clothes, thereby making a statement about the nobility of western democracy. Its romance is between Virginia (Ginger) MacVeagh, part Scottish and part Spanish, owner and manager of a southern California cattle ranch, and the eastern Brahmin Dean Wolcott. Dean, a tenderfoot shell-shocked by the war, makes a fool of himself in Virginia's eyes when he can't ride a difficult horse. He realizes that he's "the failure here. These people were integral parts of the virile picture; they fitted strongly into the high brown hills and the blue mountains far beyond, into the wide dry valleys and the deep cañons; he belonged on the pavement, in the shadow of grave buildings, art galleries, quiet clubs, dignified offices" (79). In Ginger he sees "a highly colored and careless young woman who fitted so snugly into the rough western picture that he doubted the possibility of ever seeing her against a different background' (93–94). Later he becomes a forest ranger at Big Sur and toughens up enough to win the heroine. The connections between the ranch and San Francisco where Ginger's aunt lives, and between both these places and New York City, and between all these places and Big Sur begins to map out a nation connected from coast to coast and California as one not two states.

Madge Morris Wagner's 1917 collection of poems, *The Lure of the Desert Land* (see Chapter 4 for poems about northern California), contains a couple of poems rejecting the desert cult; "Not Acclimated," a brief lyric, begins: "I hate you, Southland of the southern West. . . . Your wide hot mouth / Breathes only scorching desolated drouth" (76). A relatively long poem, "At San Diego," reflects on the long history of Spanish failure there, but ends by saying that nothing has been lost after all, because "Progress to the old new West / has turned her face and set her sail" (108). A second book of poetry, entirely about southern California, is Sarah Bixby-Smith's *My Sagebrush Garden* (1924). Having grown up on a big sheep ranch outside Los Angeles and then moved to the city, she writes nostalgically of the past. In "Return" an "empty ranch I used to know" is now "cut into farms and swarming towns / Where we buy and sell and sub-divide. / The long smooth beach whose lonely tide, / Unseen, unknown, would ebb and flow... / Is crowded with shops" (36). "Return" also detests the oil industry: "oil makes all things ugly and black" (36) as does "Signal Hill," which calls oil the "black magic of today" (40).

Bixby-Smith also wrote the only woman's memoir I've found from the region. *Adobe Days* (1925, revised in 1926 and again in 1931) remembers a nineteenth-century western childhood. "The sum of child happiness in California could not be told. How good it is to wander in the sun, smelling wild celery, or the cottonwood leaves, nibbling yellow, pungent mustard blossoms while pushing through the tangle; how good to feel a pulled tule give as the crisp, white end comes up from the mud and water, or to bury one's face in the flowing sulphur well. . . . How good to wander in the sun, to be young and tireless, to have cousins and ranches!" (123–24). The memoir uses family papers to recount the original emigration of three male Bixby cousins from Maine to the California mines before the Civil War, their return to Maine, their purchase of sheep which they drive cross-country, their settling first in the northern and then the southern part of the state. Bixby-Smith describes the ranch of her childhood—Los Ceritos (now a state historical site)—its architecture and interior design, furniture, household routines, cuisine, pastimes. When they move to Los Angeles, not only childhood, but California itself, vanishes: "The pastoral life gave way to the agricultural, and that in turn to the town and city. There is Long Beach. Once it was a cattle range, then sheep pasture, then, when I first knew it, a barley field with one small house and shed standing about where Pine and First Streets cross. And the beach was our own private, wonderful beach; we children felt that our world was reeling when it was sold" (134).

10

The Southwest

Women who published books about Arizona and New Mexico tried to substitute their narrative of peaceful progress toward prosperity for the stories of violence that characterized this region even more than the High Plains. They described the Hispanic groups that had long populated Arizona and New Mexico as the original pioneers who made it safe for Anglos by subduing—often-used word—the Indians. Yet, it was difficult for women writers to ignore the national consensus that the Southwest was the least "American" and most lawless region of the country. Cowboys flourished here after they had more or less vanished from the plains; representing them as progressives not outlaws occupied at least some of women writers. Their army accounts and anthropological findings presented a region inhabited mainly by Apaches, Comanches, Navajos, and pueblo dwellers, with little evidence that white women were anything but outsiders in the Southwest. To write about the Southwest was, in large measure, to write about men.

An example of all-male boosterism is Helen Haines's *History of New Mexico*, published in 1891. This book was written on commission when the author was barely nineteen years old, and she had not been in the Southwest at all. The source of the assignment is not explained in the various biographical dictionaries, which concentrate on Haines's later career as an important publicizer of libraries and books. Haines's publisher—New Mexico Historical Publishing—never brought out another book. I speculate that because Haines's father had been a wool broker, New Mexican territorial interests were involved here, especially because the narrative compilation is followed by over 140 celebratory biographies of New Mexican businessmen and ranchers compiled by a G. E. Yerger (whom I haven't been able to identify). Like booster books from other parts of the West—Storke for Santa Barbara, Sanders for Montana, Forter for Marshall County in Kansas,

Hill for Colorado—the volume advertises the territory's resources and remarkable development. The biographies include many men with Spanish surnames; the historical obstacle to Americanizing the territory is not the Hispanics who had so obsessed Texas women writers, but Indians. This is the narrative, too, in Ann E. Hughes's scholarly *The Beginnings of the Spanish Settlement in the El Paso District* (1914), which sees El Paso as virtually a separate province (301), more New Mexican than Texan; "At the most critical period in the early history of New Mexico, El Paso became the bulwark of the New Mexican colonists against the ravages of the Pueblo Indians, and made it possible eventually for Spanish arms to repossess the abandoned province" (391).

Janie Chase Michaels's *A Natural Sequence: A Story of Phoenix, Arizona* (1895) is a simple schoolteacher-rancher romance showing turn-of-the-century Phoenix as peaceful, sophisticated, and socially stratified, with a substantial Anglo population. The publication of this little book in Bangor, Maine, suggests that the author, like her main character, was the daughter of a Maine seafaring man who'd gone west to help the family finances. In the southwestern stories in Josephine Clifford McCrackin's collections: *Overland Tales* (1877), *Another Juanita* (1893), and *"The Woman Who Lost Him," and Tales of the Army Frontier* (1913), southwestern space and isolation imprison women whether they live on army posts or ranches. *Overland Tales* contains four fine nonfiction sketches about the overland journey: "Crossing the Arizona Deserts," "Marching with a Command," "To Texas, and by the Way," and "My First Experience in New Mexico." The title story in *Another Juanita* takes place in Albuquerque, a town of "low, flat-roofed houses . . . scattered, without order or system, in among the sand" (4). In "San Xaviar del Bac" the narrator says "Traveling in Arizona is not like traveling in a respectable Christian country, where houses, farms, cattle, stables, cabins are to be seen now and then. Anyone may take up a line of march here and continue in any direction he chooses for weeks and not see a solitary human being all this time" (53–54). In "Toby," a wife trying to escape an abusive marriage contends against both the terrain and its inhabitants: "There was nothing in this country then save military posts at long intervals and a very few poverty stricken Mexican towns and settlements, separated by hundreds of miles of waterless sand-deserts and barren rocks, with Indians of different tribes, but all alike hostile sprinkled over the whole" (109). *The Woman Who Lost Him* has a wonderful four-page sketch, "A Picture of the Plains," narrating the New Mexico trail meeting of two exotic caravans: one led by Jewish merchants, the other an army train.

Ellen Williams's 1885 army memoir of the all-volunteer Colorado unit (see Chapter 6) follows the soldiers to New Mexico and describes Santa Fe where they were posted during part of the Civil War. Frances Mullen Boyd's *Cavalry Life in Tent and Field* (1894, reissued with an introduction by Darlis A. Miller in

1982) complains about the hardships of army life for officers' wives, yet grants that "there is a rare and nameless charm in the contemplation of those extended prairies, with their soft gray tints, dreary to Eastern people, but so dearly loved by those who become imbued with the deep sentiment their vast expanse inspires. I shall never become reconciled to localities where the eye cannot look for miles and miles beyond the spot where one stands. . . . Oh, I love the West, and dislike to think that the day will surely come when it will teem with human life and all its warring elements!" (175–76).

Ellen McGowan Biddle's peripatetic *Reminiscences of a Soldier's Wife* (1907), set in Nevada, Texas, and Kansas and focused on six years in Arizona—their longest posting (the book was reissued with an introduction by Peter Cozzens in 2002)—says Arizona "was an unknown country then to the majority of people, as indeed it now is to many, and though most interesting to all who have sojourned there, none know what the development of this wonderful country will be" (189–90). She writes about Indian scares and female loneliness; when they arrive in Arizona "we seemed to be the only living people on the planet. . . . The desert seemed a wonderful place. . . . The road was lined with cactus of every description, wonderful and beautiful to me" (154). There was incredible beauty in the "blue skies, the wonderful rugged mountains, and the mystery of the desert" (168).

In Prescott at that time "There was a plaza, or park, in the center of the town and stores on the four sides of it. One side was given up to the saloons; but it was fairly orderly, considering it was a mining town. There was a good element from the beginning. . . . I never saw a place grow so rapidly and improve in every way as it did during the five and a half years we lived near it. There was an excellent society—lawyers, mining engineers, and their families, and other business men; also a great number of miners" (162). Like all army wives she reminds readers of their debt to the frontier army, which "made it possible for the great railways to be built across the Continent. . . . The isolated army post made it practicable for the pioneer and early settler to take up ground" (208).

The most literary army memoir, the only one to circulate widely, was Martha Summerhayes's *Vanished Arizona: Recollections of the Army Life of a New England Woman* (1908, second edition 1911, and reissued with an introduction by Dan L. Thrapp in 1979). The memoir recalls the arduous steamer trip up the Colorado River and then overland to their Arizona post. At the first campsite "there was not a tree nor a shrub to give shade. The only thing I could see, except sky and sand, was a ruined adobe enclosure, with no roof" (49). The horrible heat overwhelms her memories and dominates the narrative, as she enviously remembers the loose dress and simple cookery of the Mexican residents. But to her own surprise, the memories induce nostalgia: "I did not see much to admire in the desolate waste lands through which we were traveling. I did not dream of the power of the desert, nor that I should ever long to see it again. But as I write, the longing possesses me, and the pictures then indelibly printed upon my mind, long forgotten amidst the scenes and events of half a lifetime, unfold themselves like a panorama before my vision and call me to come back, to look upon them once more" (57). "Sometimes I hear the still voices of the Desert; they seem to be calling me through the echoes of the Past. . . . The wheels of the ambulance crunching the small broken stones of the *malapais* . . . the rattle of the ivory rings on the harness of the six-mule team. . . . But how vain these fancies! Railroad and automobile have annihilated distance, the army life of those years is past and gone, and Arizona, as we knew it, has vanished from the face of the earth" (291).

* * *

The earliest woman anthropologist to work in this region was Matilda Coxe Stevenson, who went West with her archeologist husband and stayed on after his death. *The Zuni Indians: Their Mythology, Esoteric Fraternities, and Ceremonies* (1905), ignores the "scientific" rule that evidence gatherers should not intrude into the situations they are researching; to the contrary it makes her interference an example of how civilized people should connect with Native culture. "It is possible," she says late in the book, "if these people are managed in the right way, to overcome their miserable superstitions. . . . Primitive man must be approached according to his understanding; thus the prime requisite for improving the conditions of the Indian is familiarity with Indian thought and customs. Those possessing superior intelligence and a love for humanity, and only such, may lead our Indians from darkness into light. The Indian will never be driven" (406). The Zuni try to keep her out of their lives, but in her own narrative she's unstoppable. "Near midnight the writer was notified that this man was to be put to death. It seemed too terrible to believe. . . . The position of the writer was a delicate one. The man must be saved" (397). After some palaver, "the unfortunate was released. This was brought about by a declaration on the part of the writer that she had deprived the man of his power of sorcery" (398).

Unlike Stevenson, Natalie Curtis hoped to preserve Native traditions in her *Indians' Book* (1907), which collected and translated Indian songs and put them in context, as much for the Indians (she claimed) as for white people. Although she worked mostly with plains groups, she also included a few southwestern tribes. The considerably more professional Elsie Clews Parsons followed Stevenson's lead in *Notes on Zuni* (1917), asserting that Zuni life was controlled by religious ceremony which, in turn, was controlled by belief in witchcraft, magic, and shamanistic (i.e., unscientific and fraudulent, since the shamans in her view certainly knew they were faking it) medicine. Parsons edited and contributed to *American Indian Life, by Several of Its Students* (1922); her sketch describes a

Zuni woman's typical life from birth to her death in early middle age. She also refers to the "berdach," the cross-dressed male, whom Stevenson had earlier discussed. Parsons's *The Pueblo of Jemez* (1925) conceded what many anthropologists chose not to admit: the observers' knowledge was at best partial for many reasons including Native unwillingness to describe sacred practices to outsiders (8). Parsons's *Tewa Tales* (1926—reissued with an introduction by Barbara A. Babcock in 1994) transcribes and compares tales from Tewa-speaking New Mexico pueblos and Tewa speakers living among the Hopi in Arizona, arguing that the New Mexico versions are more authentic because more pure—they lack Spanish and Hopi elements.

Parsons places Natives lower on the ladder of civilization than Anglos, but doesn't think they are children, which is the idea behind Katharine Berry Judson's *Myths and Legends of California and the Old Southwest* (1912, reissued in 1994 with an introduction by Peter Iverson), as well as Elizabeth Willis DeHuff's *Taytay's Tales* and *Taytay's Memories* (1922, 1924) and Aileen Nusbaum's *Zuni Indian Tales* (1926). Both Dehuff and Nusbaum were involved with Native life in the Southwest for many years, Dehuff's husband was superintendent of the Santa Fe Indian School, and she taught art to Indian youngsters to show them what authentic Native art should look like. Nusbaum's husband was long-time superintendent at Mesa Verde National Park. These women see themselves as representatives of advanced civilization, and though both Dehuff and Nusbaum know that Indians don't freely disclose tribal practices, they accept the stories they overhear Indian adults telling children as a reflection of innate Indian childishness. Nusbaum says, "This interesting people with their strange superstitions and beliefs, their childlike simplicity and rare beauty of thought, have, through their word-pictures, enabled us to see today a land of fancy that is unique" (vii).

Susan Wallace, a professional magazine writer, wife of Lew Wallace (New Mexico's Territorial Governor from 1878–81), visited many pueblos, descriptions of which she included in the 27 previously published New Mexico travel letters comprising *The Land of the Pueblos* (1888). Her sketches of Pueblo dwellers, Apaches, Pima-Maricopa, Mexicans, the *jornada del muerte* (the waterless 90-mile segment of the Camino Real), mountain and plains, mining, make the region exotic and foreign, but not glamorous. The first letter, describing arrival in Santa Fe, establishes a resolutely Anglo and judgmental perspective. "Tender the light of the evening on the mountains which encircle the ancient capital of the Pueblos. As we approach it, it is invested with indescribable romance, the poetic glamour which hovers about all places to us foreign, new, and strange. We go through a straggling suburb of low, dark adobe houses. How comfortless they look! Two Mexicans are jabbering and gesticulating, evidently in a quarrel. Swarthy women, with dismal old black shawls over their heads, sit in the porches. . . . And this is the historic city! Older than our government, older than the Spanish Conquest, it looks older than the hills surrounding it, and worn-out besides" (13).

She contrasts the fierce Apache nomad with the pueblo dweller. Apache have been "trained by their mothers to theft and murder from childhood" and "are inured to all extremes of heat and cold, hunger and thirst" (155); pueblo people are "peaceful, contented citizens, entitled to confidence and respect. . . . Their quaint primitive customs, curious myths, and legends afford rich material for the poet, and their antiquities open an endless field to the delving archeologist" (31–32). But they are also deeply conservative: "Rigid unbending adherence to old time observances sets their faces as a flint against everything new and foreign, and our mission-work seems dashing against a dead wall" (45). And, without water in the pueblos, they lead unsanitary and unhealthy lives. Even as she criticizes the inhabitants of this foreign land, Wallace advises readers to visit this "country apart from the rest of the United States" soon because "the civilizer is coming; is here. The waste lands of the wandering tribes will be divided and sold by the acre. . . . The dozing Mexican will be jostled on the elbow, and will wake from his long trance to find himself in the way" (95).

Three years later (1891) Marianna Burgess, director of the printing department at the Carlisle Indian School, published her only book, a first-person narrative by "Stiya," who tells a story of heroic resistance to traditional pueblo ways when she returns to her pueblo after five years at the school. (Burgess published as "Embe," her initials.) The unnamed pueblo, built on a high rock and barren of all vegetation, with the town of Seama nearby, can only be Acoma—a fact seemingly verified by Carlisle's record (according to Amelia Katanski) of a "real" Stiya from that pueblo. Stiya describes her reentry through a shocked, enlightenment perspective with a particular concern for cleanliness: she notices that in the pueblo clothing is washed in ditch water, dishes aren't washed at all, baths unavailable, and more. Modern domesticity is what radicalizes her— evidence, perhaps, that the work of women is absolutely central to a "civilized" politics. Stiya's political consciousness raised, she resists the governor's command to wear Indian clothing and participate in a ceremonial dance where horrible actions (unnamed) are performed. She persuades her parents to resist also; the governor causes them to be publicly whipped, after which they leave the pueblo and move into a house in Seama to enjoy the twin benefits of water and freedom of thought.

The interweaving of anthropology with pro-Indian activism is evident in Mary Katrine Sedgwick's *Acoma, the Sky City: A Study in Pueblo-Indian History and Civilization* (1926). As Sedgwick tells it, she attempted twice to enter Acoma pueblo. The first time she and her party were allowed to stay overnight in the home of a clearly reluctant hostess. The next time they were turned away.

Sedgwick uses this rebuff to speculate about Native unwillingness to share their lives with whites. Surely, she hazards, Indians would disclose details of their rituals and beliefs to a "truly interested and friendly student" as opposed to "a selfish and unscrupulous exploiter of their sacred inheritance" (31). The whole "tangle of difficulties" has been "largely created by an indifference to Indian philosophy and sensitiveness and to a misuse of power which has bred a deep sense of racial injustice" (278). Compensating for her ignorance of Acoma ways, she makes her book a synthesis of ethnographies from other pueblos arguing for an education congruent with Indian "needs and mentality . . . fostering his deft fingers in his native crafts instead of teaching him that machine-made and artificially dyed rugs are superior; that would help him to develop his innate agricultural talent by better implements and a more generous use) of soils and of irrigation. At least let him be protected from political exploitation and even from the selfishness of too ardent exploring students" (287–88).

In 1913 Agnes Laut published *Through Our Unknown Southwest,* an informal tourist guide to national forests, deserts, pueblos, and the Navajo, to Santa Fe, Taos, Mesa Verde (established as a National Park in 1906), and to Adolph Bandelier's summer camp in Frijoles Canyon. The Southwest is "a bit of old Spain picked up three centuries ago and set down here in the wilderness of New Mexico . . . a relic of the historic and the picturesque not yet sandpapered into the commonplace by the friction of progress and democracy" (51–52). A trip to the Painted Desert will teach you "that America has her own Egypt and her own Arabia and her own Persia in racial type and in handicraft and in antiquity" (103). Taos "might be part of Turkey, or Persia, or India. It is the most un-American thing in America; and yet, it is the most typical of those ancient days in America, when there was no white man" (186). Laut objects to Anglo appropriation of Mexican land and Native water: "The big irrigation companies have tapped the streams above the Indian Reserve. . . . The Pima can no longer raise crops. Slowly and very surely, he is being reduced to starvation in a country overflowing with plenty, in a country which has taken his land and his waters, in a country whose people he loyally protected as they crossed the continent to California. What are the American people going to do about it? Nothing, of course. When the wrong has been done and the tribe reduced to extermination by inches of starvation, some muckraker will rise and write an article about it, or some ethnologist a brochure about an exterminated people" (249–50).

* * *

Two southwestern poets are Sharlot Hall from Arizona and Alice Corbin Henderson from New Mexico. Hall, who served for a time as Arizona state historian, had grown up on an Arizona ranch. The 102 poems in her *Cactus and Pine: Songs of the Southwest* (1911) are tub-thumping Gringo patriotism, describing

Arizona's history as the last episode of western pioneering. In "The West" the land is "Calling, calling, calling; resistless, imperative, strong; / Soldier and priest and dreamer—she drew them, a mighty throng . . . / And she cried to the Old World cities that drowse by the Eastern main: / 'Send me your weary, house-worn broods, and I'll send you Men again'" (2). The political "Arizona" rejects the proposal for Arizona and New Mexico to enter the union as one state to amalgamate their small populations. Dense populations are un-American: "Cities we lack—and gutters where children snatch for bread; / Numbers—and hordes of starvelings, toiling but never fed. . . . / We hold to the larger measure of the men that ye forget— / The men who from trackless forests and prairies lone and far, / Hewed out the land where ye sit at ease and grudge us our fair-won star" (97–98).

Alice Corbin Henderson's *Red Earth* (1920, reissued in 2003 with an introduction by Lois Rudnick with illustrations from the New Mexico Museum of Fine Arts) is the only modernist poetry I've found in the entire western array. The title poem of *Red Earth* is about "the desert of silence, / Blinking and blind in the sun— / An old, old woman who mumbles her beads / And crumbles to stone" (37). In "Los Conquistadores" the gold-seeking Spaniards ask: "What hills are these against the sky, / What hills so far and cold? / These are the hills we have come to find, / Seeking the yellow gold. / What hills, what hills so dark and still, / What hills so brown and dry? / These are the hills of this desert land / Where you and I must die" (41). Among imagist poems of landscape are "Dust-Whorl": "The wind picks up a handful of dust, / And sets it down— / Faint spiral of lives / Lived long ago on the desert" ; "Shadow": "A deep blue shadow falls / On the face of the mountain— / What great bird's wing / Has dropped a feather?" (71); "Night": "The night is dark, and the moon / Moves heavily, dragging a cross; / Penitent peaks drip, crowned with cactus; / The wind whips itself mournfully / Through the arroyos" (73); and "Pueblo:" "The pueblo rises under the sun-bronzed noon / As if hammered out of copper; / The sky's metallic blue / Rings in the silence. / Nothing moves but the shapes / That strain without changing" (75).

*   *   *

Florence Finch Kelly, a Hearst journalist who later worked as book review editor for the *New York Times,* wrote several New Mexico fictions. Her novel of 1900, *With Hoops of Steel,* remained in print at least to 1925, when Grosset and Dunlap advertised it as the first cowboy novel. As a woman journalist keen to escape society page constraints, she wrote about men's works and lives—politics, business, cattle ranching, deploying women only for peripheral love interest (so did Ruiz de Burton, so for a long time did B. M. Bower). *With Hoops of Steel,* its title invoking Shakespeare's (or Polonius') phrase for true friendship, is about three ranchers, all with New England antecedents, all of German or Irish ancestry, all tall, lean, and muscular, and all relocated from Texas. "The dim, faintly gleaming, dusty gray of the road contracted to a lance-like point in front of them and sped onward, seeming to cleave the wall of darkness and open the way through which they galloped. The three tall, broad-shouldered, straight-backed figures sat their horses with constant grace, galloping breast to breast, neck to neck and heel to heel, without pause or slackened pace. . . . On and on through the night they went, their wiry ponies with ears closely laid and muscles strained in willing compliance, the starry sky above and the long level of the plain behind them" (66).

The novel opposes small ranchers like these men to a large cattle company; they divide politically into republican (cattle company) and democrat (as Texans, these ranchmen would be democrat although the topic of slavery never enters). The opposition introduces themes of absentee ownership and suavity versus plainspoken men of the soil—literal outsiders versus true Westerners. The villain tells Emerson, the main protagonist, that he "can't keep up this sort of thing year after year, against the resources and organization of a big company. The most distinctive commercial feature of this period is the constant growth of big interests at the expense of smaller ones. It is something that the individual members of a big concern can't help, because it is bigger than they are. Our stock-holders will undoubtedly wish to enlarge their holdings and increase their profits, and I, being only one of a number, can have no right to put my personal feelings, above their interests. You ought to see that the result is going to be inevitable in your case, just as it is everywhere else. The little fellows can't hold their own against the big ones" (190–91). But in this fiction the little fellows do hold their own. The story uses the landscape for treks across the desert, near-death from thirst. There is gunplay and two romances, one with a Mexican woman.

Kelly's *The Delafield Affair* (1909) is a love story set in New Mexico. The plot depends on the supposed ease of assuming new identities in the West. The hero, a ranch manager, is looking for the man who had ruined his father back East. The story—with crooked politics, extreme natural phenomena like drought and cloudburst, the economics of raising cattle and growing alfalfa in a harsh though beautiful environment, and the background of mountain and plain— shows a new generation of Westerners rising to the challenges and possibilities of place. The heroine, who's been East for schooling and lost her health there, becomes healthy and physically agile, learning to ride horses and even rope a steer without losing a jot of her femininity. The hero's honor is shown in his decision to support a Mexican over a corrupt Anglo for congress. Behind the story is the reality of Mexican expropriation. One character, on a train, looks out at the "little adobe houses, wondering how long these peaceful Mexican homes could withstand the pressure of the dominant American. He became aware that the men behind him were discussing the same question. 'It will be only a few years,' one of them was saying, 'until this rich valley with all this water for irrigation will be in American hands.' 'The greasers are safe enough,' said his companion, 'until they begin to borrow on mortgages. Then their fate is sealed'" (39–40).

The town of Golden, center of the action, is "the depot of supplies for the widespread miles of cattle country in the plains below, the mining regions in the mountains above, and the ranches scattered along the streams within a radius of fifty miles. As its importance increased a railway sought it out, the honor of being the county seat came to it, and the ruthless Anglo-Saxon arrived in such numbers and so energetically that its few contented and improvident Mexicans, thrust to one side, sank into hopeless nonentity" (90). "The American in the Southwest, arrogant and contemptuous as the Anglo-Saxon always is when brought face to face with a difference in race, a difference in ideals, or a difference in speech, regards the Spanish language with frank disdain and ordinarily refuses to learn it" (100).

The title story in Kelly's *Emerson's Wife, and Other Western Stories* (1911) has hard-drinking lawmen out to catch a gang of Mexican criminals in Santa Fe. "Colonel Kate's Protogee" (an Indian-white romance in Santa Fe) anatomizes the highly stratified social life in that city along with the competitive women produced by a class system; "The Kid of Apache Teju" vividly describes "the gray, cactus-dotted, heat-devoured plain, weird and fascinating, with its placid, tree-fringed lakes, that are not; its barren, jagged, turquoise-tinted mountain-peaks, born here and there of the horizon and the desert; its whirling, dancing columns of sand, which mount to mid-sky; its lying distances and deceiving levels; its silence and its fierce, white unclouded sunshine" (93).

* * *

Evelyn Raymond, who set most of her girls' novels in Southern California (see Chapter 9), placed *Carlota of the Rancho* (1909) on the New Mexico-Mexico border, with two young part-Mexican children whose Anglo mother, now dead, had been disowned by her family for marrying a Mexican (even though, as always in this type of fiction, he is wholly Castilian). Searching for their unaccountably missing father, the children have many adventures with Indians and miners—two symbols of a vanishing era. Their friendship with a brakeman brings in the railroad and gives the author a chance to show how crucial the railroad is in sparsely populated territory.

Annie Fellows Johnston, author of the popular series of Kentucky-centered "little Colonel" books for girls (in 1932 a film version of this character was played by Shirley Temple), set three books in the series partly in Arizona, which she made into a sort of hell compared to heavenly Kentucky. The fatherless Ware family from Kansas, displaced to Arizona for the mother's health, finds the place teeming with invalids seeking a warm climate. In *The Little Colonel in Arizona* (1904), one young woman cries out: "I'm sick of the desert, and of seeing nothing but invalids and sand and cactus and jack-rabbits wherever I go. And I'm sick of the prospect of living in this little hole of a mud-house, and working like a squaw, and never doing anything or being anything worth while" (21). (A long parable inserted in this novel was reissued separately as a gift book; called *In the Desert of Waiting* and set in the Arabian desert, it shows how easily the American Southwest could be thought of as a foreign land.) In *Mary Ware, the Little Colonel's Chum* (1908), Mary's life is said to have been first "limited to the narrow bounds of a Kansas village, and later to the still narrower circle of experiences in the lonely little home they had made on the edge of the desert" (14); when she visits Kentucky, "coming as she did straight from the edge of the desert, with its burning stretches of sand, its cactus and greasewood, its bare red buttes, and lank rows of cotton-wood trees, this Eden of green and bloom had a double charm for her" (23). The first part of *Mary Ware's Promised Land* (1912) shows the protagonist unable to find gainful or useful work s in Arizona; she eventually returns to the "promised land" of Kentucky.

Yet a third writer for young people is Grace May North, who wrote for the Stratemeyer syndicate. One of three southwestern novels is *Adele Doring on a Ranch* (1920), about a club of eastern schoolgirls summering on an Arizona ranch. On the train, one of them witnesses an apparent hold-up and kidnapping; but it's only a movie being filmed. Elsie, a ranch neighbor, exemplifies the western girl; in the house she's "as pretty and ladylike as any girl could be, and no one can excel her in cooking; but when she has on her cowgirl togs and is astride her horse, she can throw a rope or drive a bunch of cattle as well as a boy" (138–39). Note the "astride" there, because eastern women rode sidesaddle. Two North novels from 1924, both with Indian themes, were *Virginia of V. M. Ranch* and *Virginia's Ranch Neighbors*. The V. M. Ranch story is mostly about cowboys, who, to the visiting Margaret, are "really like moving pictures" (233). There are also Indian neighbors, "just as friendly as one could wish neighbors to be. Forty years ago, it is true, we would not have cared to remain all night with the red men of the desert, but, after all, they were unfriendly merely because they believed the white man to be treacherous, and were they not right? The pale face came and drove them from their happy hunting grounds with his superior cunning and the force of arms. My sympathy has always been largely with the Indians, but come, let's have an early lunch that we may soon be on our northward way" (242–43). *Ranch Neighbors* has two marriages between Papago (Tohono O'odum) and white people. Winona marries white Harry, overcoming his mother's opposition by her beauty and character. "You know Harry likes nothing better than to ride far away into the mountains studying the rocks and trying to read the messages of the ages in the different formations. . . . Our Winona is the very first girl who has ever appealed to him as a companion" (126). The book describes the layout of an Arizona ranch: "There in the valley was the big rambling low-built adobe house, beyond it were the bunk houses, the hen yard, the wrangling corral, the pens for the cattle that needed temporary sheltering, the small adobe house nearer the dry creek bottom . . . and towering above them all was the huge red windmill, the great wings of which were slowly turning in the gentle breeze that was blowing from the west" (15).

Mary Austin's *The Trail Book* (1918) is a collection of children's stories set in a New Mexico natural history museum where, after closing time, siblings Oliver and Dorcas Jane are instructed by the animals and Indians in the dioramas. Each story involves a particular trail, trails being for Austin—as in *The Land of Little Rain*—the threads that bind the planet. The stories are told by buffalo, mammoth, puma, coyote, condor, egret, road-runner, and Indians. She explains autobiographically that her connection with the desert "began when . . . I was transplanted from a Middle Western college town to that portion of the American desert which I have described in *The Land of Little Rain* and *Lost Borders*. Here the problem of aboriginal life and its relation to the environment was the only meat upon which the avid appetite of youth could feed. I lapped up Indians as a part of the novelist's tormented and unremitting search for adequate concepts of life and society, and throve upon them" (38). In an appendix giving "facts" as the Anglo mind understands the term, the author explains to her child readers: "Without an appendix you might not discover that all of the important things in this book really *are* true. All the main traveled roads in the United States began as animal or Indian trails. There is no map that shows these roads as they originally were, but the changes are not so many as you might think. Railways have tunneled under passes where the buffalo went over, hills have been cut away and swamps filled in, but the general direction and in many places the actual grades covered by the great continental highways remain the same" (287).

There are a few army-based fictions, something not seen in other parts of the West. The earliest is Florence Kimball Russel's boys' novel, *Born to the Blue* (1906), Jack, son of an army officer, lives the first nine years of his life in Sioux territory and, when the Sioux wars end, moves to a "little four-company post in Arizona, sixty miles from anywhere—a post that has long since been abandoned, and which with little difficulty resolved itself into the surrounding miles of alkali prairie, broken only by the gray of sage-brush and gaunt cactus" (156). Within the protected environment of army posts he learns how to be a true man. Donnelly, the Irish sergeant who becomes Jack's closest pal (there are no children his own age) opines that "the real test of a good soldier is garrison life, for it's a mighty poor stick of a man that doesn't amount to sumpin when he knows his scalp may pay the bill for his worthlessness" (126). Indians, continually breaking out of their reservations, must sometimes be killed. Jack's manhood is tested when he shoots an Indian to save Donnelly's life.

Gwendolen Overton, a captain's daughter who moved to Los Angeles in the 1890s and became a literary professional, lived on army posts in Texas, Arizona and New Mexico until she was fourteen. The female protagonist of her bleak novel, *The Heritage of Unrest* (1901), suffers from the innate conflicts of her triracial mixture: white soldier father, Apache-Mexican mother. The novel, fitting extreme emotion to extreme landscape, attacks corrupt reservation agents, local politicians, Washington ignorance, and newspapers that manipulate frontier news for their editors' benefit. In a horrific set piece, ranch hands run off stock for their own benefit when Apaches attack, leaving the rancher family to be massacred. After the father is shot, the mother kills her children and then herself to evade Apache brutality. The army as Overton depicts it has little resemblance to the army honored by women memoirists. It's replete with dishonest officers, dissolute soldiers, idle and frivolous wives. Though Mexicans and Apaches are victimized and brutalized by neglect or policies that have their destruction in view, their retaliative atrocities put them well outside the bounds of the human. The heroine's unrest is the region's unrest, the outcome of competing ethnicities for control.

Overton's *The Captain's Daughter* (1903), a girls' book earlier serialized in the *Youth's Companion,* is much more lighthearted. Sixteen-year-old Marian, on an army post in Apache territory, decides to help a recruit whom she has seen stealing from her father, the Captain, by giving him a chance to replace the money. This well-meant deed produces many unforeseen and disturbing complications, teaching young readers that it's unwise to act without consulting one's elders. Indian danger in this book is mainly a figment of the overheated settler imagination; the settlers are greatly agitated when the army doesn't dash off at every rumored Indian threat. The author uses events for instructional purposes: a fire leads to an inventory of an officer's home furnishings as they are rescued from the burning building, a theft produces a discussion of army pay, runaway mules inspire a discourse on army transportation. Overton's attractively produced and atmospherically saturated novella, *The Golden Chain* (1903 and perhaps meant as a gift book), takes place mostly in the real New Mexico town of Terra Blanca; the story concerns a young rancher who falls in love with a traveling actress and saves her from false accusations. It has a pure and strong hero, a pure and vulnerable female amid bad company, and a love story with a happy ending.

Another captain's daughter, Forrestine Cooper Hooker, grew up on posts in Oklahoma and Arizona, married the son of Arizona's first and leading cattle baron, Henry C. Hooker, lived with her adult children after this marriage dissolved, and began writing (apparently at her children's urging) in middle age. Her first book, *The Long Dim Trail* (1920), was a packed cowboy-rustler-outlaw story whose main characters are an abused wife and her alcoholic husband. Because Arizona law gives the child to the father, and Katherine has a little boy, she stays on, representing long-suffering femininity in a book dominated by male action. The alcoholic husband is also a criminal, part of a gang that changes brands, rustles, holds up trains. There are cowboy pranks, cowboy yarns, a roundup, drought, storms, scenery, horses, dogs, cattle, gunplay, drinking, cursing—a full-dress western performance. Facts about Arizona climate, terrain, and the ranching that depends on it, are made essential to the story. A few Mexicans figure in the book, portrayed patronizingly but without hostility; Apaches are wrongly accused of murder; the really bad characters are all white men.

Hooker's *The Little House on the Desert* (1925—I've been unable to establish a connection between this title and Laura Ingalls Wilder's books, which came later) is a juvenile about homesteading in Arizona near Willcox (where the Hooker ranch was located). In one chapter, a moving picture company settles on the land where a young orphan lives with her grandparents. They are filming a story about Arabia, and the Arizona desert is a convincing substitute for the Arabian Desert. There are segments on homesteading law, land values, and railroads, descriptions of the nearest town (60 miles away), adobe architecture, and Mexican cuisine. More important than all these is the railroad, whose crew always looks out for this isolated family group, and whose presence is often the only link to the outside world. Hooker set her most popular juvenile—*Star: The Story of an Indian Pony* (1922)—in the 1880s. It is narrated from the perspective of the Comanche pony owned by Songbird, daughter of Quanah Parker. Because Quanah Parker surrendered to Hooker's father and brought his band to live on the army post, her view of the Comanche is entirely favorable. They don't kill white soldiers, but confuse and defeat them by stealing their horses. They fight because they are hungry and thirsty; they are hungry and thirsty because whites are killing the buffalo and diverting the streams. The book has a preface by the famous Indian fighter, General Nelson Miles, who says: "In vain might we search history for the record of a people who contended as valiantly against a superior race, overwhelming numbers, and who defended their country until finally driven towards the setting sun, a practically subjugated nation and race. The art of war among the white people is called strategy, or tactics; when practiced by the Indians it is called treachery" (vii); "If the Indians had always been humanely and honestly dealt with, there would have been but few of the troubles which have occurred in the many years gone by" (xi).

A second Hooker book for young people is the lovely *Cricket: A Little Girl of the Old West* (1925), about the life of an army child on three posts during the 1870s, the days of Satanta the Kiowa and other famous Native warriors. *Just George* (1926) combines settler/ranching with the army in a boy's book dedicated to her grandchildren, hoping "that some day they may come to understand the spirit of the now long-vanished West that I, in childhood, knew." George, a lawless, homeless orphan in Kansas City, is unofficially adopted by a ranch foreman and transformed by ranch work. His heroic ride during the 1881 assault on Fort Apache helps frustrate the Apache plot to "menace every white person in Arizona territory" (309), and in the end he graduates from West Point with honors.

Hooker's *When Geronimo Rode* (1924), a novel for grownups, is set at the end of the Geronimo campaign (1886) with a love story centered on Bonita Duncan, an orphan returning to her uncle and aunt at Fort Grant after five years at a convent school. There are two men, one good but thought to be bad, one bad but thought to be good, and the question is which has fathered a Mexican woman's illegitimate child. Bonita ends up with the wrongly accused good man, while the not-so-bad-man after all marries his Mexican sweetheart. The Geronimo campaign is recounted in detail; and except for the villainous Geronimo himself the Apache get sympathetic treatment. One character says: "The Indians have not been given a square deal. Ever since the first settlers it has been a policy of civilization by extermination, and they come back at us in the only way they know how. . . . Our unintelligent handling of the Indians—a mixture of sentimentality and merciless punishment—is a black page of American history. We punish the innocent with the guilty, and the end will only come when the Indians have ceased to exist as a race" (85).

*   *   *

Pauline Bradford Mackie's *The Voice in the Desert* (1903) is a meditative novel about the inner lives and interrelationships of five people who constitute the entire upper class of Sahuaro, Arizona—an Episcopalian minister and his wife, a rich woman born in the territory devoted to the memory of her soldier-father, a mining tycoon, and a sojourner from the East. After fifteen years in the desert the minister has come to love it. His wife hates it—"There is no peace in this desert, still as it is. Everything is fighting for its life. Even the flowers are armed" (113). But when she returns to New England she finds the people stingy and provincial: "They bored me, and I was wild to get home" (227). The novel is more interested in the tenacious, energetic town, slowly developing from its one block of stores and saloons toward an urban future, than it is in the characters. It has skillful desert descriptions, with tremendous spring floods and violent sandstorms.

Adeline Knapp's *The Well in the Desert* (1908) is an action romance in which Gard, a wrongly jailed man, breaks out of prison and has many adventures, encountering diverse western types: a tough woman with a heart of gold, a lovely young Mexican dancer, a clever, detective-like Chinese house servant, and a strong-hearted cowboy sidekick. Eventually innocence is demonstrated, villains are routed, and Gard can marry the rancher's daughter (who went to Radcliffe for four years but is happy to be home again) and work his fabulously rich mine. The book's core resides in the hero's two-year solitary sojourn in the desert as he learns to live in it and recognize its cleansing clarity. "The armed vegetation, grotesque and menacing; the preying creatures of the plain; the sand-laden wind that was constantly tearing down and rebuilding the shifting scene—were not all these but a commentary upon the mad, devouring human world about him? But the wind that laid bare the earth's nakedness clothed and healed as well, purifying the air and cleansing the waste. The give as well as the take of life was there. Death was in the desert, but not decay. Gard, feeling it all in the whirl of his emotions, knew that the grim plain which mothered the whole fierce brood had mothered him as well, giving him back health and strength from her own burning heart, and he loved her, as her children must" (212).

Marah Ellis Ryan pursued what had now become her project of bringing earlier cultures to life in their extreme otherness, especially their archaic and violence-saturated religious practices. Insofar as these practices continued to thrive among Native people, it would be no surprise to her that they were zealously hidden from Anglo eyes. The beautiful decorations and illustrations in Ryan's books might be seen as an indirect statement of the artistry inherent in paganism. In *Indian Love Letters* (1907), still in print twenty years later, a Native graduate of an eastern college back on the reservation writes to a woman student he'd fallen in love with. Recognizing that she thinks of him—if at all—only as a possible convert to Christianity, he tries to explain Indian religion as a phenomenon of the desert. But, permanently alienated from reservation life by his education, he kills himself at the book's end. *The Flute of the Gods* (1909—with more than twenty photographic illustrations by Edward S. Curtis) tells the life story of a sixteenth-century pueblo culture hero. Tanté, a light-skinned man with dark blue eyes, is born to a "virgin" mother. The story begins with his birth in 1529 and ends when he's exiled from the Tewa pueblo after being forced to kill his sweetheart (thought to be a witch) as a blood sacrifice. Tanté warns the pueblo people that the Spanish are not to be trusted: "You will be trapped by fair words. . . . The Flute of the Gods will be silenced in the land. Your Te-hua daughters will be slaves for the men of the iron! The sacred places will be feeding lands for their animals" (320–21). Convinced that violence and religion are inseparable, Ryan interprets the prevalence of murderous cruelty among Natives and Mexicans as an aspect of their Aztec belief.

Ryan's *The House of the Dawn* (1914), another historical novel, is set around the time of the Pueblo revolt (1680) and told in the first person by a young

Spanish page who goes with his mistress Sancha—the protagonist—from Spain to Mexico to New Mexico. Sancha is looking for her fiancé, Marco, whom she (mistakenly) thinks she's in love with while the man she *really* loves is Tristan, a Jewish outcast. The journey takes them north from Mexico up through all the New Mexico pueblos and tribes: Pima, Navaho, Jemez, Puyé, San Ildefonso, Pecos. As the novel describes these in anthropological and historical terms, Sancha becomes wiser. "Instead of argument or resentment at new things and pagan ideas, she grew thoughtful of them until at times she fairly divined the Indian meanings before they could be explained to her. Thus, almost without our being aware of change in her, Sancha was one in the Brotherhood of the Desert at last" (274). The novel, like *The Flute of the Gods,* is critical of Christianity. Its philosemitism is unique; not only is Tristan Jewish, but he explains that Jews financed the explorations of the New World, that Christ and his mother were Jews, even that Columbus was Jewish (133). The novel culminates with the Pueblo revolt, from which Tristan and Sancha—now a thorough-going pagan—escape to take up a happy, wandering life.

Ryan's *The Treasure Trail: A Romance of the Land of Gold and Sunshine* (1918) responds to the entrance into World War I. A heroic cowboy novel, it has an up-to-date tomboy heroine who nevertheless does nothing but wait on the sidelines. Kit, the cowboy, goes to Mexico looking for gold but gets involved with war and politics in connection with feared collusion between Mexico and Germany and a possible invasion across the border. Two abutting ranches on each side of the border—the Mexican ranch managed by a German—involve arms dealings, slaves, and sabotage (horses sent to France are given feed with ground glass in it, for example). The American pair are ideal, free of history in contrast to Mexicans and Indians who are imprisoned by it.

A somewhat different approach to Mexican–U.S. relations can be seen in Launa M. Smith's *American Relations with Mexico* (1924), published in Oklahoma City, dedicated to her mother, and most likely originating in an M.A. dissertation mainly citing the Congressional Record. Smith identifies two sources for Mexican- tension. First is the fact that more than nine-tenths of Mexican oil and mining interests are foreign owned because the Mexican "has no confidence in his own government" (228)—nor should he have. Second is continual border anarchy, which began after the Mexican War, whose "most immediate effect . . . was to give the United States a 'border.' The United States has had boundary lines before. There had always been one between her and Canada but it was not a frontier with all the sinister connotations of the word as the Mexican 'border' became" (37). Despite the underlying racism of Smith's account, according to which Mexicans are historically behind Anglos because of the significant strain of Indian blood in their veins, she believes in national autonomy and therefore argues that revolutionaries no less than the standing government are entitled to purchase arms from whatever source is willing to sell them. The ultimate solution for Mexico, which will be long in coming, is "education and real religion" (3).

Caroline Lockhart (see Chapter 8) set a couple of her novels in the Southwest. In *Me—Smith* (1911) a criminal on the run compounds his crimes by killing an Indian. He hides at a ranch owned by an "Indian woman" (who is never named). The protagonist is this woman's sixteen-year-old "breed" daughter Susie, a "game kid." Among many side characters is middle-aged fussy bachelor Peter McArthur from New England, an anthropologist looking for fossils, who turns out to be related to Susie and eventually takes her East to get educated and refined. The titular antihero was much appreciated by reviewers, but Susie's ascent drives the story. In *The Full of the Moon* (1914) Easterner Nan Galbraith—wealthy, cultivated, and twenty-one years old—wants a western fling before settling down with boring Bob, her wealthy fiancé. She chooses Hopedale, Arizona, where "Mexicans from the placers jogged in on their half-starved horses; cowboys from distant ranges came whooping in with a clatter of hoofs and a whirl of dust; footsore prospectors turned their pack-burros loose in the streets and made a bee-line for the nearest bar, and later the men in overalls from the ore-mills came to swell the Saturday night throng" (38–39). Except for Nan, women coming to Hopedale on their own have "relatives in the vicinity, deluded notions concerning Hopedale as a fertile field for canvassing for something, or the quite frank purpose of a temporary sojourn at Dona Marianna's dance-hall" (28–29).

Nan is attracted to a working-class, handsome cowboy Ben, "the embodiment of the spirit of the cowboy, an incarnation of the sand and brawn and grit of the far West, and, as such he made a mighty appeal to the primitive in the girl, to her youth, imagination and markedly romantic nature" (218). A sojourn in a Mexican border town to get away from an overly persistent suitor introduces her to "the picturesque life with its indolence and idleness. . . . In the cool of the mornings she saddled her horse and followed the trails along the river, flushing great coveys of quail, startling innumerable jack-rabbits . . . and enjoying to the utmost the wonderful colorings of the plains and distant ranges. . . . She ate the tortillas . . . and assiduously cultivated a taste for the hot chili-sauce. . . . In the evening she sauntered with the populace in the plaza, or sat in her own doorway listening to the roar of the Rio Grande and the tinkle of guitars" (145–46). Bob comes looking for her, quickly acquires Western "vigor and vim" (244), purchases a cattle company, sets Ben up as his foreman, and wins Nan back. She understands that she had only imagined herself in love with Ben when what she really loved was "the life which he typifies" (266).

* * *

Most of Honoré Willsie's western novels were set in Arizona, where she lived for four years while married to a civil engineer. *The Heart of the Desert,* published first in 1912 as *Kut-Le of the Desert,* is a version of the romance formula where women are taken in hand by masterful men. Rhoda, an invalid visiting a New Mexico ranch with her fiancé, is kidnapped by Yale graduate Charley Cartwell, who is part Apache, part Mohave, part Pueblo (his Indian name is Kut-Le). He forces her to live in the desert until she recovers her health because though he loves her, he finds her unworthy of him. "I love you for the possibilities that I see in you. I wouldn't think of marrying you as you are. It would be an insult to my good blood" (63). As an engineer working on an irrigation project—which is how they meet—he enjoys his profession because "a civil engineer has tremendous opportunities to do really big things" and "the whites make no discrimination against an Indian in the professions" (45). Rhoda and her fiancé had never known an Indian before and "most of their ideas of the race were founded on childhood reading of Cooper. Kut-le was quite as cultured, quite as well-mannered and quite as intelligent as any of their Eastern friends. But in many other qualities he differed from them. He possessed a frank pride in himself and his blood that might have belonged to some medieval prince . . . a habit of truthfulness . . . a habit of valuing persons and things at their intrinsic worth" (39).

His tough love works: "Long years after she was to catch the afterglow of that day of her rebirth. Suddenly she realized that never could a human have found health in a setting more marvelous. . . . She drank to the full this strange mad joy of life" (204); "The silent nights of stars, the laborious crests that tossed sudden and unspeakable views before the eyes, the eternal cañons that led beneath ranges of surpassing majesty, roused in her a passion of delight that could find expression only in her growing physical prowess. She lived and ate like a splendid boy. . . . Tenderly reared creature of an ultracivilization as she was, she learned the intricate lore of the aborigines, learned what students of the dying people would give their hearts to know" (205). In the end, saving Kut-Le from a posse, she chooses him over her fiancé.

Willsie's *Still Jim* (1915) establishes her hero's New England bona fides and takes him first to the Pacific Northwest for an apprenticeship, then to Arizona where he fulfills his commitment to blood and nation by joining the Reclamation Service. "For the first time, his Anglo-Saxon race, his race of empire builders, was finding its voice in him" (36). "That's the greatest work in the world—getting out into the wilderness and finding the right spot for civilization to come and thrive. There's where you get a sense of power that makes you feel like a Pilgrim Father" (83). More important than any particular engineering problem is the service commitment to the "building of small democracies that may become the living nuclei for the rebirth of all that America once stood for" (316). In Willsie's

The Forbidden Trail (1919), Midwesterner Roger Moore, who wants to invent a machine run by solar power, sees Arizona as a potential empire: "Mineral resources beyond the dreams of avarice, four or five crops a year of food-stuffs. Why, man, millions of people could come in here and be self-sustaining. . . . A cheap fuel would open up Arizona, New Mexico, Southern California and Northern old Mexico as no one can conceive who's not studied the subject. If I can put over my experiment, I shall add to the potential wealth of this country as no single individual has ever done" (110).

He explores the desert with a group of friends: "The more intense the heat grew, the more intense, it seemed to Roger, grew the weird beauty of the desert. The midnight stars seemed hardly to have blossomed before dawn turned the desert world to a delicate transparent yellow, deepening at the zenith to blue and on the desert floor to orange. As the sun rose, the yellow changed suddenly to scarlet and for a few moments earth and sky quivered in a lambent red fire. When the sun had shot clear of the mountains, details of landscape and contrasts of color were accented. Clear black of peaks, crimson of canyons, purples of rifts in the ranges, bright moss green of cactus dots on the yellow desert floor. And always to the west that far melting loveliness of blue and gold and black that was the River Range. And always the quivering, parching air that burned against the body like a furnace blast" (207–8). The plot turns political when friend Ernie (of German background), is transformed by the war from a Germanophile to Germanophobe. He says, in the novel's longest exhortation, "Patriotism is to a man's community life what religion is to his moral life. I want to love a country, and I couldn't see, when I got down to brass tacks, why that country should be Germany. This is the land that bred me and fed me. Actually I'm a physical part of the soil of America" (371).

Willsie's *The Enchanted Canyon* (1921) is a rags-to-riches and captain-of-industry novel. Enoch Huntingdon is rescued from the slums by a millionaire lawyer who leaves him at the Grand Canyon with a guide named Frank Allen. Their descent into the Canyon produces a rebirth such that twenty-two years later, at age thirty-six, he's secretary of the interior. A conservationist, not preservationist, he says: "The time is approaching when oil, gas, and coal will not supply the power needed in America. We shall have to turn more and more to electricity produced by water power. There is enough water in the streams of this country to turn every wheel in every district. But it must be harnessed, and after it is harnessed it must be sold to the people at a just price. What I want to do is to produce all the available water power latent in our waterways. Then I want the poorest people in America to have access to it. . . . My policy aims to embody the idea that the men who develop the water power of America shall not develop for themselves and their associates a water power monopoly" (59–60). There's a romance between Enoch and Frank's daughter, Diana, a photographer of Indians and Indian landscape and ruins, who has been trying "to make a last-ing pictorial record of the Indians and their ways" (75); "I was conscious of the great loss to the world in the disappearance of the spiritual side of Indian life. . . . I knew the Indians well and the beauty of their ceremonies was even then more or less merged in my mind with the beauty of the Cañon. Their mysticism was the Cañon's mysticism" (101).

Grace MacGowan Cooke's desert novel, *The Joy Bringer; A Tale of the Painted Desert* (1913), contains pages of information about the Hopi. A spoiled beauty from Kentucky marries the wrong brother (who turns out to be the right brother) by mistake, and goes with him for appearance's sake to Oraibi on the Hopi res-ervation, where they live apart chastely. The West and the Indians are sources of unconventionality and directness available to whites, so that at the end the couple can unite on the grounds of a higher and at the same time more elemental passion than that which dominates conventional life.

Cora Marsland, a teacher at the Kansas State Normal School in Emporia, published a pietistic novel, *The Angel of the Gila: A Tale of Arizona,* in 1911. The New England protagonist, from a background of reformers who advocate for "everything that makes for righteousness" (48), means to become an urban social worker but, meeting an Arizona ranching family, goes instead to Gila as a teacher. She learns about local issues and puts her reformer heritage to good use. "Her magazine articles on the Indian first drew attention to her. Then her address at the Mohonk Conference brought her into further prominence. She was asked to speak before the Indian Commission. Later, she was sent by the Government to visit Indian schools, and report their condition. . . . What she has done for the Indians, she has also done for the cause of general education in Arizona" (287). Happily married as well, she is now "an educational and moral force in the Southwest" (289). Her Indian ward, Wathema, has gone to Carlisle and Harvard and plans to take a doctorate, after which he'll dedicate himself to the "uplift" of his race (292).

Katharine Sharp's *Jocelyn West: A Tale of the Grand Cañon* (1912) is a bi-zarre tale of grand, doomed passion in the Canyon with a few pages satiriz-ing tourists incapable of appreciating the sublime scenery, which she also describes. An adulterous couple takes refuge in a cave along the trail down into the Canyon, where they are hemmed in by the pursuing husband. Faced with certain death, the man takes his sleeping lover in his arms and jumps into the canyon. The sublimity of the Canyon is perhaps misused to signify nothing more than the dangers of adultery, but in general the Canyon defied, and defies, fictional treatment.

Christian romance-writer Grace Livingston Hill wrote two southwestern novels. In *The Man of the Desert* (1914), New Hampshire missionary John Brownleigh is still charmed by the "wonder of the desert" after three years in

Arizona. "Below him were ledges of rocks in marvelous colours. . . . Beyond was a stretch of sand, broken here and there by sage-brush, greasewood, or cactus rearing its prickly spines grotesquely" (24–25). He and socialite Hazel Radcliffe meet; various obstacles keep them apart until love and the desert conquer all. "It seemed to Hazel's city bred eyes as though the kingdom of the whole world lay spread before her awed gaze" (99). Like many a scholarly hero before and after, John woos his love with information: telling "of the Indian hogans, little round huts built of logs on end . . . of the medicine-men, the ignorance and superstition, the snake dances and heathen rites, the wild, poetic, conservative man of the desert with his distrust, his great loving heart, his broken hopes and blind aspirations until Hazel began to see that he really loved them, that he had seen the possibility of greatness in them, and longed to help develop it" (108–9). John writes to his mother about Walpi, "its only access a narrow neck of land less than a rod wide. . . . He explained that Spanish explorers found these Hopis in 1540, long before the pilgrims landed at Plymouth Rock" (175); "then he went on to describe a remarkable meeting that had been held in which the Indians had manifested deep interest in spiritual things, and had asked many curious questions about life, death and the hereafter" (176).

Hill's *A Voice in the Wilderness* (1916) begins when Margaret Earle, novice schoolteacher in Arizona, mistakenly gets off the train at the wrong place and is left alone in "this wild Western land" (10). She is rescued by Gardley, the "Kid," an Easterner working as a cowboy. She asks him: "Does it always seem so big here—so—limitless? . . . It is so far to everywhere it takes one's breath away, and yet the stars hang close, like a protection. It gives one the feeling of being alone in the great universe with God" (20). Gardley tells Margaret about "Arizona in its early ages, including a detailed description of the cliff-dwellers and their homes, which were still to be seen. . . . He told her of the petrified forest just over some low hills off to the left. . . . He described the coloring of the brilliant days in Arizona, where you stand on the edge of some flat-topped mesa and look off through the clear air to mountains that seem quite near" (23–24).

* * *

In *The Phantom Herd* (1915), B. M. Bower brings the Happy Family from the Flying U to New Mexico to work in western films. Luck, the director, who idolizes realism, has been searching vainly in Wyoming for real cowboys—the fence has done them in—until he finds the Flying U still in business. Recognizing that the Old West is truly dead, that the Flying U is a relic, he employs the Happy Family for a film bringing the past back to life authentically. The crew settles on a ranch outside Albuquerque owned by the old codger, Applehead, for a cattle film, a man's story with women in deliberately subordinate roles. (Though Bower had begun to use women protagonists, she saw them as creations of the New West inappropriate for a story about the Old West.) A huge blizzard through which cattle and cowboys must struggle makes the film's key scene unusually realistic. Luck takes his finished film to the Cattlemen's Association meeting in El Paso where the cattlemen endorse its authenticity.

In Bower's *The Heritage of the Sioux* (also 1916) bank robbers, aided by some members of the film crew, disguise a real heist as a movie shoot. Luck feels responsible for catching these criminals; he and the Happy Family enter the Navaho reservation where they are mistaken for pursuers of renegade Nava-hos. The whole tribe cooperates, using age-old tricks to erase the trail, which gives Bower the chance to point out that white people really know nothing about Indians. The metaphor for all these intersections of real and imaginary is that great desert apparition, the mirage. In the meantime, the one important woman character, a young Sioux horsewoman named Annie Manyponies, having inadvertently cooperated with the criminals, kills herself in accordance with supposed tribal values.

In *Starr, of the Desert* (1917) Bower leaves the Happy Family, following an undercover secret service agent looking for a revolutionary group colluding with Germans who plan to reclaim New Mexico, Arizona, and Texas for Mexico. According to the villain, "When Mexico joins with Germany against the damned English and French . . . our friends will sweep over from Mexico and gather in all these border states—which were once hers—and will again be hers through the strong mailed hand of Germany!" (93). The romance is between Starr and Helen May, a young woman from Los Angeles reluctantly homesteading with her brother to regain her health. "Helen May stood on the knobby, brown rock pinnacle that formed the head of Sunlight Basin and stared resentfully out over the baked desert and the forbidding hills and the occasional grassy hollows that stretched away and away to the skyline. . . . She felt its bigness and its wildness; and she who had lived the cramped life of the town resented both, because she had no previous experience by which to measure any part of it" (63). But the desert wins out; it "put a clear, steady look into her eyes in place of the glassy shine of fever. It was beginning to fill out that hollow in her neck, so that it no longer showed the angular ends of her collar bones. It had put a resilient quality into her walk, firmness into the poise of her head" (73). Eventually Helen May discovers "that this wild, strange land was beautiful. . . . The reddened clouds that rimmed the purple were the radiant shores of a wonderful, bottomless sea, where the stars were the mast lights on ships hull down in the distance. She lifted her chest and drew in long breaths of clean, sweet air that is like no other air, and she remembered all at once that she had not coughed since daylight. She breathed again, deep and long, and felt that she was drawing some wonderful, healing ether into her lungs" (85).

Vingie Roe published three action-packed southwestern novels whose women protagonists are fine horsewomen and shooters. *Tharon of Lost Valley* (1919) is a cattle-rustling, gun-slinging story in which Tharon, a rancher's daughter, faces down Buck Courtrey, owner of the adjacent and competing ranch. Courtrey's specialties are cattle rustling, homesteader terrorizing, and cowboy killing, but as the biggest landowner around, he is above the law. Into this situation comes Kenset, from D.C. and the Forest Service. Kenset "had read romances of the great West in his youth and felt a vague regret that he had not lived in the rollicking days of '49. Now as he rode his new domain he smiled to himself and thought that out of a modern college he had been set back half a century. Here was the rule of might, if he was not mistaken. Here was romance in its most vital and appealing form" (119). The twist making this an untraditional woman's novel is that Tharon, a fine shot, ultimately shoots the horse ridden by the fleeing Courtrey, which kills him too.

Roe's 1921 *Val of Paradise* is set on the Arizona-Mexico border in the fictional town of Santa Leandra—an "ancient dame among towns. Three generations back she had sent out her wagons with their freight of gold, brought them back laden with supplies for the two stores. Today the wagons still creaked over the many miles of bunch-grass plain that lay between her and the railroad—the railroad that would never come nearer—and they still carried a slender freight of gold, still brought back supplies. For Santa Leandra, though seemingly of the past, was very much of the present" (9–10). Val Hannon, the angelic-heroic protagonist, daughter of John Hannon who owns the largest ranch and has wonderful horses, is a true Western heroine because of her skill with horses and guns. The novel includes a dramatic night ride, skillful scene-setting description of ranch, town, gambling, the mission, Mexicans, cowboy yarns, and a great deal of serious riding. Roe's *Nameless River* (1923) pits cattle ranching (bad) against homesteading (good), with two women opponents—"Cattle Kate," the dark-haired owner of the Skyline ranch and Nance Allison, the blonde-haired, bible-reading homesteader who lives on the flats with her mother and disabled brother trying to farm the property while keeping it out of Kate's clutches.

Ethel Dorrance (in collaboration with James Dorrance) published two Arizona ranch novels (1920, 1926) where women exchange bad local boyfriends for good Easterners who combine western virility with eastern culture and ethics. The breezy style uses western stereotypes while mocking them. In *Glory Rides the Range* (1920), a hero's statue has a "real 'old-timer' of a gun clutched against his imitation side . . . a reminder of past dangers conquered in combat for the benefit of a new generation. Through the sky-blue paint with which, by way of verisimilitude, his eyeballs had been colored, seemed to look the indomitable courage that, in olden times, had helped the dead to die gallantly—that should, in these still stressful present-days, help the quick to live aright" (97–98). The title of *Glory Rides the Range* refers to the protagonist, Gloriana directly; and indirectly to her love of horses. She helps a stranger get his automobile out of a ditch, commenting that "when the motor craze honked over the country it looked as though we horse folks were doomed to become also-rans. A world war was necessary to re-establish our importance in the big scheme of things" (37). This hapless automobile driver is working for the government, looking for water and posting signs when he finds it; he replaces Glory's churlish neighbor as her suitor.

In *The Rim O' The Range* (1926), the heroine lives with her uncle on a border ranch (the Arizonamex, it's called), which attracts outsiders eager to buy it because they rightly assume the uncle is in financial trouble. He is in fact "in the position of seventy-five per cent of the live-stock growers of the West at that moment—broke" (36). "On every hand throughout the West, both cow and sheepmen were in trouble, many of them unable to provide gasoline for the high-priced limousines they had bought with the tremendous profits made at the beginning of the World War period. Their heavy losses, potential or real, had foundation in three years' protraction of an unprecedented drouth. . . . Always have stockmen been large borrowers of money, and from them in the past most regional bankers had waxed fat. But this time, loans on both cattle and sheep had been made at the peak of valuation, and now that prices had tumbled and freights had risen beyond endurance they were finding their bargains bad" (41–42).

In *Widening Waters* (1924), Kansas novelist Margaret Hill McCarter brought the grandson of one of her early Kansas characters, Baronet, to New Mexico as an engineer building an irrigation dam for a settler colony. There's a love story featuring Faith, an American girl in her ideal western version: a great horse-woman, attractively natural although unconscious of her charm, interested in the world around her, entirely unselfish, whose appreciation of Indian spirituality reflects "her deeper, finer nature" (153)—for once McCarter abandons her anti-Indian perspective. The book's real center is the dam-builder, the modern pioneer. "It is real history-making, where a man puts his own brain against the everlasting granite; a different kind of enemy, but as real a one as my father had in Kansas back in the 'sixties" (141). Irrigation means agriculture, which means "a community, a church, a schoolhouse, increased land values, more revenue in the state treasury from taxable property—and homesteads, and prosperity" (176). "The sunny, waterless plains; the still, tall mesas; the gigantic mountain peaks, the deep-riven canons—were setting for all the overmastering elements that shape life to nobler ends or dwarf it to sordid uselessness" (273).

Blanche C. Grant, an artist from the Northeast, moved to Taos in 1920 and became a booster of the town and region. She started editing the *Taos Valley News* in 1922 and published several books beginning in 1925. *Taos Indians* (127 pages),

One Hundred Years Ago in Old Taos (31 pages), and *Taos Today* (47 pages) explain the attractions, dwell on the Taos colony of artists, and instruct tourists on how to appreciate what they see. The approach to the Indians is both respectful and patronizing; she calls them "our Indians" and quotes one person to the effect that "you may pick out one thousand of the best Americans in New Mexico, and one thousand of the best Mexicans in New Mexico, and one thousand of the worst pueblo Indians, and there will be found less, vastly less, murder, robbery, theft or other crimes among the thousand of the worst pueblo Indians than among the thousands of the best Mexicans or Americans in New Mexico" (86–87). *One Hundred Years Ago* memorializes the earliest entrance of Americans into Taos, and Grant tries to show the town—not the pueblo—exactly as it was at that time, using long excerpts from Spanish and American sources, and praising such early-entering mountain men as Jim Bridger, for whom Taos served as entrance to southern Colorado. In *Taos Today* the author takes an airplane trip over the Taos valley, and writes about the Penitentes, Kit Carson (she later published his dictated life story), and the artist colony: "It must ever be remembered that Taos is home of the serious artist in Taos because of the valley where there's "Color, color everywhere!" (14,15). The sketches in Mary Austin's *The Land of Journey's Ending* (1924, reissued with an introduction by Melody Graulich in 2003) are based on a summer automobile trip around the Southwest. The essays publicize the Taos and Santa Fe art colonies, and says a truly American art will ultimately emerge from New Mexico, "still a place in which the miraculous may happen" (337). A capsule history of New Mexico is informed by a complicated (and now, risible) race theory beginning with nomad Indians and ending with the incoming Anglos, an "energetic blond engrafture" (443) that can bypass the centuries of Hispanic life to connect directly with the aboriginals.

In 1927, Elinore Cowan Stone published *The Laughingest Lady,* an episodic novel about a teacher in a New Mexico mill town, tracing her romance with the town's mayor and mill manager as well as her success as a third-grade teacher of Mexican students. The town has its Mexican quarter—"here pastel patches of blue, salmon and mauve that were the walls of small houses peeking through luxurious draperies of wild cucumber and hop vines; here, illumined by the morning sun against the gray crumbling plaster wall just opposite an open door, a gorgeous image of the Virgin" (26)—and its American quarter, with "wide, graveled streets that swept from the great wall sand smokestacks of the ore mills at the extreme left edge of town . . . [with] demure rows of low, square white cottages, identical to the window-pane, and placed with geometrical precision in the centers of square lots. Each yard was surrounded by a barbed wire fence with a white picket gate; each house had a neat gravel walk leading to its front door and a coal shed in the extreme left corner of the back yard" (27). Though the children's dialect is hard to follow, inviting a reader to dismiss the book as an exercise in patronizing chauvinism, it shows the children's sturdy personalities and the teacher's respect for them. Late in the novel the students, assigned to an unpleasant new teacher and understanding after all what being American means, go on strike. They demonstrate with slogans, placards, and marches against this newly arrived Southerner who calls them greasers to their face; and they win.

* * *

Willa Cather's *The Professor's House* (1925) inserts the long, separately written "Tom Outland's Story" as Book II of her Midwestern tale of a professor facing a sort of midlife crisis. Tom and a friend have discovered mesa-top ruins; his attempts to interest the US government in preserving them fail; the priceless find is eventually translated into dollars when Tom's partner sells the "curios" to a German trader. (Perhaps the trader's nationality is a belated instance of Germanophobia.) If the story is thematically about a form of corruption when the priceless gets a price tag, it is also obliquely about what is and what isn't really "American," with the truly American identified with the West. "I see them here, isolated, cut off from other tribes, working out their destiny, making their mesa more and more worthy to be a home for man, purifying life by religious ceremonies and observances, caring respectfully for their dead" (233). "I feel a reverence for this place. Wherever humanity has made that hardest of all starts and lifted itself out of mere brutality, is a sacred spot" (234).

Cather's ultimate southwest book is her incomparable *Death Comes for the Archbishop* (1927). Though inspired by William J. Howlett's 1908 biography of Archbishop Lamy's partner, Machebeuf, and based on a great deal of research, its renaming of Lamy as Latour and Machebeuf as Vaillant tells readers that her subject is not the real history of the region. The sheer number of what editors of the Library of America edition have called mistakes in the book shows that Cather was not concerned with factual accuracy. In her view, it was always the artist who invented a group's legends, which is to say a group's truths, and she ambitiously set herself to represent this process in her novel about Santa Fe and the whole of New Mexico. *Death Comes for the Archbishop,* in part about a friendship between two men lived mostly in the imagination, since they are mostly separated, tells the story of Latour's great ambition, which like that of any artist is to transcend death. The book encompasses Mexicans and Indians— Isleta, Laguna, Pecos, Taos, Santo Domingo, Acoma, the Penitentes of Abiquiu, the Navajo. Kit Carson is there, changing from a hero into the "misguided" man who imprisoned the Navajo at Bosque Redondo. Latour, dying, remembers how for many years he had wondered "if there would ever be an end to the Indian wars while there was one Navajo or Apache left alive. Too many traders and manufacturers made a rich profit out of that warfare; a political machine and immense capital were employed to keep it going" (454); but he concludes that "God has been very good to let me live to see a happy issue to those old wrongs. I do not believe, as I once did, that the Indian will perish. I believe God will preserve him" (458).

Latour's ambition to forestall death by constructing a great cathedral in the French style in Santa Fe is, after all, a demonstration of his own "white" blood: "Father Latour judged that, just as it was the white man's way to assert himself in any landscape, to change it, make it over a little (at least to leave some mark or memorial of his sojourn), it was the Indian's way to pass through a country without disturbing anything: to pass and leave no trace, like fish through the water, or birds through the air" (419). "They seemed to have none of the European's desire to 'master' nature, to arrange and re-create. . . . They ravaged neither the rivers nor the forest . . . not attempting to improve it, they never desecrated it" (420). What Cather seems to be implying here—it cannot be accidental that Latour shares this ambition—is that white people resist death while Native people accept it within the flow of nature. The earth wins; it's no accident that the first word of the title is "death."

11

On the Trail, On the Road

Most women's western books were about the place, not getting to it. Even some books named for the trail are only incidentally about it. Those books that are true journey books fall into three categories. First are army and overland accounts, many written long after the events they narrate, shaped by a sense of western history, by fallible memory, by needs and desires to spin the story in the writer's or her family's favor. Second are railroad travel books, examples of a short-lived genre that came into existence a decade or so after the completion of the transcontinental railroad in 1869. These followed the itineraries of the popular excursion companies and thus repeated many particulars, all the more because many literary travelers were moralistic New Englanders worried about western behaviors. In the twentieth century women began to go West by automobile, and wrote to celebrate auto travel as much as to describe the West.

Railroad and auto books shaped the "West" as an imaginative reappearance of earlier days, referring what they saw on the ground to ideas about the West they had begun with. Writing quite specifically to bring the dead back to life, Lydia Spencer Lane's 1893 *I Married a Soldier* (reissued in 1987 with an introduction by Darlis Miller) says: "To-day there is no 'frontier;' the wilderness blossoms as the rose; our old deadly enemy, the Indian, is educated, clothed, and almost in his right mind; railroads run hither and yon, and the great trains of army wagons and ambulances are things of the past, whatever civilization may follow. The hardy, adventurous element in those early pioneer days will ever possess an interest of its own, and I venture to hope that the record of my own experiences will contribute somewhat to the history of those heroic times" (13).

In earlier chapters I have talked about some books set mainly in one place that also had extensive travel sections. Elizabeth Cornelia Woodcock Ferris's *The Mormons at Home* (1856), for example, contributed to Utah writing but ultimately positions Salt Lake City along the way to Sacramento and the gold rush. Women who went overland to the Pacific Northwest or to the California gold fields sometimes had sections about the journey there, almost always recalling it as a nightmarish interlude.

The earliest of what might be thought of as wholly road-oriented books are three dime novels from the 1860s, frank fantasies directed, surprisingly for those who think of the dime novel as a masculine genre, toward women readers. Ann Sophia Stephens's *Esther: A Story of the Oregon Trail* (1862) has Mormons, Sioux, a beautiful Indian maiden, and a Byronic plainsman recovering from an unhappy love affair masquerading as an Indian. The protagonist is traveling the Oregon trail with her uncle. The stories make the road into a place for men to have adventures and women to find romance. Stephens says that the prairie life of "constant changes and excitement . . . is a school, the like of which there is not elsewhere on earth, for training men to be self-reliant, brave to recklessness, scornful of privation, uncaring for hardship, and steady and unquailing in the hour of strife" (65). (One may remember that books set entirely on the prairie seldom saw life there as exciting.) And Stephens does mean "men." The novel endorses Manifest Destiny, and waxes nostalgic over the vanishing Indian: "The star that leads civilization westward shines sadly upon the graves of a people almost extinct—a people that have been hunted ruthlessly from their greenwood haunts till every year has seen their graves multiplying thicker and thicker in the wilderness. Then the Anglo-Saxon comes to plow it up and plant corn above the dead warriors, stopping now and then to pick up a stone arrowhead from his furrow, and examine it curiously, as if he did not know what soil his sacrilegious plow was upturning. . . . Yon star that leads westward has no halting place for him till it sets on the calm Pacific, writing on its blue waters the history of a people that have perished" (9).

Metta Victoria Victor's two western dime novels are *The Gold Hunters* (1863) and *The Two Hunters; or, The Cañon Camp, A Romance of the Santa Fe Trail* (1865). *The Gold Hunters* takes place on the trail to Pike's Peak. Amid storms, fires, Indians, captures, rescues, and daring feats, a father meets his long-lost daughter on the trail and cedes her to the pioneer scout Nat, in reality an aristocrat in disguise. The father takes a typical antimining, profarming stance, advising that "there was a hundred-fold more gold to be found in carrots and corn and potatoes, than in the quartz of the ravines. The rich character of the land immediately at the foot of the mountain, and the fabulous prices which fruits and vegetables would bring for years to come, would insure a fortune to any farmer who would give his attention to the cultivation of articles needed in the market" (99). *The Two Hunters* features another aristocrat in disguise, this one on the trail trying to forget a love affair gone wrong. The end point of Santa Fe sets the book up geographically, but the exotic Santa Fe described, of glittering domes and minarets, has nothing in common with any Santa Fe seen by eyewitnesses. At the end, the reunited lovers and others in their party return to St. Louis, where they began; the road in this kind of novel is the fairy-tale space of nowhere.

*   *   *

E. D. E. N. Southworth's comic romance, *An Unrequited Love* (1883), is a sequel to another novel of that year, *For Woman's Love.* In the first, the popular and prolific novelist, whose books used and gently satirized the conventions of dime novels and the news of the day, managed to delay the happy conclusion to the story of a couple separated by mutual misunderstandings on their wedding day by following several other troubled romances within the heroine's family. The heroine, believing that her missing husband had been killed by Comanches on the prairie, decides to go West with her soldier brother to Fort Farthermost on the Texas frontier, where she plans to open a school for Indian children. A little group gathers around her, led by her bachelor uncle Mr. Clarence, who goes merely for a whim, not having "enlisted in the army" nor "received any appointment as post trader or Indian agent from the government, nor missionary or schoolmaster from any Christian association" (271). The story is set before the Civil War, which allows for a little family of Clarence's black servants to join the group: writes Southworth, "I know that since the days of which I write this section of the country has been wonderfully developed, and the wilderness has been made to 'bloom and blossom as the rose' but in those days it was still laid down on the maps as 'The Great American Desert'" (264). After Fort Leavenworth, the little group launches out across the Kansas prairie, where the vanished husband is discovered in the guise of a plainsman, "a majestic man, cloaked in coat of buckskin, faced and bordered with fur, leggings of buckskin and sandals of buffalo hide" (284). The novel includes an encounter with friendly Indians (Pawnees) who come to beg and barter and describes the prairie's autumn beauty, "now rising to a smooth, gradual elevation that revealed the circle of the whole horizon where it met the sky; now descending into a wide, shallow hollow, where the rising ground around inclosed them as in an amphitheater; but everywhere along the trail, the prairie grass, dried and burnished by the autumn's suns and winds, burned like gold" (277).

Many late-life trail books celebrate the covered wagon people less for the heroic events they participated in than for the grinding monotony and physical hardship they endured. Sarah Raymond Herndon's 1902 *Days on the Road: Crossing the Plains in 1865* republishes an overland diary she had serialized in a magazine twenty years before. (It was reissued with an introduction by Mary Barmeyer O'Brien in 2003.) Herndon, her widowed mother, and two of her three brothers, head to Virginia City on the crowded Platte River trail "with about two hundred wagons in sight" (30). "More than one thousand men, women and children, and I cannot guess how many wagons and tents. The wagons have been crossing all day" (50). She is awed by mountains, bored by the plains—"let those whose tastes are on a level with the ground they tread feel proud of and admire their prairie fields, but give to me a mountain home" (93)—and contemptuous of the Indians, "the most wretched-looking creatures I ever saw, nothing majestic, dignified, or noble-looking" (43). She describes fears of Indian atrocities (which don't happen) and swindles by fellow whites (which do). Men "throw a very poor excuse of a bridge across a stream that could be easily forded if let alone, but they spoil the crossing by digging ditches and throwing in bush and timbers to obstruct the fording, then build a cabin, close to the bridge, and squat to make a fortune by extorting large toll from emigrants, who have not the time to stop and contend for their rights. It seems a shameful business" (95).

Lavinia Honeyman Porter's family published her manuscript, *By Ox-Team to California in 1860* in 1910, the year she died. The family asserted that they were issuing a manuscript prepared for publication. Some historians, like John Mack Faragher, have used the book to show that women found the westering experience distasteful; others, like Sandra Myres, cite it for its demonstration of female fascination with the grand western landscape. To me, this book is best viewed as artful embellishment rather than evidence of anything that actually happened. Supposedly based on the stories she told her grandchildren (not, after all, good evidence of their accuracy!), said by the author to have been derived from a no-longer-extant journal supplemented by her memories, it collapses every kind of westering experience into the lives of one couple on the trail. It's a very readable compilation of entertaining trail stories.

Sarah J. Cummins's 1914 *Autobiography and Reminiscences* briefly rehearses her horrific overland journey to Oregon in 1845, when the starving group was saved by Marcus Whitman, who guided them to friendly Indians. She writes "we were surely taking a wild and inconsiderate step. . . . My husband had a copy of the 'Lewis and Clark' report and from that it was decided that our route lay along the banks of the Missouri river, although no definite idea was given, as making the journey in wagons and carriage was so different from the one made by Clark and Lewis" (34). "We continued our daily journeying, listening to the regular tramping of the poor four-footed beasts over the plain and through the dust, the midsummer sun beaming through the cloth roofs and the look of stern desperation setting in the countenances of the most refined and self sacrificing. A weary sameness seemed to characterize each, giving the look of similarity to the outline" (42). "The daily routine of work was now becoming almost beyond the strength of our poor teams to accomplish and yet it was impossible to stop.

We must either forge our way or take the risk of staying over winter in these lone wild mountains" (49). Before the trip is over, several in the wagon train have starved or frozen to death.

The trail also inspired a few novels. Mary Hallock Foote's *A Picked Company* (1912) installs New Englanders as the core of the best western type. A New England minister gathers said picked company for Oregon travel to realize the perfect life, just as the New England Puritans had gathered for travel to the New World. These voyagers have no interest in Natives, who pry, pilfer, run off cattle, and beg; they are "feathered Gentlemen of the Road" with faces blacked for murder (114), sinister suppliants "dangerous to refuse" (283). The noble goal is linked to the antislavery cause, a connection not seen in the writing of any Oregon woman I found. According to this novel, in response to the antislavery clause in the Oregon constitution submitted to Congress, the North "did not wait to win the fight in Congress" but "sent men of brains and character, who moved their families out there, on the ground, making the venture a species of crusade. They were helping to anchor the future State in principles of a nation's faith as dear to them as their fathers' religion. . . . The great pathway had been cut from ocean to ocean; toil of countless feet of men and cattle with sweat and blood had worn it wider, every year" (405–6). Marcus Whitman—who couldn't possibly have met this group at the time they are said to have been crossing the plains (but the historical novel as a genre almost always introduces historical counterfactuals like this; it must do so because its characters are otherwise fictive) arrives on the scene to assure the group that whatever negatives they've heard about Oregon emanate from Hudson's Bay Company propaganda designed to discourage American emigration. En route the picked company is augmented by gamblers, sexually loose women, and killers; bitter rivalries emerge, people are expelled from the train, there are murders. Two couples represent the virtuous and the vicious, and at the fork in the road past Fort Laramie, the undesirables opt for California while the New Englanders remain true to Oregon: "builders for the Northwest, gamblers for California" (406), says the narrator; "we think that the builders will always have the last word in any true story or one that pretends to be true,—though the gamblers shall be there, foremost in every race for achievement or possession: they run as torch-bearers, and end as incendiaries who perish in their own fires" (401). So Oregon is posited as New England, while California is written off the map.

Because the Santa Fe trail ran through Kansas, and because the Kansas DAR made it a project to mark the trail across the state, a couple of Kansans wrote trail stories mostly about Kansas. I suggested in Chapter 7 that this endeavor defended in part against the redefinition of Kansas and Nebraska as Midwestern, a designation depriving them of all western glamour. Kate Aplington's *Pilgrims of the Plains: A Romance of the Santa Fe Trail* (1913) takes the form of a journal kept by a woman on the trail, who goes because her seventeen-year-old invalid brother needs care. She finds romance with a German scientist looking for botanical specimens. The story involves furtive and treacherous Mexicans, stolid and vengeful Indians, upstanding ethical Scots, singing Negroes. Standard landscape descriptions include tornado, rainstorm, heat, and fine pure prairie air. "The wide prairies are glorious! The wind salutes us with a sweet, fresh kiss as it passes. . . . The rank grasses are already more than waist high. . . . And this lovely country hasn't even a name!" (130). At the end of the journey, the protagonist looks "upon the men grouped about us, and they were not as I had seen them day by day. I saw them as those who are yet to be born will see them! They are Heroes,—the *Conquerors of the Wilderness* . . . men strong and courageous, born with a feverish unrest in their hearts, with a divine frenzy in their souls, that urged them ever to tread out for themselves the new strange pathway. All the obstacles that Nature puts in their way are to them as nothing. Seas may not stay them, nor forests affright, nor deserts dismay! Bold and rough and daring they are, but they know what gentleness and tenderness mean" (210–11).

Margaret Hill McCarter expanded her Kansas repertory with *Vanguards of the Plains* (1917), a book using plot devices extracted from Southworth's *An Unrequited Love*, extolling businessmen as the real creators of a region's prosperity, and coming close to redefining Santa Fe as an outpost of Kansas City. The orphaned narrator-protagonist arrives in Kansas when he is ten, to live with his kindly uncle Esmond Clarenden (a version of Southworth's Uncle Clarence). Esmond is an unusual hero—fat, short, maternal, and commercial—but he is also the "real man," compared to whom soldier and plainsman are "but shadows." Esmond, foreseeing the Mexican War, wants to get to Santa Fe before it is ceded to the US. The war, he says, "won't last long, and we are sure to take over a big piece of ground there when it is over. And when that is settled commerce must do the real building-up of the country. I want to be a part of that thing and grow with it" (17). The book recounts four treks across the plains from the Missouri River to Santa Fe. On the first, around 1844, Esmond gathers a representative group including a Yankee, an African American woman (who admirably knows how to keep her place), and others. They encounter wily Mexicans, ferocious Apaches, a noble Hopi maiden, and in Santa Fe a lovely blonde child who becomes Esmond's ward and the narrator's love interest. The second segment of the novel travels the trail as it develops throughout the 1850s. The third part takes place after the Civil War and follows the 18th Kansas Cavalry as it wrests the state from Indians who fight "foot by foot, for supremacy against the out-reaching civilization of the dominant Anglo-American. The lonely trails were measured off by white men's graves. The vagrant winds that bear the odor of alfalfa, and of orchard bloom to-day, were laden often with the smoke of burning homes, and often, too, they bore that sickening smell of human flesh, once caught, never to be forgotten. The story of that struggle for supremacy is a tragic drama of heroism and endurance" (329–30). In the last section, "Remembering the Trail," the story jumps to the present as the now elderly narrator and his wife travel the trail by rail (including a stop at the Grand Canyon) to appreciate the "empire builded on the commerce of the land . . . empire of bridged rivers, quick transportation on steel-marked trails that girdle harvest fields and fruitful pastures; empire of homes and schools and sacred shrines. . . . Glad am I to have been a vanguard of its trails upon the Kansas prairies and the far Western plains" (397).

A couple of stagecoach narratives, written after the stage had been supplanted by the railroad, mainly show how lucky people are to have railroads. Feminist editor Caroline Churchill's 1909 *Active Footsteps* recalls travel around the western states, especially California, when she was angling for magazine subscribers. The book seems designed partly to show the writer's independence as she works on behalf of respect for women in a mainly male society. Churchill also makes a point of how much better trains are than stagecoaches—how much better, in effect, it is for women today than it was yesterday. "The interior hotels of California were not the best places in the world to regain lost flesh and retain it. . . . Spanish beef from wild cattle makes very cheap but wretchedly poor meat" (67). "Potatoes, grown year after year without cultivation, makes a very coarse tuber. . . . The coffee and tea were wretched; in fact, nothing but the bills were first class. This was thirty years ago or it would not be related here; out of pure national pride the story would be suppressed. . . . The appearance of the railroad has changed this petty rascality, from which there was no appeal, to a more respectable order on a larger scale" (68–69).

Carrie Adell Strahorn's *Fifteen Thousand Miles by Stage* (1911) is a massive stagecoach travel book about journeying with her husband, who worked for the railroad—publicly to tout the advantages of settling and secretly to choose sites for railroad towns. This book reminds one that the supposed voluntary hegira of the wretched of the earth to the land of the free was significantly orchestrated by those who stood to profit from it. Strahorn's search for good railroad towns "veiled under the popular use of the hunt for statistics to induce immigration" resulted in "some of the best known and most profitable railway lines in the West" (325). Carrie credits him for making "history never to be undone" because the work "started a trail of homeseekers" (459). The day of startup railroads is over; in rhetoric simultaneously praising the present and regretting the disappearance of the past, she writes that the "West of thirty-four years ago is now only a tradition. . . . The bird's-eye view of to-day looks down upon thousands of miles of railways, flourishing towns, substantial cities, and millions of acres of land green with cultivation where only yesterday were the dreary solitudes of sandy waste. . . . I have endeavored to give a picture of the Old West, to tell of the efforts which a Westward marching population made to establish homes on the border line of civilization and beyond, enduring hardships and privations with the courage of heroes. I have tried to restore the picturesque condition of what was the great homeless frontier of our Western country" (v). The West, Strahorn believes, needed women; and the railroad is by far the best way to get women there. "The frontier was a fact and not fiction in the '70's. A woman in the far West was a blessing sent direct from Heaven, or from the East, which was much the same in those days. Almost everywhere away from the more favored ox freight lines the modes of living were crude and often far from tempting. . . . With the coming of the dainty matron, the real homemakers, the whole western world brightened" (89).

*   *   *

Because railroad books followed the itinerary of the excursion companies, and the Raymond Company organized the most popular excursions from New England, four of the six railroad books I've found were by New Englanders and are suffused with the New England mindset. The railroad allowed women to see the wicked west safely—allowed them to see it as wicked, and to judge it without consequences. Earliest in the genre is Sara Jane Lippincott's *New Life in New Lands; Notes of Travel* (1873). In this book Lippincott, a prolific magazinist writing as Grace Greenwood, republished a series of letters she'd done for the *New York Times,* covering parts of Colorado, Utah, Nevada, and California. She strongly, and typically, preferred agriculture to mining, reporting that Greeley, Colorado, is "a really wonderful place. Established on a purely agricultural basis, with an inexhaustible capital of intelligence, energy, economy, and industry, it has thriven steadily, constantly, with no wild leaps of speculation, or fever-heats of ambition and greed. With an orderly and virtuous population, it has had to pass through none of the dark and dire and tempestuous scenes of pioneer life, such as are found in mountain mining towns" (38–39). Abandoned mining towns signify the dangers of speculation, but one neat and clean mining town passes muster: Caribou, Colorado, is congratulated for "the orderly, moral, and intelligent character of its people. Born after the evil reign of excitement and reckless speculation was past, mining life here is sober and laborious and law-abiding; we, at least, saw no gambling, no drunkenness, no rudeness, no idleness. A New England village . . . could not present a more quiet and decorous aspect" (81).

Even though the scenery and climate of Southern California send her into raptures—"I cannot see enough of this picturesque land. I cannot drink in enough of the quickening sunshine, and the balmy, healing air of this strange new summer, of this vast new sea. The very springs of life seem renewed here" (192)—she is more comfortable being critical: "I cannot see how, in a country so enticingly picturesque, where three hundred days out of every year invite you forth into the open air . . . any considerable number of sensible, healthy men and women can ever be brought to buckle down to study of the hardest, most persistent sort." California "will always produce brilliant men and women of society, wits, and ready speakers; but I do not think she will ever be the rival of bleak little Massachusetts or stony old Connecticut in thorough culture, in the production of classical scholars, great jurists, theologians, historians, and reformers. The conditions of life are too easy" (251–52).

During an eleven-day stop in Salt Lake City, Lippincott meets Brigham Young, who impresses her with his dignified courtesy. Nor is she surprised that Mormon women support polygamy, since they are enmeshed in the system. It would be cruel to take "from hundreds of Mormon wives the little title to the world's tolerance they now possess, destroy their self-respect, and drive them from their— from the places they call home." Naturally enough Mormon women "oppose a measure which would scatter and bastardize their children" (159, 160).

The western segment of Helen Hunt Jackson's 1878 *Bits of Travel at Home* has essays on Salt Lake, Colorado, and California. In Salt Lake she sees the evil of polygamy everywhere: "Each woman's face, each baby's laugh, rouses thoughts hard to bear" (20). Her hostility toward nomadic (or what she thinks of as nomadic) California Indian women makes a startling contrast to her view of the settled Natives in *Ramona*—but of course *Ramona* was several years in the future, and Ramona herself, though half Indian, was also half Scottish and brought up by Castilians. "Towards night of this day we saw our first Indian woman. We were told it was a woman. . . . It moved about on brown, bony, stalking members . . . ; it mopped, and mowed, and gibbered, and reached out through the air with more brown, bony, clutching members. . . . I shut my eyes and turned away" (9). The Chinese are equally awful: "There she is, the Chinese woman. . . . Could she be uglier? And her children. . . . When they go by, hand-in-hand, there is something pathetic in the monstrosity of them" (64). How disappointing to find such unapologetic prejudice in an author revered for her progressiveness! Crossing the Sierras, Jackson finds abandoned mining towns and their surroundings "dismal beyond description. The earth has been torn up with pick-axes, and gullied by forced streams. . . . No green thing grows for acres" (89). She wonders why Sierra mining towns aren't "clean, well-ordered, and homelike" (251); "There could hardly be a sharper contrast than that from the gorgeous color and fairy-like spectacle on which we had been feasting at the top of the hill, to the dank, dark hollow into which a few moments brought us, to the low, flat-roofed cabins, and the sad, worn face of the woman [*sic*] who stood in their doorway" (268). "A sadder and deeper thought took possession of me. . . . Fiery as the tests through which the metals pass, must be the tests of life in such a spot. How much must be consumed and perish for ever, that the pure silver be refined!" (285).

At this point in her life Jackson sees future national glory emerging in the interior West: "there is to be born of these plains and mountains, all along the great central plateaus of our continent, the very best life, physical and mental, of the coming centuries. There are to be patriarchal families, living with their herds, as patriarchs lived of old on the eastern plains. Of such life, such blood, comes culture a few generations later, a culture all the better because it comes spontaneously and not of effort, is a growth and not a graft. It was in the east that the wise men saw the star; but it was westward to a high mountain, in a lonely place, that the disciples were led for the transfiguration!" (233).

In 1881 Caroline Healey Dall published *My First Holiday; or, Letters Home from Colorado, Utah, and California,* about a railroad trip extended with appropriate stops over three months. Leadville, where "A surging mass of villainous faces swayed up and down before me" (34), is "doomed. Such a town can exist but a very short time at the best" with its "licentiousness, gambling, and drinking" countenanced by an acquiescent press (42–43). She finds diphtheria and scarlet fever in Colorado Springs. Denver streets are dirty, with "many inexplicable bad odors in the lower sections" (67). Salt Lake City lacks "all proper sanitary regulations. The irrigation made necessary by the dry climate has its own dangers"; "diphtheria and typhoid malaria" run rampant because of "stagnant pools" and household garbage around the home sites (81). Taking a break from her sanitary obsessions, she grudgingly admires Brigham Young's handling of his people, not because he is so clever but because they are so benighted. "A single glimpse of any congregation gathered in Salt Lake City reveals the source of his power. All his energy, all his plain speaking, was required to penetrate the dense nature of the people with whom he had to deal" (92–93). "Perhaps no one in the United States thought the presence of the Mormon church on its soil a greater disgrace than I did before I went to Utah," she ruminates, but visiting the place "has changed my position in many ways. . . . The moment we see that these people never were American citizens, that they were far more degraded than any class we know, and that the Mormon church even with this drawback has really led them on and up, and made decent citizens out of turbulent animals, the . . . predicament becomes endurable" (107).

San Francisco to Dall is "still little else than an old mining port, in which the ignorant, unscrupulous, lawless class opposed to all decency and order still have their way. . . . Gambling in mines and stocks, and all operations of uncertain tendency, affect the character of the banks" (118). Dupont Street's red-light district is "far worse than anything I ever saw among the Mormons; for this is evidence of fearfully disordered life, while polygamy at the worst is only a mistaken, or perhaps it would be better to say an anachronistic, *order*" (123—emphasis hers). The streets are gloomy, the atmosphere foggy, the strange food tastes bad. The whole population "gave me an extraordinary conviction of great physical depression and general disease" (173). The entire moral situation of the far West is encompassed in the Chinese problem: "So long as the men of San Francisco are unwilling to close their own houses of assignation, their gambling dens, and their brothels, they have no power either human or divine, to close those of the Chinese. If they will not stop drinking on every street-corner, they will hardly undertake to drag the opium-eater from his quiet den" (382).

Bostonian Mary Elizabeth Blake's *On the Wing: Rambling Notes of a Trip to the Pacific* (1883), stops at Denver and its mountain surroundings; Santa Fe; Los Angeles; the Yosemite; San Francisco with excursions to Monterey; the Sierra mining country; and Salt Lake City. Blake is anti-Indian, anti-Mexican, anti-Mormon, but also antilabor and therefore pro-Chinese: "It is in vain to point out what inestimable help the Chinese have given, and are giving, in public works which white labor could never accomplish. . . . The very people who cry out most loudly, the very lower class who are being driven to the wall by this tremendous competition, employ Chinese washerwomen because they do their work for quarter the price" (159–60). In the mining camps "as elsewhere, the Chinese are hewers of wood and drawers of water. Whatever is too hard or too heavy for white men's bone and muscle, falls to the lot of these helots of the west. . . . Their patience, their endurance, and their most frugal habits, enable them to live and thrive where the most prudent pale-face would starve miserably" (174–75). In San Francisco "the hills are gray, the streets windy and forlorn, whirlwinds of dust rush and rise at every corner, and the first aspect is almost one of desolation. . . . Remembering the glory of June in New-England, its sweetness, its beauty, its tenderness of unfolding life; remembering, too, the dreams we have dreamed, and stories we have heard, of the opulent wealth of this Western land, the first feeling is one of unreasoning disappointment" (136).

For Blake, the exceeding beauty of the Salt Lake Valley doesn't compensate for the "glaring contempt for the beauties and amenities of life" (187) in the city. "The classes from which, in the main, Mormonism receives its recruits, would partly explain this lack of animation, of interest. Probably, no set of people in the world are more material, or on a lower mental plain, than the operatives of large English manufacturing towns, the miners of Wales, and the laborers in small German farming villages. It is largely to these overburdened lives, in which existence resolves itself into a constant struggle . . . that the preachers of this new religion come with a gospel more of the body than the spirit" (193–94).

Home at last, and what a pleasure! "The low, rounded hills were covered with trees and verdure, the meadows were fresh as an English lawn; the beautiful bright air of the brooks and creeks sparkling and flashing in the sunshine, made the memory of the muddy Western streams like a bad nightmare. What ease and comfort about the pretty house; what home-like thrift about the small farms; what nestling peace surrounding the church-crowned villages. Ah! Let them say what they will about the newer world towards the setting sun! There is more room there, and chance for prosperity, more material for brawn and muscle, more money-making and hoarding up of richer, broader lands and softer climates; but here, here in New York and Massachusetts, is the place, after all, for the white man to live in" (214–15).

Bostonian and psychic Susie C. Clark's *The Round Trip from the Hub to the Golden Gate* (1890) is mainly a California trip. She goes west via Salt Lake City and returns through Denver, stopping at San Francisco, the Yosemite, and the southern California coast from Santa Barbara to Los Angeles. Her views, like those of the other railroad travelers, are extremely critical; she may have hoped to keep New Englanders from emigrating. Especially, she disputes the idea that western women are more emancipated than their sisters in the East. In Salt Lake City "we have never seen such lack of intelligence in human faces, or countenances so utterly devoid of expression of any kind, as on the women and children of this Mormon kingdom. That feminine snap of the eye and carriage of the head common to the woman who has a mind and will of her own and claims the right to its exercise, we did not once discover outside the ranks of their Eastern visitors. We met no Mormon child who was capable of answering a question" (159).

A more sophisticated railroad book is Miriam F. Leslie's 1877 *California: A Pleasure Trip from Gotham to the Golden Gate.* Leslie, wife of Frank Leslie the media mogul, herself an editor and journalist, traveled from New York to California in a private railroad car with a large party. She comments on the frontier West (Cheyenne), mining territory (Virginia City and the Sierras), Mormon country, and northern and southern California, always emphasizing settlement and the emerging New West. A lively stylist, she displays an ecumenical, tolerant, and outgoing personality. She admires western men "not only as men of strength, purpose, and ability, but conspicuous for that genial heartiness of manner, and the gentle kindness of feeling which makes the Western gentleman a new and charming type of his class" (54). She records the "smiling industry" she finds everywhere in Utah, where "the barren plains become verdant fields, the squalid cabin of the usual Western settler becomes a neat cottage, with flowers and garden-produce growing at its doors; the odious sage-brush disappears before the system of irrigation. . . . Men, women, and children are better fed, better dressed, and better mannered. . . . School-houses, with cleanly and comfortable troops of children about them, are a symptom of more advanced civilization than lonely shanties with only fever-and-ague and whisky therein" (71). She finds Brigham Young attractive and worldly. Alone among these writers she actually likes Mormon women. Eliza Snow tells her that "We consider ourselves among the finest women in the world, and aim to compete with our sisters elsewhere in every pursuit and every branch of education" (79).

In San Francisco she notes the bad climate, the monstrously oversized dwellings of the plutocracy, and the Chinese, whose lifestyles appall and who raise issues of prostitution and cheap labor. "Whether we like him or not, the Chinaman in California has become a fixed fact. . . . All that remains is, for us to make the best of it as it is, and treating John liberally as a man and a brother, cultivate such of his qualities as we esteem, deal with what we do not like, justly, impartially, and honorably, and wait for Time, the great assimilator, to soften the differences, subdue the Heathen's vices, and elevate the Christian's charity until it becomes the law of the individual and of the State" (173–74).

* * *

Railroad travel books by women who did not like what they found in the West give way early in the twentieth century to automobile tourism, wherein the West becomes the fantasy playground we all know so well. The earliest automobile book I've found is a novel by Grace Sartwell Mason, who worked with Percy F. Megargel, an automobile racer, to plot *The Car and the Lady* (1908) around a 1905 race from New York to Portland, Oregon, that Megargel had participated in. The All-American hero, Jerry Fleming, competes against the suave Italian Vanunnici, each driving a prototype of the auto he's designed. The protagonist-heroine Betty Albright's father, Hiram, has chosen the Italian model for his factory to manufacture, while Jerry has a Michigan factory producing his. Betty is entranced by Italian suaveness (a mistake) while Hiram thinks the Italian car is mechanically superior (another mistake). Jerry's winning the race saves the day for love, commerce, and national self-respect. The novel treats automobile travel as the modern equivalent of the old covered wagon, and makes the covered wagon an object of nostalgic glamour. Wagons broke down on the trail; so do cars. Roads had to be cut; so do they here. "Beginning that morning with the fir tree which they had chopped in two sections to get the car through, they had hewn their path through the trunks of six trees, which had fallen across the trail, and had built two sections of corduroy road over a slimy swamp" (257). At the start there are only two in the automobile, Jerry and his mechanic Sid; but more characters accumulate: Jacinta, a fiery (of course!) Mexican running away from her fiancé (she ends up with Sid in a cross-ethnic romance), papa Hiram, Betty—who abandons her eastern standoffishness and is reborn as the athletic western girl. Jerry gets the girl and his partners telegraph him: "Win or lose, your trip has sold more cars than we can build in a year. Hurry back and help us fill orders" (272).

In the book's foreword, the authors make a point of the accuracy of "particulars of equipment and the description of difficulties met and overcome," hoping that "with the progress of good highways across this fascinating continent of ours, more motorists may feel the lure of the American road. If this class of traveler finds in 'The Car and the Lady' a timely word which will make the way easier they will feel that they have been justified in supplementing the purely romantic interest of their story with wisdom gained in the school of experience." West in this novel is defined as the interior West, especially Wyoming, where though it's too late for Indians, one can encounter hostilities between sheepmen and cowmen, gambling brawls, wide-open towns, storms, and mud. "West of Cheyenne there are two-hundred-mile stretches where you won't find enough sweet water to fill a teacup; where the trail fades out and you will have to chop your way through sage brush. You'll sleep in your clothes many a night and go hungry many a day. And then, when you've made perhaps three-quarters of the way, a broken axle or cracked cylinder may lose you your race by twenty-four hours" (25). Sid is alarmed by "the West's incalculable distances. . . . To his city-bred soul there was something oppressive in this silent following of a deserted trail up and down, up and down, meeting no living soul, seeing no living thing except a little cottontail whisking into its burrow or a rattler coiled in a warm patch of sand beside the trail. The miraculous clearness of the atmosphere, the burning white sunlight, gave a sharpness of outline which was as unreal to Eastern eyes as a painted forest on the stage" (81–82). But to Fleming "the bigness and loneliness were like a stimulant. As mile after mile the trail unwound before him he felt the exhilaration of the mariner steering through strange seas; the unquenchable spirit of youth rose within him to meet the demands of the adventure" (82).

Effie Price Gladding's *Across the Continent by the Lincoln Highway* (1915), published just two years after the highway opened, recounts a trip on that road. Gladding conveys the atmosphere of a trip at once lonely and sociable, as she and her husband stop along the road for meals, camp with other motorists, are helped by farmers when they get stuck in the mud, and so on. The mishaps of an auto trip become reenactments of pioneer overland travel. Like Mason, she tends to discount California's westernness; only when they leave Stockton does "the great adventure" really begin (111). Many times, she observes, "I thought of the 'Forty-niners,' as we saw the sign, 'Overland Trail.' In coming along the Lincoln Highway, we are simply traversing the old overland road along which the prairie schooners of the pioneers passed. How much heartache, heartbreak, and hope deferred this old trail has seen! I think of it as we bowl along so comfortably over the somewhat rough but yet very passable road" (171). Western openness and lack of conventionality please her: "This custom which permits men to be at ease in public places and in the presence of ladies without coat or waist-coat in hot weather; the custom which permits ladies to sit in church without their hats; these and others which belong to the free West, the Easterner has to become accustomed to and to take kindly. Several times in California, and in Nevada, when we asked a question we received the cheerful, unconventional response, 'You bet!'. . . . These somewhat startling responses simply indicated a most cheerful spirit and a hearty readiness to do you any favor possible" (203).

In 1916 Emily Post, her career as the nation's etiquette expert still ahead, published *By Motor to the Golden Gate* about a trip taken with her adult son (chauffeur and mechanic) and a friend from New York City to San Francisco. For her too the contrast with the original overlanders is inescapable: "Compared with crossing the plains in the fifties, the worst stretch of our most uninhabited country is today the easiest road imaginable. To the rugged sons of the original pioneers, comments upon 'poor roads'—that are perfectly defined and traveled-over highways—or 'poor hotels'—where you can get not only a room to yourself, but steam heat, electric light, and generally a private bath—must seem an irritatingly squeamish attitude" (vii–viii). On the plains, she sees what she came for: "The interminable distance was itself an unforgettably wonderful experience. It gave us an impression of the lavish immensity of our own country as nothing else could. Think of driving on and on and on and yet the scene scarcely changing, the flat road stretching as endlessly in front of you as behind" (113–14). Later, thinking about the "endless plains, you forget the wearying journey and feel keenly the beauty of their very endlessness. . . . You feel as though mean little thoughts, petty worries, or skulking gossip whispers, could never come into your wind-swept mind again. That if you could only live with such vastness of outlook before you, perhaps your own puny heart and mind and soul might grow into something bigger, simpler, worthier than is ever likely otherwise" (115).

In Colorado she meditates on the symbols of pioneers and cowboys as they still affect those who live there: "Colorado people love the very name 'cowboy' with an almost personal sentiment, just as, in their love for them, they seem personally to appropriate the 'mountains,' and from both, in spite of the luxury which many have brought from Europe or the Atlantic Coast, and in contrast to their mere recklessness, they have acquired directness of outlook, fearless, open-air customs of living, and an unhampered freedom from unimportant trifles" (129–30). The Southwest is a revelation: we, "to whom the antiquities and wonders of far countries are perfectly familiar, did not even know that the wonders of our Southwest existed!" (155). "Stupendous in its desolation, sublime in its awfulness, it mystifies and dumbfounds at every turn." (177). California north and south is "Light-hearted, happy, basking in the sunshine, her eyes not dreamily gazing into the past, nor avariciously peering into the future, but dancing with the joy of today. . . . It is not only the sun of heaven shining upon California that makes her the garden-land of the world, but the sun radiating from the hearts of her people" (198).

Eighty years earlier Mary Austin Holley had expiated on the West's transformation of women; Post does the same she meets some of her relocated eastern friends: "This same woman who used to be scared to death in a house full of people, with neighbors all around, now sleeps tranquilly in a ground-floor bungalow with every door unlocked, every window open, and her servants' quarters half a mile away. She . . . thinks nothing of dining with a neighbor fifteen or twenty miles distant and coming home at night through Mexican settlements alone!" (216). "We saw our fastidious friend in heavy solid boots, a drill skirt, flannel shirt, kneeling beside a campfire cooking flapjacks. She used to be beautiful but rather anemic. . . . She looked younger than she had at twenty and she put more life and energy in her waving of her frying-pan in greeting than she would have put in a whole New York season of how-do-you-do's" (217). As Post looks back on her journey, she decides she has "acquired from the great open West a more direct outlook, a simpler, less encumbered view of life. . . . Even in a short while you find you have sloughed off the skin of Eastern hidebound dependence upon ease and luxury, and that hitherto indispensable details dwindle—at least temporarily—to unimportance" (240).

Four years later (1920), Beatrice Larned Massey, inspired she says by Post's book, published *It Might Have Been Worse: A Motor Trip from Coast to Coast*, about a drive across North Dakota, Nevada, Salt Lake, into San Francisco. There's much assessment of hotels and eating places, with the idea that the more information tourists have, the more improvement one can expect in tourist amenities. She is also attuned to western women in connection with a predetermined idea of the "real" West: "The farther we went into the real West, the West of the movies and the early days pictured by Bret Harte, we realized what part these Western women had played, and were still playing, in their unselfish, brave, industrious, vital lives, in the opening and developing of that vast territory, and in making such a trip as ours comfortable, safe, and even possible" (46). "I was especially impressed by the women. They think for themselves on the public questions of the hour, and voice their opinions in no uncertain terms" (63). And she ends with what was already standard advice: "If you want to see your country, to get a little of the self-centered, self-satisfied Eastern hide rubbed off, to absorb a little of the fifty-seven (thousand) varieties of people and customs, and the alert, open-hearted, big atmosphere of the West, then try a motor trip" (143).

Winifred Hawkridge Dixon's 1921 *Westward Hoboes: Ups and Downs of Frontier Motoring* is about a six-month trip taken with the daughter of a friend. The spectacle of two women on their own calls out chivalry and amazement across a landscape of manly motoring. Beginning in Galveston, they planned to "follow the old trails, immigrant trails, cattle trails, traders' routes,—mountain roads which a long succession of cliff dwellers, Spanish friars, gold seekers, Apache marauders, prospectors, Mormons and scouts had trod in five centuries. . . . The

Southwest has been explored afoot and on horse, by prairie schooners, burro, and locomotive; the modern pioneer rattles his weather beaten flivver on business between Gallup and Santa Fe, Tucson and El Paso, and thinks nothing of it, but the country is still new to the motoring tourist" (4). Most of the book is about the Southwest, emphatically not about California; the need to declare which western place is, and which is not, truly West is central to her presentation. "California was the West, dehorned; it possessed climate, boulevards and conveniences" (4). "With a thrill we realized we were viewing the beginnings of the Rockies. For the first time in my life, I felt I had all the room I wanted. We basked in the hot sun, expanding physically and spiritually in the immensity of the uncrowded landscape" (49). "Hardly had we crossed the political line dividing sand and sage brush from sage brush and sand before we sensed New Mexico;—a new wildness, a hint of lawlessness, a decade nearer the frontier, Old Spain enameled on the wilderness" (62). In Arizona, the green country created by the new Roosevelt Dam, where "the Water-God has turned this colorless ache of heat to emerald green" (100), is dismissed as unwestern. "Before a week passed all this artificial fertility and prettiness palled. It was not Arizona" (101). Phoenix, too, is inauthentic, is "Arizona denatured. It had taken its boom seriously, and the arch crime of self-consciousness possessed it. For the first time since the Aztecs one can find Arizonans trying to do what other people do, rather than what they dam-please. And it set, oh, so heavily on Phoenix and the Phoenicians and on the Easterners and Californians who had come there to be as western as they dared" (103).

Homeward bound, she misses the West. Entering Minnesota they see "the West fade, and give place to the East. The easy-going, slap-dash, restless, generous, tolerant, gossipy, plastic, helpful, jealous West was departing, not to reappear even sporadically. In its place we began to encounter caution, neatness, method, the feeling for property and the fear of strangers, that we were brought up with. We were clicking back into the groove of precedent and established order" (367). In sum, the overwhelming theme of *Westward Hoboes*—and in some sense of all these automobile books, not to mention western tourism in the twentieth and perhaps the twenty-first century—is to discover on the ground the real West that is in fact the imaginary West, the West of big spaces and correspondingly big people. Even as she eliminates the California coast and Phoenix and every place except the Rocky Mountains and the desert Southwest from the true West, she observes Westerners themselves trying to reimagine the very sort of West that she herself is seeking, and laughs at them for it: "The West clings pathetically to these proofs that its old romantic life is not yet extinct, even though it is but the wriggle which dies at sunset. Stories like those . . . are still told with gusto even amid the strangest familiarity with Victrolas—though the saloon is replaced by the soda fountain, and the only real cowboys are on film, and the hardy tenderfoot now rides so well, shoots so well and knows his West so well that he is an easy mark for the native" (141). It begins to seem that the "West" we think we know is the creation of tourists, while those on the ground told very different stories—or did so until they came to see the advantage in telling the story that people came to the West to see for themselves.

Sarah Emilia Olden's *Little Slants at Western Life: A Note Book of Travel and Reflection* (1927) augments the journal of a western trip by railroad and automobile with a great deal of history and, in line with Olden's interest in Native Americans, with much information about American Indians. Her stops include New Mexico (Santa Fe and Taos with history including Kit Carson and the art colony), Salt Lake (Mormons with history back to Joseph Smith's vision in Palmyra), Orleans on the Klamath River (Karoc and Urok as she spells the tribes' names); Portland, Oregon; Wind River and Cheyenne, Wyoming; Montana (the Little Big Horn battle). On to California with a base at Oakland (and taking in San Francisco and Berkley) stretching out to Carmel (art colony), Monterey (the Del Monte hotel and the cannery), Santa Barbara, and Pasadena. Next in Phoenix she addresses a convocation of Episcopalians and has much to say about Apache cruelty: "Nothing can be said in defense of the conduct of the whites as a whole in their dealings with these or with many other Indian tribes. . . . We were fully as treacherous as they, and there was much reckless killing of Indians west of the Rocky Mountains without any provocation, except the wildness of the race as a whole. We must ever keep in mind that they were plain, savage, unenlightened aborigines, fighting in defense of their own land and themselves" (205). Then comes Yosemite, San Diego (a quick drop into Tijuana, and throughout the Southwest many observations on "swarthy" Hispanics), and Oklahoma (the developing oil industry). The point is to write a history/description of the entire West.

Thus, the book displays all the continuing and unresolved contradiction of this entire body of women's literature. There is some measure of sympathy for victims of Anglo rapacity along with thrilled delight in the country that has become "ours" on account of that very rapacity. The book begins: "Our great and glorious West! As a friend of mine said to me the other day: 'Well, you are never so happy, so positively buoyant, as when you are just about to step on a western-bound train!'. . . I always am thrilled when I think of the rugged, massive, lofty, snow-capped mountain-ranges, the mighty ranches golden with ripening grain, and the billowy horizon-bordered prairies affording food to thousands of horses and cattle: the openness, the freedom, the immensity of it all deepens and expands the genial current of one's soul" (1). And it ends: "I must confess there is no other region on the face of the earth like our great West: towering mountain ranges . . . majestic tumultuous roaring rivers . . . mighty jewel-like lakes; the giant aeon-old sequoias; the countless square miles of stately pines and spruces and fire, with a grassy floor beneath as clean as a carefully groomed lawn and decked with lovely wild flowers and ferns. Then there are the quaint poplar-shadowed villages with houses of indomitable ranchers, and vast mineral and jewel deposits, and pools containing barrels of oil. The soils and climate are as varied as the tastes of men. . . How varied is this broad, magnificent land in its production and unlimited capabilities" (241–42). And so any number of us continue to feel, regardless of all we know.

12

The Authors

For some of these women authors there's substantial biographical and critical literature, for others not even dates are currently available; occasional allusions in the authors' books are sometimes the only informational source. The capsule biographies below are synthesized from a range of sources and are inevitably incomplete.

Annie Heloise Abel (later Henderson). 1873–1947. English-born, emigrated with her parents to Kansas when she was 11, graduated from the University of Kansas, got a Ph.D. in history from Yale in 1905, taught at various colleges, lived in Australia 1922–23 (the year she was married to an Australian). Retired to the state of Washington. Her three-volume history of the slaveholding Indians appeared between 1915 and 1925.

Emma H. Adams. 1827?–1917. Originally from Cleveland; published travel letters in a Cleveland newspaper about California, the Pacific Coast, the Southwest, the far north (1887, 1888); also doctrinal biographies for children (Martin Luther, Savonarola, John of Wycliffe) and didactic children's stories. Buried in Inglewood, California.

Ednah Robinson Aiken. 1872–1960. Novelist, journalist, playwright, clubwoman, she lived in San Francisco; married Charles Sedgwick Aiken (1863–1911), editor of the Southern Pacific Railroad's Sunset magazine. Her 1911 novel *The River* is set in California's Imperial Valley. In 1919 she was working as an educational assistant for the California Naturalization and Education Association.

Bess Streeter Aldrich. 1881–1954. From Cedar Falls, Iowa; graduated from Iowa State Normal School 1901; taught for four years; married and moved to Elmwood, Nebraska, where her husband went into banking and died suddenly in

1925. Had won a short story contest, now wrote to support herself and four children, becoming one of the best-paid magazine writers of her time. Almost 200 stories and nine novels, mostly about small town Nebraska life. Biographies by Abigail Ann Martin (1992) and Carol Miles Peterson (1995).

Emma S(arah) Allen. 1859–?. Originally from Indiana; attended California schools in Marysville and Modesto; taught in several California towns; married James Monroe Allen in 1882; published in eastern denominational journals; set several novels in northern California.

Margaret V. Allen. ?–?. Secretary, then president of the San Diego Pioneer Society (1916); the 64-page *Ramona's Homeland* (1914) her only book.

Ada Woodruff Anderson. 1861–1956. Born in San Francisco; her widowed mother took her and her sister to the Puget Sound region around 1865. She taught at the Yelm County school (basis for her first novel); married Oliver Phelps Anderson (1869–1941), a prominent Seattle businessman whose father was a president of the University of Washington; they lived on Mercer Island outside Seattle. She published in magazines; three regional novels (1908, 1909, 1915) about the Pacific Northwest.

Mabel Washbourne Anderson. 1863–1949. Cherokee; paternal grandfather founded the Dwight Mission; maternal grandfather was John Ridge, leader of the Removal-accepting Treaty Party. Graduated from the Cherokee Female Seminary in 1883, became a teacher and speaker, married in 1891; published in local, Indian Territory, and Oklahoma magazines and newspapers. Published a biography of Confederate General Stand Watie (grandfather's cousin) in 1915, expanded in 1931.

Kate Adele Aplington. 1859–1928. Moved with her husband from Illinois to Kansas in 1880. A painter and photographer, also clubwoman, suffragist, and lecturer, she founded the Kansas State Traveling Art Gallery in 1900; died in Miami, Florida; published a Santa Fe trail novel, *Pilgrims of the Plains* (1913).

Anna E. Arnold. 1879–1942. Native Kansan; school teacher and administrator who published two text books about Kansas (1912, 1915); moved to Portland, Oregon, in 1917 as principal of Girls Polytechnic.

Gertrude Franklin Horne Atherton. 1857–1948. Born in San Francisco, grew up with her mother in a boarding house; married unhappily into a mixed Anglo-Californio family, had a daughter; was widowed early. Ambitious and prolific, she specialized at first in California subjects, especially San Francisco; moved later to NYC, traveled widely, wrote less about California. Memoir published in 1932; biography by Emily Wortis Leider (1991).

Mary Hunter Austin. 1868–1934. Illinois native from Carlinville; graduated from Blackburn College; moved to the San Joaquin Valley with her mother and brother at age 20. Married Wallace Austin in 1891; moved to the Owens Valley where she taught, he worked on irrigation projects. Left the desert and her husband after publishing *Land of Little Rain* in 1903 (they eventually divorced); institutionalized her severely autistic daughter. Lived in Carmel, NYC, Europe, retired to Santa Fe; sketches, stories, novels with many settings on many subjects. An autobiography (*Earth Horizon*) in 1932; biographies by Augusta Fink (1983), Esther F. Lanigan (1989).

Mae Lacy Baggs. 1865–1922. From Independence, Missouri; lived in Toledo after her marriage in 1916. A book about Jack London in Hawaii (1917), and a Colorado tourist book for a "See America First" series (1918).

Alice Ward Bailey. 1857–?. Born in Amherst, Massachusetts, attended Smith College, married in 1884; published poetry, stories, and novels; a 1906 Nevada novel is supposedly based on the life of George Wharton James.

Margaret Jewett Bailey. 1821?–1882. Methodist missionary in Oregon territory, originally a New Englander; her two-volume fictionalized autobiography (1854) is said to be the earliest women's publication in Oregon. Long assumed lost, one each of the two volumes was found in different research libraries and assembled in 1986 by Evelyn Leasher and Robert J. Frank.

Mary E. Bamford. 1857–?. A Baptist missionary working in San Francisco; published Christian-themed juveniles teaching tolerance for Asian immigrants (1899, 1917).

Helen Elliott Bandini. ?–1911. Born in Indianapolis, went to California in 1874 with her family; her father, Thomas Elliott, organized and was president of the Indiana Colony, which established Pasadena. Married author Arturo Bandini, from a prominent Californio family that had sided with the US in the Mexican-American War. California historical essays published in newspapers and magazines including *Out West* and *Overland Monthly*; wrote a California school history with help from her schoolteacher sister (1908).

Anna Maynard Barbour. ?–1941. Apparently born in NYC and orphaned as a child; lived in Montana, married an Englishman, eventually became an Episcopalian deaconess working in Boston and other eastern cities. Earlier (beginning late 1890s) she published popular action thrillers; also a Colorado mining novel (1897).

Nettie Garmer Barker. ?–?. Lived in Kansas City; published a little book about Kansas women writers in 1915 and a book of poems jointly with her husband in 1952. Active in the Masons.

Josephine Barnaby. 1863?–1915. Omaha Native, educated at Presbyterian Mission Seminary and Hampton Institute 1884–87. Teacher, nurse, head of the hospital at Standing Rock reservation; returned to the Omaha reservation ca. 1890, married and lived in Harmon, Nebraska. The American Missionary Society published her (undated) pamphlet about the Sioux and Omaha, "The Present Condition of My People."

Amelia Barr. 1831–1919. English-born daughter of a Methodist minister; came to the US in the 1850s with her Scottish husband Robert Barr, an accountant. Lived in Austin for a decade beginning 1856 (he was city bookkeeper); moved to Galveston postwar; her husband and two surviving sons (one had died earlier) died in the yellow fever epidemic of 1867. She ran a boarding house, taught, then went to NYC with her three daughters and became a successful author of historical fictions, two about Texas (1884, 1888); also novels about England, Scotland, and eighteenth-century New York. A memoir (1913).

Dolly Bryant Bates (Mrs. D. B.). 1826–1908. From Kingston, Massachusetts; published a book (1857) about her sea voyage to California plus three years in the gold country. Had gone with her ship-captain husband, returned alone because (the book implies) he found another woman. Back in Kingston, she worked as a dressmaker and remarried.

Josephine White Bates. ?–1934. Originally Canadian; married Lindon Wallace Bates, a prominent hydraulic engineer, in Portland in 1881 where she lived for several years; her son was also an engineer. Listed in the Social Register; active in the women's National Preparedness Movement (pro-armament), publishing a 20-page pamphlet, "Make America Safe," in 1916. Died in New York State.

Emma Pow Bauder. 1848–1901. A missionary and reformer originally from Michigan, worked in and wrote about San Francisco.

Delilah L. Beasley. 1872–1934. African American from Cincinnati; as a teenager wrote for the *Cleveland Gazette* and Cincinnati *Sunday Enquirer*; moved to California in 1910 and, late in that decade, began writing Sunday columns on the Black community for the *Oakland Tribune*. *Negro Trail Blazers of California* (1919) is her one book. Biography by Lorraine J. Crouchett (1990).

Ellen McGowan Biddle. 1847–1922. Daughter of a navy officer, married Union army officer James Biddle (1830–1910) at age seventeen. After the Civil War he served in the frontier army, retiring in 1896. Her army memoir published 1907.

Sarah Bixby-Smith. 1871–1935. From a Maine family that moved to southern California; born at the family sheep ranch (Los Cerritos); moved to Los Angeles age six; a book of poetry (1924) and a memoir (1925).

Mary Elizabeth (McGrath) Blake. 1840–1907. Irish-born poet and travel writer; emigrated to Massachusetts with her parents around 1850; attended Emerson's school and the Academy of the Sacred Heart (Manhattanville, New York); settled in Boston; interested in female reform (but not suffrage), a pacifist; travel account published in 1883.

Nellie Blessing-Eyster. 1836–1922. Born in Fredrick, Maryland; a Quaker missionary; moved to San Francisco in 1876; active in the WCTU, first president of the Pacific Coast Women's Press Association, a founder of the California auxiliary chapter of the League of American Pen Women; author of books about the Chinese.

Geraldine Bonner. 1870–1930. Said to have been born in a Colorado mining town, she became a San Francisco journalist and prolific novelist; published mysteries, working-girl novels, plays, San Francisco social fiction, mining fiction from 1900 to 1917.

Bertha Muzzie Bower (B. M. Bower and occasionally, later, B. M. Sinclair). 1871–1940. Minnesota-born, moved with her family to Montana in 1888, taught in Grand Falls, married ranchman Clayton J. Bower in 1890 (first of three husbands). Published ca. sixty-eight western novels beginning in 1904 as well as short stories; after moving to southern California, she also wrote screenplays. Biography by Orrin Engin (1973).

Frances Anne Mullen Boyd. 1848–1926. New Yorker; married Lt. Orsemus Bronson Boyd in 1867; accompanied him to posts in Nevada, Arizona, New Mexico, and Texas. Widowed at thirty-seven, she lived in the East thereafter; army memoir published 1894.

Kate Boyles (later Bingham). 1876–1959. Born in Olivet, Dakota Territory; attended Yankton College, taught fourth grade in Yankton and, later, English at a business college in Mitchell. Coauthored four South Dakota novels with her brother, Virgil D. Boyles (a court reporter, he did the research, she the writing) between 1907 and 1922. They were the best-known South Dakota novelists of their day.

Therese Broderick. ?–?. Published one novel under this name (*The Brand: A Story of the Flathead Reservation*) 1909; was also known as "Tin Schreiner." Mourning Dove criticizes the novel in *Cogewea*, but gets many details wrong.

Elizabeth Brooks. ?–?. Her *Prominent Women of Texas* (1896) profiled 153 women.

Clara Ellis Spalding Brown. 1853–1935. From Massachusetts; went with her husband to San Diego in 1878; lived in Tombstone 1880–1882, sending regular dispatches to the *San Diego Union* (journalism collected by Lynn R. Bailey, 1998). Moved next to Los Angeles; published in the *Overland Monthly, Denver Post,* and *Detroit Free Press;* was also cofounder and president of the Southern California Women's Press Club. In 1900 after her husband died, she married Edward Sylvester Ellis, author of dime novels; relocated to his New Jersey home. Widowed again in 1916, she went back to southern California; her only book (1895) collects previously published short stories about southern California and Arizona.

Jane W. Bruner. 1845–1909. Probably from Pennsylvania; published a melodramatic novel set in Grass Valley, California (1877) dedicated to her sister in San Francisco.

Emma F(rances) Jay Bullene. ?–?. Became a traveling trance speaker around 1858; in the 1880s she lived in NYC; her psychometric interpretation of the cliff dwellers begun in 1893 was published in Denver (1905).

Marianna Burgess. 1853–1931. Pennsylvanian from a Quaker family; Katanski (citing a 1978 dissertation by Genevieve Bell) says her father, a printer, was Indian Agent for the Pawnee during removal. 1880–1910, taught at Carlisle Indian School, then ran the school print shop. Wrote *Stiya* (1891), about a Native girl returning to her pueblo home, for Carlisle students.

Katharine Newlin Burt. 1882–1977. Published many female romance novels (some still in print) including two set in Wyoming (1919, 1920) and a third about a cowboy in the city (1922); she and her husband, writer Maxwell Struthers Burt (1882–1954) operated a dude ranch in Jackson Hole (the Bar BC) from 1912 onward.

S(ophia) Alice Callahan. 1868–1894. Muscogee Creek from Oklahoma; her father fought with the Confederacy, later was superintendent of a Methodist boarding school for Creek children. Educated in Virginia; became a teacher; died of a lung infection. *Wynema: A Child of the Forest* (1891) is the earliest known novel by a Native American woman.

Sarah E. Carmichael. 1838–1901. English; came with her Mormon convert parents to Salt Lake Valley in 1850; began publishing poetry in 1858 in the *Deseret News.* A book of her poems was published outside Utah in 1866, the year she married army surgeon Jonathan Williamson stationed at nearby Fort Douglas; apparently had a nervous breakdown in 1867 and stopped publishing.

Sarah Pratt Carr. 1850–1935. Maine-born; brought to California, where her father supervised railroad construction, as a baby. The family lived along the line throughout her childhood. Became a Unitarian minister (trained under Oakland minister Charles Wendte), organized and/or served churches in the

San Joaquin Valley. Published *The Iron Way* (1907), a novel about building the Central Pacific railroad; also children's books and the libretto for her composer-daughter's 1911 opera, *Narcissa; or, The Cost of Empire*, about the Whitman Massacre.

Frances C. (Grummond) Carrington. 1845–1911. General Carrington's second wife; her first husband, an army lieutenant, was killed in the Fetterman massacre; memoir published the year she died.

Margaret I. Carrington. 1831–1870. First wife of General Henry B. Carrington, published an army account/settler guide in 1868, defending her husband after the so-called "Fetterman Massacre" of 1867 in Wyoming territory.

Willa Cather. 1873–1947. Came from Virginia to Red Cloud, Nebraska, before she was ten; attended the University of Nebraska; went east for a literary career as an editor and journalist, first in Pittsburgh then NYC; traveled widely. After 1910 lived with Edith Lewis. Six of her novels between 1913 and 1927 are set mainly in Nebraska, Colorado, or New Mexico. Her war novel, *One of Ours*, won the Pulitzer Prize in 1922. There is a huge amount of criticism; University of Nebraska Press publishes scholarly editions of her novels; biographies by James Woodress (1987) and Janis Stout (2000).

Jane McManus Storms Cazneau. 1807–1878. Born near Troy, New York; journalist, author, land promoter, and speculator; unofficial diplomat during the Mexican War (possibly a spy); vigorous advocate of US expansion. Divorced in 1831 after five years of marriage, was later named correspondent in divorce suit by Aaron Burr's wife. Married Texas entrepreneur William Cazneau in 1849; published books encouraging Texas settlement (1845, 1852). Trying to establish colonies for black people, the couple moved in 1852 to the Dominican Republic, then to Jamaica. Biography by Linda S. Hudson (2001).

Katherine Chandler. ?–? Librarian associated with the Pacific Northwest and California (Lake Tahoe, Pacific Grove); in the first decade of the twentieth century she published books for second- and third-grade schoolchildren about California wildflowers, Native folktales, Sacagawea, and (uniquely) William Clark's servant York.

Catharine Hopkins Chapman. 1872–1930. Apparently a southerner (almost all her books are set in the south); one novel (1911) set in Idaho.

Mary Ellen Chase. 1887–1973. Born in Maine; a literary critic and scholar; taught at the University of Minnesota and Smith College specializing in the Bible as literature. Two Wyoming girls' novels (1916, 1917).

Lydia Maria Child. 1802–1880. From Maine, then Massachusetts, then NYC; married David Child in 1828. A professional writer—novels, magazine work—she became one of the nation's most outspoken abolitionists. Biography by Carolyn L. Karcher (1994).

Caroline N. Churchill. 1833–1926. Canadian born, emigrated to the US for her husband's health; he died soon after they arrived. Settling in Denver, she founded the *Colorado Antelope* (woman suffrage magazine), which she edited until her death. In the 1870s traveled around the West to get journal subscriptions; published travel books.

Esther M. Clark (later Hill). 1876–1932. Native Kansan, born on a farm; English major at the University of Kansas, worked in University Extension, published in newspapers and magazines. Two small poetry books (1911, 1921) featured her popular poem, "The Call of Kansas."

Susie C(hampney) Clark. 1856–?. Boston spiritualist writer; published two travel books (1890, 1892) based on Raymond Company excursion tours.

Kate M. Cleary. 1863–1905. Daughter of Irish immigrants who emigrated to New Brunswick. She grew up in Chicago, married in 1883, lived in Hubbell, Nebraska, from 1884 to 1898; several of her children died very young. Wrote for newspapers; published many short stories and a Nebraska novel in 1897. Back in Chicago, she lived mostly apart from her husband and surviving children; institutionalized twice for mental illness. Biography with selections by Susanne George Bloomfield (1997).

Mabel Goodwin Cleland. 1876–?. Born in Arkansas; B.S. from Arkansas College; married John Irvin Cleland in 1896. Widowed, she moved to San Francisco; published in and about the Pacific Northwest: feature articles in the *Seattle Star, The Tacoma News Tribune, The Oregonian* (Portland), and national magazines. Children's book of historical stories (1923).

Bertha Browning Barnes Cobb. 1867–1951. With her husband, owned the Arlo Company of Newton, Massachusetts, publisher of educational children's books including her own *Anita: A Story of the Rocky Mountains* (1920).

Alice Rollit Coe. ?–?. Pacific Northwest poetry book (1908).

Septima Maria Levy Collis. 1842–1917. From a Charleston, South Carolina, Jewish banking family that moved to Philadelphia where she met and married Charles H. T. Collis (1838–1901), Irish-born immigrant (1853), a Union Army officer; accompanied him during the war. *A Woman's War Record* (1889), *A Woman's Trip to Alaska* (1890).

Miriam Davis Colt. 1817–?. Her 1862 hard luck story about living briefly in Kansas contains all that's known about her.

Sarah Comstock. 1875–1960?1965?. Born in Athens, Pennsylvania; attended school in Kansas City, Missouri; got her B.A. from Stanford; a staff writer for the San Francisco *Call* (1899–1903); moved to NYC for a freelance magazine career, publishing articles and stories in *Harper's* and other journals. Along with other books, published a Kansas novel (1912) and a Dakota novel (1927).

Mary Cone. 1855–?. From Marietta, Ohio; divorced; *Two Years in California* 1876; other books.

Belle W. Cooke. 1834–1919. From Connecticut; married at 16, went overland with her parents and husband to Oregon in 1851 or 1852. Had five children; taught music, art, literature; ran a private school in her Salem home. Husband, Edwin Cooke, taught at Willamette University and elsewhere. She was the first woman clerk in the Oregon Legislature; published the first book of Oregon poems by a woman (1871).

Grace MacGowan Cooke. 1863–1944. A professional popular author who often collaborated with sister, Alice MacGowan; was best known for Appalachian and southern Illinois settings. Born in Grand Rapids, moved with her family to Chattanooga in 1865, left her husband in 1907 for NYC, moved to Carmel with her mother and sister in 1908. *The Joy Bringer* (1913) takes place mostly on the Hopi Reservation.

Ina Coolbrith. 1842–1928. Born in Nauvoo, daughter of Don Carlos Smith (younger brother of Joseph Smith) and Agnes Moulton Coolbrith. With her mother and stepfather she went to California in 1850, settling in Los Angeles. Divorced; moved to San Francisco and became central to its literary culture, coediting the *Overland Monthly*, mentoring aspiring writers, publishing poetry. Worked as a librarian in Oakland (is said to have helped Jack London there). One poetic miscellany published in her lifetime (1895), one posthumously. Biography by Josephine DeWitt Rhodehamel and Raymund Francis Wood (1973).

Mary Roberts Coolidge. 1860–1945. Born in Indiana; grew up in Ithaca, New York, where her father was professor, then dean, of Agriculture; received her B.A. there; taught school, married an engineer and moved to Palo Alto in 1890; quickly divorced and remarried archeologist Dane Coolidge; Ph.D. in sociology from Stanford in 1896; taught at Stanford and later at Mills College. Published on diverse social and reform topics: Chinese immigration, women in California almshouses, middle class femininity, southwestern Native Americans, American charities.

Amelia Sheffield Peckham Cordry. 1865–?. Elected historian of the Kansas DAR in 1910; campaigned to mark the Santa Fe trail across Kansas.

Hannah Last Cornaby. 1822–1905. English-born, married Samuel Cornaby in 1851; they became Mormons in 1852; went to Salt Lake via the Mississippi route: New Orleans to Keokuk, then overland. Moved to Spanish Fork in 1856; he taught, she was active in the Relief Society and other women's enterprises. Bedridden for several years; published a combination memoir and poetic miscellany in 1881.

Isabel Crawford. 1865–1961. Canadian-born, youngest of four girls, father a Baptist preacher who worked for six years in North Dakota. She trained as a Baptist missionary in Chicago, 1891–93; sent to the Kiowa in Indian territory, first Elk Creek, then Saddle Mountain missions; raised money for building a church, trained Native pastors, was recalled over a doctrinal dispute in 1906, reassigned to NYC. Retired to Grimsby in Canada (1929), living with nieces. Buried in the Kiowa church at Saddle Mountain. Wrote about her life among the Kiowa (1915); anecdotal autobiography 1951.

Augusta Joyce Crocheron. 1844–1915. Went with her parents to San Francisco at age two in Samuel Brannan's group on the ship *Brooklyn;* later moved to Salt Lake City and became a plural wife, poet, and celebrant of Mormon women.

[Mattie] Ruth Cross. 1887–1981. Born in rural Lamar County, Texas; Phi Beta Kappa at the University of Texas, worked her way through school teaching in small Texas and Oklahoma towns. Went north; succeeded as a literary professional, publishing stories and novels; a story about cotton-field workers was made into a film (1922). A best-selling Texas novel (*The Golden Cocoon*) published 1924; married horticulturist and financier George W. Palmer and lived in Connecticut.

Sarah J. Cummins. 1828–1919. Memoir of an 1845 overland journey published in 1914.

Maud Cuney-Hare. 1874–1936. Lived in Galveston as a child, spent much of her adult life in Boston as a teacher, musician, and writer; published a celebratory biography of her father (1913), the most prominent African American Republican statesman of his era, also a businessman and philanthropist.

Emma Ghent Curtis. 1860–1918. Suffragist; lived in Canon City Colorado; published a newspaper (*The Royal Gorge*) to "promote woman suffrage among farm and labor families." Two Colorado novels (1888, 1889).

Natalie Curtis. 1875–1921. From NYC; studied to be a concert pianist but after visiting Arizona refocused on musicology, working first with Native American materials and, later, with African American.

Elizabeth Bacon Custer. 1842–1933. From Michigan, widow of George Armstrong Custer; the most famous of the army officer wives, the only one to write professionally. After Custer's death she moved to NYC, supported herself with magazine essays; collected some of these in three books about Custer set in Kansas and the Dakotas (1885, 1890, 1890). Biography by Shirley A. Leckie (1993).

Katie Litty Daffan. 1874–1951. A native Texan; grew up in and died in Ennis; attended the University of Texas and the University of Chicago; journalist and literary editor for the *Houston Chronicle,* also a teacher, president of the United Daughters of the Confederacy, politically active democrat, and writer. Her father was an official for the Houston and Texas Central railroad, and she was briefly married. Her Texas school text appeared in 1924.

Mary Stewart Daggett. 1856–1922. Born in Morristown, Ohio; graduated from Steubenville College in 1873. After moving to Pasadena, she and her husband Charles were prominent in the city's development. She wrote for newspapers and magazines; also fiction about southern California (1895, 1911, 1914).

Caroline Healey Dall. 1822–1912. New England Unitarian woman of letters, lecturer, lay preacher, contributing editor to Paulina Wright Davis's feminist magazine *Una.* Her best known book, *The College, the Market, and the Court* (1867) derived from her public lectures on female superiority. Her minister-husband went to Egypt for 30 years, abandoning her and their two children. In 1879 she moved to D.C. where her scientist-son worked at the Smithsonian. Newspaper railroad travel letters collected as a book in 1881.

Esther Birdsall Darling. ?–1965. Possibly Canadian-born, lived in Nome, Alaska from 1907–17; with her husband owned a kennel that raised prizewinning malamute racers. Published a book of Alaska poetry in 1912 and several dog books beginning 1916.

Mary (Mollie) Evelyn Moore (M. E. M.) Davis. 1844–1909. The best-known Texas writer of her generation, she published thirteen books in all. Moved with her family from Alabama to Texas in 1855, settled in Galveston in 1867; married Houston journalist Thomas E. Davis in 1874; they went to New Orleans in 1879 when he joined the staff of the *Times.* A social and literary leader, she became editor of the *Picayune* in 1889 but continued to write about Texas.

Emma Frances Dawson. 1839–1926. Born in Bangor, Maine; grew up in Massachusetts; moved with her divorced and ailing mother to Sacramento around 1873, then to San Francisco. Taught music, translated, published Poe-like magazine stories about San Francisco, some collected in an 1897 book. After her mother's death and the earthquake she moved to Palo Alto and stopped writing. Stories collected with a biography by Robert Eldridge (2007).

Sara Dean. 1870–?. *Travers* (1908), her first novel, is thought to be the earliest women's book about the San Francisco earthquake. Second novel an 18th century romance.

Elizabeth Willis DeHuff. 1886?1892?–1983. Originally from Georgia, where she returned after her husband's death. Studied at the Lucy Cobb Institute in Athens and Barnard College; taught in the Philippines from 1910 to 1913, where she met and married John David DeHuff (1872–1945), another teacher. They went to his post at the Carlisle Indian School (1913), then to Santa Fe (1916) when he became superintendent of the Indian School. She taught Native children what she considered the authentic Indian style of painting; also wrote, lectured locally (e.g., for Indian Detours at La Fonda hotel); published books of Indian children's stories (1922, 1924).

Elizabeth Dejeans. 1873–1928. Pseudonym of Frances Elizabeth Janes Budgett. Conflicting information; was probably born in Philadelphia, may or may not have traveled widely, had settled in southern California by 1909, died in Ohio (possibly a suicide) on a family visit. Wrote romance novels and screenplays; in 1920 adapted her 1917 novel, *The Tiger's Coat,* for the movies. Great Plains and southern California fiction.

Emily Inez Denny. 1853–1918. A professional painter, from a family among the earliest settlers of what became Seattle. Collected pioneer stories and memorialized her parents in *Blazing the Way* (1909).

Adina De Zavala. 1861–1955. Granddaughter of Lorenzo De Zavala, who was for a few months the first vice-president of the Republic of Texas; founded the "De Zavala Sisters" dedicated to preserving Texas historical monuments, especially the Alamo and other missions; quarreled with other preservationists about what, precisely, to save in the Alamo complex. Book of Texas mission tales (1917).

Luella Dickenson. ?–? Her California book recounts the overland journey of her husband and father-in-law, the latter a Pennsylvanian and an early settler in Stanislaus County. Seems to have lived in Merced.

Annie L. (La Porte) Diggs. 1848–1916. Canadian-born, her family moved to New Jersey in 1855; she taught school, moved to Lawrence Kansas in 1873 and married Alvin S. Diggs, a postal clerk; three children. Politically active (organized meetings, wrote editorials, orated) beginning 1877 on behalf of grangerism, populism, woman suffrage. With her husband ran the newspaper *The Kansas Liberal*; also published columns in the *Lawrence Journal*. Elected Kansas State Librarian (1898); president of the Kansas Women's Press Association (1905); retired in 1906; two books; moved to Detroit (1912) to live with a son.

Winifred Hawkridge Dixon. 1880?–?. Married English immigrant Joseph Kossuth Dixon, a minister who became a photographer working for Kodak; son Rollin Lester Dixon also a photographer and filmmaker. Traveled with them and on her own, published in magazines; 1921 account of a southwestern automobile tour with the daughter of a friend.

Ethel Dorrance. 1880–?. No information beyond that she wrote novels, stories, and screenplays, often collaborating with James Dorrance. One bibliography suggests that both "Ethel" and "James" were pen-names. Two Arizona novels (1920, 1926).

Amanda Douglas. 1831–1916. Lived in NYC and Newark, a friend of Louisa May Alcott, never married, published more than seventy books including the popular, instructional "Little Girl" historical books set in cities around the country.

Mary Osborn Douthit. 1840?–?. Emigrated with her parents to Oregon territory in 1853, lived in Linn, Oregon; compiled and partly authored a feminist tribute to Oregon Territory women in 1905.

Clara Driscoll. 1881–1945. Wealthy civic activist, she grew up on a Texas ranch, worked to preserve the Alamo, eventually took over the family businesses and practiced philanthropy. Texas novels in 1905 and 1906; had a play, *Mexicana,* produced in NYC. Was working on a novel at the time of her death. Biography by Martha Anne Turner (1979).

Constance Goddard Du Bois. ?–1934. Born in Zanesville, Ohio, never married, settled in Connecticut in 1889, published successful novels from 1890 onward, began traveling to southern California in the late 1890s. A self-taught ethnologist, she published on the Luiseno and Diegueno Indians of southern California; also an Indian novel (1900).

Abigail Scott Duniway. 1834–1915. Suffragist lecturer, editor, and writer; went overland to Oregon with her family in her teens; her mother died on the trail. Early married, she attributed her feminism to female pioneer hardship; established and edited a suffragist journal, *The New Northwest;* split with many suffragists because she was antitemperance. Brother Harvey W. Scott edited the Portland *Oregonian,* the territory's most influential newspaper and opposed to woman suffrage. Biography by Ruth B. Moynihan (1983).

Eva Emery Dye. 1855–1947. Originally from Illinois; an Oberlin graduate, she married a classmate; they taught until he got a law degree, settled in Oregon City in 1890. Civic activists, they founded the Oregon Chautauqua society. A prominent suffragist, she split with Duniway over temperance. Author of popular historical novels and school histories about Oregon territory. During the Lewis and Clark centennial, worked to make Sacagawea a heroine. Biography by Sheri Bartlett Browne (2004).

Ida Casey Dyer (Mrs. D. B.). 1849–1922. From Illinois, she married another Illinoisan—an Indian reservation agent—in 1870. They were divorced, remarried, divorced again. She lived in Kansas, Oklahoma, Missouri, and Georgia, collected Native American artifacts. Book about Oklahoma territory (1896).

Edith Maud Eaton (Sui Sin Far). 1865–1914. English-born, her father English, her mother a Chinese adopted by missionaries; oldest daughter and second of fourteen children. Grew up in Montreal, never married, left school to help support her family; lived in San Francisco, Seattle (worked as a journalist in Chinatown), Boston (worked as a legal secretary); in 1912 published *Mrs. Spring Fragrance,* story collection about the immigrant Chinese in Seattle. Died in Montreal. Biography by Annette White-Parks (1995).

Rachel Caroline Eaton. 1869–1938. Cherokee, born in the Cherokee nation (Oklahoma); graduated from the Cherokee Female Seminary (1887), from Drury College, Missouri (1895), M.A. and Ph.D. from the University of Chicago. Teacher and school superintendent, active clubwoman, honored in 1936 as an outstanding woman of Oklahoma by the Oklahoma Memorial Association. Published a biography of John Ross (1914).

Rose L. Ellerbe. 1862–1928. Born in New York, went to the University of Chicago; never married; moved to Los Angeles and published fiction, historical essays; southern California books (1916, 1925).

Maud Howe Elliot. 1854–1948. Daughter of Julia Ward and Samuel Gridley Howe; a writer and lecturer on art, travel, and biography. Married John Elliott, a painter, in 1887, three years after publishing a California novel. Jointly with her sister won a Pulitzer Prize (1915) for a biography of their mother.

Mary Katharine Jackson English. ?–?. Grew up at Fort Washakie (Wyoming Indian Post); her father was a captain. Went to an English boarding school for two years, lived in Denver as an adult, published an undated army memoir said to be recollections from 1899.

Alma Estabrook. 1871–?. Born in Greenfield, Indiana; attended Oxford College, Ohio. Married William Chester Estabrook; was widowed, then married author Paul Ellerbe, who worked for immigration/naturalization service in Denver. A professional writer, mainly of magazine stories. A Colorado novel (1909).

Eliza Farnham. 1815–1864. From New York State, advocate for and exponent of female moral superiority, especially interested in prison reform. In 1836 married professional travel writer Thomas Jefferson Farnham (1804–1848), who died in San Francisco. In California to settle his estate, she bought a farm in Santa Cruz County, married a second time (divorced within five years); published *California Indoors and Out* (1856) to encourage emigration of virtuous women to the state.

Elizabeth Cornelia Woodcock (Mrs. B. G.) Ferris. 1809–1903. Born in Ithaca, New York; her husband Benjamin was president of Ithaca College and also Utah's first territorial secretary for six months in 1853; they returned to Ithaca via California. A travel book featuring Salt Lake City (1856).

Mary C. Ferris. 1842–?. A reform novel about San Francisco and gold rush country published 1898.

Alice C. Fletcher. 1838–1923. From Brooklyn, New York. Collaborating with Francis La Flesche, an Omaha Native, she published a history/analysis of the Omaha tribe (1881); other Native-focused books appeared for more than twenty years. Also worked for the federal government as an allotment assessor on the Nez Percé Reservation after passage of the Dawes Act. Retired to Washington, D.C. Biography by Joan Mark (1988).

Mary Hallock Foote. 1847–1938. From a Quaker farm family in rural New York State; attended Cooper Union and became a successful illustrator for *Harper's* and *Scribner's*. Married Arthur De Wint Foote, a civil engineer from Connecticut, in 1876; they were often apart but she went with him to New Almaden, California; Leadville, Colorado, southern Idaho, and Grass Valley, California, publishing western regional novels and stories from the 1880s into the 1920s, often illustrating them. They retired to a daughter's home in Massachusetts. Biographies by James H. Maguire (1972), Darlis A Miller (2002).

Harrie Rebecca Piper Smith Forbes (Mrs. A[rmitage] S. C.). 1861–1951. Historian, clubwoman, preservationist; presided over the El Camino Real Association and the California History and Landmarks Club. With her husband, cofounded and co-owned the California Bell Company, producer of replica bells for historical sites and for tourists; beginning in 1903 brought out a many-times reissued and updated guide to the California missions; a book of mission stories (1909).

Emma E. C. (Elizabeth Calderhead) Forter. 1857–?. Born in Ohio, went with her parents to Kansas at age twelve, taught, and settled in Marysville, Kansas. Married Swiss-born Samuel Forter (a blacksmith) in 1884; her two sons attended the University of Kansas and became civil engineers. An active clubwoman, president of several women's groups, she published a massive history of Marshall County, Kansas, in 1917.

Caroline H. W. (Holcombe Wright) Foster. 1864–1929. Published a book of fanciful historical short stories about southern California (1906).

Ruth May Fox. 1853–1958. English-born daughter of Mormon converts, emigrated to the US with her widowed father around 1865; they went to Salt Lake City in 1867. Worked in woolen mills in Salt Lake City and Ogden, married Jesse Fox in 1873, had twelve children. He took a second wife (apparently without Ruth's knowledge) in 1888, leaving Ruth to support herself and the children. An active suffragist, Republican, member of the Women's Press Club, and various boards. A book of poems, 1923.

Jessie Benton Fremont. 1824–1902. Daughter of Senator Thomas Hart Benton of Missouri, the premier advocate for expansionist policies. Married celebrity western explorer John Fremont in her teens, helped him write his influential reports. When his business ventures and mining investments failed, she wrote for magazines; eventually collected four books of sketches (two about the gold rush era) between 1878 and 1891. Widowed, she lived in Los Angeles. Biography by Pamela Herr (1987).

Jennie Anderson Froiseth. 1849–1930. Irish-born immigrant, moved to Utah with her brother, Finley Anderson, reporter for the *New York Herald*; married Bernard Froiseth, railroad engineer and cartographer. In 1879, established and edited the short-lived *Anti-Polygamy Standard*, from which she derived a much-reissued book in 1882; also an active clubwoman and informal social worker: orphan's home, women's retirement home, etc.

Jennet Blakeslee Frost. ?–?. Apparently from Connecticut, lived in California mining towns, published a gold rush potboiler (1866) and a book critical of California development (1879).

Anna Fuller. 1853–1916. New England local color author, resident of Cambridge; began publishing in newspapers and magazines around 1872. Girls' stories; Colorado novella *A Literary Courtship under the Auspices of Pike's Peak* (1893); also a Colorado story collection (1894).

Emeline L. Fuller. 1847–1923?. From Wisconsin; went overland to Oregon Territory in 1862, surviving an Indian attack en route; returned to Wisconsin after her husband died; in 1892 published a memoir augmented by corroborative materials collected by friends.

Frances I. Sims Fulton. ?–?. From Bradford, Pennsylvania; went to northern Nebraska planning to homestead in 1884 but changed her mind as soon as she saw the place. Published her perceptions of the state as observed during her return railroad trip. Later married a minister (name unknown); may have published under her married name.

Eleanor Gates. 1875–1951. Born in Minnesota, lived in the Dakotas, and died in Los Angeles, achieving fame and fortune with *Poor Little Rich Girl* (1912). Comic and serious western fiction set in the Dakotas, Oklahoma, and northern California from 1902 to 1910.

Susa Young Gates. 1856–1933. A daughter of Brigham Young, editor, author, active in the Women's Relief Society and the Young Ladies Mutual Improvement Association; founded and edited the *Young Woman's Journal*. Married Alma Bailey Dunford at age 16, divorced five years later; her daughter from that marriage, Leah D. Widtsoe, collaborated on some of her books. Attended Brigham Young University and eventually became a trustee, published pro-Mormon history after she was fifty years old, as well as the only novel I found by a Mormon woman (1909).

Marianne Gauss. 1873–1966. From Boonesville, Missouri; moved to Denver, a novel about contemporary Denver 1925; later published nature books, died in Greeley.

Charlotte Perkins Gilman. 1860–1935. Feminist, writer, editor, lived for a time in California; known now for *Women and Economics* (1898) and *Herland* (1912). Serialized many of her novels in her magazine, *The Forerunner*, also republished a few individually including *The Crux* (1911), set in Colorado. Married, divorced, remarried, she moved between the East Coast and Pasadena where her daughter lived. Biography by Mary A. Hill (1980).

Stella Gilman. 1870?–?. Introduction to her 1901 Dakotas story collection says she went from Philadelphia as a small child to Dakota Territory in 1878 and stayed there.

Effie Price Gladding. 1865–1947. Originally from Ohio, published a motor-tour book of the newly opened Lincoln Highway (1915).

Mary W[illis] Glascock. ?–?. Born in Nevada City, California; lived in Oakland and published stories in California journals; a San Francisco novel (1882).

S. Anna Gordon. ?–?. An 1863 article in the *Wisconsin Journal of Education* suggests she was a teacher. Married to a physician, she published a tourist book about Colorado in 1879.

Effie Graham. ?–?. According to Nettie Barker (see above), she came from Ohio, had some postgraduate education at California, Chicago, and Harvard. Headed the mathematics department at Topeka High school and wrote two vernacular books about African Americans in Kansas (1912, 1916).

Margaret Collier Graham. 1850–1910. From Keokuk, Iowa; moved to Los Angeles in 1876 with her husband and brother. They invested in land, establishing

Wildomar and Elisinore in Riverside Country. Two books of collected short stories about southern California (1895, 1905).

Blanche Chloe Grant. 1874–1948. Originally from Kansas; went to Vassar, studied art in Boston, Philadelphia, and NYC; moved to Taos in 1920; published about Taos and the Taos Indians for tourists and potential residents.

Annie Maria Green. ?–?. Emigrated with her family from Franklin, Pennsylvania to Greeley, Colorado; her memoir is the only biographical information I've found.

Irene Welch Grissom. 1873–1946. Born in Greeley, Colorado; graduate of Colorado State Teacher's College; moved to Idaho; appointed Idaho's first poet laureate in 1923 (Idaho poems published 1923). Two novels about the Pacific Northwest timber industry (1910, 1918).

Helen Elizabeth Haines. 1872–1961. From Brooklyn, New York; daughter of a wool broker, was home schooled, and in 1891 published a promotional history of New Mexico at age 19 (written on commission). In 1892 became managing editor of Bowker's *Library Journal,* wrote numerous articles and a few books about librarianship and reading; moved to Pasadena in 1908.

Josie Briggs Hall. 1869–1935. African-American, born in Waxahachie, Texas; taught, married, had five children; two didactic books for the elevation of black people published in 1905.

Sharlot Mabridge Hall. 1870–1943. Moved to an Arizona ranch from Kansas with her parents when she was eleven; served as territorial historian (1909–12); in 1929 received a life lease on the governor's mansion in Prescott to restore it as a museum of territorial history. Biographer Margaret F. Maxwell (1982) identified more than 500 published articles, poems, and stories, plus edited books and contributions to books.

Mina Dean Halsey. 1873–?. A New Yorker whose sketches (1909) satirized tourists in southern California.

Katherine B. Hamill. 1877–?. Published a historical novel about Monterey before the American takeover in 1923.

Alice Harriman. 1861–1925. Author and publisher, born in Newport, Maine where she went to school; became a travel writer for *Northwest Magazine* (1897–1902); married a Mr. Browne and published some works as Alice Harriman-Browne; seems to have been widowed; moved to Seattle around 1905; established her own publishing company there in 1907, which she relocated to NYC, 1910–13. A Christian Scientist, writing teacher, translator, and clubwoman; died in Hollywood. Diverse writings include two Montana books (1903, 1910), a book about Yellowstone (1907), three books of poems.

Mattie Austin Hatcher. 1880?–1940?. Graduated from the University of Texas in 1902; became UT library archivist in 1913; published articles in the 1920s and 1930s and a scholarly book of Texas history in 1927.

Mary Jane Hayden. 1830–1919. She and her husband arrived in Oregon territory in 1850; overland and pioneer memoir (1915).

Grace Raymond Hebard. 1861–1936. Scharff, citing a 1960 dissertation by Janelle M. Wenzell, says she was from Iowa, daughter of a Presbyterian minister; got a B.S. in Engineering in 1882 from what was then called the State University of Iowa (first woman to do so). Moved with her family to Cheyenne in 1882, joined the University of Wyoming faculty in 1891, serving as librarian, political economist, historian, and woman's advocate for more than forty years. Lived with Agnes Wergeland, Norwegian poet and academic, from 1900 to Wergeland's death in 1912; published several books of Wyoming history between 1904 and 1922.

Mary Sherwood Wightman Helm. 1807–1886. Born in Herkimer county, New York; married her former teacher Elias Wightman in 1828, with whom she founded Matagorda after emigrating to Texas that year. In 1841 they moved to Kentucky on account of Elias's poor health; he died, she remarried, went with new husband to Indiana. Wrote newspaper articles about Texas history by request, published them as a book in 1884.

Alice Corbin Henderson. 1881–1949. Born in St. Louis, went to Illinois with her family at age three, attended the University of Chicago, became an editor of *Poetry* magazine and a modernist poet. With artist-husband William Penshallow Henderson, moved to Santa Fe in 1916 on account of her bad health; recovering, she stayed on, working to publicize folk art, Native art, and Santa Fe. Published a modernist book of southwestern poetry in 1920. Biography by T. M. Pearce (1969).

Sarah Raymond Herndon. 1840–1914. Went overland to Montana in 1862 with her widowed mother and two brothers; trail memoir appeared first in a magazine (1882), then as a book ten years later.

Charlotte Bronte Herr. 1875–1963. Born in Indianapolis; moved with her family to Illinois around 1900 and later to Pasadena, where she taught. Primarily a children's writer; published two short romances about southern California (1921, 1924).

Elizabeth Higgins. 1874–?. Born in Columbus, Nebraska; married in Omaha; worked for the *Omaha Bee* and Chicago dailies, was active in suffrage and horticulture, lived in Washington D.C. and Mobile, Alabama. Populist Nebraska novel, *Out of the West*, 1902.

Ella Higginson. 1861–1940. Best-known Pacific Northwest woman writer of her day, published widely in eastern magazines; appointed Washington State's poet laureate in 1931; collections of short stories (1896, 1897), a novel (1902), an Alaskan travel book (1908).

Alice Polk Hill. 1834–1921. A journalist, active clubwoman, and Colorado poet laureate 1919–21; moved to Denver with her family around 1872. Biographies of Colorado pioneers (1884, 1915).

Emma Shepard Hill. 1851–?. Her 1914 memoir implies that she was from Ohio, adopted as a child by an uncle and aunt with only one son because her father had died and her siblings were much older than she. With her adoptive family went overland to Colorado in 1864; her uncle/father managed a mine; she married a sawmill manager and became active in church work.

Grace Livingston Hill (later, for a while, Lutz). 1865–1947. From Pennsylvania, author of over sixty books, considered to have invented the modern Christian female romance merging love, adventure, and piety. Her father was a minister, as was her first husband, who died seven years after their marriage; a second husband left the family after ten years. She wrote for Christian magazines; reached a national audience with *The Girl from Montana* (1908); two novels set in Arizona (1914, 1916). Biography by Robert Munce (1986).

Abbie B. (Rich) Hillerman. 1856–1945. Born into a Quaker family in Indiana, moved to Kansas age 17, attended Kansas State and State Normal college. Married Phineas P. Hillerman, an attorney; had two daughters and one son. Moved to Oklahoma territory in 1890; active in the WCTU from Kansas days onward, president of Oklahoma Territory WCTU 1903–1907; lectured on behalf of temperance and other social causes. Oklahoma Hall of Fame 1938; president of Tulsa chapter of WCTU from 1932 to her death.

Mary E. Hitchcock. 1849–1920. Born in Virginia, married a naval officer; as a wealthy widow, traveled with a friend to Alaska; Alaska travel book in 1899.

Frances Chamberlain Holley. ?–?. A Dakota history (1891).

Mary Austin Holley. 1784–1846. Originally from New England, cousin of the Texas impresario Stephen F. Austin. Widowed and working in Kentucky as a governess, she visited Austin's colony on the Brazos, acquired land there, and hoped to sell it by attracting settlers to Texas via two promotional books (1833, 1836). Biography by Rebecca Smith Lee (1962).

Forrestine Cooper Hooker. 1867–1932. Her father, Brigadier General Charles L. Cooper of the Tenth Cavalry (African American soldiers), was involved in Apache and Comanche warfare in the Southwest. Married Edwin Hooker, son of Henry Clay Hooker, cattle baron of southeastern Arizona, at age 18; divorced him sixteen years later. In her fifties, apparently at her children's urging, she began writing Arizona fiction. Manuscript memoir posthumously edited by Dave Wilson (2003).

Lucile Hooper. ?–?. Studied with Alfred Kroeber; published her research on the Cahuilla Indians of southern California in 1920.

Alice Merrill Horne. 1868–1948. One of fourteen children, born in Fillmore, Utah; moved to Salt Lake City at age 9 to live with her widowed grandmother. Graduated from the University of Deseret (later the University of Utah) in 1887 with a degree in pedagogy, married banker George H. Horne, had six children. Chaired the Utah Liberal Arts Committee for the 1893 Columbian Exposition in Chicago, supervised the Utah women's exhibitions in Woman's Building. The second woman elected (1898) to the Utah House of Representatives, she sponsored bills on art education; was active in the International Congress of Women, International Peace Committee, Daughters of the Utah Pioneers, DAR, etc. Published a book about Utah artists (1914); also a play about pioneering (1922) .

Eliza P. Houghton. ?–?. A survivor of the Donner party, she wrote about it and her life in California in a memoir covering 1847 to 1861.

Mary W. Hudson. 1840–1930. Wife of a Topeka newspaper editor who served in the Union army; published a widely circulated anti-Mormon novel, *Esther the Gentile*, in 1888.

Ann Eugenia Hughes. ?–?. As a student (M.A.?) at Berkeley, she published a scholarly study of early settlement in El Paso, based on numerous Spanish-language documents.

Mary A. Vance Humphrey. ?–?. Married to a judge; active in women's clubs, Board of Education, libraries; a Kansas novel (1883).

May Arkwright Hutton. 1860–1915. From Ohio; went to Idaho in 1883 after a couple of early failed marriages; worked as a cook, hotel dining room manager, and other mining-related service jobs. Married railroad engineer Levi Hutton in 1887; his imprisonment during mining strikes in 1899 inspired her pro-labor novel *Coeur d-Alene* (1900). In 1901 they were successful with the Hercules mine; moved in 1907 to Spokane where she became involved in suffrage and philanthropy. Biography by James W. Montgomery (1974, reissue 1985).

Sara White Isaman. ?–?. Iowa-born, she moved to Los Angeles and joined the Southern California Women's Club, Press Club, League of American Pen Women. Three books of humorous sketches about tourists in southern California (1907, 1914, 1917).

Ellen E. Jack. 1842–1921. An English immigrant; married a naval officer in 1860; widowed, seems to have gone west around 1883. Died in Colorado Springs; a fanciful memoir published 1910.

Helen Hunt Jackson. 1830–1885. From Amherst, daughter of a professor of classics, well known for New England fiction and poetry under the initials "H. H." After the sudden deaths of her husband and son, she went to Colorado for her health, married a railroad executive, began publishing travel sketches; became interested in injustices to the Indians; *A Century of Dishonor* (1881) followed by literary- and California-history-making *Ramona* (1884). Biography by Kate Phillips (2003).

Mary E. Jackson. 1852–1893. Went with her family from Indiana to Kansas in 1855, settled in Osawatomie; became a teacher and moved to Topeka, publishing Kansas novels (1881, 1886) and Topeka publicity (1890).

Annie Fellows Johnston. 1863–1931. Born in Indiana, daughter of New Englanders. In 1888 married her much older widower cousin whose three children were being raised by an aunt in Kentucky. He died in 1892. *The Little Colonel* (1896) and other novels in a popular series for girls—more than fifty books selling together more than a million copies—took place mostly in Kentucky; five books published between 1904 and 1912 were set in Texas (where she lived for eight years) and Arizona (which she visited in 1901).

Katharine Berry Judson. ?–?. Born in Poughkeepsie, graduated from Cornell in 1904, worked as a librarian in Kalispell and Seattle, got an M.A. from the University of Washington in 1911 with a thesis on the fur trade, joined the University of Washington faculty. Published school histories (1909, 1916), a forest fire novel set in Washington (1912), and beginning in 1910 six books of Native American legends from around the West.

Phoebe Goodall Judson. 1832–1926. Went overland to Oregon Territory with her husband and child in 1853; moved frequently before settling in Washington's far north. A memoir, mostly completed by 1899, appeared in 1925.

Elizabeth Wood Kane. 1836–1909. Daughter and spouse of influential eastern abolitionists with Mormon sympathies who negotiated between the US government and the Mormon establishment. Her Utah book (1874) was assembled by her father from her letters and diaries.

Fanny Kelly. 1845–1904. Five months a captive of the Sioux, she retrieved her Dakotas narrative from the Larimers (see below) and published it in 1871 as part of a campaign for compensation from the US government.

Florence Finch Kelly. 1858–1939. A Kansan, graduate of the University of Kansas, she became a journalist, married Allen Kelly (reporter and editorial writer), and worked for Hearst, living in San Francisco, Los Angeles, and New Mexico. Published New Mexico stories and New Mexico novels (1900, 1909, 1911). Later, she edited the *New York Times* book review section for thirty years. Her memoir, *Flowing Stream,* appeared in 1939.

Hannah Tapfield King. 1807–1886. Born in England, where she published poetry; became a Mormon in 1849, emigrated with her family to Salt Lake via Keokuk in 1853. Active in Utah women's organizations, she published two collections of poems and a book about women of the Bible, also an epic poem about Mormon church history (1884).

Adeline Knapp. 1860–1909. Born in Buffalo, she went to California at age twenty-seven as a journalist and editor, working in San Francisco and Oakland. She lived with Charlotte Perkins Gilman (then Stetson) from 1891–93. The *New York Times* says she returned to NYC for good around 1902; Wikipedia says she died in San Francisco. Published a little nature book about San Francisco environs (1897) and an Arizona novel (1908).

Frances Knapp. 1869–1965. Born in Middlebury, Vermont, graduated from Wellesley in 1890. When her father, Lyman E. Knapp, became territorial governor of Alaska, she worked in Sitka for three years as his secretary, then moved to Seattle. Book about the Tlingit, which she spells Thlinkit (1896).

Jessie Juliet Knox. 1867–?. Born in Tennessee; father was a minister. After high school graduation in 1884, moved to San Jose; married banker Charles W. Knox in 1890. Began publishing sympathetic stories and articles about the immigrant Chinese mainly for children (two collections 1904, 1911). Lectured and was president of the Pacific Short Story Club of California; friendship with the Chinese Consul General to San Francisco introduced her to the wealthy Chinese community. Divorced, she became a welfare worker in Oakland.

Lydia Spencer Lane. 1836–1909. From Pennsylvania; married army officer William Bartlett Lane in 1854, crossed the plains seven times in fifteen years. He retired in 1870; her army memoir was published in 1893.

Rose Wilder Lane. 1886–1968. Daughter of Laura Ingalls Wilder, whom she helped with the *Little House* books (some think she was the series' actual author). Trained as a telegrapher, she went to San Francisco from Missouri around 1910, married, worked with her husband as a real estate agent, and after their divorce, on her own. Began writing for newspapers; was an overseas reporter (Albania) during World War I. In the 1930s she settled in Connecticut, publishing articles, nonfiction books, short stories, novels; became deeply conservative around the mid-1930s. Her novel *Diverging Roads* (1919), set in gold rush country and San Francisco, is partly autobiographical. Biography by William Holtz (1993).

Sarah L. Larimer. 1840?–?. Went from Kansas to Idaho territory with her husband and son in 1864. In the Dakotas she and her son were captured in the same attack as Fanny Kelly (see above); they escaped within a few days. She and her husband appropriated Kelly's narrative for reasons unknown, which led to a court case (they lost). Her captivity account was published in 1870.

A(gnes) C. Laut. 1871–1936. Canadian émigré, much interested in the fur trade and eventually a publicist for the fur industry; published books about the Pacific Northwest, Montana, and the Southwest for over twenty years beginning in 1900.

Caroline C. Leighton. 1838–?. Massachusetts born, she moved with her husband, a customs agent, to Washington Territory from 1865–75; then to San Francisco for six years, then back to New England. *Life on Puget Sound* (1883) appeared soon after she returned to the East.

Miriam Follin Leslie. 1836–1914. Early married, briefly on the stage, with her second husband Ephraim Squiers she worked for publisher Frank Leslie as an editor and fashion writer; divorced Squiers and married Leslie in 1874. After his death in 1880 she took over his publishing business, sold it in 1889 but continued as editor and contributor; her railroad journey book appeared in 1877.

Sara Jane Clarke Lippincott. 1823–1904. Massachusetts journalist who published as "Grace Greenwood." Reported on congressional sessions in D.C.; was a committed Congregationalist, Republican, woman's righter, abolitionist, pro–big business, pro-capital, anti-Indian. Her railroad journey book appeared in 1873.

Caroline Lockhart. 1870–1962. A journalist, originally from Illinois; as a young girl she may have spent some years in Philadelphia with relatives. Settled in Cody; edited the local newspaper; worked to refashion this agricultural community into an icon of the Old, Wild West. Never married, she enjoyed being unconventional; claimed to have had a dozen affairs; published several novels about Wyoming and Arizona between 1911 and 1921. Biographies by Lucille Patrick Hicks (1984), Necah Stewart Furman (1994), Norris Yates (1994), and John Clayton (2007).

Mae Van Norman Long. 1870–?. A theosophist and author; a southern California novel (1926).

Maria S. Lopez de Cummings. 1852–?. A Californio, she married a forty-niner turned rancher. In 1889, they opened the Cummings Hotel to entertain their rancho guests in what is now eastern Los Angeles. *Claudio and Anita* (1921) celebrates her great-grandfather and the San Gabriel Mission.

Elizabeth Laughlin Lord. 1841–1913. Missouri-born, went to Oregon with her parents and settled in The Dalles at around age nine; married a local businessman in 1861. The *Illustrated History of Central Oregon* says she was a Christian Scientist and Sorosis member who wrote a number of articles and books; World Cat has only her 1903 memoir.

Flora Haines Loughead. 1855–1943. Born in Milwaukee, educated at Lincoln College, Illinois; as a journalist went west and wrote for the San Francisco *Examiner, Chronicle, Argonaut;* also the section on California journalism for Mighels's *Story of the Files* (1893). Published more than 150 stories as well as California novels (1887, 1893, 1898) and nonfiction (1878). Married three times and had several children (her sons changed the spelling of the last name and founded Lockheed aircraft). Later she farmed and mined for opals.

Hattie Horner Louthan. 1865–?. Born in Quincy, Illinois, moved with her family to Kansas, graduated in 1883 from the Normal School in Emporia, moved to Denver where she taught (published a textbook about short story writing). Married in 1893; husband died in 1906. She was an editor of the *Great Southwest,* on the staff of the *Denver Republican,* published poetry, travel, and two Colorado-set novels (1906, 1910).

Margaret Lynn. 1890?–1958. From Iowa or Illinois, settled in Kansas; was a professor of English at the University of Kansas. Two Kansas novels (1920, 1927).

Alice MacGowan. 1858–1932. A popular novelist, born in Grand Rapids, moved to Chattanooga in 1865. After a brief marriage she worked as a governess on a Texas ranch. Wrote some books collaboratively with her sister, Grace MacGowan Cooke; moved with Grace and their mother to Carmel in 1908. Texas novels (1902, 1924).

Pauline Bradford Mackie (later Hopkins). 1873–1956. Daughter of an Episcopalian minister, born in Fairfield, Connecticut; grew up in Ohio, attended Toledo High School, studied art, wrote for the *Toledo Blade.* Married Herbert Muller Hopkins, an instructor in Latin (1870–1910) in 1899. They went to Berkeley where he taught for three years, then to Hartford (Trinity College), and finally NYC where he had a pastorate. Wrote a "princess" series of historical novels for girls; set one girls' novel in northern California (1902) and a novel for adults (1903) in Arizona.

Mary MacLane. 1881–1929. Her family moved from Canada to Minnesota and, after her father died and mother remarried, to Butte. Began writing in 1898; *The Story of Mary MacLane* was her first book, followed after she left the West by *I, Mary* (1917), and essays. Known for Bohemian nonconformity and (after leaving the West) for her sexual outspokenness, she lived in Chicago, Massachusetts, Greenwich Village; died in Chicago.

Florence Lee Mallinson. ?–?. Welsh-born, lived with her husband in Alaska 1904–1913; published an Alaskan travel memoir in 1914.

Caroline (Carrie) Louise Marshall. 1849–?. Born in Wisconsin; married an Iowa physician in 1879; contributed serials and short stories to magazines, published textbooks, some books under a man's name (Carl Louis Kingsbury), also two girls' novels about Wyoming (1898, 1899). Eventually settled in Lamar, Colorado.

Cora Marsland. 1859–?. In 1911 was on the faculty of the Kansas State Normal School; published a pietistic Arizona novel (1911) and occasional poetry about Kansas and Colorado.

Grace Sartwell Mason. 1876–1966. Originally from Rochester, New York; with her husband Redfern Mason lived in Carmel 1912–14. After their divorce he went to San Francisco, became a prominent journalist and music reviewer for the *San Francisco Examiner.* She went to NYC, published many novels and more than eighty short stories for mass circulation magazines, some made into movies. Unpublished dissertation/biography by Diane W. Moul (1998).

Beatrice Larned Massey. ?–?. An account of automobile travel published 1920 says her childhood city had been Detroit.

Amanda Chase Mathews. 1866–?. Arriving in California in 1877, attended the University of California; a teacher and settlement house worker who seems to have taught in Mexico City, also worked in Los Angeles and NYC. Published about Mexican immigrants in Los Angeles (1906), Italian schoolchildren in NYC.

Mary McNair Mathews. 1934–1903. From New York State; went to Virginia City as a widow with her young son to claim her brother's mining properties. Back in New York, she published *Ten Years in Nevada* (1880); later returned to California, joining her son who had become an actor; died in Ukiah.

Mary Katherine Maule. 1861–?. From Illinois, she moved to Nebraska, married in 1878, had three children, began publishing in 1898; to Denver in 1900 (edited the *Colorado Times* woman's department 1900–1905). Belonged to several suffrage associations, the Denver Woman's Club, Sorosis, Cliff Dweller's Association, social clubs, Denver Press Club. One juvenile about covered wagon travel (1910), another about Wyoming (1920).

Mary A. Maverick. 1818–1898 (and Rena Maverick Green, her granddaughter, 1874–1962). A South Carolinian, arrived in Texas in 1836 at age 18, bride of Samuel A. Maverick, a developer of commercial property in San Antonio, who had fought in the Texas Revolution. Fear of Mexican invaders sent them into exile for five years in Matagorda in 1842. Her memoir, originally published in only six copies, was edited and republished by granddaughter Rena Maverick Green in 1921. Biography by Paula Mitchell Marks (1989).

Celeste Ball May. 1850–?. According to successive editions of Thomas William Herringshaw's biographical summaries, she was born in Lee County Iowa and later moved to Nelson, Nebraska. Herringshaw also says she was an active temperance lecturer. The Oklahoma handbook of writers (1939) names her as a resident of Blackwell, Oklahoma, but gives no further information. A book of poems, *Sounds of the Prairie* (1886) published in Topeka; autobiographical allusions imply she married at age 20 and lost a child in infancy.

Florence Land May. ?–?. Louisiana born, daughter of state Supreme Court judge Augustus May; married Louisiana Judge A. D. Land; divorced by 1907 in a locally well-publicized case. By 1910, according to her preface in *Lyrics from Lotus Land* (1911), she had lived in California for six years. A muckraking San Francisco novel (1910).

Kate McBeth. 1832–1915. Her family emigrated from Scotland; after her father's death she and older sister Sue became teachers. Sue (d. 1893) went first to the Choctaw and then the Nez Percé Reservation, joined by Kate in 1873. Kate taught women and children, Sue more controversially taught men. A missionary history of the Nez Percé, 1908. Biography by Allen Conrad Morrill and Eleanor Dunlap Morrill (1978).

Margaret Hill McCarter. 1860–1938. From Indiana; attended Earlham College and the State Normal School in Terre Haute. In 1884 moved to Topeka as head of the English Department at Topeka High School; married a physician in 1890; had three children. An active clubwoman and lecturer, she began writing for publication when her children were in school, publishing her first novel in 1910; became the best-known and best-paid Kansas novelist of her day.

Virginia Donaghé McClurg. 1857–1931. A journalist who moved to Colorado Springs from Morristown, New Jersey, at the age of 20; married Gilbert McClurg—writer, lecturer, and railroad publicist also from Morristown—in 1889.

The first white woman to explore Mesa Verde, she publicized it nationally. The couple lived in Colorado and Connecticut. Two years after her death, Gilbert collected her Colorado poems published before 1915.

Josephine Clifford McCrackin. 1838–1920. Prussian émigré, came with her family to St. Louis in 1846; married an army officer (apparently an abusive drunk) whom she accompanied to several southwestern posts. Divorced, she moved to San Francisco around 1869, began publishing in California journals. Married Jackson McCrackin in 1882, a former miner and Arizona legislator. A clubwoman, suffragist, and conservationist interested especially in saving the redwoods. Widowed in 1904, she moved to Santa Cruz, wrote for the *Santa Cruz Sentinel.* Three collections of stories set in Arizona and California (1877, 1893, 1913).

Frances McElrath. ?–?. Daughter and granddaughter of NYC editors, she published stories in eastern magazines and one Wyoming novel (1902).

Marie L. McLaughlin. 1842–?. Part Sioux, born in Minnesota; married Indian Agent Major James McLaughlin in Mendota, Minnesota, in 1864; was his official interpreter at Standing Rock. A book of Sioux stories (1916).

Grace E. Meredith. 1976–1946. From California; wrote her aunt's Texas captivity story and published it in Los Angeles (1927).

Florence A. Merriam (later Bailey). 1863–1948. Originally from New York, an ornithologist and nature writer. Her brother Clinton became first head of the US Biological Survey. Published scientific works and two popular ornithology books with a western focus (southern California 1894, Utah 1896). She was an associate, then the first woman Fellow of the American Ornithologist's Union. Biography by Harriet Kofalk (1989).

Janie Chase Michaels. 1864?–1959. Probably from Maine with a sea captain father, likely a teacher. Published a short novel set in Phoenix (1895), a second set in the southern California oilfields (1917).

Miriam Michelson. 1870–1942. Her parents were Jewish immigrants but sources differ about whether from Alsace, Prussia, or Poland. She was born either in Calaveras or Murphys (both in California), grew up in Virginia City, Nevada. Her brother Albert won a Nobel Prize in physics in 1907; she became a journalist for the *San Francisco Call;* she also worked in film, published stories, novels, plays; collected stories set in Virginia City (1904); novels about California journalism (1905, 1906) and a history of Virginia City (1934). Her most popular novel, *In the Bishop's Carriage* (1904), was a slang narrative set in Philadelphia.

Ella Sterling Cummins Mighels. 1854–1924. Born in the Sierras, schooled in Sacramento, twice married and twice widowed. Except for four years in London with her second husband, she lived in California lifelong, writing stories, plays, novels, a California literary history (*Story of the Files,* 1893, publishing as Cummins), an anthology. Memoir (1929).

Olive Thorne Miller. 1831–1918. Born in New York State, moved to Chicago after marriage and ultimately to Los Angeles. A nature writer on botany and ornithology, with a book about birding in Colorado (1894).

Ruth Comfort Mitchell. 1882–1954. A San Franciscan; began publishing poems in her teens, married Sanborn Young in 1914, moved to NYC where they cultivated a large circle of literary, political, and celebrity friends. In California they were active in civic enterprises and conservative Republican politics; he was in the California State Senate. California novels (1923, 1927); a San Francisco play (1913, republished 1927).

Anne Shannon Monroe. 1873–1942. Born in Missouri, moved to Yakima with her parents in 1887, and when her father died (1889) to Tacoma. A teacher and reporter for the *Tacoma News,* she went to Chicago and then Manhattan to become a literary professional; returned to Montana after she was successful enough to continue as a freelancer. Pacific Northwest novels (1900, 1916, 1925) and a memoir (1928).

Sallie B. Morgan. ?–?. Carolyn Perry's book on southern writers cites *The Journalist* (1889) saying Morgan was living in the Pacific Northwest, writing for newspapers and working as a correspondent for the *Clarion Ledger* of Jackson, Mississippi; and that she was a former staff writer for the Nashville *World,* a native of Mississippi, and granddaughter of its territorial governor, Robert William. A novel, *Tahoe* (1881).

Harriet C. Morse. ?–?. Probably a sister of Samuel F. B. Morse III, she published the Texas novel *A Cowboy Cavalier* in 1908, which he illustrated.

Mourning Dove (Christine Quintasket). 1888–1936. A member of the Okanogan tribe, married and divorced, worked seasonally off the reservation. Her Montana novel, *Cogewea,* to which Lucullus Virgil McWhorter contributed in unknown but probably major ways, was finished before World War I but not published until 1927. Later she published Indian stories, became an Indian activist. Memoir edited posthumously by Jay Miller (1990).

Dell H. Munger. 1860?–1932. A 1913 article by George Wharton James says she was a Kansan, a "farmer's daughter and farmer's wife"; moved to Carmel and published a successful Kansas novel in 1912.

Lois Lovina Abbott Murray. 1826–?. Her *Incidents of Frontier Life* (1880) tells her life story, especially her eighteen years in Kansas. Born in Granville Ohio; family moved to Indiana; married Samuel Murray in 1851, lived in Indiana until 1860 and then moved to Kansas where she remained another dozen years after her husband's death in 1866; three children.

Fannie E. Newberry. 1848–1942. Author of Christian books for girls including one set in Colorado (1891).

Emma Mersereau Newton. ?–?. Published three novels, one about a winter in Florida (1881), a second set in southern California (1902), and a third set in Boston during the American Revolution (1926).

Kathleen Norris. 1880–1966. A San Francisco author of best-selling romances (the first in 1911, many placed in and around San Francisco), said to have been the highest-paid woman writer of her time. Married Charles Gilman Norris, a journalist and author (younger brother of Frank) in 1909. They lived in NYC and California.

Grace May North. 1876–1960. Born in Utica, New York, she moved to California, wrote for a Santa Barbara newspaper; in the 1920s published Stratemeyer series novels set in the Southwest. She married an advertising man with a son before 1930.

Mary Myers North. ?–?. Born and raised in Washington, D.C., she married a minister, had three sons. *Who's Who* of 1915 says she was president of the American Woman's Press Association, vice president of the League of American Pen Women, historian for the National Association of Patriotic Instructors, recording secretary for the Woman's National Rivers and Harbors Congress, Chairman of the Press Commission of the National Council of Women. One Kansas novel (1902).

Aileen (O'Bryan) Nusbaum. 1889–?. Born in Las Vegas, New Mexico; studied art in Paris for a dozen years, was married to Jesse Nusbaum—archeologist and superintendent of Mesa Verde—from 1920 to 1939. At Mesa Verde she designed the hospital and staged Indian pageants. Also an illustrator and photographer, she was an organizer of and contributor to the 1940 WPA survey of New Mexico. A book of Zuni children's stories (1926).

Mary Hamilton O'Connor. 1872–1959. Born in St. Paul, she moved to Portland and later worked as a screenwriter; buried in Los Angeles. A young people's novel of the Pacific Northwest (1905).

Sarah Emilia Olden. ?–?. An Episcopalian lay speaker and a teacher, she visited reservations and published books about Sioux, Shoshone, and Karoc Indians; a history/travel book about the West (1927).

Cora Miranda Baggersly (Mrs. Fremont) Older. 1875–1968. Born in New York, she became a reporter, married San Francisco journalist and editor Fremont Older (1856–1935) in 1893 (nineteen years her senior); California political novels (1903, 1905).

Kate Alma Orgain. 1838–1913. From Illinois; moved with her mother to Louisiana; moved again with husband John Henry Orgain to Salado, Texas. An artist, musician, librarian and writer, she taught at Salado College and the local high school, belonged to the DAR and Texas Women's Press Club. Collected previously published Texas stories (1901).

Gwendolen Overton. 1876–?. Back matter in her novella, *The Golden Chain*, says she was the daughter of Captain Gilbert Overton, born at Fort Hayes but taken as an infant to Arizona, grew up at several army posts in Arizona and New Mexico, went east to school and also lived with her family in France, Washington, D.C. Eventually settled in Los Angeles. Walker's *Literary History of Southern California* says she became part of Charles Lummis's literary circle.

Narcissa Owen. 1831–1911. From a slaveholding Cherokee family that went west before Removal—first Arkansas, then Oklahoma; married a white railroad executive; lived in Virginia during the Civil War. Lived with her younger son, Robert, in Washington D.C. after he became Oklahoma's first elected senator; known as a painter. Her older son, in the army, served in Oregon under the Indian fighter General Nelson Miles. Moved back to Oklahoma, published a memoir, 1907.

Bethenia Owens-Adair. 1840–1926. Went overland with her parents in the first big group on the Oregon trail. Married at age fourteen (on account of Donation Act's provision of double allotments for married couples), divorced five years later, worked at many odd jobs, went to Philadelphia and University of Michigan to become a doctor. Remarried in 1884, she retired in 1905; published a combined memoir and Oregon history 1906.

Cornelia (Mrs. A[lonzo] G.) Paddock. 1840–1898. Wife of a mining man, moved to Utah and became an active anti-Mormon; Utah novels (1879, 1881).

Elizabeth M. Page. ?–?. Field Secretary for the Women's Board of Domestic Missions of the Dutch Reformed Church, active in the Friends of the Indian Mohonk Conferences; Oklahoma missionary history (1915).

Frances Parker. 1875–?. Three novels set in Montana and Idaho (1903, 1904, 1910).

Elsie Clews Parsons. 1874–1941. From a wealthy NYC family, graduate of Barnard, 1896; an M.A. (1897) and Ph.D. (1899) from Columbia; married in 1900 and had four children. Helped found the New School and taught there occasionally, but mostly did anthropological and sociological research. Many publications about pueblo culture, 1917 to 1926.

Elia Wilkinson Peattie. 1862–1935. From Michigan; moved to Chicago (1871–88 and again beginning 1896); married Chicago journalist Robert Burns Peattie in 1883, lived in Omaha 1888–96. Worked for several newspapers in Chicago and Omaha; published in numerous genres; a collection of Nebraska stories (1896). Biography with selected letters by Susanne George Bloomfield (2005).

Anna J. Hardwicke Pennybacker. 1861–1938. Born in Virginia, moved to Texas, married in 1884, had three children, was early widowed. A clubwoman, suffragist, and lecturer, nationally active in democratic politics (a good friend of Eleanor Roosevelt). A Texas history textbook was published in 1888, revised 1900.

Edna Brush Perkins. 1880–1930. Cleveland native from a wealthy family; attended (but didn't finish) college, married epidemiologist Roger Griswold Perkins in 1905, had four sons. Was active in the suffrage movement, did volunteer social work. Travel account of Death Valley (1922).

Eleanor Hodgman Porter. 1868–1920. Born in New Hampshire, trained as a singer; married a businessman and became a writer, eventually publishing fourteen novels and four books of short stories, including the best-seller *Pollyanna* (serialized 1912, book 1913). A Texas novel (1913).

Lavinia Honeyman Porter. 1836–1910. Born in West Virginia, moved to Missouri in childhood. Married in 1854—her husband worked as a bank cashier, teller, bookkeeper—and went west overland in 1860. Her fanciful overland memoir, ready for the publisher when she died, was published 1910.

Rebecca N(ewman) Porter. 1883–?. Born in Chicago, lived in Brazil (father a coffee importer), settled in California. Described in publisher advertising as a "well-known regional California writer." California novels (1920, 1922).

Emily Price Post. 1872 -1960. Raised in NYC, socially well connected; divorced, she began to publish for self-support; novels, short stories, essays, a motoring book (1916) and in 1922 an etiquette book that became the standard.

Alice Day Pratt. 1872–1963. Grew up in New England and South Dakota where her father homesteaded. Never married, she taught school and homesteaded on her own in eastern Oregon from 1911 to 1929; published her homesteading account in 1922. After returning to New England she published essays and juveniles about animals.

Melinda Rankin. 1811–1888. A Presbyterian missionary and teacher raised in New Hampshire, settled in Texas near the Mexican border in the 1840s, teaching in Huntsville and then Brownsville, writing for religious publications. After the Civil War she taught in Mexico for a few years; retired to Bloomington, Illinois. Published about Texas (1850); also a memoir (1875).

Emma J. Ray. 1859–1930. African American from St. Louis; moved with her husband, a bricklayer, to Seattle where they both worked as evangelicals. Memoir (1926).

Evelyn Hunt Raymond. 1843–1910. Born in Watertown, New York; attended Mount Holyoke; lived in Baltimore; was widowed. She wrote for Stratemeyer; also a series of girls' books about "Dorothy," and, between 1892 and 1909, several southern California and Arizona novels for girls.

Clarice E. Richards. 1875–1949. From Dayton, Ohio, she married a former minister turned Colorado rancher and moved to his Elbert County ranch in 1900. In 1907 they went to Denver where she became an active clubwoman. A fictionalized Colorado memoir appeared in 1920.

Louisa (Lula) Greene Richards. 1849–1944. Born in Iowa, great niece of Brigham Young, came to Utah with her family when she was three; they settled in Cache County. Taught school, married, published poems in the *Salt Lake Herald* and the *Deseret News;* also didactic stories; was the *Woman's Exponent's* first editor (1872–77).

Mary Roberts Rinehart. 1876–1958. From Pennsylvania, author of many female romance-mysteries, a highly successful author. Married a physician, had several children, had a home in Bar Harbor and a ranch in Wyoming. *The Circular Staircase* (1908), probably her most popular book, used the so-called "dark house" formula. Worked overseas as a war correspondent in World War I; two travel books set in Montana and the Cascades, advancing the cause of the National Parks and National Forests, published in 1915 and 1917; also a cowboy romance, serialized then published as a book in 1927. Biography by Jan Cohn (1980).

Sara T. L. Robinson. 1827–1911. Born in Belchertown, Massachusetts, daughter of a lawyer; married Dr. Charles Robinson in 1851. He organized a free soil group for the New England Emigrant Society and they went to Kansas in 1855. Imprisoned by the US government, he was Kansas's first (unofficially, since it was still a territory) elected governor. Her polemical *Kansas: Its Interior and Exterior Life* (1856) had ten editions.

Frances M(arie) A(ntoinette) Roe. 1850?–1920. Originally from New York State, she married Fayette Washington Roe (1850–1916), a Virginian from a navy family and a West Point graduate, in 1871. They retired to Florida in 1888; *Army Letters from an Officer's Wife* (1909) is set in Colorado and Oklahoma.

Vingie E. (Eve) Roe. 1879–1958. According to Marable and Boylan, she was the most widely known early Oklahoma writer. Born in Kansas, went to Oklahoma as a child (father a physician); published poetry as a teenager. Married Raymond C. Lawton in 1907, moved to California; divorced, she stayed in California. First novel came out in 1912, last novel well after my cutoff date; western novels were set from the Pacific Northwest to Arizona.

Aurelia Spencer Rogers. 1834–1922. Born in Connecticut; her parents converted to Mormonism and started west. Mother died en route; father was sent on a mission to England 1846–49; the children were shepherded to Salt Lake by Brigham Young. Married at age seventeen; moved to Farmington, Utah. In 1878 she organized the first Primary association, the church auxiliary for children. Family memoir published in 1898.

Alice Wellington Rollins. 1847–1897. Born in Boston; taught before marrying a New York businessman in 1876. Was an active clubwoman, published poetry, magazine articles, novels including *Uncle Tom's Tenement* (1888) about NYC. A book about her brother's Kansas ranch (1885); another about Yellowstone Park (1887). Retired to Bronxville, New York.

Hannah Anderson Ropes. 1809–1863. Born in New Gloucester, Maine; her father and two of her brothers were lawyers. Married William H. Ropes in 1834 (a teacher and school principal); lived in Waltham. In 1855 the marriage ended and her eighteen-year-old son began homesteading in Kansas. She joined her son for six months, published a book about it in 1856; also a novel about the (generalized) West (1859). A volunteer nurse at Union Hotel Hospital in Washington, D.C. beginning July 1862; died seven months later, probably from typhoid.

Mary Jane Ross. 1827–1908. Cherokee, Tennessee-born, moved to Oklahoma and married Cherokee educator, editor, and statesman William P. Ross in 1846. After his death in 1891 she collected his addresses and published them as a "Life and Times" book with an introductory biography (1893).

Maria Amparo Ruiz de Burton. 1832–1895. Born in Baja California; married an American army officer at age 16, was widowed at age 35. Published a novel about the confusion of black-white identity in 1872 (*Who Would Have Thought It?*) under the name C. Loyal. Attempts to innovate agriculturally on southern California property and also to claim land in Baja, failed. Supported the Texas Pacific Railroad, which failed in its attempts to secure a government contract. *The Squatter and the Don* (1885) is the first known novel by a Mexican-American woman.

Florence Kimball Russel. ?–?. Daughter, sister, and wife of army officers; born and raised on frontier posts. Published a boys' novel about southwestern army post life (1906); the next year, *A Woman's Journey through the Philippines* (travel book connected with laying the cable; her husband was in the signal corps). Two more boys' army novels (not western) published before 1914.

Marah Ellis Ryan. 1860–1934. A Pennsylvanian, she married a much older Irish actor on the New York stage, probably had a brief acting career herself. Many novels from 1892 onward set from Montana into Mexico, unusually beautifully decorated and illustrated. Also fiction about the Druids and other religions she considered archaic. Settled in Los Angeles and became a "Friend of the Indian."

Kate Sanborn. 1839–1917. New Englander, daughter of a Dartmouth professor; popular public lecturer and writer known for humorous accounts of farming in New England. Published a tourist book about southern California after wintering there (1893).

Helen Fitzgerald Sanders. 1883–1955. Her Mississippi family went to southern California after the Civil War; father became a state Supreme Court justice (1893 and 1894) and, moving to San Francisco, state attorney general (1895–99). They then moved to Montana where she married a son of Wilbur Fiske Sanders, a prominent early Montana settler; used his papers for her three-volume history of Montana (1913); also novels and sketches about California and Montana.

Mary P. Sawtelle. ?–?. Douthit (see above) says she was "probably the first woman in the Pacific Northwest to practice regular medicine." She lived in Salem, Oregon, in the early '70s, then moved to California, editing the monthly *Medico-Literary Journal* in San Francisco 1878–89. An Oregon novel, 1891, was mistakenly advertised by her own publishers as a California novel.

Dorothy Scarborough. 1878–1935. Texas-born, grew up in Sweetwater and Waco, graduated from Baylor, where she taught for many years after getting a Ph.D. from Columbia. Scholarly books about folklore; ghost stories; southern sketches; Texas novels (1923, 1925).

Eliza Ruhamah Scidmore. 1856–1928. From Madison, Wisconsin; attended Oberlin College for a year, moved to Washington D.C., became a journalist, professional travel writer, and photographer. Joined the National Geographic Society in 1890, held many administrative positions in the society. Visited what were then out-of-the-way places, sometimes traveling with her brother, a career diplomat. Published on Alaska (1885), Japan (1891), Java (1897), China (1900), India (1903). Said to have originated the idea of planting cherry trees in Washington D.C.; died in Geneva, Switzerland.

Mary Katrine (Mrs. William T.) Sedgwick. ?–?. Married William T. Sedgwick (1855–1921), a biologist, epidemiologist, and specialist in public health. A book about Acoma pueblo (1926).

Grace Gallatin Seton-Thompson. 1872–1959. Born in Sacramento, she worked for San Francisco newspapers, married Ernest Thompson Seton—author, artist, founder of the US Boy Scouts—in 1896 (they divorced), and published books of travel sketches including two with a western focus (1900, 1907).

Katharine Sharp. ?–?. Published one romantic action novel set partly in the Grand Canyon (1912).

Luella Shaw. 1886–?. In a book containing narratives of three Colorado pioneers (1909), she calls herself "a true daughter of Colorado" whose "ancestors were among the pioneers of Colorado."

Alice Jack (Dolan) Shipman (Mrs. O. L.). 1889–?. A local historian, native West Texan, daughter of cattleman and Texas Ranger Pat Dolan. Her history of southwest Texas published 1926; in 1933 began editing a short-lived magazine of Big Bend history.

Constance Lindsay Skinner. 1877–1939. Canadian born; her father was a Hudson's Bay Company agent. Went to California at age sixteen for her health to live with an aunt; stayed on in the US as a journalist and freelance writer. Many books of popular history, an edited series on American rivers; one book on the fur trade in Old Oregon (1921).

Alice Prescott Smith. 1868?–?. A California journalist, wrote three novels, two about Michigan and Canada, the third (1904) set in San Francisco and a nearby rural town.

Launa M[aria] Smith. 1894–1994. Based on material from Rootsweb and official Missouri documents I surmise that she was born in Missouri (probably Otterville), attended college in Columbia, Missouri, taught in the history department of Oklahoma City High School, married Logan Wycliffe Cary (b. 1884) in 1924, the year her one book—on US relations with Mexico—was published, had two children, one of whom died in infancy, the other an engineer and lifelong bachelor. At least one of her husband's relatives lived in Mexico.

Eliza Roxcy Snow. 1894–1887. The "Mormon poetess"; went to Salt Lake in the first group; sealed to Joseph Smith in Nauvoo; later sealed to Brigham Young and lived in the "Lion House." A director of the Women's Relief Society, she traveled around Utah territory on its behalf; participated in the Temple's Endowment ceremonies; contributed to the *Woman's Exponent*. Published her poems in Liverpool in 1856; Edward Tullidge published segments of her overland journal in his *Women of Mormondom* (1877).

E. D. E. N. (Emma Dorothy Eliza Nevitte) Southworth. 1819–1899. Born and raised in Washington D.C., married and moved to Wisconsin in 1840; marriage dissolved and she returned to D.C. in 1844, teaching and writing to support her two children and herself. Many romantic adventure novels, first serialized in Robert Bonner's weekly story paper, *The Ledger,* beginning in 1857, made her one of the best paid, most popular, and most prolific novelists of her time.

Phebe Estelle Spalding. 1859–1937. From Vermont, she became a professor of English at Pomona College, published an "Indian Legend" of southern California (1911) and, in the 1930s, other little books about southern California places.

Dorcas James Spencer. ?–?. From Rhode Island, came to California in 1856, married and had several children; lived in Grass Valley. Cofounded the first temperance society there (1874); later worked as an organizer, superintendent, recording secretary for WCTU; lobbied the California legislature beginning 1884 for temperance-related causes. Her WCTU history/memoir appeared in 1913.

Josephine Spencer. ?–1928. Born in Salt Lake City, she helped organize one of its first literary societies; published many poems and short stories beginning in 1890. Society editor for the *Deseret Evening News,* she represented the paper at the 1893 Chicago World's Fair. A collection of short stories (1895).

Mallie Stafford. ?–?. A memoir of travel and life in California based on two periods of residence (1884).

Patience Stapleton. 1861–1893. Born in Wiscasset, Maine; maiden name Martha Armstrong Tucker; educated at the Moravian Academy in Bethlehem, moved to Colorado in 1882; wrote for the *Denver Tribune* as "Patience Thornton." Married William Stapleton, managing editor of the *Rocky Mountain News,* in 1883, thereafter publishing as Patience Stapleton. A suffragist. *New York Times* obituary says she published more than 300 short stories; two Colorado novels are *Kady* (1888) and *Babe Murphy* (1890).

Fanny (Mrs. T. B.) Stenhouse. 1829–?. English, she and her husband converted to Mormonism and emigrated, settling first in NYC and then Salt Lake City where they were among the city's elite; quarreled with Brigham Young; were harassed; left Utah for the East. Both published anti-Mormon books in the 1870s. Later they went to San Francisco, where Thomas B.H. Stenhouse died in 1882. Nothing is known of Fanny's life after that.

Ann Sophia Stephens. 1818–1886. Eastern-based editor and author of much sensational woman-centered fiction, she published the first dime novel, *Malaeska, the Indian Wife of the White Hunter,* in 1860. Two dime novels about the West (1862, 1874).

Louise Gregg Stephens. 1843–1912. From the East; moved to Oregon; her husband was the local Portland agent for the *Oregonian.* Later they settled in Corvallis. *Letters from an Oregon Ranch* (1905) was first serialized in the Sunday *Oregonian* in 1903; her obituary calls her a "well-known writer and journalist," but I haven't identified other works by her.

Matilda Coxe Stevenson. 1849–1915. Born in Texas, she grew up in the East (mainly D.C.); in 1872 married James Stevenson of the US Geological Survey, going with him on surveys in Colorado, Idaho, Wyoming, and Utah between 1879 and his death in 1888. She was the first woman employed as a government anthropologist; wrote about the Zuni (1905). She moved to New Mexico in 1904, buying a ranch near San Ildefonso pueblo; was working on a comparative study of pueblo religion at her death.

Elinore Pruitt Stewart. 1876–1933. Born in Arkansas, grew up in the Oklahoma strip, worked at service jobs, married a much older railroad engineer. Widowed with a young child, she went to Wyoming to homestead and work as a house-keeper for rancher Clyde Stewart in 1909, whom she married six weeks after arriving. Letters to a former employer, collected in two books (1914, 1915) appeared first in the *Atlantic.* Biography with letters by Susanne George (1992).

Mary E. Stickney. 1853–?. In the 1890s she published western stories in eastern magazines; a Wyoming novel (1900); a collection of Colorado and Wyoming stories (1904).

Elinore Cowan Stone. 1883–1974. Born in Michigan; a teacher, newspaper-woman, and short story writer who taught in various places in the West. An episodic novel about a teacher in a New Mexico mining/mill town (1927); also a nonwestern mystery novel in the 1930s, when she was living in Pittsburgh.

Yda Addis Storke. 1857–1902. From Kansas, she traveled in Mexico with her father, an itinerant photographer. After the Civil War they went to California. She worked as a reporter; published more than a hundred stories, never collected, but highly praised in Mighels's *Story of the Files.* In 1890 she married attorney Charles Storke, who divorced her the next year. Said to have been committed to an insane asylum from which she disappeared. Her only book (1891) is boomer publicity for three southern California counties.

Marietta Lois Bell Stow. 1830?–1902. Born in New York State, moved with farmer parents to Ohio at age two; married a Cleveland merchant. Widowed, moved to NYC, began a lecture career in 1859. Married Joseph W. Stow, wid-ower from Vermont and a San Francisco merchant, in 1866; he died in 1874. Attacked the gender inequalities of the California judicial system in *Probate Confiscation* (1876); founded and edited several journals; ran for governor of California in 1882 as an independent and for US vice president on the Equal Rights ballot in 1884.

Carrie Adell Strahorn. 1854–1925. Wrote for newspapers and accompanied her husband Robert Strahorn, former journalist working as a town locator for the Northern Pacific, around the West, publishing her account of their travels in 1911. Said she was the first white woman to visit Yellowstone.

Lilyan Corbin Stratton. 1882–1928. From Crisfield, Maryland, a several-times-married actress and writer; went to Reno for a divorce, published *Reno* in 1921.

Idah Meacham Strobridge. 1855–1932. Grew up in the desert and mining country of Nevada, ranched and prospected. Married with three sons, lost them all to disease around 1889. Taking up bookbinding, she moved to southern California with her parents. Beginning 1895, she published sketches and stories in western magazines and newspapers; three collections (1904, 1907, 1909) from her own Artemisia Bindery. Stopped writing after 1909, became an active club-woman and genealogist.

May Kellogg Sullivan. ?–?. Two books about Alaska—travel account (1903), book of sketches (1910). Travel book suggests that she was originally from Wisconsin, had taught music and painting, that her father and brother were in Alaska looking for gold when she joined them the first time (she went twice), and that though married, she had little to do with her husband. Sketchbook preface implies she was living in the East by 1910 and had been to Alaska seven times.

Martha Summerhayes. 1844–1926. From Nantucket; after a year in Germany she married a military officer from Nantucket. He was posted to Ehrenberg, Arizona, for eighteen months handling transfers of army freight from the river to the interior. After his retirement, they lived in New York State, becoming close friends with Frederic Remington, who encouraged her to write the memoir she published in 1908.

A. Jennie (Bartlett) Switzer. ?–?. An anti-Mormon novel (1882).

Louise E. Taber. 1890–?. Published a San Francisco novel (1911); in the 1930s produced radio programs about the gold rush.

Annie D. Tallent. 1827–1902. The only woman in the so-called "Gordon Party" that entered the Black Hills illegally (Dec. 1874) and was expelled by the US Army (Apr. 1875). After the Black Hills were opened to whites, settled in Deadwood, taught school, became a school superintendent; husband and son were both presidents of Deadwood's pioneer society. History/publicity book about the Black Hills (1899).

Lucy Thompson. 1853–1932. A Yurok from extreme northern California, she married Scotsman Milton James Thompson, locator and assessor of claims for homesteaders, around 1875. *To the American Indian,* a book about Yurok history and ceremonies (1916).

Rose Hartwick Thorpe. 1850–1939. Moved in childhood from Indiana to Kansas to Michigan; wrote "The Curfew Will Not Ring Tonight" when she was sixteen. Married in 1871, she and her husband moved to Grand Rapids and then San Antonio for four years; ultimately to San Diego for his health in 1887. A book of southern California Indian legends (1904).

Zoe Stratton Tilghman. 1880–1964. Born in Kansas, emigrated with her family to Oklahoma, attended the University of Oklahoma, taught school. Married William Tilghman, widower and famous US Marshall, in 1902; had three sons. After Tilghman was killed in the line of duty (1924) she turned to writing and editing for family support, including a prairie novel (1925) and a book about Tilghman's exploits (1926). Wrote for and edited *Harlow's Weekly* (leading Oklahoma periodical); worked on the Federal Writers' project in Oklahoma, later published many juveniles about Native Americans from diverse tribes; a long biography of her husband (1949) has some autobiography.

Katherine Augusta Westcott Tingley. 1847–1929. Born in Newbury, Massachusetts. Three times married; by the 1880s had become a Spiritualist and social reformer in NYC, joining the Theosophists in winter 1892–93 and succeeding William Q. Judge as president of the breakaway American Section after his death in 1896. She traveled around the world and in 1900 established the renamed society's headquarters at Point Loma; founded a school and a publishing house, and made the grounds a tourist destination, which had its heyday in the teens and twenties. Her book on the Point Loma establishment was published in 1908.

Juliet Wilbor Tompkins. 1871–1956. Popular and prolific author of novels, magazine stories, poems, and plays; a native Californian who lived with her widowed mother in the San Leandro Valley; collaborated with her brother, Gilbert Tompkins, a composer. Associated especially with *Munsey's Magazine.*

Margaret Turnbull. ?–1942. Novelist and screenwriter for the silents, born in Scotland; published at least fourteen popular novels and worked on fifty-one films beginning in 1914. Her mystery series featured Juliet Jackson, the "female ferret." *The Close-Up* (1918) is a novel about Los Angeles and the movie industry.

Charlotte Marion White Vaile. 1852–1902. Originally from Massachusetts, married Indianan Joel Fredrick Vaile in 1875; after seven years in Indiana they moved to Denver in 1882 where he practiced law, summered on their property in what is now Vail, Colorado. She wrote popular books for girls set in New England, Indiana, and Colorado (1898).

Mary T(urril) Van Denburgh. ?–?. Shows up as an author in a 1922 *Who's Who* of California women. Published on San Francisco's Chinatown (1907).

Frances Fuller Victor. 1826–1902. The premier western woman historian of her era, originally part of the New York dime novelist group writing for Beadle. Went to California with her husband; widowed, she wrote on salary, anonymously, for Bancroft's histories. Around 1890 she retired to Oregon. Books of history and stories (1870, 1872, 1877, 1891, 1894). Biography by Jim Martin (1992).

Metta Victoria Fuller Victor. 1831–1885. Like her sister, Frances, she worked for Beadle; seems not to have gone west. A novel opposing Utah statehood published in 1856; her more than twenty dime novels include two westerns (1863, 1865). Because she married her sister's brother-in-law, the two had the same last name before and after marriage.

Teresa Vielé. 1831–1906. Born in NYC, where she eventually returned, she married an army officer, spent some time in Texas, was involved in a scandalous divorce and custody suit in 1871. Book about Texas (1858).

Madge Morris Wagner. 1862–1924. Appleton's biographical encyclopedia says she was born on the plains while her parents were en route to California, but *Story of the Files* locates her in Colorado before she moved to California, where she was a journalist, editor (of the *Golden Era* magazine), and poet. She married San Francisco publisher Harr Wagner, published books of poetry in 1881, 1885, 1917; and a lost novel called *A Titled Plebeian*.

Frona Eunice Wait (later Colburn). 1859–1946. Born in Midland, California. Apparently the first woman writer on the San Francisco *Examiner,* also worked for the San Francisco *Call* and San Francisco *Chronicle.* An author and lecturer, she established the San Francisco book fair, published on diverse California subjects, was the California women's commissioner to the Columbian Exposition of 1893. Died in Washington, D.C.

C(atharine) V. Waite. 1829–1913. Canadian-born, came with her family to Iowa in 1846, attended Knox College and Oberlin, graduated 1853. Married Charles Burlingame Waite in 1853, whom Lincoln appointed a federal judge for Utah Territory in 1862; they left within a year without his having presided over any cases. In her fifties she went to law school in Chicago and was active in the bar. Two anti-Mormon books 1866, 1882.

Susan E. Wallace. 1830–1907. From a wealthy Crawfordsville, Indiana, family; married fellow Indianan Lew Wallace (1827–1905) in 1852; he was a General in the Union Army, territorial governor of New Mexico 1878–1881, author of *Ben Hur.* Published travel sketches in magazines, eventually six books including *The Land of the Pueblos* (1888).

Jeannette Walworth. 1837–1918. Settled in New Orleans as a widow after sixteen years in NYC; published at least thirty novels. *The Bar-Sinister* (1885) was a widely-circulated anti-Mormon novel.

Eliza Spalding Warren. 1837–1919. Daughter of the missionary Spalding couple who went overland with the Whitmans and settled among the Nez Percé in western Idaho, said to have been the first white child born in the Pacific Northwest. Her late-life memoir, augmented by family papers, is the only biographical source.

Emmeline B. Wells. 1828–1921. Born in Massachusetts; became a Mormon at age fourteen; married three times—1843, 1845, and 1852. Was in the exodus from Nauvoo to Salt Lake; edited the *Women's Exponent* from 1877 to 1914, represented Utah at national and international women's meetings, was general secretary of the Relief Society for more than 20 years. She collected previously published work in *Musings and Memories* (1896) (second edition, 1915).

May Wentworth (also Mary Wentworth Newman, Mary Richardson Dolliver). 1830?–1899. Born in Maine, she died in San Francisco; between 1867 and 1870 published children's fairy tales set in California and an anthology of Pacific poetry. Also invested in real estate and ran a hotel.

Leoti L. West. 1851–1933. Born in Iowa, never married, went to Colfax (Washington) to teach; taught also in Walla Walla, Rosalia, Camano; served on boards of education. Eulogized as "The Inland Empire's Most Famous Teacher," taught over 5,000 pupils; wrote her reminiscences for the Spokane *Spokesman Review* and published them as a book in 1927.

Helen Cody Wetmore. 1850–?. Youngest sister of Buffalo Bill Cody; married a rancher whom she met while visiting her brother at Fort McPherson in 1871. Widowed with a young daughter by 1877, she was supported by her brother for many years. Remarried in 1893, to Hugh Wetmore, editor of the *Duluth Press.* Cody's continuing support included his commissioning her to write (and market) his 1899 biography.

Lu Wheat. ?–?. Widowed by 1898 (husband, Thomas H. Smith, was an attorney), lived and traveled in Japan and China, settled in Los Angeles and Pasadena. Novels with legal themes (1906, 1908) about northern and southern California.

Helen Mar (Kimball) Whitney. 1828–1896. Daughter of Heber Kimball, an early LDS President; in 1843 was sealed to Joseph Smith in Nauvoo, probably his youngest wife. Married Horace Whitney 1844 (he died in 1884), went to Salt Lake City 1848; became a plural wife in 1850. One of her 11 children, Orson, became a prominent Mormon Bishop. Published reminiscences in the *Woman's*

Exponent 1880–1886 (collected in 1997); two books defending plural marriage 1882 (now very rare) and 1884; her articles about early church history collected and published 1997; diary of her life as a widow published 2003.

Martha S. Whitten. 1842–1917. Daughter of a Texas judge, wife of a prominent architect and builder, lived most of her life in Austin; lauded in the *Austin Daily Statesman* as "one of the oldest and most respected pioneers of this city." A book of poetry (1866) in which autobiographical poems say her husband fought with the Confederacy and a brother was murdered by persons unknown on a mining expedition in Mexico.

Leah D. Widtsoe. 1864–1964. Daughter of Susa Young Gates; granddaughter of Brigham Young. Earned a degree in domestic science from BYU in 1898; taught; married John A. Widtsoe, professor of agriculture at BYU. Collaborated on doctrinal works with her mother and with her husband; in 1931 collaborated with her mother on a biography of Brigham Young.

Kate Douglas Wiggin. 1856–1923. From Maine, moved with parents to Santa Barbara as a child; later, involved in the kindergarten movement, went to San Francisco. Twice married; relocated to NYC in 1884, traveled and lectured widely. Her *Rebecca of Sunnybrook Farm* (1904) is one of the most popular girls' books of all time. *Summer in a Cañon* (1889) is set in the hills outside Santa Barbara.

Bernice Love Wiggins. 1897–?. African American poet originally from Austin; grew up with an aunt in El Paso after her mother died in 1902. Self-published *Tuneful Tales* in 1925; is said to have moved to California in the early 1930s.

Emma Hart Willard. 1787–1870. From Massachusetts, an educator who settled in Troy, New York, where she established a prestigious girls' school; also a historian, especially of the US. In 1849 she synthesized available materials into a book on the Mexican War and California, *Last Leaves of American History.*

Madeline Deaderick Willard. ?–?. A historical novel about southern California, *The King's Highway,* 1913.

Ellen Williams. ?–?. Wife of a bugler in the Second Colorado Cavalry in the Civil War which, at Glorieta in New Mexico, stopped the confederate advance into the West. *Three Years and a Half in the Army* (1885) memorializes the regiment.

Mary H. Wills. ?–?. Her 1889 travel book about southern California implies that she lived in Norristown, Pennsylvania, was a grandmother when she published the book, and worked in a newspaper or magazine office.

Honoré Willsie (later Morrow). 1880–1940. Born in Iowa, graduated from the University of Wisconsin, married an engineer in 1901 and went with him to Arizona, where she wrote stories and novels (six western novels published between 1915 and 1923). They separated; she edited the Chicago-based women's magazine *The Delineator,* 1914–1919; divorced from Willsie in 1921, she married publisher William Morrow in 1923; moved permanently to England after his death in 1931. In the late 1920s began publishing about Abraham Lincoln and the Civil War.

Augusta Evans Wilson. 1835–1909. From Georgia; after father's bankruptcy in 1845, the family moved to San Antonio for a few years, then settled in Alabama. *Inez, a Tale of the Alamo* appeared anonymously in 1855, under her own name in 1864. A strong Confederate partisan, she married Lorenzo Madison Wilson, twenty-seven years older than she, in 1868; a leading social presence in Mobile and a famous gardener. Several novels set in the South; her *St. Elmo* (1866) sold a million copies in its first four months. Biography by William Perry Fidler (1951).

Sarah Winnemucca (Hopkins). 1844?–1891. A Northern Paiute, an interpreter for her people, reservation agents, and the army. She lived with white ranchers as a young girl, married a white man, lectured on the East Coast. Mary Mann and Elizabeth Peabody, her Boston hosts, suggested she write a memoir; *Life among the Piutes,* edited by Mann, appeared in 1884. Returning west, she lived with relatives and taught school until her sudden death. Biographies by Gae Whitney Canfield (1983) and Sally Zanjani (2001).

Alice S. Wolf. ?–?. One of eleven children, a member of San Francisco's well-to-do Jewish community. Father died in 1878; mother kept the family together; one brother became president of the city's grain exchange. She taught, published in California journals. A San Francisco society novel, *A House of Cards* (1896).

Emma Wolf. 1865–1932. Sister of Alice, trained as a teacher but never taught, apparently because of a physical disability. Published five California novels, two about San Francisco's Jewish community, between 1892 and 1916.

Ruth Kedzie Wood. 1880?–1950. A professional tourist writer and traveler; her first book, *Honeymooning in Russia,* appeared in 1911. Published on Eastern Canada, the American and Canadian northwest (1918), California (1914), Spain and Portugal, and elsewhere; was a fellow of the Royal Geographic Society.

Abby Johnson Woodman. 1828–1921. Born in New Hampshire, a cousin of John Greenleaf Whittier; lived at Oak Knoll in Danvers, where Whittier spent summers after 1878. He wrote a brief introduction to her Alaska travel book (1889).

Sarah Chauncey Woolsey. 1835–1905. Grew up in Cleveland and the Northeast; never married, worked as a nurse during the Civil War; settled in the family home in Newport, Rhode Island, after the war and began to write under the pen name Susan Coolidge. Her popular five-book *What Katy Did* series for girls had two novels—*Clover* (1888) and *In the High Valley* (1890)—with Colorado scenes.

Pauline Wilson Worth. 1887–?. Published short stories; one book collection, *Death Valley Slim and Other Stories* (1909).

Muriel H. Wright. 1889–1975. An Oklahoman; her father was part Choctaw, her mother a white Presbyterian missionary. She was first a teacher, then a distinguished historian, writing textbooks for the Oklahoma public schools beginning 1923; for thirty years (1943–73) edited and contributed to *Chronicles of Oklahoma,* quarterly journal of the Oklahoma Historical Society. Also active in Choctaw politics. Biography by Patricia Loughlin (2005).

Ann Eliza Young. 1844–?. One of Brigham Young's wives, she apostatized and sued for divorce, lecturing widely on her Mormon life. An autobiography, *Wife No. 19 (1875).* Biography by Irving Wallace (1961).

Margaret G. Young. ?–?. An Idaho novel, *Homestead Ranch* (1922).

Zitkala-Sa (Gertrude Bonnin). 1876–1938. Sioux activist and writer born on the Yankton Reservation; Sioux mother, white father. At age eight she went to a Quaker boarding school in Wabash, Indiana, for three years; later attended the Santee Normal Training School and Earlham College; began teaching at Carlisle in 1898; married part-Sioux Raymond Bonnin in 1902; they worked on Sioux reservations and eventually went to D.C. to work for Indian welfare. Assembled two books from materials published mostly at the turn of the century: folklore (*Old Indian Legends,* 1901), sketches, stories, autobiography (*American Indian Stories,* 1921).

Acknowledgments

Many people helped me as I worked on this book. I owe special thanks to:

Susan Armitage for help with Phoebe Goodall Judson.

Katie Armitage for connecting me to Pat Michaelis of the Kansas State Historical Society, who helped me with Mary E. Jackson. Also, from the Kansas State Historical Society, Lin Fredericksen who helped me with Annie Diggs's birth and death dates.

Dale Bauer for suggesting two novels by E. D. E. N. Southworth and Kathleen Norris's *Foolish Virgin*.

Venice Beske of the Wyoming State Library for help with Sarah Emilia Olden.

Susanne George Bloomfield for directing me to Elia Peattie, Kate M. Cleary, and Patience Stapleton.

James Crisp for help with Adina De Zavala, Mary Austin Holley, and Texas history.

Charles Davis for discovering Mary Cone and Caroline Churchill in a California bookstore.

Bethany Eisenlohr for research on Helen Fitzgerald Sanders and for taking notes on Sanders's *History of Montana*; Jill Bergman and Brady Harrison for finding Bethany Eisenlohr.

Eric Gardner for directing me to Maud Cuney-Hare, Delilah Beasley, Josie Briggs Hall, and Bernice Love Wiggins.

Susan Goodman for help with Mary Austin.

James Keeline for directing me to Grace May North and for help with Evelyn Raymond.

Arnold Krupat for help with Zitkala-Sa and Native American writers in general.

Karen Kunz at Coren Printing for finding me a copy of their reprint of Annie Green's *Sixteen Years on the Great American Desert.*

Victoria Lamont for directing me to Emma Ghent Curtis and for conversations about Frances McElrath.

Paula Mitchell Marks for help with Mary Maverick.

Jeanne Moskel for directing me to Melinda Rankin.

Diane Moul for help with Grace Sartwell Mason's life and for directing me to Mason's *The Lady and the Car.*

Robert Dale Parker for directing me to Mabel Washbourne Anderson and Marianna Burgess.

Karen Ramirez for help with Helen Hunt Jackson.

Jeanne Reesman for help with Rose Wilder Lane.

The late Merrill Skaggs for help with Willa Cather.

Sharon Snyder for directing me to Sharlot Hall, Alice Corbin Henderson, and Frona Wait; Sharon Snyder and Richard Anderson for sharing their unpublished paper, "In Pursuit of Marah Ellis Ryan" (copyright 2004) with me.

Mandy Wescott, my RA for one semester, for biographical sleuthing.

Rusty Yerxa of the National Park Service at Glacier Bay for help with Eliza Scidmore.

For comments on an earlier, longer draft of the introduction, thanks to Dale Bauer, Margaret Bolsterli, Lawrence Buell, Robert Levine, Vivian Narehood, Frederick Newberry, and Richard Powers.

Richard Powers's generosity helped me survive several computer glitches.

The Andrew Mellon foundation supported travel and book purchases through an Emeritus Fellowship.

Without the library of the University of Illinois, the English Department of the University of Illinois, and funds from my Swanlund Endowed Chair at the University of Illinois, this book couldn't have been written.

Bibliography

Selected Women's Western Books through 1927

Abel, Annie Heloise. *The Slaveholding Indians*. Vol. I, *The American Indian as Slave-holder and Secessionist* (Cleveland: Arthur H. Clark, 1915); Vol. II, *The American Indian as Participant in the Civil War* (Cleveland: Arthur H. Clark, 1919); Vol. III, *The American Indian under Reconstruction* (Cleveland: Arthur H. Clark, 1925). Vol. III also published the same year as *The American Indian and the End of the Confederacy, 1863–1866*.

Adams, Emma H. *To and Fro in Southern California, with Sketches in Arizona and New Mexico*. Cincinnati: W. M. B. C. Press, 1887.

———. *To and Fro, Up and Down in Southern California, Oregon, and Washington Territory, with Sketches in Arizona, New Mexico, and British Columbia*. Cincinnati: Cranston and Howe, 1888.

Aiken, Ednah. *The River*. Indianapolis: Bobbs, Merrill, 1914.

Aldrich, Bess Streeter. *Mother Mason*. New York: D. Appleton, 1924.

———. *The Rim of the Prairie*. New York: A. L. Burt, 1925.

———. *The Cutters*. New York: D. Appleton, 1926.

———. *A Lantern in Her Hand*. New York: D. Appleton, 1928.

Allen, Emma S. *The Awakening of the Hartwells: A Tale of the San Francisco Earthquake*. New York: American Tract Society, 1913.

———. *Afterwards*. New York: Edward J. Clode, 1914.

———. *The High Road*. New York: Meridian, 1917.

Allen, Margaret V. *Ramona's Homeland*. Chula Vista: Denrich Press, 1914.

Anderson, Ada Woodruff. *The Heart of the Red Firs*. Boston: Little, Brown, 1908.

———. *The Strain of White*. Boston: Little, Brown, 1909.

———. *The Rim of the Desert*. New York: A. L. Burt, 1915.

Anderson, Mabel Washbourne. *Life of General Stand Watie, The Only Indian Brigadier General of the Confederate Army and the Last General to Surrender*. Pryor, Okla.: Mayes

County Republican, 1915. Facsimile edition with new material, Harrah, Oklahoma: Brandy Station Bookshelf, 1995.

Aplington, Kate A. *Pilgrims of the Plains: A Romance of the Santa Fe Trail.* Chicago: F. G. Browne, 1913.

Arnold, Anna E. *Civics and Citizenship: A Textbook for the Boys and Girls of Kansas Which Is Intended Not Merely to Give Them Information, but to Assist Them in Developing a Quality of Citizenship That Will Make Them Worthy of Their Heritage.* Cottonwood Falls, Kansas: A. E. Arnold, 1912. Revised edition. Topeka: State of Kansas, 1917.

———. *A History of Kansas.* Topeka: State of Kansas, 1915.

Atherton, Gertrude. *Los Cerritos: A Romance of the Modern Time.* New York: John W. Lovell, 1890.

———. *The Doomswoman: An Historical Romance of Old California.* Philadelphia: J. B. Lippincott, 1892.

———. *A Whirl Asunder.* New York: Frederick A. Stokes, 1895.

———. *The Californians.* New York: J. Lane, 1898.

———. *The Valiant Runaways.* New York: Dodd, Mead, 1898.

———. *A Daughter of the Vine.* New York: J. Lane, 1899.

———. *The Splendid Idle Forties.* New York: Macmillan, 1902.

———. *Rezanov.* New York: Frederick A. Stokes, 1906.

———. *Ancestors.* New York: Harper and Brothers, 1907.

———. *California: An Intimate History.* New York: Harper and Brothers, 1914. Revised edition. New York: Horace Liveright, 1927.

———. *Perch of the Devil.* New York: Frederick A. Stokes, 1914.

———. *The Avalanche: A Mystery Story.* New York: Frederick A. Stokes, 1919.

———. *The Sisters-in-Law; A Novel of Our Time.* New York: Frederick A. Stokes, 1921.

———. *Sleeping Fires.* New York: Frederick A. Stokes, 1922.

Austin, Mary. *The Land of Little Rain.* Boston: Houghton, Mifflin, 1903. Reissue, together with *Lost Borders* in *Stories from the Country of Lost Borders,* ed. Marjorie Pryse. New Brunswick: Rutgers University Press, 1987.

———. *The Basket Woman: A Book of Fanciful Tales for Children.* Boston: Houghton, Mifflin, 1904. (1910 edition called *Indian Tales for Children;* either title may appear in reissue.) Facsimile reissue titled *A Book of Indian Tales,* with a foreword by Mark Schlenz. Reno: University of Nevada Press, 1999.

———. *Isidro.* Boston: Houghton, Mifflin, 1905.

———. *The Flock.* Boston: Houghton, Mifflin, 1906. Reissue with an afterword by Barney Nelson. Reno: University of Nevada Press, 2001.

———. *Santa Lucia: A Common Story.* New York: Harper and Brothers, 1908.

———. *Lost Borders.* New York: Harper and Brothers, 1909. Reissue, together with *Land of Little Rain* in *Stories from the Country of Lost Borders,* ed. Marjorie Pryse. New Brunswick: Rutgers University Press, 1987.

———. *California: The Land of the Sun.* New York: Macmillan, 1914.

———. *The Man Jesus, Being a Brief Account of the Life and Teaching of the Prophet of Nazareth.* New York: Harper, 1915.

———. *The Ford.* Boston: Houghton, Mifflin, 1917. Reissue with a foreword by John Walton. Berkeley: University of California Press, 1997.

———. *The Trail Book.* Boston: Houghton, Mifflin, 1918.

———. *The American Rhythm.* New York: Harcourt, Brace, 1923.

———. *The Land of Journey's Ending.* New York: Century, 1924. Facsimile with an introduction by Melody Graulich. Urbana: University of Illinois Press, 2003.

Baggs, Mae Lacy. *Colorado: The Queen Jewel of the Rockies: A Description of Its Climate and of Its Mountains, Rivers, Forests, and Valleys; An Account of Its Explorers; A Review of Its Indians—Past and Present; A Survey of Its Industries, with Some Reference to What It Offers of Delight to the Automobilist, Traveller, Sportsman and Health Seeker; Together with a Brief Resume of Its Influence upon Writers and Artists, and a Short Account of Its Problems and How Met, and of Its Inexhaustible Resources and Their Development.* Boston: Page, 1918.

Bailey, Alice Ward. *Sage Brush Parson.* Boston: Little, Brown, 1906.

Bailey, Margaret Jewett. *The Grains; or, Passages in the Life of Ruth Rover, with Occasional Pictures of Oregon, Natural and Moral.* Portland, Ore.: Carter and Austin, 1854. New edition prepared by Evelyn Leasher and Robert J. Frank. Corvallis: Oregon State University Press, 1986.

Bamford, Mary: *Angel Island: The Ellis Island of the West.* Chicago: Woman's American Baptist Home Mission Society, 1917.

Bamford, Mary E. *Ti: A Story of Chinatown.* Chicago: David C. Cook, 1899.

Bandini, Helen Elliott. *History of California.* New York: American Book Company, 1908.

Barbour, A(nna) Maynard. *Told in the Rockies: A Pen Picture of the West* (also published as *The Award of Justice; or, Told in the Rockies*). Chicago: Rand, McNally, 1897.

Barker, Nettie Garmer. *Kansas Women in Literature.* Kansas City, Kans.: S. I. Mesereaull and Son, 1915.

Barnaby, Josephine. *The Present Condition of My People.* New York: American Missionary Association, n.d.

Barr, Amelia. *The Hallam Succession.* New York: Philips and Hunt, 1884.

———. *Remember The Alamo.* New York: Dodd, Mead, 1888.

———. *All the Days of My Life: An Autobiography; The Red Leaves of a Human Heart.* New York: D. Appleton, 1913.

Bates, Mrs. D. B. (Dolly Bryant). *Incidents on Land and Water, or Four Years on the Pacific Coast. Being a Narrative of the Burning of the Ships Nonantum, Humayoon and Fanchon, together with Many Startling and Interesting Adventures on Sea and Land.* Boston: J. French, 1857.

Bates, Josephine. *A Blind Lead: The Story of a Mine.* Philadelphia: J. B. Lippincott, 1888.

Bates, Josephine White. *A Nameless Wrestler.* Philadelphia: J. B. Lippincott, 1889.

———. *Bunch-Grass Stories.* Philadelphia: J. B. Lippincott, 1895.

Bauder, Emma Pow. *Ruth and Marie: A Fascinating Story of the Nineteenth Century.* Chicago: Monarch, 1895.

Beasley, Delilah L. *The Negro Trail Blazers of California: A Compilation of Records from the California Archives in the Bancroft Library at the University of California, in Berke-*

ley; and from the Diaries, Old Papers and Conversations of Old Pioneers in the State of California. It Is a True Record of Facts, as They Pertain to the History of the Pioneer and Present Day Negroes of California. Los Angeles: Times Mirror Printing and Binding House, 1919. Facsimile, New York: Negro Universities Press, 1969.

Biddle, Ellen McGowan. Reminiscences of a Soldier's Wife. Philadelphia: J. B. Lippincott, 1907. Reissue with an introduction by Peter Cozzens. Mechanicsburg, Pa.: Stackpole, 2002.

Bixby-Smith, Sarah. My Sagebrush Garden. Cedar Rapids: Torch Press, 1924.

———. Adobe Days. Cedar Rapids: Torch Press, 1926. Reissue with a foreword by Gloria Ricci Lothrop. Lincoln: University of Nebraska Press, 1987.

Blake, Mary Elizabeth. On the Wing: Rambling Notes of a Trip to the Pacific. Boston: Lee and Shepard, 1883.

Blessing-Eyster, Nellie. A Chinese Quaker: An Unfictitious Novel. New York: Fleming H. Revell, 1902.

Bonner, Geraldine. Hard Pan: A Story of Bonanza Fortunes. New York: Century, 1900.

———. Tomorrow's Tangle. Indianapolis: Bobbs, Merrill, 1903.

———. The Pioneer: A Tale of Two States. Indianapolis: Bobbs, Merrill, 1905.

———. Rich Men's Children. Indianapolis: Bobbs, Merrill, 1907.

———. The Emigrant Trail. New York: Duffield, 1910.

———. Treasure and Trouble Therewith: A Novel of California. New York: D. Appleton, 1917.

Bower, B. M. The Lonesome Trail. New York: G. W. Dillingham, 1904.

———. Chip of the Flying U. New York: Street and Smith, 1904.

———. The Range Dwellers. New York: G. W. Dillingham, 1906.

———. Rowdy of the Cross L. New York: G. W. Dillingham, 1907.

———. Her Prairie Knight. New York: G. W. Dillingham, 1906.

———. The Lure of the Dim Trails. New York: G. W. Dillingham, 1907.

———. The Long Shadow. New York: G. W. Dillingham, 1909.

———. Good Indian. Boston: Little, Brown, 1912.

———. The Lonesome Land. New York: A. L. Burt, 1912.

———. The Gringos. Boston: Little, Brown, 1913.

———. The Uphill Climb. Boston: Little, Brown, 1913.

———. Flying U Ranch. New York: G. W. Dillingham, 1914.

———. Jean of the Lazy A. New York: A. L. Burt, 1915.

———. The Flying U's Last Stand. Boston: Little, Brown, 1915.

———. The Phantom Herd. Boston: Little, Brown, 1915.

———. The Heritage of the Sioux. Boston: Little, Brown, 1916.

———. Starr, of the Desert. Boston: Little, Brown, 1917.

———. The Lookout Man. Boston: Little, Brown, 1917.

———. Cabin Fever. Boston: Little Brown, 1918.

———. Rim7 O' the World. Boston: Little, Brown, 1919.

———. The Quirt. Boston: Little Brown, 1920.

———. Cow-Country. Boston: Little, Brown, 1921.

——. *The Parowan Bonanza.* Boston: Little, Brown, 1923.

——. *The Bellehelen Mine.* Boston: Little, Brown, 1924.

——. *The Eagle's Wing.* Boston: Little, Brown, 1924.

——. *Desert Brew.* Boston: Little, Brown, 1925.

Boyd, Frances Mullen (Mrs. Orsemus B.). *Cavalry Life in Tent and Field.* New York: J. S. Tait, 1894. Reissue with an introduction by Darlis A. Miller. Lincoln: University of Nebraska Press, 1982.

Boyles, Kate and Virgil D. *Langford of the Three Bars.* New York: A. L. Burt, 1907.

——. *The Homesteaders.* New York: A. L. Burt, 1909.

——. *The Spirit Trail.* Chicago: A. C. McClurg, 1910.

——. *A Daughter of the Badlands.* Boston: Stratford, 1922.

Broderick, Therese. *The Brand: A Tale of the Flathead Reservation.* Seattle: Alice Harriman, 1909.

Brooks, Elizabeth. *Prominent Women of Texas.* Akron, Ohio: Werner, 1896.

Brown, Clara Spalding. *Life at Shut-In Valley, and Other Pacific Coast Tales.* Franklin, Ohio: Editor Publishing, 1895.

Bruner, Jane W. *Free Prisoners: A Story of California Life.* Philadelphia: Claxton, Remsen and Haffelfinger, 1877.

Bullene, Emma Frances Jay. *The Psychic History of the Cliff Dwellers: Their Origin and Destruction.* Denver: Reed Publishing, 1905.

Burgess, Marianna (pseudonym Embe). *Stiya, a Carlisle Indian Girl at Home; Founded on the Author's Actual Observations.* Cambridge: Riverside, 1891.

Burt, Katharine Newlin. *The Branding Iron.* Boston: Houghton, Mifflin, 1919.

——. *Hidden Creek.* Boston: Houghton, Mifflin, 1920.

——. *Q.* Boston: Houghton, Mifflin, 1922.

Callahan, S. Alice. *Wynema: A Child of the Forest.* Chicago: H. J. Smith, 1891. Reissue with introduction and notes by A. LaVonne Brown Ruoff. Lincoln: University of Nebraska Press, 1997.

Carmichael, Sarah E. *Poems; A Brief Selection Published by Permission of the Authoress, for Private Circulation.* San Francisco: Towne and Bacon, 1866.

Carr, Sarah Pratt. *The Iron Way: A Tale of the Builders of the West.* Chicago: A. C. McClurg, 1907.

Carrington, Frances C. *My Army Life and the Fort Phil. Kearney Massacre, with an Account of the Celebration of "Wyoming Opened."* Philadelphia: J. B. Lippincott, 1910. Reissue with an introduction by Shannon Smith Calitri. Lincoln: University of Nebraska Press, 2004.

Carrington, Margaret Irvin. *Absaraka, Home of the Crows: Being the Experience of an Officer's Wife on The Plains, and Marking the Vicissitudes of Peril and Pleasure during the Occupation of the New Route to Virginia City, Montana, 1866–7, and the Indian Hostility Thereof; with Outlines of the Natural Features and Resources of the Land, Tables of Distances, Maps, and Other Aids to the Traveler; Gathered from Observation and Other Reliable Sources.* Philadelphia: J. B. Lippincott, 1868. Facsimile, Lincoln: University of Nebraska Press, 1983.

Cather, Willa. *O Pioneers!* Boston: Houghton, Mifflin, 1913. Scholarly edition ed. Charles Mignon and Susan J. Rosowski. Lincoln: University of Nebraska Press, 1999.

———. *The Song of the Lark.* Boston: Houghton, Mifflin, 1915.

———. *My Antonia.* Boston: Houghton, Mifflin, 1918. Scholarly edition ed. Charles Mignon and Kari A. Ronning. Lincoln: University of Nebraska Press, 2003.

———. *A Lost Lady.* New York: A. A. Knopf, 1923. Scholarly edition ed. Charles Mignon, Kari A. Ronning, and Frederick M. Link. Lincoln: University of Nebraska Press, 2003.

———. *The Professor's House.* New York: A. A. Knopf, 1925. Scholarly edition ed. Charles Mignon and Frederick M. Link. Lincoln: University of Nebraska Press, 2002.

———. *Death Comes for the Archbishop.* New York: A. A. Knopf, 1927. Scholarly edition ed. John J. Murphy. Lincoln: University of Nebraska Press, 1999.

Cazneau, Jane. *Texas and Her Presidents; with a Glance at Her Climate and Agricultural Capabilities.* New York: E. Winchester, 1845.

———. *Eagle Pass; or, Life on the Border.* New York: G. P. Putnam, 1852.

———. *The Coast of Chance.* Indianapolis: Bobbs, Merrill, 1908.

Chandler, Katherine. *The Bird-Woman of the Lewis and Clark Expedition: A Supplementary Reader for the First and Second Grades.* New York: Ginn, 1905.

———. *In the Reign of Coyote: Folklore from the Pacific Coast.* New York: Ginn, 1905.

Chapman, Katharine Hopkins. *The Fusing Force: An Idaho Idyll.* Chicago: A. C. McClurg, 1911.

Chase, Mary Ellen. *The Girl from the Big Horn Country.* New York: A. L. Burt, 1916.

———. *Virginia of Elk Creek Valley.* New York: A. L. Burt, 1917.

Child, Lydia Maria. "The Kansas Emigrants." *Autumnal Leaves.* New York: C. S. Francis, 1857: 302–63.

Churchill, Caroline Nichols. *Over the Purple Hills; or, Sketches of Travel in California of Important Points Usually Visited by Tourists.* Chicago: Hazlitt and Reed, 1877.

———. *Active Footsteps.* Colorado Springs: Mrs. C. N. Churchill, 1909. Reissue New York: Arno Press, 1990.

Clark, Esther M. *The Call of Kansas and Other Verses.* Second edition. Lawrence: Windmill Press, 1911.

———. *The Call of Kansas and Later Verse.* Cedar Rapids: Torch Press, 1921.

Clark, Susie C. *The Round Trip from the Hub to the Golden Gate.* Boston: Lee and Shepard, 1890.

———. *Lorita: An Alaskan Maiden.* Boston: Lee and Shepard, 1892.

Cleary, Kate M. *Like a Gallant Lady.* Chicago: Way and Williams, 1897.

Cleland, Mabel Goodwin. *Early Days in the Fir Tree Country.* Seattle: Washington Printing Co., 1923.

Cobb, Bertha B. and Ernest Cobb. *Anita: A Story of the Rocky Mountains.* Boston: Arlo, 1920.

Coe, Alice Rollit. *Lyrics of Fir and Foam.* Seattle: Alice Harriman, 1908.

Collis, Septima M. *A Woman's Trip to Alaska: Being an Account of a Voyage through the Inland Seas of the Sitkan Archipelago in 1890.* New York: Cassell Publishing, 1890.

Colt, Miriam Davis. *Went to Kansas; Being a Thrilling Account of an Ill-fated Expedition* to *That Fairy Land, and Its Sad Results; Together with a Sketch of the Life of the Author, and How the World Goes with Her.* Watertown, New York: L. Ingals, 1862.

Comstock, Sarah. *The Soddy.* New York: Doubleday, Page, 1912.

———. *The Valley of Vision.* New York: Doubleday, Page, 1919.

———. *Speak to the Earth.* New York: Doubleday, Page, 1927.

Cone, Mary. *Two Years in California.* Chicago: S. C. Griggs, 1876.

Cooke, Belle W. *Tears and Victory.* Salem, Ore.: E. M. Waite, 1871.

Cooke, Grace MacGowan. *The Joy Bringer: A Tale of the Painted Desert.* New York: Doubleday, Page, 1913.

Cooke, Grace MacGowan and Alice MacGowan. *Aunt Huldah: Proprietor of the Wagon-Tire House and Genial Philosopher of the Cattle Country.* Indianapolis: Bobbs, Merrill, 1904.

Coolbrith, Ina. *Songs from the Golden Gate.* Boston: Houghton, Mifflin, 1895.

Coolidge, Mary Roberts. *Chinese Immigration.* New York: Henry Holt, 1909.

Coolidge, Susan. See Woolsey, Sarah.

Cordry, Almira Sheffield Peckham (Mrs. T. A.). *The Story of the Marking of the Santa Fe Trail by the Daughters of the American Revolution in Kansas and the State of Kansas.* Topeka: Crane and Co., 1915.

Cornaby, Hannah. *Autobiography and Poems.* Salt Lake City: J. C. Graham, 1881.

Crawford, Isabel. *Kiowa: The History of a Blanket Indian Mission.* New York: Fleming H. Revell, 1915. Reissued as *Kiowa: A Woman Missionary in Indian Territory,* with an introduction by Clyde Ellis. Lincoln: University of Nebraska Press, 1988.

Crocheron, Augusta Joyce. *Wild Flowers of Deseret: A Collection of Efforts in Verse.* Salt Lake City: Juvenile Instructor Office, 1881.

———. *Representative Women of Deseret: A Book of Biographical Sketches.* Salt Lake City: J. C. Graham, 1884.

Cross, Ruth. *The Golden Cocoon.* New York: A. L. Burt, 1924.

Cummins, Sarah J. *Autobiography and Reminiscences.* La Grande, Oregon: La Grande Printing Co., 1914. Reissue Fairfield, Wash.: Ye Galleon Press, 1999.

Cuney-Hare, Maud. *Norris Wright Cuney: A Tribune of the Black People.* New York: Crisis Publishing, 1913. Reissue with an introduction by Tera W. Hunter. New York: G. K. Hall, 1995.

Curtis, Emma Ghent. *The Fate of a Fool.* New York: John A. Berry, 1888.

———. *The Administratrix.* New York: John Alden, 1889.

Curtis, Natalie. *The Indians' Book: An Offering by the American Indians of Indian Lore, Musical and Narrative, to Form a Record of the Songs and Legends of Their Race.* New York: Harper, 1907.

Custer, Elizabeth Bacon. *Boots and Saddles; or, Life in Dakota with General Custer.* New York: Harper, 1885. Reissue with an introduction by Jane R. Stewart. Norman: University of Oklahoma Press, 1961.

———. *Tenting on the Plains; or, General Custer in Kansas and Texas.* New York: C. L. Webster, 1887. Reissue with a foreword by Shirley A. Leckie and an introduction by Jane R. Stewart. Norman: University of Oklahoma Press, 1994.

———. *Following the Guidon.* New York: Harper, 1890. Reissue with an introduction by Shirley A. Leckie. Lincoln: University of Nebraska Press, 1994.

Daffan, Katie. *Texas Hero Stories: an Historical Reader for the Grades.* Boston: B. H. Sanborn, 1908. Republished as *Texas Heroes: a Reader for Schools.* Boston: B. H. Sanborn, 1912.

Daggett, Mary Stewart. *Mariposilla.* Chicago: Rand, McNally, 1895.

———. *The Higher Court.* Boston: Gorham Press, 1911.

———. *The Yellow Angel.* Chicago: Browne and Howell, 1914.

Dall, Caroline Healey. *My First Holiday; or, Letters Home from Colorado, Utah, and California.* Boston: Roberts Brothers, 1881.

Darling, Esther Birdsall. *Up in Alaska.* Sacramento: Jo Anderson Press, 1912.

———. *Baldy of Nome.* Philadelphia: Penn Publishing, 1916.

Davis, M. E. M. (Mary Evelyn Moore). *Under the Man-Fig.* Boston: Houghton, Mifflin, 1895. Reissue with an afterword by Sylvia Ann Grider. Fort Worth: Texas Christian University Press, 2000.

———. *An Elephant's Track, and Other Stories.* New York: Harper and Brothers, 1897.

———. *Under Six Flags: The Story of Texas.* Boston: Ginn, 1897. Also published as *Texas under Six Flags.*

———. *The Wire-Cutters.* Boston: Houghton, Mifflin, 1899.

Dawson, Emma Frances. *An Itinerant House, and Other Stories.* San Francisco: William Doxey, 1897.

Dean, Sara. *Travers: A Story of the San Francisco Earthquake.* New York: Frederick A. Stokes, 1908.

DeHuff, Elizabeth Willis. *Taytay's Tales, Collected and Retold.* New York: Harcourt, Brace, 1922.

———. *Taytay's Memories, Collected and Retold.* New York: Harcourt, Brace, 1924.

Dejeans, Elizabeth. *The Heart of Desire.* Philadelphia: J. B. Lippincott, 1910.

———. *The Life-Builders.* New York: Harper, 1915.

———. *The Tiger's Coat.* Indianapolis: Bobbs, Merrill, 1917.

Denny, Emily Inez. *Blazing the Way; or, True Stories, Songs and Sketches of Puget Sound and Other Pioneers.* Seattle: Rainier Printing Company, 1909.

De Zavala, Adina. *History and Legends of the Alamo and Other Missions in and around San Antonio.* San Antonio: Adina De Zavala, 1917. Edited with an introduction by Richard Flores. Houston: Arte Publico, 1996.

Dickenson, Luella. *Reminiscences of a Trip across the Plains in 1846 and Early Days in California.* San Francisco: Whittaker and Ray, 1904. Reissue Fairfield, Wash.: Ye Galleon Press, 1977.

Diggs, Annie L. *The Story of Jerry Simpson.* Wichita: Jane Simpson, 1908.

Dixon, Winifred Hawkridge. *Westward Hoboes: Ups and Downs of Frontier Motoring.* New York: Charles Scribner's Sons, 1921.

Dorrance, Ethel and James Dorrance. *Glory Rides the Range.* New York: A. L. Burt, 1920.

———. *The Rim O' The Range.* New York: Chelsea House, 1926.

Douglas, Amanda M. *A Little Girl in Old San Francisco.* New York: A. L. Burt, 1905.

Douthit, Mary Osborn. *The Souvenir of Western Women.* Portland, Ore.: Anderson and Duniway Company, 1905.

Driscoll, Clara. *The Girl of La Gloria.* New York: G. P. Putnam's Sons, 1905.

——. *In the Shadow of the Alamo, and Other Texas Tales.* New York: G. P. Putnam's Sons, 1906.

Du Bois, Constance Goddard. *A Soul in Bronze: A Novel of Southern California.* Chicago: Herbert S. Stone, 1900.

——. *The Condition of the Mission Indians of Southern California.* Philadelphia: Office of the Indian Rights Association, 1901.

——. *The Religion of the Luiseño Indians of Southern California.* Berkeley: University of California Press, 1908.

Duniway, Abigail Scott. *Captain Gray's Company; or, Crossing the Plains and Living in Oregon.* Portland, Ore.: S. T. McCormick, 1859.

——. *From the West to the West.* Chicago: A. C. McClurg, 1905.

——. *Path Breaking: An Autobiographical History of the Equal Suffrage Movement in Pacific Coast States.* Portland, Ore.: James, Kerns and Abbott, 1914. Reissue with an introduction by Eleanor Flexnor. New York: Schocken, 1971.

Dye, Eva Emery. *McLoughlin and Old Oregon.* Chicago: A. C. McClurg, 1900.

——. *Stories of Oregon.* San Francisco: Whitaker and Ray, 1900.

——. *The Conquest: The True Story of Lewis and Clark.* Chicago: A. C. McClurg, 1902.

——. *McDonald of Oregon: A Tale of Two Shores.* Chicago: A. C. McClurg, 1906.

Dyer, Ida Casey (Mrs. D. B.). *Fort Reno; or, Picturesque Cheyenne and Arrapahoe Army Life, before the Opening of Oklahoma.* New York: G. W. Dillingham, 1896. Reissue with an introduction by David Dary. Machanicsburg, Pa.: Stackpole, 2005.

Eaton, Rachel Caroline. *John Ross and the Cherokee Indians.* Menasha, Wis.: George Banta, 1914.

Ellerbe, Rose L. *Tales of California Yesterdays.* Los Angeles: Warren T. Potter, 1916.

——. *Ropes of Sand.* Hollywood: David Graham Fischer, 1925.

Elliot, Maud Howe. *The San Rosario Ranch.* Boston: Roberts Brothers, 1884.

English, Mary Katharine Jackson. *Prairie Sketches; or Fugitive Recollections of an Army Girl of 1899.* n.d., n.p. (read in microform: Western Americana: Frontier History of the Trans-Mississippi West, 1550–1900, reel 176, no. 1837. New Haven, Conn.: Research Publications, 1975).

Estabrook, Alma. *The Rule of Three: A Story of Pike's Peak.* Boston: Small, Maynard, 1909.

Farnham, Eliza W. *California, In-Doors and Out; or, How We Farm, Mine, and Live Generally in the Golden State.* New York: Dix, Edwards, 1856. Facsimile reissue with an introduction by Madeleine B. Stern. Niewkoop, Netherlands: B. DeGraaf, 1972.

——. *The Ideal Attained: Being the Story of Two Steadfast Souls and How They Won Their Happiness and Lost It Not.* New York: C. M. Plumb, 1865.

Ferris, (Mrs.) B. G. *The Mormons at Home; with Some Incidents of Travel from Missouri to California, 1852–3. In a Series of Letters.* New York: Dix and Edwards, 1856. Reprint New York: AMS Press, 1971.

Ferris, Mary C. *As a Man Lives.* Cincinnati: Editor Publishing, 1898.

Fletcher, Alice C. *Indian Education and Civilization.* Washington: Government Printing Office, 1888. Reprint Milwood, N.Y.: Kraus, 1973.

Fletcher, Alice and Francis La Flesche. *The Omaha Tribe.* Washington, D.C.: Government Printing Office, 1911.

Foote, Mary Hallock. *The Led-Horse Claim: A Romance of a Mining Camp.* Boston: Houghton, Mifflin, 1883.

———. *John Bodewin's Testimony.* Boston: Houghton, Mifflin, 1885.

———. *The Chosen Valley.* Boston: Houghton, Mifflin, 1892.

———. *In Exile, and Other Stories.* Boston: Houghton, Mifflin, 1894.

———. *Coeur d'Alene.* Boston: Houghton, Mifflin, 1895.

———. *The Cup of Trembling, and Other Stories.* Boston: Houghton, Mifflin, 1895.

———. *The Prodigal.* Boston: Houghton, Mifflin, 1900.

———. *The Desert and the Sown.* Boston: Houghton, Mifflin, 1902.

———. *A Touch of Sun and Other Stories.* Boston: Houghton, Mifflin, 1903.

———. *A Picked Company: A Novel.* Boston: Houghton, Mifflin, 1912.

———. *The Valley Road.* Boston: Houghton, Mifflin, 1915.

———. *Edith Bonham.* Boston: Houghton, Mifflin, 1917.

———. *The Ground-Swell.* Boston: Houghton, Mifflin. 1919.

Forbes, Mrs. A(rmitage) S. C. (Harrie Rebecca Piper Smith). *California Missions and Landmarks, and How to Get There.* Los Angeles, n.p. 1903.

Forbes, Harrie R. P. (Smith) Forbes (Mrs. A. S. C). *Mission Tales in the Days of the Dons.* Chicago: A. C. McClurg, 1909.

Forbes, Mrs. A(rmitage) S. C. (Harrie Rebecca Piper Smith). *California Missions and Landmarks: El Camino Real.* Los Angeles, n.p. 1915 (third edition, revised, enlarged, renamed).

———. *California Missions and Landmarks: El Camino Real.* Los Angeles, n.p. 1925 (eighth and last edition, revised and enlarged).

Forter, Emma E. *History of Marshall County, Kansas: Its People, Industries and Institutions.* Indianapolis: R. F. Bowen, 1917.

Foster, Caroline H. W. *Little Stories of Yesterday.* Los Angeles: Arroyo Press, 1906.

Fox, Ruth May. *May Blossoms.* Salt Lake City: Young Ladies' Mutual Improvement Association, 1923.

Fremont, Jessie Benton. *A Year of American Travel.* New York: Harper and Brothers, 1878.

———. *Far-West Sketches.* Boston: D. Lothrop. 1890.

Froiseth, Jennie Anderson. *The Women of Mormonism; or, The Story of Polygamy as Told by the Victims Themselves.* Detroit: C. G. G. Paine, 1882; San Francisco, Wm. Garretson, 1884.

Frost, (Mrs.) J(ennett) Blakeslee. *The Gem of the Mines; A Thrilling Narrative of California Life. Composed of Scenes and Incidents Which Passed under the Immediate Observation of the Author during Five Years Residence in That State in the Early Days.* Hartford: by the authoress, 1866.

Frost, Jennett Blakeslee. *California's Greatest Curse.* San Francisco: J. Winterburn, 1879.

Fuller, Anna. *A Literary Courtship under the Auspices of Pike's Peak.* New York: G. P. Putnam's Sons, 1893.

———. *Peak and Prairie: From a Colorado Sketch-Book.* New York: G. P. Putnam's Sons, 1894.

Fuller, Emeline L. *Left by the Indians.* Mt. Vernon, Iowa: Hawk-Eye Station, 1892. Reprint with additional material, Fairfield, Wash.: Ye Galleon Press, 1988.

Fulton, Frances I. Sims. *To and Through Nebraska, by a Pennsylvania Girl.* Lincoln, Neb.: Journal Company, 1884.

Gates, Eleanor. *The Biography of a Prairie Girl.* New York: Century, 1902.

———. *The Plow-Woman.* New York: McClure, Philips, 1906.

———. *Alec Lloyd, Cowpuncher.* New York: Curtis, 1907. (Also published as *Cupid, the Cow-Punch.* New York: McClure, Philips, 1907.)

———. *The Justice of Gideon.* New York: Macaulay, 1910.

Gates, Susa Young. *John Stevens' Courtship: A Story of the Echo Canyon War.* Salt Lake City: Deseret News, 1909.

———. *History of the Young Ladies' Mutual Improvement Association of the Church of Jesus Christ of Latter-Day Saints from November 1859 to June 1910.* Salt Lake City: Deseret News, 1911.

Gauss, Marianne. *Danae.* New York: Harper, 1925.

Gilman, Charlotte Perkins. *The Crux.* New York: Charlton, 1911. Reissue ed. Jennifer S. Tuttle, Newark: University of Delaware Press, 2002.

Gilman, Stella. *That Dakota Girl.* New York: United States Book Company, 1892.

———. *A Gumbo Lily, and Other Tales.* New York: Abbey Press, 1901.

Gladding, Effie Price. *Across the Continent by the Lincoln Highway.* New York: Brentano's, 1915.

Glascock, Mary W. *Dare.* San Francisco: California Publishing Co., 1882.

Gordon, S. Anna. *Camping in Colorado, with Suggestions to Gold-Seekers, Tourists and Invalids.* New York: Authors' Publishing Co., 1879.

Graham, Effie. *The Passin'-on Party.* Chicago: A. C. McClurg, 1912.

———. *Aunt Liza's "Praisin' Gate."* Chicago: A. C. McClurg, 1916.

Graham, Margaret Collier. *Stories of the Foot-hills.* Boston: Houghton, Mifflin, 1895.

———. *The Wizard's Daughter and Other Stories.* Boston: Houghton, Mifflin, 1905.

Grant, Blanche C. *One Hundred Years Ago in Old Taos.* Taos, n.p. 1925.

———. *Taos Indians.* Taos, n p. 1925.

———. *Taos Today.* Taos, n .p. 1925.

Green, Annie Maria. *Sixteen Years on the Great American Desert; or, The Trials and Triumphs of a Frontier Life.* Titusville, Pa.: T. W. Truesdell, 1887. Reissue Windsor, Colo: Coren, 1983.

Grissom, Irene Welch. *The Superintendent.* New York: Alice Harriman, 1910.

———. *A Daughter of the Northwest.* Boston: Cornhill, 1918.

———. *The Passing of the Desert.* Garden City: Country Life Press, 1923.

Haines, Helen. *History of New Mexico.* New York: New Mexico Historical Publishing, 1891.

Hall, Josie Briggs. *Hall's Moral and Mental Capsule for the Economic and Domestic Life of the Negro, as a Solution of the Race Problem.* Dallas: R. S. Jenkins, 1905.

Hall, Sharlot M. *Cactus and Pine: Songs of the Southwest.* Boston: Sherman, French, 1911.

Halsey, Mina Dean. *When East Comes West.* New York: L. L. Little and Ives, 1909.

Hamill, Katherine B. *A Flower of Monterey.* Boston: Page, 1921.

Harriman, Alice. *Pacific History Stories, Montana Edition.* San Francisco: Whitaker and Ray, 1903.

———. *Chaperoning Adrienne: A Tale of the Yellowstone National Park.* Seattle: Metropolitan Press, 1907.

———. *A Man of Two Countries.* New York: Alice Harriman, 1910.

———. *Wilt Thou Not Sing? A Book of Verses.* New York: Alice Harriman, 1912.

Hatcher, Mattie Austin. *The Opening of Texas to Foreign Settlement, 1801–1821.* Austin: University of Texas Press, 1927.

Hayden, Mary Jane. *Pioneer Days.* San Jose: Murgotten Press, 1915. Reissue Fairfield, Wash.: Ye Galleon Press, 1979.

Hebard, Grace Raymond. *The Government of Wyoming: The History, Constitution and Administration of Affairs.* San Francisco: Whittaker and Ray, 1904.

———. *The Pathbreakers from River to Ocean: The Story of the Great West from the Time of Coronado to the Present.* Chicago: Lakeside Press, 1911.

Hebard, Grace Raymond and E. A. Brininstool. *The Bozeman Trail: Historical Accounts of the Blazing of the Overland Routes into the Northwest, and the Fights with Red Cloud's Warriors.* Cleveland: Arthur H. Clark, 1922.

Helm, Mary S. Wightman. *Scraps of Early Texas History.* Austin: for the author, 1884. Facsimile reissue Austin: Eakin Press, 1987.

Henderson, Alice Corbin. *Red Earth.* Chicago: Ralph Fletcher Seymour, 1920. Reissue with an introduction by Lois Rudnick and illustrations from the New Mexico Museum of Fine Arts. Albuquerque: University of New Mexico Press, 2003.

Herndon, Sarah Raymond. *Days on the Road: Crossing the Plains in 1865.* New York: Burr, 1902. Reissue with an introduction by Mary Barmeyer O'Brien. Guilford, Connecticut: Globe Pequot Press, 2003.

Herr, Charlotte. *Their Mariposa Legend: A Romance of Santa Catalina.* Pasadena: Post, 1921.

———. *San Pasqual: A Tale of Old Pasadena.* Pasadena, n.p. 1924.

Higgins, Elizabeth. *Out of the West.* New York: Harper, 1902.

Higginson, Ella. *The Flower That Grew in the Sand, and Other Stories.* Seattle: Calvert, 1896.

———. *From the Land of the Snow-Pearls: Tales from Puget Sound.* New York: Macmillan, 1897. Reprint Freeport, New York: Books for Libraries Press, 1970.

———. *Mariella of Out-West.* New York: Macmillan, 1902.

———. *Alaska: The Great Country.* New York: Macmillan, 1908.

Hill, Alice Polk. *Tales of the Colorado Pioneers.* Denver: Pierson and Gardner, 1884.

———. *Colorado Pioneers in Picture and Story.* Denver: Brock-Haffner, 1915. Reprint Bowie, Md.: Heritage Classic, 2002.

Hill, Emma Shepard. *A Dangerous Crossing and What Happened on the Other Side.* Denver, n.p. 1914.

Hill, Grace Livingston. *The Girl from Montana.* Wheaton, Ill.: Tyndale House, 1908.

———. *A Voice in the Wilderness.* Wheaton, Ill.: Tyndale House, 1916.

Hill, Grace Livingston [Lutz]. *The Man of the Desert.* Wheaton, Ill.: Tyndale House, 1914.

Hillerman, Abbie B. *History of the Woman's Christian Temperance Union of Indian Territory, Oklahoma Territory, State of Oklahoma; 1888–1925.* Sapulpa, Okla.: Jennings Printing & Stationery Co., 1925.

Hitchcock, Mary E. *Two Women in the Klondike: The Story of a Journey to the Gold-Fields of Alaska.* New York: Putnam, 1899.

Holley, Frances Chamberlain. *Once Their Home; or, Our Legacy from the Dahkotahs. Historical, Biographical, and Incidental from Far-off Days, down to the Present.* Chicago: Donohue and Henneberry, 1891.

Holley, Mary Austin. *Notes on Texas. Observations, Historical, Geographical and Descriptive, in a Series of Letters, Written during a Visit to Austin's Colony, with a View to a Permanent Settlement in That Country, in the Autumn of 1831. With an Appendix, Containing Specific Answers to Certain Questions, Relative to Colonization in Texas, Issued Some Time Since by the London Geographical Society. Also, Some Notice of the Recent Political Events in that Quarter.* Baltimore: Armstrong and Plaskitt, 1833. Reissue with an introduction by Marilyn McAdams Sibley. Austin: Texas State Historical Association, 1985.

———. *Notes on Texas.* Lexington, Ky.: Y. J. Clarke, 1836.

Hooker, Forrestine C. *The Long Dim Trail.* New York: A. L. Burt, 1920.

———. *Star: The Story of an Indian Pony,* with a foreword by Lieut.-General Nelson A. Miles, U.S.A. Garden City: Doubleday and Page, 1922.

———. *When Geronimo Rode.* Garden City: Doubleday, Page, 1924.

———. *Cricket: A Little Girl of the Old West.* Garden City: Doubleday, Page, 1925.

———. *The Little House on the Desert.* Garden City: Doubleday, Page, 1925.

———. *Just George.* Garden City: Doubleday, Page, 1926.

Hooper, Lucile. *The Cahuilla Indians.* Berkeley: University of California Press, 1920.

Horne, Alice Merrill. *Devotees and Their Shrines: A Hand Book of Utah Art.* Salt Lake City: Deseret News, 1914.

———. *Columbus, Westward Ho! A Dramatic Production.* Salt Lake City, for the author, 1922.

Houghton, Eliza P. Donner. *The Expedition of the Donner Party and Its Tragic Fate.* Chicago: A. C. McClurg, 1911. Reissue with an introduction by Kristin Johnson. Reno: University of Nevada Press, 1988.

Hudson, Mary W. *Esther the Gentile.* Topeka: Geo. W. Crane, 1888.

Hughes, Ann E. *The Beginnings of the Spanish Settlement in the El Paso District.* Berkeley: University of California Publications in History I (1914): 295–392.

Humphrey, Mary A. *The Squatter Sovereign, or Kansas in the '50s. A Life Picture of the Early Settlement of the Debatable Ground. A Story, Founded upon Memorable, and Historical Events, Whose Characters Have Been Carefully Chosen to Represent the Various Types of Men and Women Who Met upon the Kansas Plains Intent on Settling the Vexed Question as to Whether the Territory Should Come into the Union as a Free, or Slave State.* Chicago: Corburn and Newman, 1883.

Hutton, May Arkwright. *The Coeur d'Alenes; or, A Tale of the Modern Inquisition in Idaho.* Wallace, Idaho: M. A. Hutton, 1900. Facsimile reprint bound together with James Montgomery, *Liberated Woman: A Life of May Arkwright Hutton.* Fairfield, Wash.: Ye Galleon Press, 1985: 135–400.

Isaman, Sara White. *Tourist Tales of California.* Chicago: Reilly and Britton, 1907.

———. *Sophisticating Uncle Hiram: A Book of Fun and Laughter.* Chicago: Reilly and Britton, 1912.

———. *Uncle Hiram in California: More Fun and Laughter with Uncle Hiram and Aunt Phoebe.* New York: H. K. Fly, 1917.

Jack, Ellen E. *The Fate of a Fairy; or, Twenty Seven Years in the Far West.* Chicago: W. B. Conkey, 1910.

Jackson, Helen Hunt. *Bits of Travel at Home.* Boston: Roberts Brothers, 1878.

———. *Nelly's Silver Mine: A Story of Colorado Life.* Boston: Roberts Brothers, 1878.

———. *A Century of Dishonor.* New York: Harper and Brothers, 1881. Reissue with appendixes 1885; 1885 edition facsimile reissue with an introduction by Valerie Sherer Mathes. Norman: University of Oklahoma Press, 1995.

———. *Ramona: A Story.* Boston: Roberts Brothers, 1884.

———. *Glimpses of Three Coasts.* Boston: Roberts Brothers, 1886.

Jackson, Mary E. *The Spy of Osawatomie; or, the Mysterious Companions of Old John Brown.* St. Louis: W. S. Bryan, 1881.

———. *The Life of Nellie C. Bailey: A Romance of the West.* Topeka: G. W. Crane, 1886.

———. *Topeka Pen and Camera Sketches.* Topeka: G. W. Crane, 1890.

Johnston, Annie Fellows. *In the Desert of Waiting.* Boston: L. C. Page, 1904.

———. *The Little Colonel in Arizona.* Boston: L. C. Page, 1904.

———. *Mary Ware, the Little Colonel's Chum.* Boston: L. C. Page, 1908.

———. *Mary Ware in Texas.* Boston: L. C. Page, 1910.

———. *Mary Ware's Promised Land.* Boston: L. C. Page, 1912.

Judson, Katharine Berry. *Montana: The Land of Shining Mountains.* Chicago: A .C. McClurg, 1909.

———. *Myths and Legends of the Pacific Northwest, Especially Washington and Oregon.* Chicago: A. C. McClurg, 1910. Reissue with an introduction by Jay Miller. Lincoln: University of Nebraska Press, 1997.

———. *Myths and Legends of Alaska.* Chicago: A. C. McClurg, 1911.

———. *Myths and Legends of California and the Old Southwest.* Chicago: A. C. McClurg, 1912. Reissue with an introduction by Peter Iverson. Lincoln: University of Nebraska Press, 1994.

———. *When the Forests Are Ablaze.* Chicago: A. C. McClurg, 1912.

———. *Myths and Legends of the Great Plains.* Chicago: A. C. McClurg, 1913.

———. *Early Days in Old Oregon.* Chicago: A. C. McClurg, 1916.

Judson, Phoebe Goodall. *A Pioneer's Search for an Ideal Home.* Bellingham: Union Printing, 1925. Reissue with a foreword by Susan Armitage. Lincoln: University of Nebraska Press, 1984.

Kane, Elizabeth Wood. *Twelve Mormon Homes Visited in Succession on a Journey through Utah to Arizona.* Philadelphia, n.p., 1874. Reissue with an introduction and notes by Everett L. Cooley. Salt Lake: University of Utah Library, 1974.

Kelly, Fanny. *Narrative of My Captivity among the Sioux Indians; with a Brief Account of General Sully's Indian Expedition in 1864, Bearing upon Events Occurring in My Captivity.* Hartford, Connecticut: Mutual Publishing Company, 1871. Revised edition. Chicago: R. R. Donnelley, 1891. Reissue with annotations and an introduction by Clark Spence and Mary Lee Spence. Chicago: R. R. Donnelley and Sons, 1990.

Kelly, Florence Finch. *With Hoops of Steel.* Indianapolis: Bowen-Merrill, 1900.

———. *The Delafield Affair.* Chicago: A. C. McClurg, 1909.

———. *Emerson's Wife, and Other Western Stories.* Chicago: A .C. McClurg, 1911.

King, Hannah Tapfield. *An Epic Poem. A Synopsis of the Rise of the Church of Jesus Christ of Latter-Day Saints, from the Birth of the Prophet Joseph Smith to the Arrival on the Spot Which the Prophet Brigham Young Pronounced to Be the Site of the Future Salt Lake City.* Salt Lake City: Juvenile Instructor Office, 1884.

Knapp, Adeline. *This Then Is Upland Pastures: Being Some Out-door Essays Dealing with the Beautiful Things That the Spring and Summer Bring.* East Aurora, New York: Roycroft, 1897.

———. *The Well in the Desert.* New York: Century, 1908.

Knapp, Frances and Rheta Louise Childe Dorr. *The Thlinkets of Southeastern Alaska.* Chicago: Stone and Kimball, 1896.

Knox, Jesse Juliet. *Little Almond Blossoms: A Book of Chinese Stories for Children.* Boston: Little, Brown, 1904.

———. *In the House of the Tiger.* Cincinnati: Jennings and Graham, 1911.

Lane, Lydia Spencer. *I Married a Soldier.* Philadelphia: J. B. Lippincott, 1893. Reissue with an introduction by Darlis A. Miller. Albuquerque: University of New Mexico Press, 1987.

Lane, Rose Wilder. *Diverging Roads.* New York: Century, 1919.

———. *He Was A Man.* New York: Harper, 1925.

Larimer, Sarah. *The Capture and Escape; or, Life among the Sioux.* Philadelphia: Claxton, Remsen and Haffelfinger, 1870.

Laut, A(gnes) C. *The Story of the Trapper.* New York: D. Appleton, 1902.

———. *The Freebooters of the Wilderness.* New York: Moffat, Yard, 1910.

———. *Through Our Unknown Southwest: The Wonderland of the United States—Little Known and Appreciated—The Home of the Cliff Dweller and the Hopi, the Forest Ranger and the Navajo—The Lure of the Painted Desert.* New York: McBride, Nast, 1913.

———. *The Fur Trade of America.* New York: Macmillan, 1921.

———. *Enchanted Trails of Glacier Park.* New York: Robert M. McBride, 1926.

———. *The Conquest of Our Western Empire.* New York: Robert M. McBride, 1927.

Leighton, Caroline. *Life at Puget Sound, with Sketches of Travel in Washington Territory, British Columbia, Oregon, and California 1865–1881.* Boston: Lee and Shepard, 1883.

Leslie, Miriam Follin (Mrs. Frank). *California: A Pleasure Trip from Gotham to the Golden Gate.* New York: Carleton, 1877.

Lippincott, Sara Jane (Clarke) (Grace Greenwood). *New Life in New Lands: Notes of Travel.* New York: J. B. Ford, 1873.

Lockhart, Caroline. *Me—Smith.* Philadelphia: J. B. Lippincott, 1911.

———. *The Lady Doc.* Philadelphia: J. B. Lippincott, 1912.

———. *The Full of the Moon*. Philadelphia: J. B. Lippincott, 1914.

———. *The Man from the Bitter Roots*. New York: A. L. Burt, 1915.

———. *The Fighting Shepherdess*. Boston: Small, Maynard, 1919.

———. *The Dude Wrangler*. Garden City: Doubleday, Page, 1921.

Long, Mae Van Norman. *The Canyon of the Stars*. Hollywood: David Graham Fisher, 1926.

Lopez de Cummings, Maria S. *Claudio and Anita: A Historical Romance of San Gabriel's Early Days*. Los Angeles: J. F. Rowny, 1921.

Lord, Elizabeth. *Reminiscences of Eastern Oregon*. Portland, Ore.: Irwin-Hodson, 1903.

Loughead, Flora Haines (publishing as Flora Haines Apponyi). *The Libraries of California; Containing Descriptions of the Principal Private and Public Libraries throughout the State*. San Francisco: A. L. Bancroft, 1878.

Loughead, Flora Haines. *The Man Who Was Guilty*. Boston: Houghton, Mifflin, 1886.

———. *The Abandoned Claim*. Boston: Houghton, Mifflin, 1893.

———. *The Black Curtain*. Boston: Houghton, Mifflin, 1898.

Louthan, Hattie Horner. *This Was a Man: A Romance*. Boston: C. M. Clark, 1906.

———. *A Rocky Mountain Feud*. Boston: C. M. Clark, 1910.

Lynn, Margaret. *Free Soil*. New York: Macmillan, 1920.

———. *The Land of Promise*. Boston: Little, Brown, 1927.

MacGowan, Alice. *The Last Word*. Boston: L. C. Page, 1902.

———. *A Girl of the Plains Country*. New York: Frederick A. Stokes, 1924.

Mackie, Pauline Bradford. *The Story of Kate: A California Story for Girls*. Boston: L. C. Page, 1902.

———. *The Voice in the Desert*. New York: McClure, Philips, 1903.

MacLane, Mary. *The Story of Mary MacLane, by Herself*. Chicago: Herbert H. Stone, 1902. Reissue with an introduction by Julia Weston. Helena: Riverbend, 2002. Included in *Tender Darkness: A Mary MacLane Anthology* edited with an introduction and notes by Elisabeth Pruitt. Belmont, Calif.: Abernathy & Brown, 1993.

Mallinson, Florence Lee. *My Travels and Adventures in Alaska*. Seattle: Seattle-Alaska Co., 1914.

Marshall, Carrie. *The Girl Ranchers of the San Coulee: A Story for Girls*. Philadelphia: Penn Publishing, 1897.

———. *Two Wyoming Girls and Their Homestead Claim*. Philadelphia: Penn Publishing, 1899.

Marsland, Cora. *The Angel of the Gila: A Tale of Arizona*. Boston: Richard G. Badger, 1911.

Mason, Grace Sartwell and Percy F. Megargel. *The Car and the Lady*. New York: Baker and Taylor. 1908.

Mason, Grace Sartwell and John Northern Hilliard. *The Golden Hope*. New York: Appleton, 1916.

Massey, Beatrice Larned. *It Might Have Been Worse: A Motor Trip from Coast to Coast*. San Francisco: Harr Wagner, 1920.

Mathews, Amanda. *The Hieroglyphics of Love*. Los Angeles: Artemesia Bindery, 1906.

Mathews, Mary McNair. *Ten Years in Nevada; or, Life on the Pacific Coast*. Buffalo: Baker,

Jones, 1880. Reissue with an introduction by Clark Spence and Mary Lee Spence. Lincoln: University of Nebraska Press, 1985.

Maule, Mary K. *The Little Knight of the X Bar B.* Boston: Lothrop, Lee and Shepard, 1910.

———. *A Prairie Schooner Princess.* Boston: Lothrop, Lee and Shepard, 1920.

Maverick, Mary A. *Memoirs,* ed. Rena Maverick Green. San Antonio: Alamo Printing Co., 1921.

May, Celeste. *Sounds of the Prairie.* Topeka: Geo. W. Crane, 1886.

May, Florence Land. *The Broken Wheel.* Boston: C. M. Clark, 1910.

———. *Lyrics from Lotus Land.* Boston: Poet Lore, 1911.

McBeth, Kate. *The Nez Percés since Lewis and Clark.* New York: Fleming H. Revell, 1908. Reissue with an introduction by Peter Iverson and Elizabeth James. Moscow: University of Idaho Press, 1993.

McCarter, Margaret Hill. *The Price of the Prairie: A Story of Kansas.* New York: A. L. Burt, 1910.

———. *The Peace of Solomon Valley.* Chicago: A. C. McClurg, 1911.

———. *A Wall of Men.* Chicago: A. C. McClurg, 1912.

———. *A Master's Degree.* Chicago: A. C. McClurg, 1913.

———. *Winning the Wilderness.* Chicago: A. C. McClurg, 1914.

———. *Vanguards of the Plains: A Romance of the Santa Fe Trail.* New York: Harper and Brothers, 1917.

———. *The Reclaimers.* New York: Harper, 1918.

———. *Widening Waters.* New York: Harper, 1924.

McClurg, Virginia Donaghé. *Collected Poems,* ed. Gilbert McClurg. Colorado Springs: Colorado College Publications, 1933. [all poems pre-1915]

McCrackin, Josephine Clifford. *Overland Tales.* Philadelphia: Claxon, Remsen and Haffelfinger, 1877.

———. *"Another Juanita" and Other Stories.* Buffalo: Charles Wells Moulton, 1893.

———. *"The Woman Who Lost Him," and Tales of the Army Frontier.* Pasadena: George Wharton James, 1913.

McElrath, Frances. *The Rustler: A Tale of Love and War in Wyoming.* New York: Funk and Wagnells, 1902. Reissue with an introduction by Victoria Lamont. Lincoln: University of Nebraska Press, 2002.

McLaughlin, Marie L. *Myths and Legends of the Sioux.* Bismarck: Bismarck Tribune, 1916. Reissue Lincoln: University of Nebraska Press, 1990.

Meredith, Grace E. *Girl Captives of the Cheyennes; A True Story of the Capture and Rescue of Four Pioneer Girls.* Los Angeles: Gem Publishing, 1927.

Merriam, Florence A. *My Summer in a Mormon Village.* Boston: Houghton, Mifflin, 1894.

———. *A-Birding on a Bronco.* Boston: Houghton, Mifflin, 1896.

Michaels, Janie Chase. *A Natural Sequence: A Story of Phoenix, Arizona.* Bangor, Maine: Charles B. Glass, 1895.

———. *Polly of the Midway-Sunset.* San Francisco: Harr Wagner, 1917.

Michelson, Miriam. *The Madigans.* New York: Century, 1904.

———. *A Yellow Journalist*. New York: D. Appleton, 1905.

———. *Anthony Overman*. New York: Doubleday, Page, 1906.

Mighels, Ella Sterling (publishing as Ella Sterling Cummins). *The Story of the Files: A Review of California Writers and Literature*. San Francisco: Cooperative Print, 1893. Reissue with an introduction by Oscar Lewis. San Leandro: Yosemite Collections, 1982.

———. *The Full Glory of Diantha*. Chicago: Forbes and Company, 1909.

———. *Literary California: Poetry Prose and Portraits*. San Francisco: Harr Wagner, 1918.

———. *Wawona: An Indian Story of the Northwest*. San Francisco: Harr Wagner, 1921.

Miller, Olive Thorne. *A Bird-Lover in the West*. Boston: Houghton, Mifflin, 1894.

Mitchell, Ruth Comfort. *Narratives in Verse*. New York: D. Appleton, 1923.

———. *Corduroy*. New York: D. Appleton, 1924.

———. *Call of the House*. New York: D. Appleton, 1927.

Monroe, Anne Shannon. *Eugene Norton: A Tale of the Sagebrush Land*. Chicago: Rand, McNally, 1900.

———. *Happy Valley; A Story of Oregon*. Chicago: A. C. McClurg, 1916. Reissue with an introduction by Karen Blair. Corvallis: Oregon State University Press, 1991.

———. *Behind the Ranges*. Garden City, New Jersey: Doubleday, Page, 1925.

Morgan, Sallie B. *Tahoe; or, Life in California*. Atlanta: Jas. P. Harrison, 1881.

Morse, Harriet C. *A Cowboy Cavalier*. Boston: C. M. Clark, 1908.

Mourning Dove. *Cogewea, the Half-Blood, Given through Sho-pow-tan with Notes and Biographical Sketch by Lucullus Virgil McWhorter*. Boston: Four Seas Company, 1927. Reissue with an introduction by Dexter Fisher. Lincoln: University of Nebraska Press, 1981.

Munger, Dell H. *The Wind before the Dawn*. Garden City: Doubleday, Page, 1912.

Murray, Lois. *Incidents of Frontier Life. In Two Parts. Containing Religious Incidents and Moral Comment, Relating to Various Occurrences, Evils of Intemperance, and Historical and Biographical Sketches*. Goshen, Ind.: Evangelical United Mennonite Publishing House, 1880.

Newberry, Fannie E. *Mellicent Raymond: The Impress of a Gentlewoman*. New York: A. L. Burt, 1891

Newton, Emma Mersereau. *The Veil of Solana*. New York: Frank F. Lovell, 1902.

Norris, Kathleen. *The Rich Mrs. Burgoyne*. Garden City: Doubleday, Page, 1912.

———. *Saturday's Child*. Garden City: Doubleday, Page, 1914.

———. *The Story of Julia Page*. Garden City: Doubleday, Page, 1915.

———. *Martie the Unconquered*. Garden City: Doubleday, Page, 1917.

———. *Sisters*. Garden City: Doubleday, Page, 1919.

———. *Certain People of Importance*. Garden City: Doubleday, Page, 1922.

———. *Rose of the World*. Garden City: Doubleday, Page, 1924.

———. *The Foolish Virgin*. New York: A. L. Burt, 1927.

North, Grace May. *Adele Doring on a Ranch*. Boston: Lothrop, Lee and Shepard, 1920.

———. *Virginia of V. M. Ranch*. New York: A. L. Burt, 1924.

———. *Virginia's Ranch Neighbors*. New York: A. L. Burt, 1924.

North, Mary M. *A Prairie Schooner: A Romance of the Plains of Kansas.* Washington, D.C.: Neale, 1902.

Nusbaum, Aileen. *Zuni Indian Tales.* New York: G. P. Putnam, 1926.

O'Connor, Mary Hamilton. *The "Vanishing Swede": A Tale of Adventure and Pluck, in the Pine Forests of Oregon.* New York: Robert Grier Cooke, 1905.

Olden, Sarah Emilia. *The People of Tipi Sapa (The Dakotas).* Milwaukee: Morehouse, 1918.

———. *Karoc Indian Stories.* San Francisco: Harr Wagner, 1923.

———. *Little Slants at Western Life: A Note Book of Travel and Reflection.* New York: Harold Vinal, 1927.

Older, Cora Miranda Baggersley (Mrs. Fremont Older). *The Socialist and the Prince.* New York: Funk and Wagnalls, 1903.

Older, Mrs. Fremont. *The Giants.* New York: D. Appleton, 1905.

Orgain, Kate Alma. *A Waif from Texas.* Austin: Ben C. Jones, 1901.

Overton, Gwendolen. *The Heritage of Unrest.* New York: Macmillan, 1901.

———. *The Captain's Daughter.* New York: Macmillan, 1903.

———. *The Golden Chain.* New York: Macmillan, 1903.

Owen, Narcissa. *Memoirs.* Washington D.C., n.p. 1907. Reissue with an introduction by Karen L. Kilcup. Gainesville: University of Florida Press, 2005.

Owens-Adair, Bethenia. *Some of Her Life Experiences.* Portland, Ore.: Mann and Breach, 1906.

Paddock, Cornelia (Mrs. A[lonzo]. G.). *In the Toils; or, Martyrs of the Latter Days.* Chicago: Shepard, Tobias, 1879.

———. *The Fate of Madame La Tour, A Tale of the Great Salt Lake.* New York: Fords, Howard and Hulbert, 1881.

Page, Elizabeth M. *In Camp and Tepee: An Indian Mission Story.* New York: Fleming H. Revell, 1915.

Parker, Frances. *Marjie of the Lower Ranch.* Boston: C. M. Clark, 1903.

———. *Hope Hathaway: A Story of Western Ranch Life.* Boston: C. M. Clark, 1904.

———. *Winding Waters: The Story of a Long Trail and Strong Hearts.* Boston: C. M. Clark, 1909.

Parsons, Elsie Clews. *Notes on Zuni.* American Anthropological Association, 1917.

———. *The Pueblo of Jemez.* New Haven: Yale University Press, 1925.

———. *Tewa Tales.* New York: American Folk-lore Society, 1926. Reissue with an introduction by Barbara A. Babcock. Tucson: University of Arizona Press, 1994.

———, ed. and contributor. *American Indian Life.* New York: B. W. Huebsch, 1922; "Waiyautitsa of Zuni, New Mexico": 157–73.

Peattie, Elia W[ilkinson]. *A Mountain Woman.* Chicago: Way and Williams, 1896.

Pennybacker, Anna J. Hardwicke. *A New History of Texas; for Schools, Also for General Reading and for Teachers Preparing Themselves for Examination.* Revised edition. Austin: Mrs. Percy B. Pennybacker, 1900. (Originally self-published in Tyler, Tex., 1888.)

Perkins, Edna Brush. *The White Heart of Mojave.* New York: Boni and Liveright, 1922. Reissue with an afterword by Peter Wild. Baltimore: Johns Hopkins University Press, 2001.

Porter, Eleanor H. *Six Star Ranch*. Boston: L. C. Page, 1913.

Porter, Lavinia Honeyman. *By Ox Team to California: A Narrative of Crossing the Plains in 1860*. Oakland: Oakland Enquirer Publishing Co., 1910. Reissue Chicago: R. R. Donnelley and Sons, 1989.

Porter, Rebecca N. *The Girl from Four Corners: A Romance of California Today*. New York: Henry Holt, 1920.

———. *The Rest Hollow Mystery*. New York: Century, 1922.

Post, Emily. *By Motor to the Golden Gate*. New York: D. Appleton, 1916.

Pratt, Alice Day. *A Homesteader's Portfolio*. New York: Macmillan, 1922. Reissue with an introduction by Molly Gloss. Corvallis, Ore.: State University Press, 1991.

Rankin, Melinda. *Texas in 1850*. Boston: Damrell and Moore, 1850.

———. *Twenty Years among the Mexicans: A Narrative of Missionary Labor*. Cincinnati: Chase and Hall, 1875.

Ray, Emma J. *Twice Sold, Twice Ransomed: Autobiography of Mr. and Mrs. L. P. Ray*. Chicago: Free Methodist Publishing House, 1926. Reissue with an introduction by C. E. McReynolds. Freeport, N.Y: Books for Libraries Press, 1971.

Raymond, Evelyn. *Monica, the Mesa Maiden*. New York: Thomas Y. Crowell, 1892.

———. *The Little Lady of the Horse*. Boston: Roberts Brothers, 1894.

———. *A Daughter of the West*. Boston: W. A. Wilde, 1899.

———. *A Yankee Girl in Old California*. Philadelphia: Penn Publishing, 1901.

———. *Jessica Trent: Her Life on a Ranch*. Racine: Whitman Publishing, 1902.

———. *Polly the Gringo*. Philadelphia: Penn Publishing, 1905.

———. *Carlota of the Rancho*. Philadelphia: Penn Publishing, 1909.

———. *Dorothy on a Ranch*. New York: Hurst, 1909.

Richards, Clarice E. *A Tenderfoot Bride: Tales from an Old Ranch*. New York: Fleming H. Revell, 1920. Reissue with an introduction by Maxine Benson. Lincoln: University of Nebraska Press, 1988.

Richards, Louisa L. Greene. *Branches That Run over the Wall: A Book of Mormon Poem, and Other Writings*. Salt Lake City: Magazine Printing Company, 1904.

Rinehart, Mary Roberts. *Through Glacier Park: Seeing America First with Howard Eaton*. Boston: Houghton, Mifflin, 1916.

———. *Tenting To-Night: A Chronicle of Sport and Adventure in Glacier Park and the Cascade Mountains*. Garden City: Doubleday, Doran, 1918.

———. *Lost Ecstasy*. New York: George H. Doran, 1927.

Robinson, Sara T. L. *Kansas; Its Interior and Exterior Life. Including a Full View of Its Settlement, Political History, Social Life, Climate, Soil, Productions, Scenery, etc.* Boston: Crosby, Nichols, 1856.

Roe, Frances M(arie). A(ntoinette). *Army Letters from an Officer's Wife*. New York: D. Appleton, 1909. Reissue with an introduction by Sandra Myres. Lincoln: University of Nebraska Press, 1981.

Roe, Vingie E. *The Heart of Night Wind: A Story of the Great North West*. New York: Dodd, Mead, 1913.

———. *Tharon of Lost Valley*. New York: Dodd, Mead, 1919.

———. *Val of Paradise.* New York: Dodd, Mead, 1921.

———. *Nameless River.* New York: A. L. Burt, 1923.

———. *The Splendid Road.* New York: Duffield, 1925.

Rogers, Aurelia Spencer. *Life Sketches of Orson Spencer and Others and the History of Primary Work.* Salt Lake City: George Cannon, 1898.

Rollins, Alice Wellington. *The Story of a Ranch.* New York: Cassell, 1885.

———. *The Three Tetons: A Story of the Yellowstone.* New York: Cassell, 1887.

Ropes, Hannah A. *Six Months in Kansas, by a Lady.* Boston: John P. Jewett, 1856.

———. *Cranston House: A Novel.* Boston: O. Clapp, 1859.

Ross, Mary Jane. *The Life and Times of Hon. William P. Ross.* Fort Smith, Ark.: William and Weldon, 1893.

Ruiz de Burton, Maria Amparo. *The Squatter and the Don.* San Francisco: S. Carson, 1885. Reissue with an introduction and notes by Rosaura Sanchez and Beatrice Pita. Houston: Arte Publico, 1997.

Russel, Florence Kimball. *Born to the Blue: A Story of the Army.* Boston: L. C. Page, 1906.

Ryan, Marah Ellis. *Told in the Hills.* Chicago: Rand, McNally, 1891.

———. *Squaw Elouise.* Chicago: Rand, McNally, 1892.

———. *That Girl Montana.* Chicago: Rand, McNally 1901.

———. *Miss Moccasins.* Chicago: Rand, McNally, 1904.

———. *For the Soul of Rafael.* Chicago: A. C. McClurg, 1906.

———. *Indian Love Letters.* Chicago: A. C. McClurg, 1907.

———. *The Flute of the Gods.* New York: Frederick A. Stokes, 1909.

———. *The Woman of the Twilight.* Chicago: A. C. McClurg, 1913.

———. *The House of the Dawn.* Chicago: A. C. McClurg, 1914.

———. *The Treasure Trail: A Romance of the Land of Gold and Sunshine.* Chicago: A. C. McClurg, 1918.

Sanborn, Kate. *A Truthful Woman in Southern California.* New York: D. Appleton, 1893.

Sanders, Helen Fitzgerald. *Trails through Western Woods.* New York: Alice Harriman, 1910.

———. *The White Quiver.* New York: Duffield, 1913.

———. *A History of Montana.* 3 Volumes. Chicago: Lewis Publishing, 1913.

———. *The Dream Maker.* Boston: Cornhill, 1918.

Sawtelle, Mary P. *The Heroine of '49: A Story of the Pacific Coast.* San Francisco: Mrs. M. P. Sawtelle, M.D., 1891.

Scarborough, Dorothy. *In the Land of Cotton.* New York: Macmillan, 1923.

———. *The Wind.* New York: Harper, 1925.

Scidmore, E[liza] Ruhamah. *Alaska: Its Southern Coast and the Sitkan Archipelago.* Boston: D. Lothrop, 1885.

Scidmore, Eliza Ruhama. *Guide-Book to Alaska and the Northwest Coast.* New York: D. Appleton, 1893.

Sedgwick, Mary Katrine [Mrs. William T.]. *Acoma, The Sky City: A Study in Pueblo-Indian History and Civilization.* Cambridge: Harvard University Press, 1926.

Seton-Thompson, Grace Gallatin. *A Woman Tenderfoot.* New York: Doubleday, Page, 1900.

———. *Nimrod's Wife.* New York: Doubleday, Page, 1907.

Sharp, Katharine. *Jocelyn West: A Tale of the Grand Cañon.* New York: Goodhue, 1912.

Shaw, Luella. *True History of Some of the Pioneers of Colorado.* Hotchkiss, Colo.: W. S. Coburn, John Patterson, and A. K. Shaw, 1909.

Shipman, Alice Jack (Dolan) (Mrs. O. L.). *Taming the Big Bend: A History of the Extreme Western Portion of Texas from Fort Clark to El Paso.* Austin: Von Boeckmann-Jones, 1926.

Skinner, Constance Lindsay. *Adventurers of Oregon: A Chronicle of the Fur Trade.* New Haven: Yale University Press, 1921.

Smith, Alice Prescott. *Off the Highway.* Boston: Houghton, Mifflin, 1904.

Smith, Launa M. *American Relations with Mexico.* Oklahoma City: Harlow Publishing, 1924.

Snow, Eliza R. *Poems, Religious, Historical, and Political.* Liverpool: P. D. Richards, 1856.

Southworth, E. D. E. N. *For Woman's Love.* New York: A. L. Burt, 1883.

———. *An Unrequited Love.* New York: A. L. Burt, 1883.

Spalding, Phebe Estelle. *The Tahquitch Maiden: A Tale of the San Jacintos.* San Francisco: Paul Elder, 1911.

Spencer, Dorcas James. *A History of the Woman's Christian Temperance Union of Northern and Central California.* Oakland: West Coast Printing Company, 1913.

Spencer, Josephine. *The Senator from Utah and Other Tales of the Wasatch.* Salt Lake City: George G. Cannon, 1895.

Stafford, (Mrs.) Mallie. *"The March of Empire" through Three Decades, Embracing Sketches of California History.* San Francisco: George Spaulding, 1884.

Stapleton, Patience. *Kady.* Chicago: Belford, Clarke, 1888.

———. *Babe Murphy.* Chicago: Belford, Clarke, 1890.

Stenhouse, Fanny (Mrs. T. B). *Tell It All; The Story of a Life's Experience in Mormonism; An Autobiography.* Hartford: A. D. Worthington, 1874.

Stephens, Ann Sophia. *Esther: A Story of the Oregon Trail.* New York: Beadle, 1862.

———. *The Outlaw's Wife; or, the Valley Ranche. A Tale of California Life.* New York: Beadle and Adams, 1874.

Stephens, Louise Gregg. *Letters from an Oregon Ranch, by "Katharine."* Chicago: A. C. McClurg, 1905.

Stevenson, Matilda Coxe. *The Zuni Indians: Their Mythology, Esoteric Fraternities, and Ceremonies.* Washington, D.C.: Government Printing Office, 1905.

Stewart, Elinore Pruitt. *Letters of a Woman Homesteader.* Boston: Houghton, Mifflin, 1914. Reissue with a foreword by Jessamyn West. Lincoln: University of Nebraska Press, 1961.

———. *Letters on an Elk Hunt.* Boston: Houghton, Mifflin, 1915. Reissue with a foreword by Elizabeth Fuller Ferris. Lincoln: University of Nebraska Press, 1979.

Stickney, Mary E. *Brown of Lost River: A Story of the West.* New York: D. Appleton, 1900.

———. *Ouray Jim, and Other Stories.* Longmont, Colo.: Ledger, 1904.

Stone, Elinore Cowan. *The Laughingest Lady.* New York: D. Appleton, 1927.

Storke, Yda Addis. *A Memorial and Biographical History of the Counties of Santa Barbara, San Luis Obispo and Ventura, California; Containing a History of This Important Section of the Pacific Coast from the Earliest Period of Its Occupancy to the Present Time, Together with Glimpses of Its Prospective Future; with Profuse Illustrations of Its Beautiful Scenery, Full-Page Steel Portraits of Its Most Eminent Men, and Biographical Mention of Many of Its Pioneers and Also of Prominent Citizens of To-day.* Chicago: Lewis Publishing, 1891.

Stow, Marietta L. Bell (Mrs. J. W.). *Probate Confiscation: Unjust Laws Which Govern Women.* San Francisco: Bacon, 1876.

Strahorn, Carrie Adell. *Fifteen Thousand Miles by Stage; A Woman's Unique Experience during Thirty Years of Path Finding and Pioneering from the Missouri to the Pacific and from Alaska to Mexico.* Two volumes. New York: G. P. Putnam's Sons, 1911. Reissue with an introduction by Judith Austin. Lincoln: University of Nebraska Press, 1988.

Stratton, Lilyan. *Reno.* Newark: Colyer Printing, 1921.

Strobridge, Idah Meacham. *In Miner's Mirage-Land.* Los Angeles: Artemisia Bindery, 1904.

———. *The Loom of the Desert.* Los Angeles: Artemisia Bindery, 1907.

———. *The Land of Purple Shadows.* Los Angeles: Artemisia Bindery, 1909.

Sui Sin Far (Edith Maude Eaton). *Mrs. Spring Fragrance.* Chicago: A. C. McClurg, 1912. Reissue with an introduction by E. Catherine Falvey. Albany: NCUP, 1994.

Sullivan, May Kellogg. *A Woman Who Went to Alaska.* Boston: James H. Earle, 1902.

———. *The Trail of a Sourdough: Life in Alaska.* Boston: Richard H. Badger, 1910.

Summerhayes, Martha. *Vanished Arizona: Recollections of the Army Life of a New England Woman.* Second edition. Salem, Mass.: Salem Press, 1911. Reissue with an introduction by Dan L. Thrapp. Lincoln: University of Nebraska Press, 1979.

Switzer, A. Jennie (Bartlett). *Elder Northfield's Home; or Sacrificed on the Mormon Altar: A Story of the Blighting Curse of Polygamy.* New York: J. Howard Brown, 1882.

Taber, Louise E. *The Flame.* New York: Alice Harriman, 1911.

Tallent, Annie D. *The Black Hills, or Last Hunting Grounds of the Dakotas.* St. Louis: Nixon-Jones, 1899. Reissued with an introduction by Virginia Driving Hawk Sneve. Sioux Falls, S. Dak.: Brevet Press, 1974.

Thompson, Lucy. *To the American Indian.* Eureka: Cummins Print Shop, 1916. Reissue edited by Peter E. Palmquist with an introduction by Julian Lang. Berkeley: Heyday Books, 1991.

Thorpe, Rose Hartwick. *The White Lady of La Jolla.* San Diego: Grandier, 1904.

Tilghman, Zoe. *The Dugout.* Oklahoma City: Harlow Publishing, 1925.

———. *Outlaw Days: A True History of Early-Day Oklahoma Characters.* Oklahoma City: Harlow Publishing, 1926.

Tingley, Katherine. *Lomaland.* Point Loma: Aryan Theosophical Press, 1908.

Tompkins, Juliet Wilbor. *Dr. Ellen.* New York: Baker and Taylor, 1908.

Turnbull, Margaret. *The Close-Up.* New York: Harper and Brothers, 1918.

Vaile, Charlotte M. *The M. M. C.: A Story of the Great Rockies.* Boston: W. A. Wilde, 1898.

Van Denburgh, Mary T. *Ye On's Ten Hundred Sorrows and Other Stories*. San Francisco: Murdock, 1907.

Victor, Frances Fuller. *Alicia Newcome; or, The Land Claim, A Tale of the Upper Missouri*. New York: Beadle, 1862.

———. *The River of the West. Life and Adventure in the Rocky Mountains and Oregon; Embracing Events in the Life-time of a Mountain-man and Pioneer; with the Early History of the North-Western Slope, Including an Account of the Fur Traders, and Indian Tribes, the Overland Immigration, the Oregon Missions, and the Tragic Fate of Rev. Dr. Whitman and Family. Also, a Description of the Country, Its Condition, Prospects and Resources; Its Soil, Climate, and Scenery; Its Mountains, Rivers, Valleys, Deserts, and Plains; Its Inland Waters, and Natural Wonders*. Hartford, Conn.: R. W. Bliss, 1870.

———. *All Over Oregon and Washington; Observations on the Country, Its Scenery, Soil, Climate, Resources, and Improvements, with an Outline of Its Early History. Also Hints to Immigrants and Travelers Concerning Routes, the Cost of Travel, the Price of Land, etc*. San Francisco: J. H. Carmony, 1872.

———. *The New Penelope and Other Stories and Poems*. San Francisco: A. L. Bancroft, 1877.

———. *Atlantis Arisen; or, Talks of a Tourist about Oregon and Washington*. Philadelphia: J. B. Lippincott, 1891.

———. *Early Indian Wars of Oregon; Compiled from the Oregon Archives and Other Original Sources, with Muster Rolls*. Salem, Ore.: Frank C. Baker, State Printer, 1894.

Victor, Metta Victoria. *Mormon Wives: A Narrative of Facts Stranger than Fiction*. New York: Derby and Jackson, 1856. Also published as *Lives of Female Mormons; A Narrative of Facts Stranger than Fiction*. Philadelphia: G. G. Evans, 1860.

———. *The Gold Hunters*. New York: Beadle, 1863. (Published under varying titles.)

———. *The Two Hunters; or, the Cañon Camp, A Romance of the Santa Fe Trail*. New York: Beadle, 1865.

Vielé, Teresa Griffin. *Following the Drum: A Glimpse of Frontier Life*. New York: Rudd and Carleton, 1858. Reissue with a foreword by Sandra J. Myres. Lincoln: University of Nebraska Press, 1984.

Wagner, Madge Morris. *The Lure of the Desert Land, and Other Poems*. San Francisco: Harr Wagner, 1917.

Wait, Frona Eunice (Mrs. Frederick Colburn). *Wines and Vines of California; or, A Treatise on the Ethics of Wine Drinking*. San Francisco: Bancroft, 1889.

———. *Yermah the Dorado; The Story of a Lost Race*. San Francisco: William Doxey, 1897.

———. *The Stories of El Dorado*. San Francisco, n.p. 1904.

———. *The Kingship of Mt. Lassen*. San Francisco: Nemo Publishing, 1922.

Waite, C(atharine) V. *The Mormon Prophet and His Harem; or, An Authentic History of Brigham Young, His Numerous Wives and Children*. Cambridge: Riverside Press, 1866.

Waite, Mrs. C. V. *Adventures in the Far West; and Life among the Mormons*. Chicago: C. V. Waite and Company, 1882.

Wallace, Susan E. *The Land of the Pueblos*. New York: John B. Alden, 1888.

Walworth, Jeannette H. *The Bar-Sinister: A Mormon Study.* New York: Mershon, 1885.

Warren, Eliza Spalding. *Memoirs of the West: The Spaldings.* Portland, Ore.: Marsh Printing Company, 1916.

Wells, Emmeline B. *Charities and Philanthropies, Women's Work in Utah.* Salt Lake City: G. Q. Canon, 1893.

———. *Musing and Memories.* Salt Lake: Deseret News, 1896. Second expanded edition, 1915.

Wentworth, May (later Mary Wentworth Newman), ed. *Poetry of the Pacific.* San Francisco: Pacific Publishing Company, 1867.

———. *Fairy Tales from Gold Lands.* San Francisco: A. Roman, 1867.

———. *Fairy Tales from Gold Lands, second series.* San Francisco: A. Roman, 1868.

———. *The Golden Dawn and Other Stories.* San Francisco: A. Roman, 1870.

West, Leoti L. *The Wide Northwest: Historic Narrative of America's Wonder Land as Seen by a Pioneer Teacher.* Spokane: Shaw and Borden, 1927. Reissue with an introduction by Brenda K. Jackson. Lincoln: University of Nebraska Press, 2005.

Wetmore, Helen Cody. *The Last of the Great Scouts: The Life Story of Col. William F. Cody, "Buffalo Bill."* Chicago: Duluth Press, 1899.

Wheat, Lu. *The Third Daughter: A Story of Chinese Home Life.* Los Angeles: Oriental Publishing Co., 1906. Abridged as *Ah Moy, The Story of a Chinese Girl.* New York: Grafton Press, 1908.

———. *Helen: A Story of Things to Be.* New York: Grafton Press, 1908.

Whitney, Helen Mar. *Why We Practice Plural Marriage.* Salt Lake City: Juvenile Instructor Office, 1884.

Whitten, Martha E. *Author's Edition of Texas Garlands.* Austin: Triplett and Hutchings, 1886.

Wiggin, Kate Douglas. *A Summer in a Cañon: A California Story.* Boston: Houghton, Mifflin, 1889.

Wiggins, Bernice Love. *Tuneful Tales.* El Paso, n.p. 1925. Reissue edited by Maceo C. Dailey Jr. and Ruthe Winegarten. Lubbock: Texas Tech University, 2002.

Willard, Emma Hart. *Last Leaves of American History, Comprising Histories of the Mexican War and California.* New York: Putnam, 1849.

Willard, Madeline Deaderick. *The King's Highway.* Los Angeles: Grafton, 1913.

Williams, Ellen. *Three Years and a Half in the Army; or, History of the Second Colorados.* New York: for the author by Fowler and Wells, 1885.

Wills, Mary H. *A Winter in California.* Norristown, Pa., n.p. 1889.

Willsie, Honoré. *Kut-Le of the Desert.* New York: A. L. Burt, 1912. Reissued as *The Heart of the Desert.* New York: A. L. Burt, 1913.

———. *Still Jim.* New York: Frederick A. Stokes, 1915.

———. *The Forbidden Trail.* New York: Frederick A. Stokes, 1919.

———. *The Enchanted Canyon.* New York: A. L. Burt, 1921.

———. *Judith of the Godless Valley.* New York: Frederick A. Stokes, 1922.

———. *The Exile of the Lariat.* New York: Frederick A. Stokes, 1923.

Willsie, Honoré (publishing as Honoré Morrow). *We Must March: A Novel of the Winning of Oregon.* New York: A. L. Burt, 1925.

Wilson, Augusta Evans. *Inez, a Tale of the Alamo.* New York: Harper, 1855.

Winnemucca, Sarah. *Life among the Piutes: Their Wrongs and Claims.* New York: G. P. Putnam's Sons, 1883. Reissue Reno: University of Nevada Press, 1994.

Wolf, Alice S. *A House of Cards.* Chicago: Stone and Kimball, 1896.

Wolf, Emma. *Other Things Being Equal.* Chicago: A. C. McClurg, 1892; revised 1916. Revised edition reissued with an introduction by Barbara Cantalupo. Detroit: Wayne State University Press, 2002.

———. *A Prodigal in Love.* New York: Harper and Brothers, 1894.

———. *The Joy of Life.* Chicago: A. C. McClurg, 1896.

———. *Heirs of Yesterday.* Chicago: A. C. McClurg, 1900.

———. *Fulfillment: A California Novel.* New York: Henry Holt, 1916.

Wood, Ruth Kedzie. *The Tourist's California.* New York: Dodd, Mead, 1914.

———. *The Tourist's Northwest.* New York: Dodd, Mead, 1917.

Woodman, Abby Johnson. *Picturesque Alaska: A Journal of a Tour among the Mountains, Seas and Islands of the Northwest, from San Francisco to Sitka.* Boston: Houghton, Mifflin, 1889.

Woolsey, Sarah Chauncey (penname Susan Coolidge). *Clover.* Boston: Roberts Brothers, 1888.

———. *In the High Valley.* Boston: Roberts Brothers, 1891.

Worth, Pauline Wilson. *Death Valley Slim and Other Stories.* Los Angeles: Segnogram Press, 1909.

Wright, Muriel H. *The Story of Oklahoma.* Oklahoma City: Webb Publishing, 1924; expanded edition 1929.

Young, Ann Eliza. *Wife No. 19, or The Story of a Life in Bondage, Being a Complete Exposé of Mormonism, and Revealing the Sorrows, Sacrifices, and Sufferings of Women in Polygamy.* Hartford, Connecticut: Dustin, Gilman and Co., 1875. Reprint with introductory notes by John B. Gough and Mary A. Livermore. New York: Arno Press, 1972.

Young, Margaret G. *Homestead Ranch.* New York: D. Appleton, 1922.

Zitkala-Sa. *Old Indian Legends.* Boston: Ginn and Co., 1901. Reprint Lincoln: University of Nebraska Press, 1985.

———. *American Indian Stories.* Washington, D.C.: Hayworth Publishing House, 1921.

Secondary Bibliography: Western Women Writers

Abrams, Jeanne E. *Jewish Women Pioneering the Frontier Trail: A History in the American West.* New York: New York University Press, 2006.

Alexander, Ruth Ann. "Fictionalizing South Dakota from a Feminist Point of View: The Western Novels of Virgil D. Boyles and Kate Boyles Bingham." *South Dakota History,* 23 (1993): 244–63.

———. "Women Writers" in Hoover, Herbert et. al. *A New South Dakota History* (Sioux Falls: Pine Hills Press, 2005): 367–83.

Ammons, Elizabeth. *Conflicting Stories: American Women Writers at the Turn into the Twentieth Century.* New York: Oxford University Press, 1991.

Atherton, Gertrude. *Adventures of a Novelist.* New York: Liveright, 1932.

Austin, Mary. *Earth Horizon*. Boston: Houghton, Mifflin, 1932.

Bailey, Lynn R., ed. *Tombstone from a Woman's Point of View: The Correspondence of Clara Spalding Brown, July 7, 1880 to November 14, 1882*. Tucson: Westernlore, 1998.

Baird, Newton D., and Robert Greenwood. *An Annotated Bibliography of California Fiction, 1664–1970*. Georgetown, Calif.: Talisman Literary Research, 1971.

Bay, J. Christian. *A Heroine of the Frontier: Miriam Davis Colt in Kansas, 1856; extracts from Mrs. Colt's Diaries*. Cedar Rapids, Iowa: Torch Press, 1941.

Baym, Nina. *American Women Writers and the Work of History, 1790–1860*. New Brunswick: Rutgers University Press, 1995.

Bennion, Sherilyn Cox. "Lulu Greene Richards: Utah's First Woman Editor." *BYU Studies* 21 (1981): 155–74.

———. *Equal to the Occasion: Women Editors of the Nineteenth-Century West*. Reno: University of Nevada Press, 1990.

Bentley, Nancy. "Marriage as Treason: Polygamy, Nation, and the Novel." Donald E. Pease and Robyn Wiegman, eds. *The Futures of American Studies* (Durham: Duke University Press, 2002): 341–370.

Bernardin, Susan. "The Lessons of a Sentimental Education: Zitkala-Sa's Autobiographical Narratives." *Western American Literature* 32 (1997): 212–37.

Biedler, Peter G. "Literary Criticism in *Cogewea*: Mourning Dove's Protagonist Reads *The Brand*." *American Indian Culture and Research Journal* 19 (1995): 45–65.

Blend, Benay. "A Victorian Gentlewoman in the Rocky Mountain West: Ambiguity in the Work of Mary Hallock Foote," *Reading under the Sign of Nature: New Essays in Ecocriticism*, ed. John Tallmadge and Henry Harrington (Salt Lake City: University of Utah Press, 2000): 85–100.

Browne, Sheri Bartlett. *Eva Emery Dye: Romance with the West*. Corvallis: Oregon State University Press, 2004.

Brumble, H. David III. *American Indian Autobiography*. Berkeley: University of California Press, 1988.

Burgess-Olson, Vicky, ed. *Sister Saints*. Provo: Brigham Young University Press, 1978. See: Maureen Ursenbach Beecher, "The Eliza Enigma: The Life and Legend of Eliza R. Snow" pp. 1–19; Rebecca Foster Cornwall, "Susa Young Gates: The Thirteenth Apostle" pp. 61–93; Miriam Brinton Murphy, "Sarah Elizabeth Carmichael: Poetic Genius of Pioneer Utah" pp. 413–31; Carol Cornwall Madsen, "Louisa Lula Greene Richards: 'Remember the Women of Zion,'" pp. 433–53; Judith Rasmussen Dushku and Patricia Rasmussen Eaton-Gadsby, "Augusta Joyce Crocheron: A Representative Woman" pp. 481–94.

Canfield, Gae Whitney. *Sarah Winnemucca of the Northern Paiutes*. Norman: University of Oklahoma Press, 1983.

Cantalupo, Barbara. "Emma Wolf," in Ann R Shapiro, ed., *Jewish American Women Writers: A Bio-Bibliographical and Critical Sourcebook*, Westport: Greenwood Press, 1994: 465–72.

Carr, Glynis, ed. *The Online Archive of Nineteenth-Century U.S. Women's Writings*. http://www.facstaff.bucknell.edu/gcarr/19cUSWW/

Carter, Catherine. "Poverty, Payment, Power: Kathleen Thompson Norris and Popular Romance." *Studies in American Fiction* 38 (2008): 197–221.

Clayton, John. *The Cowboy Girl: The Life of Caroline Lockhart.* Lincoln: University of Nebraska Press, 2007.

Cohn, Jan. *Improbable Fiction: The Life of Mary Roberts Rinehart.* Pittsburgh: University of Pittsburgh Press, 1980.

Compton, Todd. *In Sacred Loneliness: The Plural Wives of Joseph Smith.* Salt Lake City: Signature, 1997.

Cragg, Barbara, Dennis M. Walsh, and Mary Ellen Walsh. *The Idaho Stories and Far West Illustrations of Mary Hallock Foote.* Pocatello: Idaho State University Press, 1988.

Crawford, Isabel. *Joyful Journey, Highlights by the Way; An Autobiography.* Philadelphia: Judson Press, 1951.

Crouchett, Lorraine J. *Delilah Leontium Beasley: Oakland's Crusading Journalist.* El Cerrito: Downey Place Publishing House, 1990.

Davis, Reda. *California Women: A Guide to Their Politics, 1886–1911.* San Francisco: California Scene, 1967.

Dearborn, Mary V. *Pocahantas' Daughters: Gender and Ethnicity in American Culture.* New York: Oxford University Press, 1986.

Egli, Ida Rae, ed. *No Rooms of Their Own: Women Writers of Early California, 1849–1869.* Berkeley: Heyday, 1992.

Eldridge, Robert. "Introduction," *An Itinerant House and Other Ghost Stories by Emma Frances Dawson.* Portland, Maine: Thomas Loring, 2007: xvii–lx.

Engin, Orrin. *Writer of the Plains: A Biography of B. M. Bower.* Culver City, Calif.: Pontine Press, 1973.

Fidler, William Perry. *Augusta Evans Wilson, 1835–1909: A Biography.* University: University of Alabama Press, 1951.

Fink, Augusta. *I-Mary: A Biography of Mary Austin.* Tucson: University of Arizona Press, 1983.

Foote, Cheryl. "'My Husband Was a Madman and a Murderer': Josephine Clifford McCrackin, Army Wife, Writer, and Conservationist." *New Mexico Historical Review* 65 (1990): 199–224.

Furman, Necah Stewart. *Caroline Lockhart: Her Life and Legacy.* Seattle: University of Washington Press, 1994.

Gay, E. Jane. *With the Nez Perces: Alice Fletcher in the Field, 1889–92.* Edited and with an introduction by Frederick E. Hoxie and Joan T. Mark. Lincoln: University of Nebraska Press, 1981.

George, Susanne K. *Adventures of the Woman Homesteader: The Life and Letters of Elinore Pruitt Stewart.* Lincoln: University of Nebraska Press, 1992.

———. *Kate M. Cleary: A Literary Biography with Selected Works.* Lincoln: University of Nebraska Press, 1997.

George Bloomfield, Susanne, ed. *Impertinences: Selected Writings of Elia Peattie, a Journalist in the Gilded Age, with a biography.* Lincoln: University of Nebraska Press, 2005.

Georgi-Findlay, Brigitte. *The Frontiers of Women's Writing: Women's Narratives and the Rhetoric of Westward Expansion.* Tucson: University of Arizona Press, 1996.

Goodburn, Amy, "Girls' Literacy in the Progressive Era: Female and American Indian Identity at the Genoa Indian School," in Greer, Jane, ed., *Girls and Literacy in America: Historical Perspective to the Present Moment.* Santa Barbara: ABC CLIO, 2003, pp. 79–102.

Goodman, Susan and Carl Dawson, eds. *Mary Austin and the American West.* Berkeley: University of California Press, 2008.

Graulich, Melody and Elizabeth Klimasmith, eds. *Exploring Lost Borders: Critical Essays on Mary Austin.* Reno: University of Nevada Press, 1999.

Griffith, Jean C. "How the West Was Whitened: 'Racial' Difference on Cather's Prairie." *Western American Literature* 41 (2007): 393–418.

Gruber, Laura Katherine. "'The Naturalistic Impulse': Limitations of Gender and Landscape in Mary Hallock Foote's Idaho Stories." *Western American Literature* 38 (2004): 330–52.

Halverson, Cathryn. *Maverick Autobiographies: Women Writers and the American West, 1900–1936.* Madison: University of Wisconsin Press, 2004.

Herr, Pamela. *Jessie Benton Fremont: A Biography.* New York: Franklin Watts, 1987.

Hicks, Lucille Patrick. *Caroline Lockhart, Liberated Lady, 1870–1962.* Cody: Pioneer Printing and Stationary, 1984.

Hill, Mary A. *Charlotte Perkins Gilman: The Making of a Radical Feminist, 1860–1896.* Philadelphia: Temple University Press, 1980.

Holtz, William. *The Ghost in the Little House: A Life of Rose Wilder Lane.* Columbia: University of Missouri Press, 1993.

Hooker, Forrestine C. and Dave Wilson, ed. *Child of the Fighting Tenth: On the Frontier with the Buffalo Soldiers.* New York: Oxford University Press, 2003.

Howe, Susan Elizabeth and Sheree Maxwell Bench. *Discoveries: Two Centuries of Poems by Mormon Women.* Provo: Association for Mormon Letters, 2004.

Hudson, Linda S. *Mistress of Manifest Destiny: A Biography of Jane McManus Storm Cazneau, 1807–1878.* Austin: Texas State Historical Association, 2001.

Iverson, Harris. "Reminiscences of Lomaland: Madame Tingley and the Theosophical Institute in San Diego." *Journal of San Diego History* 20 (1974). https://www.sandiegohistory.org/journal/74summer/lomaland.htm.

Johnson, Lee Ann. *Mary Hallock Foote.* Boston: Twayne, 1980.

Karcher, Carolyn L. *First Woman in the Republic: A Biography of Lydia Maria Child.* Durham: Duke University Press, 1994.

Kelly, Florence Finch. *Flowing Stream: The Story of Fifty-six Years in American Newspaper Life.* New York: E. P. Dutton, 1939.

Kilcup, Karen L., ed. *Native American Women's Writing, 1800–1924: An Anthology.* Oxford: Blackwell, 2000.

Kofalk, Harriet. *No Woman Tenderfoot: Florence Merriam Bailey, Pioneer Naturalist.* College Station: Texas A&M University Press, 1989.

Lawrence, Deborah. *Writing the Trail: Five Women's Frontier Narratives.* Iowa City: University of Iowa Press, 2006.

Laylander, Don. *Listening to the Raven: The Southern California Ethnography of Constance Goddard DuBois.* Salinas: Coyote Press, 2004.

Leckie, Shirley A. *Elizabeth Bacon Custer and the Making of a Myth.* Norman: University of Oklahoma Press, 1993.

Lee, L. L. and Merrill Lewis, eds. *Women, Women Writers, and the West.* Troy: Whitston, 1979.

Lee, Rebecca Smith. *Mary Austin Holley: A Biography.* Austin: University of Texas Press, 1962.

Leider, Emily Wortis. *California's Daughter: Gertrude Atherton and Her Times.* Stanford: Stanford University Press, 1991.

Loughlin, Patricia. *Hidden Treasures of the American West: Muriel H. Wright, Angie Debo, and Alice Marriott.* Albuquerque: University of New Mexico Press, 2005.

Maguire, James H. *Mary Hallock Foote.* Boise: Boise State College Press, 1972.

———. "*Coeur d'Alene* and *Angle of Repose:* Justice and the Quality of Mercy." *Weber Studies* 8 (1991) [online, n.p.].

Mainiero, Lina, ed. *American Women Writers: A Critical Reference Guide from Colonial Times to the Present.* 4 Vols. New York: Frederick Unger, 1971.

Mark, Joan. *A Stranger in Her Native Land: Alice Fletcher and the American Indians.* Lincoln: University of Nebraska Press, 1988.

Marks, Paula Mitchell. *Turn Your Eyes Toward Texas: Pioneers Sam and Mary Maverick.* College Station: Texas A&M Press, 1989.

Martin, Abigail Ann. *Bess Streeter Aldrich.* Boise, Idaho: Boise State University Press, 1992.

Martin, Jim. *A Bit of a Blue: The Life and Work of Frances Fuller Victor.* Salem, Ore.: Deep Well Publishing, 1992.

Mathes, Valerie Sherer. *Helen Hunt Jackson and Her Indian Reform Legacy.* Austin: University of Texas Press, 1990.

———, ed. *Indian Reform Letters of Helen Hunt Jackson, 1879–85.* Norman: University of Oklahoma Press, 1998.

Maxwell, Margaret F. *A Passion for Freedom: The Life of Sharlot Hall.* Tucson: University of Arizona Press, 1982.

McClure, Charlotte. *Gertrude Atherton.* Boston: Twayne, 1979.

Michelson, Miriam. *The Wonderlode of Silver and Gold.* Boston: Stratford, 1934.

Mighels, Ella Sterling. *Life and Letters of a Forty-Niner's Daughter.* San Francisco: Harr Wagner, 1929.

Miller, Darlis A. *Mary Hallock Foote: Author-Illustrator of the American West.* Norman: University of Oklahoma Press, 2002.

Miller, Jay, ed. *Mourning Dove: A Salishan Autobiography.* Lincoln: University of Nebraska Press, 1990.

Miller, Susan Cummins, ed. *A Sweet, Separate Intimacy: Women Writers of the American Frontier, 1800–1922.* Salt Lake City: University of Utah Press, 2000.

Monroe, Anne Shannon. *The World I Saw.* Garden City: Doubleday, Doran, 1928.

Montgomery, James W. *Liberated Woman: A Life of May Arkwright Hutton.* Spokane: Gingko House, 1974. Reissue Fairfield, Wash.: Ye Galleon Press, 1985 (bound together with Hutton's *Coeur d'Alene*).

Morrill, Allen Conrad and Eleanor Dunlop Morrill. *Out of the Blanket: The Story of*

Sue and Kate McBeth, Missionaries to the Nez Perces. Moscow: University of Idaho Press, 1978.

Moul, Diane W. "'A Certain Something': Reclaiming Grace Sartwell Mason." Ph.D. Dissertation, University of Rhode Island, 1998.

Moynihan, Ruth B. *Rebel for Rights: Abigail Scott Duniway.* New Haven: Yale University Press, 1983.

Munce, Robert. *Grace Livingston Hill.* Wheaton: Tyndale House, 1986.

Myres, Sandra L. "Army Women's Narrative as Documents of Social History: Some Examples from the Western Frontier, 1840–1900." *New Mexico Historical Review* 65 (1990): 175–98.

Nacy, Michele J. *Members of the Regiment: Army Officers' Wives on the Western Frontier, 1865–1890.* Westport: Greenwood Press, 2000.

Okker, Patricia. *Our Sister Editors: Sara J. Hale and the Tradition of Nineteenth-Century American Women Editors.* Athens: University of Georgia Press, 1995.

Overton, Grant. *The Women Who Make Our Novels.* Revised edition. New York: Dodd, Mead, 1928.

Pagh, Nancy. "Imagining Native Women: Feminine Discourse and Four Women Travelling the Northwest Coast," in Cavanaugh, Catherine and Randi R. Warme, *Telling Tales: Essays on Western Women's History.* Vancouver: University of British Columbia Press, 2001: 82–99.

Parezo, Nancy J., ed. *Hidden Scholars: Women Anthropologists and the Native American Southwest.* Albuquerque: University of New Mexico Press, 1993.

Patterson-Black, Sheryll and Gene Patterson-Black. *Western Women in History and Literature.* Crawford, Neb.: Cottonwood, 1978.

Pearce, T. M. *Alice Corbin Henderson.* Austin: Stack-Vaughn, 1969.

Peterson, Carol Miles. *Bess Streeter Aldrich: The Dreams Are All Real.* Lincoln: University of Nebraska Press, 1995.

Phillips, Kate. *Helen Hunt Jackson: A Literary Life.* Berkeley: University of California Press, 2003.

Ramirez, Karen E. *Reading Helen Hunt Jackson's Ramona.* Boise: Boise State University Press, 2006.

Rhodehamel, Josephine DeWitt and Raymund Francis Wood. *Ina Coolbrith: Librarian and Laureate of California.* Provo: Brigham Young University Press, 1973.

Ruoff, A. LaVonne Brown. "Early Native American Women Authors: Jane Johnston Schoolcraft, Sarah Winnemucca, S. Alice Callahan, E. Pauline Johnson, and Zitkala-Sa." in Kilcup, Karen L., ed. *Nineteenth-Century American Women Writers: A Critical Reader.* Malden: Blackwells, 1998: 81–111.

Scott, Patricia Lyn. "Jennie Anderson Froiseth and the Blue Tea." *Utah Historical Quarterly* 71 (Winter 2003): 20–35.

Senier, Siobhan. *Voices of American Indian Assimilation and Resistance: Helen Hunt Jackson, Sarah Winnemucca, and Victoria Howard.* Norman: University of Oklahoma Press, 2001.

Showalter, Elaine. *A Jury of Her Peers: American Women Writers from Anne Bradstreet to Annie Proulx.* New York: Knopf, 2009.

Smith, Christine Hill. *Social Class in the Writings of Mary Hallock Foote*. Reno: University of Nevada Press, 2009.

Stenhouse, Fanny. *Exposé of Polygamy: A Lady's Life among the Mormons*, edited and annotated by Linda DeSimone. Logan: Utah State University Press, 1988.

Stern, Madeleine B. *Purple Passage: The Life of Mrs. Frank Leslie*. Norman: University of Oklahoma Press, 1953.

Stout, Janis P. *Willa Cather: The Writer and Her World*. Charlottesville: University of Virginia Press, 2000.

Strobridge, Idah Meacham. *Sagebrush Trilogy: Idah Meacham Strobridge and her Works*, with an introduction by Richard A. Dwyer and Richard E. Lingenfelter. Reno: University of Nevada Press, 1990.

Swift, John N. and Joseph R. Urgo, eds. *Willa Cather and the American Southwest*. Lincoln: University of Nebraska Press, 2002.

Switzer, Charles. "The MacGowan Sisters: Early-twentieth-century Popular Writers." *Journal of Popular Culture* 30 (2000): 85–103.

Tilghman, Zoe A. *Marshall of the Last Frontier: Life and Services of William Matthew (Bill) Tilghman, for 50 Years One of the Greatest Peace Officers of the West*. Glendale, California: Arthur H. Clark, 1949.

———. *Oklahoma Stories*. Oklahoma City: Harlow, 1955.

Turner, Martha Anne. *Clara Driscoll: An American Tradition*. Austin: Madrona Press, 1979.

Van Dyke, Annette. "An Introduction to *Wynema, a Child of the Forest*, by Sophia Alice Callahan." *Studies in American Indian Literatures* 4 (1992): 123–28.

Viehmann, Martha L. "A Rain Song for America: Mary Austin, American Indians, and American Literature and Culture." *Western American Literature* 39 (2004): 5–36.

Wallace, Irving. *The Twenty-Seventh Wife*. New York: Simon and Schuster, 1961.

Ward, Jean M. and Elaine A. Maveety, eds. *Pacific Northwest Women, 1815–1925: Lives, Memories, and Writings*. Corvallis: Oregon State University Press, 1995.

White-Parks, Annette. *Sui Sin Far/Edith Maude Eaton: A Literary Biography*. Urbana: University of Illinois Press, 1995.

Whitney, Colleen, ed. *Worth Their Salt: Notable but Often Unnoted Women of Utah*. Logan: Utah State University Press, 1996. See Harriet Horne Arrington, "Alice Merrill Horne (1868–1948): Art Promoter and Early Utah Legislator," pp. 171–88; Miriam B. Murphy, "Sarah Elizabeth Carmichael (1838–1901): Poetic Genius of Pioneer Utah," pp. 61–75.

Whitney, Helen Mar. *A Woman's View: Helen Marr Whitney's Reminiscences of Early Church History*. Edited with an introductory essay by Jeni Broberg Holzapfel and Richard Neitzel Holzapfel. Provo: Brigham Young University Religious Studies Center, 1997.

———. *A Widow's Tale: The 1884–1896 Diary of Helen Mar Kimball Whitney*. Introduction, Notes, and Register by Todd M. Compton. Logan: Utah State University Press, 2003.

Woodress, James. *Willa Cather: A Literary Life*. Lincoln: University of Nebraska Press, 1987.

Wright, Muriel H. "Necrology: Eaton, Rachel Caroline." *Chronicles of Oklahoma* 16 (1938): 509–11.

Yates, Norris. *Caroline Lockhart*. Boise: Boise State University Press, 1994.

———. *Gender and Genre: An Introduction to Women Writers of Formula Westerns, 1900–1950*. Albuquerque: University of New Mexico Press, 1995.

Zanjani, Sally. *Sarah Winnemucca*. Lincoln: University of Nebraska Press, 2001.

Secondary Bibliography: The West

Alexander, Thomas G. *Mormonism in Transition: A History of the Latter-day Saints, 1890–1930*. Urbana: University of Illinois Press, 1986.

Allmendinger, Blake. *The Cowboy: Representations of Labor in an American Work Culture*. New York: Oxford University Press, 1992.

———. *Ten Most Wanted: The New Western Literature*. New York and London: Routledge, 1998.

Armitage, Susan and Elizabeth Jameson, eds. *The Women's West*. Norman: University of Oklahoma Press, 1987.

Aron, Cindy S. *Working at Play: A History of Vacations in the United States*. New York: Oxford University Press, 1999.

Arrington, Leonard and Jon Haupt. "Intolerable Zion: The Image of Mormonism in Nineteenth Century American Literature." *Western Humanities Review* 22 (1968): 243–60.

Arrington, Leonard J. *Great Basin Kingdom: An Economic History of the Latter-Day Saints, 1830–1900*. Reissue Urbana: University of Illinois Press, 2005.

Arrington, Leonard J., Feramorz Y. Fox, and Dean L. May. *Building the City of God: Community and Cooperation among the Mormons*. Second edition. Urbana: University of Illinois Press, 1992.

Athearn, Robert. G. *High Country Empire: The High Plains and Rockies*. New York: McGraw-Hill, 1960.

———. *The Mythic West in Twentieth-Century America*. Lawrence: University Press of Kansas, 1986.

Atherton, Lewis. *The Cattle Kings*. Bloomington: Indiana University Press, 1961.

Backhouse, Frances. *Women of the Klondike*. Vancouver: Whitecap Books, 1995.

Bagley, Will. *Blood of the Prophets: Brigham Young and the Massacre at Mountain Meadows*. Norman: University of Oklahoma Press, 2002.

Bailey, Lynn R. *Henry Clay Hooker and the Sierra Bonita*. Tucson: Westernlore Press, 1988.

Bailey, Paul. *Sam Brannan and the Mormons*. Los Angeles: Westernlore Press, 1953.

Barnett, Louise. *Touched by Fire: The Life, Death, and Mythic Afterlife of George Armstrong Custer*. New York: Henry Holt, 1996.

Barney, Garold D. *Mormons, Indians and the Ghost Dance Religion of 1890*. Lanham, Md.: University Press of America, 1986.

Barr, Alwyn. *Black Texans: A History of African Americans in Texas, 1528–1995*. Norman: Oklahoma University Press, 1996.

Barth, Gunther. *Instant Cities: Urbanization and the Rise of San Francisco and Denver.* New York: Oxford University Press, 1975.

Basso, Matthew, Laura McCall, and Dee Garceau, eds. *Across the Great Divide: Cultures of Manhood in the American West.* New York: Routledge, 2001. See Susan Lee Johnson, "Bulls, Bears, and Dancing Boys: Race, Gender, and Leisure in the California Gold Rush," pp. 45–71; Gunther Peck, "Manly Gambles: The Politics of Risk on the Comstock Lode, 1860–1880," pp. 73–96; Dee Garceau, "Nomads, Bunkies, Cross-Dressers, and Family Men: Cowboy Identity and the Gendering of Ranch Work," pp. 149–68.

Bataille, Gretchen, ed. *Native American Women: A Biographical Dictionary.* New York: Garland, 1993.

Beck, Warren A. *New Mexico: A History of Four Centuries.* Norman: University of Oklahoma Press, 1962.

Berke, Arnold. *Mary Colter: Architect of the Southwest.* New York: Princeton Architectural Press, 2002.

Bigler, David L. *Forgotten Kingdom: The Mormon Theocracy in the American West, 1847–1896.* Logan: Utah State University Press, 2005.

Bingham, Edwin R. *Charles F. Lummis, Editor of the Southwest.* San Marino: Huntington Library, 1955.

Blackhawk, Ned. *Violence over the Land: Indians and Empires in the Early American West.* Cambridge: Harvard University Press, 2006.

Bold, Christine. *Selling the Wild West: Popular Western Fiction, 1860 to 1960.* Bloomington: Indiana University Press, 1987.

Bramen, Carrie Tirado. *The Uses of Variety: Modern Americanism and the Quest for National Distinctiveness.* Cambridge: Harvard University Press, 2000.

Brickhouse, Anna. *Transamerican Literary Relations and the Nineteenth-Century Public Sphere.* Cambridge: Cambridge University Press, 2004.

Briggs, Harold E. *Frontiers of the Northwest: A History of the Upper Missouri Valley.* New York: Peter Smith, 1950.

Brinkley, Douglas. *The Wilderness Warrior: Theodore Roosevelt and the Crusade for America.* New York: Harper Collins, 2009.

Brodie, Fawn M. *No Man Knows My History: The Life of Joseph Smith.* Second edition. New York: Alfred A. Knopf, 1975.

Brooks, James F. *Captives and Cousins: Slavery, Kinship, and Community in the Southwest Borderlands.* Chapel Hill: University of North Carolina Press, 2002.

Buell, Lawrence. *The Environmental Imagination: Thoreau, Nature Writing, and the Formation of American Culture.* Cambridge: Harvard University Press, 1995.

Butler, Anne M. *Daughters of Joy, Sisters of Misery: Prostitutes in the American West, 1865–90.* Urbana: University of Illinois Press, 1985.

Cantrell, Greg and Elizabeth Hayes Turner, eds. *Lone Star Pasts: Memory and History in Texas.* College Station: Texas A&M University Press, 2007. See Laura Lyons, "Early Historians and the Shaping of Texas Memory," pp. 15–38; Greg Cantrell, "The Bones of Stephen F. Austin: History and Memory in Progressive-Era Texas," pp. 39–74; Walter L. Buenges, "Memory and the 1920s Ku Klux Klan in Texas," pp. 119–42; Andres Tijerina, "Constructing Tejano Memory," pp. 176–202; Randolph B. Campbell,

"History and Collective Memory in Texas: The Entangled Stories of the Lone Star State," pp. 270–82.

Cawelti, John G. *The Six-Gun Mystique*. Bowling Green: Bowling Green State University Popular Press, 1971.

———. *The Six Gun Mystique Sequel*. Bowling Green: Bowling Green State University Popular Press, 1999.

Chevigny, Hector. *Russian America: The Great Alaskan Venture, 1741–1867*. New York: Viking, 1965.

Coffman, Edward M. *The Old Army: A Portrait of the American Army in Peacetime, 1784–1898*. New York: Oxford University Press, 1986.

Conzen, Michael P., ed. *The Making of the American Landscape*. Boston: Unwin Hyman, 1990.

Cook, Sherburne F. *The Conflict between the California Indian and White Civilization*. Berkeley: University of California Press, 1986.

Cox, J. Randolph. *The Dime Novel Companion: A Source Book*. Westport: Greenwood Press, 2000.

Crisp, James E. *Sleuthing the Alamo: Davy Crockett's Last Stand and Other Mysteries of the Texas Revolution*. New York: Oxford University Press, 2005.

Cronon, William. *Nature's Metropolis: Chicago and the Great West*. New York: W. W. Norton, 1991.

Cronon, William, George Miles, and Jay Gitlin, eds. *Under an Open Sky: Rethinking America's Western Past*. New York: W. W. Norton, 1992.

Davis, Reda, *California Women: A Guide to Their Politics 1885–1911*. San Francisco: California Scene, 1967.

Dearborn, Mary V. *Pocahontas's Daughters: Gender and Ethnicity in American Culture*. New York: Oxford University Press, 1986.

Delo, David Michael. *Peddlers and Post Traders: The Army Sutler on the Frontier*. Salt Lake City: University of Utah Press, 1992.

Deloria, Philip J. *Playing Indian*. New Haven: Yale University Press, 1998.

Deloria, Vine. *Custer Died for Your Sins*. New York: Macmillan, 1969.

Deloria, Vine, Jr. *Singing for a Spirit: A Portrait of the Dakota Sioux*. Santa Fe: Clear Light, 1999.

Delyser, Dydia. *Ramona Memories: Tourism and the Shaping of Southern California*. Minneapolis: University of Minnesota Press, 2005.

Deming, Michael. *Mechanic Accents: Dime Novels and Working-Class Culture in America*. Revised edition. London: Verso, 1998.

De Zavala, Lorenzo. *Journey to the United States of North America*. Houston: Arte Publico Press, 2005. (Originally published 1831 in French.) Edited in English and with an introduction by John Michael Rivera.

Dozier, Edward P. *The Pueblo Indians of North America*. New York: Holt, Rinehart and Winston, 1970.

Drury, Clifford Merrill. *Where Wagons Could Go: Narcissa Whitman and Eliza Spalding*. Lincoln: University of Nebraska Press, 1997.

Dunlay, Tom. *Kit Carson and the Indians*. Lincoln: University of Nebraska Press, 2000.

Dykstra, Robert R. *The Cattle Towns*. New York: Knopf, 1968.

Eckert, Allan W. *The World of Opals*. New York: John Wiley and Sons, 1997.

Egan, Timothy. *The Big Burn: Teddy Roosevelt and the Fire That Saved America*. Boston: Houghton, Mifflin, 2009.

Elliott, Russell R. *History of Nevada*. Second edition. Lincoln: University of Nebraska Press, 1987.

Erisman, Fred and Richard W. Etulain. *Fifty Western Writers: A Bio-Bibliographical Sourcebook*. Westport: Greenwood Press, 1982.

Fabian, Ann. *The Unvarnished Truth: Personal Narratives in Nineteenth-Century America*. Berkeley: University of California Press, 2000.

Faragher, John Mack. *Women and Men on the Overland Trail*. Second edition. New Haven: Yale University Press, 2001.

Fite, Gilbert C. *The Farmers' Frontier, 1865–1900*. New York: Holt, Rinehart and Winston, 1966.

Flores, Dan. *The Natural West: Environmental History in the Great Plains and Rocky Mountains*. Norman: University of Oklahoma Press, 2001.

Flores, Richard R. *Remembering the Alamo: Memory, Modernity, and the Master Symbol*. Austin: University of Texas Press, 2002.

Foote, Stephanie. *Regional Fictions: Culture and Identity in Nineteenth-Century American Literature*. Madison: University of Wisconsin Press, 2001.

Forsyth, George A. *The Story of the Soldier*. New York: D. Appleton, 1909.

Fowler, Arlen L. *The Black Infantry in the West, 1869–1891*. Westport: Greenwood Press, 1971.

Frazer, Robert W. *Forts of the West: Military Forts and Presidios and Posts Commonly Called Forts West of the Missouri River to 1898*. Norman: University of Oklahoma Press, 1965.

Gard, Wayne. *The Chisholm Trail*. Norman: University of Oklahoma Press, 1954.

Gardner, Eric. *Unexpected Places: Relocating Nineteenth-Century African American Literature*. Jackson: University Press of Mississippi, 2009.

Gates, Susa Young and Leah D. Widtsoe. *Women of the "Mormon" Church*. Independence, Mo.: Zion's Printing and Publishing Company, 1928.

——. *The Life of Brigham Young*. New York: Macmillan, 1930.

George Bloomfield, Susanne and Eric Melvin Reed, eds. *Adventures in the West: Stories for Young Readers*. Lincoln: University of Nebraska Press, 2007.

Germic, Stephen. *American Green: Class, Crisis, and the Deployment of Nature in Central Park, Yosemite, and Yellowstone*. Oxford: Lexington Books, 2001.

Gibson, Arrel Morgan. *Oklahoma: A History of Five Centuries*. Second edition. Norman: University of Oklahoma press, 1981.

Givens, Terryl L. *The Viper on the Hearth: Mormons, Myths, and the Construction of Heresy*. New York: Oxford University Press, 1997.

Goetzmann, William H. and William N. Goetzmann. *The West of the Imagination*. New York: W. W. Norton, 1986.

Goins, Charles Robert and Danney Goble. *Historical Atlas of Oklahoma*. Fourth edition. Norman: University of Oklahoma Press, 2006.

Goldman, Marion S. *Gold Diggers and Silver Miners: Prostitution and Social Life on the Comstock Lode.* Ann Arbor: University of Michigan Press, 1981.

Goodman, Audrey. *Translating Southwestern Landscapes: The Making of an Anglo Literary Region.* Tucson: University of Arizona Press, 2002.

Gordon, Sarah Barringer. *The Mormon Question: Polygamy and Constitutional Conflict in Nineteenth-Century America.* Chapel Hill: University of North Carolina Press, 2002.

Graham, Don B. "Texas Historical Literature." www.rootsweb.com/~txdonley/txhistory .html.

Grattan, Virginia L. *Mary Colter: Builder upon the Red Earth.* Grand Canyon, Ariz.: Grand Canyon Natural History Association, 1992.

Graulich, Melody and Stephen Tatum, eds. *Reading* The Virginian *in the New West.* Lincoln: University of Nebraska Press, 2003.

Graves, Richard S. *Oklahoma Outlaws: A Graphic History of the Early Days in Oklahoma; the Bandits Who Terrorized the First Settlers and the Marshals Who Fought them to Extinction; Covering a Period of Twenty-five Years.* Oklahoma City: State Printing and Publishing Co., 1915.

Green, Rayna. "The Pocahontas Perplex: The Image of the Indian Woman in American Culture." *Massachusetts Review* 16 (1975): 698–714.

Gregg, Josiah. *Commerce of the Prairies; or, The Journal of a Southwest Trader.* New York: G. Langley, 1844. Edited and annotated by Max L. Moorhead. Norman: University of Oklahoma Press, 1954.

Grusin, Richard. *Culture, Technology, and the Creation of America's National Parks.* Cambridge: Cambridge University Press, 2004.

Hall, Roger A. *Performing the American Frontier, 1870–1906.* Cambridge: Cambridge University Press, 2001.

Hall, Thomas D. *Social Change in the Southwest, 1350–1880.* Lawrence: University Press of Kansas, 1989.

Hammalainen, Pekka. *The Comanche Empire.* New Haven: Yale University Press, 2008.

Handley, William R. *Marriage, Violence, and the Nation in the American Literary West.* Cambridge: Cambridge University Press, 2002.

Henderson, George. *California and the Fictions of Capital.* New York: Oxford University Press, 1999.

Hittman, Michael. *Wovoka and the Ghost Dance.* Expanded edition. Lincoln: University of Nebraska Press, 1990.

Horgan, Paul. *Lamy of Santa Fe.* New York: Farrar, Straus and Giroux, 1975.

Horsman, Reginald. *Race and Manifest Destiny.* Cambridge: Harvard University Press, 1981.

Hough, Emerson. *The Story of the Cowboy.* New York: Appleton, 1897.

Howard, Kathleen L. and Diana Pardue. *Inventing the Southwest: The Fred Harvey Company and Native American Art.* Flagstaff, Ariz.: Northland Publishing, 1996.

Howard, Thomas Frederick. *Sierra Crossing: First Roads to California.* Berkeley: University of California Press, 1998.

Hoxie, Frederick E. *A Final Promise: The Campaign to Assimilate the Indians, 1880–1920.* Lincoln: University of Nebraska Press, 1984.

———. *Parading through History: The Making of the Crow Nation in America, 1805–1935.* Cambridge: Cambridge University Press, 1995.

Hoyer, Mark T. *Dancing Ghosts: Native American and Christian Syncretism in Mary Austin's Work.* Reno: University of Nevada Press, 1998.

Hutner, Gordon. *What America Read: Taste, Class, and the Novel, 1920–1960.* Chapel Hill: University of North Carolina Press, 2009.

Hutton, Paul Andrew. *Phil Sheridan and His Army.* Lincoln: University of Nebraska Press, 1985.

Hyde, Anne F. *An American Vision: Far Western Landscape and National Culture, 1820–1920.* New York: New York University Press, 1990.

Isenberg, Andrew C. *The Destruction of the Bison: An Environmental History, 1750–1920.* Cambridge: Cambridge University Press, 2000.

Iversen, Joan Smyth. *The Antipolygamy Controversy in U.S. Women's Movements, 1880–1925.* New York: Garland, 1997.

Iverson, Peter. *When Indians Became Cowboys: Native Peoples and Cattle Ranching in the American West.* Norman: University of Oklahoma Press, 1994.

———. *Diné: A History of the Navajos.* Albuquerque: University of New Mexico Press, 2002.

Jackson, Brenda K. *Domesticating the West: The Re-creation of the Nineteenth-Century American Middle Class.* Lincoln: University of Nebraska Press, 2005.

Jacobs, Margaret D. *Engendered Encounters: Feminism and Pueblo Cultures, 1879–1934.* Lincoln: University of Nebraska Press, 1999.

James, Edward T., Janet Wilson James, and Paul S. Boyer. *Notable American Women: A Biographical Dictionary.* 3 Vols. Cambridge: Harvard University Press, 1971.

James, Ronald M. and E. Elizabeth Raymond, eds. *Comstock Women: The Making of a Mining Community.* Reno: University of Nevada Press, 1998.

Jameson, Elizabeth and Susan Armitage, eds. *Writing the Range: Race, Class, and Culture in the Women's West.* Norman: University of Oklahoma Press, 1997.

Jeffrey, Julie Roy. *Frontier Women: The Trans-Mississippi West, 1840–1880.* New York: Hill and Wang, 1979.

———. *Converting the West: A Biography of Narcissa Whitman.* Norman: University of Oklahoma Press, 1991.

Jenkins, John H. *Basic Texas Books: An Annotated Bibliography of Selected Works for a Research Library.* Austin: Jenkins Publishing, 1983.

Jenson, Joan M. and Darlis A. Miller. *New Mexico Women: Intercultural Perspectives.* Albuquerque: University of New Mexico Press, 1986.

Johannsen, Robert W. *To the Halls of the Montezumas: The Mexican War in the American Imagination.* New York: Oxford University Press, 1985.

Johnson, David Alan. *Founding the Far West: California, Oregon, and Nevada, 1840–1890.* Berkeley: University of California Press, 1992.

Johnson, Deidre. *Edward Stratemeyer and the Stratemeyer Syndicate.* New York: Twayne, 1993.

Johnson, Michael L. *Hunger for the Wild: America's Obsession with the Untamed West.* Lawrence: University Press of Kansas, 2007.

Johnson, Susan Lee. *Roaring Camp: The Social World of the California Gold Rush*. New York: W. W. Norton, 2000.

Jones, Daryl. *The Dime Novel Western*. Bowling Green: Popular Press, 1978.

Jordan, Teresa. *Cowgirls: Women of the American West*. Garden City, New York: Anchor Press, 1982.

Joseph, Philip. *American Literary Regionalism in a Global Age*. Baton Rouge: Louisiana State University Press, 2007.

Kaplan, Amy. *The Anarchy of Empire in the Making of U.S. Culture*. Cambridge: Harvard University Press, 2002.

Kasson, Joy. *Buffalo Bill's Wild West: Celebrity, Memory, and Popular History*. New York: Hill and Wang, 2000.

Katanski, Amelia V. *Learning to Write "Indian": The Boarding-School Experience and American Indian Literature*. Norman: University of Oklahoma Press, 2005.

Katz, Friedrich. *The Secret War in Mexico: Europe, the United States, and the Mexican Revolution*. Chicago: University of Chicago Press, 1981.

Kaufman, Polly Welts. *Women Teachers on the Frontier*. New Haven: Yale University Press, 1984.

———. *National Parks and the Woman's Voice: A History*. Albuquerque: University of New Mexico Press, 1996.

King, Geoff. *Mapping Reality: An Exploration of Cultural Cartographies*. New York: St. Martin's, 1996.

Kirkley, Evelyn A. "'Starved and Treated like Convicts': Images of Women in Point Loma Philosophy." *Journal of San Diego History* 43 (1997). https://www.sandiegohistory.org/journal/97winter/theosophical.htm.

Knack, Martha C. *Boundaries Between: The Southern Paiutes, 1775–1995*. Lincoln: University of Nebraska Press, 2001.

Knight, Grant C. *The Strenuous Age in American Literature*. Chapel Hill: University of North Carolina Press, 1954.

Knight, Oliver. *Following the Indian Wars: The Story of the Newspaper Correspondents among the Indian Campaigners*. Norman: University of Oklahoma Press, 1960.

———. *Life and Manners in the Frontier Army*. Norman: University of Oklahoma Press, 1978.

Koopman, LeRoy. *Taking the Jesus Road: The Ministry of the Reformed Church in America among Native Americans*. Grand Rapids: William B. Eerdmans, 2005.

Krech, Shepard. *The Ecological Indian: Myth and History*. New York: W. W. Norton, 1999.

Kropp, Phoebe S. *California Vieja: Culture and Memory in a Modern American Place*. Berkeley: University of California Press, 2006.

Krupat, Arnold. *Ethnocriticism: Ethnography, History, Literature*. Berkeley: University of California Press, 1992.

———. *Red Matters: Native American Studies*. Philadelphia: University of Pennsylvania Press, 2002.

Lack, Paul D. *The Texas Revolutionary Experience: A Political and Social History, 1835–1836*. College Station: Texas A&M University Press, 1992.

LaFeber, Walter. *The New Empire: An Interpretation of American Expansion, 1860–1898.* Ithaca: Cornell University Press, 1963.

Lamar, Howard R. *Dakota Territory, 1861–1889: A Study of Frontier Politics.* Third edition. New Haven: Yale University Press, 1966.

———. *The Far Southwest, 1846–1912: A Territorial History.* Revised edition. Albuquerque: University of New Mexico Press, 2000.

Larson, Gustive O. *The "Americanization" of Utah for Statehood.* San Marino: Huntington Library, 1971.

Larson, John Lauritz. *Bonds of Enterprise: John Murray Forbes and Western Development in America's Railway Age.* Expanded ed. Iowa City: University of Iowa Press, 2001.

Lavender, David. *Bent's Fort.* Garden City: Doubleday, 1954.

Leckie, William H. *The Buffalo Soldiers: A Narrative of the Negro Cavalry in the West.* Norman: University of Oklahoma Press, 1967.

Leonard, John William, editor-in-chief. *Woman's Who's Who of America, 1914–1915.* New York: American Commonwealth Company, 1914.

Leonard, Stephen J. and Thomas J. Noel. *Denver: Mining Camp to Metropolis.* Niwot, Colo.: University Press of Colorado, 1990.

Levy, Joann. *They Saw the Elephant: Women in the California Gold Rush.* Hamden, Conn.: Archon, 1990.

Lewis, Nathaniel. *Unsettling the Literary West: Authenticity and Authorship.* Lincoln: University of Nebraska Press, 2003.

Littlefield, Daniel F., Jr. and James W. Parins. *A Bibliography of Native American Writers, 1772–1924.* Metuchen, New Jersey: Scarecrow, 1981.

Livingston, Dorothy Michelson. *The Master of Light: A Biography of Albert A. Michelson.* New York: Charles Scribner's Sons, 1973.

Lockwood, Frank C. *The Apache Indians.* New York: Macmillan, 1938. Reissue Lincoln: University of Nebraska Press, 1987.

Lutes, Jean Marie. *Front Page Girls: Women Journalists in American Culture and Fiction, 1880–1930.* Ithaca: Cornell University Press, 2006.

Lutz, Tom. *Cosmopolitan Vistas: American Regionalism and Literary Value.* Ithaca: Cornell University Press, 2004.

Lynn, Karen. "Sensational Virtue: Nineteenth-Century Mormon Fiction and American Popular Taste." *Dialogue: A Journal of Mormon Thought* 14 (1981): 101–11.

Major, Mabel and T. M. Pearce. *Southwest Heritage: A Literary History with Bibliographies.* Revised and enlarged. Albuquerque: University of New Mexico Press, 1948.

Malone, Michael P. *The Battle for Butte: Mining and Politics on the Northern Frontier, 1864–1906.* Seattle: University of Washington Press, 1981.

Malone, Michael P., Richard B. Roeder, and William A. Lang. *Montana: A History of Two Centuries.* Revised edition. Seattle: University of Washington Press, 1991.

Marable, Mary Hays and Elaine Boylan. *A Handbook of Oklahoma Writers.* Norman: University of Oklahoma Press, 1939.

Mardock, Robert Winston. *The Reformers and the American Indian.* Columbia: University of Missouri Press, 1971.

Mattes, Merrill J. *The Great Platte River Road.* Lincoln: University of Nebraska Press, 1987.

McCallum, Henry D. and Frances T. McCallum. *The Wire That Fenced the West.* Norman: University of Oklahoma Press, 1965.

McClelland, Linda Flint. *Building the National Parks.* Baltimore: Johns Hopkins University Press, 1998.

McFeely, Eliza. *Zuni and the American Imagination.* New York: Hill and Wang, 2001.

McLagan, Elizabeth. *A Peculiar Paradise: A History of Blacks in Oregon, 1788–1940.* Portland: Georgian Press, 1980.

McWilliams, Carey. *Southern California Country: An Island on the Land.* New York: Duell, Sloan and Pearce, 1946.

Meinig, D. W. *Imperial Texas: An Interpretive Essay in Cultural Geography.* Austin: University of Texas Press, 1969.

———. *Southwest: Three Peoples in Geographical Change, 1600–1970.* New York: Oxford University Press, 1971.

———. *The Shaping of America: A Geographical Perspective on 500 Years of History, Vol. 3 (Transcontinental America, 1850–1915).* New Haven: Yale University Press, 1998.

Meldahl, Keith Heyer. *Hard Road West: History and Geology along the Gold Rush Trail.* Chicago: University of Chicago Press, 2007.

Merchant, Carolyn. *American Environmental History: An Introduction.* New York: Columbia University Press, 2007.

Meserve, John Bartlett. "Chief William Potter Ross." *Chronicles of Oklahoma* 15 (1937): 21–29.

Meyer, Roy W. *History of the Santee Sioux: United States Indian Policy on Trial.* Lincoln: University of Nebraska Press, 1967.

Miller, Darlis A. *Soldiers and Settlers: Military Supply in the Southwest, 1861–1885.* Albuquerque: University of New Mexico Press, 1989.

Milton, John R. *The Literature of South Dakota.* Vermillion: Dakota Press, 1976.

———. *The Novel of the American West.* Lincoln: University of Nebraska Press, 1980.

Miner, H. Craig and William E. Unrau. *The End of Indian Kansas: A Study of Cultural Revolution, 1854–1871.* Lawrence: University of Kansas Press, 1978.

Mitchell, Lee Clark. *Witnesses to a Vanishing America: The Nineteenth-Century Response.* Princeton: Princeton University Press, 1981.

Mormon Literature Database, Brigham Young University. http://www.mormonlit.lib.byu.edu.

Morrill, Susanna. *White Roses on the Floor of Heaven: Mormon Women's Popular Theology, 1880–1920.* New York: Routledge, 2006.

Moses, L. G. *Wild West Shows and the Images of American Indians, 1883–1933.* Albuquerque: University of New Mexico Press, 1996.

Mott, Frank Luther. *Golden Multitudes: The Story of Best Sellers in the United States.* New York: Macmillan, 1947.

Mowry, George E. *The Era of Theodore Roosevelt.* New York: Harper and Brothers, 1958.

Moynihan, Ruth B., Susan Armitage, and Christiane Fischer Dichamp, eds. *So Much to Be Done: Women Settlers on the Mining and Ranching Frontiers.* Lincoln: University of Nebraska Press, 1990.

Muir, John. *Our National Parks.* Boston: Houghton Mifflin Company, 1901.

Murphy, Mary. *Mining Culture: Men, Women, and Leisure in Butte, 1914–41.* Urbana: University of Illinois Press, 1997.

Myres, Sandra L. *Westering Women and the Frontier Experience, 1800–1915.* Albuquerque: University of New Mexico Press, 1982.

Nelson, Barney. *The Wild and the Domestic: Animal Representation, Ecocriticism, and Western American Literature.* Reno: University of Nevada Press, 2000.

News Notes of California Libraries 9 (April 1914), "Fiction in the State Library Having a Local Coloring," pp. 227–42.

News Notes of California Libraries 13 (October 1918), "Supplementary List of Fiction in the State Library Having a California Coloring," pp. 874–77.

Nicholas, Liza J. *Becoming Western: Stories of Culture and Identity in the Cowboy State.* Lincoln: University of Nebraska Press, 2006.

Nichols, Jeffrey. *Prostitution, Polygamy, and Power: Salt Lake City, 1847–1918.* Urbana: University of Illinois Press, 2002.

Nissen, Axel. *Manly Love: Romantic Friendship in American Fiction.* Chicago: University of Chicago Press, 2009.

Nixon, Oliver W. *How Marcus Whitman Saved Oregon.* Chicago: Star Co., 1895.

Ohmann, Richard M. *Selling Culture: Magazine, Markets and Class at the Turn of the Century.* New York: Verso, 1996.

Older, Fremont and Cora Older. *George Hearst: California Pioneer.* Los Angeles: privately published, 1933. Reprint Los Angeles: Westernlore, 1966.

Olson, James C. and Ronald C. Naugle. *History of Nebraska.* Third edition. Lincoln: University of Nebraska Press, 1997.

Ortiz, Alfonso. *The Tewa World: Space, Time, Being, and Becoming in a Pueblo Society.* Chicago: University of Chicago Press, 1969.

Osgood, Ernest Staples. *The Day of the Cattleman.* Chicago: University of Chicago Press, 1929.

Pascoe, Peggy. *Relations of Rescue: The Search for Female Moral Authority in the American West, 1874–1939.* New York: Oxford University Press, 1990.

Paul, Rodman W. *The Far West and the Great Plains in Transition, 1859–1900.* New York: Harper and Row, 1988.

Paul, Rodman Wilson. *Mining Frontiers of the Far West, 1848–1880.* Revised and expanded by Elliott West. Albuquerque: University of New Mexico Press, 2001.

Perez, Vincent. *Remembering the Hacienda: History and Memory in the Mexican American Southwest.* College Station: Texas A&M University Press, 2006.

Perry, Carolyn and Mary Louise Weaks, eds. *History of Southern Women's Literature.* Baton Rouge: Louisiana State University Press, 2002.

Peterson, Richard H. *The Bonanza Kings: The Social Origins and Business Behavior of Western Mining Entrepreneurs, 1870–1900.* Lincoln: University of Nebraska Press, 1971.

Pilkington, William T. *Critical Essays on the Western American Novel*. Boston: G. K. Hall, 1980.

Pisani, Donald J. *From the Family Farm to Agribusiness: The Irrigation Crusade in California and the West, 1850–1931*. Berkeley: University of California Press, 1984.

——. *To Reclaim a Divided West: Water, Law, and Public Policy, 1848–1902*. Albuquerque: University of New Mexico Press, 1992.

Pletcher, David M. *The Diplomacy of Annexation: Texas, Oregon, and the Mexican War*. Columbia: University of Missouri Press, 1973.

Poling-Kempes, Lesley. *The Harvey Girls: Women Who Opened the West*. New York: Marlowe, 1991.

Pomeroy, Earl. *In Search of the Golden West: The Tourist in Western America*. Lincoln: University of Nebraska Press, 1957.

——. *The Pacific Slope: A History of California, Oregon, Washington, Idaho, Utah, and Nevada*. Seattle: University of Washington Press, 1965.

Powers, Alfred. *History of Oregon Literature*. Portland: Metropolitan Press, 1935.

Priest, Loring Benson. *Uncle Sam's Stepchildren: The Reformation of United States Indian Policy, 1865–1887*. New Brunswick: Rutgers University Press, 1942.

Reese, Linda Williams. *Women of Oklahoma, 1890–1920*. Norman: University of Oklahoma Press, 1997.

Reid, Stuart. *The Secret War for Texas*. College Station: Texas A&M University Press, 2007.

Reisner, Marc. *Cadillac Desert: The American West and Its Disappearing Water*. New York: Viking, 1986.

Richards, Leonard L. *The California Gold Rush and the Coming of the Civil War*. New York: Alfred A. Knopf, 2007.

Riley, Glenda. "The Specter of a Savage: Rumors and Alarmists on the Overland Trail." *Western Historical Quarterly* 15 (1984): 427–44.

——. *The Female Frontier: A Comparative View of Women on the Prairie and the Plains*. Lawrence: University Press of Kansas, 1988.

——. *Women and Nature: Saving the "Wild" West*. Lincoln: University of Nebraska Press, 1999.

——. *Confronting Race: Women and Indians on the Frontier, 1815–1915*. Albuquerque: University of New Mexico Press, 2004.

Robbins, William G. *Colony and Empire: The Capitalist Transformation of the American West*. Lawrence: University Press of Kansas, 1994.

Rochlin, Harriet and Fred Rochlin. *Pioneer Jews: A New Life in the Far West*. Boston: Houghton, Mifflin, 1984.

Rollins, Philip Ashton; *The Cowboy: His Characteristics, His Equipment, and His Part in the Development of the West*. New York: Scribners, 1924. Reissue New York: Skyhorse, 2007.

Rosenbaum, Robert J. *Mexicano Resistance in the Southwest*. Second edition. Dallas: Southern Methodist University Press, 1998.

Rydell, Robert W. *All the World's a Fair: Visions of Empire at American International Expositions, 1876–1916*. Chicago: University of Chicago Press, 1984.

Sabin, Edwin L. *Kit Carson Days (1809–1868)*. Revised edition. Lincoln: University of Nebraska Press, 1935.

Saxton, Alexander. *The Rise and Fall of the White Republic: Class Politics and Mass Culture in Nineteenth-Century America*. London: Verso, 1990.

Scharff, Virginia. *Twenty Thousand Roads: Women, Movement, and the West*. Berkeley: University of California Press, 2003.

Schell, Herbert S. *History of South Dakota*. Fourth edition. Pierre: State Historical Society, 2004.

Schlissel, Lillian, Vicki L. Ruiz, and Janice Monk, eds. *Western Women: Their Land, Their Lives*. Albuquerque: University of New Mexico Press, 1988.

Schrems, Suzanne H. *Who's Rocking the Cradle? Women Pioneers of Oklahoma Politics from Socialism to the KKK, 1900–1930*. Norman: Horse Creek Publications, 2004.

Schwantes, Carlos Arnaldo. *The Pacific Northwest: An Interpretive History*. Revised and enlarged edition. Lincoln: University of Nebraska Press, 1996.

Shaffer, Marguerite S. *See America First: Tourism and National Identity, 1880–1940*. Washington D.C.: Smithsonian, 2001.

Shannon, Fred A. *The Farmer's Last Frontier: Agriculture, 1860–1897*. New York: Rinehart, 1945.

Shaver, F. A., et al. *An Illustrated History of Central Oregon, Embracing Wasco, Sherman, Gilliam, Wheeler, Crook, Lake, and Klamath Counties*. Spokane: Western Historical Publishing, 1905.

Shipps, Jan. *Mormonism: The Story of a New Religious Tradition*. Urbana: University of Illinois Press, 1985.

Sicherman, Barbara and Carol Hurd Green, eds. *Notable American Women: The Modern Period*. Cambridge: Harvard University Press, 1980.

Silbey, Joel H. *Storm over Texas: The Annexation Controversy and the Road to the Civil War*. New York: Oxford University Press, 2005.

Simmons, Marc. *New Mexico: An Interpretive History*. Second edition. Albuquerque: University of New Mexico Press, 1988.

Simmons, Virginia McConnell. *The Ute Indians of Utah, Colorado, and New Mexico*. Boulder: University of Colorado Press, 2000.

Simonson, Jane E. *Making Home Work: Domesticity and Native American Assimilation in the American West, 1860–1919*. Chapel Hill: University of North Carolina Press, 2006.

Slotkin, Richard. *The Fatal Environment: The Myth of the Frontier in the Age of Industrialization, 1800–1890*. New York: Macmillan, 1992.

Smith, Duane A. *Rocky Mountain West: Colorado, Wyoming, and Montana, 1859–1915*. Albuquerque: University of New Mexico Press, 1992.

Smith, Geoffrey D. *American Fiction, 1901–1925: A Bibliography*. Cambridge: Cambridge University Press, 1997.

Smith, Helena Huntington. *The War on Powder River: The History of an Insurrection*. New York: McGraw Hill, 1966.

Smith, Sherry L. *The View from Officers' Row: Army Perception of Western Indians*. Tucson: University of Arizona Press, 1990.

———. *Reimagining Indians: Native Americans through Anglo Eyes, 1880–1940.* New York: Oxford University Press, 2000.

Spence, Clark C. *Mining Engineers and the American West: The Lace-Boot Brigade, 1849–1932.* New Haven: Yale University Press, 1970.

Stallard, Patricia Y. *Glittering Misery: Dependents of the Indian Fighting Army.* San Rafael: Presidio, 1978.

Starr, Kevin. *Americans and the California Dream, 1850–1915.* New York: Oxford, 1973.

———. *Inventing the Dream: California through the Progressive Era.* New York: Oxford, 1985.

———. *Material Dreams: California through the 1920s.* New York: Oxford, 1990.

Stenhouse, Thomas B. H. *The Rocky Mountain Saints: A Full and Complete History of the Mormons, from the First Vision of Joseph Smith to the Last Courtship of Brigham Young . . . and the Development of the Great Mineral Wealth of the Territory of Utah.* New York: D. Appleton, 1873.

Stillson, Richard T. *Spreading the Word: A History of Information in the California Gold Rush.* Lincoln: University of Nebraska Press, 2006.

Streeby, Shelley. *American Sensations: Class, Empire, and the Production of Popular Culture.* Berkeley: University of California Press, 2002.

Sutton, Walter. *The Western Book Trade: Cincinnati as a Nineteenth-Century Publishing and Book-Trade Center.* Columbus: Ohio State University Press, 1961.

Tate, Michael L. *The Frontier Army in the Settlement of the West.* Norman: University of Oklahoma Press, 1999.

Taylor, Quintard. *In Search of the Racial Frontier: African Americans in the American West, 1528–1990.* New York: W. W. Norton, 1998.

Texas State Historical Association. *Handbook of Texas Online.* http://www.tshaonline.org/handbook/online/.

Thurman, Melvena K., ed. *Women in Oklahoma: A Century of Change.* Oklahoma City: Oklahoma Historical Society, 1982.

Tobias, Henry J. *A History of the Jews in New Mexico.* Albuquerque: University of New Mexico Press, 1990.

Tong, Benson. *Unsubmissive Women: Chinese Prostitutes in Nineteenth-Century San Francisco.* Norman: University of Oklahoma Press, 1994.

———. *Susan La Flesche Picotte, M.D.: Omaha Indian Leader and Reformer.* Norman: University of Oklahoma Press, 1999.

Trachtenberg, Alan. *The Incorporation of America: Culture and Society in the Gilded Age.* New York: Hill and Wang, 1982.

Trimble, Marshall. *Arizona: A Cavalcade of History.* Revised edition. Tucson: Rio Nuevo, 2003.

Tullidge, Edward W. *The Women of Mormondom.* New York, n.p. 1877.

Tuveson, Ernest Lee. *Redeemer Nation: The Idea of America's Millennial Role.* Chicago: University of Chicago Press, 1968.

United States Air Force Academy. *American Military on the Frontier: The Proceedings of the Seventh Military History Symposium, USAF Academy, 1976.* Washington: Office of Air Force History, 1978.

Unruh, John D., Jr. *The Plains Across: The Overland Emigrants and the Trans-Mississippi West, 1840–1860.* Urbana: University of Illinois Press, 1993.

Utley, Robert M. *The Last Days of the Sioux Nation.* New Haven: Yale University Press, 1963.

———. *Frontiersmen in Blue: The United States Army and the Indian, 1848–1865.* New York: Macmillan, 1967.

———. *Frontier Regulars: The United States Army and the Indian, 1866–1891.* New York: Macmillan, 1973.

———. *The Indian Frontier of the American West, 1846–1890.* Albuquerque: University of New Mexico Press, 1984.

———. *A Life Wild and Perilous: Mountain Men and the Paths to the Pacific.* New York: Henry Holt, 1997.

———. *Cavalier in Buckskin: George Armstrong Custer and the Western Military Frontier.* Revised edition. Norman: University of Oklahoma Press, 2001.

Van Wagoner, Richard S. *Mormon Polygamy: A History.* Salt Lake City: Signature, 1986.

Vestal, Stanley. *Joe Meek, The Merry Mountain Man.* Caldwell, Idaho: Caxton, 1952.

Walker, Cheryl. *Indian Nation: Native American Literature and Nineteenth-Century Nationalisms.* Durham: Duke University Press, 1997.

Walker, Don D. *Clio's Cowboys: Studies in the Historiography of the Cattle Trade.* Lincoln: University of Nebraska Press, 1981.

Walker, Franklin. *San Francisco's Literary Frontier.* New York: Alfred A. Knopf, 1939.

———. *A Literary History of Southern California.* Berkeley: University of California Press, 1950.

———. *The Seacoast of Bohemia.* Santa Barbara: Peregrine Smith, 1973.

Walker, Henry Pickering. *The Wagonmasters: High Plains Freighting from the Earliest Days of the Santa Fe Trail to 1880.* Norman: University of Oklahoma Press, 1966.

Walker, Ronald W. *Wayward Saints: The Godbeites and Brigham Young.* Foreword by Jan Shipps. Urbana: University of Illinois Press, 1998.

Walker, Ronald W. et al. *Mormon History.* Urbana: University of Illinois Press, 2001.

Wallace, Ernest and E. Adamson Hoebel. *The Comanches: Lords of the Southern Plains.* Norman: University of Oklahoma Press, 1952.

Wallis, Michael. *The Real Wild West: The 101 Ranch and the Creation of the American West.* New York: St. Martin's, 1999.

Warfel, Harry R. *American Novelists of Today.* New York: American Book Company, 1951.

Warman, Cy. *The Story of the Railroad.* New York: D. Appleton, 1902.

Warren, Louis S. *Buffalo Bill's America: William Cody and the Wild West Show.* New York: Knopf, 2005.

Watters, Leon L. *The Pioneer Jews of Utah.* New York: American Jewish Historical Society, 1952.

Weaver, Jace. *That the People Might Live: Native American Literatures and Native American Community.* New York: Oxford University Press, 1997.

Webb, Walter Prescott. *The Great Plains.* Boston: Ginn, 1931. Reissue Lincoln: University of Nebraska Press, 1981.

———. *The Texas Rangers: A Century of Frontier Defense*. Boston: Houghton Mifflin, 1935.

Weber, David J. *The Mexican Frontier, 1821–1846: The American Southwest under Mexico*. Albuquerque: University of New Mexico Press, 1982.

Weigle, Marta and Kyle Fiore. *Santa Fe and Taos: The Writer's Era, 1916–1941*. Santa Fe: Ancient City Press, 1982.

West, Elliott. *Growing Up with the Country: Childhood on the Far Western Frontier*. Albuquerque: University of New Mexico Press, 1989.

———. *The Way to the West: Essays on the Central Plains*. Albuquerque: University of New Mexico Press, 1995.

———. *The Contested Plains: Indians, Goldseekers, and the Rush to Colorado*. Lawrence: University Press of Kansas, 1998.

White, G. Edward. *The Eastern Establishment and the Western Experience: The West of Frederic Remington, Theodore Roosevelt, and Owen Wister*. New Haven: Yale University Press, 1968.

White, Richard. *The Roots of Dependency: Subsistence, Environment, and Social Change among the Choctaws, Pawnees, and Navajos*. Lincoln: University of Nebraska Press, 1983.

Wild, Peter. *Desert Literature, The Middle Period: J. Smeaton Chase, Edna Brush Perkins, and Edwin Corle*. Boise: Boise State University Press, 1999.

Willard, Frances E. and Mary A. Livermore, eds. *A Woman of the Century: Fourteen Hundred-Seventy Biographical Sketches Accompanied by Portraits of Leading American Women in All Walks of Life*. Buffalo: Charles Wells Moulton, 1893.

Willard, James F., ed. *The Union Colony at Greeley, Colorado, 1869–1871*. Boulder: W. F. Robinson, 1918.

Winther, Oscar Osburn. *The Transportation Frontier: Trans-Mississippi West, 1865–1890*. New York: Holt, Rinehart and Winston, 1964.

Wishart, David J. *The Fur Trade of the American West, 1807–1840: A Geographical Synthesis*. Lincoln: University of Nebraska Press, 1979.

———. *An Unspeakable Sadness: The Dispossession of the Nebraska Indians*. Lincoln: University of Nebraska Press, 1994.

Wooster, Robert. *The Military and United States Indian Policy, 1865–1903*. New Haven: Yale University Press, 1988.

———. *Nelson A. Miles and the Twilight of the Frontier Army*. Lincoln: University of Nebraska Press, 1993.

Worster, Donald. *Rivers of Empire: Water, Aridity, and the Growth of the American West*. New York: Pantheon, 1985.

Wright, Lyle H. *American Fiction, 1876–1900: A Contribution toward a Bibliography*. San Marino: Huntington Library, 1972.

Wright, Muriel H. *A Guide to the Indian Tribes of Oklahoma*. Norman: University of Oklahoma Press, 1951.

Wrobel, David M. *Promised Lands: Promotion, Memory, and the Creation of the American West*. Lawrence: University Press of Kansas, 2002.

Wrobel, David M. and Michael C. Steiner, eds. *Many Wests: Place, Culture, and Regional*

Identity. Lawrence: University Press of Kansas, 1997. See Peter Boag. "Mountain, Plain, Desert, River: The Snake River Region as a Western Crossroads," pp. 177–204; Elizabeth Raymond, "When the Desert Won't Bloom: Environmental Limitation and the Great Basin," pp. 71–92; Anne F. Hyde, "Round Pegs in Square Holes: The Rocky Mountains and Extractive Industry," pp. 93–113.

Wyckoff, William. *Creating Colorado: The Making of a Western American Landscape, 1860–1940.* New Haven: Yale University Press, 1999.

Zornow, William Frank. *Kansas: A History of the Jayhawk State.* Norman: University of Oklahoma Press, 1957.

Zuckerman, Mary Ellen. *A History of Popular Women's Magazines in the United States, 1792–1995.* Westport: Greenwood Press, 1998.

Index

NINA BAYM is a professor emeritus of English at the University of Illinois at Urbana-Champaign. The general editor of *The Norton Anthology of American Literature*, she has written several books on nineteenth-century women writers, beginning with *Woman's Fiction: A Guide to Novels by and about Women in America, 1820–70*.

The University of Illinois Press
is a founding member of the
Association of American University Presses.

Composed in 10.5/13 Adobe Minion Pro
by Celia Shapland
at the University of Illinois Press
Manufactured by Sheridan Books, Inc.

University of Illinois Press
1325 South Oak Street
Champaign, IL 61820-6903
www.press.uillinois.edu